Marketing Scales Handbook

A Compilation of Multi-Item Measures

Volume II

Marketing Scales Handbook

A Compilation of Multi-Item Measures

Volume II

Gordon C. Bruner II   •   Paul J. Hensel

American Marketing Association
Chicago, Illinois USA

Library of Congress Cataloging-in-Publication Data

Bruner, Gordon C., 1954-
    Marketing scales handbook : a compilation of multi-item measures /
Gordon C. Bruner and Paul J. Hensel.
      p.   cm
    Includes index.
    1. Marketing research—Statistical methods—Handbooks, manuals,
etc. 2. Scaling (Social sciences)—Handbooks, manuals, etc.
I. Hensel, Paul J. II. Title.
HF5415.3.B785   1992
658.8'3028—dc20   92-18858
                                                      CIP

ISBN 0-87757-261-5

Published by American Marketing Association
250 S. Wacker Drive
Chicago, Illinois 60606, U.S.A.

Francesca Van Gorp, Editor
Marilyn Stone, Copy editor

Cover design by Mary Kushmir

Manufactured in the United States of America.

Table of Contents
. . . .

Scale No.	Advertising Scales	Page No.

Scale No.	**Organizational, Salesforce, and Miscellaneous Scales**	Page No.

Acknowledgments

....

We express our appreciation to the many researchers who developed, used, and/or reported the measures on which this book is based. Many authors were contacted by mail and some were contacted by phone and e-mail when more information was needed about a scale. Not all responded but the following are among those who wrote back to us and provided information that enabled us to produce a more complete description than there otherwise would have been. Our gratitude is extended to:

Chris T. Allen
University of Cincinnati

Julie Baker
University of Texas at Arlington

Hans Baumgartner
Penn State University

Richard F. Beltramini
Wayne State University

Robert L. Berl
University of Memphis

James M. Carman
University of California at Berkeley

Elizabeth Cooper-Martin
Georgetown University

Carolyn L. Costley
University of Miami

Scott Dawson
Portland State University

Alan Dick
State University of New York at Buffalo

John F. Dickson
University of Puget Sound

Glen Fischer
York University

Robert J. Fisher
University of Southern California

Jule Gassenheimer
University of Kentucky

Ronald Goldsmith
Florida State University

Kent Granzin
University of Utah

James K. Harvey
George Mason University

Jeffrey Inman
University of Wisconsin

Scott W. Kelly
University of Kentucky

Patricia A. Knowles
Clemson University

Donald R. Lichtenstein
University of Colorado at Boulder

Durairaj Maheswaran
New York University

Lawrence J. Marks
Kent State University

Anil Mathur
Hofstra University

Stephen W. McDaniel
Texas A&M University

Edward F. McQuarrie
Santa Clara University

Paul W. Miniard
Florida International University

Christine Moorman
University of Wisconsin

George Moschis
Georgia State University

Darrel D. Muehling
Washington State University

Keith B. Murray
Bryant College

Richard G. Netemeyer
Louisiana State University

Roobina Ohanian
Emory University

Robert A. Peterson
University of Texas

A. Parasuraman
Texas A&M University

Brian T. Ratchford
State University of New York at Buffalo

Marsha L. Richins
University of Missouri

Alan G. Sawyer
University of Florida

Anusorn Singhapakdi
Old Dominion University

Deepak Sirdeshmukh
Case Western Reserve University

M. Joseph Sirgy
Virginia Tech

Robert E. Smith
Indiana University

Meera Venkatraman
Suffolk University

Joe L. Welch
University of North Texas

Tommy E. Whittier
University of Kentucky

Robert E. Widing II
University of Melbourne

At Southern Illinois University, we are grateful to Letty Workman and Scott Thorne who successively managed the **Office of Scale Research**. At University of New Orleans, thanks go to Shelly Verma and Devesh Desai who managed the office. We also appreciate the support provided by our respective departments and colleges. In addition, the work at the University of New Orleans could not have been accomplished without a generous grant from the Louisiana Education Quality Support Fund.

We express our indebtedness to the American Marketing Association. We are proud that the discipline and the organization continue to value our efforts. In particular, at AMA our thanks are extended to Francesca Van Gorp. As our editor, she has coordinated the printing, promotion, and sales of both the first and second volumes of this series.

Finally, as with the first volume, much personal time was taken from our families to create this second volume. Again we thank our wives, Lesa and Victoria, and our children for their patience and support.

Gordon C. Bruner II
Southern Illinois University

Paul J. Hensel
University of New Orleans

Introduction
· · · · · · · · · · · · · · · ·

The first volume of this series was published just four years ago and it quickly became one of the American Marketing Association's best sellers. It is evident that researchers of marketing-related issues value the kind of information the book provides about multi-item scales. Because of that, work began on the second volume soon after it was clear that the first volume was well received.

This second volume focuses on the scales that were reported in articles published from 1990 to 1993. Technically, this new book is not a revised edition, because material from the first volume was not automatically included in the second volume; thus our decision to title it **Volume II**. As is discussed subsequently, the contents of this second volume are predominately new. Scales from the time frame covered by Volume I (1980–1989) were not reported again unless they were used again or they were not included in the earlier volume (e.g., the addition of *Journal of Personal Selling and Sales Management*). The first volume has hundreds of scales not contained here and therefore should not be viewed as superseded.

The reader may wonder why this new volume covers a shorter period than was true of the previous volume. Simply, scales are reported in journals more frequently in the 1990s than they were in the 1980s. Also, two more journals have been added to the domain of review: *Journal of Retailing* and *Journal of Personal Selling and Sales Management*. Not only are they among the top journals in the field, but they cover important topics (and scales) that may not be as likely to appear in the other journals. These two journals join the six already included in the first volume: *Journal of Advertising, Journal of Advertising Research, Journal of the Academy of Marketing Science, Journal of Consumer Research, Journal of Marketing,* and *Journal of Marketing Research*. We could have cherry picked scales from other publications but felt that such a selection process would be too subjective. Again, our reasoning for limiting the domain to this particular set of journals was that if a scale was important to the field, then it should have been used at least once during the period under examination in one of these eight top journals. If instead it appeared for the first time in another journal not part of our review and if it is viewed as useful, then it will eventually be used in research reported in one of these journals and will be included in future volumes of this series.

To better appreciate the growth that has occurred in scale usage, some characteristics of the consumer behavior sections of volume one and volume two can be compared. The first volume contained 283 substantially different consumer-related scales that came from six major marketing journals over a ten-year period. This volume has 310 scales from eight journals over a four-year period. (Although eight journals were reviewed, no consumer-related scales were found for the 1990 to 1993 time frame from the *Journal of Personal Selling and Sales Management*.) Although a comparison of these two periods is awkward because of the different number of journals and years, some conclusions can still be drawn. First, multi-item scales are used more in the 1990s than they were in the 1980s. Second, of the 283 different scales reported in the first volume, only 39 were used again in the 1990 to 1993 period. Therefore, 271 of the consumer-related scales included in this volume were not part of the first volume. Although this number may be off a little given oversights and other errors, it is obvious to us that the majority of scales used during the more recent period are new. This means that the majority of the scales reported in the first volume were not used again in the domain reviewed. To what extent researchers have developed new scales when "good" ones already existed or have created new scales because no scales existed will only be understood with further examination of this database.

As with the first volume, only multi-item scales have been reviewed. One difference between the two books, however, is that the first volume routinely included two-item scales, whereas this volume primarily reports scales with at least three items. Not only did this make the number of scales for review more manageable, but it is also more in line with the spirit of what is meant by "multi-item" scales. Furthermore, a minimum amount of information was required for a scale to be described. The most important information was scale items and reliability. Although we wanted to discuss a scale's validity and origin, such information was much less likely to be reported in articles and was not considered critical. Also, this volume is more likely than the first to provide references for scale uses that are not fully described because of missing information but that appear to deserve the reader's attention.

Readers are urged to take care in the selection of scales. Naive scale users would do well to read up on psychometrics to improve their ability to evaluate alternative measures and make a selection. A suggested reading list is provided at the end of the book from which a rich explanation of psychometric issues can be found.

This second volume is laid out similar to volume one. The largest section covers scales related to consumer behavior. The second section, the smallest, is related to advertising measures. Many of these scales could have been put in the consumer behavior section but were considered important enough to deserve a separate section. The third section is composed of scales used in something other than consumer research. The majority of the scales come from studies of sales people, marketing management, or product distributors.

We have attempted to describe scales of like constructs that use similar sets of items together. Generally, if scales appear to be measuring the same thing and have half or more items in common, then they were written up together. Some scales were not amenable to that approach, however. Specifically, the semantic differential versions of Attitude Toward the Brand and Attitude Toward the Ad (#33 and # 330, respectively) have been measured dozens of ways with dozens of items. Although these have been the most popular constructs to measure through multi-item scales, there has been little agreement on how to measure them. The hodgepodge of bi-polar adjectives used to measure the constructs thwarted our efforts to determine which scales were essentially the same and which ones were different enough to deserve separate treatment. Therefore, many measures have been written up together because, at least on the surface, they appeared to be measuring the same construct in roughly the same way.

Finally, the structure of our scale descriptions remains the same as it was in the first volume and is generally described in the table.

Table
Description of Scale Write-Up Format

SCALE NAME: A short, descriptive name of the construct being measured.

SCALE DESCRIPTION: A sentence or two describing the physical structure of the measure(s) and the psychological construct apparently being assessed. The number of items, the number of points on the scale, and its Likert or semantic differential type are typically specified. If significantly different names were used by authors of articles, they are usually noted here.

SCALE ORIGIN: This provides some limited information about the creation of the scale, if known. Most of the scales originated in one article in the domain and were not known to have been used again.

SAMPLES: For all known uses of the scale in the domain, separate descriptions are provided of their samples but are limited, in most cases, to what was available in the journals' articles. Sample size is provided in almost every case with some information about subject characteristics and study designs, if known.

RELIABILITY: For the most part, reliability is described in terms of Cronbach's alpha, a measure of internal consistency. If known, other issues related to reliability were mentioned as well, such as item-total and test-retest correlations.

VALIDITY: The validity section was among the most difficult to write. The vast majority of scale uses in the domain did not report examining validity at all. Some studies simply performed factor analyses, which may offer some limited evidence of dimensionality. In rare cases, scale authors assessed convergent or discriminant validity. In some instances, the nomological or face validity of scales could be commented on even if scale authors provided little or no other information.

ADMINISTRATION: This section describes the manner in which a scale was administered to a sample. In the overwhelming majority of cases, scales were of the paper-and-pencil variety and were part of self-administered question-naires. In many instances, the interpretation of scale scores is described as well.

MAJOR FINDINGS: A brief discussion of the results associated with a scale, study by study, is given in this section. Though the information offers the reader an idea of previous research findings related to a specific scale, it is not intended to replace a thorough review of the relevant literature.

COMMENTS: This field is not always used. Occasionally something signifi-cant was observed in writing up a scale that we felt should be pointed out to readers. If the psychometric characteristics of a scale were judged to be poor, then it was mentioned. Also, when other studies were considered to be potentially relevant to the scale's usage but were not fully described for some reason, they were cited here as ''see also.''

REFERENCES: Every source cited in the write-up is referenced here using the *Journal of Marketing* style. Titles of the eight primary journals from which scales were taken are abbreviated as follows.

Journal of the Academy of Marketing Science = JAMS
Journal of Advertising = JA
Journal of Advertising Research = JAR
Journal of Consumer Research = JCR
Journal of Marketing = JM
Journal of Marketing Research = JMR
Journal of Personal Selling & Sales Management = JPSSM
Journal of Retailing = JR

Titles of other cited journals and sources are referenced less frequently and are written out in full.

SCALE ITEMS: The scale items used in published research are listed here as are the directions for administering the scale, if known. Also, in most cases there is an indication of the graphic scale that was used to record responses to items. Where an item is followed by (r), it means that the numerical response to the item should be reverse coded when calculating scale scores. Other idiosyncrasies may be noted as well. For example, when slightly different versions of the same scale are discussed in the same write-up, then an indica-tion is given as to which items were used in particular studies.

Part I

Consumer Behavior Scales

SCALE NAME: Ability to Process (Nutritional Information)

SCALE DESCRIPTION:

A four-item, seven-point summated ratings scale measuring the degree to which people say they are confident in their ability to understand and use specified nutritional information on food packaging.

SCALE ORIGIN:

As specified in personal correspondence, the scale was developed by Moorman (1990).

SAMPLES:

The sample used by Moorman (1990) came from the staff at a northeastern U.S. university. A systematic sample was gleaned from a list of staff, and subjects were contacted by mail. (Because of the nature of the research, those employed in health-related areas were dropped from the list.) Of the 274 employees sent a letter, **180** completed the experiment. Incentives to participate were in the form of dollar bills in each of the initial letters of contact and eligibility to win more money if subjects cooperated fully.

RELIABILITY:

An alpha of **.76** was reported by Moorman (1990) for the scale.

VALIDITY:

Because the research was based on personal correspondence, the only validation of the scale came from using principal components analysis with Varimax rotation. The items composing the scale loaded high on a single factor and not on factors used to compose other scales.

ADMINISTRATION:

The scale was included along with several other measures on a questionnaire completed by subjects after an experimental activity. Higher scores on the scale would appear to indicate that respondents have the ability and confidence to use nutrition-related information supplied on some specific food package to which they have been exposed.

MAJOR FINDINGS:

Moorman (1990) examined the influence of consumer and stimulus characteristics on the use of nutrition information. In general, both types of characteristics were found to affect information processing and decision quality. Among the many findings were that age and enduring ability to process nutritional information were positively related and education was negatively related to the ability to process specific nutritional information in a particular experimental circumstance.

REFERENCES:

Moorman, Christine (1990), ''The Effects of Stimulus and Consumer Characteristics on the Utilization of Nutrition Information,'' *JCR*, 17 (December), 362-74.

SCALE ITEMS: ABILITY TO PROCESS (NUTRITIONAL INFORMATION)*

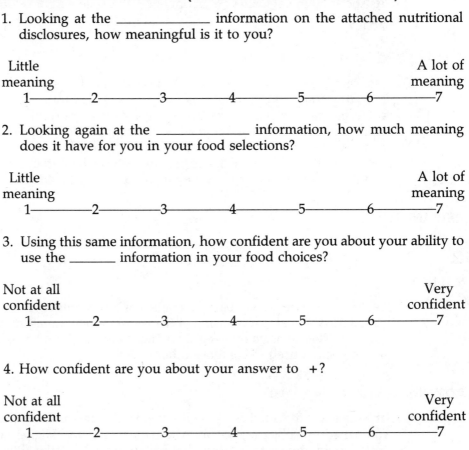

1. Looking at the _____ information on the attached nutritional disclosures, how meaningful is it to you?

Little   A lot of
meaning   meaning
1————2————3————4————5————6————7

2. Looking again at the _____ information, how much meaning does it have for you in your food selections?

Little   A lot of
meaning   meaning
1————2————3————4————5————6————7

3. Using this same information, how confident are you about your ability to use the _____ information in your food choices?

Not at all   Very
confident   confident
1————2————3————4————5————6————7

4. How confident are you about your answer to +?

Not at all   Very
confident   confident
1————2————3————4————5————6————7

* The blanks in items 1-3 should be filled with the name of a nutrient of interest, such as sodium. Also, the verbal anchors for the response scales were not specified in the article but would appear to have been something like those provided here.

\+ Subjects were asked previously to state the ideal level of a specific nutrient (e.g., sodium) for a specific food (e.g., single hot dog).

SCALE NAME: Adoption Intention

SCALE DESCRIPTION:

A four-item, seven-point Likert-type scale measuring the inclination to buy a new product as soon as it is available. There is also a sense of urgency to purchase the product earlier than other people (referents). There are direct and indirect versions of the scale; as shown in "Scale Items," the difference between the two has to do with whether the items are responded to in the first person (direct version) or the third person (indirect version).

SCALE ORIGIN:

Although not specifically stated by Fisher (1993; Fisher and Price 1992), the scale is original (Fisher 1994). Items composing this scale were refined along with items intended to measure four other constructs. No information about this scale in a particular was provided. In general, item-to-total correlations had to be higher than .50 and items had to load on hypothesized factors. Items that did not fit these criteria were eliminated before use in the main study.

SAMPLES:

The convenience sample analyzed by Fisher and Price (1992) was a mixed gender group of **172** undergraduate students. Fisher (1993) reported on three studies though the scale was only used in study two. Further, study two was a two-group experiment: one received direct questioning and the other indirect questioning. The former group was identical to the sample used by Fisher and Price (1992) except that it had **170** students, two students being dropped because of missing data (Fisher 1994). The group receiving indirect questioning had **182** subjects.

RELIABILITY:

An alpha of **.93** was reported for the scale by Fisher (1993; Fisher and Price 1992) for the group receiving direct questioning, and for the group receiving indirect questioning, it was **.81** (Fisher 1993).

VALIDITY:

The validity of the scale was not specifically addressed by Fisher (1993; Fisher and Price 1992). However, Fisher and Price (1992) did state that the variance extracted for the scale was .79, which provides some evidence of its unidimensionality.

ADMINISTRATION:

The scale was administered to subjects along with other measures after they had been exposed to experimental stimuli (Fisher 1993; Fisher and Price 1992).

A high score on the direct version of the scale suggests that a respondent has a strong intention to purchase the new product as soon as it is on the market. A high score on the indirect version of the scale indicates that a respondent believes the typical member of the referent group (e.g., student) would want very much to be among the first to adopt the product.

MAJOR FINDINGS:

The purpose of the study by Fisher and Price (1992) was to investigate the impact of perceived consumption visibility and superordinate group influence on the development of new product **adoption intentions**. Perceived personal and normative outcomes both had significant positive effects on **adoption intention**.

Using three studies, Fisher (1993) examined the ability of indirect questioning to reduce the influence of social desirability bias on self-report measures. As noted previously, **adoption intentions** was only used in study two. There it was found that the association between **adoption intentions** and perceived normative outcomes was significantly higher for the group receiving indirect questioning versus the group receiving direct questioning.

COMMENTS:

Fisher (1993) used the scale to measure students' intentions regarding a fictional new product idea: cordless headphones. If a group other than students is studied then the term *student* should be replaced with a word/phrase that describes an important reference group of which the respondents are members, such as professors, employees, housewives. If a general term such as *persons* is used then it changes the meaning of the scale somewhat.

REFERENCES:

Fisher, Robert J. (1994), personal correspondence.

———— (1993), "Social Desirability Bias and the Validity of Indirect Questioning," *JCR*, 20 (September), 303-15.

———— and Linda L. Price (1992), "An Investigation into the Social Context of Early Adoption Behavior," *JCR*, 19 (December), 477-86.

SCALE ITEMS: ADOPTION INTENTIONS*

Strongly disagree ____ : ____ : ____ : ____ : ____ : ____ : ____ Strongly agree
       0   1   2   3   4   5   6

Direct version of scale:

1. I would like to buy a _____ today, if possible.
2. I will try to buy one of the products as soon as I can.
3. I am likely to be one of the first students to buy a _____.

4. I will probably purchase one of the new products soon after they are on the market.

Indirect version of scale:

THE TYPICAL STUDENT WILL . . .

1. . . . want to buy a _____ today, if possible.
2. . . . try to buy one of the products as soon as s/he can.
3. . . . want to be among the first students to buy a _____.
4. . . . probably purchase one of the new products soon after they are on the market.

* The items were supplied by Fisher (1994). Also, the generic name of the product should be placed in the blanks.

SCALE NAME: Affect (Music)

SCALE DESCRIPTION:

Three one-word descriptors measuring the degree to which one likes some stimulus and perceives it to be ''good.'' Although the study reported here used the scale with respect to musical stimuli it is possible to use it for other stimuli as well. The construct was referred to by MacInnis and Park (1991) as ''likability.''

SCALE ORIGIN:

Although not stated explicitly, it appears that the scale was original to the work of MacInnis and Park (1991).

SAMPLES:

The scale was apparently used in just the pretest stage of the study by Mac-Innis and Park (1991). The sample was composed of **20** subjects. Although undescribed, they were likely to have been similar to those used in the final experiment (college students).

RELIABILITY:

MacInnis and Park (1991) reported an alpha of **.91**.

VALIDITY:

MacInnis and Park (1991) reported no examination of scale validity or unidimensionality.

ADMINISTRATION:

The scale was self-administered along with other measures in a pretest. High scores on the scale suggest that respondents like a particular musical stimulus, and low scores imply that respondents neither like a stimulus nor feel that it is good.

MAJOR FINDINGS:

MacInnis and Park (1991) examined the influence of two dimensions of music on low- and high-involvement ad processing: the music's fit with the ad message and the music's links to past emotion-laden experiences (indexicality). As noted previously, the scale was used in the pretest to investigate the relationship between indexicality and **affect**. Twenty-six songs were rated by subjects, with the results indicating that those songs characterized by high indexicality were more likable.

COMMENTS:

Because the scale has been used only with music stimuli, some adjustment may be necessary if used with different stimuli.

REFERENCE:

MacInnis, Deborah J. and C. Whan Park (1991), ''The Differential Role of Characteristics of Music on High- and Low-Involvement Consumers' Processing of Ads,'' *JCR*, 18 (September), 161-73.

SCALE ITEMS: AFFECT (MUSIC)

1. good
2. pleasant
3. likable

SCALE NAME: Affect (Negative)

SCALE DESCRIPTION:

A ten-item, five-point scale measuring the degree of negative affect one has toward some specified stimulus. As noted in the next section, several versions of the scale that were created and tested vary in their temporal instructions. Therefore, the items can be used to measure one's mood state at a particular point in time or, at the other extreme, reference to a year's time can be used as something more like a trait measure of affect.

SCALE ORIGIN:

The scale used by Mano and Oliver (1993) was developed by Watson, Clark, and Tellegen (1988). The ten negative and ten positive items compose the Positive and Negative Affect Schedule (PANAS). Sharing the same items, seven versions of the scale were tested varying in whether the time period of interest was ''right now'' or ''during the last year.'' Alphas ranged from .84 to .87 using data from college students. Stability of each of these versions were tested using 101 students and with eight-week intervals. The resulting test-retest correlations ranged from .39 to .71. A factor analysis of the ten positive and ten negative items indicated that the positive items all had high loadings (>.50) on the same factor. Evidence of the scale's validity was also provided. By design, the scales were supposed to be independent (uncorrelated), and the evidence bore this out.

SAMPLES:

Data were collected by Mano and Oliver (1993) from **118** undergraduate business students attending a midwestern U.S. university.

RELIABILITY:

Mano and Oliver (1993) reported an alpha of **.87** for the scale.

VALIDITY:

Mano and Oliver (1993) did not specifically address the validity of the scale.

ADMINISTRATION:

The scale was part of a longer questionnaire self-administered by students in a classroom (Mano and Oliver 1993). A high score suggests that a stimulus has evoked a very negative affective reaction in a respondent.

MAJOR FINDINGS:

Mano and Oliver (1993) examined the dimensionality and causal structure of product evaluation, affect, and satisfaction. Among the many findings involving emotion was that **negative affectivity** was significantly greater for subjects in a high-involvement manipulation.

REFERENCES:

Mano, Haim and Richard L. Oliver (1993), ''Assessing the Dimensionality and Structure of the Consumption Experience: Evaluation, Feeling, and Satisfaction,'' *JCR*, 20 (December), 451-66.

Watson, David, Lee Anna Clark, and Auke Tellegen (1988), ''Development and Validation of Brief Measures of Positive and Negative Affect: The PANAS Scales,'' *Journal of Personality and Social Psychology*, 54 (6), 1063-70.

SCALE ITEMS: AFFECT (NEGATIVE)

Not at all   Very much

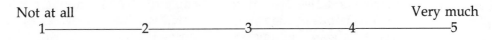

1——————2—————3—————4—————5

1. scared
2. afraid
3. upset
4. distressed
5. jittery
6. nervous
7. ashamed
8. guilty
9. irritable
10. hostile

SCALE NAME: Affect (Positive)

SCALE DESCRIPTION:

A ten-item, five-point scale measuring the degree of positive affect one has toward some specified stimulus. As noted in the following section, several versions of the scale that were created and tested vary in their temporal instructions. Therefore, the items can be used to measure one's mood state at a particular point in time or, at the other extreme, reference to a year's time may be used as something more like a trait measure of affect.

SCALE ORIGIN:

The scale used by Mano and Oliver (1993) was developed by Watson, Clark, and Tellegen (1988). The ten positive and ten negative items compose the Positive and Negative Affect Schedule (PANAS). Sharing the same items, seven versions of the scale were tested varying in whether the time period of interest was "right now" or "during the last year." Alphas ranged from .86 to .90 using data from college students. Stability of each of these versions were tested using 101 students and with eight-week intervals. The resulting test-retest correlations ranged from .47 to .68. A factor analysis of the ten positive and ten negative items indicated that the positive items all had high loadings (> .50) on the same factor. Evidence of the scale's validity was also provided. By design, the scales were supposed to be independent (uncorrelated) and the evidence bore this out.

SAMPLES:

Data were collected by Mano and Oliver (1993) from **118** undergraduate business students attending a midwestern U.S. university.

RELIABILITY:

Mano and Oliver (1993) reported an alpha of **.90** for the scale.

VALIDITY:

Mano and Oliver (1993) did not specifically addressed the validity of the scale.

ADMINISTRATION:

The scale was part of a longer questionnaire self-administered by students in a classroom (Mano and Oliver 1993). A high score suggests that a stimulus has evoked a very positive affective reaction in a respondent.

MAJOR FINDINGS:

Mano and Oliver (1993) examined the dimensionality and causal structure of product evaluation, affect, and satisfaction. Among the many findings involving emotion was that **positive affectivity** was significantly greater for subjects in a high-involvement manipulation.

REFERENCES:

Mano, Haim and Richard L. Oliver (1993), ''Assessing the Dimensionality and Structure of the Consumption Experience: Evaluation, Feeling, and Satisfaction,'' *JCR*, 20 (December), 451-66.

Watson, David, Lee Anna Clark, and Auke Tellegen (1988), ''Development and Validation of Brief Measures of Positive and Negative Affect: The PANAS Scales,'' *Journal of Personality and Social Psychology*, 54 (6), 1063-70.

SCALE ITEMS: AFFECT (POSITIVE)

Not at all   Very much
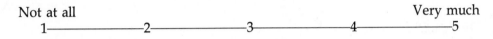
1————————2————————3————————4————————5

1. enthusiastic
2. interested
3. determined
4. excited
5. inspired
6. alert
7. active
8. strong
9. proud
10. attentive

SCALE NAME: Alienation (Consumer)

SCALE DESCRIPTION:

A seven-item, six-point Likert-type scale measuring the degree to which a consumer has negative beliefs about business in general and is alienated from it.

SCALE ORIGIN:

The scale is original to Singh (1990), but he notes that he drew on the work of Allison (1978). The latter developed a 35-item measure of consumer alienation. Although the two scales have some similar items and measure the same construct, they are not the same scale, and one is not a subset of the other.

SAMPLES:

Data were collected from four samples by Singh (1988, 1990). Four slightly different survey instruments were used, varying in the dissatisfying experience referred to. One thousand households were sent a questionnaire for each of the four service categories studied: car repairs, grocery stores, medical care, and banking. Response rates were estimated to be more than 50% for each category given that only around 30% of the random samples had dissatisfying experiences worthy of reporting on a questionnaire.

Ultimately, usable data ranged from **116** respondents in the repair service sample to **125** in the medical care sample. Detailed demographic information for each of the four samples is provided in the article; it is difficult to summarize the four profiles given that they varied somewhat, most likely because the instrument itself indicated that the questionnaire was to be completed by the one in the household dealing most with the specified service category. For example, men mostly filled out the questionnaire regarding auto repair (67%), whereas women filled out the one pertaining to grocery shopping (73%).

RELIABILITY:

Singh (1990) reported an alpha of **.80** for the car repair version of the scale.

VALIDITY:

The items in this scale were analyzed using common factor analysis. The results were interpreted as showing evidence of unidimensionality with the main factor explaining 47% of the total variance.

ADMINISTRATION:

The scale was administered in a mail survey instrument along with many other scales and measures. High scores on the scale indicate that respondents believe businesses in general do not care about them, whereas low scores indicate that respondents are likely to have more positive beliefs about business.

MAJOR FINDINGS:

In a detailed study of consumer complaint behavior, Singh (1990) concluded that there were four consumer clusters with distinct response styles: passives, voicers, irates, and activists. Profiles were developed for each cluster. **Alienation** was found to significantly discriminate between the clusters such that activists and irates were more likely to be **alienated** from the marketplace than voicers and passives.

COMMENTS:

As noted previously, four transactions were examined in the study by Singh (1990). However, only the items relating to the car repair were reported. To the extent that one wished to use the scale to study complaints in a non-repair context, one of the other three versions of the scale might be more appropriate.

REFERENCES:

Allison, Neil K. (1978), ''A Psychometric Development of a Test for Consumer Alienation from the Marketplace,'' *JMR*, 15 (November), 565-75.

Singh, Jagdip (1988), ''Consumer Complaint Intentions and Behaviors: Definitional and Taxonomical Issues,'' *JM*, 52 (January), 93-107.

_____ (1990), ''A Typology of Consumer Dissatisfaction Response Styles,'' *JR*, 66 (Spring), 57-97.

SCALE ITEMS: ALIENATION (CONSUMER)

Strongly disagree	Moderately disagree	Slightly disagree	Slightly agree	Moderately agree	Strongly agree
1	2	3	4	5	6

1. Most companies care nothing at all about the consumer.
2. Shopping is usually an unpleasant experience.
3. Consumers are unable to determine what products will be sold in the stores.
4. In general, companies are plain dishonest in their dealings with the consumer.
5. Business firms stand behind their products and guarantees. **(r)**
6. The consumer is usually the least important consideration to most companies.
7. As soon as they make a sale, most businesses forget about the buyer.

SCALE NAME: Anger

SCALE DESCRIPTION:

A three-item, five-point summated ratings scale assessing the experience a person has had with anger-related emotions. The directions and response scale can be worded so as to measure the intensity of the emotional state at the present time, or they can be adjusted to measure the frequency with which a person has experienced the emotional trait during some specified time period. One-word items were used in the study by Westbrook and Oliver (1991), and phrases based on those same items were used by Allen, Machleit, and Kleine (1992).

SCALE ORIGIN:

The measure was developed by Izard (1977) and is part of the Differential Emotions Scale (DES II). The instrument was designed originally as a measure of a person's emotional "state" at a particular point in time, but adjustments in the instrument's instructions allow the same items to be used in the assessment of emotional experiences as perceived over a longer time period. The latter was viewed by Izard as measure of one's emotional "trait" (1977, p. 125). Test-retest reliability for the anger subscale of the DES II was reported to be .68 (n = 63) and item-factor correlations were .74 and above (Izard 1977, p. 126).

Beyond this evidence, several other studies have provided support for the validity of the scale, even in consumption settings (e.g., Westbrook 1987). The items in DES II were composed solely of one word. In contrast, the items in DES III are phrases describing the target emotion. They were developed by Izard, although the first published validity testing was conducted by Kotsch, Gerbing, and Schwartz (1982). A study by Allen, Machleit, and Marine (1988) provides some insight to the factor structure of both DES II and III. The results indicate that when presented with the other DES items, the anger items tended to load with other items such as sadness and disgust. Because of this, the scale may have low discriminant validity.

SAMPLES:

The data used by Allen, Machleit, and Kleine (1992) came from a stratified sample of people of diverse experience with blood donation. Nine hundred questionnaires were mailed and **361** usable forms were returned. Given that all respondents had donated blood previously, limited information was known about them and allowed a comparison with nonrespondents. Respondents were a little older, less likely to be male, and more likely to be heavier donors than nonrespondents.

The data for the study conducted by Westbrook and Oliver (1991) came from a judgmental area sample. Convenience samples were taken at four shopping centers in a large northeastern city and were limited to persons who had purchased a new or used car in the past year. Complete and usable questionnaires were obtained from **125** respondents. A majority (74%) of the

sample was male. The average respondent had an income in the $25,000 to $40,000 range and was 33 years of age.

The frequency version of the scale was used in this study. Two samples were used in the study by Oliver (1993), one examining satisfaction with cars and the other examining course satisfaction. The one involving cars is the same as the one described previously in Westbrook and Oliver (1991). The other sample was composed of students who volunteered from nine sections of a required marketing class. Usable questionnaires were provided by 178 students. The intensity version of the scale was used in this study.

RELIABILITY:

Alphas of **.89** and **.92** were calculated for the scale by Allen, Machleit, and Kleine (1992; Allen 1994) and Westbrook and Oliver (1991), respectively. Oliver (1993) reported alphas of **.94** (n = 125) and **.86** (n = 178).

VALIDITY:

No specific examination of the scale's validity was reported in any of the studies.

ADMINISTRATION:

The scale was included with many other measures in the instruments used by Allen, Machleit, and Kleine (1992), Oliver (1993), and Westbrook and Oliver (1991). High scores on the frequency version of the scale suggest that a respondent perceives him/herself as having experienced the anger-related emotional trait very often in some specified time period. A high score on the intensity version of the scale indicates that he/she is feeling very angry at the time of measurement.

MAJOR FINDINGS:

Allen, Machleit, and Kleine (1992) examined whether emotions affect behavior through attitudes or instead are viewed better as having a separate and distinct impact. Although several emotions were found to play a key role in predicting behavior, **anger** (DES III) was not found to have a significant relationship, at least with regard to donating blood.

The separate roles of positive and negative affect, attribute performance, and disconfirmation were examined by Oliver (1993) for their impact on satisfaction. Negative affect was viewed as a function of several emotions, **anger** being one of them. For both samples, negative affect as found to have direct influence on satisfaction.

Westbrook and Oliver (1991) studied the correspondence of the consumption emotional responses and satisfaction judgments that occur in the postpurchase period of the consumer decision process. **Anger** had its highest correlation with disgust (r = .85) and its lowest correlation with joy (r = −.22). **Anger** was also found to be a primary emotional trait linked to the cluster of consumers who had the lowest satisfaction in their car buying experiences.

REFERENCES:

Allen, Chris T. (1994), personal correspondence.

_____, Karen A. Machleit, and Susan Schultz Kleine (1992), ''A Comparison of Attitudes and Emotions as Predictors of Behavior at Diverse Levels of Behavioral Experience,'' *JCR*, 18 (March), 493-504.

_____, _____, and Susan S. Marine (1988), ''On Assessing the Emotionality of Advertising Via Izard's Differential Emotions Scale,'' in *Advances in Consumer Research*, Vol. 11, Tom Kinnear, ed. Provo, UT: Association for Consumer Research, 226-31.

Izard, Carroll E. (1977), *Human Emotions*. New York: Plenum Press.

Kotsch, William E., Davis W. Gerbing, and Lynne E. Schwartz (1982), ''The Construct Validity of the Differential Emotions Scale as Adapted for Children and Adolescents,'' in *Measuring Emotions in Infants and Children*, Carroll E. Izard, ed. New York: Cambridge University Press, 251-78.

Oliver, Richard L. (1993), ''Cognitive, Affective, and Attribute Bases of the Satisfaction Response,'' *JCR*, 20 (December), 418-30.

Westbrook, Robert A. (1987), ''Product/Consumption-based Affective Responses and Postpurchase Processes,'' *JMR*, 24 (August), 258-70.

_____ and Richard L. Oliver (1991), ''The Dimensionality of Consumption Emotion Patterns and Consumer Satisfaction,'' *JCR*, 18 (June), 84-91.

SCALE ITEMS: ANGER

POSSIBLE DIRECTIONS FOR FREQUENCY VERSION OF SCALE: Below is a list of words that you can use to show how you feel. We want you to tell us how often you felt each of these feelings _____.* You can tell us how often you felt each of these feelings on the list by marking one of the numbers next to each question.

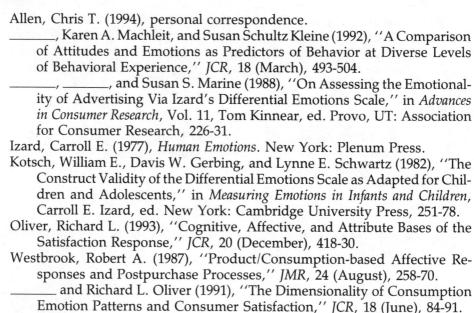

```
Almost                                              Very
never    ____ : ____ : ____ : ____ : ____           often
          1      2      3      4      5
```

POSSIBLE DIRECTIONS FOR INTENSITY VERSION OF SCALE: Below is a list of words that you can use to show how you feel. We want you to tell us how strongly you feel. You can tell us how strongly you feel each of these feelings on the list by marking one of the numbers next to each question.

```
Very                                                Very
weak     ____ : ____ : ____ : ____ : ____           strong
          1      2      3      4      5
```

DES II
1. enraged
2. angry
3. mad

DES III
1. feel like screaming at somebody or banging on something
2. feel angry, irritated, annoyed
3. feel so mad you're about to blow up

* The blank should be used to specify the time period of interest such as "during the last week."

SCALE NAME: Anonymity of Responses

SCALE DESCRIPTION:

A four-item, seven-point Likert-type scale measuring the degree to which a person who has filled out a questionnaire perceives that his/her responses will remain anonymous.

SCALE ORIGIN:

Although not specifically stated by Fisher (1993), the scale is assumed to be original to his study.

SAMPLES:

Fisher (1993) reported on three studies, though the scale was only used in the first one. The study was a two-group experiment: one group received a *direct* version of the scale and the other an *indirect* version. The sample was composed of male and female undergraduate students, with 92 subjects being assigned to each group.

RELIABILITY:

An alpha of .71 was calculated for the scale (Fisher 1994).

VALIDITY:

No direct examination of the scale's validity was reported by Fisher (1993). However, some degree of criterion validity was evidenced given that the subjects in the anonymous experimental condition group scored significantly higher on the scale than those in the unanonymous group. Those in the former group were told that their responses would be anonymous, whereas those in the latter group were told to put their identification numbers on their survey forms and that they might have to discuss their responses with a researcher.

ADMINISTRATION:

The scale(s) were administered to the subjects after they had been exposed to experimental stimuli (Fisher 1993). Higher scores on the scale suggest that respondents believe that the information they have provided on a survey will be known and traced to them specifically.

MAJOR FINDINGS:

Fisher (1993) examined the ability of indirect questioning to reduce the influence of social desirability bias on self-report measures. The measure of **anonymity** was used as a manipulation check and, as noted previously, those in the group who were told that their responses would be **anonymous** were as a group more likely to express that they perceived their information was anonymous compared with those in the **unanonymous** group.

REFERENCES:

Fisher, Robert J. (1994), personal correspondence.
_____ (1993), ''Social Desirability Bias and the Validity of Indirect Questioning,'' *JCR*, 20 (September), 303-15.

SCALE ITEMS: ANONYMITY OF RESPONSES

Strongly
disagree   ____ : ____ : ____ : ____ : ____ : ____ : ____   Strongly
agree
          0   1   2   3   4   5   6

1. My responses on this survey are anonymous. **(r)**
2. My responses on this survey can be traced back to me.
3. It's likely I'll be contacted by someone about my responses.
4. Once I hand this survey to the researcher, no one will know who filled out this particular survey. **(r)**

SCALE NAME: Anxiety

SCALE DESCRIPTION:

A three-item, five-point scale measuring the degree to which one reports a stimulus making him/her feel nervous and fearful. Mano and Oliver (1993) referred to the scale as Distress.

SCALE ORIGIN:

Although an item and inspiration were drawn from the work of Watson, Clark, and Tellegen (1988), the three items used by Mano and Oliver (1993) appear to have been used first as a summated scale by Mano (1991). With 224 college students, the scale was reported to have an alpha of .83. Cluster and factor analyses grouped these three items together by themselves.

SAMPLES:

Data were collected by Mano and Oliver (1993) from **118** undergraduate business students attending a midwestern U.S. university.

RELIABILITY:

Mano and Oliver (1993) reported an alpha of **.82** for the scale.

VALIDITY:

Mano and Oliver (1993) did not specifically address the validity of the scale.

ADMINISTRATION:

The scale was part of a longer questionnaire self-administered by students in a classroom (Mano and Oliver 1993). A high score suggests that some stimulus has caused a person to feel nervous and fearful.

MAJOR FINDINGS:

Mano and Oliver (1993) examined the dimensionality and causal structure of product evaluation, affect, and satisfaction. Among the many findings involving the **anxiety** emotion was that it was significantly greater for subjects in a high-involvement manipulation.

REFERENCES:

Mano, Haim (1991), ''The Structure and Intensity of Emotional Experiences: Method and Context Convergence,'' *Multivariate Behavioral Research*, 26 (3), 389-411.

_____ and Richard L. Oliver (1993), ''Assessing the Dimensionality and

Structure of the Consumption Experience: Evaluation, Feeling, and Satisfaction,'' *JCR*, 20 (December), 451-66.

Watson, David, Lee Anna Clark, and Auke Tellegen (1988), ''Development and Validation of Brief Measures of Positive and Negative Affect: The PANAS Scales,'' *Journal of Personality and Social Psychology*, 54 (6), 1063-70.

SCALE ITEMS: ANXIETY

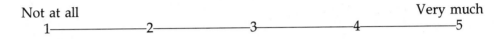

Not at all   Very much

1————————2————————3————————4————————5

1. anxious
2. fearful
3. nervous

SCALE NAME: Anxiety (Social)

SCALE DESCRIPTION:

A 30-item true-false scale measuring the extent to which a person expects to be evaluated negatively by others and avoids evaluative situations. A person scoring high on this scale should *not* necessarily be assumed to have a negative self-image. The measure was referred to as Fear of Negative Evaluation (FNE) by the originators (Watson and Friend 1969) as well as Bearden and Rose (1990).

SCALE ORIGIN:

The scale originally was constructed along with a similar measure by Watson and Friend (1969). Initially, 145 items were selected from a much larger pool and administered to 297 undergraduate students. Thirty items survived the testing to compose the FNE scale. The mean item-total correlation for the scale was **.72** and the KR-20 was **.94**. A one-month test of the scale's stability was made. A test-retest correlation of **.78** was found on the basis of data from 154 students. The scale had a negative correlation (−.25, p < .01) with the Marlowe-Crowne measure of social desirability (Crowne and Marlowe 1960).

SAMPLES:

The article by Bearden and Rose (1990) reported the use of several studies and samples. The only study in which the self-esteem scale was used involved data collected from **99** undergraduate business students.

RELIABILITY:

earden and Rose (1990) reported an alpha of **.89** for the scale.

VALIDITY:

The validity of the scale was not directly examined by Bearden and Rose (1990). However, some idea of its nomological validity can be found in the findings discussed subsequently.

ADMINISTRATION:

The scale was administered to students by Bearden and Rose (1990) in a larger survey instrument. Scores can range from 0 to 30. High scores on the scale indicate that respondents are fearful of social evaluation, whereas low scores suggest a lack of anxiety about others' evaluations.

MAJOR FINDINGS:

Bearden and Rose (1990) conducted a series of studies to investigate the reliability and validity of a measure of attention to social comparison information (ATSCI) and the extent to which this construct is a moderator of interpersonal influence. The measure of **social anxiety** was found to have significant positive relationships with measures of conformity motivation and public self-consciousness.

REFERENCES:

Bearden, William O. and Randall L. Rose (1990), ''Attention to Social Comparison Information: An Individual Difference Factor Affecting Consumer Conformity,'' *JCR*, 16 (March), 461-71.

Crowne, Douglas P. and David Marlowe (1960), ''A New Scale of Social Desirability Independent of Psychopathology,'' *Journal of Consulting Psychology*, 24 (August), 349-54.

Watson, David and Ronald Friend (1969), ''Measurement of Social-Evaluative Anxiety,'' *Journal of Consulting and Clinical Psychology*, 33 (4), 448-57.

SCALE ITEMS: ANXIETY (SOCIAL)*

1. I rarely worry about seeming foolish to others. **(F)**
2. I worry about what people will think of me even when I know it doesn't make any difference. **(T)**
3. I become tense and jittery if I know someone is sizing me up. **(T)**
4. I am unconcerned even if I know people are forming an unfavorable impression of me. **(F)**
5. I feel very upset when I commit some social error. **(T)**
6. The opinions that important people have of me cause me little concern. **(F)**
7. I am often afraid that I may look ridiculous or make a fool of myself. **(T)**
8. I react very little when other people disapprove of me. **(F)**
9. I am frequently afraid of other people noticing my shortcomings. **(T)**
10. The disapproval of others would have little effect on me. **(F)**
11. If someone is evaluating me I tend to expect the worst. **(T)**
12. I rarely worry about what kind of impression I am making on someone. **(F)**
13. I am afraid that others will not approve of me. **(T)**
14. I am afraid that people will find fault with me. **(T)**
15. Other people's opinions of me do not bother me. **(F)**
16. I am not necessarily upset if I do not please someone. **(F)**
17. When I am talking to someone, I worry about what they may be thinking about me. **(T)**
18. I feel that you can't help making social errors sometimes, so why worry about it. **(F)**
19. I am usually worried about what kind of impression I make. **(T)**
20. I worry a lot about what my superiors think of me. **(T)**
21. If I know someone is judging me, it has little effect on me. **(F)**
22. I worry that others will think I am not worthwhile. **(T)**
23. I worry very little about what others may think of me. **(F)**
24. Sometimes I think I am too concerned with what other people think of me. **(T)**

25. I often worry that I will say or do the wrong things. **(T)**
26. I am often indifferent to the opinions others have of me. **(F)**
27. I am usually confident that others will have a favorable impression of me. **(F)**
28. I often worry that people who are important to me won't think very much of me. **(T)**
29. I brood about the opinions my friends have about me. **(T)**
30. I become tense and jittery if I know I am being judged by my superiors. **(T)**

* When a respondent provides the indicated answer, a point is received; for example, answering "false" to item 1 would give a person a point.

SCALE NAME: Arousal

SCALE DESCRIPTION:

A three-item, five-point scale measuring one's excitement-related emotional reaction to an environmental stimulus.

SCALE ORIGIN:

Although the idea for the scale and one item come from the work of Mehrabian and Russell (1974), the scale as a whole is original to Dawson, Bloch, and Ridgway (1990).

SAMPLES:

The sample collected by Dawson, Bloch, and Ridgway (1990) came from a large arts and crafts market in a major West Coast city. Shoppers were approached over four summer days by trained survey administrators and asked to participate. Those who did participate were paid $1. The analysis was based on data from **278** respondents. The only significant difference noted between the sample and that of the surrounding SMSA was that the former contained more females.

RELIABILITY:

Dawson, Bloch, and Ridgway (1990) reported an alpha of **.64** for the scale.

VALIDITY:

Dawson, Bloch, and Ridgway (1990) performed an exploratory factor analysis on the items composing this scale as well as four other items composing a Pleasure scale. Although the items loaded highest on their respective factors, it was mentioned that one item (happy) had split loadings.

ADMINISTRATION:

The scale was self-administered as part of a larger survey instrument in the field study conducted by Dawson, Bloch, and Ridgway (1990). High scores on the scale suggest that respondents feel excitement because of some specified stimulus, whereas low scores imply that they are bored and/or not aroused by the stimulus.

MAJOR FINDINGS:

Dawson, Bloch, and Ridgway (1990) investigated the role played by shopping motives in shaping the emotions triggered during a retail shopping experience. The clearest finding involving the construct measured by this scale was that the **arousal** experienced by shoppers at the market had a significant positive relationship with their experience-related shopping motives and, to a lesser extent, their product-related motives.

REFERENCES:

Dawson, Scott, Peter H. Bloch, and Nancy M. Ridgway (1990), ''Shopping Motives, Emotional States, and Retail Outcomes,'' *JR*, 66 (Winter), 408-27.

Mehrabian, Albert and James A. Russell (1974), *An Approach to Environmental Psychology*. Cambridge, MA: The MIT Press.

SCALE ITEMS: AROUSAL

Directions: People experience a variety of feelings or moods in different types of situations and at different points in time. For example, spending time at the market is a situation that may produce one set of feelings. Similarly, you may not have the same types of feelings during your visit to the market today that you had during an earlier visit. Please indicate below the extent to which each word describes your **feelings at this moment.**

Does not describe at all		Describes somewhat		Describes a great deal
1	2	3	4	5

1. surprised
2. excited
3. rewarded

SCALE NAME: Arousal

SCALE DESCRIPTION:

A three-item, five-point scale measuring one's surprise-related emotional reaction to some specified stimulus.

SCALE ORIGIN:

Although drawing in general from the work of Watson, Clark, and Tellegen (1988), the items used by Mano and Oliver (1993) appear to have been used first as a summated scale by Mano (1991). With 224 college students, the scale was reported to have an alpha of .72. A factor analysis did *not* find the three items loading on the same factor although a cluster analysis grouped them together with few *elation*-related items.

SAMPLES:

Data were collected by Mano and Oliver (1993) from **118** undergraduate business students attending a midwestern U.S. university.

RELIABILITY:

Mano and Oliver (1993) reported an alpha of **.60** for the scale.

VALIDITY:

Mano and Oliver (1993) did not specifically address the validity of the scale.

ADMINISTRATION:

The scale was part of a longer questionnaire self-administered by students in a classroom (Mano and Oliver 1993). A high score suggests that a respondent is feeling surprised by some stimulus.

MAJOR FINDINGS:

Mano and Oliver (1993) examined the dimensionality and causal structure of product evaluation, affect, and satisfaction. Among the many findings involving the **arousal** emotion was that it was significantly greater for subjects in a high involvement manipulation.

REFERENCES:

Mano, Haim (1991), ''The Structure and Intensity of Emotional Experiences: Method and Context Convergence,'' *Multivariate Behavioral Research*, 26 (3), 389-411.

_____ and Richard L. Oliver (1993), ''Assessing the Dimensionality and

Structure of the Consumption Experience: Evaluation, Feeling, and Satisfaction," *JCR*, 20 (December), 451-66.

Watson, David, Lee Anna Clark, and Auke Tellegen (1988), "Development and Validation of Brief Measures of Positive and Negative Affect: The PANAS Scales," *Journal of Personality and Social Psychology*, 54 (6), 1063-70.

SCALE ITEMS: AROUSAL

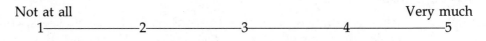

Not at all   Very much

1————————2————————3————————4————————5

1. aroused
2. astonished
3. surprised

SCALE NAME: Arousal

SCALE DESCRIPTION:

A six-item, six-point summated ratings scale measuring the arousal-related emotional reaction one has to an environmental stimulus. The scale focuses on the person's feelings rather than being a direct description of the stimulus.

SCALE ORIGIN:

The scale used by Baker, Levy, and Grewal (1992) is a modified version of one developed by Russell and Pratt (1980). Specifically, the latter constructed a five-item measure of the "sleepy" quality of a place. This scale was reported to have an alpha of **.82** (n = 241). Baker, Levy, and Grewal (1992) used those items plus one from the "arousing" quality scale also developed by Russell and Pratt (1980). Therefore, the scale could be described more accurately as measuring the "sleepy" quality of places, except that by reversing scores on five of the items, it appears instead to measure the arousal dimension.

SAMPLES:

The data analyzed by Baker, Levy, and Grewal (1992) came from an experiment using **147** undergraduate students. The study used a 2 (store ambient levels) × 2 (store social levels) between subjects factorial design with 35-39 subjects per cell.

RELIABILITY:

Baker, Levy, and Grewal (1992) reported an alpha of **.80** for the scale.

VALIDITY:

Evidence of the scale's validity was provided by Baker, Levy, and Grewal (1992). Specifically, the intra-item correlations within the scale were higher than the intercorrelations with items from a related scale (pleasure). Moreover, confirmatory factor analysis indicated that a two-factor model (pleasure and arousal) fit the data better than a one-factor model.

ADMINISTRATION:

The scale was self-administered by subjects as part of a questionnaire after exposure to experimental stimuli (Baker, Levy, and Grewal 1992). High scores on the scale suggest that respondents consider some specified stimulus to make them feel active and alert, whereas low scores imply that they feel drowsy and slow.

MAJOR FINDINGS:

Baker, Levy, and Grewal (1992) examined the effects of two retail atmospheric factors—ambient and social cues—on respondents' pleasure, **arousal**, and shopping intentions. Overall, the results led the authors to conclude that store environment influences consumers' **arousal** emotion, which enhances shopping intentions.

REFERENCES:

Baker, Julie, Michael Levy, and Dhruv Grewal (1992), ''An Experimental Approach to Making Retail Store Environmental Decisions,'' *JR*, 68 (Winter), 445-60.

Russell, James A. and Geraldine Pratt (1980), ''A Description of Affective Quality Attributed to Environments,'' *Journal of Personality and Social Psychology*, 38 (February), 311-22.

SCALE ITEMS: AROUSAL

Directions: Below is a list of words that can be used to describe places. We would like you to rate how accurately each word below described this place. Use the following rating scale for your answer.*

Extremely
inaccurate   ____ : ____ : ____ : ____ : ____ : ____   Extremely
accurate
           1   2   3   4   5   6

1. alive
2. inactive **(r)**
3. drowsy **(r)**
4. idle **(r)**
5. lazy **(r)**
6. slow **(r)**

* These are the directions as reported by Russell and Pratt (1980).

SCALE NAME: Arousal-Seeking Tendency

SCALE DESCRIPTION:

A scale measuring the level of stimulation and arousal a person prefers. The scale has been used with several different numbers of items and response alternatives. Two long versions have been offered by the originator (see following). Also, a five-item subset of the longer scales was used by Dawson, Bloch, and Ridgway (1990) and referred to as "stimulation seeking." Dawson, Bloch, and Ridgway (1990) and Steenkamp and Baumgartner (1992) used five-point response scales, and a nine-point version was used by Mehrabian (1978; and Russell 1974).

SCALE ORIGIN:

The 40-item version of the scale was constructed by Mehrabian and Russell (1974). Three studies with three separate samples of University of California undergraduates (203, 316, and 214) were conducted to arrive at the final 40-item inventory. An initial set of items was generated from similar measures such as curiosity, change-seeking, and sensation-seeking. Some items were written to augment those borrowed from past studies and to tap into dimensions not represented by the other measures. Among other things, the final scale consisted of those items that had the best item-total correlations, the highest factor loadings, and the lowest correlations with social desirability. Scores on the 40-item version had a correlation of **.96** with a larger 125 item version. A Kuder-Richardson reliability coefficient of **.87** was reported for the 40-item set. A test-retest correlation of **.88** was calculated for a group of 78 students. A pattern of correlations with measures of other personality constructs provided evidence of construct validity.

The 32-item version of the scale has 25 items in common with the longer version and 7 new items. A brief description of its development is provided by Mehrabian, who says it "has greater internal consistency and somewhat different theoretical properties" than the earlier scale (1978, p. 724). The reliability (KR) was said to be .93 and evidence of the scale's discriminant validity was given.

SAMPLES:

The sample collected by Dawson, Bloch, and Ridgway (1990) came from a large arts and crafts market in a major West Coast city. Shoppers were approached over four summer days by trained survey administrators and asked to participate. Those who did participate were paid $1. The analysis was based on data from **278** respondents. The only significant difference noted between the sample and that of the surrounding SMSA was that the former contained more females.

Analysis in Goodwin and Etgar (1980) was based on data collected from **180** students enrolled in business courses in a northeastern state university. A 2 × 3 × 3 factorial between-subjects design was used, with 10 subjects per cell. (There were two types of products, three levels of product attributes, and three different message appeals.)

Convenience samples of homemakers and students in undergraduate business courses were used by Raju (1980). The scale was administered to groups of various sizes in an initial study, with the homemaker groups ranging between 30 and 39 and the student groups ranging between 51 and 69. In a larger follow-up study, there were **336** homemakers and **105** students.

The sample used by Steenkamp and Baumgartner (1992) was composed of **223** volunteers from undergraduate marketing courses at a university. A lottery with cash prizes was used to help motivate students to participate.

RELIABILITY:

Dawson, Bloch, and Ridgway (1990) reported an alpha of **.76** for their short version of the scale. A reliability (LISREL) of **.89** was reported for the version of the scale used by Steenkamp and Baumgartner (1992). The other two studies did not provide any information regarding the scale's reliability.

VALIDITY:

No examination of scale validity was reported by either Dawson, Bloch, and Ridgway (1990) or Goodwin and Etgar (1980). Raju (1980) used the scale to construct a related scale that measured consumer exploratory tendencies. The correlation between the two scales was reported to be **.53** for homemakers (n = 336) and **.51** for students (n = 105). This provides some evidence of the scale's convergent validity.

Although the principal components factor analysis conducted by Steenkamp and Baumgartner (1992) produced at least five factors with eigenvalues greater than one, the authors concluded that the scale was basically unidimensional because of scree plots of the eigenvalues. Scores on the scale had correlations of between .46 and .76 with three other measures of optimum stimulation level, which provides some evidence of convergent validity. A confirmatory factor analysis of all four scales also provided some evidence of convergent validity, because Arousal-Seeking Tendency not only loaded significantly on the underlying construct but it was also the second highest standardized factor loading (.85) of the four measures tested.

ADMINISTRATION:

The scale was self-administered as part of a larger survey instrument in the field study conducted by Dawson, Bloch, and Ridgway (1990). Subjects in the Goodwin and Etgar (1980) study completed the scale along with several other self-administered measures one month prior to the experiment. Raju (1980) had subjects self-administer the scale along with other measures. The scale was administered by Steenkamp and Baumgartner (1992) as part of a larger questionnaire composed primarily of four scales that measured optimum stimulation level in various ways. High scores on the scale suggest a person prefers a high level of optimum stimulation, whereas low scores imply the person has a low level of optimum arousal.

MAJOR FINDINGS:

Dawson, Bloch, and Ridgway (1990) investigated the role played by shopping motives in shaping the emotions triggered during a retail shopping experience. **Arousal-seeking tendency** was examined merely as a moderating variable given that it was possible for it to moderate the influence of shopping motives on transient emotions experienced during a retail visit. Very little evidence was found to support the potential influence of this variable on the model hypothesized.

The communication effectiveness of three ad appeals were investigated by Goodwin and Etgar (1980). **Arousal-seeking** was one of several personality variables included as a covariate in the analysis to be able to minimize error variation in the findings. None of the personality variables was found to have a significant influence on the relative effectiveness of the three appeals.

Raju (1980) examined optimum stimulation level and numerous personality, demographic, and consumer-related characteristics. Among the many findings were that **arousal seeking tendency** had (1) significant positive correlations with such consumer behaviors as risk taking, brand switching, and innovativeness; (2) significant negative correlations with age, employment status, rigidity, and intolerance of ambiguity; and (3) no significant correlations with dogmatism and household income.

Steenkamp and Baumgartner (1992) studied the role of optimum stimulation level in exploratory consumer behavior. A weighted composite of the **Arousal-Seeking Tendency** scale and three other well-known measures were used to examine people's desire for stimulation. Beyond the information provided previously regarding reliability and validity, the authors did not discuss the findings of any one scale (findings can be obtained from the authors). The authors did conclude that the **Arousal-Seeking Tendency** scale was one of the best scales in terms of reliability and validity and its relatively short length made it more convenient to use than the other scales.

REFERENCES:

Dawson, Scott, Peter H. Bloch, and Nancy M. Ridgway (1990), ''Shopping Motives, Emotional States, and Retail Outcomes,'' *JR*, 66 (Winter), 408-27.

Goodwin, Stephen and Michael Etgar (1980), ''An Experimental Investigation of Comparative Advertising: Impact of Message Appeal, Information Load, and Utility of Product Class,'' *JMR*, 17 (May), 187-202.

Mehrabian, Albert (1978), ''Characteristic Individual Reactions to Preferred and Unpreferred Environments,'' *Journal of Personality*, 40 (December), 717-31.

———— and James A. Russell (1974), *An Approach to Environmental Psychology*. Cambridge, MA: MIT Press.

Raju, P. S. (1980), ''Optimum Stimulation Level: Its Relationship to Personality, Demographics, and Exploratory Behavior,'' *JCR*, 7 (December), 272-82.

Steenkamp, Jan-Benedict E. M. and Hans Baumgartner (1992), ''The Role of Optimum Stimulation Level in Exploratory Consumer Behavior,'' *JCR*, 19 (December), 434-48.

SCALE ITEMS: AROUSAL-SEEKING TENDENCY*

Please use the following scale to indicate the degree of your agreement or disagreement with each of the following statements.

+4 = very strong agreement
+3 = strong agreement
+2 = moderate agreement
+1 = slight agreement
 0 = neither agreement nor disagreement
−1 = slight disagreement
−2 = moderate disagreement
−3 = strong disagreement
−4 = very strong disagreement

1. Designs or patterns should be bold and exciting.
2. I feel best when I am safe and secure.(r)
3. I would like the job of a foreign correspondent for a newspaper.
4. I don't pay much attention to my surroundings.(r)

The Arousal-Seeking Tendency scale is copyrighted by Dr. Albert Mehrabian. The additional 43 items can be obtained by writing for permission to: Albert Mehrabian, Ph.D., 1130 Alta Mesa Road, Monterey, CA 93940. Telephone: (408) 649-5710. The items here were used with permission.

SCALE NAME: Attitude Toward a Brand of Beer (Comparative)

SCALE DESCRIPTION:

A four-item, five-point summated ratings scale measuring the attitude and intention one has toward a specific brand of beer compared with the one the person drinks most often.

SCALE ORIGIN:

The scale was original to Sirgy and colleagues (1991).

SAMPLES:

The scale was adapted for use with eight different products in study 4 described by Sirgy and colleagues (1991). That study was composed of **83** college students who filled out a questionnaire about beer drinking for extra credit.

RELIABILITY:

Sirgy and colleagues (1991) reported an alpha of **.92** for the scale.

VALIDITY:

Sirgy and colleagues (1991) provided no information regarding the scale's validity.

ADMINISTRATION:

The scale was included by Sirgy and colleagues (1991) as part of a larger survey instrument self-administered by students. The scale followed an exercise in which students were asked to indicate on a list the brand of beer they drank most as well as another brand with which they were familiar. High scores on the scale indicate that respondents like a brand of beer with which they are familiar compared with the one they drink the most, whereas a low score suggests that consumers have a poor attitude toward the brand with which they are simply familiar.

MAJOR FINDINGS:

Four studies were conducted by Sirgy and colleagues (1991) to test the hypothesis that consumer behavior is influenced more by functional congruity than self-congruity. As a test of this hypothesis, it was found that functional congruity more strongly and significantly predicted **brand attitudes** than did self-congruity.

REFERENCE:

Sirgy, M. Joseph, J.S. Johar, A.C. Samli, and C.B. Claiborne (1991), ''Self-Congruity Versus Functional Congruity: Predictors of Consumer Behavior,'' *JAMS*, 19 (Fall), 363-75.

SCALE ITEMS: ATTITUDE TOWARD A BRAND OF BEER (COMPARATIVE)

1. Indicate the extent to which the beer brand you checked appeals to you compared with the beer brand you drink most often.

Does not appeal to me at all	Does not appeal to me much	Neutral	Slightly appeals to me	Appeals to me much
1	2	3	4	5

2. Indicate the extent you like or dislike the beer brand you checked compared with the beer brand you drink most often.

I dislike very much	I dislike somewhat	Neutral	I like somewhat	I like very much
1	2	3	4	5

3. Indicate the extent to which you prefer or do not prefer the beer brand you checked compared with the beer brand you drink most often.

I do not prefer at all	I do not prefer that much	Neutral	I prefer somewhat	I prefer very much
1	2	3	4	5

4. Indicate the extent to which you intend or do not intend to purchase and drink the beer brand you checked.

I do not intend to at all	I do not intend that much	Neutral	I intend to somewhat	I intend to very much
1	2	3	4	5

SCALE NAME: Attitude Toward a Country

SCALE DESCRIPTION:

A nine-item, seven-point Likert-type scale designed to measure a person's attitude toward some specified country.

SCALE ORIGIN:

The scale by Netemeyer, Durvasula, and Lichtenstein (1991) is a nine-item version of the ten-item measure constructed by Parameswaran and Yaprak (1987). The latter drew on even earlier work by Boddewyn (1981) when developing the items. Six versions of the scale were tested by Parameswaran and Yaprak (1987): two languages (English and Turkish) and three countries of origin (West Germany, Japan, and Italy). There was some slight variation in reliability across countries of origin, none between samples (Turkish and American), resulting in a grand mean of .70.

SAMPLES:

Netemeyer, Durvasula, and Lichtenstein (1991) used undergraduate students studying business in four different countries. The sample consisted of **76** subjects from two universities in Japan, **70** subjects from a college in France, **73** subjects from a college in Germany, and **71** subjects from a major state university in the United States.

RELIABILITY:

Netemeyer, Durvasula, and Lichtenstein (1991) found reliabilities ranging from **.71** to **.83** for the scale across countries.

VALIDITY:

Some idea of the scale's discriminant validity can be ascertained because it was used in the assessment of the CETSCALE's (#102) validity. The evidence indicated that the two scales were measuring related though distinct constructs.

ADMINISTRATION:

Netemeyer, Durvasula, and Lichtenstein (1991) administered the scale as part of a larger questionnaire during class time. High scores on the scale suggest that respondents have a strong positive attitude about a specified country, whereas low scores indicate that they hold very bad attitudes.

MAJOR FINDINGS:

The purpose of the study by Netemeyer, Durvasula, and Lichtenstein (1991) was to examine the psychometric properties of the CETSCALE using homogeneous samples from four countries that actively trade with each other. The Attitude Toward a Country scale was employed in the study just to help assess the CETSCALE's discriminant validity as described previously. The two scales were found to have positive and significant correlations for three of the four countries, yet other evidence indicated that they were measuring different constructs.

REFERENCES:

Boddewyn, Jean J. (1981), "Comparative Marketing: The First Twenty—Five Years," *Journal of International Business Studies*, 12 (Spring/Summer), 61-80.

Netemeyer, Richard G. Srinvas Durvasula, and Donald R. Lichtenstein (1991), "A Cross-National Assessment of the Reliability and Validity of the CETSCALE," *JMR*, 28 (August), 320-27.

Parameswaran, Ravi and Attila Yaprak (1987), "A Cross-National Comparison of Consumer Research Measures," *Journal of International Business Studies*, 18 (Spring), 35-49.

SCALE ITEMS: ATTITUDE TOWARD A COUNTRY*

Strongly
agree   ____ : ____ : ____ : ____ : ____ : ____ : ____   Strongly
disagree

      7   6   5   4   3   2   1

1. The people of the _____ are well educated.
2. The people of the _____ emphasize technical/vocational training.
3. The people of the _____ are hard working.
4. The people of the _____ are creative.
5. The people of the _____ are friendly and likable.
6. The technical skills of the _____ work force are high.
7. The _____ actively participates in international affairs.
8. The people of the _____ are motivated to raise living standards.
9. The people of the _____ are proud to achieve high standards.

* The name of the country being studied should be put in the blanks (e.g., U.S.).

SCALE NAME: Attitude Toward Complaining (Personal Norms)

SCALE DESCRIPTION:

A multi-item Likert-type scale measuring a consumer's attitude toward the personal reasons for complaining after a dissatisfying transaction has occurred. Richins (1983) used a four-item, five-point scale whereas Singh (1990) used a five-item, six-point scale. Although the two scales are not exactly the same, they have two items in common and appear to measure the same construct.

SCALE ORIGIN:

The origin of the scale used by Richins (1983) is provided in Richins (1983), which shares the same database. Thirty-one items were generated using depth interviews with 16 consumers and tested using a convenience sample of 43 student and 14 adult consumers. A final group of 15 items was factor analyzed, which resulted in three complaint-related factors, one of which is the four-item scale discussed here.

Singh (1990) modified the Richins version of the scale: Three items were added and two were dropped. Two of the three items added by Singh were slight modifications of items used in the ten-item measure described by Day (1984).

SAMPLES:

The sample used by Richins (1982, 1983) was composed of respondents from one of three groups: 400 questionnaires were mailed to a random sample of residents of a western SMSA, 212 were mailed to members of a consumer protection group residing in the same area, and 198 were sent to people who had in the past year registered a complaint with either the government or a private consumer protection group. After this mailing and a reminder postcard, **356** usable forms were returned for analysis.

Data were collected from four samples by Singh (1988, 1990). Four slightly different survey instruments were used, which varied in the dissatisfying experience referred to. One thousand households were sent a questionnaire for each of the four service categories studied: car repairs, grocery stores, medical care, and banking. Response rates were estimated to be more than 50% for each category given that only around 30% of the random samples had dissatisfying experiences worthy of reporting on a questionnaire. Ultimately, usable data ranged from **116** respondents in the repair service sample to **125** in the medical care sample.

Detailed demographic information for each of the four samples is provided in the article. However, it is difficult to summarize the four profiles given that they varied somewhat, most likely because the instrument itself indicated that the questionnaire was to be completed by the one in the household dealing most with the specified service category. For example, men mostly filled out the questionnaire regarding auto repair (67%), whereas women filled out the one pertaining to grocery shopping (73%).

RELIABILITY:

Alphas of **.62** and **.67** were reported by Richins (1983) and Singh (1990), respectively.

VALIDITY:

Information regarding the unidimensionality of the scale used by Richins (1983) is provided in Richins (1982) as described in the "Origin" section.

Singh (1990) factor analyzed eight items: those five from his version of this scale and the three items from the Societal Benefits version of the scale. A two-factor structure with negligible cross-loadings resulted.

ADMINISTRATION:

The scale was self-administered in mail surveys along with several other measures. Low scores on the scale suggest that respondents perceive complaining to be an acceptable and justified behavior, whereas high scores imply that respondents think it is inappropriate to complain.

MAJOR FINDINGS:

The study by Richins (1983) reports on the construction of consumer assertiveness and aggressiveness scales. Furthermore, the findings indicated that consumers can be divided into four categories depending on the strategies they use to interact with marketers and their representatives: there are consumers high on both traits, some low on both traits, and some low on one trait and high on the other. Those consumers who perceived **complaining to be the most acceptable** were also the most aggressive, whereas those who thought it was **the least appropriate** were low on aggressiveness and assertiveness.

In a detailed study of consumer complaint behavior, Singh (1990) concluded that there were four consumer clusters with distinct response styles: passives, voicers, irates, and activists. Profiles were developed for each cluster. Activists were described as being the group with the most positive **attitude about complaining due to personal norms,** whereas the passives were the least positive.

REFERENCES:

Day, Ralph L. (1984), "Modeling Choices Among Alternative Responses to Dissatisfaction," in *Advances in Consumer Research*, Vol. 11, Tom Kinnear, ed. 496-99.

Richins, Marsha L. (1982), "An Investigation of Consumers' Attitudes Toward Complaining," in *Advances in Consumer Research*, Vol. 9, Andrew Mitchell, ed. Ann Arbor, MI: Association for Consumer Research, 502-6.

_____ (1983), "An Analysis of Consumer Interaction Styles in the Marketplace," *JCR*, 10 (June), 73-82.

Singh, Jagdip (1990), "A Typology of Consumer Dissatisfaction Response Styles," *JR*, 66 (Spring), 57-97.

SCALE ITEMS: ATTITUDE TOWARD COMPLAINING (PERSONAL NORMS)*

Strongly agree	Agree	Neutral	Disagree	Strongly disagree
1—————	—2—————	—3—————	—4—————	—5

1. Most people don't make enough complaints to businesses about unsatisfactory products.
2. I feel a sense of accomplishment when I have managed to get a complaint to a store taken care of satisfactorily.
3. People are bound to end up with unsatisfactory products once in a while, so they shouldn't complain [about them]. (r)
4. It bothers me quite a bit if I don't complain about an unsatisfactory product [when I know I should].
5. It sometimes feels good to get my dissatisfaction and frustration with the product off my chest by complaining.
6. I often complain when I'm dissatisfied with business or products because I feel it is my duty to do so.
7. I don't like people who complain to stores because usually their complaints are unreasonable. (r)

* Richins (1982, 1983) used items 1 and 2 and the long versions of items 3 and 4. Singh (1990) used a six-point scale along with items 5, 6, and 7 and the short versions of items 3 and 4.

SCALE NAME: Attitude Toward Complaining (Societal Benefits)

SCALE DESCRIPTION:

A three-item, six-point Likert-type scale measuring a consumer's attitude toward the social benefits of complaining after a dissatisfying transaction has occurred.

SCALE ORIGIN:

The origin of the items used by Singh (1990) is Richins (1982). Thirty-one items were generated using depth interviews with 16 consumers and tested using a convenience sample of 43 student and 14 adult consumers. A final group of 15 items was factor analyzed, which resulted in three complaint-related factors, one of which is the three-item scale discussed here. The items used by Singh are slightly modified versions of those used by Richins.

SAMPLES:

Data were collected from four samples by Singh (1988, 1990). Four slightly different survey instruments were used, which varied in the dissatisfying experience referred to. One thousand households were sent a questionnaire for each of the four service categories studied: car repairs, grocery stores, medical care, and banking. Response rates were estimated to be more than 50% for each category given that only around 30% of the random samples had dissatisfying experiences worthy of reporting on a questionnaire. Ultimately, usable data ranged from **116** respondents in the repair service sample to **125** in the medical care sample.

Detailed demographic information for each of the four samples is provided in the article. However, it is difficult to summarize the four profiles given that they varied somewhat, most likely because the instrument itself indicated that the questionnaire was to be completed by the one in the household dealing most with the specified service category. For example, men mostly filled out the questionnaire regarding auto repair (67%), whereas women filled out the one pertaining to grocery shopping (73%).

RELIABILITY:

Singh (1990) reported an alpha of **.66**.

VALIDITY:

Singh (1990) factor analyzed eight items: the three items composing this scale and the five items from the Personal Norms version of the scale. A two-factor structure with negligible cross-loadings resulted.

ADMINISTRATION:

The scale was self-administered in mail surveys along with several other measures. High scores on the scale suggest that respondents perceive complaining to be a socially redeeming behavior, whereas low scores imply that respondents think it does society little good to complain.

MAJOR FINDINGS:

In a detailed study of consumer complaint behavior, Singh (1990) concluded that there were four consumer clusters with distinct response styles: passives, voicers, irates, and activists. Profiles were developed for each cluster. Activists were described as being the group with the most positive **attitude about complaining due to it social benefits,** whereas the passives expressed the least positive attitude.

REFERENCES:

Richins, Marsha L. (1982), "An Investigation of Consumers' Attitudes Toward Complaining," in *Advances in Consumer Research*, Vol. 9, Andrew Mitchell, ed. Ann Arbor, MI: Association for Consumer Research, 502-6.

Singh, Jagdip (1990), "A Typology of Consumer Dissatisfaction Response Styles," *JR*, 66 (Spring), 57-97.

SCALE ITEMS: ATTITUDE TOWARD COMPLAINING (SOCIETAL BENEFITS)

Strongly disagree	Moderately disagree	Slightly disagree	Slightly agree	Moderately agree	Strongly agree
1	2	3	4	5	6

1. By making complaints about unsatisfactory products, in the long run the quality of products will improve.
2. By complaining about defective products, I may prevent other consumers from experiencing the same problem.
3. People have a responsibility to tell stores when a product they purchase is defective.

SCALE NAME: Attitude Toward Gambling (Negative Beliefs)

SCALE DESCRIPTION:

A five-item, four-point Likert-like scale measuring a person's agreement about the negative effects of legalized casino gambling in his/her city.

SCALE ORIGIN:

The article by Mascarenhas (1990) indicates that the scale was developed after brainstorming sessions with city officials and other concerned parties in the city where casino gambling was being considered (Detroit). Several pretests also were conducted with adult citizens to finalize the survey form containing the scale.

SAMPLES:

Mascarenhas (1990) collected his data from an established eight-county metropolitan household panel. He indicates that panel membership was rotated regularly and checked for its representativeness of the eight-county area. Of the 1050 panel households contacted by mail, only **569** responses were received and deemed to be complete enough for inclusion in the analysis.

RELIABILITY:

Mascarenhas (1990) reported an alpha of **.85** for the scale.

VALIDITY:

Several pieces of evidence regarding the scale's validity were provided. Among the findings were that an exploratory factor analysis of 16 gambling-related items showed the five items composing this scale loaded highest on the same factor. Also, as predicted, gamblers scored significantly higher on the scale than did nongamblers. (Because of reverse coding, higher scale scores implied less agreement that gambling would have negative effects in the community.)

ADMINISTRATION:

The scale was administered to panel members as part of a larger mail survey questionnaire. Because of reverse coding of all the items, higher scores on the scale suggest that citizens do not believe gambling would have specific negative effects on their community.

MAJOR FINDINGS:

The exploratory study by Mascarenhas (1990) focused on the development of scales to help in ethically assessing such socio-moral phenomena as legalized casino gambling. A 16-item attitude-toward-gambling scale was developed consisting of three subscales: 9 items measuring positive beliefs, 5 items measuring **negative beliefs**, and 2 items related to the distribution of surplus casino profits. In addition to the findings described regarding validity (discussed previously), a measure of gaming behavior (dollars spent on lotteries, racing, football, bingo) did not significantly explain variance in **attitudes about the negative effects of gambling**. This suggests that **negative beliefs** do not directly or substantially affect the daily gaming habits of people.

COMMENTS:

The author chose not to have a midpoint on the scale so that he could force respondents to "take a stand." However, he admits a concern that this could have led to higher nonresponse rates if the lack of a midpoint led to people simply choosing not to answer.

REFERENCE:

Mascarenhas, Oswald A. J. (1990), "An Empirical Methodology for the Ethical Assessment of Marketing Phenomena Such as Casino Gambling," *JAMS*, 18 (Summer), 209-20.

SCALE ITEMS: ATTITUDE TOWARD GAMBLING (NEGATIVE BELIEFS)*

A = I fully (say 100%) believe what this statement affirms.
B = I believe more (say 75%) than disbelieve (say 25%) what this statement affirms.
C = I disbelieve more (say 75%) than believe (say 25%) what this statement affirms.
D = I fully (say 100%) disbelieve what this statement affirms.

1. Casino Gambling will increase unorganized small crime in the metro area. **(r)**
2. Casino Gambling will increase social crimes (prostitution) in the state. **(r)**
3. Casino Gambling will disrupt family life in the metro area. **(r)**
4. Casino Gambling will increase substance abuse in the area. **(r)**
5. Casino Gambling would impact on the metro youth negatively. **(r)**

* As presented in the article, all references to the specific city were eliminated from the items. With slight modification the scale can be made specific for a state, city, county, or other area of interest.

SCALE NAME: Attitude Toward Gambling (Positive Beliefs)

SCALE DESCRIPTION:

A nine-item, four-point Likert-like scale measuring a person's agreement about the positive benefits of legalized casino gambling in his/her city.

SCALE ORIGIN:

The article by Mascarenhas (1990) indicates that the scale was developed after brainstorming sessions with city officials and other concerned parties in the city where casino gambling was being considered (Detroit). Several pretests also were conducted with adult citizens to finalize the survey form containing the scale.

SAMPLES:

Mascarenhas (1990) collected his data from an established eight-county metropolitan household panel. He indicates that panel membership was rotated regularly and checked for its representativeness of the eight-county area. Of the 1050 panel households contacted by mail, only **569** responses were received and deemed to be complete enough for inclusion in the analysis.

RELIABILITY:

Mascarenhas (1990) reported an alpha of **.91** for the scale.

VALIDITY:

Several pieces of evidence regarding the scale's validity were provided. Among the findings were that an exploratory factor analysis of 16 gambling-related items showed the nine items composing this scale loaded highest on the same factor. Also, as predicted, gamblers scored significantly higher on the scale than did nongamblers.

ADMINISTRATION:

The scale was administered to panel members as part of a larger mail survey questionnaire. High scores on the scale suggest that citizens believe that gambling can have specific benefits for their community.

MAJOR FINDINGS:

The exploratory study by Mascarenhas (1990) focused on the development of scales to help in ethically assessing such socio-moral phenomena as legalized casino gambling. A 16-item attitude-toward-gambling scale was developed consisting of three subscales: nine items measuring **positive beliefs**, five items measuring negative beliefs, and two items related to the distribution of surplus casino profits. In addition to the findings described regarding validity (discussed previously), a measure of gaming behavior (dollars spent on lotteries, racing, football, bingo) significantly explained variance in **attitudes about the positive benefits of gambling**.

COMMENTS:

The author chose not to have a midpoint on the scale so that he could force respondents to "take a stand." However, he admits a concern that this could have led to higher nonresponse rates if the lack of a midpoint led to people simply choosing not to answer.

REFERENCE:

Mascarenhas, Oswald A. J. (1990), "An Empirical Methodology for the Ethical Assessment of Marketing Phenomena Such as Casino Gambling," *JAMS*, 18 (Summer), 209-20.

SCALE ITEMS: ATTITUDE TOWARD GAMBLING (POSITIVE BELIEFS)*

A = I fully (say 100%) believe what this statement affirms.
B = I believe more (say 75%) than disbelieve (say 25%) what this statement affirms.
C = I disbelieve more (say 75%) than believe (say 25%) what this statement affirms.
D = I fully (say 100%) disbelieve what this statement affirms.

1. Casino Gambling in my city would develop its entertainment industry much to my liking.
2. Casino Gambling in my city would encourage its residents to stay within the state rather than visit Las Vegas or Atlantic City.
3. Casino Gambling will attract more attendance at our metro sports events.
4. Casino Gambling will create more than 50,000 new jobs for our city residents.
5. Casino Gambling will reduce the number of city households on welfare.
6. Casino Gambling will reduce illegal gambling in my city.
7. Casino Gambling would generate more revenues for inner-city improvements.
8. Casino Gambling will offer year-round jobs for our metro youth.
9. Additional personal income from Casino Gambling can significantly increase church contributions.

* As presented in the article, all references to the specific city were eliminated from the items. With slight modification the scale can be made specific for a state, city, county, or other area of interest.

SCALE NAME: Attitude Toward the Product Endorser

SCALE DESCRIPTION:

> A four-item, seven-point Likert-type scale measuring the extent to which a person believes a party that has evaluated and endorsed a new product is viewed favorably by others. The measure was referred to as "superordinate group influence" by Fisher and Price (1992).

SCALE ORIGIN:

> Although not specifically stated by Fisher and Price (1992), the scale is original (Fisher 1994). Items composing this scale were refined along with items intended to measure four other constructs. No information about this scale in particular were provided. In general, item-to-total correlations had to be more than .50 and items had to load on hypothesized factors. Items that didn't fit these criteria were eliminated before use in the main study.

SAMPLES:

> The convenience sample analyzed by Fisher and Price (1992) was a mixed-gender group of **172** undergraduate students.

RELIABILITY:

> Fisher and Price (1992) reported an alpha of **.86** for the scale.

VALIDITY:

> The validity of the scale was not specifically addressed by Fisher and Price (1992). However, they did state that the variance extracted for the scale was .60, which provides some limited evidence of its unidimensionality.

ADMINISTRATION:

> The scale was administered to subjects along with other measures after they had been exposed to experimental stimuli (Fisher and Price 1992). A high score on the scale suggests that a person strongly believes that others have a positive view of a party that has tested and endorsed a new product.

MAJOR FINDINGS:

> The purpose of the study by Fisher and Price (1992) was to investigate the impact of perceived consumption visibility and superordinate group influence on the development of new product purchase intentions. Superordinate group influence (**attitude toward endorser**) was found to have a significant positive effect on perceived visibility of product usage.

COMMENTS:

As written, the scale indicates that the endorser is a group. However, the items could be easily modified to accommodate an individual endorser by merely replacing the words "group" and "people" with "person."

REFERENCES:

Fisher, Robert J. (1994), personal correspondence.
_____ and Linda L. Price (1992), "An Investigation Into the Social Context of Early Adoption Behavior," *JCR*, 19 (December), 477-86.

SCALE ITEMS: ATTITUDE TOWARD THE PRODUCT ENDORSER*

Strongly disagree ___ : ___ : ___ : ___ : ___ : ___ : ___ Strongly agree

      0   1   2   3   4   5   6

1. The group endorsing the product is admired or respected by others.
2. The people testing the new product are perceived favorably by others.
3. The people evaluating the product are thought of highly by others.
4. The group evaluating the new product has characteristics that others wish they had.

* The items were supplied by Fisher (1994).

SCALE NAME: Attitude Toward Self-Service Stores

SCALE DESCRIPTION:

A three-item, five-point Likert-type scale measuring the degree to which a consumer prefers a personalized shopping experience rather than self-service stores where there is little personal interaction between salespeople and customers. The scale was referred to by Forman and Sriram (1991) as ''Attitude Toward Perceived Depersonalization'' (APD).

SCALE ORIGIN:

The scale is original to the study by Forman and Sriram (1991).

SAMPLES:

A convenience sample of 327 adults in a large, northeastern U.S. metropolitan area was used by Forman and Sriram (1991). Respondents were asked to return questionnaires by mail to ensure anonymity. The median age was 44 years old, and 59% of the sample was female. About 43% of the sample was married and 32% had completed some college.

RELIABILITY:

Forman and Sriram (1991) reported an alpha of .71 for the scale. Item-total correlations ranged from .51 to .67.

VALIDITY:

Forman and Sriram (1991) conducted a factor analysis of the items composing the scale and examined the intercorrelations of several scales used in their study. The findings provided some evidence of the scale's unidimensionality as well as its convergent and discriminant validities.

ADMINISTRATION:

The scale was administered as part of a larger questionnaire apparently through personal interviews (Forman and Sriram 1991). Low scores on the scale indicate that respondents prefer stores that are more self-service oriented, whereas high scores suggest that they do not like stores that depersonalize the shopping experience.

MAJOR FINDINGS:

Forman and Sriram (1991) examined the affect of automated retailing systems on lonely consumers. As expected, nonlonely consumers were found to have better **attitudes towards self-service stores** than were lonely consumers.

REFERENCE:

Forman, Andrew M. and Ven Sriram (1991), ''The Depersonalization of Retailing: Its Impact on the 'Lonely' Consumer,'' *JR*, 67 (Summer), 226-43.

SCALE ITEMS: ATTITUDE TOWARD SELF-SERVICE STORES

Strongly disagree	Disagree	Neutral	Agree	Strongly agree
1——————	—2——————	—3——————	—4——————	—5

1. Self-service stores are more pleasant. **(r)**
2. Self-service stores are foreboding.
3. I prefer dealing with machines rather than people. **(r)**

SCALE NAME: Attitude Toward Store Background Music

SCALE DESCRIPTION:

A three-item, seven-point Likert-type scale measuring a shopper's attitude about the background music played in a store. Although Baker, Levy, and Grewal (1992) described the scale as measuring "the store ambient factor," it is clear from an examination of the items that only the music aspect of the retail atmosphere is assessed.

SCALE ORIGIN:

The scale used by Baker, Levy, and Grewal (1992) was original to their study (Baker 1993).

SAMPLES:

The data analyzed by Baker, Levy, and Grewal (1992) came from an experiment using **147** undergraduate students. The study used a 2 (store ambient levels) × 2 (store social levels) between-subjects factorial design with between 35 and 39 subjects per cell.

RELIABILITY:

Baker, Levy, and Grewal (1992) reported an alpha of **.91** for the scale.

VALIDITY:

Baker, Levy, and Grewal (1992) reported no examination of the scale's validity.

ADMINISTRATION:

The scale was self-administered by subjects as part of a larger questionnaire after exposure to experimental stimuli (Baker, Levy, and Grewal 1992). A high score on the scale indicates that a respondent has a positive opinion about a store's background music, whereas a low score suggests that a respondent considers it to be unpleasant and inappropriate.

MAJOR FINDINGS:

Baker, Levy, and Grewal (1992) examined the effects of two retail atmospheric factors—ambient and social cues—on respondents' pleasure, arousal, and shopping intentions. Measurement of **attitude toward background music** was used only as a check on an experimental treatment and, indeed, the results indicated that the manipulation was perceived as intended.

COMMENTS:

Subjects responded to the scale items after viewing a video of a retail interior. Some slight modification in the wording of items 1 and 2 is necessary if the scale is used with actual shoppers, as noted subsequently.

REFERENCES:

Baker, Julie (1993), personal correspondence.
_____, Michael Levy, and Dhruv Grewal (1992), "An Experimental Approach to Making Retail Store Environmental Decisions," *JR*, 68 (Winter), 445-60.

SCALE ITEMS: ATTITUDE TOWARD STORE BACKGROUND MUSIC*

Strongly ____ : ____ : ____ : ____ : ____ : ____ : ____ Strongly
disagree   1   2   3   4   5   6   7   agree

1. The background music (in the video would) make shopping in this store pleasant.
2. (If I shopped at this store,) the background music (that I heard on the video would bother) bothered me. **(r)**
3. The background music was appropriate.

* If the items were used with actual shoppers then the phrases in parentheses would not be necessary.

SCALE NAME: Attitude Toward the Act

SCALE DESCRIPTION:

A scale that measures the favorableness of a person's attitude toward some specified behavior. The scale has mixed characteristics in that the four items have varying statements as well as different bipolar adjectives in which to respond. The act studied by Maheswaran and Meyers-Levy (1990) was taking a diagnostic blood test.

SCALE ORIGIN:

The article by Maheswaran and Meyers-Levy (1990) did not specify the origin of the scale.

SAMPLES:

The study conducted by Maheswaran and Meyers-Levy (1990) used a sample of **98** undergraduate students who received extra course credit for participating. The data were gathered from small groups of students (five to seven at a time) and then analyzed as a 2 × 2 factorial design.

RELIABILITY:

Maheswaran and Meyers-Levy (1990) reported the scale to have an alpha of .82.

VALIDITY:

Maheswaran and Meyers-Levy (1990) provided no evidence of the scale's validity.

ADMINISTRATION:

The scale was administered by Maheswaran and Meyers-Levy (1990) along with several other measures in an experiment after subjects had read some test material. A high score on the scale indicates that a respondent thinks favorably of some advocated behavior, whereas a low score suggests that he/she considers it to be a bad idea.

MAJOR FINDINGS:

Maheswaran and Meyers-Levy (1990) examined the persuasiveness of different ways to frame a message and the role played by issue involvement. The results indicated that more favorable **attitudes toward the act** were produced in the high-involvement condition when the message was stated negatively. In contrast, more favorable **attitudes toward the act** were produced in the low-involvement condition when the message was stated positively.

REFERENCE:

Maheswaran, Durairja and Joan Meyers-Levy (1990), ''The Influence of Message Framing and Issue Involvement,'' *JMR*, 27 (August), 361-67.

SCALE ITEMS: ATTITUDE TOWARD THE ACT*

Directions: We are interested in your attitudes about the information provided to you and about the _____. For each of the following questions, please indicate how you feel by circling the one number on each of the scales that best represents the way you feel about it.

1. How useful do you feel it would be to take a _____?

not at all useful   ____ : ____ : ____ : ____ : ____ : ____ : ____   extremely useful
     1   2   3   4   5   6   7

2. Would you say your overall opinion about the _____ is:

extremely unfavorable   ____ : ____ : ____ : ____ : ____ : ____ : ____   favorable
     1   2   3   4   5   6   7

3. Would you say the _____ is:

an extremely bad idea   ____ : ____ : ____ : ____ : ____ : ____ : ____   an extremely good idea
     1   2   3   4   5   6   7

4. Would you say that regularly taking the _____ is:

not at all important   ____ : ____ : ____ : ____ : ____ : ____ : ____   very important
     1   2   3   4   5   6   7

* The stimulus of interest should be placed in the blanks.

SCALE NAME: Attitude Toward the Act (Semantic Differential)

SCALE DESCRIPTION:

A semantic differential presumed to measure a person's overall attitude about using some specified item. Sawyer and Howard (1991) used a four-item, eight-point version with reference to a product featured in an ad. Bagozzi, Baumgartner, and Yi (1992) used a three-item, seven-point version with reference to the use of grocery coupons in the coming week.

SCALE ORIGIN:

No information regarding the scale's origin was provided by Sawyer and Howard (1991) or Bagozzi, Baumgartner, and Yi (1992), but it is likely that the scale was developed for use in their individual studies. Either the similarity of the measures is coincidental or the same previous work was being built upon by both parties though not cited.

SAMPLES:

The data for the study by Bagozzi, Baumgartner, and Yi (1992) were collected in two questionnaires, administered a week apart to female staff members of a major university. **One hundred forty-nine** women completed both questionnaires and provided complete information. To encourage subjects to participate in the study, a lottery with several cash prizes was used.

The scale was used in both experiments described by Sawyer and Howard (1991) and samples were taken in each case from the same subject pool. Both were composed of undergraduate college students with the sample sizes being **110** and **142** for experiments one and two, respectively.

RELIABILITY:

The scale was used in both experiments by Sawyer and Howard (1991) and a mean alpha of **.96** for the two uses was reported. A composite reliability of **.86** was calculated for the scale by Bagozzi, Baumgartner, and Yi (1992; Bagozzi 1994).

VALIDITY:

No information about the scale's validity was reported in either study. Bagozzi, Baumgartner, and Yi (1992) did make a general observation that all of their measures had an average variance extracted of more than .50, with the mean being .74.

ADMINISTRATION:

The scale was administered by Bagozzi, Baumgartner, and Yi (1992) in the first questionnaire of two sent by campus mail to staff members of a university. In the Sawyer and Howard (1991) study, the scale was administered along with other questions after subjects were exposed to a product in an ad. High scores on the scale suggest that respondents have a positive attitude toward using a specified item (product, brand, coupon), whereas low scores indicate that they have a bad attitude about it.

MAJOR FINDINGS:

Bagozzi, Baumgartner, and Yi (1992) investigated the role played by decision action control in moderating relationships in the theory of reasoned action. This was studied in the context of coupon usage. It was found that the paths from **attitudes** to intentions to behavior were positive and direct despite one's type of decision action control (state versus action orientation).

Sawyer and Howard (1991) examined the effect of an audience's level of involvement and the open-endedness of an ad on several attitudinal variables such as **attitude toward the act** of using the advertised product. The clear results were that open-ended ads produced significantly more positive **attitudes** than closed-ended ones, but only for the involved subjects.

COMMENTS:

The scale bears some similarity to scales referred to elsewhere in the book as Attitude Toward the Product/Brand because the former's items are among those that have been used to measure the latter. In fact, Sawyer and Howard (1991) sometimes called the variable they measured "brand attitude." However, it is treated here as Attitude Toward the Act because the authors themselves clearly stated that the scale was used to measure "attitude toward using the advertised brand" (p. 471).

REFERENCES:

Bagozzi, Richard P. (1994), personal correspondence.

————, Hans Baumgartner, and Youjae Yi (1992), "State Versus Action Orientation and the Theory of Reasoned Action: An Application to Coupon Usage," *JCR*, 18 (March), 505-18.

Sawyer, Alan G. and Daniel J. Howard (1991), "Effects of Omitting Conclusions in Advertisements to Involved and Uninvolved Audiences," *JMR*, 28 (November), 467-74.

SCALE ITEMS: ATTITUDE TOWARD THE ACT (SEMANTIC DIFFERENTIAL)*

Directions: Please give your overall feelings or impressions toward using _____.

1. bad ___ : ___ : ___ : ___ : ___ : ___ : ___ : ___ good
           1   2   3   4   5   6   7   8

2. unsatisfactory ___ : ___ : ___ : ___ : ___ : ___ : ___ : ___ satisfactory
           1   2   3   4   5   6   7   8

3. unfavorable   ____ : ____ : ____ : ____ : ____ : ____ : ____ : ____ favorable
                 1   2   3   4   5   6   7   8

4. negative   ____ : ____ : ____ : ____ : ____ : ____ : ____ : ____ postitive
                 1   2   3   4   5   6   7   8

5. unpleasant   ____ : ____ : ____ : ____ : ____ : ____ : ____ : ____ pleasant
                 1   2   3   4   5   6   7   8

* Bagozzi, Baumgartner, and Yi (1992) used items 1, 3, and 5, whereas Sawyer and Howard (1991) used items 1-4.

SCALE NAME: Attitude Toward the Act (Semantic Differential)

SCALE DESCRIPTION:

A scale characterized by several bipolar adjectives presumed to measure the subject's overall evaluation of a purchase activity. The various versions of the scale discussed here have between three and five items. They are similar in that they have at least two items in common with every other version, and most share three items in common with at least one other scale usage. Although all users did not describe the number of points on their scales, it is still clear that the majority employed seven-point scales.

SCALE ORIGIN:

Oliver and Bearden cite Ajzen and Fishbein (1980) as the source of their scale. Although none of the other studies were as explicit in describing the origins of their measures, the overlap between their sets of items and those offered in Ajzen and Fishbein (1980, pp. 261, 262, and 267) is too similar to be coincidental. Two of the following items (1 and 4) are also among the set of items recommended by Osgood, Suci, and Tannenbaum (1957) for measuring the evaluative dimension of semantic judgment.

SAMPLES:

The data used by Allen, Machleit, and Kleine (1992) came from a stratified sample of people of diverse experience with blood donation. Nine hundred questionnaires were mailed and **361** usable forms were returned. Given that all respondents had previously donated blood, limited information was known about them and allowed a comparison with nonrespondents. Respondents were a little older, less likely to be male, and more likely to be heavier donors than nonrespondents.

Bagozzi (1982) used **136** students, **7** faculty, and **27** staff members chosen from a variety of places and times at a university. A quota sample was used in that recruitment for each category of respondent was halted once it reached the proportion characteristic of previous blood drives at the university. The sample included both genders.

The sample used by Gardner, Mitchell, and Russo (1985) was composed of **25** male and female volunteers on a university campus, most of whom were students or recent graduates.

Little is known about the sample used by Grossbart, Muehling, and Kangun (1986) beyond that it was composed of **111** undergraduate students randomly assigned to treatment conditions. The groups were described as similar in their product class experience and demographics.

Hastak (1990) used **160** undergraduate student subjects in a four-way ($2 \times 2 \times 2 \times 2$) factorial design. There were 10 subjects per cell.

Mitchell (1986) used **69** students volunteers who were recruited from undergraduate business classes and paid $4 each for their participation. There were either 17 or 18 subjects in each of the four cells of the design.

Mitchell and Olson (1981) used **71** upperclassperson volunteers of both sexes from an introductory marketing course. Subjects were paid for participation in the study. All that is known about the sample used by Muehling (1987) is that it was composed of **133** students randomly assigned to one of six treatment conditions.

The experiment conducted by Netemeyer and Bearden (1992) was based on data from a sample of **372** undergraduate students. They were randomly assigned to a 2 (informational influence) × 2 (normative influence) design. The sample was split approximately in half to test two different models of Behavioral Intention. Therefore, there were four cells per model tested, with each cell having between 46 and 49 subjects.

Oliver and Bearden (1985) used data from **353** members of a bi-state consumer panel that responded to two questionnaires and had received a four-week supply of appetite suppressant capsules between the two questionnaires. Panel members were selected to be representative of urban and suburban households with family incomes greater that $10,000 annually. Subjects were typically white (89%), female (56%), and had at least some education beyond high school (70%).

Raju and Hastak (1983) used **61** undergraduate student volunteers ranging in age from 19 to 23 years. Subjects were assigned randomly to one of three groups and were paid $4 each for participating in the study.

Many samples of varying characteristics were used in the studies reported by Shimp and Sharma (1987), but the one in which the Attitude Toward the Act scale was used had **145** college students, about 60% of whom were male and with a mean age of 21.5 years.

RELIABILITY:

LISREL estimates of scale reliability were **.95** in Bagozzi (1982) and **.86** in Oliver and Bearden (1985). Two models were tested by Netemeyer and Bearden (1992) and the alphas were separately calculated as **.90** and **.89**. The following alphas were reported in the other studies: **.72** (Allen, Machleit, and Kleine 1992); **.97** (Gardner, Mitchell, and Russo 1985); **.95** (Grossbart, Muehling, and Kangun 1986); greater than **.90** (Hastak (1990); **.85** and **.88** (Mitchell 1986); **.85** (Mitchell and Olson 1981); **.90** and **.95** (Muehling 1987); **.87** (Raju and Hastak 1983); and **.92** and **.90** (Shimp and Sharma 1987).

VALIDITY:

Bagozzi (1981, 1982) provided some evidence of convergent validity for his six-item version of the scale. Using the same items as Bagozzi, Allen, and Machleit, Kleine (1992) used LISREL to confirm the scale's unidimensionality. The scale was used by Shimp and Sharma (1987) to provide evidence of their CETSCALE's nomological validity. Beyond that, little or no direct testing of this scale's validity was described clearly in any of the other articles.

ADMINISTRATION:

The following phrases were used in the cited studies to lead into the sets of bipolar adjectives: ''Donating blood for me would be (is) ...'' Bagozzi (1981,

1982); "Taking (this appetite suppressant) is ..." (Oliver and Bearden 1985); "From your perspective, buying foreign-made products is ..." (Shimp and Sharma 1987). The typical scenario for administering the scale was as part of a larger questionnaire filled out by subjects after being exposed to a product in an ad. High scores on the scale suggest that respondents have a positive attitude toward some act such as purchasing a specified product, whereas low scores indicate that they have a bad attitude about it.

MAJOR FINDINGS:

The study by Allen, Machleit, and Kleine (1992) examined whether emotions effect behavior through attitudes or are better viewed as having a separate and distinct impact. Among the many findings was that emotions can have a direct effect on behavior (e.g., donating blood) that is not captured by attitude (e.g., **attitude toward the act**.)

Using LISREL, Bagozzi (1982) found strong evidence that **attitude toward the act** influences behavioral intention but does not directly influence behavior. The results also indicated that the overall expectancy-value judgment directly determines behavioral intentions and **attitude toward the act** but does not directly affect future behavior.

Gardner, Mitchell, and Russo (1985) conceptualized involvement as having two dimensions: intensity (amount of attention) and direction (type of processing strategy). They conducted an experiment that varied the direction component of involvement and noted its effect on **attitude toward the act** of purchasing and using the product. As hypothesized, those in the low-involvement condition retained less correct brand knowledge than those in the high-involvement condition but expressed more positive attitudes toward buying and using the brand.

The relative effectiveness of various comparative and noncomparative ads were examined by Grossbart, Muehling, and Kangun (1986). A confusing array of attitudinal effects were found depending on the type of comparison made in the ads. **Attitude toward the act** of buying the advertised product was examined only as a covariate and was not found to have a significant effect on the findings.

Hastak (1990) reported on some effects of taking thought measurements immediately after ad exposure. The findings indicated that thought measurement could increase correlations between an expectancy-value measure and other post-exposure types of measures such as **attitude toward the act.** The degree of the impact appeared to be affected by the product category and was especially greater for those subjects who were high in message-response involvement. The study by Mitchell (1986) examined the influence of the visual and verbal components of ads on attitudes toward the brand and the ad. It was found that affect-laden ads had a significant effect on both attitudes which was not attributable to product attribute beliefs. This visual manipulation was evaluated as having only a marginal effect on **attitude toward the act** of purchasing and using the product shown in the ad.

In a now classic study, Mitchell and Olson (1981) examined whether product attribute beliefs are the only determinants of brand attitude. Their results suggested that attitude toward the ad has its greatest effect on attitude toward the brand and **attitude toward the act** of purchasing with less of an impact on behavioral intentions. In contrast, **attitude toward the act** was found to be the major influence on behavioral intention, as predicted by Fishbein theory.

Muehling (1987) tested the effect of five different comparative advertising treatment conditions on **attitude toward the acts** of purchasing the sponsor's as well as the competitor's brand. For each type of comparative advertisement tested, the attitude toward the ad had a significant, positive influence on attitude toward purchasing the sponsor's brand, but no significant effect was found on attitude toward purchasing the competitor's brand.

Netemeyer and Bearden (1992) conducted an experiment to compare the causal structure and predictive ability of the models of Behavioral Intentions by Ajzen and Fishbein (1980) and Miniard and Cohen (1983). Some evidence was found that higher perceptions of information source expertise are associated with better **attitudes toward the act,** and this was especially true with the Miniard and Cohen model.

Oliver and Bearden (1985) examined a extension of the crossover path in the Fishbein behavioral intention model. Both **attitude toward the act** and subjective norm were found to have a significant impact on behavioral intentions, the impact of the former being much greater. The authors concluded that a person's attitude toward an act is strengthened the more one believes significant others also support it.

Raju and Hastak (1983) studied the influence of coupons on pretrial cognitive structure. Significant intercorrelations were found among **attitude toward the act** of buying the brand, attitude toward the brand, belief structure, and behavioral intentions. The results indicated that the magnitude of a coupon has a significant impact on behavioral intention but little if any effect on belief structure, attitude toward the brand, and attitude toward buying the brand.

The purpose of the studies described by Shimp and Sharma (1987) were to introduce the concept of consumer ethnocentrism and to validate a scale for its measurement (CETSCALE). As part of the validation process, **attitude toward the act** of buying foreign-made products was found to be negatively related to consumer ethnocentrism.

REFERENCES:

Ajzen, Icek and Martin Fishbein (1980), *Understanding Attitudes and Predicting Social Behavior*. Englewood Cliffs, NJ: Prentice-Hall, Inc.

Allen, Chris T., Karen A. Machleit, and Susan Schultz Kleine (1992), ''A Comparison of Attitudes and Emotions as Predictors of Behavior at Diverse Levels of Behavioral Experience,'' JCR, 18 (March), 493-504.

Bagozzi, Richard P. (1981), ''Attitudes, Intentions, and Behavior: A Test of Some Key Hypotheses,'' *Journal of Personality and Social Psychology*, 41 (4), 607-27.

———— (1982), ''A Field Investigation of Causal Relations Among Cognitions, Affect, Intentions, and Behavior,'' JMR, 19 (November), 562-84.

Gardner, Meryl Paula, Andrew A. Mitchell, and J. Edward Russo (1985),

"Low Involvement Strategies for Processing Advertisements," *JA*, 14 (2), 44-56.

Grossbart, Sanford, Darrel D. Muehling, and Norman Kangun (1986), "Verbal and Visual References to Competition in Comparative Advertising," *JA*, 15 (1), 10-23.

Hastak, Manoj (1990), "Does Retrospective Thought Measurement Influence Subsequent Measures of Cognitive Structure in an Advertising Context?" *JA*, 19 (3), 3-13.

Miniard, Paul W. and Joel B. Cohen (1983), "Modeling Personal and Normative Influences on Behavior," *JCR*, 10 (September), 169-80.

Mitchell, Andrew A. (1986), "The Effect of Verbal and Visual Components of Advertisements on Brand Attitudes and Attitude Toward the Advertisement," *JCR*, 13 (June), 12-24.

_____ and Jerry C. Olson (1981), "Are Product Attribute Beliefs the Only Mediator of Advertising Effects on Brand Attitude?" *JMR*, 18 (August), 318-32.

Muehling, Darrel D. (1987), "Comparative Advertising: The Influence of Attitude-Toward-the-Ad on Brand Evaluation," *JA*, 16 (4), 43-49.

Netemeyer, Richard G. and William O. Bearden (1992), "A Comparative Analysis of Two Models of Behavioral Intention," *JAMS*, 20 (Winter), 49-59.

Oliver, Richard L. and William O. Bearden (1985), "Crossover Effects in the Theory of Reasoned Action: A Moderating Influence Attempt," *JCR*, 12 (December), 324-40.

Osgood, Charles E., George J. Suci, and Percy H. Tannenbaum (1957), *The Measurement of Meaning*. Urbana, IL: University of Illinois Press.

Raju, P. S. and Manoj Hastak (1983), "Pre-Trial Cognitive Effects of Cents-Off Coupons," *JA*, 12 (2), 24-33.

Shimp, Terence A. and Subhash Sharma (1987), "Consumer Ethnocentrism: Construction and Validation of The CETSCALE," *JMR*, 24 (August) 280-89.

SCALE ITEMS: ATTITUDE TOWARD THE ACT (SEMANTIC DIFFERENTIAL)*

1. bad   1———2———3———4———5———6———7 good

2. foolish   1———2———3———4———5———6———7 wise

3. harmful   1———2———3———4———5———6———7 beneficial

4. unpleasant 1———2———3———4———5———6———7 pleasant

5. unsafe   1———2———3———4———5———6———7 safe

6. punishing   1———2———3———4———5———6———7 rewarding

* The items used in particular studies are indicated following with reference to the numbered bi-polar adjectives listed here:

Allen, Machleit, and Kleine (1992): 1, 2, 4, 5, 6
Bagozzi (1982): 1, 2, 4, 5, 6
Gardner, Mitchell, and Russo (1985): 1, 2, 3
Grossbart, Muehling, and Kangun (1986): 1, 2, 3
Hastak (1990): 1, 2, 3, 4
Mitchell (1986): 1, 2, 3
Mitchell and Olson (1981): 1, 2, 3
Muehling (1987): 1, 2, 3
Netemeyer and Bearden (1992): 1, 2, 3
Oliver and Bearden (1985): 1, 2, 4
Raju and Hastak (1983): 1, 2, 3, 4
Shimp and Sharma (1987): 1, 2, 3

SCALE NAME: Attitude Toward the Brand

SCALE DESCRIPTION:

A three-item, five-point Likert-type summated ratings scale measuring a consumer's evaluation of a brand. The scale is appears to capture one's affect toward a brand and does not attempt to assess cognitions related to particular product characteristics. The scale was referred to as a measure of "prior brand evaluation" by Chattopadhyay and Basu (1990).

SCALE ORIGIN:

No information regarding the scale's origin was provided by Chattopadhyay and Basu (1990).

SAMPLES:

Chattopadhyay and Basu (1990) had a sample of **80** subjects. Although it appears that they were college students, that fact is not specified in the article. Cell sizes in the 2 × 2 between-subjects factorial design experiment ranged from 18 to 22. However, when subjects came to the experimental laboratory, they participated in groups of 2 to 5. Subjects were paid for their participation.

RELIABILITY:

Chattopadhyay and Basu (1990) reported an alpha of **.94** for the scale.

VALIDITY:

Chattopadhyay and Basu (1990) reported no information regarding the scale's validity.

ADMINISTRATION:

The scale was administered to subjects in the experiment conducted by Chattopadhyay and Basu (1990) after they were exposed to some information in order to determine if the manipulation of attitudes was successful. High scores on the scale indicate that respondents have more favorable attitudes toward a specified brand, whereas low scores suggest that they have poor attitudes about the brand.

MAJOR FINDINGS:

The purpose of the experiment by Chattopadhyay and Basu (1990) was to examine the relationship between prior brand evaluation and humorous advertising. It was found that when prior **attitude toward the brand** is positive, exposure to a humorous ad yields significantly better ad and brand attitudes and greater purchase intent than when exposed to a nonhumorous ad. In contrast, when prior **attitude toward the brand** is unfavorable, exposure to a humorous ad produced worse brand attitudes than when exposed to a nonhumorous ad.

REFERENCE:

> Chattopadhyay, Amitava and Kunal Basu (1990), ''Humor in Advertising: The Moderating Role of Prior Brand Evaluation,'' *JMR*, 27 (November), 466-76.

SCALE ITEMS: ATTITUDE TOWARD THE BRAND*

strongly
disagree ___ : ___ : ___ : ___ : ___ : ___ : ___ : ___ : ___ strongly agree
       1   2   3   4   5   6   7   8   9

1. I like the _____.
2. I think it is a good _____.
3. I think it is a nice _____.

* Chattopadhyay and Basu (1990) used the word ''pen'' in these sentences. To make the items amenable for use when studying other products, place the generic name of the product category in the blanks.

SCALE NAME: Attitude Toward the Brand (Comparative)

SCALE DESCRIPTION:

A four-item, five-point summated ratings scale measuring the attitude and intention one has toward a focal brand of a product compared with the some referent brand.

SCALE ORIGIN:

The scale is original to Sirgy and colleagues (1991).

SAMPLES:

The scale was adapted for use with eight different products in study 3 described by Sirgy and colleagues (1991). That study was composed of **428** college students who were given the questionnaire and asked to take it home and fill it out for extra credit. Students responded to one product each, and the number of students examining each of the eight products varied from 35 to 70.

RELIABILITY:

Alphas for the eight products ranged from .72 to .98 (Sirgy et al. 1991).

VALIDITY:

Sirgy and colleagues (1991) provided no information regarding the scale's validity.

ADMINISTRATION:

Sirgy and colleagues (1991) included the scale as part of a larger survey instrument self-administered by students outside of class. A high score on the scale indicates that a respondent likes a specified focal brand better than some specified referent brand, whereas a low score suggests that a respondent has a poor attitude toward the specified focal brand.

MAJOR FINDINGS:

Sirgy and colleagues (1991) conducted four studies to test the hypothesis that consumer behavior is influenced more by functional congruity than by self-congruity. As a test of this hypothesis, it was found that functional congruity more strongly and significantly predicted **brand attitudes** than did self-congruity.

REFERENCE:

Sirgy, M. Joseph, J. S. Johar, A. C. Samli, and C. B. Claiborne (1991), ''Self-Congruity Versus Functional Congruity: Predictors of Consumer Behavior,'' *JAMS*, 19 (Fall), 363-75.

SCALE ITEMS: ATTITUDE TOWARD THE BRAND (COMPARATIVE)*

Strongly disagree	Disagree	Neutral	Agree	Strongly agree
1	2	3	4	5

1. I like _____ better than _____.
2. I would use _____ more than I would _____.
3. _____ is my preferred brand over _____.
4. I would be inclined to buy a _____ over _____.

* For each statement, the name of the focal brand should be inserted in the first blank and the name of some referent brand in the second.

SCALE NAME: Attitude Toward the Company

SCALE DESCRIPTION:

> A six-item, seven-point summated ratings scale measuring a person's attitude toward the manufacturer of a product with emphasis on the quality of its image and long-term probability of remaining in business. Boulding and Kirmani (1993) referred to the scale as "warranty bond credibility"; however, it was not evident from the information provided in the article that the scale was inherently related to warranties.

SCALE ORIGIN:

> The origin of the scale was not described by Boulding and Kirmani (1993), but it appears to have been developed for their study.

SAMPLES:

> Little description was provided about the sample used by Boulding and Kirmani (1993) except that it was composed of **150** MBA students. They were randomly assigned to one of eight treatments in a $2 \times 2 \times 2$ between-subjects design, and cell sizes were 18 or 19.

RELIABILITY:

> Boulding and Kirmani (1993) reported an alpha of **.85** for the scale.

VALIDITY:

> Boulding and Kirmani (1993) reported no examination of the scale's validity.

ADMINISTRATION:

> Subjects completed the scale along with other measures after being exposed to experimental stimuli (Boulding and Kirmani 1993). A high score on the scale indicates that a respondent has a good attitude toward a company and believes it will be around for the long run.

MAJOR FINDINGS:

> Boulding and Kirmani (1993) explored consumer perceptions of warranties as quality cues within the framework of economic signaling theory. **Attitude toward the company** was successfully used as a manipulation check: **attitudes** were significantly higher for those in treatments that were told that the company's previous products had been rated average or well above average by *Consumer Reports*.

REFERENCE:

Boulding, William and Amna Kirmani (1993), ''A Consumer-Side Experimental Examination of Signaling Theory: Do Consumers Perceive Warranties as Signals of Quality?'' *JCR*, 20 (June), 111-23.

SCALE ITEMS: ATTITUDE TOWARD THE COMPANY

1. unreputable   ___ : ___ : ___ : ___ : ___ : ___ : ___   reputable
    1   2   3   4   5   6   7

2. financially
    unstable   ___ : ___ : ___ : ___ : ___ : ___ : ___   financially stable
    1   2   3   4   5   6   7

3. untrustworthy   ___ : ___ : ___ : ___ : ___ : ___ : ___   trustworthy
    1   2   3   4   5   6   7

4. fly-by-night   ___ : ___ : ___ : ___ : ___ : ___ : ___   established
    1   2   3   4   5   6   7

5. short-run
    oriented   ___ : ___ : ___ : ___ : ___ : ___ : ___   long-run
    1   2   3   4   5   6   7   oriented

6. How likely is _____ to be in business seven years from now?*

    very unlikely   ___ : ___ : ___ : ___ : ___ : ___ : ___   very likely
    1   2   3   4   5   6   7

* The name of the business goes in the blank.

SCALE NAME: Attitude Toward the Offer

SCALE DESCRIPTION:

A five-item, nine-point summated ratings scale measuring a person's attitude about a certain product offered at a certain price. The scale is composed of four bipolar adjectives and one agree-disagree item, each measured on a nine-point graphic scale. A three-item, seven-point version of the scale has also been used (Biswas and Burton 1993; Lichtenstein, Burton, and Karson 1991).

SCALE ORIGIN:

There is no information to indicate that the scale originated elsewhere than in the study reported in both Burton and Lichtenstein (1988) and Lichtenstein and Bearden (1989).

SAMPLES:

Biswas and Burton (1993) reported on two studies in their article. In the first, data were collected from **392** undergraduate business students. Little more is said about the sample except that there were nearly equal portions of each gender and participants were randomly assigned to one of the 12 treatments. The second sample was composed of **303** nonstudents who were recruited by students in a marketing course. All of those in the sample were 18 years of age or older with a median of 40 years. A little more than half were female (56%), and the median household income was $35,000.

Analyses in Burton and Lichtenstein (1988) and Lichtenstein and Bearden (1989) were based on the same data collected from **278** undergraduate business students. The students were assigned randomly to one of 12 treatment conditions in a 2 × 2 × 3 experimental design. There were between 21 and 28 students per cell.

Lichtenstein, Burton, and Karson (1991) used **830** undergraduate business majors and randomly assigned each of them to one of 31 conditions in a 5 × 6 (plus control group) between-subjects experimental design. There were between 22 and 29 subjects per cell.

RELIABILITY:

Alphas of **.92** and **.95** were reported for the scale as used by Burton and Lichtenstein (1988; Lichtenstein and Bearden 1989) and Lichtenstein, Burton, and Karson (1991), respectively. Biswas and Burton (1993) reported alphas of **.95** and **.94** in their first and second studies, respectively.

VALIDITY:

No specific examination of scale validity was reported in any of the studies. However, in Biswas and Burton (1993) it was mentioned that though **attitude toward the offer** was highly correlated with a measure of the **perceived value**

of the offer, confirmatory factor analysis provided evidence of a two-factor rather than one-factor model.

ADMINISTRATION:

The scale was self-administered by subjects along with several other measures after exposure to experimental stimuli. High scores on the scale imply that respondents hold a positive attitude about some specified deal (price and product), whereas low scores suggest that respondents have unfavorable attitudes about an offer.

MAJOR FINDINGS:

Biswas and Burton (1993) investigated the impact of three different price claims on various perceptions and intentions. Among the many findings was that **attitude toward the offer** was better for larger discount ranges than for smaller.

The study reported by Burton and Lichtenstein (1988; Lichtenstein and Bearden 1989) examined the influence of merchant-supplied reference prices, ad distinctiveness, and ad message consistency on perception of source credibility, value of the deal, and attitude toward the deal. In Burton and Lichtenstein (1988), the findings indicated that both the cognitive and affective components of attitude toward the ad were significant predictors of **attitude toward the offer** beyond that which could be explained by other components examined. Among many other findings reported in Lichtenstein and Bearden (1989), **attitude toward the offer** was better for plausible-high merchant-supplied prices than for implausible-high merchant-supplied prices.

Lichtenstein, Burton, and Karson (1991) studied the way reference price ads are phrased (semantic cues) and consumer's price-related responses. High distinctiveness semantic cues indicate the difference between the advertised price and what is charged by competitors, whereas low consistency cues compare prices charged at other times by the same retailer. Among the many findings was that for implausibly high external reference prices, semantic cues that suggest high distinctiveness produced significantly better **attitudes toward the offer** than low consistency cues.

REFERENCES:

Biswas, Abhijit and Scot Burton (1993), "Consumer Perceptions of Tensile Price Claims in Advertisements: An Assessment of Claim Types Across Different Discount Levels," *JAMS*, 21 (Summer), 217-29.

Burton, Scot and Donald R. Lichtenstein (1988), "The Effect of Ad Claims and Ad Context on Attitude Toward the Advertisement," *JA*, 17 (1), 3-11.

Lichtenstein, Donald R. and William O. Bearden (1989), "Contextual Influences on Perceptions of Merchant-Supplied Reference Prices," *JCR*, 16 (June), 55-66.

_____, Scot Burton, and Eric J. Karson (1991), ''The Effect of Semantic Cues on Consumer Perceptions of Reference Price Ads,'' *JCR*, 18 (December), 380-91.

SCALE ITEMS: ATTITUDE TOWARD THE OFFER*

My attitude toward this deal is:

1. favorable ___ : ___ : ___ : ___ : ___ : ___ : ___ : ___ : ___ unfavorable **(r)**
       1 2 3 4 5 6 7 8 9

2. bad ___ : ___ : ___ : ___ : ___ : ___ : ___ : ___ : ___ good
       1 2 3 4 5 6 7 8 9

3. harmful ___ : ___ : ___ : ___ : ___ : ___ : ___ : ___ : ___ beneficial
       1 2 3 4 5 6 7 8 9

4. attractive ___ : ___ : ___ : ___ : ___ : ___ : ___ : ___ : ___ unattractive **(r)**
       1 2 3 4 5 6 7 8 9

5. poor ___ : ___ : ___ : ___ : ___ : ___ : ___ : ___ : ___ excellent
       1 2 3 4 5 6 7 8 9

6. I like this deal:

strongly disagree ___ : ___ : ___ : ___ : ___ : ___ : ___ : ___ : ___ strongly agree
       1 2 3 4 5 6 7 8 9

* Lichtenstein and Bearden (1989) used all these items except item 5. Biswas and Burton (1993) and Lichtenstein, Burton, and Karson (1991) used items 1, 2, and 5 in a seven-point response format.

SCALE NAME: Attitude Toward the Product/Brand

SCALE DESCRIPTION:

A seven-item, seven-point semantic differential measuring a consumer's evaluation of a product.

SCALE ORIGIN:

The origin of the scale was not described by Maheswaran and Sternthal (1990). However, to the extent that only two of the seven items are known to have been used before in other measures of Attitude Toward the Ad, this version of the measure would appear to be original.

SAMPLES:

Little demographic information was provided about the sample used by Maheswaran and Sternthal (1990). It is known that the sample was composed of 155 graduate business students. They were paid $5 each for their participation and were also eligible for a $100 lottery. Experimental treatments were run with groups of five to eight subjects.

RELIABILITY:

Maheswaran and Sternthal (1990) reported the scale to have an alpha of .81.

VALIDITY:

The validity of the scale was not directly examined by Maheswaran and Sternthal (1990). However, there was evidence of the scale's unidimensionality because a factor analysis showed that all seven items loaded on a single factor.

ADMINISTRATION:

The scale was included as part of a booklet in the study conducted by Maheswaran and Sternthal (1990). The booklet contained a description of the study's apparent purpose, a description of the product, and the dependent variables. Therefore, the scale was administered to subjects after exposure to one of three message stimuli and one of two motivation manipulations. High scores on the scale indicate that respondents view the product as being good if not better than competing brands.

MAJOR FINDINGS:

Maheswaran and Sternthal (1990) used an experiment to examine the effects of knowledge, motivation, and type of message on information processing. The results indicated that one's **product evaluation** depended on several things: whether one was an expert or a novice; whether motivation to process was high or low; and whether the message described only product attributes, only benefits, or both. Among the many findings, for example, was that the attributes-only message produced higher **brand attitudes** when motivation to process was low.

REFERENCE:

Maheswaran, Durairaj and Brian Sternthal (1990), ''The Effects of Knowledge, Motivation, and Type of Message on Ad Processing and Product Judgments,'' *JCR*, 17 (June), 66-73.

SCALE ITEMS: ATTITUDE TOWARD THE PRODUCT/BRAND

bad	___ : ___ : ___ : ___ : ___ : ___ : ___	good
	1 2 3 4 5 6 7	

bad   ___ : ___ : ___ : ___ : ___ : ___ : ___   good
                   1   2   3   4   5   6   7

outmoded   ___ : ___ : ___ : ___ : ___ : ___ : ___   advanced
                   1   2   3   4   5   6   7

inferior   ___ : ___ : ___ : ___ : ___ : ___ : ___   superior
                   1   2   3   4   5   6   7

not as good as
competing brands   ___ : ___ : ___ : ___ : ___ : ___ : ___   as good as competing brands
                   1   2   3   4   5   6   7

not useful   ___ : ___ : ___ : ___ : ___ : ___ : ___   useful
                   1   2   3   4   5   6   7

a product I'll not
try   ___ : ___ : ___ : ___ : ___ : ___ : ___   a product I'll try
                   1   2   3   4   5   6   7

not a good value   ___ : ___ : ___ : ___ : ___ : ___ : ___   a good value
                   1   2   3   4   5   6   7

SCALE NAME: Attitude Toward the Product/Brand (Hedonic)

SCALE DESCRIPTION:

A seven-point semantic differential scale measuring the pleasure-related aspects of a consumer's attitude toward some specific product. Stayman and Batra (1991) used a four-item version in Study 1 and a six-item version in Study 2.

SCALE ORIGIN:

The original development and testing of this scale appears to have been reported first in a working paper by Batra and Ahtola (1988).

SAMPLES:

Stayman and Batra (1991) used the scale in Study 1 on a sample of **79** undergraduate business students at the University of Texas. The experiment took place in a behavioral laboratory, with groups of two to five students who received class credit for volunteering. In Study 2 the scale was administered to **239** undergraduate business students attending the University of Texas and recruited from student organizations. The organizations as well as the students were given $3 each for their participation.

RELIABILITY:

The four- and six-item versions of the scale were reported to have alphas of **.85** and **.96**, respectively (Stayman and Batra 1991).

VALIDITY:

Although not mentioned in Stayman and Batra (1991), a little insight about the scale's validity comes from a footnote in Batra and Stayman (1990); there it is mentioned that confirmatory factor analysis indicated that a ten-item measure of Brand Attitude could be analyzed as two separate factors. One of the factors was composed of the six-item version of the scale described here.

ADMINISTRATION:

The four-item version of the scale was administered to students on a computer along with several other measures in Study 1 of Stayman and Batra (1991) after being exposed to the advertising stimulus. The six-item version of the scale was administered to subjects in Study 2 of Stayman and Batra (1991) after a mood manipulation stimulus had been presented. High scores on the scale indicate that respondents believe that a product is pleasant and good, whereas low scores suggest that they believe a product is bad and disagreeable.

MAJOR FINDINGS:

The general purpose of Stayman and Batra (1991) was to investigate the connection in memory between affect evoked by an ad and brand name. In both studies reported in the article, two ad executions resulted in similar overall brand attitudes, but the affective ad was associated with higher **hedonic attitudes** whereas the argument-based ad had higher utilitarian attitudes. (These differences were not statistically different except for utilitarian attitudes in Study 2.)

COMMENTS:

Stayman and Batra (1991) also used the items in this scale with four utilitarian items to produce an overall measure of brand attitude. Alphas of .90 and .94 were reported for the eight-item (Study 1) and ten-item (Study 2) versions of the scale, respectively. See also Batra and Stayman (1990) for further discussion of the ten item Brand Attitude measure.

REFERENCES:

Batra, Rajeev and Stayman (1990), "The Role of Mood in Advertising Effectiveness," *JCR*, 17 (September), 203-14.

Stayman, Douglas M. and Rajeev Batra (1991), "Encoding and Retrieval of Ad Affect in Memory," *JMR*, 28 (May), 232-39.

SCALE ITEMS: ATTITUDE TOWARD THE PRODUCT/BRAND (HEDONIC)*

bad	___ :	___ :	___ :	___ :	___ :	___ :	___ good
	1	2	3	4	5	6	7
unfavorable	___ :	___ :	___ :	___ :	___ :	___ :	___ favorable
	1	2	3	4	5	6	7
disagreeable	___ :	___ :	___ :	___ :	___ :	___ :	___ agreeable
	1	2	3	4	5	6	7
unpleasant	___ :	___ :	___ :	___ :	___ :	___ :	___ pleasant
	1	2	3	4	5	6	7
negative	___ :	___ :	___ :	___ :	___ :	___ :	___ positive
	1	2	3	4	5	6	7
dislike	___ :	___ :	___ :	___ :	___ :	___ :	___ like
	1	2	3	4	5	6	7

* The last two items listed were used only in Study 2 of Stayman and Batra (1991).

SCALE NAME: Attitude Toward the Product/Brand (Semantic Differential)

SCALE DESCRIPTION:

Scales consisting of various bipolar adjectives presumed to measure the subject's overall evaluation of the product or brand. The various versions of the scale are similar in that they are not specific to any particular product or brand under investigation, although certain adjectives may not be appropriate in some cases.

SCALE ORIGIN:

There is no common origin for these scales and many of them are unique in that the sets of items of which they are composed have been used as a set in just one or two studies. Some items have been used much more than others, but **good/bad** is by far the most commonly used bipolar adjective. Most of the scales have also used **favorable/unfavorable** and/or **pleasant/unpleasant.** At the other extreme, there are several items (e.g., item 22–26) that appear to have been used just once.

SAMPLES:

The main experiment conducted by Anand and Sternthal (1990) had a sample of **109** undergraduate students. The experiment was run with small groups of subjects.

Batra and Ray (1986) used **120** female subjects recruited from Palo Alto, California area. Subjects were randomly assigned to one of ten treatment groups. The sample used by Batra and Stayman (1990) was composed of **251** undergraduate business students attending the University of Texas and recruited from student organizations. The organizations as well as the students were given $3 each for their participation.

Bello, Pitts, and Etzel (1983) used **138** male and **79** female undergraduate student subjects randomly assigned to experimental treatment groups. The sample was considered by the authors as appropriate given that the subjects' age groups represented the largest groups of buyers of the product category under examination (jeans).

Berger and Mitchell (1989) used **52** male and **52** female students randomly assigned by sex to one of four experimental conditions. Subjects were paid $5 each for participation.

Two experiments were discussed in the article by Bone and Ellen (1992). The sample for the first experiment was composed of **127** college students and the second **179**. Both experiments were similar in their collection of data and took place in an audiovisual lab with students randomly assigned to treatments.

Chattopadhyay and Basu (1990) had a sample of **80** subjects. Although it appears that they were college students, that fact is not specified in the article. Subjects were paid for their participation. Chattopadhyay and Nedungadi (1992) obtained usable data from **160** subjects who were students in continuing education courses at a major northeastern U.S. university. Students were paid $15 for participating in two one-hour sessions.

Cox and Cox (1988) used **240** student subjects recruited from MBA classes at a large southwestern university. Most subjects were employed on a full-time basis and attended the MBA program on a part-time basis. The ages of subjects ranged from 21 to 62, with a median age of 26. Forty-five percent of the respondents were female. Cox and Locander (1987) used **240** part-time graduate business student subjects from a large southwestern urban area. Age of the subjects ranged from 21 to 62 years, with a mean of 31, and 55% of the subjects were male. Subjects were assigned randomly to treatment groups.

Darley and Smith (1993) used the mall intercept method of recruiting respondents. The final number of subjects was not directly specified, but it was said that "thirty subjects were randomly assigned to each treatment" of the 3 × 2 factorial design. Given this, it is assumed that analysis was based on data from about 180 subjects. All respondents were 18 years of age or older with only 27% being 45 years of age or older. The sample was split almost evenly on gender (51% male) and marital status (56% married).

Droge (1989) used a total of **178** student subjects, 89 in each of two experimental treatment groups. Edell and Keller (1989) used **243** undergraduate student subjects. Participation in the study was required to fulfill a course requirement.

Gardner, Mitchell, and Russo (1985) used **10** female and **20** male volunteers recruited through direct interrupt on a university campus. Twenty-six of the subjects were either current students or recent graduates, and four were university employees. Gelb and Zinkhan (1986) used **120** employed adult subjects enrolled in graduate or undergraduate business classes on a part-time basis. Ninety-six of the 120 subjects were used in the final analysis.

Gill, Grossbart, and Laczniak (1988) used **109** undergraduate students randomly assigned to one of two treatment groups. Goodstein (1993) collected data in two phases from the respondents. All that was reported about the sample was that it was composed of **302** students who were recruited from undergraduate marketing classes at three major southeastern U.S. universities.

Very little description was provided about the sample used by Gotlieb and Swan (1990). The study was a 2 × 2 × 2 factorial experiment with 126 college students. Fifty-nine percent of the students had visited a lawyer in the last five years. Grossbart, Muehling, and Kangun (1986) used **111** undergraduate student subjects, with approximately 22 subjects per cell in a five cell design.

Hastak and Olson (1989; Hastak 1990) used **160** undergraduate student subjects in a four-way (2 × 2 × 2 × 2) factorial design. There were 10 subjects per cell. Two experiments were reported in the article by Herr, Kardes, and Kim (1991), but the brand attitude scale appears to have been used only in the first one. The sample in the first experiment was **84** undergraduate students randomly assigned to one of four treatments in a 2 × 2 factorial design.

The scale was used in two experiments reported on by Homer (1990). The sample in the first experiment was composed of **268** undergraduate communication students who were randomly assigned to levels of experimental treatments. The second experiment was based on data from **144** business and communication students. In both experiments the students participated voluntarily. Data were gathered by Homer and Kahle (1990) from **234** undergraduate students who volunteered for the study. The sample was composed of both males and females who were assigned randomly to treatment levels.

Iyer (1988) used **200** subjects recruited at a shopping mall, with 25 subjects randomly assigned to each of eight treatments. Subjects ages ranged from 16 to 70 years, with the mean age at 29. Fifty-six percent of the subjects were male, and 40% of the subjects were married. Sixty-one percent had at least a college degree, and average income was slightly under $26,000.

Two experiments were conducted by Kardes and Kalyanaram (1992). Little is known about the samples except that they were composed of students, possibly MBAs. Analyses for both experiments were apparently based on data from **40** subjects drawn independently from the student population at the university.

The study by Keller (1991a) was based on data collected from **103** adults who were either members of a local PTA or employees of a large private university. A majority of the sample was female (89%), half had at least a college degree, and half were older than forty. For their participation subjects either received a small fee and participated in a lottery or a contribution was made to their organization. Subjects were assigned randomly to experimental conditions. Keller (1991b) conducted an experiment using data collected from **145** undergraduate students attending a large west coast U.S. university. Involvement was required for credit in a basic marketing course.

Kelleris, Cox, and Cox (1993) collected data from **231** students in upper-level business classes at an urban university. The sample was 55.6% male, most (80%) of them worked full- or part-time, and their ages ranged from 20 to 40 years.

Data were gathered by Laczniak and Muehling (1993) from **280** students in introductory marketing classes. The experiment took place in an college auditorium and students were randomly assigned to one of 12 treatment conditions.

Loken and Ward (1990) indicate that 115 undergraduate marketing students participated in pretests and 466 completed the measures in the main study. It is not clear, however, what sample size the analyses involving the scale were based on. The authors do say that between 10 and 12 students completed each individual measure.

Machleit, Madden, and Allen (1990) gathered data from students in two sections of a college marketing course. **Eighty** students completed both the pre- and post-exposure questionnaires. Forty-two watched a Pepsi ad, and 38 were exposed to a Levi's ad. Data were gathered in the experiment by MacInnis and Park (1991) from **178** female undergraduates. Subjects received course credit for their participation and were randomly assigned to treatments.

MacKenzie and Lutz (1989) used a sample of **203** student subjects from a major midwestern university. Subject ages ranged from 20 to 25 years, and subjects were balanced for gender. A validation sample was also used, containing **120** student subjects from a major university in southern California. Subject ages in the validation sample ranged from 20 to 32 years, and 60% of the subjects were male.

MacKenzie, Lutz, and Belch (1986) used the scale in two experiments. In the first, **260** people were recruited from two church organizations. They ranged in age from 18 to 75 years, and 69% were female. The subjects in the second experiment were **225** undergraduate and master's-level business students who volunteered for the study. The study by MacKensie and Spreng (1992) used data collected from **360** undergraduate and MBA students. The sample was almost equally split between males and females and ages ranged from 20 to 32 years.

Macklin, Bruvold, and Shea (1985) used **127** subjects recruited from a festival held at a public elementary magnet school in a large midwestern city. Subjects were given free tickets (valued at $1.00) for participating in the study.

Two experiments were reported by McQuarrie and Mick (1992). All that is known about the sample used in the first experiment was that it was composed of **112** undergraduate students. In contrast, the second experiment was composed of a range of age groups but deliberately excluded full-time college students. Usable data were received from **98** subjects. Half of the sample was male and a little more than half (51%) were 35 years of age or younger.

The experiment conducted by Mick (1992) was based on data collected from **161** (53% female) undergraduates attending a large U.S. university. Students received extra credit for their participation and were also eligible for the drawing of a new CD player. The data gathered by Miller and Marks (1992) came from **124** undergraduate marketing students attending a large midwestern U.S. university. Volunteers were compensated for their participation with extra credit points.

The sample used by Miniard, Bhatla, and Rose (1990) was the same as the one described as the first experiment of Miniard and colleagues (1991). It was composed of **170** students in an undergraduate business course at a midwestern U. S. university. The second experiment of Miniard and colleagues (1991) had **62** subjects, equally split between males and females. The subjects were students enrolled in an undergraduate marketing course, and they participated in the study for extra credit. Three experiments were reported by Miniard, Sirdeshmukh, and Innis (1992) with sample sizes of **72**, **151**, and **126** for the first, second, and third experiments, respectively. The samples were similar in that they each included males and females recruited from undergraduate marketing classes. It is not known whether they were all from the same school or if any students were in more than one of the experiments.

Mitchell (1986) used **69** undergraduate student subjects who were each paid $4 for their participation. There were either 17 or 18 subjects in each of the four cells of the design. Mitchell and Olson (1981) used **71** junior and senior undergraduate students of both sexes who were recruited from an introductory marketing course. Subjects were paid for participation in the study reported here.

Mittal (1990) reported on two studies. In the first he collected data from **83** undergraduate students meeting in a large auditorium. Students saw two ads of research interest, one for wine and the other for shampoo. In the second study, data were gathered from 60 more students, but in this case only half saw the wine ad and the other half saw the shampoo ad.

Muehling, Laczniak, and Stoltman (1991) used a sample composed of **105** undergraduate business students. Munch and Swasy (1988) used **249** undergraduate student subjects from a large eastern university. Subjects were paid $3 for their participation in the study.

Complete and usable data were received from **999** members of a national mail panel by Peterson, Wilson, and Brown (1992). Respondents averaged 44 years of age, 64% were married, 53% were female, and 27% were college graduates. Raju and Hastak (1983) used **61** undergraduate student subjects ranging in age from 19 to 23 years. Subjects were randomly assigned to one of three groups, and each subject was compensated $4 for participating in the study.

Raju and Hastak (1983) used **61** undergraduate student subjects ranging in age from 19 to 23 years. Subjects were randomly assigned to one of three groups, and each subject was compensated $4 for participating in the study.

Rossiter and Percy (1980) used **88** adult subjects (44 female) recruited in intercept interviews at a midwestern shopping center. All subjects were consumers of the product used in the study (beer). Sanbonmatsu and Kardes (1988) used **136** undergraduate student subjects (58 male). Participation was voluntary, and subjects were each paid $3. All subjects were screened for health problems prior to the study (which required physical exertion by subjects). Assignment of subjects to the eight treatment groups were made on a random basis.

Data were collected by Singh and Cole (1993) from **138** undergraduate students. Students were assigned randomly to treatment cells, and the order of commercials within cells was randomly assigned as well. Subjects were exposed to the ads in groups of five to seven.

For the experiment conducted by Smith (1993), students were recruited from classes at a major university. Twenty-one subjects were assigned randomly to each of seven treatments. Three subjects guessed the true purpose of the study and were eliminated, leaving a sample of **144** on which to base the analysis. The students were paid $5 for their participation.

Stout and Burda (1989) used a total of **163** male and female undergraduate volunteers from undergraduate communication classes. Subjects were offered extra credit for their participation.

Sujan and Bettman (1989) used **46** undergraduate and graduate business student subjects at a large eastern university. Announcements were made in classes asking for volunteers, with a $100 lottery as an incentive to participate. The sample was divided into two groups, and experimental conditions were conducted on them in two large classrooms. Two studies using the scale were conducted Sujan, Bettman, and Baumgartner (1993). Study 1 and 2 were composed of **72** and **164** junior and senior business students, respectively.

Data were collected by Wansink and Ray (1992) from 239 adults living in the northern California area. Analysis seems to have been based on the **219** who were defined as users of the product. Subjects were recruited through PTA groups, and $6 was donated to the respective organizations for each volunteer. Most of the subjects (80%) were between 30 and 45 years of age, and most were not working outside the home.

The sample employed by Ward, Bitner, and Barnes (1992) was composed of **86** undergraduate students attending a large southwestern U.S. university. In groups of 5 to 11, the students were taken by a researcher to three fast-food restaurants for "taste tests" and later returned to a laboratory environment to respond to a set of questions regarding the interior and exterior environments they encountered. In total, 15 restaurants were used in the study. Students received credit for their participation in the research.

The scale was used in two studies described by Whittler (1991). The first one was administered to **160** white undergraduate students. All that is said about the second sample is that the subjects were 160 white adults from the southeastern United States. This appears to be the same sample as described by Whittler and DiMeo (1991), who indicated that their study was based on data from **160** adults who were compensated for their participation. All of the subjects were white and the mean age was 35.9. The majority were married (82%) and attended college or had obtained college degrees (86%).

Yi (1990a) gathered data from **72** undergraduate students who were recruited from introductory business courses. Little more was said about the subjects except that they were randomly assigned to one of four treatment groups. The article by Yi (1990b) described the scale being used in two experiments. The first had a sample of **40** college students and the second had **120** students recruited from several business classes.

Zinkhan and colleagues (1986) used **420** subjects recruited by an advertising agency, with 21 subjects assigned to each of 20 cells. Each subject participated in three sessions, and subjects were compensated an unspecified amount at the end of the experiment.

RELIABILITY:

Cronbach's alphas were reported to be: **.91** (Anand and Sternthal 1990); **.80** and **.93** for the five-and four-item versions, respectively, by Batra and Ray (1986); **.94** (Batra and Stayman 1990); **.86** (Bello, Pitts, and Etzel 1983); **.94** by Berger and Mitchell (1989) for the entire sample and **.95**, **.89**, **.95**, and **.91** for each experimental condition; **.86** and **.82** in experiments 1 and 2, respectively, by Bone and Ellen (1992); **.93** (Chattopadhyay and Basu 1990); **.87** (Chattopadhyay and Nedungadi 1992); **.94** (Cox and Cox 1988); **.90** (Cox and Locander 1987); **.83** (Darley and Smith 1993); **.942** and **.941** for comparative and noncomparative treatment groups, respectively, in Droge (1989); **.94** (Gardner, Mitchell, and Russo 1985); **.91** (Gelb and Zinkhan 1986); **.95** (Gill, Grossbart, and Laczniak 1988); **.97** and **.98** by Goodstein (1993) for the pre- and post- administrations of the scale in his study; **.93** (Gotlieb and Swan); **.96** and **.97** in two repetitions of the same scale by Grossbart, Muehling, and Kangun (1986); **.90** or better for each of two measures used by Hastak and Olson (1989; Hastak 1990); **.95** (Herr, Kardes, and Kim 1991); **.85** and **.91** were reported by Homer (1990) for use of the scale in experiments 1 and 2, respectively; **.86** (Homer and Kahle 1990); **.698** by Iyer (1988); greater than **.92** and **.94** for the three brands evaluated in experiments 1 and 2, respectively (Kardes and Kalyanaram 1992); **.94** and **.90** by Keller (1991a, 1991b), respectively; **.91** (Kelleris, Cox, and Cox 1993); **.94** (Laczniak and Muehling 1993); **.95** (MacInnis and Park 1991); **.86** (MacKenzie and Lutz 1989); **.92** in both experiments by MacKenzie, Lutz, and Belch (1986); **.85** (MacKensie and Spreng 1992); **.83** (Macklin, Bruvold, and Shea 1985); **.88** and **.92** (McQuarrie and Mick 1992); **.87** (Mick 1992); **.84** (Miller and Marks (1992); **.97** (Miniard, Bhatla, and Rose 1990); **.95** (Miniard et al. 1991); **.89** to **.92** by Mitchell (1986); **.88** (Mitchell and Olson 1981); **.93** (Muehling, Laczniak, and Stoltman 1991); **.89** by Munch and Swasy (1988); **.80** (Peterson, Wilson, and Brown 1992); **.90** (Raju and Hastak 1983); **.86** (Rossiter and Percy 1980); **.98** (Sanbonmatsu and Kardes 1988); **.95** (Singh and Cole 1993); **.97** (Smith 1993); **.75** (Stout and Burda 1989); **.94** (Sujan and Bettman 1989); **.97** and **.98** (Sujan, Bettman, and Baumgartner 1993) for their studies 1 and 2, respectively; **.936** (Wansink and Ray 1992); **.95** (Ward, Bitner, and Barnes 1992); **.91** and **.88** in the two studies described by Whittler (1991); **.88** (Whittler and DiMeo 1991); **.92** and **.90** (Yi 1990a, 1990b); and **.93** (Zinkhan et. al 1986).

The correlation between the two scale items used by Edell and Keller (1989) was .97. Loken and Ward (1990) reported an alpha of **.979** for the scale. This appears to have been averaged across 16 product categories with 15 members each (240).

Machleit, Allen, and Madden (1993) reported alphas of **.96** and **.85** for pre-and post-exposure measures, respectively, regarding Levi's. Likewise, alphas of **.86** and **.96** were reported for pre- and post-measures, respectively, involving Pepsi.

Two measures of brand attitude were used by Miniard, Sirdeshmukh, and Innis (1992) in three experiments; however, only the alphas for the first two experiments were reported. For the measure they referred to as "initial brand attitude," the reliabilities were **.97** in both cases. For the "final brand attitude" measure, the alphas were **.91** for the first experiment and .94 for the second.

In study 1 (n = 83), Mittal (1990) reported construct reliabilities of **.74** for both shampoo and wine. In study 2, alphas of **.81** (n = 30) and **.90** (n = 30) were reported for shampoo and wine, respectively.

VALIDITY:

Little if any evidence of scale validity was provided in the majority of the studies. A few studies conducted some testing, however. The factor analyses reported by Anand and Sternthal (1990) as well as MacInnis and Park (1991) indicated that the sets of items they used were unidimensional.

Batra and Stayman (1990) performed confirmatory factor analysis on their ten-item scale and indicated that there were two factors, one more hedonic and the other more utilitarian. However, because using the two scales separately led to findings not significantly different from those of the combined items, the latter was not discussed any further in the article.

Darley and Smith (1993) conducted several tests to determine if the three multi-item measures they used (**brand attitude**, ad attitude, and ad credibility) were sufficiently representative of their respective latent constructs. Among the findings was that a three-factor model fit the data better than a one-factor model. This provides some evidence of the scale's discriminant validity.

Although not specifically examining the validity of **brand attitude**, Machleit, Allen, and Madden (1993) used confirmatory factor analysis to provide evidence that another somewhat similar measure, brand interest, and **brand attitude** were not measures of the same construct (discriminant validity). Miller and Marks (1992) performed a factor analysis of nine items expected to measure either attitude toward the ad or **attitude toward the brand.** All of the items had loadings of .65 or higher on the expected factors, providing some evidence of each scale's discriminant validity. Munch and Swasy analyzed validity through statistically significant (p < .01) correlations with dependent variable sets, and factor analysis.

ADMINISTRATION:

Respondents typically complete the scale as part of a longer instrument administered in a survey or experimental context. Subjects are asked to evaluate a specific brand or product using some set of bipolar adjectives and marking the scales appropriately. The overwhelming majority of scales employ seven-point response alternatives. Scores on the overall scale can be calculated as the sum or the mean of numeric responses to the individual items. Higher scores indicate a better attitude toward some specified product/brand.

MAJOR FINDINGS:

Anand and Sternthal (1990) examined the ability of the two-factor theory (positive habituation and liking) to explain advertising repetition effects. Three message treatments were varied in their comprehension difficulty ranging from an ad using just a dramatic reading of the message to two other treatments that had varying levels of music and singing. As expected, the varying treatments led to significantly different **brand evaluations** when the messages were repeated three, five, and eight times. Specifically, **brand evaluations** for the easiest message decreased then increased with more exposures; they increased then decreased for the message of moderate difficulty; and they continually increased for the most difficult message.

Batra and Ray (1986) measured both immediate and delayed brand attitudes (one week later). They found that SEVA (surgency, elation, vigor/activation) and social affection are significant predictors of **brand attitude** but that the effect of these two responses drops to a nonsignificant level when attitude toward the ad as well as support and counterarguments are considered.

Batra and Stayman (1990) investigated the influence of mood on **brand attitudes.** Specifically, it was found that when subjects processed an ad in a positive rather than neutral mood, they had more positive **brand attitudes**.

Bello, Pitts, and Etzel (1983) examined the effect and interactions of using ads with controversial sexual content within different types of programs. The findings indicate that **brand attitude** and purchase intention are highly correlated. Although the controversial attitude produced greater interest than the noncontroversial ad, it did not produce a significantly better attitude.

Berger and Mitchell (1989) found the **attitude toward the product** (candy bar) and behavior consistency significantly lower for single ad exposure than for direct product, three or four ad exposure conditions. **Brand attitude** was significantly higher in the four exposure condition than any other condition.

Bone and Ellen (1992) investigated the influence that imagery has on recall, **brand attitudes,** and purchase intentions. Two experiments were conducted, and both showed that imagery-related variables had significant positive impacts on attitude toward the ad but not on **brand attitudes** or purchase intentions.

The purpose of the experiment by Chattopadhyay and Basu (1990) was to examine the relationship between prior **brand evaluation** and humorous advertising. It was found that when prior **brand evaluation** is positive, exposure to a humorous ad yields significantly better ad and **brand attitudes** and greater purchase intent than when exposed to a nonhumorous ad.

The persistence and durability of ad-attitude effects was investigated by Chattopadhyay and Nedungadi (1992). The authors found that, given low attention to an ad and then a delay, those exposed to a more likable ad had lower **brand attitudes** than those originally exposed to a more neutral ad.

Cox and Cox (1988) found that exposures (two exposures versus one) have a positive and statistically significant effect on **brand attitude. Brand attitude** was found to increase with an increase in exposures (from one to two) for both simple and complex ads, even though simple ads did not experience a significant gain in attitude with exposure. Cox and Locander (1987) found that for familiar products, 26% of the variance in **brand attitude** was explained by attitude toward the ad.

The objectivity of claims made in advertising as well as media type (print or radio) were examined by Darley and Smith (1993). Among the findings was that both the degree of claim objectivity and type of media had significant main effects on **brand attitudes** but their interaction did not.

In Droge (1989), structural equation modeling via LISREL was utilized to support the dual mediation hypothesis regarding the causal relationship between attitude toward the ad and **attitude toward the brand** for noncomparative ads (relatively less central processing) and the lack thereof for comparative ads (relatively more central processing). **Attitude toward the brand** was found to be significantly linked with cognitive measures of intention to try and information search intentions. This was true for both the comparative and noncomparative conditions for the former and only for the comparative for the latter.

Edell and Keller (1989) found that there is a significant effect for a media exposure condition (television and radio) on **attitude toward the brand.** Differences in **attitude toward the brand** were attributed to exposure to at least one television advertisement treatment (as compared with exposure to only radio advertisements).

The effect of involvement on processing of ad information was studied by Gardner, Mitchell, and Russo (1985). Those in the low-involvement manipulation had worse memory of brand information but more positive **brand attitudes** than those in the high-involvement group.

Gelb and Zinkhan (1986) found that humor is positively related to **brand attitude. Brand attitude** also was found to have significant correlations with purchase intention probability and choice behavior.

Gill, Grossbart, and Laczniak (1988) found that **brand attitude** had a strong, direct effect on purchase intention. Commitment was found to be negatively associated with **brand attitude.** Ajzen and Fishbein's summation of beliefs and their evaluation aspects were found to be significantly related to **brand attitude**.

The purpose of the study by Goodstein (1993) was to examine the influence of an ad's fit with an ad schema evoked in memory on the intensity of processing. One of the study's many findings was that **brand attitudes** are less positive for those products featured in atypical ads (those that do not fit well within the product type ad schema).

Gotlieb and Swan (1990) investigated the influence of price savings on motivation to process a message. As hypothesized, only when subjects had both product experience and were offered a large price savings did source credibility have a significant impact on **attitude toward the product**.

Grossbart, Muehling, and Kangun (1986) found that comparative ads containing only verbal cues to the competition generated more positive **attitude** toward the sponsor's brand than comparative ads with both visual and verbal references to the competition. Noncomparative ads were found to provoke more positive **brand attitudes** than comparative ads using both verbal and visual cues to the competition.

Hastak and Olson (1989) found that brand cognitive responses displayed significant correlations with **brand attitudes.** Subjects with ad evaluation goals (as opposed to subjects with brand evaluation goals) were found to have weaker correlations between target attribute cognitive responses and an overall expectancy value index of beliefs and attitude toward the brand. With the same database, Hastak (1990) reported on some effects of taking thought measurements immediately after ad exposure. The findings indicated that thought measurement could increase correlations between expectancy-value measures and other post-exposure types of measures such as **brand attitude**. The degree of the impact appeared to be affected by the product category and was especially greater for those subjects who were high in message-response involvement.

The experiments reported by Herr, Kardes, and Kim (1991) examined the influence of word-of-mouth (WOM) communications and product attribute information on product evaluations. They found positive WOM anecdotal information produced higher **brand attitudes** than similar information in printed form.

In two experiments, Homer (1990) used structural equations to compare and test competing models of the mediating role of attitude toward the ad. The Dual Mediation Hypothesis provided the best fit of the four models in both experiments. Specifically, evidence was found to support the notion that ad attitudes have a direct effect on **brand attitudes** as well as an indirect effect through brand cognitions.

Homer and Kahle (1990) studied the interrelationships of source expertise, timing of source identification, and ad involvement. Among the findings was that when involvement was low, **brand attitudes** were significantly higher if expert sources were identified at the end (rather than the beginning) of a message.

Iyer (1988) found that **brand attitude** was influenced by verbal content of a message. Purchase intention, however, was not influenced by verbal content.

Kardes and Kalyanaram (1992) investigated aspects of the "pioneering advantage"—specifically, what impact a brand's order of entry to the market has on consumer learning about products and the consequences of these effects on judgments. The findings indicated that the order of market entry does effect learning, which in turn leads to better positive **attitudes** toward the pioneering **brand**.

Keller (1991a) tested three propositions regarding conditions under which retrieval cues should work. In general, the results indicated that processing goal and retrieval cues influence how cognitive responses are associated with **brand attitudes**. In a similar study, Keller (1991b) examined how competitive advertising and retrieval cues influence memory and **brand judgments**. Interference effects on **brand attitudes** were found for both good and bad target ads when subjects also were exposed to three competing ads but not when they were exposed to just one competing ad.

Kelleris, Cox, and Cox (1993) examined the congruency of meanings communicated by ad copy (verbal) and music (nonverbal). **Brand attitude** was measured but not directly relevant to the study's hypotheses. It was merely noted that the experimental treatments did not produce significant main or interaction affects on **brand attitude**.

Several manipulations of advertising message involvement were tested by Laczniak and Muehling (1993). They were compared for their ability to place people into high- and low-involvement groups. Of the six manipulations evaluated, only one produced results consistent with theory; that is, brand beliefs and attitude toward the ad had significant impacts on **brand attitudes** under high-involvement conditions but only attitude toward the ad affected it under low-involvement conditions.

Loken and Ward (1990) examined the determinants of typicality as well as the relationship between typicality and **attitude** using eight superordinate and eight subordinate product categories. **Attitude** was also found to correlate with typicality for most product categories and was a significant predictor even when several potentially mediating variables were accounted for.

Machleit, Allen, and Madden (1993) proposed and examined a new model of advertising effects that introduced brand interest as a key component of the hierarchy of effects for mature brands. Indeed, the findings indicated that ad-evoked affect affected brand interest but not **brand attitude**.

MacInnis and Park (1991) examined the influence of two dimensions of music on low- and high-involvement ad processing: the music's fit with the ad message and the music's links to past emotion-laden experiences (indexicality). As expected, attitude toward the ad had a strong positive impact on **brand attitude** for both low- and high-involvement subjects.

MacKenzie and Lutz (1989) found that **brand attitude** is strongly influenced by attitude toward the ad and is not influenced by brand perceptions. Ad credibility was unexpectedly found to have a weak influence on **brand attitude.**

MacKenzie, Lutz, and Belch (1986) examined four competing models of attitude toward the ad's role as a mediator of ad influence on **brand attitudes** and purchase intentions. The dual mediation hypothesis was found to be the superior model and provides strong evidence of attitude toward the ad's direct effect on **brand attitude** as well as its indirect effect via brand cognitions.

Among other relationships, the study by MacKensie and Spreng (1992) examined the process through which motivation moderates the influence of **brand attitudes** on purchase intentions. As predicted, motivation was found to strengthen the effect of **brand attitudes** on behavioral intentions.

Macklin, Bruvold, and Shea (1985) found that when the concreteness of verbal messages was held constant, the readability level of advertisements was not found to have a significant effect on **attitude toward the brand.**

The purpose of the two experiments reported by McQuarrie and Mick (1992) was to investigate advertising "resonance," wordplay accompanied by a relevant picture. In both experiments it was found that **brand attitude** was significantly more positive for resonant ads than for nonresonant ads.

The experiment by Mick (1992) studied the levels of subjective comprehension in terms of its effect on various attitudes and memory. It was found that deep comprehension levels had stronger relationships with positive changes in **brand attitude** than more shallow levels did.

Miller and Marks (1992) investigated the impact of sound effects on processing and reactions to advertisements. The findings indicated that ads with imagery-producing sound effects did not produce significantly different **brand attitudes** than those ads without sound effects.

The study by Miniard, Bhatla, and Rose (1990) challenged the typical view of attitude toward the ad as simply being a peripheral cue with little causal impact on **attitude toward the brand** in central route processing. Unique to their study was the decomposition of attitude toward the ad into claim and nonclaim components. Much of the effect of attitude toward the ad on **brand attitude** came through the claim rather than the nonclaim component.

The study reported by Miniard and colleagues (1991) involved two experiments, with the first being the same as that reported by Miniard, Bhatla, and Rose except that some different relationships were explored. Specifically, **attitude toward the brand** was significantly worse in the unfavorable picture condition than in favorable picture condition when involvement was manipulated to be low. In a high-involvement manipulation, **attitude toward the brand** was significantly better when claims were strong than when they were weak. Among the findings in the second experiment was that **attitude toward the brand** was significantly greater with relevant pictures in the ads than with irrelevant pictures.

Using three experiments, Miniard, Sirdeshmukh, and Innis (1992) investigated the effect of peripheral advertising cues on brand choice. Among the many findings was that **attitudes** were significantly more positive for brands that were shown with attractive peripheral cues than with unattractive visuals.

Mitchell (1986) studied **brand attitude** and attitude toward purchasing and using the product. The results indicated that the use of affect-laden photographs in advertisements that also contain copy has an effect on **brand attitudes** when individuals execute a brand processing strategy. Negatively evaluated photographs resulted in less favorable attitudes than positively or neutrally evaluated photographs.

In a classic study, Mitchell and Olson (1981) questioned whether brand beliefs were the only mediators of **attitude toward the brand.** Their results showed that not only were brand beliefs mediating the formation of **brand attitudes** but so was a "new" construct they called attitude toward the ad.

The two studies reported on by Mittal (1990) examined the effect of image-related brand beliefs on **brand attitudes**. For two products and two studies it was shown that image beliefs add substantially to utilitarian beliefs in explaining the variance in **brand attitude**.

Muehling, Laczniak, and Stoltman (1991) examined the moderating effect of ad message involvement (AMI) in the context of **brand attitude** formation. Attitude toward the ad was always found to have a significant impact on **brand attitudes,** but brand cognitions had a significant impact only when a measure of "cognitive structure" was used rather than a measure of "cognitive response."

Munch and Swasy (1988) found a significant effect for argument strength on **attitude toward the product** (message acceptance). For all types of strong arguments, **attitude toward the product** decreased as the frequency of summarizing rhetorical questions in the argument increased.

The primary issue investigated by Peterson, Wilson, and Brown (1992) was the effect advertised claims of customer satisfaction had on consumer attitudes and intentions. The findings indicated that there were no significant differences in **brand attitudes** between those consumers exposed to ads with various claims of customer satisfaction and those exposed to ads with no such claims.

Raju and Hastak (1983) found that **attitude toward the brand** was significantly correlated with attitude toward the act, the summation of beliefs and evaluation, and behavioral intention.

Rossiter and Percy (1980) found that ads with a high visual emphasis and explicit verbal claims produced a significantly greater **product attitude** rating than ads with a low visual emphasis and implicit verbal claims.

Sanbonmatsu and Kardes (1988) found that **brand attitude** was more positively related to strong arguments than weak ones. **Brand attitude** was also found to be significantly greater when celebrity endorsers were used (as opposed to non-celebrity endorsers).

Singh and Cole (1993) evaluated the relative effectiveness of 15-second and 30-second commercials. Among the findings was that length did not appear to make a significant difference in attitude toward the ad, **brand attitude**, or purchase intention.

The purpose of the study by Smith (1993) was to investigate how consumers integrate new brand information from product trial and advertising. The findings indicated that when consumers get product information from both trial and advertising, the ability of cognitive evaluations of the product to mediate **brand attitude** is significantly enhanced in comparison with what happens in ad-only situations.

In Stout and Burda (1989), **brand attitude** was used as a measure of advertising effectiveness for zipped commercials. The results indicated that the speed of the commercial significantly affected **attitude toward the brand.** Viewers in the zip speed conditions had more neutral attitudes than those in normal speed conditions.

Sujan and Bettman (1989) investigated the influence of advertising strongly versus moderately discrepant information on brand positioning, brand perceptions, and category perceptions. Greater correlation was found between focal attribute importance and **brand attitude** in the strong discrepancy condition than in the moderate discrepancy condition.

Sujan, Bettman, and Baumgartner (1993) examined the influence of autobiographical memories on attitudes toward ads and brands. The results indicated that subject's **brand attitudes** are shaped more heavily by affect transfer from memories than by product feature analysis.

Wansink and Ray (1992) compared different measures of attitudes and consumption to determine the one that best predicted later consumption for those consumers who already were using the brand. On the basis of the results, the authors concluded that **brand attitude** was a weak predictor of consumption. Interestingly, it was a better predictor of the average monthly consumption of light users than for heavy users.

The study by Ward, Bitner, and Barnes (1992) focused on the influence of external and internal environmental attributes in evaluating the prototypicality of fast-food restaurants. They found that **attitude** was significantly related to exterior environmental resemblance as well as typicality.

Processing of racial cues in advertising was examined in both Whittler (1991) and Whittler and DiMeo (1991). Among the findings were that **brand attitudes** were better for products advertised with white rather than black actors and for those of high rather than low prejudice.

Yi (1990a) examined how exposure to magazine articles can effect processing of ads in the magazine. **Brand attitude** was directly affected by the cognitive context and indirectly affected by the affective context. Similarly, Yi (1990b) investigated the possibility that prior exposure to certain contextual materials can prime certain product characteristics in ads and thereby influence development of **brand attitudes** and intentions. Indeed, the results indicated that a primed product attribute was more cognitively accessible and resulted in better **brand attitudes**.

Zinkhan and colleagues (1986) found that attitude toward the ad and **attitude toward the brand** are strongly related to aided brand recall and recognition. The authors state that **attitude toward the brand** appears to be largely cognitive in nature.

COMMENTS:

See also Debevec and Iyer (1986), Holmes and Crocker (1987), Kamins and Marks (1987), Prakash (1992), Sheffet (1983), and Smith and Swinyard (1983) for other uses of the scale, which were excluded here due to a lack of critical information. Some variations on the scale can also be found in Batra and Stayman (1990) and Stayman and Batra (1991).

As is obvious from the material presented here, a wide variety of bipolar adjectives have been used over the years to measure **brand attitude.** No one set of items has been declared the optimal scale. Definitive studies of the psychometric quality of alternative versions of the measure are certainly needed. In the meantime, it is clear that some items are much more widely used than others, and one should strongly consider using a set that has been used before rather than generating yet another unique set that may not be easily comparable to previous studies of the construct.

REFERENCES:

Anand, Punam and Brian Sternthal (1990), ''Ease of Message Processing as a Moderator of Repetition Effects in Advertising,'' *JMR*, 27 (August). 345-53.

Batra, Rajeev and Michael L. Ray (1986), ''Affective Responses Mediating Acceptance of Advertising,'' *JCR*, 13 (September) 234-49.

_____ and Stayman (1990), ''The Role of Mood in Advertising Effectiveness,'' *JCR*, 17 (September), 203-14.

Bello, Daniel C., Robert E. Pitts, and Michael J. Etzel (1983), ''The Communication Effects of Controversial Sexual Content in Television Programs and Commercials,'' *JA*, 12 (3) 32-42.

Berger, Ida E. and Andrew A. Mitchell (1989), ''The Effect of Advertising on Attitude Accessibility, Attitude Confidence, and the Attitude-Behavior Relationship,'' *JCR*, 16 (December) 269-79.

Bone, Paula Fitzgerald and Pam Scholder Ellen (1992), ''The Generation and Consequences of Communication-Evoked Imagery,'' *JCR*, 19 (June), 93-104.

Chattopadhyay, Amitava and Kunal Basu (1990), ''Humor in Advertising: The Moderating Role of Prior Brand Evaluation,'' *JMR*, 27 (November), 466-76.

_____ and Prakash Nedungadi (1992), ''Does Attitude Toward the Ad Endure? The Moderating Effects of Attention and Delay,'' *JCR*, 19 (June), 26-33.

Cox, Dena Saliagas and Anthony D. Cox (1988), "What Does Familiarity Breed? Complexity as a Moderator of Repetition Effects in Advertisement Evaluations," *JCR*, 15 (June) 111-16.

_____ and William B. Locander (1987), "Product Novelty: Does It Moderate the Relationship Between Ad Attitudes and Brand Attitudes," *JA*, 16 (3) 39-44.

Darley, William K. and Robert E. Smith (1993), "Advertising Claim Objectivity: Antecedents and Effects," *JM*, 57 (October), 100-113.

Debevec, Kathleen and Easwar Iyer (1986), "The Influence of Spokespersons in Altering a Product's Gender Image: Implications for Advertising Effectiveness," *JA*, 15 (4) 12-20.

Droge, Cornelia (1989), "Shaping the Route to Attitude Change: Central Versus Peripheral Processing Through Comparative Versus Noncomparative Advertising," *JMR*, 26 (May), 193-204.

Edell, Julie and Kevin Lane Keller (1989), "The Information Processing of Coordinated Media Campaigns," *JMR*, 26 (May) 149-63.

Gardner, Meryl Paula, Andrew A. Mitchell, and J. Edward Russo (1985), "Low Involvement Strategies for Processing Advertisements," *JA*, 14 (2), 4-12, 56.

Gelb, Betsy G. and George M. Zinkhan (1986), "Humor and Advertising Effectiveness After Repeated Exposures to a Radio Commercial," *JA*, 15 (2) 15-20.

Gill, James D., Sanford Grossbart, and Russel N. Laczniak (1988), "Influence of Involvement, Commitment, and Familiarity on Brand Beliefs and Attitudes of Viewers Exposed to Alternative Advertising Claim Strategies," *JA*, 17 (2) 33-43.

Goodstein, Ronald C. (1993), "Category-Based Applications and Extensions in Advertising: Motivating More Extensive Ad Processing," *JCR*, 20 (June), 87- 99.

Gotlieb, Jerry B. and John E. Swan (1990), "An Application of the Elaboration Likelihood Model," *JAMS*, 18 (Summer), 221-28.

Grossbart, Sanford, Darrel D. Muehling, and Norman Kangun (1986), "Verbal and Visual References to Competition in Comparative Advertising," *JA*, 15 (1) 10-23.

Hastak, Manoj (1990), "Does Retrospective Thought Measurement Influence Subsequent Measures of Cognitive Structure in an Advertising Context?" *JA*, 19 (3), 3-13.

_____ and Jerry C. Olson (1989), "Assessing the Role of Brand Related Cognitive Responses as Mediators of Communication Effects," *JCR*, 15 (March) 444-56.

Herr, Paul M., Frank R. Kardes, and John Kim (1991), "Effects of Word-of-Mouth and Product Attribute Information on Persuasion: An Accessibility-Diagnosticity Perspective," *JCR*, 17 (March), 454-62.

Holmes, John H. and Kenneth E. Crocker (1987), "Predispositions and the Comparative Effectiveness of Rational, Emotional, and Discrepant Appeals for Both High Involvement and Low Involvement Products," *JAMS*, 15 (Spring) 27-35.

Homer, Pamela M. (1990), "The Mediating Role of Attitude Toward the Ad: Some Additional Evidence," *JMR*, 27 (February), 78-86.

_____ and Lynn R. Kahle (1990), "Source Expertise, Time of Source Identification, and Involvement in Persuasion: An Elaborative Processing Perspective," *JA*, 19 (1), 30-39.

Iyer, Easwar S. (1988), "The Influence of Verbal Content and Relative Newness on the Effectiveness of Comparative Advertising," *JA*, 17 (3) 15-21.

Kamins, Michael A. and Lawrence J. Marks (1987), " Advertising Puffery: The Impact of Using Two-Sided Claims on Product Attitude and Purchase Intention," *JA*, 16 (4) 6-15.

Kardes, Frank R. and Gurumurthy Kalyanaram (1992), "Order-of-Entry Effects on Consumer Memory and Judgment: An Information Integration Perspective," *JMR*, 29 (August), 343-57.

Keller, Kevin Lane (1991a), "Cue Compatibility and Framing in Advertising," *JMR*, 28 (February), 42-57.

_____ (1991b), "Memory and Evaluation Effects in Competitive Advertising Environments," *JCR*, 17 (March), 463-76.

Kelleris, James J., Anthony D. Cox, and Dena Cox (1993), "The Effect of Background Music on Ad Processing: A Contingency Explanation," *JM*, 57 (October), 114-25.

Laczniak, Russell N. and Darrel D. Muehling (1993), "The Relationship Between Experimental Manipulations and Tests of Theory in an Advertising Message Involvement Context," *JA*, 22 (September), 59-74.

Loken, Barbara and James Ward (1990), "Alternative Approaches to Understanding the Determinants of Typicality," *JCR*, 17 (September), 111-26.

Machleit, Karen A., Chris T. Allen, and Thomas J. Madden (1993), "The Mature Brand and Brand Interest: An Alternative Consequence of Ad-Evoked Affect," *JM*, 57 (October), 72-82.

MacInnis, Deborah J. and C. Whan Park (1991), "The Differential Role of Characteristics of Music on High- and Low-Involvement Consumers' Processing of Ads," *JCR*, 18 (September), 161-73.

MacKenzie, Scott B. and Richard J. Lutz (1989), "An Empirical Examination of the Structural Antecedents of Attitude Toward the Ad in an Advertising Pretesting Context," *JM*, 53 (April) 48-65.

_____ , _____ , and George E. Belch (1986), "The Role of Attitude Toward the Ad as a Mediator of Advertising Effectiveness: A Test of Competing Explanations," *JMR*, 23 (May), 130-43.

_____ and Richard A. Spreng (1992), "How Does Motivation Moderate the Impact of Central and Peripheral Processing on Brand Attitudes and Intentions," *JCR*, 18 (March), 519-29.

Macklin, M. Carole, Norman T. Bruvold, and Carole Lynn Shea (1985), "Is It Always as Simple as 'Keep It Simple'?" *JA*, 14 (4), 28-35.

McQuarrie, Edward F. and David Glen Mick (1992), "On Resonance: A Critical Pluralistic Inquiry into Advertising Rhetoric," *JCR*, 19 (September), 180-97.

Mick, David Glen (1992), "Levels of Subjective Comprehension in Advertising Processing and Their Relations to Ad Perceptions, Attitudes, and Memory," *JCR*, 18 (March), 411-24.

Miller, Darryl W. and Lawrence J. Marks (1992), "Mental Imagery and Sound Effects in Radio Commercials," *JA*, 21 (4), 83-93.

Miniard, Paul W., Sunil Bhatla, and Randall L. Rose (1990), "On the Formation and Relationship of Ad and Brand Attitudes: An Experimental and Causal Analysis," *JMR*, 27 (August), 290-303.

———, ———, Kenneth R. Lord, Peter R. Dickson, and H. Rao Unnava (1991), "Picture-Based Persuasion Processes and the Moderating Role of Involvement," *JCR*, 18 (June), 92-107.

———, Deepak Sirdeshmukh, and Daniel E. Innis (1992), "Peripheral Persuasion and Brand Choice," *JCR*, 19 (September), 226-39.

Mitchell, Andrew A. (1986), "The Effect of Verbal and Visual Components of Advertisements on Brand Attitudes and Attitude Toward the Advertisement," *JCR*, 13 (June) 12-24.

——— and Jerry C. Olson (1981), " Are Product Attribute Beliefs the Only Mediator of Advertising Effects on Brand Attitude? " *JMR*, 18 (August), 318-32.

Mittal, Banwari (1990), "The Relative Roles of Brand Beliefs and Attitude Toward the Ad as Mediators of Brand Attitude: A Second Look," *JMR*, 27 (May), 209-19.

Muehling, Darrel D., Russell N. Laczniak, and Jeffrey J. Stoltman (1991), "The Moderating Effects of Ad Message Involvement: A Reassessment," *JA*, 20 (June), 29-38.

Munch, James M. and John L. Swasy (1988), "Rhetorical Question, Summarization Frequency, and Argument Strength Effects on Recall," *JCR*, 15 (June) 69-76.

Peterson, Robert A., William R. Wilson, and Steven P. Brown (1992), "Effects of Advertised Customer Satisfaction Claims on Consumer Attitudes and Purchase Intentions," *JAR*, 32 (March/April), 34-40.

Prakash, Ved (1992), "Sex Roles and Advertising Preferences," *JAR*, 32 (May/June), 43-52.

Raju, P.S. and Manoj Hastak (1983), "Pre-Trial Cognitive Effects of Cents-Off Coupons," *JA*, 12 (2), 24-33.

Rossiter, John R. and Larry Percy (1980), "Attitude Change Through Visual Imagery in Advertising," *JA*, 9 (2) 10-16.

Sanbonmatsu, David and Frank R. Kardes (1988), "The Effects of Physiological Arousal on Information Processing and Persuasion," *JCR*, 15 (December) 379-85.

Sheffet, Mary Jane (1983), "An Experimental Investigation of the Documentation of Advertising Claims," *JA*, 12 (1) 19-29.

Singh, Surendra N. and Catherine Cole (1993), "The Effects of Length, Content, and Repetition on Television Commercial Effectiveness," *JMR*, 30 (February), 91-104.

Smith, Robert E. (1993), "Integrating Information From Advertising and Trial: Processes and Effects on Consumer Response to Product Information," *JMR*, 30 (May), 204-19.

——— and William R. Swinyard (1983), "Attitude-Behavior Consistency: The Impact of Product Trial Versus Advertising," *JMR*, 20 (August) 257-67.

Stayman, Douglas M. and Rajeev Batra (1991), "Encoding and Retrieval of Ad Affect in Memory," *JMR*, 28 (May), 232-39.

Stout, Patricia and Benedicta L. Burda (1989), "Zipped Commercials: Are They Effective?" *JA*, 18, Number 4, 23-32.

Sujan, Mita and James R. Bettman (1989), ''The Effects of Brand Positioning Strategies on Consumers' Brand and Category Perceptions: Some Insights from Schema Research,'' *JMR*, 26 (November) 454-67.

_____, _____, and Hans Baumgartner (1993), ''Influencing Consumer Judgments Using Autobiographical Memories: A Self-Referencing Perspective,'' *JMR*, 30 (November), 422-36.

Wansink, Brian and Michael L. Ray (1992), ''Estimating and Advertisement's Impact on One's Consumption of a Brand,'' *JAR*, 32 (May/June), 9-16.

Ward, James C., Mary Jo Bitner, and John Barnes (1992), ''Measuring the Prototypicality and Meaning of Retail Environments,'' *JR*, 68 (Summer), 194- 220.

Whittler, Tommy E. (1991), ''The Effects of Actors' Race in Commercial Advertising: Review and Extension,'' *JA*, 20 (1), 54-60.

_____ and Joan DiMeo (1991), ''Viewers' Reactions to Racial Cues in Advertising Stimuli,'' *JAR*, 31 (December), 37-46.

Yi, Youjae (1990a), ''Cognitive and Affective Priming Effects of the Context for Print Advertisements,'' *JA*, 19 (2), 40-48.

_____ (1990b), ''The Effects of Contextual Priming in Print Advertisements,'' *JCR*, 17 (September), 215-22.

Zinkhan, George M., William B. Locander, and James H. Leigh (1986), ''Dimensional Relationships of Aided Recall and Recognition,'' *JA*, 15 (1) 38-46.

SCALE ITEMS: ATTITUDE TOWARD THE PRODUCT/BRAND (SEMANTIC DIFFERENTIAL)

Scale items used in specific studies are listed subsequently with an indication the number of response alternatives, if known. Some authors have used scale anchors that have essentially the same meaning but with minor semantic differences, such as ''like/not like'' instead of ''like very much/dislike very much.'' For purposes of parsimony, one version is reported and slight variations are noted with an asterisk. Finally, for ease of reporting, the positive anchors are listed on the left.

Anand and Sternthal (1990): 1, 2, 3, 13, 15; seven-point
Batra and Ray (1986): 1, 3, 16, 18, 19; seven-point
Batra and Ray (1986): 3, 16, 18, 19
Batra and Stayman (1990): 1, 2, 3, 4*, 5, 9, 12, 16, 20, 21
Bello, Pitts, and Etzel (1983): 1*, 4*, 7*, 8*, 10*, 16*, 17*; seven-point
Berger and Mitchell (1989): 1, 2*; seven-point
Bone and Ellen (1992): 1, 7, 9, 16
Chattopadhyay and Basu (1990): 1, 2, 18*; nine-point
Chattopadhyay and Nedungadi (1992): 1, 2, 18*; nine-point
Cox and Cox (1988): 1, 2*, 3; nine-point
Cox and Locander (1987): 1, 2*, 3; nine-point
Darley and Smith (1993): 1, 4, 11*
Droge (1989): 1, 3, 5, 6*, 7, 8; seven-point
Edell and Keller (1989): 1*, 2*; seven-point
Gardner, Mitchell, and Russo (1985): 1, 2*, 4

Gelb and Zinkhan (1986): 1, 6*, 9
Gill, Grossbart, and Laczniak (1988): 1*, 2*, 9*, 21*; seven-point
Goodstein (1993): 1, 9, 11; seven-point
Gotlieb and Swan (1990): 1, 6*, 9
Grossbart, Muehling, and Kangun (1986): 1, 9, 12; seven-point
Hastak and Olson (1989; Hastak 1990): 1, 2, 4 seven-point
Herr, Kardes, and Kim (1991): 1, 9, 17; 11-point
Homer (1990): 1, 2, 9; nine-point
Homer and Kahle (1990): 1, 6*, 17
Iyer (1988): 1, 8, 16; seven-point
Kardes and Kalyanaram (1992): 1*, 6, 9*; 11-point
Keller (1991a): 1, 3, 4, 5, 8, 11, 16, 18, 19; seven-point
Keller (1991b): 1, 3, 4, 11; seven-point
Kelleris, Cox, and Cox (1993): 1, 2, 11*, 28*, 29; seven-point
Laczniak and Muehling (1993): 1*, 2*, 4, 9*, 21; seven-point
Loken and Ward (1990): 1, 4, 6*; 11-point

Machleit, Allen, and Madden (1993): 1, 7*, 17; seven-point
MacInnis and Park (1991): 1*, 9, 11*, 30; seven-point
MacKenzie and Lutz (1989): 1, 3, 9; seven-point
MacKenzie, Lutz, and Belch (1986): 1, 7, 9; seven-point
MacKenzie and Spreng (1992): 1, 3, 9; seven-point
Macklin, Bruvold, and Shea (1985): 1, 3, 18, 21, 27, 28; seven-point
McQuarrie and Mick (1992): 1*, 4*, 21; seven-point
Mick (1992): 1, 3, 21; nine-point
Miller and Marks (1992): 1, 2*, 3, 4, 25; seven-point
Miniard, Bhatla, and Rose (1990): 2, 9, 12; seven-point
Miniard et al. (1991): 2*, 9, 12; seven-point
Miniard, Sirdeshmukh, and Innis (1992) initial measure: 9, 12, 30; 11-point
Miniard, Sirdeshmukh, and Innis (1992) final measure: 1, 14, 17; seven-point
Mitchell (1986): 1, 2, 3; seven-point
Mitchell and Olson (1981): 1, 2*, 3, 4; five-point
Mittal (1990): 1, 2, 17; seven-point
Muehling, Laczniak, and Stoltman (1991): 1, 9, 12; seven-point
Munch and Swasy (1988): 1, 3, 12; seven-point

Peterson, Wilson, and Brown (1992): 4, 16*, 17*, 23, 24
Raju and Hastak (1983): 1, 2*, 4; seven-point
Rossiter and Percy (1980): 1, 3, 27, 28; seven-point
Sanbonmatsu and Kardes (1988): 1, 6, 9; nine-point
Singh and Cole (1993): 2*, 8*, 15, 16, 19, 21, 26; seven-point
Smith (1993): 1, 3, 9
Smith and Swinyard (1983): 1, 3, 5, 6; seven-point
Stout and Burda (1989): 2, 9; seven-point
Sujan and Bettman (1989): 1, 9, 12; seven-point
Sujan, Bettman, and Baumgartner (1993): 1, 3, 9, 12; nine-point
Wansink and Ray (1992): 1*, 4*, 11, 22; seven-point
Ward, Bitner, and Barnes (1992): 1, 4, 6*; 11-point
Whittler and DiMeo (1991): 1, 4*, 6*; 15-point

Whittler (1991): 1, 4*, 6*; 15-point
Yi (1990a): 1, 2, 3; seven-point
Yi (1990b): 1, 2, 9; seven-point
Zinkhan, Locander, and Leigh (1986): 1, 3, 21; eight-point

1. good / bad
2. like / dislike
3. pleasant / unpleasant
4. high quality / poor quality
5. agreeable / disagreeable
6. satisfactory / dissatisfactory
7. wise / foolish
8. beneficial / harmful
9. favorable / unfavorable
10. distinctive / common
11. likable / dislikable
12. positive / negative
13. buy / would not buy
14. attractive / unattractive
15. enjoyable / unenjoyable
16. useful / useless
17. desirable / undesirable
18. nice / awful
19. important / unimportant
20. beneficial / not beneficial
21. valuable / worthless
22. appetizing / unappetizing
23. unique / not unique
24. expensive / inexpensive
25. needed / not needed
26. fond of / not fond of
27. superior / inferior
28. interesting / boring
29. tasteful / tasteless
30. appealing / unappealing

SCALE NAME: Attitude Toward the Product/Brand (Utilitarian)

SCALE DESCRIPTION:

A four-item, seven-point semantic differential scale measuring the value-related aspects of a consumer's attitude toward some specific product.

SCALE ORIGIN:

The original development and testing of this scale appears to have been reported in a working paper by Batra and Ahtola (1988).

SAMPLES:

The scale was used in Study 1 by Stayman and Batra (1991) on a sample of **79** undergraduate business students at the University of Texas. The experiment took place in a behavioral laboratory with groups of two to five students who received class credit for volunteering. The scale used in Study 2 was composed of **239** undergraduate business students attending the University of Texas and recruited from student organizations. The organizations as well as the students were given $3 a piece for their participation.

RELIABILITY:

The scale was reported to have alphas of **.85** and **.87** for Studies 1 and 2, respectively (Stayman and Batra 1991).

VALIDITY:

Although not mentioned in Stayman and Batra (1991), a little insight about the scale's validity comes a footnote in Batra and Stayman (1990), where it is mentioned that confirmatory factor analysis indicated that a ten-item measure of Brand Attitude could be analyzed as two separate factors. One of the factors was composed of the four-item version of the scale described here.

ADMINISTRATION:

The scale was administered to students on a computer along with several other measures in Study 1 of Stayman and Batra (1991) after being exposed to the advertising stimulus. In Study 2, the scale was administered to subjects after a mood manipulation stimulus had been presented. High scores on the scale indicate that respondents believe that a product is useful and valuable, whereas low scores suggest that they believe a product is worthless and of low quality.

MAJOR FINDINGS:

The general purpose of Stayman and Batra (1991) was to investigate the connection in memory between affect evoked by an ad and brand name. In both studies reported in the article, two ad executions resulted in similar overall brand attitudes, but the affective ad was associated with higher hedonic attitudes whereas the argument-based ad had higher **utilitarian attitudes**. (These differences were not statistically different except for **utilitarian attitudes** in Study 2.)

COMMENTS:

Stayman and Batra (1991) also used the items in this scale with some hedonic items to produce an overall measure of brand attitude. Alphas of .90 and .94 were reported for the eight-item (Study 1) and ten-item (Study 2) versions of the scale, respectively. See also Batra and Stayman (1990) for further discussion of the ten-item Brand Attitude measure.

REFERENCES:

Batra, Rajeev and Olli T. Ahtola (1988), "Hedonic and Utilitarian Antecedents of Consumer Attitudes," working paper, Columbia University.

_____ and Stayman (1990), "The Role of Mood in Advertising Effectiveness," *JCR*, 17 (September), 203-14.

Stayman, Douglas M. and Rajeev Batra (1991), "Encoding and Retrieval of Ad Affect in Memory," *JMR*, 28 (May), 232-39.

SCALE ITEMS: ATTITUDE TOWARD THE PRODUCT/BRAND (UTILITARIAN)

Useless   ___ : ___ : ___ : ___ : ___ : ___ : ___   Useful
                1   2   3   4   5   6   7

Not beneficial   ___ : ___ : ___ : ___ : ___ : ___ : ___   Beneficial
                1   2   3   4   5   6   7

Low quality   ___ : ___ : ___ : ___ : ___ : ___ : ___   High quality
                1   2   3   4   5   6   7

Worthless   ___ : ___ : ___ : ___ : ___ : ___ : ___   Valuable
                1   2   3   4   5   6   7

SCALE NAME: Attitude Toward the Product Idea

SCALE DESCRIPTION:

A four-item, eight-point summated rating scale measuring a consumer's attitude toward some new product concept.

SCALE ORIGIN:

The scale is original to Ratneshwar and Chaiken (1991).

SAMPLES:

The scale was used in two experiments reported by Ratneshwar and Chaiken (1991). Complete and useable information for the first experiment came from **105** male and female undergraduate college students. They were assigned randomly to small groups in a 2 (source expertise) × 2 (comprehensibility) between-subjects design. Similarly, the subjects for the second experiment were **125** college students.

RELIABILITY:

The alpha was reported to be **.90** in both uses of the scale (Ratneshwar and Chaiken 1991).

VALIDITY:

Ratneshwar and Chaiken (1991) reported no direct examination of the scale's validity.

ADMINISTRATION:

The scale was self-administered by subjects after they were exposed to the experimental stimuli (Ratneshwar and Chaiken 1991). A high score on the scale indicates that someone has a very positive attitude toward a new product idea and would strongly consider buying it when it is available.

MAJOR FINDINGS:

Ratneshwar and Chaiken (1991) examined the roles of message comprehension and source expertise on persuasion. Findings among the two experiments led the authors to conclude that subjects who received information difficult to comprehend expressed more favorable **new product attitudes** when the source of the information was perceived to be an expert than when it was attributed to a novice.

REFERENCE:

Ratneshwar, S. and Shelly Chaiken (1991), "Comprehension's Role in Persuasion: The Case of Its Moderating Effect on the Persuasive Impact of Source Cues," *JCR*, 18 (June), 52-62.

SCALE ITEMS: ATTITUDE TOWARD THE PRODUCT IDEA

Directions: You just read the description of a new product idea. We would like you to answer a few questions that ask for your opinions about this invention. In each case please circle the number on the scale that best represents the way you feel about the product.

1. If this product were to be manufactured and made available in the market at a reasonable price, would you say that it is likely that:

You would definately not consider buying it ___ : ___ : ___ : ___ : ___ : ___ : ___ : ___ : ___ You would definately consider buying it
$-4 \quad -3 \quad -2 \quad -1 \quad 0 \quad +1 \quad +2 \quad +3 \quad +4$

2. Do you feel that the product is:

Not at all useful ___ : ___ : ___ : ___ : ___ : ___ : ___ : ___ : ___ Very useful
$-4 \quad -3 \quad -2 \quad -1 \quad 0 \quad +1 \quad +2 \quad +3 \quad +4$

3. Would you say that your overall opinion of the product is:

Very unfavorable ___ : ___ : ___ : ___ : ___ : ___ : ___ : ___ : ___ Very favorable
$-4 \quad -3 \quad -2 \quad -1 \quad 0 \quad +1 \quad +2 \quad +3 \quad +4$

4. Would you say that the product is:

Very bad ___ : ___ : ___ : ___ : ___ : ___ : ___ : ___ : ___ Very good
$-4 \quad -3 \quad -2 \quad -1 \quad 0 \quad +1 \quad +2 \quad +3 \quad +4$

SCALE NAME: Attitude Toward Trying to Lose Weight

SCALE DESCRIPTION:

A four-item, seven-point semantic differential measuring how a person feels about attempting to lose weight during the upcoming week.

SCALE ORIGIN:

Although not specifically stated so, the scale would appear to be original to the work by Bagozzi and Warshaw (1990).

SAMPLES:

Data in the study by Bagozzi and Warshaw (1990) were collected from undergraduate business students at two Canadian universities. Survey forms were filled out on three separate occasions, one week apart, with 240 complete sets being obtained. Participation was required as part of the course requirements.

RELIABILITY:

Bagozzi and Warshaw (1990; Bagozzi 1994) calculated an alpha of .89 for the scale.

VALIDITY:

Bagozzi and Warshaw (1990) reported that the scale had correlations greater than .50 with two other weight loss-related scales. Strangely, these correlations were offered as evidence of discriminant validity rather than convergent validity. As further evidence of discriminant validity, the scale was not significantly correlated with the social desirability scale (Crowne and Marlowe 1960), indicating that respondents were not just answering in socially acceptable ways. Specific evidence regarding convergent validity was not detailed in the article, but the scale was among others generally described as having been based on analysis of a MTMM using structural equations models.

ADMINISTRATION:

The scale was administered by Bagozzi and Warshaw (1990) along with several other measures on two occasions, a week apart. It is not clear whether students completed the questionnaires in class or were allowed to do them outside of class. A low score on the scale indicates that making an effort to lose weight during the upcoming week would make a person feel good, and a high score suggests that anticipating such an experience would not be pleasant.

MAJOR FINDINGS:

The study by Bagozzi and Warshaw (1990) examined the pursuit of goals, planned behavior, and the role of "trying" in the context of weight-loss planning. Models based on the theories of goal pursuit and planned behavior explained significant amounts of variance in **attitude toward trying** but the explanatory power was even stronger when past trying variables were included.

REFERENCES:

Bagozzi, Richard P. (1994), personal correspondence.

_____ and Paul R. Warshaw (1990), ''Trying to Consume,'' *JCR*, 17 (September), 127-40.

Crowne, Douglas P. and David Marlowe (1960), ''A New Scale of Social Desirability Independent of Psychopathology,'' *Journal of Consulting Psychology*, 24 (August), 349-54.

SCALE ITEMS: ATTITUDE TOWARD TRYING TO LOSE WEIGHT

All things considered, my trying to lose weight during the next week would make me feel . . .

pleasant	____ : ____ : ____ : ____ : ____ : ____ : ____	unpleasant
	1 2 3 4 5 6 7	
good	____ : ____ : ____ : ____ : ____ : ____ : ____	bad
	1 2 3 4 5 6 7	
enjoyable	____ : ____ : ____ : ____ : ____ : ____ : ____	disgusting
	1 2 3 4 5 6 7	
satisfying	____ : ____ : ____ : ____ : ____ : ____ : ____	unsatisfying
	1 2 3 4 5 6 7	

SCALE NAME: Autonomy (Female)

SCALE DESCRIPTION:

A ten-item, seven-point Likert-type scale measuring the degree to which a person professes support for the freedom of women from subordinate and traditional roles.

SCALE ORIGIN:

The scale was constructed and tested by Arnott (1972), who apparently took many of the items from a much earlier work by Kirkpatrick (1936). The content validity of the items was judged by a group of sociology doctoral students. Criterion validity was checked using the "known groups" technique and items discriminating the two groups least clearly were eliminated. The six-week stability (test-retest) of the scale was estimated to be .78 using a sample of 15 sociology students.

SAMPLES:

Three mutually exclusive samples were drawn by Ford and LaTour (1993). **Ninety-four** usable questionnaires were received from members of the League of Women Voters; **130** usable responses were received from members of the National Organization of Women; and **150** completed surveys were obtained from a random sample of adult women. The authors provided demographic profiles of each of these samples and concluded that they generally fit the groups they were supposed to represent.

RELIABILITY:

Ford and LaTour (1993) reported an alpha of **.8731** for the scale.

VALIDITY:

The validity of the scale was not directly addressed by Ford and LaTour (1993). However, the three groups had predictably different scores on the scale such that those who were expected to be the most "radical" (members of NOW) had the highest score on the scale whereas those from the random sample had the lowest mean score. This provides some evidence of the scale's criterion (predictive) validity.

ADMINISTRATION:

The scale was self-administered by respondents as part of a larger survey instrument (Ford and LaTour 1993). A higher score on the scale indicates that a person believes women should have a great deal of autonomy in the way they live their lives and not be dependent on men and traditional roles.

MAJOR FINDINGS:

Ford and LaTour (1993) studied how women from different interest groups viewed portrayals of females in advertising. A significant positive association was found between attitude about **female autonomy** and the level of advertising criticism.

COMMENTS:

See also Green and Cunningham (1975) as well as Venkatesh (1980) for previous uses of the scale in consumer research. The latter reports an alpha for the scale of .75.

REFERENCES:

Arnott, Catherine C. (1972), ''Husbands' Attitude and Wives' Commitment to Employment,'' *Journal of Marriage and the Family*, 34 (November), 673-81.

Ford, John B. and Michael S. LaTour (1993), ''Differing Reactions to Female Role Portrayals in Advertising,'' *JAR*, 33 (5), 43-52.

Green, Robert T. and Isabella C.M. Cunningham (1975), ''Feminine Role Perceptions and Family Purchasing Decisions,'' *JMR*, 12 (August), 325-32.

Kirkpatrick, Clifford (1936), ''The Construction of a Belief-Pattern Scale for Measuring Attitudes Toward Feminism,'' *Journal of Social Psychology*, 7, 421-37.

Venkatesh, Alladi (1980), ''Changing Roles of Women: A Lifestyle Analysis,'' *JCR*, 7 (September), 189-97.

SCALE ITEMS: AUTONOMY (FEMALE)

strongly disagree	___ : ___ : ___ : ___ : ___ : ___ : ___	strongly agree
	1 2 3 4 5 6 7	

1. The word ''obey'' should be removed from the marriage service.
2. Girls should be trained to be homemakers and boys for an occupation suited to their talents. **(r)**
3. The initiative in courtship should come from men. **(r)**
4. A woman should expect just as much freedom of action as a man.
5. Women should subordinate their career to home duties to a greater extent than men. **(r)**
6. Motherhood is the ideal ''career'' for most women. **(r)**
7. Within their marriage, women should be free to withhold or initiate sex intimacy as they choose.
8. The husband should be regarded as the legal representative of the family group in matters of law. **(r)**
9. The decision whether to seek an abortion should rest with the wife.
10. Her sex should not disqualify a woman from any occupation.

SCALE NAME: Behavioral Intention

SCALE DESCRIPTION:

A multi-point semantic differential measuring the stated inclination of a person to engage in a specified behavior. In most of the studies described subsequently, the behavior was a purchase, but the items are general enough to refer to nonpurchase behaviors as well (e.g., likelihood of shopping at a store, paying attention to an ad, using a coupon). One version of the scale used by Machleit, Allen, and Madden (1993) (referred to as *contact intention*) measured the motivation to try the brand if in the market for the product. The various versions of the scale differ in the number and set of items employed. However, the uses were similar in that they had at least two items in common (see the ''Scale Items'' section).

SCALE ORIGIN:

No specific information was provided in any of the studies about the origin of the particular sets of items they used. Because it is unlikely that they would have arrived independently at such similar sets of items, instead they must have built on some unspecified source and from each other. The books by Fishbein (Ajzen and Fishbein 1980; Fishbein and Ajzen 1975) are possible sources, although only item 1 figures prominently in those books as a way to measure **Behavioral Intention.**

SAMPLES:

Chattopadhyay and Basu (1990) had a sample of **80** subjects. Although it appears that they were college students, that fact is not specified in the article. Cell sizes in the 2 × 2 between-subjects factorial design experiment ranged from 18 to 22. However, when subjects came to the experimental laboratory, they participated in groups of 2 to 5. Subjects were paid for their participation.

The sample used by Gill, Grossbart, and Laczniak (1988) was described only as being **109** students recruited from undergraduate classes. Little is known about the sample used by Grossbart, Muehling, and Kangun (1986) beyond that it was composed of **111** undergraduate students randomly assigned to treatment conditions. The groups were described as similar in their product class experience and demographics.

Survey instruments were completed by **148** subjects in the experiment conducted by Gotlieb and Sarel (1991). The subjects were all selected from a pool of upperclasspersons attending a large urban university and were assigned randomly to treatments in a 2 × 2 × 2 factorial experimental design. The sample used by Gotlieb and Sarel (1992) was similar in that it was composed of responses from **113** upperclasspersons and graduate students attending a large urban university. As in the previous study, subjects were assigned randomly to treatments in a 2 × 2 × 2 factorial design.

Machleit, Allen, and Madden (1993) gathered data from students in two sections of a college marketing course. **Eighty** students completed both the pre- and post-exposure questionnaires. Forty-two watched a Pepsi ad and 38 were exposed to a Levi's ad.

MacKenzie, Lutz, and Belch (1986) used the scale in two experiments. In the first experiment, **260** people were recruited from two church organizations. They ranged in age from 18 to 75 years, and 69% were female. The subjects in the second experiment were **225** undergraduate and master's-level business students who volunteered for the study.

The study by MacKenzie and Spreng (1992) used data collected from **360** undergraduate and MBA students. The sample was almost equally split between males and females, and ages ranged from 20 to 32 years.

The experiment conducted by Netemeyer and Bearden (1992) was based on data from a sample of **372** undergraduate students. They were assigned randomly to a 2 (informational influence) × 2 (normative influence) design. The sample was split approximately in half to test two different models of Behavioral Intention. Therefore, there were four cells per model tested, with each cell composed of 46-49 subjects.

Oliver and Bearden (1985) used data from **353** members of a bi-state consumer panel who responded to two questionnaires and had received a four-week supply of appetite suppressant capsules between the two questionnaires. Panel members were selected to be representative of urban and suburban households with family incomes greater that $10,000 annually. Subjects were typically white (89%), female (56%), and had at least some education beyond high school (70%).

Many samples of varying characteristics were used in the studies reported by Shimp and Sharma (1987), but the one in which this **Behavioral Intention** scale used had **145** college students with a mean age of 21.5 years, about 60% of whom were male.

Singh and Cole (1993) collected data from **138** undergraduate students. Students were assigned randomly to treatment cells, and the order of commercials within cells was assigned randomly as well. Subjects were exposed to the ads in groups of 5 to 7.

Yi (1990a) gathered data from **72** undergraduate students who were recruited from introductory business courses. Little more was said about the subjects, except that they were assigned randomly to one of four treatment groups.

Yi's second study (1990b) described the scale being used in two experiments. The first had a sample of **40** college students and the second had **120** students recruited from several business classes.

RELIABILITY:

Alphas of **.93**, **.861**, **.89**, **.93**, **.88**, **.84**, and **.93** were reported by Chattopadhyay and Basu (1990), Gill, Grossbart, and Laczniak (1988), Gotlieb and Sarel (1991, 1992), MacKensie and Spreng (1992), Shimp and Sharma (1987), and Singh and Cole (1993), respectively. Grossbart, Muehling, and Kangun reported alphas of **.95** and **.94** for the two-item version of the scale and an alpha of **.92** for the three-item version. Machleit, Allen, and Madden (1993) reported the alphas to be above **.95** for both the purchase and contact intention versions of the scale for two different products. Alphas of **.88** and **.90** were reported by MacKenzie, Lutz, and Belch (1986) for their first and second experiments, respectively. The LISREL estimate of reliability was **.87,** as reported by Oliver and Bearden (1985). Two models of Behavioral Intention were tested by Netemeyer and Bearden (1992) and alphas were separately calculated as **.91** and **.90.** Yi (1990a) reported an alpha of **.89.** An alpha of **.92** was reported by Yi (1990b) for use of the scale in experiment 1; no reliability information was reported for the scale's use in experiment 2.

VALIDITY:

None of the studies specifically addressed the matter of scale validity. Although not specifically examining the validity of **behavioral intention**, Machleit, Allen, and Madden (1993) used confirmatory factor analysis to provide evidence that another measure (brand interest) and two measures of **behavioral intention** (purchase and contact) were not measures of the same construct (discriminant validity).

A correlation matrix was provided by MacKenzie and Spreng (1992) between the items in the Behavioral Intention scale as well as several others that sheds some limited light on the issue of validity. For example, the intercorrelations of the Intention scale items ranged from .47 to .88, which provides some evidence that the items are measuring the same thing. In contrast, the correlations between the Intention items and items measuring related but theoretically distinct constructs were much lower.

ADMINISTRATION:

Administration was similar in several of the studies in that the scale was given to subjects as part of a larger questionnaire after they had viewed a test stimulus (Chattopadhyay and Basu 1990; Gill, Grossbart, and Laczniak 1988; Gotlieb and Sarel 1991, 1992; Grossbart, Muehling, and Kangun 1986; MacKenzie, Lutz, and Belch 1986; MacKenzie and Spreng 1992; Netemeyer and Bearden 1992; Shimp and Sharma 1987; Singh and Cole 1993; Yi 1990a and b). In contrast, Oliver and Bearden (1985) included the scale on a questionnaire sent to panel subjects before they received a test stimulus. In the study by Machleit, Allen, and Madden (1993), subjects filled out the measure both before and after being exposed to an ad. A high score on the scale would indicate that a person plans on engaging in a certain behavior, whereas a low score suggests that a person is unlikely to do something.

MAJOR FINDINGS:

The purpose of the experiment by Chattopadhyay and Basu (1990) was to examine the relationship between prior brand evaluation and humorous advertising. It was found that when prior brand evaluation is positive, exposure to a humorous ad yields significantly greater purchase **intent** than when exposed to a nonhumorous ad.

Gill, Grossbart, and Laczniak (1988) found that Fishbein's summation of beliefs and evaluations was linked directly to attitude toward the ad, which subsequently affected purchase intention. This relationship was found to be consistent regardless of whether subjective-only claims were used in a treatment advertisement or a combination of both objective and subjective claims were used. Attitude had a stronger, direct effect on **behavioral intention** in the case of the former treatment.

Gotlieb and Sarel (1991) studied the role of involvement and source credibility on the influence of comparative advertising. The findings indicated that when there is high involvement with a product and high credibility of the message's source, comparative advertising for a new brand has a greater positive impact than do noncomparative ads on **purchase intentions**. Gotlieb and Sarel (1992) examined the impact of comparative advertising, price, and source credibility on perceived quality of a new brand. Two main effects (ad type and brand price) as well as a three-way interaction (ad type, source credibility, and brand price) were found to have significant influences on **behavioral intention.**

Grossbart, Muehling, and Kangun (1986) examined the relative effectiveness of various comparative and noncomparative ads. A confusing array of attitudinal effects were found depending on the type of comparison made in the ads. As expected, alternative ad formats did not result in significantly different **behavioral intentions** toward the sponsor's brand. However, the authors speculated that the lack of behavioral differences in the formats may have occurred because the number of ad exposures was limited.

Machleit, Allen, and Madden (1993) proposed and examined a new model of advertising effects that introduced brand interest as a key component of the hierarchy of effects for mature brands. Indeed, the findings indicated that ad-evoked affect affected brand interest (but not brand attitude) and that brand interest influenced **contact intention** (but not **purchase intention**).

MacKenzie, Lutz, and Belch (1986) examined four competing models of Attitude Toward the Ad's role as a mediator of ad influence on **brand attitudes** and purchase intentions. The dual mediation hypothesis was found to be the superior model and provides evidence that attitude toward the ad does not have a significant direct effect on **behavioral intentions.**

Among other relationships, the study by MacKensie and Spreng (1992) examined the process through which motivation moderates the influence of brand attitudes on purchase **intentions**. As predicted, motivation was found to strengthen the effect of brand attitudes on **behavioral intentions**.

Netemeyer and Bearden (1992) conducted an experiment to compare the causal structure and predictive ability of the models of Behavioral Intentions by Ajzen and Fishbein (1980) and Miniard and Cohen (1983). The former was much better than the latter at predicting **behavioral intention.**

Oliver and Bearden (1985) examined a extension of the crossover path in the Fishbein behavioral intention model. Both attitude toward the act and subjective norm were found to have a significant impact on **behavioral intentions**, with the impact of the former being much greater. Moreover, the results indicated that **behavioral intention** had significant impact on self-reported behavior.

The **behavioral intention** scale was used in one of the Shimp and Sharma (1987) studies as one of many variables to provide evidence of their CETS-CALE's nomological validity. Little was reported except that the CETSCALE had a significant though moderate correlation with intentions to purchase American-made apparel.

Singh and Cole (1993) evaluated the relative effectiveness of 15- and 30-second commercials. Among the findings was that length did not appear to make a significant difference in attitude toward the ad, brand attitude, or **purchase intention**.

Yi (1990a) examined how exposure to magazine articles can effect processing of ads in the magazine. **Intention** was indirectly affected by the cognitive and affective contexts. Similarly, Yi (1990b) investigated the possibility that prior exposure to certain contextual materials can prime certain product characteristics in ads and thereby influence development of brand attitudes and **intentions**. Indeed, the results indicated that a primed product attribute was more cognitively accessible and increased purchase **intentions**.

COMMENTS:

See also Oliver, Robertson, and Mitchell (1993) and Prakash (1992) for other uses of this scale.

REFERENCES:

Ajzen, Icek and Martin Fishbein (1980), *Understanding Attitudes and Predicting Social Behavior.* Englewood Cliffs, NJ: Prentice-Hall Inc.

Chattopadhyay, Amitava and Kunal Basu (1990), ''Humor in Advertising: The Moderating Role of Prior Brand Evaluation,'' *JMR*, 27 (November), 466-76.

Fishbein, Martin and Icek Ajzen (1975), *Belief, Attitude, Intention, and Behavior: An Introduction to Theory and Research.* Reading, MA: Addison-Wesley.

Gill, James D., Sanford Grossbart, and Russell N. Laczniak (1988), ''Influence of Involvement, Commitment and Familiarity on Brand Beliefs and Attitudes of Viewers Exposed to Alternative Claim Strategies,'' *JA*, 17 (2) 33-43.

Gotlieb, Jerry B. and Dan Sarel (1991), ''Comparative Advertising Effectiveness: The Role of Involvement and Source Credibility,'' *JA*, 20 (1), 38-45.

_____ and _____ (1992), ''The Influence of Type of Advertisement, Price, and Source Credibility on Perceived Quality,'' *JAMS*, 20 (Summer), 253-60.

Grossbart, Sanford, Darrel D. Muehling, and Norman Kangun (1986), ''Verbal and Visual References to Competition in Comparative Advertising,'' *JA*, 15 (1) 10-23.

Machleit, Karen A., Chris T. Allen, and Thomas J. Madden (1993), ''The Mature Brand and Brand Interest: An Alternative Consequence of Ad-Evoked Affect,'' *JM*, 57 (October), 72-82.

MacKenzie, Scott B., Richard J. Lutz, and George E. Belch (1986), ''The Role of Attitude Toward the Ad as a Mediator of Advertising Effectiveness: A Test of Competing Explanations,'' *JMR*, 23 (May), 130-43.

_____ and Richard A. Spreng (1992), ''How Does Motivation Moderate the Impact of Central and Peripheral Processing on Brand Attitudes and Intentions?'' *JCR*, 18 (March), 519-29.

Miniard, Paul W. and Joel B. Cohen (1983), ''Modeling Personal and Normative Influences on Behavior,'' *JCR*, 10 (September), 169-80.

Netemeyer, Richard G. and William O. Bearden (1992), ''A Comparative Analysis of Two Models of Behavioral Intention,'' *JAMS*, 20 (Winter), 49-59.

Oliver, Richard L. and William O. Bearden (1985), ''Crossover Effects in the Theory of Reasoned Action: A Moderating Influence Attempt,'' *JCR*, 12 (December) 324-40.

_____, Thomas S. Robertson, and Deborah J. Mitchell (1993), ''Imaging and Analyzing in Response to New Product Advertising,'' *JA*, 22 (December), 35-50.

Prakash, Ved (1992), ''Sex Roles and Advertising Preferences,'' *JAR*, 32 (May/June), 43-52.

Shimp, Terence A. and Subhash Sharma (1987), ''Consumer Ethnocentrism: Construction and Validation of The CETSCALE,'' *JMR*, 24 (August) 280-89.

Singh, Surendra N. and Catherine Cole (1993), ''The Effects of Length, Content, and Repetition on Television Commercial Effectiveness,'' *JMR*, 30 (February), 91-104.

Yi, Youjae (1990a), ''Cognitive and Affective Priming Effects of the Context for Print Advertisements,'' *JA*, 19 (2), 40-48.

_____ (1990b), ''The Effects of Contextual Priming in Print Advertisements,'' *JCR*, 17 (September), 215-22.

SCALE ITEMS: BEHAVIORAL INTENTION*

1. Unlikely   1———2———3———4———5———6———7 Likely

2. Non-existant   1———2———3———4———5———6———7 Existent

3. Improbable   1———2———3———4———5———6———7 Probable

4. Impossible   1———2———3———4———5———6———7 Possible

5. Uncertain   1———2———3———4———5———6———7 Certain

* The scales used by Chattopadhyay and Basu (1990); Gotlieb and Sarel (1991, 1992); Machleit, Allen, and Madden (1993); MacKenzie, Lutz, and Belch (1986); MacKenzie and Spreng (1992); Netemeyer and Bearden (1992); Singh and Cole (1993); and Yi (1990a, 1990b) were composed of items 1, 3, and 4. Gill, Grossbart, and Laczniak (1988) used items 1, 2, 3, and 4. Grossbart, Muehling, and Kangun (1986) made three uses of the scale employing items 1 and 3; item 5 was used in one of those instances. Oliver and Bearden (1985) used items 1, 3, 4, and 5. Shimp and Sharma (1987) used items 1, 3, and 5. They also used the word ''very'' before each set of the bipolar adjectives.

SCALE NAME: Behavioral Intention (Blood Test)

SCALE DESCRIPTION:

A three-item, seven-point summated ratings scale attempting to assess a person's stated likelihood of getting a diagnostic blood test in the future.

SCALE ORIGIN:

The article by Maheswaran and Meyers-Levy (1990) did not specify the origin of the scale, but it is likely to have been developed for use in their study.

SAMPLES:

The study conducted by Maheswaran and Meyers-Levy (1990) used a sample of **98** undergraduate students who received extra course credit for participating. The data were gathered from small groups of students (5 to 7 at a time) and then analyzed as a 2 × 2 factorial design.

RELIABILITY:

Maheswaran and Meyers-Levy (1990) reported the scale to have an alpha of .73.

VALIDITY:

Maheswaran and Meyers-Levy (1990) provided no evidence of the scale's validity.

ADMINISTRATION:

The scale was administered by Maheswaran and Meyers-Levy (1990) along with several other measures in an experiment after subjects had read some test material. A high score on the scale indicates that a person is strongly inclined to have a blood test in the near future whereas a low score suggests that one does not plan on doing such a thing, at least not soon.

MAJOR FINDINGS:

Maheswaran and Meyers-Levy (1990) examined the persuasiveness of different ways to frame a message and the role played by issue involvement. The results indicated that more favorable **behavioral intentions** were produced in the high involvement condition when the message was stated negatively. In contrast, more favorable **behavioral intentions** were produced in the low involvement condition when the message was stated positively.

REFERENCE:

Maheswaran, Durairja and Joan Meyers-Levy (1990), ''The Influence of Message Framing and Issue Involvement,'' *JMR*, 27 (August), 361-67.

SCALE ITEMS: BEHAVIORAL INTENTION (BLOOD TEST)

Directions: We are interested in your attitudes about the information provided to you and about the diagnostic blood test. For each of the following questions, please indicate how you feel by circling the one number on each of the scales that best represents the way you feel about it.

1. If the diagnostic test were to be made available in your area at a reasonable price, to what extent would you consider taking it *soon*?

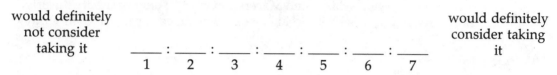

would definitely not consider taking it ___ : ___ : ___ : ___ : ___ : ___ : ___ would definitely consider taking it

    1   2   3   4   5   6   7

2. If the diagnostic blood test were to be made available in your area at a reasonable price, to what extent would you consider taking it in the *future*?

would definitely not consider taking it ___ : ___ : ___ : ___ : ___ : ___ : ___ would definitely consider taking it

    1   2   3   4   5   6   7

3. Did going through the materials about cholesterol and coronary heart disease today make you more or less likely to take the diagnostic blood test in the future?

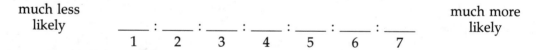

much less likely ___ : ___ : ___ : ___ : ___ : ___ : ___ much more likely

    1   2   3   4   5   6   7

SCALE NAME: Belief Confidence

SCALE DESCRIPTION:

A three-item, eleven-point summated rating scale that can provide an idea about the certainty with which a consumer perceives he/she has been able to accurately reflect his/her evaluation of a brand.

SCALE ORIGIN:

The measure is original to Kardes (1994).

SAMPLES:

Two experiments were conducted by Kardes and Kalyanaram (1992). Little is known about the samples except that they were composed of students, possibly MBAs. Analyses for both experiments were apparently based on data from **40** subjects drawn independently from the student population at the university.

RELIABILITY:

The scale apparently was filled out for three brands in each of the experiments, and all that is known about the reliability is that the alphas were higher than .93 in each case (Kardes and Kalyanaram 1992).

VALIDITY:

Kardes and Kalyanaram (1992) reported no examination of the scale's validity.

ADMINISTRATION:

The scale was administered at least with a brand attitude measure after subjects were exposed to experimental stimuli. A high score on the scale suggests that a person has a lot of confidence in an evaluation he/she has made of a brand.

MAJOR FINDINGS:

Kardes and Kalyanaram (1992) investigated aspects of the pioneering advantage. Specifically, what impact a brand's order of entering the market has on consumer learning about products and the consequences of these effects on judgments. Among the findings was that the order of market entry does affect learning such that **confidence** in brand attitudes was higher for the pioneering **brand** than it was for later entrants.

COMMENTS:

Note that this scale is constructed in such a way that it can not be used by itself. The items are exactly the same and depend, therefore, on items composing another measure such as brand attitude. In that sense, then, these items can be used with many other scales as a simple means of measuring a person's confidence in the judgment he/she has expressed.

REFERENCES:

Kardes, Frank R. and Gurumurthy Kalyanaram (1992), "Order-of-Entry Effects on Consumer Memory and Judgment: An Information Integration Perspective," *JMR*, 29 (August), 343-57.
_____ (1994), personal correspondence.

SCALE ITEMS: BELIEF CONFIDENCE*

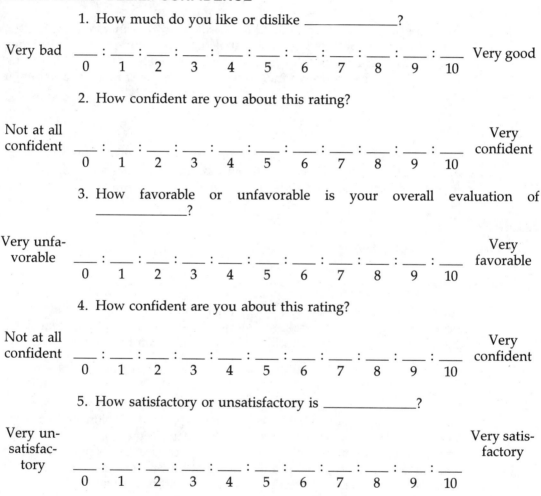

1. How much do you like or dislike _____?

Very bad __ : __ : __ : __ : __ : __ : __ : __ : __ : __ : __ Very good
      0   1   2   3   4   5   6   7   8   9   10

2. How confident are you about this rating?

Not at all
confident __ : __ : __ : __ : __ : __ : __ : __ : __ : __ : __ Very confident
      0   1   2   3   4   5   6   7   8   9   10

3. How favorable or unfavorable is your overall evaluation of _____?

Very unfavorable __ : __ : __ : __ : __ : __ : __ : __ : __ : __ : __ Very favorable
      0   1   2   3   4   5   6   7   8   9   10

4. How confident are you about this rating?

Not at all
confident __ : __ : __ : __ : __ : __ : __ : __ : __ : __ : __ Very confident
      0   1   2   3   4   5   6   7   8   9   10

5. How satisfactory or unsatisfactory is _____?

Very unsatisfactory __ : __ : __ : __ : __ : __ : __ : __ : __ : __ : __ Very satisfactory
      0   1   2   3   4   5   6   7   8   9   10

6. How confident are you about this rating?

Not at all
confident   __ : __ : __ : __ : __ : __ : __ : __ : __ : __ : __   Very
                    0   1   2   3   4   5   6   7   8   9   10   confident

* The items that are exactly the same (items 2, 4, and 6) compose the Confidence scale. As noted in the "Comments" section, other items are required for the scale to make any sense but not necessarily those (items 1, 3, 5) that were used by Kardes and Kalyanaram (1992).

SCALE NAME: Belief Confidence (Soft Drink)

SCALE DESCRIPTION:

A three-item, seven-point summated rating scale intended to measure the certainty with which a consumer perceives he/she has been able to reflect his/her evaluation of a soft drink accurately.

SCALE ORIGIN:

Smith (1993) drew on the form of similar scales that had been developed previously to measure confidence in evaluations, possibly originating in marketing with Bettman, Capon, and Lutz (1975). The version of the scale for use with soft drinks appears to be original to Smith (1993).

SAMPLES:

For the experiment conducted by Smith (1993), students were recruited from classes at a major university. Twenty-one subjects were assigned randomly to each of seven treatments. Three subjects guessed the true purpose of the study and were eliminated, leaving a sample of **144** upon which the analysis was based. The students were paid $5 for their participation.

RELIABILITY:

Smith (1993) reported an alpha of **.70** for the scale.

VALIDITY:

Smith (1993) reported no examination of the scale's validity.

ADMINISTRATION:

The scale was administered to students along with other measures after they had been exposed to experimental manipulations (Smith 1993). A high score on the scale suggests that a person has a lot of confidence in the evaluations he/she has made of a soft drink.

MAJOR FINDINGS:

The purpose of the study by Smith (1993) was to investigate how consumers integrate new brand information from product trial and advertising. Among the findings was that a combination of exposure to advertising and positive trial of the product (regardless of sequence) did not significantly increase subjects' **belief confidence** beyond that achieved from positive trial alone.

COMMENTS:

Although some direct analysis was made of the data provided the scale, its primary purpose was use with a *brand beliefs* scale (#46). Specifically, scores on the *brand beliefs* scale were multiplied by scores a person had on the **belief confidence** scale, producing a measure of *total expectancy*. Given the way the scale stem is stated presently, it can not be used alone and must follow a *brand beliefs* scale.

REFERENCES:

Bettman, James R., Noel Capon, and Richard J. Lutz (1975), ''Multiattribute Measurement Models and Multiattribute Attitude Theory: A Test of Construct Validity,'' *JCR*, 1 (March), 1-14.

Smith, Robert E. (1993), ''Integrating Information From Advertising and Trial: Processes and Effects on Consumer Response to Product Information,'' *JMR*, 30 (May), 204-19.

SCALE ITEMS: BRAND CONFIDENCE (SOFT DRINK)*

How confident are you that the likelihood estimate you just provided is accurate?

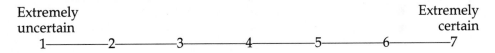

Extremely uncertain

Extremely certain

1———2———3———4———5———6———7

1. great taste
2. no aftertaste
3. not watery

* The items were not explicitly provided in the article but are reconstructed here using the descriptions provided.

SCALE NAME: Benefit Perception (Composite)

SCALE DESCRIPTION:

A six-item, seven-point summated ratings scale measuring the probability that a consumer perceives the purchase of some specified product to be associated with six types of gain.

SCALE ORIGIN:

The scale was developed by Murray (1985) in his dissertation research. The same data are used by Murray and Schlacter 1990. The six items used by Murray (1985; Murray and Schlacter 1990) are adaptations of six items developed by Peter and Tarpey (1975).

SAMPLES:

The sample was composed of **256** students attending Arizona State University. Nearly 53% of the sample was female, and the mean age was nearly 24 years of age. Students were assigned randomly to one of 15 different treatments systematically varied in terms of the "serviceness" of the three products to which they responded.

RELIABILITY:

A mean alpha of **.878** was reported for the scale averaged over 15 different products. For products with high, moderate, and low service attributes, mean alphas of .804, .839, and .814, respectively, were reported.

VALIDITY:

No information regarding the scale's validity was reported.

ADMINISTRATION:

The scale was administered as part of a larger questionnaire to students in a classroom setting. High scores on the scale suggest that consumers perceive most if not all the types of gain to be associated with the purchase of some specified product, whereas low scores indicate that expectations of positive consequences are low.

MAJOR FINDINGS:

The purpose of the study by Murray and Schlacter (1990) was to examine how products placed along a goods-services continuum vary in the kind and amount of prechoice risk perceived. **Product benefit** was examined only indirectly, as part of a product variability measure. Variability was apparently calculated by noting the absolute difference between scores on the **perceived benefit** scale and a perceived risk scale. Their findings indicated that there are differences in the variability perceived in the purchase of goods and services such that products high in service attributes have more variability associated with them than products low in serviceness.

REFERENCES:

Murray, Keith B. (1985), "Risk Perception and Information Source Use for Products Differing in Service Attributes," doctoral dissertation, Arizona State University: Tempe, Arizona.

_____ and John L. Schlacter (1990), "The Impact of Services Versus Goods on Consumers' Assessment of Perceived Risk and Variability," *JAMS*, 18 (Winter), 51-65.

Peter, J. Paul and Lawrence X. Tarpey, Sr. (1975), "A Comparative Analysis of Three Consumer Decision Strategies," *JCR*, 2 (June), 29-37.

SCALE ITEMS: BENEFIT PERCEPTION (COMPOSITE)

Circle the number that best describes your reaction to each statement if you were considering the purchase of a _____.

Extremely = 1   Slightly = 5
Moderately = 2   Moderately = 6
Slightly = 3   Extremely = 7
Neither = 4

Improbable   ____ : ____ : ____ : ____ : ____ : ____ : ____   Probable
         1   2   3   4   5   6   7

1. What is the probability that a purchase of an unfamiliar alternative for a _____ will lead to a FINANCIAL GAIN for you because it would function extremely well and exceed your expectations relative to the amount of money required to pay for it?
2. What is the probability that a purchase of an unfamiliar alternative for a _____ will lead to a PERFORMANCE GAIN for you because it would function extremely well and it would serve your needs, desires, and expectations very well?
3. What is the probability that a purchase of an unfamiliar alternative for a _____ will lead to a PHYSICAL GAIN for you because it would be safe and very beneficial?
4. What is the probability that a purchase of an unfamiliar alternative for a _____ will lead to a PSYCHOLOGICAL GAIN for you because it would fit in well with your self image or self-concept?
5. What is the probability that a purchase of an unfamiliar alternative for a _____ will lead to a SOCIAL GAIN for you because your friends and family would think more highly of you?
6. What is the probability that a purchase of an unfamiliar alternative for a _____ will lead to a GAIN IN CONVENIENCE because you wouldn't have to waste a lot of time and effort before having your needs satisfied?

SCALE NAME: Black Racial Identification

SCALE DESCRIPTION:

A 13-item summated ratings scale measuring the degree to which a person expresses a sense of belonging to the African-American ethnic group by accepting attitudes and behaviors supportive of that group.

SCALE ORIGIN:

The scale appears to be original to Whittler with the construction and testing of the scale described in Whittler, Calantone, and Young (1991). A preliminary 35-item version was tested on 34 students, and item analysis led to only 13 items being kept. The alpha of that set was .82, and some evidence of its criterion validity was found. A more recent study using 160 students found an alpha of .73, but there was evidence of a two-factor structure. Another study used responses from 170 blacks from the population at large to perform a confirmatory factor analysis of the scale. The results indicated that there were two factors, and there was only weak evidence of convergent and discriminant validity.

SAMPLES:

The scale was administered in the first of two studies described by Whittler (1991). All that is said about those who filled out the scale was that the sample was composed of **140** black undergraduate students.

RELIABILITY:

Whittler (1991) reported an alpha of **.72** for the scale.

VALIDITY:

No examination of the scale's validity was reported by Whittler (1991), but he did indicate that a factor analysis yielded two factors.

ADMINISTRATION:

The scale was administered along with other measures in an experimental setting (Whittler 1991). A high score on the scale indicates that a person appears to strongly identify with African-American subculture.

MAJOR FINDINGS:

Processing of racial cues in advertising was examined by Whittler (1991). Among the findings was that high-**identification** blacks had a significantly greater perception of similarity with black actors in ads than did blacks scoring low on the **racial identification** scale.

COMMENTS:

The combined evidence of the studies described here show rather clearly that the scale is bidimensional, not unidimensional. It may make more sense, therefore, to score the dimensions separately. The two factors have been described as *cross-race attraction* and *support for black causes*, with the former explaining more variance and having greater internal consistency. The items composing these subscales were not specified by Whittler, Calantone, and Young (1991) although it was stated that each had four items (p. 464).

REFERENCES:

Whittler, Tommy E. (1991), ''The Effects of Actors' Race in Commercial Advertising: Review and Extension,'' *JA*, 20 (1), 54-60.
_____, Roger J. Calantone, and Mark R. Young (1991), ''Strength of Ethnic Affiliation: Examining Black Identification with Black Culture,'' *Journal of Social Psychology*, 131 (4), 461-67.

SCALE ITEMS: BLACK RACIAL IDENTIFICATION*

1. Black men should not date white women.
2. I am less likely to buy a product if it is promoted by Whites than if it is promoted by Blacks.
3. Profit-making organizations should not be required to meet quotas for hiring minorities. **(r)**
4. I have voted for those candidates who are sensitive to the concerns of Blacks.
5. I would rather not have Blacks live in the same apartment building I live in. **(r)**
6. In order to preserve the best of the culture and heritage of both the Blacks and Whites, the two races should not intermarry.
7. Black celebrities and professionals should not date Whites.
8. Blacks should purchase goods and services from Black-owned businesses.
9. I would not mind at all if my only friends were White. **(r)**
10. It does not really matter whether Black parents purchase Black or White dolls for their children. **(r)**
11. I would feel comfortable attending an all-White church. **(r)**
12. There is nothing wrong with Black women dating White men. **(r)**
13. Black people should not associate with leaders who talk tough since they will only make it harder for Blacks to make real progress. **(r)**

* The response scale was not identified by Whittler (1991) or Whittler, Calantone, and Young (1991) but it is likely to have been a five- or seven-point Likert-type scale.

SCALE NAME: Brand Beliefs (35mm Camera)

SCALE DESCRIPTION:

A five-item, seven-point summated ratings scale measuring the extent to which several statements that are made about the features of a specified brand of 35mm camera are true.

SCALE ORIGIN:

The scale appears to have been developed by Laczniak and Muehling (1993) for use in their study.

SAMPLES:

Data were gathered by Laczniak and Muehling (1993) from **280** students in introductory marketing classes. The experiment took place in an college auditorium, and students were randomly assigned to one of 12 treatment conditions.

RELIABILITY:

Laczniak and Muehling (1993) reported an alpha of **.85** for the scale.

VALIDITY:

Laczniak and Muehling (1993) reported no examination of the scale's validity.

ADMINISTRATION:

The scale was administered to students, along with other measures, after they had been exposed to experimental manipulations (Laczniak and Muehling 1993). A high score on the scale indicates that a person believes it is very likely that a specified brand of camera has certain positive characteristics.

MAJOR FINDINGS:

Several manipulations of advertising message involvement were tested by Laczniak and Muehling (1993). They were compared for their ability to place people into high- and low-involvement groups. Of the six manipulations evaluated, only one produced results consistent with theory; that is, **brand beliefs** and attitude toward the ad had significant impacts on brand attitudes under high-involvement conditions, but only attitude toward the ad affected it under low-involvement conditions.

REFERENCES:

Laczniak, Russell N. and Darrel D. Muehling (1993), ''The Relationship Between Experimental Manipulations and Tests of Theory in an Advertising Message Involvement Context,'' *JA*, 22 (September), 59-74.

SCALE ITEMS: BRAND BELIEFS (35mm CAMERAS)

Directions: We would like to know your beliefs about the _____ 35mm camera (the one advertised in the booklet you looked at.) We are *not* asking if you think the following statements were made in the ad. What we want to know is the extent to which *you believe* the following statements are true about the _____ 35mm camera.

How likely is it that the _____ 35mm camera has the following features?

```
Very                                                              Very
unlikely                        Neither                          likely
    1————————2————————3————————4————————5————————6————————7
```

1. Wide range of shutter speeds compatible with many lenses of every type
2. Fast automatic film rewind
3. Fast film advance
4. Many different types of exposure modes
5. Many precise metering systems

SCALE NAME: Brand Beliefs (Shampoo)

SCALE DESCRIPTION:

A five-item, seven-point summated ratings scale measuring how probable a person believes several statements about the features of a specified brand of shampoo are.

SCALE ORIGIN:

Although not stated explicitly, it appears that the scale was original to the work of MacInnis and Park (1991).

SAMPLES:

Data were gathered in the experiment by MacInnis and Park (1991) from **178** female undergraduates. Subjects received course credit for their participation and were randomly assigned to treatments.

RELIABILITY:

MacInnis and Park (1991) reported an alpha of **.79** for the scale.

VALIDITY:

No examination of scale validity or unidimensionality was reported by MacInnis and Park (1991).

ADMINISTRATION:

The scale was administered to students along with other measures after they had been exposed to experimental stimuli (MacInnis and Park 1991). A high score on the scale indicates that a person believes it is very likely that a specified brand of shampoo has certain positive characteristics.

MAJOR FINDINGS:

MacInnis and Park (1991) examined the influence of two dimensions of music on low- and high-involvement ad processing: the music's fit with the ad message and the music's links to past emotion-laden experiences (indexicality). Attitude toward the ad had a much stronger positive impact on brand attitude for both low- and high-involvement subjects than did **brand beliefs**.

REFERENCES:

MacInnis, Deborah J. and C. Whan Park (1991), "The Differential Role of Characteristics of Music on High- and Low-Involvement Consumers' Processing of Ads," *JCR*, 18 (September), 161-73.

SCALE ITEMS: BRAND BELIEFS (SHAMPOO)*

Improbable ___ : ___ : ___ : ___ : ___ : ___ : ___ Probable
      1   2   3   4   5   6   7

1. The shampoo is natural.
2. The shampoo has a herbalescent formula.
3. The shampoo makes hair shiny.
4. The shampoo makes hair soft.
5. The shampoo makes hair healthy looking.

* The items are reconstructed here on the basis of descriptions provided in the article but may not be phrased exactly as MacInnis and Park (1991) used them.

SCALE NAME: Brand Beliefs (Soft Drink)

SCALE DESCRIPTION:

A three-item, seven-point summated ratings scale measuring the likelihood that a particular brand of a soft drink has several specified characteristics that are typically considered to be desirable.

SCALE ORIGIN:

Smith (1993) drew on the form of similar scales that had been developed previously to measure confidence in evaluations, possibly originating in marketing with Bettman, Capon, and Lutz (1975). The version of the scale for use with soft drinks appears to be original to Smith (1993).

SAMPLES:

For the experiment conducted by Smith (1993), students were recruited from classes at a major university. Twenty-one subjects were assigned randomly to each of seven treatments. Three subjects guessed the true purpose of the study and were eliminated, leaving a sample of **144** upon which the analysis was based. The students were paid $5 for their participation.

RELIABILITY:

Smith (1993) reported an alpha of **.73** for the scale.

VALIDITY:

Smith (1993) reported no examination of the scale's validity.

ADMINISTRATION:

The scale was administered to students along with other measures after they had been exposed to experimental manipulations (Smith 1993). A high score on the scale indicates that a person believes it is very likely that a specified brand of soft drink has certain positive characteristics.

MAJOR FINDINGS:

The purpose of Smith's (1993) study was to investigate how consumers integrate new brand information from product trial and advertising. Among the findings was that a combination of exposure to advertising and positive trial of the product (regardless of sequence) did not significantly increase subjects' **brand beliefs** beyond that achieved from positive trial alone.

COMMENTS:

Although some direct analysis was made of the data provided the scale, its primary purpose was use with a *belief confidence* scale (#41). Specifically, scores on the **brand beliefs** scale were multiplied by scores a person had on the *belief confidence* scale producing a measure of *total expectancy*.

REFERENCES:

Bettman, James R., Noel Capon, and Richard J. Lutz (1975), ''Multiattribute Measurement Models and Multiattribute Attitude Theory: A Test of Construct Validity,'' *JCR*, 1 (March), 1-14.

Smith, Robert E. (1993), ''Integrating Information From Advertising and Trial: Processes and Effects on Consumer Response to Product Information,'' *JMR*, 30 (May), 204-19.

SCALE ITEMS: BRAND BELIEFS (SOFT DRINK)*

How likely is it that the soft drink has the following attributes?

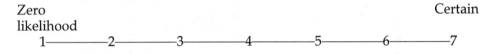

```
Zero                                                        Certain
likelihood
   1--------2--------3--------4--------5--------6--------7
```

1. great taste
2. no aftertaste
3. not watery

* The scale stem and the items were not explicitly provided in the article but are reconstructed here using the descriptions provided.

SCALE NAME: Brand Beliefs (Tape Player)

SCALE DESCRIPTION:

A seven-point Likert-like measure of the beliefs a person reports having regarding five attributes of a specified brand of a product. Muehling, Laczniak, and Stoltman (1991) referred to this measure as *cognitive structure index* and used it to examine a fictitious brand of cassette player.

SCALE ORIGIN:

The scale was original to Muehling, Laczniak, and Stoltman (1991), although inspiration was attributed to MacKenzie and Lutz (1989).

SAMPLES:

Muehling, Laczniak, and Stoltman (1991) used a sample composed of **105** undergraduate business students.

RELIABILITY:

Muehling, Laczniak, and Stoltman (1991) reported an alpha of **.64** for the scale.

VALIDITY:

Muehling, Laczniak, and Stoltman (1991) reported no examination for the scale's validity.

ADMINISTRATION:

The scale was administered to students as part of a larger survey instrument after they read a booklet that contained the test ad (Muehling, Laczniak, and Stoltman 1991). A high score on the scale indicates that a person believes it is extremely likely that the specified brand has the (assumably) positive characteristics specified in the statements.

MAJOR FINDINGS:

Muehling, Laczniak, and Stoltman (1991) examined the moderating effect of ad message involvement (AMI) in the context of brand attitude formation. The approach to **brand beliefs** measurement, though suggested by MacKenzie and Lutz (1989), was considered to be new. Two models of brand attitude formation were compared: dual mode persuasion (DMP) and contextual evaluation transfer (CET). The findings showed that when levels of ad execution involvement and AMI are high (DMP model) that the significance of some relationships depends on the way constructs are measured. In particular, brand perceptions' impact on brand attitudes was significant only when measured with the scale shown subsequently, not with another measure referred to as *cognitive response*.

COMMENTS:

A database and analysis similar to what is described in Muehling, Laczniak, and Stoltman (1991) was examined by Muehling and Laczniak (1988), and more discussion of the **brand beliefs** scale can be found there.

REFERENCES:

MacKenzie, Scott B. and Richard J. Lutz (1989), ''An Empirical Examination of the Structural Antecedents of Attitude Toward the Ad in an Advertising Pretesting Context,'' *JM*, 53 (April) 48-65.
Muehling, Darrel D. (1994), personal correspondence.
_____ and Russell N. Laczniak (1988), ''Advertising's Immediate and De-layed Influence on Brand Attitudes: Considerations Across Message-Involvement Levels,'' *JA*, 17 (4), 23-34.
_____, _____, and Jeffrey J. Stoltman (1991), ''The Moderating Effects of Ad Message Involvement: A Reassessment,'' *JA*, 20 (June), 29-38.

SCALE ITEMS: BRAND BELIEFS*

Directions: We would like to know your **beliefs** about the *Polysound* cassette player (the brand advertised in the booklet you looked at.) We are *not* asking if you think the following statements were made in the ad. What we want to know is the extent to which you believe the following statements are true about the *Polysound* cassette player.

Extremely unlikely	___ : ___ : ___ : ___ : ___ : ___ : ___	Extremely likely
	-3 -2 -1 0 1 2 3	

The *Polysound* personal stereo cassette player with headphones . . .
1. is extremely lightweight.
2. delivers high-quality sound.
3. has headphones that are comfortable.
4. is built to last.
5. is low priced.

* These directions and items were provided by Muehling (1994).

SCALE NAME: Brand Popularity

SCALE DESCRIPTION:

A four-item, seven-point semantic differential measuring the degree of popularity that a specified brand is perceived to have. The scale was used by Mishra, Umesh, and Stem (1993) with reference to a "decoy" brand and was referred to as *perceived decoy popularity*.

SCALE ORIGIN:

The scale appears to be original to the research reported by Mishra, Umesh, and Stem (1993). A pretest estimated that the scale was internally consistent (= .90, n = 27) and had some discriminant validity given that scores were significantly different between those who had been presented with a very popular brand and those who received less popular ones.

SAMPLES:

The sample used by Mishra, Umesh, and Stem (1993) was composed of undergraduate and graduate students attending a large university. The mean age of the subjects was 22 years and ranged from 19 to 45. Credit was given for participation in the study. The final sample sizes used in the analyses were **359** for beer and television sets and **330** for cars.

RELIABILITY:

Alphas for the products studied by Mishra, Umesh, and Stem (1993) were **.89**, **.93**, and **.95** for beer, cars, and television sets, respectively.

VALIDITY:

Mishra, Umesh, and Stem (1993) did not specifically examine the validity of the scale.

ADMINISTRATION:

The scale was self-administered along with other measures after subjects had been exposed to stimulus information (Mishra, Umesh, and Stem 1993). A high score on the scale suggests that a person believes a brand is very popular.

MAJOR FINDINGS:

Mishra, Umesh, and Stem (1993) performed a causal analysis of the attraction effect that occurs when the introduction of a relatively inferior "decoy" brand increases (rather than decreases) choice probability of an existing target brand. Indeed, the results showed that for three different products the attraction effect increases as the **popularity** of the decoy brand increases.

REFERENCE:

Mishra, Sanjay, U.N. Umesh, and Donald E. Stem, Jr. (1993), ''Antecedents of the Attraction Effect: An Information-Processing Approach,'' *JMR*, 30 (August), 331-49.

SCALE ITEMS: BRAND POPULARITY

Rate your perception of the popularity of _____.*

Not industry leader	___ : ___ : ___ : ___ : ___ : ___ : ___	Industry leader
	1 2 3 4 5 6 7	
Not at all popular	___ : ___ : ___ : ___ : ___ : ___ : ___	Very popular
	1 2 3 4 5 6 7	
Not widely accepted	___ : ___ : ___ : ___ : ___ : ___ : ___	Widely accepted
	1 2 3 4 5 6 7	
Few like it	___ : ___ : ___ : ___ : ___ : ___ : ___	Many like it
	1 2 3 4 5 6 7	

* The name of the brand should be placed in the blank.

SCALE NAME: Brand Preference

SCALE DESCRIPTION:

A three-item, 100-point summated scale measuring the relative preference a consumer has between two competing brands of a product.

SCALE ORIGIN:

Although the items may have been used previously by others, there is no information to indicate that these items have been used together as a summated ratings scale other than by Costley and Brucks (1992). A six-item version was initially tested with 34 student respondents and resulted in alphas from .91 to .97 (Costley 1993). However, the authors desired a shorter version and ultimately settled for the three items listed here.

SAMPLES:

The sample used for the experiment by Costley and Brucks (1992) was composed of 387 undergraduate college students from 12 different classes. Students were assigned randomly to experimental treatments. However, the alpha was based on data from a pretest sample of 34 students.

RELIABILITY:

Six analyses of the scale yielded alphas ranging from **.90** to **.97** (Costley 1993).

VALIDITY:

Costley and Brucks (1992) did not discuss information regarding the scale's validity.

ADMINISTRATION:

The scale was administered to subjects on the second day of testing in the study by Costley and Brucks (1992). Responses to each item are quantified and summed, and the total divided by three. Scale scores can range from 0 to 100, with a high score on the scale indicating that a person very much favors Brand 2 (specified) over Brand 1 and a low score suggesting the opposite.

MAJOR FINDINGS:

Costley and Brucks (1992) examined the relationship between memory and the use of information to make brand judgments. The primary finding was that greater recallability only improves the chances of information being used to compare brands when other information is unavailable or inadequate. Specifically, the form in which brand information was presented in an ad was found to affect recallability but not usage in making **brand preference** decisions.

COMMENTS:

Lines of 100-millimeter length were used by Costley and Brucks (1992) to record responses for each of the scale's three items. Quantitative scores were then determined by using a ruler with millimeter markings. Hypothetically, this would make the scale more sensitive than one with 5 to 7 points, but its effect on reliability and validity is unknown.

REFERENCES:

Costley, Carolyn L. (1993), personal correspondence.
_____ and Merrie Brucks (1992), "Selective Recall and Information Use in Consumer Preferences," *JCR*, 18 (March), 464-74.

SCALE ITEMS: BRAND PREFERENCE

Directions: Please compare the two brands as if you were choosing between them. Draw a vertical line on the scale to indicate how "good" Brand 1 is compared with how "good" Brand 2 is. The midpoint indicates equally good brands. The nearer you place your mark toward one end, the more you lean toward the brand on that end of the scale.

1. Good brand
Brand 1 :____.____.____.____: Brand 2

2. Like the brand
Brand 1 :____.____.____.____: Brand 2

3. Would buy the brand
Brand 1 :____.____.____.____: Brand 2

SCALE NAME: Buy American-Made Products (Importance)

SCALE DESCRIPTION:

A four-item, six-point, Likert-type scale measuring a consumer's willingness to try to buy American-made brands in a specified product category. The scale was referred to as *willingness to help* by Olsen, Granzin, and Biswas (1993). It is called something a little different here because the items emphasize the extra effort one tries to make to purchase domestically produced brands and is *not* measuring a person's willingness to buy American-made products in order to help American workers.

SCALE ORIGIN:

Although not stated specifically in the article, the scale appears to be original to these authors (Olsen, Granzin, and Biswas 1993) if not to this particular piece of research.

SAMPLES:

The data for the study by Olsen, Granzin, and Biswas (1993) was apparently gathered from a large southern metropolitan area. The sample was taken to represent the general population in terms of age and gender on the basis of the most recent census of the area's MSA. The quota sample resulted in responses from **243** adults.

RELIABILITY:

Olsen, Granzin, and Biswas (1993) reported a LISREL construct reliability of **.803** for the scale.

VALIDITY:

Olsen, Granzin, and Biswas (1993) did not specifically examine the scale's validity.

ADMINISTRATION:

The scale was just one part of a larger self-administered questionnaire (Olsen, Granzin, and Biswas 1993). A high score on the scale indicates that an American consumer is eager to try to buy domestically produced brands from within some specified class of products.

MAJOR FINDINGS:

The purpose of the study by Olsen, Granzin, and Biswas (1993) was to propose and test a model of what affects consumers' willingness to **buy American-made products**. Attitudes about the following two issues had the strongest positive direct effects on the **importance of buying American-made products**:

foreign competition damages domestic industries and *Americans shouldn't buy foreign brands.*

COMMENTS:

Olsen, Granzin, and Biswas (1993) used the scale with reference to the purchase of clothing, but the scale seems amenable for use with other product categories after some modification. The changes are simple with items 2 and 3, and none are needed with item 1. The fourth item would require more rephrasing to make it relevant to the product category of interest.

REFERENCE:

Olsen, Janeen E., Kent L. Granzin, and Abhijit Biswas (1993), "Influencing Consumers' Selection of Domestic Versus Imported Products: Implications for Marketing Based on a Model of Helping Behavior," *JAMS*, 21 (Fall), 307- 21.

SCALE ITEMS: BUY AMERICAN-MADE PRODUCTS (IMPORTANCE)*

Strongly
disagree ____ : ____ : ____ : ____ : ____ : ____   Strongly agree
      1   2   3   4   5   6

1. I will shop first at retail stores that make a special effort to sell American-made products.
2. When I buy _____ I will try as much as I can to buy U.S. brands.
3. I am willing to always buy American made _____.
4. I am willing to take the time to look on labels so I know where the _____ I wear were made.

* The name of the product category should be placed in the blanks. See also the "Comments" section.

SCALE NAME: Calmness

SCALE DESCRIPTION:

A three-item, five-point scale measuring one's calmness-related emotional reaction to some specified stimulus.

SCALE ORIGIN:

Although not expressly indicated, the items used by Mano and Oliver (1993) appear to have been used first as a summated scale by Mano (1991). With 224 college students, the scale was reported to have an alpha of .80. A cluster analysis grouped these three items together by themselves, but in a factor analysis the items loaded along with three more related to *quietness*.

SAMPLES:

Data were collected by Mano and Oliver (1993) from **118** undergraduate business students attending a midwestern U.S. university.

RELIABILITY:

Mano and Oliver (1993) reported an alpha of **.77** for the scale.

VALIDITY:

Mano and Oliver (1993) did not specifically address the validity of the scale.

ADMINISTRATION:

The scale was part of a longer questionnaire self-administered by students in a classroom (Mano and Oliver 1993). A high score suggests that some stimulus has evoked a restful feeling.

MAJOR FINDINGS:

Mano and Oliver (1993) examined the dimensionality and causal structure of product evaluation, affect, and satisfaction. Among the many findings involving the **calmness** emotion was that it was slightly higher for subjects in a low-involvement manipulation.

REFERENCES:

Mano, Haim (1991), ''The Structure and Intensity of Emotional Experiences: Method and Context Convergence,'' *Multivariate Behavioral Research*, 26 (3), 389-411.

———— and Richard L. Oliver (1993), ''Assessing the Dimensionality and Structure of the Consumption Experience: Evaluation, Feeling, and Satisfaction,'' *JCR*, 20 (December), 451-66.

SCALE ITEMS: CALMNESS

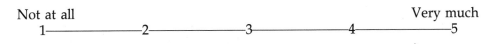

Not at all   Very much

1————————2————————3————————4————————5

1. calm
2. at rest
3. relaxed

SCALE NAME: Change Seeker Index

SCALE DESCRIPTION:

A scale composed of 95 items using a five-point, Likert-type response scale. The scale is intended to measure a personality characteristic concerned with the desire for change and variation in stimuli. The originators of the scale have said that **change seeking** ''is an habitual, consistent pattern of behavior which acts to control the amount and kind of stimulus input a given organism receives'' (Garlington and Shimota 1964, p. 920).

SCALE ORIGIN:

The scale used by Steenkamp and Baumgartner (1992) was adapted from a scale constructed by Garlington and Shimota (1964). The former used a Likert-type response format, whereas the latter used a dichotomous format (like/dislike).

Garlington and Shimota (1964) indicated that they developed the instrument because at that time there was no structured test specifically designed to measure the need for variation. Split-half reliabilities for two different samples were .85 and .80. One-week stability with one sample was estimated as .91, and for another group the three-month stability was .77. Other testing led the authors to conclude that change seeking was not related to IQ but might have some moderate association with age.

SAMPLES:

The sample used by Steenkamp and Baumgartner (1992) was composed of 223 volunteers from undergraduate marketing courses at a university. A lottery with cash prizes was used to help motivate students to participate.

RELIABILITY:

Steenkamp and Baumgartner (1992) reported a reliability (LISREL) of **.915** for the scale.

VALIDITY:

Although the principal components factor analysis conducted by Steenkamp and Baumgartner (1992) produced at least five factors with eigenvalues greater than one, the authors concluded that the scale was basically unidimensional due to scree plots of the eigenvalues. Scores on the scale had correlations of between .41 and .76 with three other measures of optimum stimulation level, which provides some evidence of convergent validity. A confirmatory factor analysis of all four scales also provided some evidence of convergent validity in that the Change Seeker Index not only loaded significantly on the underlying construct but it was the highest standardized factor loading (.89) of the four measures tested.

ADMINISTRATION:

The scale was administered by Steenkamp and Baumgartner (1992) as part of a larger questionnaire composed primarily of four scales that measured optimum stimulation level in various ways. The questionnaire was handed out to students in class, and they were asked to bring the completed form back at the next class period. High scores on the scale indicate that respondents engage in behaviors that bring about variation in stimuli input, whereas low scores indicate respondents dislike such experiences.

MAJOR FINDINGS:

Steenkamp and Baumgartner (1992) studied the role of optimum stimulation level in exploratory consumer behavior. A weighted composite of the **Change Seeker Index** and three other well-known measures were used to examine people's desire for stimulation. Beyond the information provided previously regarding reliability and validity, the authors did not discuss the findings of any one scale (however, they can be obtained from the authors). The authors did conclude that though the **Change Seeker Index** was one of the best scales in terms of reliability and validity, its length made it less convenient to use than one of the other scales that tested well.

REFERENCES:

Garlington, Warren K. and Helen E. Shimota (1964), ''The Change Seeker Index: A Measure of the Need for Variable Stimulus Input,'' *Psychological Reports*, 14, 919-24.

Steenkamp, Jan-Benedict E. M. and Hans Baumgartner (1992), ''The Role of Optimum Stimulation Level in Exploratory Consumer Behavior,'' *JCR*, 19 (December), 434-48.

SCALE ITEMS: CHANGE SEEKER INDEX*

Strongly disagree	Disagree	Neither agree nor disagree	Agree	Strongly agree
−2	−1	0	1	2

1. I think a strong will power is a more valuable gift than a well-informed imagination. **(r)**
2. I like to read newspaper accounts of murders and other forms of violence.
3. I like to conform to custom and to avoid doing things that people I respect might consider unconventional. **(r)**
4. I would like to see a bullfight in Spain.
5. I would prefer to spend vacations in this country, where you know you can get a good holiday, than in foreign lands that are colorful and ''different.'' **(r)**
6. I often take pleasure in certain non-conforming attitudes and behaviors.

7. In general, I would prefer a job with a modest salary but guaranteed security rather than one with large but uncertain earnings. **(r)**
8. I like to feel free to do what I want to do.
9. 2. I like to follow instructions and to do what is expected of me. **(r)**
10. Because I become bored easily, I need plenty of excitement, stimulation, and fun.
11. I like to complete a single job or task at a time before taking on others. **(r)**
12. I like to be independent of others in deciding what I want to do.
13. I am well described as a meditative person, given to finding my own solutions instead of acting on conventional rules.
14. I much prefer symmetry to asymmetry. **(r)**
15. I often do whatever makes me feel cheerful here and now, even at the cost of some distant goal.
16. I can be friendly with people who do things that I consider wrong.
17. I tend to act impulsively.
18. I like to do routine work using a good piece of machinery or apparatus. **(r)**
19. People view me as a quite unpredictable person.
20. I think society should be quicker to adopt new customs and throw aside old habits and mere traditions.
21. I prefer to spend most of my leisure hours with my family. **(r)**
22. In traveling abroad I would rather go on an organized tour than plan for myself the places I will visit. **(r)**
23. I like to have lots of lively people around me.
24. I like to move about the country and to live in different places.
25. I feel that what this world needs is more steady and ''solid'' citizens rather than ''idealists'' with plans for a better world. **(r)**
26. I like to dabble in a number of different hobbies and interests.
27. I like to avoid situations where I am expected to do things in a conventional way.
28. I like to have my life arranged so that it runs smoothly and without much change in my plans. **(r)**
29. I like to continue doing the same old things rather than to try new and different things. **(r)**
30. I would like to hunt lions in Africa.
31. I find myself bored by most tasks after a short time.
32. I believe that it is not a good idea to think too much. **(r)**
33. I always follow the rule: business before pleasure. **(r)**
34. I enjoy gambling for small stakes.
35. Nearly always I have a craving for more excitement.
36. I enjoy doing ''daring,'' foolhardy things ''just for fun.''
37. I see myself as an efficient, businesslike person. **(r)**
38. I like to wear clothing that will attract attention.
39. I cannot keep my mind on one thing for any length of time.
40. I enjoy arguing even if the issue isn't very important.
41. It bothers me if people think I am being too unconventional or odd.
42. I see myself as a practical person. **(r)**
43. I never take medicine on my own, without a doctor's ordering it. **(r)**

44. From time to time, I like to get completely away from work and anything that reminds me of it.
45. At times, I have been very anxious to get away from my family.
46. My parents have often disapproved of my friends.
47. There are several areas in which I am prone to doing things quite unexpectedly.
48. I would prefer to be a steady and dependable worker than a brilliant but unstable one. **(r)**
49. In going places, eating, working, etc., I seem to go in a very deliberate, methodical fashion rather than rush from one thing to another. **(r)**
50. It annoys me to have to wait for someone.
51. I get mad easily and then get over it soon.
52. I find it hard to keep my mind on a task or job unless it is terribly interesting.
53. For me planning one's activities well in advance is very likely to take most of the fun out of life.
54. I like to go to parties and other affairs where there is lots of loud fun.
55. I enjoy lots of social activity.
56. I enjoy thinking up unusual or different ideas to explain everyday events.
57. I seek out fun and enjoyment.
58. I like to experience novelty and change in my daily routine.
59. I like a job that offers change, variety, and travel, even if it involves some danger.
60. In my job, I appreciate constant change in the type of work to be done.
61. I have the wanderlust and am never happy unless I am roaming or traveling about.
62. I have periods of such great restlessness that I cannot sit long in a chair.
63. I like to travel and see the country.
64. I like to plan out my activities in advance, and then follow the plan.
65. I like to be the center of attention in a group.
66. When I get bored, I like to stir up some excitement.
67. I experience periods of boredom with respect to my job.
68. I admire a person who has a strong sense of duty to the things he believes in more than a person who is brilliantly intelligent and creative. **(r)**
69. I like a job that is steady enough for me to become expert at it rather than one that constantly challenges me. **(r)**
70. I like to finish any job or task that I begin. **(r)**
71. I feel better when I give in and avoid a fight than I would if I tried to have my own way. **(r)**
72. I don't like things to be uncertain and unpredictable. **(r)**
73. I am known as a hard and steady worker. **(r)**
74. I would like the job of a foreign correspondent for a newspaper.
75. I used to feel sometimes that I would like to leave home.
76. I find my interests change quite rapidly.
77. I am continually seeking new ideas and experience.
78. I like continually changing activities.
79. I get a lot of bright ideas about all sorts of things—too many to put into practice.
80. I like being amidst a great deal of excitement and bustle.

81. I feel a person just can't be too careful. **(r)**
82. I try to avoid any work which involves patient persistence.
83. Quite often I get "all steamed up" about a project, but then lose interest in it.
84. I would rather drive 5 miles under the speed limit than 5 miles over it. **(r)**
85. Most people bore me.
86. I like to find myself in new situations where I can explore all the possibilities.
87. I much prefer familiar people and places. **(r)**
88. When things get boring, I like to find some new and unfamiliar experience.
89. If I don't like something, I let people know about it.
90. I prefer a routine way of life to an unpredictable one full of change.
91. I feel that people should avoid behavior or situations that will call undue attention to themselves. **(r)**
92. I am quite content with my life as I am now living it. **(r)**
93. I would like to be absent from work (school) more often than I actually am.
94. Sometimes I wanted to leave home, just to explore the world.
95. My life is full of change because I make it so.

* Garlington and Shimota (1964) used dichotomous response alternatives (true/false). In contrast, Steenkamp and Baumgartner (1992) used a five-point scale ranging from "completely false" (–2) to "completely true" (+2).

SCALE NAME: Cognitive Age

SCALE DESCRIPTION:

A four-item, seven-point summated ratings scale measuring a person's perception of their nonchronological age rather than the number of years lived. Although not the same thing, there is a strong correlation between cognitive and chronological age.

SCALE ORIGIN:

The scale was constructed by Barak and Schiffman (1981), on the basis of earlier work by Kastenbaum and colleagues (1972). The latter used lengthy personal interviews to examine four age dimensions. Barak and Schiffman (1981) tested a scale version of that longer measure using 324 older (55) females. A three-week test-retest correlation was .88 (n = 15). Guttman, Lambda, and Spearman-Brown split-half tests were .86 and .85, respectively (n = ?). Thus, these three measures of reliability provided evidence of the scale's internal consistency and stability.

SAMPLES:

Data were collected by Wilkes (1992) from **363** females from three cities in a southwestern state. The ages of respondents ranged from 60 to 79 years. Private, religious, and civic groups were contacted followed by identification of additional groups and eventually the individuals who were asked to participate. Questionnaires apparently were delivered to respondents' homes and then picked up within a week.

RELIABILITY:

Wilkes (1992) reported a composite reliability of **.89**. Reliabilities under the congeneric model for each of the four items were .79 (item 1), .48 (item 2), .72 (item 3), and .65 (item 4).

VALIDITY:

Wilkes (1992) tested three measurement-error models using LISREL 7. The evidence supported the congeneric model, suggesting that the four items are measuring the same latent variable though not with equal reliabilities or validities.

ADMINISTRATION:

Data were gathered through self-administered questionnaires in the study by Wilkes (1992). Scores are computed by calculating the average of the decade midpoints for the four items. A high score indicates that a person perceives him/herself to have a high cognitive age.

MAJOR FINDINGS:

Wilkes (1992) studied the measurement characteristics of **cognitive age** and its association with demographic antecedent variables as well as lifestyle-related consequential factors. Among the many significant findings was that **cognitively younger** women were more work-oriented, had greater fashion interest, and had higher self-confidence than cognitively older females. No significant relationship was found between the **cognitive age** of women and their social involvement.

COMMENTS:

It appears that by adding more decade columns at the lower end one could use the scale to study age perception among younger groups such as teenagers. However, with such a revised instrument and a very different population of interest, the psychometric quality of the scale would have to be reassessed completely.

REFERENCES:

Barak, Benny and Leon G. Schiffman (1981), ''Cognitive Age: A Nonchronological Age Variable,'' in *Advances in Consumer Research*, Vol. 8, Kent B. Monroe, ed. Ann Arbor, MI: Association for Consumer Research, 602-6.

Kastenbaum, Roger, Valerie Derbin, Paul Sabatini, and Steven Artt (1972), '' 'The Ages of Me': Towards Personal and Interpersonal Definitions of Functional Aging,'' *Aging and Human Development*, 3 (2), 197-211.

Wilkes, Robert E. (1992), ''A Structural Modeling Approach to the Measurement and Meaning of Cognitive Age,'' *JCR*, 19 (September), 292-301.

SCALE ITEMS: COGNITIVE AGE

Instructions: Most people seem to have other ''ages'' besides their official or ''date of birth'' age. The questions which follow have been developed to find out about your ''unofficial'' age. Please specify which age group you feel you really belong to: twenties, thirties, forties, fifties, sixties, seventies, or eighties.

	20s	30s	40s	50s	60s	70s	80s
1. I *feel* as though I am in my ____.	___	___	___	___	___	___	___
2. I *look* as though I am in my ____.	___	___	___	___	___	___	___
3. I *do* most things as if I am in my ____.	___	___	___	___	___	___	___
4. My *interests* are mostly those of a ____.	___	___	___	___	___	___	___

SCALE NAME: Cognitive Effort (Choice)

SCALE DESCRIPTION:

A five-item, Likert-type summated ratings scale measuring the cognitive resources such as attention and concentration a person reports bringing to bear on a recently completed consumption-related choice activity.

SCALE ORIGIN:

The scale is original to the work of Cooper-Martin (1993, 1994a).

SAMPLES:

A convenience sample of **36** women was used by Cooper-Martin (1993). The women were from the New York City area and were paid $25 for participating. The mean age was 34 and ranged from 18 to 70 years.

RELIABILITY:

Cooper-Martin (1993) reported an alpha of **.93** for the scale.

VALIDITY:

The validity of the scale was not specifically addressed by Cooper-Martin (1993), although it was said that a factor analysis indicated that this scale and another scale (*intention to choose best alternative*) were independent. In work not reported in the article, a factor analysis was performed on seven items and indicated that the five listed here loaded on the same factor (Cooper-Martin 1994a). However, a more in-depth analysis of the same data set as described here led to a different set of items to be recommended (Cooper-Martin 1994b). It is not clear, therefore, that this set of five is the most valid measure of the construct.

ADMINISTRATION:

The scale was administered along with other measures after subjects had been exposed to experimental stimuli. A high score on the scale indicates that a person believes that a great amount of cognitive resources was expended on some particular choice activity he/she had engaged in.

MAJOR FINDINGS:

Cooper-Martin (1993) examined how the degree of similarity among product alternatives may affect **cognitive effort** and intention to choose the best alternative. Among the findings was that **cognitive effort** (besides comparisons) was lower for a similar set of alternatives than for a dissimilar set.

REFERENCES:

Cooper-Martin, Elizabeth (1993), ''Effects of Information Format and Similarity Among Alternatives on Consumer Choice Processes,'' *JAMS*, 21 (Summer), 239-46.

_____ (1994a), personal correspondence.

_____ (1994b), ''Measures of Cognitive Effort,'' *Marketing Letters*, 5 (1), 43-56.

SCALE ITEMS: COGNITIVE EFFORT (CHOICE)*

1. How much effort did you put into making this decision?

Very little effort	____ : ____ : ____ : ____ : ____ : ____ : ____	A great deal of effort
	1 2 3 4 5 6 7	

Items 2 to 5 use the following response scale:

Strongly disagree	____ : ____ : ____ : ____ : ____ : ____ : ____	Strongly agree
	1 2 3 4 5 6 7	

2. I concentrated a lot while making this choice.
3. I was careful about which _____ I choose.
4. I thought very hard about which _____ I choose.
5. I didn't pay much attention while making this choice. **(r)**

* Items were supplied by Cooper-Martin (1994a). The name of the product category should be placed in the blanks.

SCALE NAME: Communion With Nature

SCALE DESCRIPTION:

A six-item, seven-point, Likert-type summated ratings scale measuring the degree to which a person who has just experienced an outdoor adventure describes it as an escape from his/her previous "world" for a time and enjoy another more natural one.

SCALE ORIGIN:

The origin of the scale was not specified by Arnould and Price (1993), but it appears that it was developed in a series of stages described in their article. An earlier version of the scale with a different item for item 4 had an alpha of .84 and a correlation of .70 with a measure of trip satisfaction.

SAMPLES:

Very little information was provided by Arnould and Price (1993) regarding their sample. The respondents are described simply as a stratified random sample of people taking multi-day river trips with one of three clients' rafting companies. A total of **137** clients filled out post-trip questionnaires, but only 97 of those had completed pre-trip surveys.

RELIABILITY:

Arnould and Price (1993) reported an alpha of **.86** for the scale.

VALIDITY:

A considerable amount of research in the form of participant observation and focus groups was conducted by Arnould and Price (1993) in preparation for development of the scale and probably improved the scale's content validity. A factor analysis of the items in this scale and two others showed that its items for had loadings of at least .64 on the same factor and no greater than .36 on either of the other two factors.

ADMINISTRATION:

The scale was self-administered by respondents as part of a larger survey after they had finished the rafting trip (Arnould and Price 1993). High scores on the scale suggest that respondents have experienced something involving nature that has enabled them to feel like they have truly escaped their previous "world" for a while.

MAJOR FINDINGS:

Arnould and Price (1993) explored the impact of several experiential variables on satisfaction with an extraordinary hedonic experience. There was a strong and significant correlation (r = .61) between one's feeling that the experience had produced a **communion with nature** and overall satisfaction with the trip.

REFERENCES:

Arnould, Eric J. and Linda L. Price (1993), "River Magic: Extraordinary Experience and the Extended Service Encounter," *JCR*, 20 (June), 24-45.

SCALE ITEMS: COMMUNION WITH NATURE*

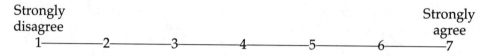

Strongly
disagree
1————2————3————4————5————6————7
Strongly
agree

I felt:
1. harmony with nature.
2. like I explored new worlds.
3. I escaped into a different world.
4. I got a new perspective on nature.
5. freedom from obligations.
6. like I was getting away from it all.

* A short description of the activity should go in the blank (e.g., *rafting trip*).

SCALE NAME: Communion With Others

SCALE DESCRIPTION:

A six-item, seven-point, Likert-type summated ratings scale measuring the degree to which a person who has just gone through an experience with other people describes feeling closer to them because of the events and activities they shared. Arnould and Price (1993) referred to the construct measured as *Communitas*.

SCALE ORIGIN:

The origin of the scale was not specified by Arnould and Price (1993), but it appears that it was developed in a series of stages described in their article.

SAMPLES:

Very little information was provided by Arnould and Price (1993) regarding their sample. The respondents are described simply as a stratified random sample of people taking multi-day river trips with one of three clients' rafting companies. A total of **137** clients filled out post-trip questionnaires, but only 97 of those had completed pre-trip surveys.

RELIABILITY:

Arnould and Price (1993) reported an alpha of **.90** for the scale.

VALIDITY:

A considerable amount of research in the form of participant observation and focus groups was conducted by Arnould and Price (1993) in preparation for development of the scale and probably improved the scale's content validity. A factor analysis of the items in this scale and two others showed that the items for this scale had loadings of at least .67 on the same factor and no greater than .38 on either of the other two factors.

ADMINISTRATION:

The scale was self-administered by respondents as part of a larger survey after they had finished the rafting trip (Arnould and Price 1993). High scores on the scale suggest that respondents have experienced something that has caused them to feel like they have grown closer to the others who shared the same experience.

MAJOR FINDINGS:

Arnould and Price (1993) explored the impact of several experiential variables on satisfaction with an extraordinary hedonic experience. There was a strong and significant correlation (r = .55) between one's feeling that the experience had produced a **communion with others** and overall satisfaction with the trip.

REFERENCES:

Arnould, Eric J. and Linda L. Price (1993), "River Magic: Extraordinary Experience and the Extended Service Encounter," *JCR*, 20 (June), 24-45.

SCALE ITEMS: COMMUNION WITH OTHERS*

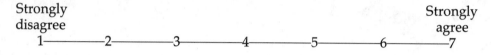

Strongly
disagree
1————2————3————4————5————6————7
Strongly
agree

I felt:
1. in harmony with others.
2. I interacted well with others.
3. I made new friends.
4. my skills were appreciated by others.
5. needed by the group.
6. I pulled my weight.

SCALE NAME: Company Reputation

SCALE DESCRIPTION:

A scale composed of four items with a common seven-point response scale measuring the image a company has with several specific publics.

SCALE ORIGIN:

Goldberg and Hartwick (1990) did not specify the origin of the scale.

SAMPLES:

The sample used by Goldberg and Hartwick (1990) was described as being composed of **416** college students in a required business course. The experiment was conducted on about sixty students at a time in eight different sections of the course. Students were assigned randomly within sections to either positive or negative reputation manipulations and sections were assigned randomly to one of four levels of ad claim extremity.

RELIABILITY:

The scale was reported to have an alpha of **.71** (Goldberg and Hartwick 1990).

VALIDITY:

Goldberg and Hartwick (1990) provided no information regarding the scale's validity.

ADMINISTRATION:

The scale was administered to students along with other questions after being exposed to experimental stimuli in a classroom setting (Goldberg and Hartwick 1990). High scores on the scale suggest that respondents believe that a certain company has a good reputation among several specified publics.

MAJOR FINDINGS:

Goldberg and Hartwick (1990) conducted an advertising experiment in which **advertiser reputation** and ad claim extremity were manipulated. The scale (**company reputation**) was used as a check on the advertiser reputation manipulation. Indeed, mean scores on the scale indicated that the positive and negative company descriptions successfully manipulated subjects' perceptions.

REFERENCES:

Goldberg, Marvin E. and Jon Hartwick (1990), ''The Effects of Advertiser Reputation and Extremity of Advertising Claim on Advertising Effectiveness,'' *JCR*, 17 (September), 172-79.

SCALE ITEMS: COMPANY REPUTATION

What sort of reputation do you think _____ has?*

a poor	____	:	____	:	____	:	____	:	____	:	____	:	____	a good
reputation	-3		-2		-1		0		1		2		3	reputation

1. with its employees?
2. with financial investors?
3. with the U.S. public?
4. with the Canadian public?

* The name of the company being studied should be placed in the blank.

SCALE NAME: Complaint Intentions (Private)

SCALE DESCRIPTION:

A three-item, six-point, Likert-like summated ratings scale measuring the likelihood that a consumer would express his/her dissatisfaction after a purchase to parties not involved in the exchange such as friends and relatives so that they also will not use that service again.

SCALE ORIGIN:

Although Singh (1988, 1990) drew on information previously written by Day (1984), the scale was original. Along with other scales developed in the study, the items were modified on the basis of data collected in a pretest of faculty and staff.

SAMPLES:

Data were collected from four samples by Singh (1988, 1990). Four slightly different survey instruments were used which varied in the dissatisfying experience referred to. One thousand households were sent a questionnaire for each of the four service categories studied: car repairs, grocery stores, medical care, and banking. Response rates were estimated to be more than 50% for each category, given that only around 30% of the random samples had dissatisfying experiences worthy of reporting on a questionnaire. Ultimately, usable data ranged from **116** respondents in the repair service sample to **125** in the medical care sample.

Detailed demographic information for each of the four samples is provided in the article. However, it is difficult to summarize the four profiles given that they varied somewhat, most likely because the instrument itself indicated that the questionnaire was to be completed by the one in the household dealing most with the specified service category. For example, men mostly filled out the questionnaire regarding auto repair (67%) whereas women filled out the one pertaining to grocery shopping (73%).

RELIABILITY:

Singh (1990) reported an alpha of **.77** for the car repair version of the scale.

VALIDITY:

Using data from the car repair sample, the items in this scale along with those for two other related complaint intentions scales (Voice and Third Party) were analyzed using exploratory factor analysis (Singh 1988, 1990). A three-factor structure was obtained and then examined using confirmatory factor analysis for the other three data sets. Results of the CFA provided further support for the three-factor structure and discriminant validity. See Singh (1988) for more validation information.

ADMINISTRATION:

The scale was administered by Singh (1988, 1990) in a mail survey instrument along with many other scales and measures. High scores on the scale indicate that respondents are very likely to express their complaints to friends and relatives after a dissatisfying experience occurs, whereas low scores indicate respondents are not as likely to say anything.

MAJOR FINDINGS:

In a detailed study of consumer complaint behavior, Singh (1990) concluded that there were four consumer clusters with distinct response styles: passives, voicers, irates, and activists. Profiles were developed for each cluster. There was significant variation among the four clusters in their **intentions to complain privately.** Specifically, about twice as many irates said they would complain privately compared with passives and voicers.

COMMENTS:

As noted previously, four transactions were examined in the study by Singh (1988, 1990). However, only the items relating to the car repair were reported. To the extent that one wished to use the scale to study complaints in a non-repair context, one of the other three versions of the scale might be appropriate.

REFERENCES:

Day, Ralph L. (1984), "Modeling Choices Among Alternative Responses to Dissatisfaction," in *Advances in Consumer Research*, Vol. 11, Tom Kinnear, ed. Provo, UT: Association for Consumer Research, 496-99.

Singh, Jagdip (1988), "Consumer Complaint Intentions and Behaviors: Definitional and Taxonomical Issues," *JM*, 52 (January), 93-107.

———— (1990), "A Typology of Consumer Dissatisfaction Response Styles," *JR*, 66 (Spring), 57-97.

SCALE ITEMS: COMPLAINT INTENTIONS (PRIVATE)

Very unlikely ____ : ____ : ____ : ____ : ____ : ____ Very likely
               1   2   3   4   5   6

How likely is it that you would:
1. decide not to use the repair shop again?
2. speak to your friends and relatives about your bad experience?
3. convince your friends and relatives not to use that repair shop?

SCALE NAME: Complaint Intentions (Third Party)

SCALE DESCRIPTION:

A four-item, six-point Likert-like summated ratings scale measuring the likelihood that a consumer would express his/her dissatisfaction after a purchase to parties not involved in the exchange but which could bring some pressure to bear on the offending marketer. Such third parties could be consumer organizations, the media, or lawyers.

SCALE ORIGIN:

Although Singh (1988, 1990) drew on information previously written by Day (1984), the scale was original. Along with other scales developed in the study, the items were modified on the basis of data collected in a pretest of faculty and staff.

SAMPLES:

Data were collected from four samples by Singh (1988, 1990). Four slightly different survey instruments were used which varied in the dissatisfying experience referred to. One thousand households were sent a questionnaire for each of the four service categories studied: car repairs, grocery stores, medical care, and banking. Response rates were estimated to be more than 50% for each category given that only around 30% of the random samples had dissatisfying experiences worthy of reporting on a questionnaire. Ultimately, usable data ranged from **116** respondents in the repair service sample to **125** in the medical care sample.

Detailed demographic information for each of the four samples is provided in the article. However, it is difficult to summarize the four profiles given that they varied somewhat, most likely because the instrument itself indicated that the questionnaire was to be completed by the one in the household dealing most with the specified service category. For example, men mostly filled out the questionnaire regarding auto repair (67%), whereas women filled out the one pertaining to grocery shopping (73%).

RELIABILITY:

Singh (1990) reported an alpha of **.84** for the car repair version of the scale.

VALIDITY:

Using data from the car repair sample, the items in this scale along with those for two other related complaint intentions scales (Voice and Private) were analyzed using exploratory factor analysis (Singh 1988, 1990). A three-factor structure was obtained and then examined using confirmatory factor analysis for the other three data sets. Results of the CFA provided further support for the three factor structure and discriminant validity. (See Singh [1988] for more validation information.)

ADMINISTRATION:

The scale was administered by Singh (1988, 1990) in a mail survey instrument along with many other scales and measures. High scores on the scale indicate that respondents are very likely to express their complaints after a dissatisfying experience to third parties not involved in the exchange in order to seek some remedy, whereas those with low scores are not likely to approach those parties.

MAJOR FINDINGS:

In a detailed study of consumer complaint behavior, Singh (1990) concluded that there were four consumer clusters with distinct response styles: passives, voicers, irates, and activists. Profiles were developed for each cluster. **Intention to complain to third parties** was the least likely type of complaining to occur for each of the clusters, but there was still some significant variation among the groups. Specifically, a greater percentage of actives were likely to complain this way, with the portion being more than three times as great as passives and voicers.

COMMENTS:

As noted previously, four transactions were examined in the study by Singh (1988, 1990). However, only the items relating to the car repair were reported. To the extent that one wished to use the scale to study complaints in a non-repair context, one of the other three versions of the scale might be appropriate.

REFERENCES:

Day, Ralph L. (1984), ''Modeling Choices Among Alternative Responses to Dissatisfaction,'' in *Advances in Consumer Research*, Vol. 11, Tom Kinnear, ed. Provo, UT: Association for Consumer Research, 496-99.

Singh, Jagdip (1988), ''Consumer Complaint Intentions and Behaviors: Definitional and Taxonomical Issues,'' *JM*, 52 (January), 93-107.

———— (1990), ''A Typology of Consumer Dissatisfaction Response Styles,'' *JR*, 66 (Spring), 57-97.

SCALE ITEMS: COMPLAINT INTENTIONS (THIRD PARTY)

Very unlikely   ____ : ____ : ____ : ____ : ____ : ____   Very likely

                  1   2   3   4   5   6

How likely is it that you would:
1. complain to a consumer agency and ask them to make the repair shop take care of your problem?
2. write a letter to a local newspaper about your bad experience?
3. report to a consumer agency so that they can warn other consumers?
4. take some legal action against the repair shop/manufacturer?

SCALE NAME: Complaint Intentions (Voice)

SCALE DESCRIPTION:

A three-item, six-point, Likert-like summated ratings scale measuring the likelihood that a consumer would aim complaints at those marketers (e.g., salespersons or managers) involved in the offending transaction.

SCALE ORIGIN:

Although Singh (1988, 1990) drew on information previously written by Day (1984), the scales are original. Along with other scales developed in the study, the items were modified on the basis of data collected in a pretest of faculty and staff.

SAMPLES:

Data were collected from four samples by Singh (1988, 1990). Four slightly different survey instruments were used which varied in the dissatisfying experience referred to. One thousand households were sent a questionnaire for each of the four service categories studied: car repairs, grocery stores, medical care, and banking. Response rates were estimated to be more than 50% for each category given that only around 30% of the random samples had dissatisfying experiences worthy of reporting on a questionnaire. Ultimately, usable data ranged from **116** respondents in the repair service sample to **125** in the medical care sample.

Detailed demographic information for each of the four samples is provided in the article. However, it is difficult to summarize the four profiles given that they varied somewhat, most likely because the instrument itself indicated that the questionnaire was to be completed by the one in the household dealing most with the specified service category. For example, men mostly filled out the questionnaire regarding auto repair (67%) whereas women filled out the one pertaining to grocery shopping (73%).

RELIABILITY:

Singh (1990) reported an alpha of **.75** for the car repair version of the scale.

VALIDITY:

Using data from the car repair sample, the items in this scale along with those for two other related complaint intentions scales (Private and Third Party) were analyzed using exploratory factor analysis (Singh 1988, 1990). A three-factor structure was obtained and then examined using confirmatory factor analysis for the other three data sets. Results of the CFA provided further support for the three-factor structure and discriminant validity. See Singh (1988) for more validation information.

ADMINISTRATION:

The scale was administered by Singh (1988, 1990) in a mail survey instrument along with many other scales and measures. High scores on the scale indicate that respondents are very likely to complain to service providers if a dissatisfying experience occurs, whereas low scores indicate respondents are more likely to do nothing.

MAJOR FINDINGS:

In a detailed study of consumer complaint behavior, Singh (1990) concluded that there were four consumer clusters with distinct response styles: passives, voicers, irates, and activists. Profiles were developed for each cluster. There was significant variation among the four clusters in their **intentions to voice complaints.** Specifically, twice as many voicers said they would voice their complaints compared with passives.

COMMENTS:

As noted previously, four transactions were examined in the study by Singh (1988, 1990). However, only the items relating to the car repair were reported. To the extent that one wished to use the scale to study complaints in a non-repair context, one of the other three versions of the scale might be appropriate.

REFERENCES:

Day, Ralph L. (1984), ''Modeling Choices Among Alternative Responses to Dissatisfaction,'' on *Advances in Consumer Research*, Vol. 11, Tom Kinnear, ed. Provo, UT: Association for Consumer Research, 496-99.

Singh, Jagdip (1988), ''Consumer Complaint Intentions and Behaviors: Definitional and Taxonomical Issues,'' *JM*, 52 (January), 93-107.

_____ (1990), ''A Typology of Consumer Dissatisfaction Response Styles,'' *JR*, 66 (Spring), 57-97.

SCALE ITEMS: COMPLAINT INTENTIONS (VOICE)

Very unlikely ____ : ____ : ____ : ____ : ____ : ____ Very likely

1   2   3   4   5   6

How likely is it that you would:
1. forget the incident and do nothing? **(r)**
2. definitely complain to the store manager on your next trip?
3. go back or call the repair shop immediately and ask them to take care of the problem.

SCALE NAME: Complaint Success Likelihood

SCALE DESCRIPTION:

A three-item, six-point Likert-like summated ratings scale measuring a consumer's degree of expectation that a complaint would be responded to in a positive way by a marketer. The construct measured by the scale is referred to as ''expectancy (voice)'' in Singh (1990a) and ''probability of a successful complaint'' in Singh (1990b). Three slightly different versions of the scale were used depending on the service category being studied.

SCALE ORIGIN:

Although Singh (1990a, 1990b) drew on similar studies by Day (1984) and Richins (1983), the scale was original. Along with other scales developed in the study, the items were modified on the basis of data collected in a pretest of faculty and staff.

SAMPLES:

Data were collected from four samples by Singh (1988, 1990a, 1990b). Four slightly different survey instruments were used which varied in the dissatisfying experience referred to. One thousand households were sent a questionnaire for each of the four service categories studied: car repairs, grocery stores, medical care, and banking. Response rates were estimated to be more than 50% for each category given that only around 30% of the random samples had dissatisfying experiences worthy of reporting on a questionnaire. Responses from the banking sample were excluded from the analysis reported in the 1990b article. Ultimately, usable data ranged from **116** respondents in the repair service sample to **125** in the medical care sample.

Detailed demographic information for each of the four samples is provided in the article. However, it is difficult to summarize the four profiles given that they varied somewhat, most likely because the instrument itself indicated that the questionnaire was to be completed by the one in the household dealing most with the specified service category. For example, men mostly filled out the questionnaire regarding auto repair (67%) whereas women filled out the one pertaining to grocery shopping (73%).

RELIABILITY:

Singh (1990b) reported composite reliabilities of **.84, .89,** and **.93** for the grocery, car repair, and medical care versions of the scale, respectively.

VALIDITY:

Using results from a LISREL analysis, the author concluded that the scale provided acceptable evidence of discriminant validity (variance extracted, variance shared) in each of the three service categories examined.

ADMINISTRATION:

The scale was administered by Singh (1988, 1990a, 1990b) in a mail survey instrument along with many other scales and measures. High scores on the scale indicate that respondents have strong expectations that if they complain after a dissatisfying experience the offending marketer will make a positive response.

MAJOR FINDINGS:

Singh (1988, 1990a, 1990b) made a detailed study of consumer complaint behavior. In the 1990b article he focused specifically on using a theoretical framework to explain and predict complaint behaviors across the service categories. Among the many findings was that higher levels of expected **complaint success** were associated with lower levels of exit and word-of-mouth complaining behaviors across all three service categories.

REFERENCES:

Day, Ralph L. (1984), ''Modeling Choices Among Alternative Responses to Dissatisfaction,'' in *Advances in Consumer Research*, Vol. 11, Tom Kinnear, ed. Provo, UT: Association for Consumer Research, 496-99.

Richins, Marsha (1983), ''Negative Word-of-Mouth By Dissatisfied Customers: A Pilot Study,'' *JM*, 47 (Winter), 68-78.

Singh, Jagdip (1988), ''Consumer Complaint Intentions and Behaviors: Definitional and Taxonomical Issues,'' *JM*, 52 (January), 93-107.

_____ (1990a), ''A Typology of Consumer Dissatisfaction Response Styles,'' *JR*, 66 (Spring), 57-97.

_____ (1990b), ''Voice, Exit, and Negative Word-of-Mouth Behaviors: An Investigation Across Three Service Categories,'' *JAMS*, 18 (Winter), 1-15.

SCALE ITEMS: COMPLAINT SUCCESS LIKELIHOOD*

Very unlikely   ____ : ____ : ____ : ____ : ____ : ____   Very likely
                   1   2   3   4   5   6

Assume you reported the incident to the _____, how likely is it that the _____ would:
1. take appropriate action to take care of your problem (refund, etc.)?
2. solve your problem and give service to you in the future?
3. be more careful in the future and everyone would benefit?

* As Singh (1990a, 1990b) did, the blanks can be filled in with an appropriate term or phrase describing the marketer being studied.

SCALE NAME: Complaint Worthiness

SCALE DESCRIPTION:

A three-item, six-point, Likert-like summated ratings scale measuring the likelihood that a consumer would complain to an offending marketer if it was expected that the latter would respond in a positive way. The construct measured by the scale is referred to as "value (voice)" in Singh (1990a) and "worthiness of complaint" in Singh (1990b). Three slightly different versions of the scale were used depending on the service category being studied.

SCALE ORIGIN:

Singh (1990a, 1990b) used the approach described by Bagozzi (1982, p. 577) to develop the scale. Along with other scales developed in the study, the items were modified on the basis of data collected in a pretest of faculty and staff.

SAMPLES:

Data were collected from four samples by Singh (1988, 1990a, 1990b). Four slightly different survey instruments were used which varied in the dissatisfying experience referred to. One thousand households were sent a questionnaire for each of the four service categories studied: car repairs, grocery stores, medical care, and banking. Response rates were estimated to be more than 50% for each category given that only around 30% of the random samples had dissatisfying experiences worthy of reporting on a questionnaire. Responses from the banking sample were excluded from the analysis reported in the 1990b article. Ultimately, usable data ranged from **116** respondents in the repair service sample to **125** in the medical care sample.

Detailed demographic information for each of the four samples is provided in the article. However, it is difficult to summarize the four profiles given that they varied somewhat, most likely because the instrument itself indicated that the questionnaire was to be completed by the one in the household dealing most with the specified service category. For example, men mostly filled out the questionnaire regarding auto repair (67%), whereas women filled out the one pertaining to grocery shopping (73%).

RELIABILITY:

Singh (1990b) reported composite reliabilities of **.84, .89,** and **.93** for the grocery, car repair, and medical care versions of the scale, respectively.

VALIDITY:

Using results from a LISREL analysis, the author concluded that the scale provided acceptable evidence of discriminant validity (variance extracted, variance shared) in each of the three service categories examined.

ADMINISTRATION:

The scale was administered by Singh (1988, 1990a, 1990b) in a mail survey instrument along with many other scales and measures. High scores on the scale indicate that respondents are likely to complain after a dissatisfying experience to the offending marketer if it is expected that the latter will make a positive response.

MAJOR FINDINGS:

Singh (1988, 1990a, 1990b) made a detailed study of consumer complaint behavior. In the 1990b article, he focused specifically on using a theoretical framework to explain and predict complaint behaviors across the service categories. Among the many findings was that the higher consumers' perception of **complaint worthiness,** the greater the tendency to voice a complaint to the offending marketers. This was found for the grocery and medical care data but not for the car repair data.

REFERENCES:

Bagozzi, Richard P. (1982), ''A Field Investigation of Causal Relations Among Cognitions, Affect, Intentions, and Behavior,'' *JMR*, 19 (November), 562-84.

Singh, Jagdip (1988), ''Consumer Complaint Intentions and Behaviors: Definitional and Taxonomical Issues,'' *JM*, 52 (January), 93-107.

_____ (1990a), ''A Typology of Consumer Dissatisfaction Response Styles,'' *JR*, 66 (Spring), 57-97.

_____ (1990b), ''Voice, Exit, and Negative Word-of-Mouth Behaviors: An Investigation Across Three Service Categories,'' *JAMS*, 18 (Winter), 1-15.

SCALE ITEMS: COMPLAINT WORTHINESS*

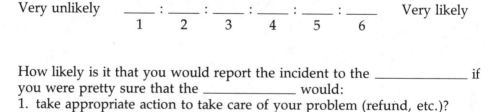

Very unlikely ___ : ___ : ___ : ___ : ___ : ___ Very likely
           1   2   3   4   5   6

How likely is it that you would report the incident to the _____ if you were pretty sure that the _____ would:
1. take appropriate action to take care of your problem (refund, etc.)?
2. solve your problem and give service to you in the future?
3. be more careful in the future and everyone would benefit?

* As Singh (1990a, 1990b) did, the blanks can be filled in with an appropriate term or phrase describing the marketer being studied.

SCALE NAME: Compulsivity (General)

SCALE DESCRIPTION:

A five-item, five-point, Likert-type summated ratings scale measuring the degree to which a person is characterized by an abnormal amount of fear, worry, and self-debasing feelings and attitudes. This measure was called *obsessive-compulsive* by O'Guinn and Faber (1989; Faber and O'Guinn 1992).

SCALE ORIGIN:

The scale represents a subset of items from scale 7 of the Minnesota Multiphasic Personality Inventory (Dahlstrom et al. 1982a). That scale is purported to measure the obsessive-compulsive syndrome and has a long history of development and use. In a variety of studies using a variety of measures, internal consistency always has been more than .80 (Dahlstrom et al. 1982b, p.260). Test-retest correlations have been estimated in numerous studies as well and seem to have been influenced by several factors the main one being the time between administrations. For example, .93 was calculated for male college students when there was a one-day interval, but .37 was reported for male adolescents with a three-year interval (Dahlstrom et al. 1982b, pp. 253-259). The items used by O'Guinn and Faber (1989) were those reported to have the highest item-total correlation (Dahlstrom 1982a, p. 213).

SAMPLES:

Two samples were employed by O'Guinn and Faber (1989). One was of **386** completed responses (out of 808 questionnaires sent) from people who previously had written an organization that aided compulsive buyers. A second group was used for comparison purposes and was intended to represent the general population. Eight hundred questionnaires were mailed to people in three Illinois areas: Chicago, Springfield, and Bloomington-Normal. Two mailings produced a total of **250** completed survey forms. The database used in Faber and O'Guinn (1992) is basically the same except that sample 1 had a few more responses (n = 388) and the second survey benefited from a third mailing (n = 292).

RELIABILITY:

Alphas of **.92** and **.85** have been reported for the scale by O'Guinn and Faber (1989) and Faber and O'Guinn (1992), respectively.

VALIDITY:

No specific examination of scale validity was made by O'Guinn and Faber (1989), but some evidence of criterion validity was found by noting that two known groups had significantly different mean scores on the scale and the differences were in the hypothesized directions (see ''Major Findings'').

ADMINISTRATION:

The scale was one of several self-administered measures used in mail survey instruments O'Guinn and Faber (1989; Faber and O'Guinn 1992). High scores on the scale indicate that respondents have a tendency to engage in compulsive behaviors, whereas those with low scores are not likely to have abnormal obsessions.

MAJOR FINDINGS:

O'Guinn and Faber (1989) studied compulsive shopping. Their results showed that a sample of compulsive shoppers scored significantly higher on the **compulsivity** scale than a general sample of consumers. Although using the same general database, Faber and O'Guinn (1992) reported on the development and testing of a scale to identify compulsive buyers.

REFERENCES:

Dahlstrom, W. Grant, George Schlager Welsh, and Leona E. Dahlstrom (1982a), *An MMPI Handbook: Clinical Interpretation (Vol. I).* Minneapolis: University of Minnesota Press.

_____, _____, and _____ (1982b), *An MMPI Handbook: Research Applications (Vol. 2).* Minneapolis: University of Minnesota Press.

Faber, Ronald J. and Thomas C. O'Guinn (1992), ''A Clinical Screener for Compulsive Buying,'' *JCR,* 19 (December), 459-69.

O'Guinn, Thomas C. and Ronald J. Faber (1989), ''Compulsive Buying: A Phenomenological Exploration,'' *JCR,* 16 (September), 147-57.

SCALE ITEMS: COMPULSIVITY (GENERAL)

Strongly disagree	Disagree	Neutral	Agree	Strongly agree
1	2	3	4	5

1. I frequently find myself worrying about something.
2. Almost everyday something happens to frighten me.
3. Even when I am with people I feel lonely much of the time.
4. Much of the time I feel as if I have done something wrong or evil.
5. I am certainly lacking in self confidence.

SCALE NAME: Compulsivity (Purchase)

SCALE DESCRIPTION:

A three-item, five-point, Likert-type summated ratings scale measuring the frequency with which a consumer buys something not so much because of a desire for the product itself but as a desire to engage in purchase activity. The scale was called *object attachment* by O'Guinn and Faber (1989; Faber and O'Guinn 1992).

SCALE ORIGIN:

The scale was apparently original to O'Guinn and Faber (1989).

SAMPLES:

O'Guinn and Faber (1989) used two samples. One was of **386** completed responses (out of 808 questionnaires sent) from people who previously had written an organization that aided compulsive buyers. A second group was used for comparison purposes and was intended to represent the general population. Eight hundred questionnaires were mailed to people in three Illinois areas: Chicago, Springfield, and Bloomington-Normal. Two mailings produced a total of **250** completed survey forms. The database used in Faber and O'Guinn (1992) is basically the same except that sample 1 had a few more responses (n = 388) and the second survey benefited from a third mailing (n = 292).

RELIABILITY:

An alpha of **.75** was reported for this scale (O'Guinn and Faber 1989; Faber and O'Guinn 1992).

VALIDITY:

Beyond a factor analysis, which indicated that the items loaded together, no specific examination of scale validity was reported (O'Guinn and Faber 1989).

ADMINISTRATION:

The scale was one of several self-administered measures used in mail survey instruments (O'Guinn and Faber 1989; Faber and O'Guinn 1992). High scores on the scale indicate that respondents frequently purchase items that they do not need out of a compulsion just to buy something, whereas low scores suggest they either do not purchase a lot or what they do buy they feel they used and needed.

MAJOR FINDINGS:

O'Guinn and Faber (1989) studied compulsive shopping. Their results showed that a sample of shoppers who were generally more compulsive also exhibited significantly more **purchase compulsion** than a general sample of consumers. This supports the position that compulsive buyers are less motivated by the desire to own the object of the purchase and more motivated by the activity of purchasing itself. Although using the same general database, Faber and O'Guinn (1992) reported on the development and testing of a scale to identify compulsive buyers.

REFERENCES:

Faber, Ronald J. and Thomas C. O'Guinn (1992), "A Clinical Screener for Compulsive Buying," *JCR*, 19 (December), 459-69.

O'Guinn, Thomas C. and Ronald J. Faber (1989), "Compulsive Buying: A Phenomenological Exploration," *JCR*, 16 (September), 147-57.

SCALE ITEMS: COMPULSIVITY (PURCHASE)*

Very infrequent	Infrequent	Sometimes	Frequent	Very frequent
1————	——2————	——3————	——4————	—5

How frequently have you experienced each of the following?
1. bought something and when I got home wasn't sure why I had bought it.
2. just wanted to buy things and didn't care what I bought.
3. my closets are full of unopened items.

* Except for the items themselves, this is the assumed structure of the rest of the scale because it was not described in the article.

SCALE NAME: Confidence (Computer Use)

SCALE DESCRIPTION:

A three-item, seven-point summated rating scale assessing the ease of using a microcomputer to perform some task that a person reports experiencing.

SCALE ORIGIN:

The origin of the scale was not specified by Ozanne, Brucks, and Grewal (1992), but there was nothing to indicate that it was developed by anyone but the authors for that particular study.

SAMPLES:

Ozanne, Brucks, and Grewal (1992) used a sample composed of 43 undergraduate business majors. The study took place at a major state university, and students agreed to participate in the study as one way to meet a course requirement.

RELIABILITY:

Ozanne, Brucks, and Grewal (1992) reported an alpha for the scale of .72.

VALIDITY:

Ozanne, Brucks, and Grewal (1992) discussed no examination of the scale's validity.

ADMINISTRATION:

The scale was employed by Ozanne, Brucks, and Grewal (1992) as a check on the similarity of subject in different treatments in their ease of performing the experimental task (see "Major Findings"). The scale was scored such that a low score meant that a person perceived him/herself to be very comfortable performing the task on the computer.

MAJOR FINDINGS:

Ozanne, Brucks, and Grewal (1992) examined the information search behavior of consumers with particular regard for the process of categorizing products that differ from previously familiar categories. The **confidence** of subjects in using the computer to perform the experimental task was checked to ensure that it was reasonably similar. No differences were found between those people randomly assigned to the luxury car and the economy car conditions.

REFERENCES:

Ozanne, Julie L., Merrie Brucks, and Dhruv Grewal (1992), "A Study of Information Search Behavior During the Categorization of New Products," *JCR*, 18 (March), 452-63.

SCALE ITEMS: CONFIDENCE (COMPUTER USE)

1. I felt _____ on the microcomputer.

Uncomfortable ____ : ____ : ____ : ____ : ____ : ____ : ____ Comfortable
                  7   6   5   4   3   2   1

2. I did _____ the computer.

Not understand ____ : ____ : ____ : ____ : ____ : ____ : ____ Understand
                 7   6   5   4   3   2   1

3. I am _____ in using the computer.

Not confident ____ : ____ : ____ : ____ : ____ : ____ : ____ Very confident
               7   6   5   4   3   2   1

SCALE NAME: Conformity Motivation

SCALE DESCRIPTION:

A 13-item, six-point summated ratings scale measuring the degree to which a person looks to others to determine how to behave and desires to act in accordance with group norms. This measure was called Attention to Social Comparison Information (ATSCI) by Lennox and Wolfe (1984) as well as Bearden and colleagues (1989).

SCALE ORIGIN:

The scale was constructed by Lennox and Wolfe (1984) in the process of refining an index of self-monitoring measures presented previously by Snyder (1974). The scale was developed in several stages, the final version being tested on 224 introductory psychology students at SUNY Genesco who were required to participate as part of a course. Testing occurred in small groups. The scale had an alpha of .83 and item-total correlations between .34 and .60. It was concluded that this should not be considered a component of the self-monitoring construct though it does seem to measure tendency to conform.

SAMPLES:

This was just one of many samples used in a series of studies by Bearden and colleagues (1989). All that is known about the sample used with respect to this scale was that it was composed of 47 undergraduate business students.

The article by Bearden and Rose (1990) reported using the scale in four different studies/samples. Each sample was apparently composed of undergraduate business students with the following sizes for studies 1 to 4, respectively: 62, 99, 63, and 85.

RELIABILITY:

Bearden and colleagues (1989) reported an alpha of .82 for the scale. Bearden and Rose (1990) reported alphas of .85, .83, .88, and .89 for the scale in studies 1 to 4, respectively.

VALIDITY:

This scale was used by Bearden and colleagues (1989) to help validate two other scales constructed in the study. Therefore, beyond the findings discussed here no other examination of its validity was reported.

In contrast, one of the purposes of the studies conducted by Bearden and Rose (1990) was to evaluate the validity of the scale. These studies provided evidence of the scale's convergent and discriminant validity.

ADMINISTRATION:

The scale was self-administered in all of the studies (Bearden et al. 1989; Bearden and Rose 1990). High scores on the scale indicate that respondents are strongly motivated to seek information from others about appropriate behavior and desire to conform to group norms.

MAJOR FINDINGS:

The purpose of the study by Bearden and colleagues(1989) was to develop scales for measuring the dimensions of consumer susceptibility to interpersonal influence. A series of studies provided support for a two-factor model (normative and informational factors). Among the many findings was that the normative factor had a significantly stronger positive correlation than the informational factor with **conformity motivation.**

Bearden and Rose (1990) conducted a series of studies to investigate the reliability and validity of a measure of attention to social comparison information (**social conformity**) and the extent to which this construct is a moderator of interpersonal influence. The results indicated that the scale was internally consistent and valid and that it moderates the influence of interpersonal considerations on behavioral intentions.

REFERENCES:

Bearden, William O., Richard G. Netemeyer, and Jesse E. Teel (1989), ''Measurement of Consumer Susceptibility to Interpersonal Influence,'' *JCR*, 15 (March), 473-81.

_____ and Randall L. Rose (1990), ''Attention to Social Comparison Information: An Individual Difference Factor Affecting Consumer Conformity,'' *JCR*, 16 (March), 461-71.

Lennox, Richard D. and Raymond N. Wolfe (1984), ''Revision of the Self-Monitoring Scale,'' *Journal of Personality and Social Psychology*, 46 (6), 1349-64.

Snyder, Mark (1974), ''The Self-Monitoring of Expressive Behavior,'' *Journal of Personality and Social Psychology*, 30 (October), 526-37.

SCALE ITEMS: CONFORMITY MOTIVATION

Respond to the statements below using the following scale:

0 = Certainly, always false
1 = Generally false
2 = Somewhat false, but with exception
3 = Somewhat true, but with exception
4 = Generally true
5 = Certainly, always true

1. It is my feeling that if everyone else in a group is behaving in a certain manner, this must be the way to behave.
2. I actively avoid wearing clothes that are not in style.

3. At parties I usually try to behave in a manner that makes me fit in.
4. When I am uncertain how to act in a social situation, I look to the behavior of others for cues.
5. I try to pay attention to the reaction of others to my behavior in order to avoid being out of place.
6. I find that I tend to pick up slang expressions from others and use them as part of my own vocabulary.
7. I tend to pay attention to what others are wearing.
8. The slightest look of disapproval in the eyes of a person with whom I am interacting is enough to make me change my approach.
9. It's important to me to fit in with the group I'm with.
10. My behavior often depends on how I feel others wish me to behave.
11. If I am the least bit uncertain as to how to act in a social situation, I look to the behavior of others for cues.
12. I usually keep up with clothing style changes by watching what others wear.
13. When in a social situation, I tend not to follow the crowd, but instead behave in a manner that suits my particular mood at the time.*

* Numerical response should be reverse coded before calculating scale scores.

SCALE NAME: Consumption Motivation (Objective)

SCALE DESCRIPTION:

A five-item, five-point summated ratings scale measuring the importance a consumer places on objective, functional, and economic issues before buying five common products. This was referred to as Economic Motivations for Consumption by Moschis (1978, 1981) and Carlson and Grossbart (1988; Grossbart, Carlson, and Walsh 1991).

SCALE ORIGIN:

The measure originates from a dissertation published by Moschis in 1978. His study, reported subsequently, is from that same dissertation research.

SAMPLES:

The data in Moschis (1981) came from **806** middle or senior high school students. There were 365 "older" adolescents (15 years of age and older) and 441 "younger" adolescents (younger than 15 years of age). The students came from 13 schools and seven towns in Wisconsin representing a wide variety of urban to rural situations. The author indicates that the sample was well balanced in terms of most demographic characteristics except for sex— nearly two-thirds of the respondents were female.

The same data set is reported on in two articles by Carlson and Grossbart (1988; Grossbart, Carlson, and Walsh 1991). The survey instrument was distributed to mothers via students at three elementary schools of an unidentified U.S. city. The schools were chosen on a convenience basis but appeared to represent a variety of socioeconomic areas of the city. A $1 contribution was made to the PTO for each completed questionnaire returned by the children. Analysis was based on **451** completed questionnaires. Ninety-three percent of the responding mothers indicated that they were the primary person in the child's socialization.

RELIABILITY:

Alphas of **.69** and **.73** were reported for the scale by Moschis (1981) and Carlson and Grossbart (1988; Grossbart, Carlson, and Walsh 1991), respectively.

VALIDITY:

No examination of scale validity was reported, although Grossbart, Carlson, and Walsh (1991) reported a beta of .69.

ADMINISTRATION:

The scale was self-administered along with other measures in the studies reported by Moschis (1981) as well as Carlson and Grossbart (1988; Grossbart, Carlson, and Walsh 1991). Scores are calculated by adding up for the five products the total number of "objective" issues a person says he/she would consider before purchasing. High scores on the scale indicate that respondents are concerned about "objective" issues before making purchases, whereas low scores suggest that they are not very much motivated by functional or economic considerations.

MAJOR FINDINGS:

The study by Moschis (1981) investigated the validity of the cognitive development approach to socialization (e.g., Piaget) to predict a wide variety of consumer-related cognitions learned during adolescence. In general, the findings indicated that the cognitive developmental model did not explain consumer socialization during adolescence very well. Older adolescents had significantly less favorable attitudes toward advertising, brands, and prices compared with younger adolescents but had significantly greater **"objective" consumptive motivations.**

Carlson and Grossbart (1988; Grossbart, Carlson, and Walsh 1991) investigated the relationship between general parental socialization styles and children's consumer socialization. **Objective motivations for consumption** significantly differentiated between several of the parental socialization styles examined. Specifically, "Authoritative" mothers scored highest on the scale and "Neglecting" mothers scored lowest.

REFERENCES:

Carlson, Les and Sanford Grossbart (1988), "Parental Style and Consumer Socialization of Children," *JCR*, 15 (June), 77-94.

Grossbart, Sanford, Les Carlson, and Ann Walsh (1991), "Consumer Socialization and Frequency of Shopping with Children," *JAMS*, 19 (Summer), 155-63.

Moschis, George P. (1978), *Acquisition of the Consumer Role By Adolescents*, Research Monograph No. 82. Atlanta, Georgia: Publishing Services Division, College of Business Administration, Georgia State University.

_____ (1981), "Patterns of Consumer Learning," *JAMS*, 9 (2), 110-26.

SCALE ITEMS: CONSUMPTION MOTIVATION (OBJECTIVE)

Strongly disagree	Disagree	Neutral	Agree	Strongly agree
1	2	3	4	5

Before purchasing a product it is important to know:

1. Guarantees on different brands.
2. Name of the company that makes the product.
3. Whether any brands are on sale.
4. Kinds of materials different brands are made of.
5. Quality of store selling a particular brand.

SCALE NAME: Consumption Motivation (Social)

SCALE DESCRIPTION:

A four-item, five-point, Likert-type summated ratings scale measuring the importance a consumer places on what others think or are doing before buying five common products. This was referred to as Social Motivations for Consumption by Moschis (1978, 1981) and Carlson and Grossbart (1988; Grossbart, Carlson, and Walsh 1991).

SCALE ORIGIN:

The measure originates from a dissertation published by Moschis in 1978. His study, reported subsequently, is from that same dissertation research.

SAMPLES:

The data in Moschis (1981) came from **806** middle or senior high school students. There were 365 "older" adolescents (15 years of age and older) and 441 "younger" adolescents (younger than 15 years of age). The students came from 13 schools and seven towns in Wisconsin representing a wide variety of urban to rural situations. The author indicates that the sample was well balanced in terms of most demographic characteristics except for sex—nearly two-thirds of the respondents were female.

The same data set is reported on in two articles by Carlson and Grossbart (1988; Grossbart, Carlson, and Walsh 1991). The survey instrument was distributed to mothers via students at three elementary schools of an unidentified U.S. city. The schools were chosen on a convenience basis but appeared to represent a variety of socioeconomic areas of the city. A $1 contribution was made to the PTO for each completed questionnaire returned by the children. Analysis was based on **451** completed questionnaires. Ninety-three percent of the responding mothers indicated that they were the primary person in the child's socialization.

RELIABILITY:

Alphas of .85 and .74 were reported for the scale by Moschis (1981) and Carlson and Grossbart (1988; Grossbart, Carlson, and Walsh 1991), respectively.

VALIDITY:

No examination of scale validity has been reported except that Grossbart, Carlson, and Walsh (1991) reported that the scale had a beta of .67.

ADMINISTRATION:

The scale was self-administered along with other measures in the studies reported by Moschis (1981) as well as Carlson and Grossbart (1988; Grossbart, Carlson, and Walsh 1991). Scores are calculated by adding up for the five products the total number of social issues a person says he/she would consider before purchasing. High scores on the scale indicate that respondents have a high sensitivity about the social visibility of their consumption, whereas low scores suggest that they are not very much motivated by social visibility considerations.

MAJOR FINDINGS:

The study by Moschis (1981) investigated the validity of the cognitive development approach to socialization (e.g., Piaget) to predict a wide variety of consumer-related cognitions learned during adolescence. In general, the findings indicated that the cognitive developmental model did not explain consumer socialization during adolescence very well. Older adolescents had significantly less favorable attitudes towards advertising, brands, and prices compared to younger children but used a significantly greater prepurchase information source usage. No significant difference was found between the two groups of adolescents based upon their **social visibility consumption motivation**.

Carlson and Grossbart (1988; Grossbart, Carlson, and Walsh 1991) investigated the relationship between general parental socialization styles and children's consumer socialization. "Neglecting" mothers exhibited more **social motivation for consumption** than any of the other four parental socialization styles examined. However, the difference was only significant in comparison to "Permissive" mothers who scored lowest on the scale.

REFERENCES:

Carlson, Les and Sanford Grossbart (1988), "Parental Style and Consumer Socialization of Children," *JCR*, 15 (June), 77-94.

Grossbart, Sanford, Les Carlson, and Ann Walsh (1991), "Consumer Socialization and Frequency of Shopping with Children," *JAMS*, 19 (Summer), 155-63.

Moschis, George P. (1978), *Acquisition of the Consumer Role By Adolescents*, Research Monograph No. 82. Atlanta, Georgia: Publishing Services Division, College of Business Administration, Georgia State University.

_____ (1981), "Patterns of Consumer Learning," *JAMS*, 9 (2), 110-26.

SCALE ITEMS: CONSUMPTION MOTIVATION (SOCIAL)

Strongly disagree	Disagree	Neutral	Agree	Strongly agree
1	2	3	4	5

Before purchasing a product it is important to know:

1. What friends think of different brands or products.
2. What kinds of people buy certain brands or products.
3. What others think of people who use certain brands of products.
4. What brands or products to buy to make good impressions on others.

SCALE NAME: Contempt

SCALE DESCRIPTION:

A three-item, five-point summated ratings scale assessing a person's experience with the contempt-related emotion. The directions and response scale can be worded so as to measure the *intensity* of the emotional state at the present time, or they can be adjusted to measure the *frequency* with which a person has experienced the emotional trait during some specified time period. One-word items were used in the study by Westbrook and Oliver (1991), and phrases based on those same items were used by Allen, Machleit, and Kleine (1992).

SCALE ORIGIN:

The measure was developed by Izard (1977) and is part of the Differential Emotions Scale (DES II). The instrument was designed originally as a measure of a person's emotional "state" at a particular point in time, but adjustments in the instrument's instructions allow the same items to be used in the assessment of emotional experiences as perceived over a longer time period. The latter was viewed by Izard as measure of one's emotional "trait" (1977, p. 125). Test-retest reliability for the contempt scale was reported to be .78 (n = 63) and item-factor correlations were .84 and higher (Izard 1977, p. 126). Beyond this evidence, several other studies have provided support for the validity of the scale, even in consumption settings (e.g., Westbrook 1987).

The items in DES II were composed solely of one word. In contrast, the items in DES III are phrases describing the target emotion. They were developed by Izard, although the first published validity testing was conducted by Kotsch, Gerbing, and Schwartz (1982). A study by Allen, Machleit, and Marine (1988) provides some insight to the factor structure of both DES II and III. The results indicate that when presented with the other DES items, the contempt items may not be unidimensional and may not have discriminant validity with other items such as those purported to measure disgust.

SAMPLES:

The data used by Allen, Machleit, and Kleine (1992) came from a stratified sample of people of diverse experience with blood donation. Nine hundred questionnaires were mailed and **361** usable forms were returned. Given that all respondents had previously donated blood, limited information was known about them and allowed a comparison with nonrespondents. Respondents were a little older, less likely to be male, and more likely to be heavier donors than nonrespondents.

The data for the study conducted by Westbrook and Oliver (1991) came from a judgmental area sample. Convenience samples were taken at four shopping centers in a large northeastern city and were limited to persons who had purchased a new or used car in the past year. Complete and usable questionnaires were obtained from **125** respondents. A majority (74%) of the sample was male. The average respondent had an income in the $25,000-

$40,000 range and was 33 years of age. The frequency version of the scale was used in this study.

Two samples were used in the study by Oliver (1993), with one examining satisfaction with cars and the other examining course satisfaction. The one involving cars is the same as the one described previously in Westbrook and Oliver (1991). The other sample was composed of students who volunteered from nine sections of a required marketing class. Usable questionnaires were provided by **178** students. The intensity version of the scale was used in this study.

RELIABILITY:

Alphas of **.88** and **.56** were reported for the versions of the scale used by Westbrook and Oliver (1991) and Allen, Machleit, and Kleine (1992), respectively. Oliver (1993) reported alphas of **.88** (n = 125) and **.85** (n = 178).

VALIDITY:

No specific examination of the scale's validity was reported in any of the studies.

ADMINISTRATION:

The scale was included with many other measures in the instrument used by Westbrook and Oliver (1991), Oliver (1993), and Allen, Machleit, and Kleine (1992). High scores on the frequency version of the scale suggest that a person perceives him/herself as having experienced the contempt-related emotional trait very often in some specified time period. A high score on the intensity version of the scale indicates that one is feeling very scornful at the time of measurement.

MAJOR FINDINGS:

The study by Allen, Machleit, Kleine (1992) examined whether emotions affect behavior via attitudes or, instead, are better viewed as having a separate and distinct impact. Among the many findings was that **contempt** (DES III) plays a key role with the act of donating blood for the least experienced donors. The relationship was negative, which means that the least experienced donors had a positive emotion linked with the behavior.

Oliver (1993) examined the separate roles of positive and negative affect, attribute performance, and disconfirmation for their impact on satisfaction. Negative affect was viewed as a function of several emotions, **contempt** being one of them. For both samples, negative affect was found to have direct influence on satisfaction.

Westbrook and Oliver (1991) studied the correspondence of the consumption emotional responses and satisfaction judgments that occur in the postpurchase period of the consumer decision process. **Contempt** (DES II) had its highest correlation with disgust (r = .92) and its lowest correlation with joy (r = −.20). **Contempt** was also found to be a primary emotional trait linked to low satisfaction in the car buying experience.

REFERENCES:

Allen, Chris T., Karen A. Machleit, and Susan Schultz Kleine (1992), ''A Comparison of Attitudes and Emotions as Predictors of Behavior at Diverse Levels of Behavioral Experience,'' *JCR*, 18 (March), 493-504.

_____, _____, and Susan S. Marine (1988), ''On Assessing the Emotionality of Advertising Via Izard's Differential Emotions Scale,'' in *Advances in Consumer Research*, Vol. 15, Michael J. Houston, ed. Provo, UT: Association for Consumer Research, 226-31.

Izard, Carroll E. (1977), *Human Emotions*. New York: Plenum Press.

Kotsch, William E., Davis W. Gerbing, and Lynne E. Schwartz (1982), ''The Construct Validity of the Differential Emotions Scale as Adapted for Children and Adolescents,'' in *Measuring Emotions in Infants and Children*, Carroll E. Izard, ed. New York: Cambridge University Press, 251-78.

Oliver, Richard L. (1993), ''Cognitive, Affective, and Attribute Bases of the Satisfaction Response,'' *JCR*, 20 (December), 418-30.

Westbrook, Robert A. (1987), ''Product/Consumption-Based Affective Responses and Postpurchase Processes,'' *JMR*, 24 (August), 258-70.

_____ and Richard L. Oliver (1991), ''The Dimensionality of Consumption Emotion Patterns and Consumer Satisfaction,'' *JCR*, 18 (June), 84-91.

SCALE ITEMS: CONTEMPT

POSSIBLE DIRECTIONS FOR FREQUENCY VERSION OF SCALE: Below is a list of words that you can use to show how you feel. We want you to tell us how often you felt each of these feelings _____.* You can tell us how often you felt each of these feelings on the list by marking one of the numbers next to each question.

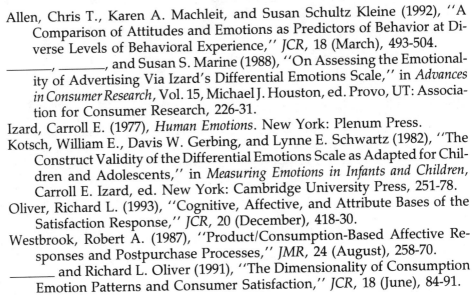

```
Almost                                          Very
never     ____ : ____ : ____ : ____ : ____      often
            1     2     3     4     5
```

POSSIBLE DIRECTIONS FOR INTENSITY VERSION OF SCALE: Below is a list of words that you can use to show how you feel. We want you to tell us how strongly you feel. You can tell us how strongly you feel each of these feelings on the list by marking one of the numbers next to each question.

```
Very                                            Very
weak      ____ : ____ : ____ : ____ : ____      strong
            1     2     3     4     5
```

DES II
1. contemptuous
2. scornful
3. disdainful

DES III
1. feel like somebody is a low-life, not worth the time of day
2. feel like somebody is a ''good-for-nothing''
3. feel like you are better than somebody

* The blank should be used to specify the time period of interest such as ''during the last week.''

SCALE NAME: Control

SCALE DESCRIPTION:

A three-item, seven-point, Likert-type scale measuring the degree to which a person would feel in control in a particular setting and able to influence outcomes.

SCALE ORIGIN:

It appears that the scale is original to Bateson and Hui (1992).

SAMPLES:

Bateson and Hui (1992) conducted two separate studies, one described as a laboratory experiment and the other a field quasi-experiment. The subjects were recruited from the streets of a southern England coastal town and randomly assigned to either a slide or a video setting. Complete data were received from **119** persons (60 with slides and 59 videos). In the second study, passengers in a major train station in London were asked to fill out a questionnaire regarding their experience at the train ticket office. Usable surveys were received from **92** people.

RELIABILITY:

Bateson and Hui (1992) reported an alpha of **.61** for the scale.

VALIDITY:

Bateson and Hui (1992) did not specifically address the validity of the scale. However, some idea of the scale's convergent validity can be taken from correlations between it and another scale used to measure the same construct. In two laboratory situations the correlations were .67 or higher, and a correlation of .42 was found in the field study. This provides some evidence that the two measures were tapping into the same construct, although this scale may be the weaker of the two given its lower reliability.

ADMINISTRATION:

The scale was self-administered by subjects along with other measures after being exposed to experimental stimuli (Bateson and Hui 1992). High scores on the scale indicate that if respondents were placed in a particular situation they would feel in command and control over what happened.

MAJOR FINDINGS:

Bateson and Hui (1992) investigated the ecological validity of slide and video presentations in controlled (laboratory) settings. The illustration of ecological validity made use of most of the same variables as used in the study by Hui and Bateson (1991) and produced similar findings. In particular, perceived **control** had a significant positive effect on pleasure.

REFERENCES:

Bateson, John E. G. and Michael K. Hui (1992), ''The Ecological Validity of Photographic Slides and Videotapes in Simulating the Service Setting,'' *JCR*, 19 (September), 271-81.

Hui, Michael K. and John E. G. Bateson (1991), ''Perceived Control and the Effects of Crowding and Consumer Choice on the Service Experience,'' *JCR*, 18 (September), 174-84.

SCALE ITEMS: CONTROL

Disagree   ____ : ____ : ____ : ____ : ____ : ____ : ____   Agree
                1   2   3   4   5   6   7

1. I would feel that everything is under my control.
2. I would feel it difficult to get my own way. **(r)**
3. I would feel able to influence the way things were.

SCALE NAME: Coviewing TV (Parent/Child)

SCALE DESCRIPTION:

A four-item, five-point, Likert-type summated rating scale measuring the degree to which a parent reports watching TV with a child and the importance of doing that in order to monitor what is watched.

SCALE ORIGIN:

The scale is indicated as being original to Carlson and Grossbart (1988; Grossbart, Carlson, and Walsh 1991).

SAMPLES:

The same data set is reported on in two articles by Carlson and Grossbart (1988; Grossbart, Carlson, and Walsh 1991). The survey instrument was distributed to mothers via students at three elementary schools of an unidentified U.S. city. The schools were chosen on a convenience basis but appeared to represent a variety of socioeconomic areas of the city. A $1 contribution was made to the PTO for each completed questionnaire returned by the children. Analysis was based on **451** completed questionnaires. Ninety-three percent of the responding mothers indicated that they were the primary person in the child's socialization.

RELIABILITY:

Carlson and Grossbart (1988; Grossbart, Carlson, and Walsh 1991) reported an alpha of **.90** and a beta of .85 for the scale.

VALIDITY:

Carlson and Grossbart (1988; Grossbart, Carlson, and Walsh 1991) reported no examination of scale validity.

ADMINISTRATION:

The scale was self-administered along with many other measures in the questionnaire used by Carlson and Grossbart (1988; Grossbart, Carlson, and Walsh 1991). High scores on the scale mean that respondents report that they often watch TV with their children, whereas low scores suggest that they do not think it is very important and do not do it often.

MAJOR FINDINGS:

The authors (Carlson and Grossbart 1988; Grossbart, Carlson, and Walsh 1991) investigated the relationship between general parental socialization styles and children's consumer socialization. In a factor analysis of scale scores, scores on the **Coviewing** scale loaded on a separate factor from the other scales. On the basis of this, a significant difference was found in the degree of parent-child communication between one of the parental socialization styles and several of the others. Specifically, ''Authoritative'' mothers reported significantly more **coviewing** than three of the other four parental styles examined.

REFERENCES:

Carlson, Les and Sanford Grossbart (1988), ''Parental Style and Consumer Socialization of Children,'' *JCR*, 15 (June), 77-94.

Grossbart, Sanford, Les Carlson, and Ann Walsh (1991), ''Consumer Socialization and Frequency of Shopping with Children,'' *JAMS*, 19 (Summer), 155-63.

SCALE ITEMS: COVIEWING TV (PARENT/CHILD)

Very seldom	Seldom	Sometimes	Often	Very often
1	2	3	4	5

I watch TV with my children on:
1. . . . weekdays.
2. . . . Saturdays.
3. . . . Sundays.
4. It is important for my child and me to watch TV together so I know what kind of programs he/she is watching.

Strongly disagree	Disagree	Neutral	Agree	Strongly agree
1	2	3	4	5

SCALE NAME: Credibility (Company)

SCALE DESCRIPTION:

A six-item, seven-point semantic differential measuring a person's attitude about the trustworthiness and expertise of a company.

SCALE ORIGIN:

No detailed information is provided by Keller and Aaker (1992) regarding the scale's origin, but it appears to have been developed for use in their study. As noted in "Validity," the final form of the scale was a combination of items from two other scales, *trustworthiness* and *expertise*.

SAMPLES:

The sample employed by Keller and Aaker (1992) was composed of **430** university employees, most of whom were female (90%). About half had a college degree, and the average age was 28 years. Respondents were paid $5 for their participation and given a chance to win cash prizes in a lottery.

RELIABILITY:

All that is said by Keller and Aaker (1992) about the reliability of their multi-item scales is that they were all in excess of .70.

VALIDITY:

Keller and Aaker (1992) reported no specific examination of the scale's validity. They did report that the correlation of scores on their *trustworthiness* and *expertise* scales was .82, which led them to treat the items as one measure of **company credibility**. More sophisticated testing is needed to determine if the scale is truly unidimensional.

ADMINISTRATION:

The scale was self-administered by subjects along with other measures after exposure to experimental manipulation information (Keller and Aaker 1992). A high score on the scale indicates that the respondent perceives a company to be trustworthy and to have high expertise in what it does, whereas a low score suggests that the respondent considers the company to have little or no credibility.

MAJOR FINDINGS:

The experiment by Keller and Aaker (1992) examined the factors influencing evaluation of proposed extensions of a core brand. The findings appeared to support the conclusion that perceived product/company fit along with company credibility mediate the impact of previous brand extensions on evaluations of a proposed extension.

COMMENTS:

The first three items compose the *expertise* subscale and the other three the *trustworthiness* subscale.

REFERENCE:

Keller, Kevin Lane and David A. Aaker (1992), ''The Effects of Sequential Introduction of Brand Extensions,'' *JMR*, 29 (February), 35-50.

SCALE ITEMS: CREDIBILITY (COMPANY)

Overall low-quality products	___ :	___ :	___ :	___ :	___ :	___ :	___	Overall high-quality products
	1	2	3	4	5	6	7	
Not at all good at manufacturing	___ :	___ :	___ :	___ :	___ :	___ :	___	Very good at manufacturing
	1	2	3	4	5	6	7	
Overall inferior products	___ :	___ :	___ :	___ :	___ :	___ :	___	Overall superior products
	1	2	3	4	5	6	7	
Not at all trustworthy	___ :	___ :	___ :	___ :	___ :	___ :	___	Very trustworthy
	1	2	3	4	5	6	7	
Not at all dependable	___ :	___ :	___ :	___ :	___ :	___ :	___	Very dependable
	1	2	3	4	5	6	7	
Not at all concerned about customers	___ :	___ :	___ :	___ :	___ :	___ :	___	Very concerned about customers
	1	2	3	4	5	6	7	

SCALE NAME: Crowding

SCALE DESCRIPTION:

A three-item, seven-point, Likert-type scale measuring the degree to which a person would feel crowded in a particular setting. The construct also carries with it the sense that perceived crowding is linked with stress and is an unpleasant subjective experience.

SCALE ORIGIN:

It appears that the scale is original to Bateson and Hui (1992).

SAMPLES:

Bateson and Hui (1992) conducted two separate studies, one described as a laboratory experiment and the other a field quasi-experiment. The subjects were recruited from the streets of a southern England coastal town and assigned randomly to either a slide or a video setting. Complete data were received from **119** persons (60 with slides and 59 videos). In the second study, passengers in a major train station in London were asked to fill out a questionnaire regarding their experience at the train ticket office. Usable surveys were received from **92** people.

RELIABILITY:

Bateson and Hui (1992) reported an alpha of **.75** for the scale.

VALIDITY:

Bateson and Hui (1992) did not specifically address the validity of the scale. However, some idea of the scale's convergent validity can be taken from correlations between it and another scale used to measure the same construct. In three different situations the correlations were .65 or higher providing evidence that the two measures were tapping into the same construct.

ADMINISTRATION:

The scale was self-administered by subjects along with other measures after being exposed to experimental stimuli (Bateson and Hui 1992). Those with high scores on the scale are indicating that if they were placed in a particular situation they would feel crowded and uncomfortable.

MAJOR FINDINGS:

Bateson and Hui (1992) investigated the ecological validity of slide and video presentations in controlled (laboratory) settings. The illustration of ecological validity made use of most of the same variables as used in the study by Hui and Bateson (1991) and produced similar findings. In particular, perceived **crowding** had a significant negative effect on pleasure.

REFERENCES:

Bateson, John E. G. and Michael K. Hui (1992), ''The Ecological Validity of Photographic Slides and Videotapes in Simulating the Service Setting,'' *JCR*, 19 (September), 271-81.

Hui, Michael K. and John E. G. Bateson (1991), ''Perceived Control and the Effects of Crowding and Consumer Choice on the Service Experience,'' *JCR*, 18 (September), 174-84.

SCALE ITEMS: CROWDING

Disagree	___ : ___ : ___ : ___ : ___ : ___ : ___	Agree
	1 2 3 4 5 6 7	

1. I would not feel crowded. **(r)**
2. I would feel that there are too many people in the setting.
3. I would feel that there is no space for me in the setting.

SCALE NAME: Crowding

SCALE DESCRIPTION:

A five-item, seven-point semantic differential scale measuring the perceived density of people in an area of space. The construct also carries with it the sense that perceived crowding is linked with stress and is an unpleasant subjective experience.

SCALE ORIGIN:

It appears that the scale was first presented by Bateson and Hui (1987). Using a convenience sample of 30 business school students, the alpha was reported to be .91. The measure was found to have high negative correlations with dominance and pleasure but no significant relationship with arousal.

SAMPLES:

Bateson and Hui (1992) conducted two separate studies, one described as a laboratory experiment and the other a field quasi-experiment. The subjects were recruited from the streets of a southern England coastal town and assigned randomly to either a slide or a video setting. Complete data were received from **119** persons (60 with slides and 59 videos). In the second study, passengers in a major train station in London were asked to fill out a questionnaire regarding their experience at the train ticket office. Usable surveys were received from **92** people.

Hui and Bateson (1991) gathered data from people between the ages of 25 and 40 years. They were recruited in London through an ad in a free local paper as well as through various churches and a public housing area. The experiment was conducted in a central location, and subjects were assigned to one of three treatment rooms. Completed questionnaires were received from **107** and **112** people for the bank and bar settings, respectively. These were the same people because subjects responded to both of the settings.

RELIABILITY:

Alphas of **.86** and **.90** were reported for the scale by Bateson and Hui (1992) and Hui and Bateson (1991), respectively.

VALIDITY:

The validity of the scale was not specifically addressed by either Bateson and Hui (1992) or Hui and Bateson (1991). However, some idea of the scale's convergent validity can be taken from correlations between it and another scale used to measure the same construct (Bateson and Hui 1992, p. 278). In three different situations the correlations were .65 or higher, providing evidence that the two measures were tapping into the same construct.

ADMINISTRATION:

The scale was self-administered by subjects, along with other measures, after being exposed to experimental stimuli (Bateson and Hui 1992; Hui and Bateson 1991). High scores on the scale indicate that respondents perceive a particular situation to be crowded.

MAJOR FINDINGS:

The purpose of the experiment by Hui and Bateson (1991) was to examine the effect of perceived control in the service encounter on the service experience. Among the findings was that perceived **crowding** was a positive function of consumer density and a negative function of perceived control.

Bateson and Hui (1992) investigated the ecological validity of slide and video presentations in controlled (laboratory) settings. The illustration of ecological validity made use of most of the same variables as used in the study by Hui and Bateson (1991) and produced similar findings.

REFERENCES:

Bateson, John E. G. and Michael K. Hui (1987), ''A Model for Crowding in the Service Experience: Empirical Findings,'' in *The Service Challenge: Integrating for Competitive Advantage*, John A. Czepiel et al., eds. Chicago: American Marketing Association, 85-90.

———— and ———— (1992), ''The Ecological Validity of Photographic Slides and Videotapes in Simulating the Service Setting,'' *JCR*, 19 (September), 271-81.

Hui, Michael K. and John E. G. Bateson (1991), ''Perceived Control and the Effects of Crowding and Consumer Choice on the Service Experience,'' *JCR*, 18 (September), 174-84.

SCALE ITEMS: CROWDING

	1	2	3	4	5	6	7	
Not stuffy	___ :	___ :	___ :	___ :	___ :	___ :	___	Stuffy
Uncrowded	___ :	___ :	___ :	___ :	___ :	___ :	___	Crowded
Uncramped	___ :	___ :	___ :	___ :	___ :	___ :	___	Cramped
Restricted	___ :	___ :	___ :	___ :	___ :	___ :	___	Free to move
Confined	___ :	___ :	___ :	___ :	___ :	___ :	___	Spacious

SCALE NAME: Crowding

SCALE DESCRIPTION:

A six-item, seven-point semantic differential measuring the level of crowding a consumer perceives there to be in some specified shopping context. The measure was referred to as *perceived retail crowding* by Eroglu and Machleit (1990).

SCALE ORIGIN:

The items originate from a study by Harrell, Hutt, and Anderson (1980), where they appear to have composed two measures of crowding: one scale had two items and an alpha of .63 and measured the degree of confined, closed feelings; the other had four items and an alpha of .69 and measured the degree to which movement was perceived as restricted.

SAMPLES:

Subjects used by Eroglu and Machleit (1990) were recruited from professional, nonprofit, and church organizations. The sample was composed of 112 adults and had the following characteristics: 58% were female, 70% were married, and 63% were between the ages of 20 and 49 years.

RELIABILITY:

The scale was completed for five slides representing different levels of retail density in the study by Eroglu and Machleit (1990). Alphas of .73, .76, .85, .90, and .80 were reported for the slides from least to most dense retail conditions, respectively.

VALIDITY:

No direct information regarding the scale's validity was reported by Eroglu and Machleit (1990). However, as noted in "Major Findings," the strong positive relationship between retail density (as determined by 15 independent judges) and crowding (as determined by the scale) provide some evidence of the scale's convergent validity.

ADMINISTRATION:

The scale was filled out by subjects after viewing each of the experimental slides. A high score on the scale indicates that a respondent perceives a lot of crowding with some specified retail environment, whereas a low score would imply that a respondent sees little crowding.

MAJOR FINDINGS:

Eroglu and Machleit (1990) examined some of the determinants and outcomes of retail crowding. There was a clear linear and positive relationship between retail density and perceived **crowding**. Only under the higher retail density conditions, however, were purchase risk and time pressure found to be significantly related to perceived **crowding**.

REFERENCES:

Eroglu, Segin A. and Karen A. Machleit (1990), "An Empirical Study of Retail Crowding: Antecedents and Consequences," *JR*, 66 (Summer), 201-21.

Harrell, Gilbert D., Michael D. Hutt, and James C. Anderson (1980), "Path Analysis of Buyer Behavior Under Conditions of Crowding," *JMR*, 17 (February), 45-51.

SCALE ITEMS: CROWDING

Confined   __ : __ : __ : __ : __ : __ : __   Spacious
           7   6   5   4   3   2   1

Too many shoppers   __ : __ : __ : __ : __ : __ : __   Too few shoppers
           7   6   5   4   3   2   1

Restricts movement   __ : __ : __ : __ : __ : __ : __   Allows free movement
           7   6   5   4   3   2   1

Crowded   __ : __ : __ : __ : __ : __ : __   Uncrowded
           7   6   5   4   3   2   1

Gives a closed feeling   __ : __ : __ : __ : __ : __ : __   Gives an open feeling
           7   6   5   4   3   2   1

Must move at a pace set by other shoppers   __ : __ : __ : __ : __ : __ : __   Can move at my own pace
           7   6   5   4   3   2   1

SCALE NAME: Customer Orientation (Customer's Perception of Salespeople)

SCALE DESCRIPTION:

A 24-item, six-point summated ratings scale that measures the degree to which a consumer perceives that retail salespeople in general engage in behaviors aimed at increasing long-term customer satisfaction rather than having low concern for customer's needs. The scale could be viewed as a measure of consumers' *attitudes toward salespeople in general,* but the emphasis is on whether salespeople are focused most on making sales or on satisfying customer needs.

SCALE ORIGIN:

The scale originally was constructed and tested by Saxe and Weitz (1982) for use with salespeople themselves. The version of the scale reviewed here is a modification of that previous scale such that customers evaluate salespeople rather than salespeople evaluating themselves.

SAMPLES:

The sample analyzed by Brown, Widing, and Coulter (1991) was composed of **348** consumers drawn from a midsize midwestern U.S. city. Four hundred phone numbers were called with three follow-up attempts, resulting in an 87% response rate. No demographic characteristics of the sample were provided.

RELIABILITY:

An alpha of **.81** was reported by Brown, Widing, and Coulter (1991). Mean inter-item correlation was .15 and mean item-total correlation was .33.

VALIDITY:

Although validity was not directly assessed, some limited evidence was provided by the factor analysis performed by Brown, Widing, and Coulter (1991). The scale is clearly bidimensional; two clear factors were found, one relating to the customer orientation and the other to the selling orientation. The former explained 41% of the variance and had factor loadings between .35 and .67. Factor 2 explained 34% of the variance and had loadings ranging from .31 to .69.

ADMINISTRATION:

The scale was administered to respondents in telephone interviews (Brown, Widing, and Coulter 1991). A high score on the scale suggests that a respondent views most salespeople as having a customer orientation, whereas a low score means that a respondent thinks most salespeople are just interested in the sale itself, not the customer's satisfaction.

MAJOR FINDINGS:

The purpose of the study by Brown, Widing, and Coulter (1991) was to determine if the SOCO scale (**customer orientation**) could be successfully modified so that consumers could evaluate salespeople. Little more substantive detail is provided by the authors about the scale beyond what is reported here regarding its psychometric qualities.

COMMENTS:

Mean total scores on the scale were reported to be 83 (Brown, Widing, and Coulter 1991, p. 349). The standard deviation was 13 and skewness was -.27.

Given that the scale is not unidimensional, some serious thought should be given to measuring the two different orientations separately. Two separate scales would likely be of higher reliability and validity than the present combined version and therefore could explain more variance.

REFERENCES:

Brown, Gene, Robert E. Widing II, and Ronald L. Coulter (1991), ''Customer Evaluations of Retail Salespeople Utilizing the SOCO Scale: A Replication, Extension, and Application,'' *JAMS*, 19 (Fall), 347-51.

Saxe, Robert and Barton A. Weitz (1982), ''The SOCO Scale: A Measure of the Customer Orientation of Salespeople,'' *JMR*, 19 (August), 343-51.

SCALE ITEMS: CUSTOMER ORIENTATION (CUSTOMER'S PERCEPTION OF SALESPEOPLE)*

DIRECTIONS USED IN TELEPHONE INTERVIEWS: I'm going to read you some statements regarding retail salesperson behaviors and would like you to tell me if you think the statement is true for:

1 = No retail salespeople
2 = Some salespeople
3 = Somewhat less than half of salespeople
4 = Somewhat more than half of salespeople
5 = A lot of salespeople
6 = All salespeople

1. Salespersons try to help me achieve my goals.
2. Salespersons try to achieve their goals by satisfying customers.
3. A good salesperson has to have a customer's best interest in mind.
4. Salespersons try to get me to discuss my needs with them.
5. Salespersons try to influence a customer with information rather than pressure.
6. Salespersons offer the product of theirs that is best suited to the customer's problem.
7. Salespersons try to find out what kind of product would be most helpful to a customer.

8. Salespersons answer a customer's questions about the product as correctly as they can.
9. Salespersons try to bring a customer with a problem together with a product that helps solve that problem.
10. Salespersons are willing to disagree with a customer in order to help him make a better decision.
11. Salespersons try to give customers an accurate expectation of what the product will do for them.
12. Salespersons try to figure out what a customer's needs are.
13. Salespersons try to sell customers all they can convince him to buy, even if customers think it is more than a wise customer would buy. r
14. Salespersons try to sell as much as they can rather than to satisfy a customer. (r)
15. Salespersons keep alert for weaknesses in a customer's personality so they can use them to put pressure on customers to buy. (r)
16. If a salesperson is not sure a product is right for a customer, he will still apply pressure to get him to buy. (r)
17. Salespersons decide what products to offer on the basis of what they can convince customers to buy, not on the basis of what will satisfy them in the long run. (r)
18. Salespersons paint too rosy a picture of their products, to make them sound as good as possible. (r)
19. Salespersons spend more time trying to persuade a customer to buy than they do trying to discover customer needs. (r)
20. Salespersons stretch the truth in describing a product to a customer. (r)
21. Salespersons pretend to agree with customers to please them. (r)
22. Salespersons imply to a customer that something is beyond their control when it is not. (r)
23. Salespersons begin the sales talk for a product before exploring a customer's needs with him. (r)
24. Salespersons treat customers as rivals. (r)

* The first 12 items measure the customer orientation, whereas the last 12 measure the selling orientation. The positive and negative items should be intermixed when put on a survey instrument.

SCALE NAME: Deal Retraction

SCALE DESCRIPTION:

A three-item, seven-point Likert-type measure assessing a consumer's tendency to not buy products unless he/she has a coupon for it or the product is on sale.

SCALE ORIGIN:

No indication is provided by Lichtenstein, Netemeyer, and Burton (1990) that the scale is anything other than original to their study.

SAMPLES:

The data for the main study by Lichtenstein, Netemeyer, and Burton (1990) came from a convenience sample of **350** nonstudent adults from a medium-size SMSA. The majority of the sample was female (57%) and married (69%). College graduates composed 40% of the sample. The median age of respondents was between 35 and 44 years and household income was between $30,000 and $39,999.

RELIABILITY:

Lichtenstein, Netemeyer, and Burton (1990) reported the reliability (LISREL estimate) of the scale to be **.50.**

VALIDITY:

Lichtenstein, Netemeyer, and Burton (1990) reported no test of validity.

ADMINISTRATION:

Lichtenstein, Netemeyer, and Burton (1990) did not describe the manner in which the scale was administered to the subjects in their study. However, it was clear that the scale was one of many measures that composed the survey instrument. High scores on the scale indicate that at least for some products, consumers only buy the products when they are on sale or have coupons to reduce the prices, whereas low scores indicate that pricing is less of an issue in purchasing products.

MAJOR FINDINGS:

The study by Lichtenstein, Netemeyer, and Burton (1990) examined the effect of both value consciousness and coupon involvement on coupon redemption behavior. One of the major findings was that coupon involvement had a much greater positive relationship with **deal retraction** (grocery products) than did value consciousness.

REFERENCE:

Lichtenstein, Donald R., Richard D. Netemeyer, and Scot Burton (1990), "Distinguishing Coupon Proneness From Value Consciousness: An Acquisition-Transaction Utility Theory Perspective," *JM*, 54 (July), 54-67.

SCALE ITEMS: DEAL RETRACTION

Strongly disagree	___ : ___ : ___ : ___ : ___ : ___ : ___	Strongly agree
	1 2 3 4 5 6 7	

1. For some products, when the manufacturer stops offering coupons, I stop buying their product.
2. Even when a manufacturer stops offering a coupon for a product, I will often keep buying the product if I like it. **(r)**
3. In general, I will not buy a product if I know it has been previously offered at a sale price.

SCALE NAME: Decision Action Control Orientation

SCALE DESCRIPTION:

A scale purported to measure a person's disposition and/or capacity toward transforming intentions into behavior-related decisions. The measure is composed of 20 forced-choice items, with one alternative in each of the items reflecting a "state" orientation and the other alternative reflecting an "action" orientation. A state orientation is a mode of control similar to wishful thinking, in which a behavior is desired but little action is taken to make it happen. In contrast, with an action orientation a person engages in tasks that bring about the desired behavior. Finally, half of the items (1-10) assess cognitive manifestations of action and state orientations with the other half (11-20) assessing behavioral manifestations.

SCALE ORIGIN:

The scale was constructed by Kuhl (1985). In a study of 115 unspecified subjects, an alpha of .79 was found for the scale. Theoretically expected correlations were found between the scale and test anxiety, extraversion, self-consciousness, achievement motivation, future orientation, and cognitive complexity. The author concluded that the moderate to low size of these correlations suggested that a considerable amount of variance in action control could not be attributable to these personality variables.

SAMPLES:

The data for the study by Bagozzi, Baumgartner, and Yi (1992) were collected in two questionnaires, administered a week apart to female staff members of a major university. **One hundred forty-nine** women completed both questionnaires and provided complete information. To encourage subjects to participate in the study, the authors used a lottery with several cash prizes.

RELIABILITY:

Bagozzi, Baumgartner, and Yi (1992) reported an alpha of .61 for the scale. Realizing that this was low, the authors also calculated alpha using polychoric correlations, more appropriate for the 20 dichotomous measures composing the scale. With this alteration, a more respectable value of .75 was found.

VALIDITY:

Using a separate sample of 56 undergraduate students, the discriminant validity of the scale was examined by Bagozzi, Baumgartner, and Yi (1992). After examining the pattern of correlations the authors concluded that there was some theoretical overlap of action control with several personality-related variables but that there was enough variance left unexplained to indicate that action control was a distinct construct.

ADMINISTRATION:

The scale was administered by Bagozzi, Baumgartner, and Yi (1992) in the first questionnaire of two sent by campus mail to staff members of a university. Scores are calculated by summing the action-oriented response alternatives selected by respondents. A high score on the scale indicates that a respondent has an action orientation, whereas a low score suggests that the respondent has a state orientation.

MAJOR FINDINGS:

Bagozzi, Baumgartner, and Yi (1992) investigated the role played by **decision action control** in moderating relationships in the theory of reasoned action. This was studied in the context of coupon usage. It was found that normative considerations were more important for those with a state orientation, whereas attitudinal considerations were more important for action-oriented people.

REFERENCES:

Bagozzi, Richard P., Hans Baumgartner, and Youjae Yi (1992), ''State Versus Action Orientation and the Theory of Reasoned Action: An Application to Coupon Usage,'' *JCR*, 18 (March), 505-18.

Kuhl, Julius (1985), ''Volitional Mediators of Cognition-Behavior Consistency: Self-Regulatory Processes and Action Versus State Orientation,'' in *Action Control: From Cognition to Behavior*, Julius Kuhl and Jeurgen Beckmann, eds. Berlin: Springer-Verlag.

SCALE ITEMS: DECISION ACTION CONTROL ORIENTATION

1. If I had to work at home
   _____ I would often have problems getting started.
   _____ I would usually start immediately.*
2. When I want to see someone again
   _____ I try to set a date for the visit right away.*
   _____ I plan to do it some day.
3. When I have a lot of important things to take care of
   _____ I often don't know where to start.
   _____ It is easy for me to make a plan and then stick to it.*
4. When I have two things that I would like to do and can do only one
   _____ I decide between them pretty quickly.*
   _____ I wouldn't know right away which was most important to me.
5. When I have to do something important that's unpleasant
   _____ I'd rather do it right away.*
   _____ I avoid doing it until it's absolutely necessary.
6. When I really want to finish an extensive assignment in an afternoon
   _____ it often happens that something distracts me.
   _____ I can really concentrate on the assignment.*

7. When I have to complete a difficult assignment
    _____ I can concentrate on the individual parts of the assignment.*
    _____ I easily lose my concentration on the assignment.
8. When I fear that I'll lose interest during a tedious assignment
    _____ I complete the unpleasant things first.
    _____ I start with the easier parts first.*
9. When it's absolutely necessary that I perform an unpleasant duty
    _____ I finish it as soon as possible.
    _____ It takes a while before I start on it.
10. When I've planned to do something unfamiliar in the following week
    _____ it can happen that I change my plans at the last moment.
    _____ I stick with what I've planned.
11. When I know that something has to be done soon
    _____ I often think about how nice it would be if I were already finished with it.
    _____ I just think about how I can finish it the fastest.*
12. When I'm sitting at home and feel like doing something
    _____ I decide on one thing relatively fast and don't think much about other possibilities.*
    _____ I like to consider several possibilities before I decide on something.
13. When I don't have anything special to do and am bored
    _____ I sometimes contemplate what I can do.
    _____ it usually occurs to me soon what I can do.*
14. When I have a hard time getting started on a difficult problem
    _____ the problem seems huge to me.
    _____ I think about how I can get through the problem in a fairly pleasant way.*
15. When I have to solve a difficult problem
    _____ I think about a lot of different things before I really start on the problem.
    _____ I think about which way would be best to try first.*
16. When I'm trying to solve a difficult problem and there are two solutions that seem equally good to me
    _____ I make a spontaneous decision for one of the two without thinking much about it.*
    _____ I try to figure out whether or not one of the solutions is really better than the other.
17. When I have to study for a test
    _____ I think a lot about where I should start.
    _____ I don't think about it too much; I just start with what I think is most important.*
18. When I've made a plan to learn how to master something difficult
    _____ I first try it out before I think about other possibilities.*
    _____ before I start, I first consider whether or not there's a better plan.
19. When I'm faced with the problem of what to do with an hour of free time
    _____ sometimes I think about it for a long time.
    _____ I come up with something appropriate relatively soon.*

20. When I've planned to buy just one piece of clothing but then see several things that I like
_____ I think a lot about which piece I should buy.
_____ I usually don't think about it very long and decide relatively soon.*

* These response alternatives reflect an action orientation.

SCALE NAME: Decision Difficulty (Electronic Decision Aid)

SCALE DESCRIPTION:

A three-item, nine-point summated ratings scale measuring a person's perception of the relative difficulty involved in making a choice decision using an electronic decision aid versus a choice made with the same information printed on paper but with the brands listed in random order.

SCALE ORIGIN:

Although drawing on several past studies, it appears that the final version of the scale was developed by Widing and Talarzyk (1993).

SAMPLES:

Widing and Talarzyk (1993) collected data from **283** volunteers from a university's marketing courses. Students received credit for their involvement. A little more than half were male (56%), and the average age was 22 years.

RELIABILITY:

Widing and Talarzyk (1993) reported an alpha of **.84** for the scale.

VALIDITY:

No detailed examination of scale validity was reported by Widing and Talarzyk (1993). However, the items composing this scale as well as the ones in a similar scale (*decision quality*, #80) were factor analyzed using maximum likelihood solution and an oblique rotation. Loadings of .54 and higher occurred on the two expected factors with very small cross-loadings. This at least provides evidence of the scale's unidimensionality.

ADMINISTRATION:

The scale was self-administered by subjects along with other measures in one of the three phases of an experiment. A high score on the scale suggests that a person perceives that the use of a computerized decision aid led to a much less difficult decision than if a more traditional unaided format had been used.

MAJOR FINDINGS:

The experiment conducted by Widing and Talarzyk (1993) compared various formats for presenting information about brand performance on multiple evaluative criteria. Among the many findings was that subjects considered both of the computer assisted formats to be have been associated with lower **decision difficulty** compared with a format in which brand information was listed in random order.

COMMENTS:

On the basis of pilot studies, Widing and Talarzyk (1993) determined that some frame of reference (e.g., sheet of paper) was necessary in the items in order to make the scale a discriminating measure.

REFERENCES:

Widing, Robert E. II (1994), personal correspondence.

_____ and W. Wayne Talarzyk (1993), ''Electronic Information Systems for Consumers: An Evaluation of Computer-Assisted Formats in Multiple Decision Environments,'' *JMR*, 30 (May), 125-41.

SCALE ITEMS: DECISION DIFFICULTY*

Directions: Please answer all questions about the ''computer format'' (the format you used) in comparison to a format presenting the same information, but with the brands listed in random order on a sheet of paper (e.g., on a magazine page).

1. How did the use of the computer format affect any *confusion* you may have experienced in decision making, in comparison to a format presenting the same information but with brands listed in random order on a sheet of paper?

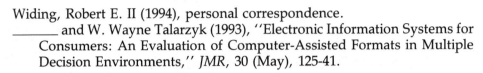

```
Greatly                                                              Greatly
increased                                                          decreased
decision                                                            decision
confusion                                                          confusion
  1———————2———————3———————4———————5———————6———————7———————8———————9
```

2. How did the use of the computer format affect any *frustration* you may have experienced in decision making, in comparison to a format presenting the same information but with brands listed in random order on a sheet of paper?

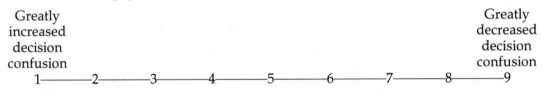

```
Greatly                                                              Greatly
increased                                                          decreased
decision                                                            decision
frustration                                                        frustration
  1———————2———————3———————4———————5———————6———————7———————8———————9
```

3. How do you feel the use of the computer format affected any *difficulty* you may have experienced in decision making, in comparison to a format presenting the same information but with brands listed in random order on a sheet of paper?

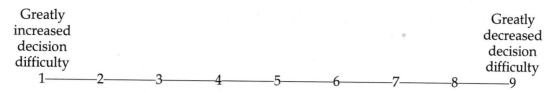

Greatly
increased
decision
difficulty

Greatly
decreased
decision
difficulty

1———2———3———4———5———6———7———8———9

* The items were provided by Widing (1994).

SCALE NAME: Decision Quality (Electronic Decision Aid)

SCALE DESCRIPTION:

A three-item, nine-point summated ratings scale measuring a person's perception of the relative quality of a choice decision that was made with an electronic decision aid versus a choice made with the same information printed on paper but with the brands listed in random order.

SCALE ORIGIN:

Although drawing on several past studies, it appears that the final version of the scale was developed by Widing and Talarzyk (1993).

SAMPLES:

Widing and Talarzyk (1993) collected data from **283** volunteers from a university's marketing courses. Students received credit for their involvement. A little more than half were male (56%) and the average age was 22 years.

RELIABILITY:

Widing and Talarzyk (1993) reported an alpha of **.81** for the scale.

VALIDITY:

Widing and Talarzyk (1993) reported no detailed examination of scale validity. However, the items composing this scale as well as the ones in a similar scale (*decision difficulty, #79*) were factor analyzed using maximum likelihood solution and an oblique rotation. Loadings of .54 and higher occurred on the two expected factors with very small cross-loadings. This at least provides evidence of the scale's unidimensionality.

ADMINISTRATION:

The scale was self-administered by subjects along with other measures in one of the three phases of an experiment. A low score on the scale suggests that a respondent perceives that the use of a computerized decision aid led to a much higher-quality decision than if a more traditional unaided format had been used.

MAJOR FINDINGS:

The experiment conducted by Widing and Talarzyk (1993) compared various formats for presenting information about brand performance on multiple evaluative criteria. Among the many findings was that subjects evaluated both of the computer assisted formats more highly on increasing **decision quality** compared with a format in which brand information was listed in random order.

COMMENTS:

On the basis of pilot studies, Widing and Talarzyk (1993) determined that some frame of reference (e.g., sheet of paper) was necessary in the items in order to make the scale a discriminating measure.

REFERENCES:

Widing, Robert E. II (1994), personal correspondence.
_____ and W. Wayne Talarzyk (1993), ''Electronic Information Systems for Consumers: An Evaluation of Computer-Assisted Formats in Multiple Decision Environments,'' *JMR*, 30 (May), 125-41.

SCALE ITEMS: DECISION QUALITY*

Directions: Please answer all questions about the ''computer format'' (the format you used) in comparison to a format presenting the same information, but with the brands listed in random order on a sheet of paper (e.g., on a magazine page).

1. How do you feel the use of the computer format affected the *accuracy* with which you made your best choice decision, in comparison to a format presenting the same information but with brands listed in random order on a sheet of paper?

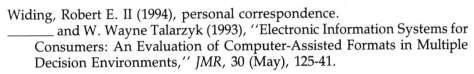

```
Greatly                                                              Greatly
improved                                                           decreased
decision                                                            decision
accuracy                                                            accuracy
  1———2———3———4———5———6———7———8———9
```

2. How do you feel the use of the computer format affected the degree of *certainty* you have that you made the best choice for you, in comparison to a format presenting the same information but with brands listed in random order on a sheet of paper?

```
Greatly                                                              Greatly
increased                                                          decreased
decision                                                            decision
certainty                                                          certainty
  1———2———3———4———5———6———7———8———9
```

3. How did the use of the computer format affect the amount of *confidence* you have that you made the best choice for you, in comparison to a format presenting the same information but with brands listed in random order on a sheet of paper?

#80 *Decision Quality (Electronic Decision Aid)*

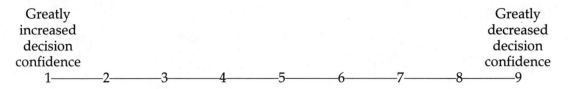

Greatly
increased
decision
confidence

Greatly
decreased
decision
confidence

1———2———3———4———5———6———7———8———9

* Only item 1 was provided in the article. The rest were provided by Widing (1994).

SCALE NAME: Derogatory Beliefs Against Blacks

SCALE DESCRIPTION:

A ten-item, seven-point, Likert-type scale measuring the degree of subtly degrading and derogatory opinions held by a person toward blacks in general. The items suggest that blacks are socially, morally, and/or educationally backward.

SCALE ORIGIN:

The items represent the Derogatory Beliefs subscale of the Multifactor Racial Inventory developed by Woodmansee and Cook (1967). The items were developed and refined in a series of studies. An alpha of .70 was reported for the scale using 317 respondents whose attitudes toward blacks was otherwise unknown. Testing was also done on people who were selected from groups expected to have certain attitudes towards blacks (criterion validity). Indeed, it was found that the groups had significantly different mean scores on the scale in the expected directions. Moreover, this finding was replicated in another part of the country.

The only modifications Whittler (1991; Whittler and DiMeo 1991) made to the items was to substitute the word *blacks* for *Negroes*.

SAMPLES:

The scale was used in two studies described by Whittler (1991). The first one was administered to **160** white undergraduate students. All that is said about the second sample is that the subjects were 160 white adults from the southeastern United States. This appears to be the same sample as described by Whittler and DiMeo (1991), who indicated that their study was based on data from **160** adults who were compensated for their participation. All of the subjects were white and the mean age was 35.9. The majority were married (82%) and attended college or had obtained college degrees (86%).

RELIABILITY:

Whittler (1991) and Whittler and DiMeo (1991) reported alphas of **.84** and **.87**, respectively, for the scale.

VALIDITY:

No direct examination of the scale's validity was reported in either of the studies.

ADMINISTRATION:

The scale was administered along with other measures in experimental settings (Whittler 1991; Whittler and DiMeo 1991). A high score on the scale indicates that a respondent holds subtle derogatory opinions about blacks, whereas a low score suggests that he/she has a very favorable attitude toward them.

MAJOR FINDINGS:

Processing of racial cues in advertising was examined in both Whittler (1991) and Whittler and DiMeo (1991). Among the findings were that brand and ad attitudes were better for whites who had high rather than low **derogatory beliefs**. Moreover, whites with high **derogatory beliefs** found it more difficult to identify with black actors than with white ones.

REFERENCES:

Whittler, Tommy E. (1991), ''The Effects of Actors' Race in Commercial Advertising: Review and Extension,'' *JA*, 20 (1), 54-60.

_____ and Joan DiMeo (1991), ''Viewers' Reactions to Racial Cues in Advertising Stimuli,'' *JAR*, 31 (December), 37-46.

Woodmansee, John J. and Stuart W. Cook (1967), ''Dimensions of Verbal Racial Attitudes: Their Identification and Measurement,'' *Journal of Personality and Social Psychology*, 7 (3), 240-50.

SCALE ITEMS: DEROGATORY BELIEFS AGAINST BLACKS

Strongly
disagree
1————2————3————4————5————6————7
Strongly
agree

1. Blacks sometimes imagine they have been discriminated against on the basis of color even when they have been treated fairly.
2. Some blacks are so touchy about getting their rights that it is difficult to get along with them.
3. Although social equality of the races may be the democratic way, a good many blacks are not yet ready to practice the self-control that goes along with it.
4. Many blacks spend money for big cars and television sets instead of spending it for better housing.
5. Even if there were complete equality of opportunity tomorrow, it would still take a long time for blacks to show themselves equal to whites in some areas of life.
6. Even though blacks may have some cause for complaint, they would get what they want faster if they were a bit more patient about it.
7. The problem of racial prejudice has been greatly exaggerated by a few black agitators.
8. Even if blacks are given the opportunity for college education it will take several generations before they are ready to take advantage of it.
9. Although social mixing of the races might be right in principle, it is impractical until blacks learn to accept more ''don'ts'' in the relations between teenage boys and girls.
10. If I were a black person, I would not want to gain entry into places where I was not really wanted.

SCALE NAME: Desire To Win

SCALE DESCRIPTION:

A three-item, five-point summated ratings scale measuring the degree to which a person describes him/herself as being competitive and as having a strong desire to win.

SCALE ORIGIN:

The items used by Corfman (1991) to measure this construct are apparently original to that study (Corfman 1994).

SAMPLES:

Data for the survey and experiment conducted by Corfman (1991) came from **61** couples from various church, school, and community groups in a major metro area. The couples received compensation for their participation. A broad range of education, age, and income groups were represented. For the survey portion of the study, two copies of the questionnaire were delivered to each couple's home, and they were told to complete the forms independently without discussing their answers during or after. The experimental sessions were conducted in the couples' homes about 19 days after filling out the questionnaire.

RELIABILITY:

The scale was reported to have an alpha of **.82** (Corfman 1991).

VALIDITY:

The items in the scale were factor analyzed along with many others used to measure other constructs. The items for all of the scales were described as loading at .69 or greater on their respective factors.

ADMINISTRATION:

The scale was self-administered by subjects along with many other measures in a questionnaire format during the survey phase of the study by Corfman (1991). High scores on the scale indicate that a person is highly motivated to compete and win.

MAJOR FINDINGS:

The purpose of Corfman's (1991) study was to identify sources of inaccuracy in measuring perceived influence of spouses in their decision making. **Desire to win** was a low but significant predictor of the inaccuracy of a spouse's global influence such that those with a greater **desire to win** were less accurate in describing their general level of relative influence in decision making.

COMMENTS:

See also Corfman and Lehmann (1987) for further analysis of this same data set.

REFERENCES:

Corfman, Kim P. (1994), personal correspondence.

Corfman, Kim P. (1991), "Perceptions of Relative Influence: Formation and Measurement," *JMR*, 28 (May), 125-36.

_____ and Donald R. Lehmann (1987), "Models of Cooperative Group Decision-Making and Relative Influence: An Experimental Investigation of Family Purchase Decisions," *JCR*, 14 (June), 1-13.

SCALE ITEMS: DESIRE TO WIN

Directions: Please rate yourself on each of the scales provided by placing an "X" in the appropriate space.

Not at all   ____ : ____ : ____ : ____ : ____   Extremely or very much
                   1   2   3   4   5

1. want to win
2. Competitive
3. dislike losing

SCALE NAME: Desired Picture Quality (Camera)

SCALE DESCRIPTION:

A three-item, seven-point summated ratings scale measuring the level of picture quality a consumer would like in a camera. *Desires* is supposed to be distinct from *expectations* because whereas the former relates to beliefs about "ideal" product performance that lead to achievement of higher-level values, the latter are beliefs about performance benefits that will occur with a specified focal brand but may be short of what is "ideal" (Spreng and Olshavsky 1993, p. 172). Thus, *desires* implies higher standards than *expectations*.

SCALE ORIGIN:

The origin of the scale was not specified by Spreng and Olshavsky (1993), but it appears to have been developed for that study.

SAMPLES:

The subjects (n = **128**) used by Spreng and Olshavsky (1993) were graduate and undergraduate students attending a major university. They were from both the business school and journalism. Cash prizes were offered as incentives to volunteer.

RELIABILITY:

Spreng and Olshavsky (1993) reported an alpha of **.97** for the scale.

VALIDITY:

Spreng and Olshavsky (1993) performed confirmatory factor analysis and other tests, and the evidence was sufficient for them to conclude that this and their other scales showed convergent and discriminant validity.

ADMINISTRATION:

The scale was administered before subjects were exposed to experimental stimuli (Spreng and Olshavsky 1993). A high score on the scale suggests that a respondent wants a camera that produces professional quality pictures, whereas a low score indicates that he/she simply desires "average" quality photos.

MAJOR FINDINGS:

Spreng and Olshavsky (1993) investigator the relative strengths of two models of satisfaction: *expectancy disconfirmation* and *desires congruency*. The results supported the latter model. **Desired picture quality** was found to have a significant indirect impact on overall satisfaction.

REFERENCE:

Spreng, Richard A. and Richard W. Olshavsky (1993), ''A Desires Congruency Model of Satisfaction,'' *JAMS*, 21 (Summer), 169-77.

SCALE ITEMS: DESIRED PICTURE QUALITY (CAMERA)

Given your individual photographic needs and desires, what would be the level of picture quality you would desire?

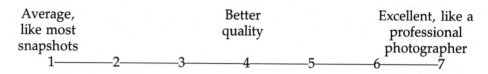

Average, like most snapshots		Better quality		Excellent, like a professional photographer
1———2———3———4———5———6———7				

1. clarity of the picture
2. sharpness of the picture
3. color of the picture

SCALE NAME: Desires Congruency (Camera Picture Quality)

SCALE DESCRIPTION:

> A three-item, seven-point summated ratings scale measuring the level of similarity in beliefs a consumer has toward a particular camera. Desires congruency refers to the results of the comparison made by a consumer of *desires* for "ideal" product performance and *actual* performance by some focal brand.

SCALE ORIGIN:

> The origin of the scale was not specified by Spreng and Olshavsky (1993), but it appears to have been developed for that study.

SAMPLES:

> The subjects (n = 128) used by Spreng and Olshavsky (1993) were graduate and undergraduate students attending a major university. They were from both the business school and journalism. Cash prizes were offered as incentives to volunteer.

RELIABILITY:

> Spreng and Olshavsky (1993) reported an alpha of **.96** for the scale.

VALIDITY:

> Spreng and Olshavsky (1993) performed confirmatory factor analysis and other tests, and the evidence was sufficient for them to conclude that this and their other scales showed convergent and discriminant validity.

ADMINISTRATION:

> The scale was administered before subjects were exposed to experimental stimuli (Spreng and Olshavsky 1993). A high score on the scale suggests that a respondent perceives that a camera has performed better than was desired.

MAJOR FINDINGS:

> Spreng and Olshavsky (1993) investigated the relative strengths of two models of satisfaction: *expectancy disconfirmation* and *desires congruency*. The results supported the latter model.

REFERENCE:

> Spreng, Richard A. and Richard W. Olshavsky (1993), "A Desires Congruency Model of Satisfaction," *JAMS*, 21 (Summer), 169-77.

SCALE ITEMS: DESIRES CONGRUENCY (CAMERA PICTURE QUALITY)

In comparison to the quality level you desired, how would you rate the performance of this camera with regard to the quality of the picture?

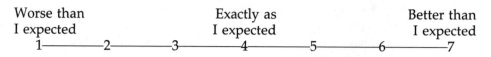

Worse than   Exactly as   Better than
I expected   I expected   I expected
  1————2————3————4————5————6————7

1. clarity of the picture
2. sharpness of the picture
3. color of the picture

SCALE NAME: Dieter (Health)

SCALE DESCRIPTION:

A six-item, seven-point summated rating scale measuring the frequency with which a person engages in several activities related to healthy nutrition. The scale was referred to by Moorman and Matulich (1993) as *Negative Diet Restriction* because the emphasis of these items is on what to limit in one's diet rather than good foods to consume.

SCALE ORIGIN:

The scale was developed by Moorman and Matulich (1993). Development and refinement of the many scales used in their study generally followed the Churchill (1979) paradigm. Measures were pretested on 67 undergraduate students. Then in the main the scales were purified further using alpha, item-total correlations, and LISREL.

SAMPLES:

Moorman and Matulich (1993) used two sampling techniques to obtain respondents who differed on the variables under examination. First, a stratified sample with low and high income as well as young and elderly strata was taken. Respondents from the two income strata were obtained by randomly selecting from lower- and higher-income neighborhoods in Milwaukee and Madison, Wisconsin. Respondents representing the elderly segment were selected randomly from adult centers and retirement communities. Data for young consumers was retained from the pretest (students in an introductory marketing class). In the second sample, survey forms were mailed to addresses of those randomly selected from the telephone books of the same two mentioned cities. The total number of usable questionnaires was **404**, indicating about a 51% overall response rate. A dollar was enclosed with the questionnaires received by all respondents as a token of appreciation and incentive to return the form.

RELIABILITY:

Moorman and Matulich (1993) reported an alpha of **.86** for the scale.

VALIDITY:

Although specific details about this scale were not provided in the article, Moorman and Matulich (1993) engaged in various purification activities in both the pretest and the main study for all their scales. At the least then it would appear that evidence was collected which indicated the scale was unidimensional and internally consistent.

#85 *Dieter (Health)*

ADMINISTRATION:

The scale was self-administered along with many other measures in a questionnaire (Moorman and Matulich 1993). A high score on the scale indicates that a person reports engaging frequently in several healthy diet-related activities.

MAJOR FINDINGS:

The study by Moorman and Matulich (1993) presented and tested a model of the impact various consumer characteristics have on some health-related behaviors. Among the findings was that people with high health motivation as well as high control engaged in significantly more **healthy diet-related activities.**

COMMENTS:

Moorman and Matulich (1993) reported the mean score of the sample on the scale to be 4.44 with a standard deviation of 1.34.

REFERENCES:

Churchill, Gilbert A., Jr. (1979), ''A Paradigm for Developing Better Measures of Marketing Constructs,'' *JMR*, 16 (February), 64-73.

Moorman, Christine and Erika Matulich (1993), ''A Model of Consumers' Preventive Health Motivation and Health Ability,'' *JCR*, 20 (September), 208-28.

SCALE ITEMS: DIETER (HEALTH)

On the scale below please indicate how much you engage in the following activities.*

None of the time   ____ : ____ : ____ : ____ : ____ : ____ : ____   All of the time
                           1   2   3   4   5   6   7

1. Reduce my sodium intake
2. Watch the amount of fat I consume
3. Moderate my sugar intake
4. Moderate my red meat consumption
5. Cut back on snacks and treats
6. Avoid foods with additives and preservatives

* The instructional statement was not provided in the article but was probably something similar to this.

SCALE NAME: Disconfirmation

SCALE DESCRIPTION:

A three-item, five-point, Likert-type scale measuring the degree to which a consumer's expectations regarding a decision are not met. The three-item version has been used most (Oliver 1993; Oliver and Swan 1989a, 1989b; Westbrook 1987), but a two-item, seven-point version has been used as well (Oliver 1980).

SCALE ORIGIN:

The three-item version of the scale was based on the two-item version developed and used originally by Oliver (1980).

SAMPLES:

Systematic random sampling was used by Oliver (1980) to select names and addresses from two sources: the telephone directory of a south-central U.S. city and preregistration data from a major university in the same city. Questionnaires were sent to those selected from the two samples. Of those returning useable forms, **291** residents and **162** students reported receiving a flu shot; **65** residents and **86** students reported that they did not get flu shots.

Two samples were used in the study by Oliver (1993), one examining satisfaction with cars and the other examining course satisfaction. The data involving cars came from a judgmental area sample. Convenience samples were taken at four shopping centers in a large northeastern city and were limited to persons who had purchased a new or used car in the past year. Complete and usable questionnaires were obtained from **125** respondents. A majority (74%) of the sample was male. The average respondent had an income in the $25,000-$40,000 range and was 33 years of age. The second sample was composed of students who volunteered from nine sections of a required marketing class. Usable questionnaires were provided by **178** students.

Findings in Oliver and Swan (1989a) were based on **415** completed questionnaires from two random samples of new car buyers. Because the two samples did not differ significantly on any demographics measured, the data sets were combined. The sample was 63% male and 30% college educated; 22% had incomes between $30,000 and $39,999; and respondents had an average of 41 years of age and had owned 7.8 cars.

Analysis in Oliver and Swan (1989b) was based on just one of the initial samples mentioned previously. Completed surveys were obtained from **184** people who had bought new cars within six months prior to the survey. The average respondent was male (67%), was college educated (32%), had an income between $20,000 and $29,999, was 43 years old, had owned 7.8 cars in his lifetime, and had purchased his latest car 4.5 months previously.

The study by Westbrook (1987) was based on two independent survey samples. One survey focused on CATV services, used area probability sampling of households in a U.S. metropolitan area, and successfully and professionally interviewed **154** adults heads of households. The other sample obtained responses from **200** vehicle owners in the same metro area using personally delivered and retrieved self-administered questionnaires. The samples were said to match their respective populations on selected demographic and product usage characteristics.

RELIABILITY:

The version of the scale used by Westbrook (1987) was reported to have an alpha of **.84**. Three LISREL estimates of the scale's reliability were made in Oliver and Swan (1989b). The consumers' disconfirmation perceptions regarding the dealer, the salesperson, and the car produced alphas of **.86**, **.87**, and **.84**, respectively. With regard to disconfirmation with a salesperson in Oliver and Swan (1989a), a LISREL estimate of **.856** was reported. No reliability information was reported by Oliver (1980). Oliver (1993) reported alphas of **.89** (n = 125) and **.65** (n = 178).

VALIDITY:

No specific examination of scale validity has been reported in any of the studies.

ADMINISTRATION:

The scale was one of many other measures that were self-administered in each of the studies. For the three-item versions of the scale, low scores on the scale suggest that results of a decision have turned out much worse than expected, whereas high scores imply that the results of a decision have turned out much better than expected.

MAJOR FINDINGS:

Oliver (1980) tested a model of consumer satisfaction that expresses satisfaction as a function of expectation and **disconfirmation**. The model was examined in the context of comparing people's expectations regarding a flu shot with their perceived benefits and problems after they had received the shot. The results indicated that **disconfirmation** was not significantly related to any preexposure measure but had the greatest impact on satisfaction of the variables studied.

The separate roles of positive and negative affect, attribute performance, and **disconfirmation** were examined by Oliver (1993) for their impact on satisfaction. For both samples, **disconfirmation** was found to have direct and very significant influence on satisfaction.

The general purpose of both Oliver and Swan (1989a and 1989b) was to examine customer perceptions of satisfaction in the context of new car purchases. Using LISREL it was determined that fairness is more important than **disconfirmation** in producing interpersonal satisfaction and advantageous inequity is unrelated to it (1989a).

The findings were the same in Oliver and Swan (1989b) with the added insight that customer satisfaction with the dealer was primarily related to the former's perception of fairness, followed by satisfaction with the salesperson, and then somewhat influenced by **disconfirmation**.

Affective responses to consumption experiences and their influence on postpurchase processes were studied by Westbrook (1987). **Disconfirmation** is a significant positive predictor of satisfaction and a significant negative predictor of complaint behavior. However, the latter relationship is fully mediated by satisfaction.

COMMENTS:

Although similarities exist between the versions of the scales used, the object of the expectations does make a difference in the phrasing of the items (as noted subsequently). However, it appears that with minimal adjustment the scale might be usable for other decisions.

REFERENCES:

Oliver, Richard L. (1980), ''A Cognitive Model of the Antecedents and Consequences of Satisfaction Decisions,'' *JMR*, 17 (November), 460-69.

_____ (1993), ''Cognitive, Affective, and Attribute Bases of the Satisfaction Response,'' *JCR*, 20 (December), 418-30.

_____ and Richard L. and John E. Swan (1989a), ''Consumer Perceptions of Interpersonal Equity and Satisfaction in Transactions: A Field Survey Approach,'' *JM*, 53 (April), 21-35.

_____ and John E. Swan (1989b), ''Equity and Disconfirmation Perceptions as Influences on Merchant and Product Satisfaction,'' *JCR*, 16 (December), 372-83.

Westbrook, Robert A. (1987), ''Product/Consumption-Based Affective Responses and Postpurchase Processes,'' *JMR*, 24 (August), 258-70.

SCALE ITEMS: DISCONFIRMATION*

1. The problems you have encountered have been:

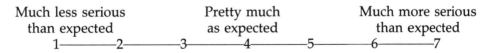

2. The benefits you have experienced have been:

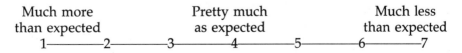

* The actual items were not provided in Oliver (1980) but, on the basis of their description, this is their assumed form. Similarly, the items in Oliver (1993) as well as Westbrook (1987) were not given but appear to be similar to these items except that they referred to the purchase of a car and included a third ''overall'' item similar to those that follow.

Much worse than expected	Worse than expected	As expected	Better than expected	Much better than expected
1	2	3	4	5

Compared to what I expected the salesperson to be like: +
1. The problems I had with him were . . .
2. His good points were . . .
3. Overall, my salesman was . . .

Compared to what I expected the dealership to be like:**
1. The problems I had were . . .
2. The benefits I expected were . . .
3. Overall, the dealer was . . .

Compared to what I expected:**
1. The car's strength's were . . .
2. The car's weaknesses were . . .
3. All things about the car were . . .

+ Used by Oliver and Swan (1989a and 1989b).
** Used by Oliver and Swan (1989b).

SCALE NAME: Disconfirmation (Camera Picture Quality)

SCALE DESCRIPTION:

A three-item, seven-point summated ratings scale measuring the level of disconfirmation in beliefs a consumer has toward a particular camera. Disconfirmation refers to the results of the comparison made by a consumer of *expectations* of product performance and *actual* performance.

SCALE ORIGIN:

The origin of the scale was not specified by Spreng and Olshavsky (1993), but it appears to have been developed for that study.

SAMPLES:

The subjects (n = **128**) used by Spreng and Olshavsky (1993) were graduate and undergraduate students attending a major university. They were from both the business school and journalism. Cash prizes were offered as incentives to volunteer.

RELIABILITY:

Spreng and Olshavsky (1993) reported an alpha of **.96** for the scale.

VALIDITY:

Spreng and Olshavsky (1993) performed confirmatory factor analysis and other tests, and the evidence was sufficient for them to conclude that this and their other scales showed convergent and discriminant validity.

ADMINISTRATION:

The scale was administered before subjects were exposed to experimental stimuli (Spreng and Olshavsky 1993). A high score on the scale suggests that the respondent perceives that a camera has performed better than was expected.

MAJOR FINDINGS:

Spreng and Olshavsky (1993) investigated the relative strengths of two models of satisfaction: *expectancy disconfirmation* and *desires congruency*. The results supported the latter model.

REFERENCE:

Spreng, Richard A. and Richard W. Olshavsky (1993), ''A Desires Congruency Model of Satisfaction,'' *JAMS*, 21 (Summer), 169-77.

SCALE ITEMS: DISCONFIRMATION (CAMERA PICTURE QUALITY)

In comparison to the quality level you expected, how would you rate the performance of this camera with regard to the quality of the picture?

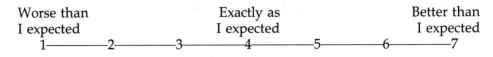

Worse than   Exactly as   Better than
I expected   I expected   I expected
1————2————3————4————5————6————7

1. clarity of the picture
2. sharpness of the picture
3. color of the picture

SCALE NAME: Discount Size

SCALE DESCRIPTION:

A three-item, seven-point summated ratings scale measuring a person's perception of the magnitude of the savings indicated in an ad for a category of products on sale.

SCALE ORIGIN:

Although it is not specifically stated, the scale apparently was developed by Biswas and Burton (1993).

SAMPLES:

Biswas and Burton (1993) reported on two studies in their article. In the first one data was collected from **392** undergraduate business students. Little more is said about the sample except there was a nearly equal portion of each gender and they were assigned randomly to one of the 12 treatments. The second sample was composed of **303** nonstudents who were recruited by students in a marketing course. All those in the sample were 18 years of age and older with a median of 40 years. A little more than half were female (56%), and the median household income was $35,000.

RELIABILITY:

Biswas and Burton (1993) reported alphas of **.71** and **.77** in their first and second studies, respectively.

VALIDITY:

Biswas and Burton (1993) reported no specific examination of the scale's validity.

ADMINISTRATION:

The scale was self-administered by subjects along with several other measures after exposure to experimental stimuli (Biswas and Burton 1993). High scores on the scale imply that respondents perceive that a discount stated in an ad represents a large amount of money that buyers would save.

MAJOR FINDINGS:

Biswas and Burton (1993) investigated the impact of three different price claims on various perceptions and intentions. Among the many findings was that **perceptions of discount size** were much greater for larger discount ranges than for smaller.

REFERENCE:

> Biswas, Abhijit and Scot Burton (1993), "Consumer Perceptions of Tensile
> Price Claims in Advertisements: An Assessment of Claim Types Across
> Different Discount Levels," *JAMS*, 21 (Summer), 217-29.

SCALE ITEMS: DISCOUNT SIZE*

1. The amount of discount that is offered on _____ represents:

A large savings   ____ : ____ : ____ : ____ : ____ : ____ : ____   No savings at all
             1   2   3   4   5   6   7

2. The amount of money that customers will save on most _____ is:

A lot   ____ : ____ : ____ : ____ : ____ : ____ : ____   A little
       1   2   3   4   5   6   7

3. The amount of discount implied in the advertisement is:

High   ____ : ____ : ____ : ____ : ____ : ____ : ____   Low
       1   2   3   4   5   6   7

* The name of the product category on sale goes in the blanks. Biswas and Burton
(1993) used *35mm cameras*, and they indicated that all three items were reverse
coded.

SCALE NAME: Disgust

SCALE DESCRIPTION:

A three-item, five-point summated ratings scale assessing the experience a person has had with disgust-related emotions. The directions and response scale can be worded so as to measure the *intensity* of the emotional state at the present time, or they can be adjusted to measure the *frequency* with which a person has experienced the emotional trait during some specified time period. One-word items were used in the study by Westbrook and Oliver (1991), whereas phrases based on those same items were used by Allen, Machleit, and Kleine (1992).

SCALE ORIGIN:

The measure was developed by Izard (1977) and is part of the Differential Emotions Scale (DES II). The instrument originally was designed as a measure of a person's emotional "state" at a particular point in time, but adjustments in the instrument's instructions enable the same items to be used in the assessment of emotional experiences as perceived over a longer time period. The latter was viewed by Izard as measure of one's emotional "trait" (1977, p. 125). Test-retest reliability for the disgust subscale of DES II was reported to be .73 (n = 63) and item-factor correlations were .78 and more (Izard 1977, p. 126).

The items in DES II were composed solely of one word. In contrast, the items in DES III are phrases describing the target emotion. They were developed by Izard, though the first published validity testing was conducted by Kotsch, Gerbing, and Schwartz (1982). A study by Allen, Machleit, and Marine (1988) provides some insight to the factor structure of both DES II and III. The results indicate that when presented with the other DES items, the disgust items were not unidimensional and tended to load with items representing other emotions such as anger and contempt. Because of this, the scale may have low validity.

SAMPLES:

The data used by Allen, Machleit, and Kleine (1992) came from a stratified sample of people of diverse experience with blood donation. Nine hundred questionnaires were mailed and **361** usable forms were returned. Given that all respondents previously had donated blood, limited information was known about them and allowed a comparison with nonrespondents. Respondents were a little older, less likely to be male, and more likely to be heavier donors than nonrespondents.

The data for the study conducted by Westbrook and Oliver (1991) came from a judgmental area sample. Convenience samples were taken at four shopping centers in a large northeastern city and were limited to persons who had purchased a new or used car in the past year. Complete and usable questionnaires were obtained from **125** respondents. A majority (74%) of the sample was male. The average respondent had an income in the $25,000–

$40,000 range and was 33 years of age. The frequency version of the scale was used in this study.

Two samples were used in the study by Oliver (1993), one examining satisfaction with cars and the other examining course satisfaction. The one involving cars is the same as the one described previously in Westbrook and Oliver (1991). The other sample was composed of students who volunteered from nine sections of a required marketing class. Usable questionnaires were provided by **178** students. The intensity version of the scale was used in this study.

RELIABILITY:

Westbrook and Oliver (1991) reported an alpha of **.91** for the scale. An alpha of **.88** was calculated by Allen, Machleit, and Kleine (1992; Allen 1994). Oliver (1993) reported alphas of **.92** (n = 125) and **.80** (n = 178).

VALIDITY:

No specific examination of the scale's validity was reported in any of the studies.

ADMINISTRATION:

The scale was included with many other measures in the instrument used by Westbrook and Oliver (1991), Oliver (1993), and Allen, Machleit, and Kleine (1992). High scores on the frequency version of the scale suggest that a person perceives him/herself as having experienced the disgust-related emotional trait very often in some specified time period. A high score on the intensity version of the scale indicates that one is feeling very disgusted at the time of measurement.

MAJOR FINDINGS:

The study by Allen, Machleit, Kleine (1992) examined whether emotions effect behavior through attitudes or are better viewed as having a separate and distinct impact. Although several emotions were found to play key roles in predicting behavior, **disgust** (DES III) was not found to have a significant relationship, at least with regard to donating blood.

The separate roles of positive and negative affect, attribute performance, and disconfirmation were examined by Oliver (1993) for their impact on satisfaction. Negative affect was viewed as a function of several emotions, **disgust** being one of them. For both samples, negative affect was found to have direct influence on satisfaction.

Westbrook and Oliver (1991) studied the correspondence of the consumption emotional responses and satisfaction judgments that occur in the postpurchase period of the consumer decision process. **Disgust** had its highest correlation with contempt (r = .92) and its lowest correlation with interest (r = .22). **Disgust** also was found to be a primary emotional trait linked to the cluster of consumers who had the lowest satisfaction in their car buying experiences.

REFERENCES:

Allen, Chris T. (1994), personal correspondence.

_____, Karen A. Machleit, and Susan Schultz Kleine (1992), ''A Comparison of Attitudes and Emotions as Predictors of Behavior at Diverse Levels of Behavioral Experience,'' *JCR*, 18 (March), 493-504.

_____, _____, and Susan S. Marine (1988), ''On Assessing the Emotionality of Advertising Via Izard's Differential Emotions Scale,'' in *Advances in Consumer Research*, Vol. 15, Michael J. Houston, ed. Provo, UT: Association for Consumer Research, 226-31.

Izard, Carroll E. (1977), *Human Emotions*. New York: Plenum Press.

Kotsch, William E., Davis W. Gerbing, and Lynne E. Schwartz (1982), ''The Construct Validity of the Differential Emotions Scale as Adapted for Children and Adolescents,'' in *Measuring Emotions in Infants and Children*, Carroll E. Izard, ed. New York: Cambridge University Press, 251-78.

Oliver, Richard L. (1993), ''Cognitive, Affective, and Attribute Bases of the Satisfaction Response,'' *JCR*, 20 (December), 418-30.

Westbrook, Robert A. and Richard L. Oliver (1991), ''The Dimensionality of Consumption Emotion Patterns and Consumer Satisfaction,'' *JCR*, 18 (June), 84-91.

SCALE ITEMS: DISGUST

POSSIBLE DIRECTIONS FOR FREQUENCY VERSION OF SCALE: Below is a list of words that you can use to show how you feel. We want you to tell us how often you felt each of these feelings _____.* You can tell us how often you felt each of these feelings on the list by marking one of the numbers next to each question.

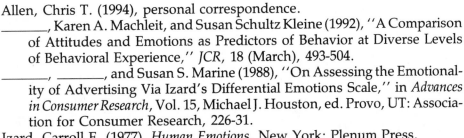

```
Almost                                          Very
never      ____ : ____ : ____ : ____ : ____     often
             1      2      3      4      5
```

POSSIBLE DIRECTIONS FOR INTENSITY VERSION OF SCALE: Below is a list of words that you can use to show how you feel. We want you to tell us how strongly you feel. You can tell us how strongly you feel each of these feelings on the list by marking one of the numbers next to each question.

```
Very                                            Very
weak       ____ : ____ : ____ : ____ : ____     strong
             1      2      3      4      5
```

DES II
1. feeling of distaste
2. disgusted
3. feeling of revulsion

DES III

1. feel like something stinks, put a bad taste in your mouth
2. feel disgusted, like something is sickening
3. feel like things are so rotten they could make you sick

* The blank should be used to specify the time period of interest such as ''during the last week.''

SCALE NAME: Dominance

SCALE DESCRIPTION:

A six-item, seven-point semantic differential summated ratings scale measuring one's dominance-related emotional reaction to an environmental stimulus.

SCALE ORIGIN:

This scale is taken from the work of Mehrabian and Russell (1974). Given previous work by others as well as their own research, they proposed that there are three factors that compose all emotional reactions to environmental stimuli: pleasure, arousal, and dominance. A series of studies were used to develop measures of each factor. A study of the ''final'' set of items used 214 University of California undergraduates, each of whom used the scales to evaluate a different subset of six situations. (The analysis was based, therefore, on 1284 observations.) A principal components factor analysis with oblique rotation was used, and the expected three factors emerged. Pleasure, arousal, and dominance explained 27%, 23%, and 14% of the available evidence, respectively. Scores on the pleasure scale had correlations of −.07 and .03 with arousal and dominance, respectively. Dominance had a correlation of .18 with arousal.

SAMPLES:

Holbrook and colleagues (1984) used **60** MBA students with a mean age of 25.6 years.

RELIABILITY:

An alpha of **.88** was reported for the scale.

VALIDITY:

No examination of the scale's validity was reported.

ADMINISTRATION:

The scale was self-administered along with several other measures in the middle of individual experimental sessions. Low scores on the scale suggest that respondents feel in control of some specified stimulus, whereas high scores imply that they are instead heavily influenced by the stimulus. Holbrook and colleagues (1984) noted that scores were normalized for each individual by subtracting the scale mean from the response to each item and then summing the corrected numeric responses.

MAJOR FINDINGS:

The study examined the role played by emotions, performance, and personality in the enjoyment of games. In general, it was found that emotions depend on personality-game congruity, perceived complexity, and prior performance. Specifically, the **dominance** expressed in playing a video game was most significantly predicted by a match between cognitive style (visualizing/verbalizing) and game format (visual/verbal) as well as the number of successful performances out of four immediately preceding plays.

COMMENTS:

As noted previously, this scale was developed along with two other scales, arousal and pleasure. Although scored separately, they typically are used together in a study.

See also Havlena and Holbrook (1986), as well as Hui and Bateson (1991) and Bateson and Hui (1992).

REFERENCES:

Bateson, John E. G. and Michael K. Hui (1992), "The Ecological Validity of Photographic Slides and Videotapes in Simulating the Service Setting," *JCR*, 19 (September), 271-81.

Havlena, William J. and Morris B. Holbrook (1986), "The Varieties of Consumption Experience: Comparing Two Typologies of Emotion in Consumer Behavior," *JCR*, 13 (December), 394-404.

Holbrook, Morris B., Robert W. Chestnut, Terence A. Oliva, and Eric A. Greenleaf (1984), "Play as a Consumption Experience: The Roles of Emotions, Performance, and Personality in the Enjoyment of Games," *JCR*, 11 (September), 728-39.

Hui, Michael K. and John E. G. Bateson (1991), "Perceived Control and the Effects of Crowding and Consumer Choice on the Service Experience," *JCR*, 18 (September), 174-84.

Mehrabian, Albert and James A. Russell (1974), *An Approach to Environmental Psychology*. Cambridge, MA: The MIT Press.

SCALE ITEMS: DOMINANCE

Controlling ___ : ___ : ___ : ___ : ___ : ___ : ___ Controlled
1 2 3 4 5 6 7

Influential ___ : ___ : ___ : ___ : ___ : ___ : ___ Influenced
1 2 3 4 5 6 7

In control ___ : ___ : ___ : ___ : ___ : ___ : ___ Cared for
1 2 3 4 5 6 7

Important ___ : ___ : ___ : ___ : ___ : ___ : ___ Awed
1 2 3 4 5 6 7

Dominant ___ : ___ : ___ : ___ : ___ : ___ : ___ Submissive
1 2 3 4 5 6 7

Autonomous ___ : ___ : ___ : ___ : ___ : ___ : ___ Guided
1 2 3 4 5 6 7

SCALE NAME: Donor Motivation (Blood)

SCALE DESCRIPTION:

A four-item, seven-point, Likert-type scale measuring the reason a person gives for donating blood. The focus of the measure is on the degree to which a person perceives his/her behavior to be self-motivated.

SCALE ORIGIN:

The scale was developed by Allen, Machleit, and Kleine (1992; Allen 1994) specifically for the study in which it was reported.

SAMPLES:

The data used by Allen, Machleit, and Kleine (1992) came from a stratified sample of people of diverse experience with blood donation. Nine hundred questionnaires were mailed, and **361** usable forms were returned. Given that all respondents previously had donated blood, limited information was known about them and enabled a comparison with nonrespondents. Respondents were a little older, less likely to be male, and more likely to be heavier donors than nonrespondents.

RELIABILITY:

Allen, Machleit, and Kleine (1992) reported an alpha of **.75** for the scale.

VALIDITY:

Allen, Machleit, and Kleine (1992) used LISREL to confirm that the scale was unidimensional.

ADMINISTRATION:

The scale was part of a larger mail questionnaire (Allen, Machleit, and Kleine 1992). A high score on the scale indicates that a respondent reports his/her blood donation activity to be intrinsically motivated, whereas a low score suggests that the respondent's behavior was influenced heavily by some extrinsic stimulus.

MAJOR FINDINGS:

The study by Allen, Machleit, and Kleine (1992) examined whether emotions effect behavior via attitudes or are better viewed as having a separate and distinct impact. Among the many findings was that **donor self-motivation** had a positive relationship with the number of blood donations during a year's time.

REFERENCES:

Allen, Chris T. (1994), personal correspondence.

_____, Karen A. Machleit, and Susan Schultz Kleine (1992), ''A Comparison of Attitudes and Emotions as Predictors of Behavior at Diverse Levels of Behavioral Experience,'' *JCR*, 18 (March), 493-504.

SCALE ITEMS: DONOR MOTIVATION (BLOOD)

Strongly disagree	___ : ___ : ___ : ___ : ___ : ___ : ___	Strongly agree
	1 2 3 4 5 6 7	

1. The last time I gave blood, someone had pressured me into it. **(r)**
2. I donate blood because I want to, not because I have to.
3. Others do not have to talk me into giving blood.
4. I am good at handling the negative aspects of giving blood.

SCALE NAME: Donor Motivation (Charity Administration Importance)

SCALE DESCRIPTION:

A nine-item, five-point summated scale measuring the importance to potential donors of various business aspects of a charity. It was described by Harvey (1990) as the *management activities* dimension of the fundraising "product."

SCALE ORIGIN:

The wording of scale items was developed along with many other measures during a preliminary focus group phase of the project.

SAMPLES:

Harvey (1990) administered his questionnaire to a convenience sample of 1000 workers in nine cities across the country, all of whom reported donating to charity in the preceding year. Survey forms were completed at the workers' job sites. The analysis was based on **857** completed questionnaires. Although some examination of demographic differences among donor clusters was made, no description of the demographics of the entire sample was provided.

RELIABILITY:

Harvey (1990) reported an alpha of **.87** for the scale.

VALIDITY:

A factor analysis of 41 donation-related items indicated that the items composing this scale all loaded on the same factor. Moreover, that factor explained more variance than any other factor in the analysis (36.8%).

ADMINISTRATION:

The scale was administered to the sample as part of a larger survey form. High scores on the scale indicate that donors believe various management-related activities of charities are very important in deciding which one(s) to support.

MAJOR FINDINGS:

The purpose of Harvey's (1990) study was to apply benefit segmentation to the market of charitable donors. On the basis of responses to the items in several scales, a sample of donors was clustered. A fifth of all the donors surveyed were labeled as "Managers" because their main concern was supporting a cause that was perceived to be managed well. This group scored highest on the **Charity Administration Importance** scale. Among the many findings about this group was that it had the highest proportion of females and non-whites. The people in this segment also reported donating the highest percentage of income and having the highest level of voluntarism.

REFERENCE:

> Harvey, James W. (1990), ''Benefit Segmentation for Fund Raisers,'' *JAMS*, 18 (Winter), 77-86.

SCALE ITEMS: DONOR MOTIVATION (CHARITY ADMINISTRATION IMPORTANCE)*

When choosing whether to give money to charity or deciding which fund-raiser to support, donors base their choices on a variety of issues. Use the following scale to indicate how important each of the following are to you when making a donation decision.

```
Not important                                             Very
   at all                                             important
   1————————2————————3————————4————————5
```

How important is:
1. assessing community needs
2. auditing operating standards
3. disbursing funds properly
4. recruiting volunteers
5. reviewing budgets
6. identifying problem solvers
7. managing volunteers
8. directing needy to agencies
9. educating the community

* The exact instructions and response scale were not provided in the article. They were likely to be similar to what is presented here on the basis of the information available.

SCALE NAME: Donor Motivation (Charity Cause Importance)

SCALE DESCRIPTION:

A seven-item, five-point summated scale measuring the importance to potential donors of the service a charity provides to the community. It was described
by Harvey (1990) as the *cause* dimension of the fundraising ''product.''

SCALE ORIGIN:

The wording of scale items was developed along with many other measures
during a preliminary focus group phase of the project.

SAMPLES:

Harvey (1990) administered his questionnaire to a convenience sample of
1000 workers in nine cities across the country, all of whom reported donating
to charity in the preceding year. Survey forms were completed at the workers'
job sites. The analysis was based on **857** completed questionnaires. Although
some examination of demographic differences among donor clusters was
made, no description of the demographics of the entire sample was provided.

RELIABILITY:

Harvey (1990) reported an alpha of **.81** for the scale.

VALIDITY:

A factor analysis of 41 donation-related items indicated that the items composing this scale all loaded on the same factor. Moreover, that factor explained
19% of the variance in the analysis.

ADMINISTRATION:

The scale was administered to the sample as part of a larger survey form.
High scores on the scale indicate that donors believe the purpose served by
a charitable organization is very important in deciding whether to support
it.

MAJOR FINDINGS:

The purpose of the study by Harvey (1990) was to apply benefit segmentation
to the market of charitable donors. On the basis of responses to the items
in several scales, a sample of donors was clustered. Twenty-two percent of
the donors surveyed were labeled as ''Crusaders,'' those who scored highest
on the **Charity Cause Importance** scale. Among the many findings about
this group was that it had the most favorable attitude toward fund raising
activities, believed that a greater percentage of donated funds actually reached
the needy, and was the most likely to give because it helped others.

REFERENCE:

> Harvey, James W. (1990), ''Benefit Segmentation for Fund Raisers,'' *JAMS*, 18 (Winter), 77-86.

SCALE ITEMS: DONOR MOTIVATION (CHARITY CAUSE IMPORTANCE)*

> When choosing whether to give money to charity or deciding which fundraiser to support, donors base their choices on a variety of issues. Use the following scale to indicate how important each of the following are to you when making a donation decision.

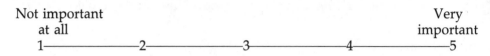

> How important is it that the charity:
> 1. has fundraising costs that are excessive **(r)**
> 2. solves problems
> 3. strengthens the community
> 4. helps people
> 5. provides quality services
> 6. assists people
> 7. doesn't serve people **(r)**

> * The exact instructions and response scale were not provided in the article. They were likely to be similar to what is presented here on the basis of the information available.

SCALE NAME: Donor Motivation (Charity Curative Services Importance)

SCALE DESCRIPTION:

A five-item, five-point summated scale measuring the importance to potential donors of a charity's support services that focus on repairing damage already done. It was described by Harvey (1990) as the *curative services dimension* of the fundraising "product."

SCALE ORIGIN:

The wording of scale items was developed along with many other measures during a preliminary focus group phase of the project.

SAMPLES:

Harvey (1990) administered his questionnaire to a convenience sample of 1000 workers in nine cities across the country, all of whom reported donating to charity in the preceding year. Survey forms were completed at the workers' job sites. The analysis was based on **857** completed questionnaires. Although some examination of demographic differences among donor clusters was made, no description of the demographics of the entire sample was provided.

RELIABILITY:

Harvey (1990) reported an alpha of **.84** for the scale.

VALIDITY:

A factor analysis of 41 donation-related items indicated that the items composing this scale all loaded on the same factor. Moreover, that factor explained 6.4% of the variance in the analysis.

ADMINISTRATION:

The scale was administered to the sample as part of a larger survey form. High scores on the scale indicate that donors believe various curative-related support activities of charities are very important in deciding which one(s) to support.

MAJOR FINDINGS:

The purpose of the study by Harvey (1990) was to apply benefit segmentation to the market of charitable donors. On the basis of responses to the items in several scales, a sample of donors was clustered. A fifth of all the donors surveyed were labeled as "Managers" because their main concern was supporting a cause that was perceived to be managed well. This group also scored highest on the **Charity Curative Services Importance** scale. Among the many findings about this group was that it had the highest proportion of females and non-whites. The people in this segment also reported donating the highest percentage of income and having the highest level of voluntarism.

REFERENCE:

Harvey, James W. (1990), ''Benefit Segmentation for Fund Raisers,'' *JAMS*, 18 (Winter), 77-86.

SCALE ITEMS: DONOR MOTIVATION (CHARITY CURATIVE SERVICES IMPORTANCE)*

When choosing whether to give money to charity or deciding which fund-raiser to support, donors base their choices on a variety of issues. Use the following scale to indicate how important each of the following are to you when making a donation decision.

Not important   Very
   at all   important
  1————————2————————3————————4————————5

How important are:
1. family counseling services
2. child welfare services
3. mental health services
4. elderly services
5. rehabilitation services

* The exact instructions and response scale were not provided in the article. They were likely to be similar to what is presented here on the basis of the information available.

SCALE NAME: Donor Motivation (Charity Fundraising Pressure Importance)

SCALE DESCRIPTION:

A four-item, five-point summated scale measuring the importance to potential donors of the pressure tactics used by a charity in its fundraising activities. It was described by Harvey (1990) as the *campaign intensity dimension* of the fundraising "product."

SCALE ORIGIN:

The wording of scale items was developed along with many other measures during a preliminary focus group phase of the project.

SAMPLES:

Harvey (1990) administered his questionnaire to a convenience sample of 1000 workers in nine cities across the country, all of whom reported donating to charity in the preceding year. Survey forms were completed at the workers' job sites. The analysis was based on **857** completed questionnaires. Although some examination of demographic differences among donor clusters was made, no description of the demographics of the entire sample was provided.

RELIABILITY:

Harvey (1990) reported an alpha of **.61** for the scale.

VALIDITY:

A factor analysis of 41 donation-related items indicated that the items composing this scale all loaded on the same factor. Moreover, that factor explained 5.7% of the variance in the analysis.

ADMINISTRATION:

The scale was administered to the sample as part of a larger survey form. High scores on the scale indicate that donors believe the pressure applied by a charitable organization in its fundraising activities is very important in deciding whether to support it.

MAJOR FINDINGS:

The purpose of the study by Harvey (1990) was to apply benefit segmentation to the market of charitable donors. On the basis of responses to the items in several scales, a sample of donors was clustered. Twenty-two percent of the donors surveyed were labeled as "Crusaders," those who scored highest on the Charity Cause Importance scale. This group also scored highest on the **Fundraising Pressure Importance** scale. Among the many findings about this group was that it had the most favorable attitude toward fund raising activities, believed that a greater percentage of donated funds actually reached the needy, and was the most likely to give because it helped others.

REFERENCE:

Harvey, James W. (1990), "Benefit Segmentation for Fund Raisers," *JAMS*, 18 (Winter), 77-86.

SCALE ITEMS: DONOR MOTIVATION (CHARITY FUNDRAISING PRESSURE IMPORTANCE)

When choosing whether to give money to charity or deciding which fund-raiser to support, donors base their choices on a variety of issues. Use the following scale to indicate how important each of the following are to you when making a donation decision.

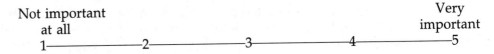

Not important at all — Very important

1———2———3———4———5

How important is:
1. fundraising pressure
2. compelled to give
3. felt pressure to give
4. receive pressure

* The exact instructions and response scale were not provided in the article. They were likely to be similar to what is presented here on the basis of the information available.

SCALE NAME: Donor Motivation (Charity Wellness Services Importance)

SCALE DESCRIPTION:

An eight-item, five-point summated scale measuring the importance to potential donors of a charity's support services that focus on preventing problems from developing. It was described by Harvey (1990) as the *preventative/facilitative services* dimension of the fundraising "product."

SCALE ORIGIN:

The wording of scale items was developed along with many other measures during a preliminary focus group phase of the project.

SAMPLES:

Harvey (1990) administered his questionnaire to a convenience sample of 1000 workers in nine cities across the country, all of whom reported donating to charity in the preceding year. Survey forms were completed at the workers' job sites. The analysis was based on **857** completed questionnaires. Although some examination of demographic differences among donor clusters was made, no description of the demographics of the entire sample was provided.

RELIABILITY:

Harvey (1990) reported an alpha of **.87** for the scale.

VALIDITY:

A factor analysis of 41 donation-related items indicated that the items composing this scale all loaded on the same factor. Moreover, that factor explained 12.5% of the variance in the analysis.

ADMINISTRATION:

The scale was administered to the sample as part of a larger survey form. High scores on the scale indicate that donors believe various preventative-related support activities of charities are very important in deciding which one(s) to support.

MAJOR FINDINGS:

The purpose of Harvey's (1990) study was to apply benefit segmentation to the market of charitable donors. On the basis of responses to the items in several scales, a sample of donors was clustered. A fifth of all the donors surveyed were labeled as "Managers" because their main concern was supporting a cause that was perceived to be managed well. This group also scored highest on the **Charity Wellness Services Importance** scale. Among the many findings about this group was that it had the highest proportion of females and non-whites. The people in this segment also reported donating the highest percentage of income and having the highest level of voluntarism.

REFERENCE:

Harvey, James W. (1990), ''Benefit Segmentation for Fund Raisers,'' *JAMS*, 18 (Winter), 77-86.

SCALE ITEMS: DONOR MOTIVATION (CHARITY WELLNESS SERVICES IMPORTANCE)*

When choosing whether to give money to charity or deciding which fund-raiser to support, donors base their choices on a variety of issues. Use the following scale to indicate how important each of the following are to you when making a donation decision.

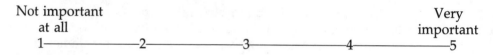

Not important
  at all

1————————2————————3————————4————————5

Very
important

How important are:
1. educational services
2. consumer services
3. legal aid services
4. employment services
5. arts & cultural services
6. housing services
7. day care services
8. family planning services

* The exact instructions and response scale were not provided in the article. They were likely to be similar to what is presented here on the basis of the information available.

SCALE NAME: Egalitarianism

SCALE DESCRIPTION:

A 17-item, five-point, summated ratings scale measuring a person's attitude about gender roles, equality of the sexes, and self-actualization for women.

SCALE ORIGIN:

The items composing the scale used by Fischer and Arnold (1990) originated in the work of Scanzoni (e.g., 1975, 1978). Although treated by the former as one summated scale, the latter treated the items as well as a few others as measures of five different gender role dimensions. The Traditional-Wife Role scale had eight items and alphas of .74 and .81 for two different administrations of the scale. Similarly, the Wife Self-Actualization scale had four items and alphas of .56 and .63. The Problematic-Husband Alterations scale had five items and alphas of .62 and .68. The Institutionalized Equality scale had two items and alphas of .68 and .74. Finally, the Traditional-Husband Role scale had two items and alphas of .20 and .38.

SAMPLES:

Data were collected using multistage cluster sampling by Fischer and Arnold (1990). The study was based on data from the **299** people who completed the questionnaire. Compared with the population from which the data were collected, the sample had fewer males but was more upscale. A $1 lottery ticket was given to respondents for participating.

RELIABILITY:

Fischer and Arnold (1990) reported an alpha of **.83**.

VALIDITY:

Although Fischer and Arnold (1990) did not report examination of the scale's validity, the former did so in personal correspondence. The results of a factor analysis indicated that items 9-11, 15, and 16 loaded together; items 12-14, and 17 loaded on another factor; and the other eight items loaded on a third factor.

ADMINISTRATION:

The scale was administered by Fischer and Arnold (1990) as part of a structured survey instrument during in-home personal interviews with respondents. High scores indicate greater belief that men and women should be equal in their approaches to work and family responsibilities, whereas lower scores suggest acceptance of more traditional gender roles.

MAJOR FINDINGS:

Fischer and Arnold (1990) studied the impact of several gender-related variables on Christmas gift shopping patterns. It was found that men who were more **egalitarian** were slightly more involved than other men in their Christmas shopping. In contrast, women who were more **egalitarian** were slightly less involved than other women in Christmas shopping.

COMMENTS:

The evidence regarding reliability and dimensionality indicate that even though the items are probably tapping into a common factor, at least three subfactors are being measured as well by the various sets of items. This lack of unidimensionality brings the scale's validity into question and suggests that caution should be exercised in its use until further testing and refinement occurs.

REFERENCES:

Fischer, Eileen and Stephen J. Arnold (1990), ''More than a Labor of Love: Gender Roles and Christmas Gift Shopping,'' *JCR*, 17 (December), 333-45.

Scanzoni, John (1975), ''Sex Roles, Economic Factors, and Marital Solidarity in Black and White Marriages,'' *Journal of Marriage and the Family*, 34 (February), 130-44.

_____ (1978), *Sex Roles, Women's Work, and Marital Conflict*. Lexington, MA: Lexington Books.

SCALE ITEMS: EGALITARIANISM*

Directions: Below are some statements concerning the responsibilities of adults. Please respond on the scale from one to five. (To clarify: a 1 means that you strongly disagree; a 2 means that you disagree somewhat; a 3 means that you both agree and disagree; a 4 means that you agree somewhat; and a 5 means that you strongly agree.)

Strongly disagree	Disagree somewhat	Both agree and disagree	Agree somewhat	Strongly agree
1	2	3	4	5

1. A married man's chief responsibility is his job.
2. If his wife works, he should share equally in household chores such as cooking, cleaning and washing.
3. If his wife works, he should share equally in the responsibilities of child care.
4. If her job requires her to be away from home overnight, this should not bother him.
5. If a child gets sick and his wife works, he should be just as willing as she to stay home from work and take care of the child.

6. If his wife makes more money than he does, this should not bother him.
7. The husband should be the head of the family. **(r)**
8. On the job, he should be willing to work for women supervisors.
9. A married woman's most important task in life should be taking care of her husband. **(r)**
10. She should realize that a mother's greatest reward and satisfaction come through her children. **(r)**
11. Having a job herself should be just as important as encouraging her husband in his job.
12. She should be able to make long range plans for her occupation in the same way her husband does for his.
13. If being a wife and mother isn't satisfying enough, she should take a job.
14. There should be more daycare centers and nursery schools so that more young mothers could work.
15. A wife should give up her job whenever it makes a hardship for her husband and children. **(r)**
16. If a mother of young children works, it should only be while the family needs money. **(r)**
17. A mother with preschoolers should be able to work just as many hours per week as their father.

* Indications of reverse coding were not provided in the published sources or in personal correspondence from Fischer (1993). The notations made are based solely on our judgment.

SCALE NAME: Elation

SCALE DESCRIPTION:

A three-item, five-point scale measuring one's excitement-related emotional reaction to some specified stimulus.

SCALE ORIGIN:

Although two items were drawn from the work of Watson, Clark, and Tellegen (1988), the items used by Mano and Oliver (1993) appear to have been used first as a summated scale by Mano (1991). With 224 college students, the scale was reported to have an alpha of .75. Factor and cluster analyses both found that two of the items (elated and excited) would group together, although in both cases items thought to represent other emotions were part of the groupings.

SAMPLES:

Data were collected by Mano and Oliver (1993) from **118** undergraduate business students attending a midwestern U.S. university.

RELIABILITY:

Mano and Oliver (1993) reported an alpha of **.71** for the scale.

VALIDITY:

Mano and Oliver (1993) did not specifically address the validity of the scale.

ADMINISTRATION:

The scale was part of a longer questionnaire self-administered by students in a classroom (Mano and Oliver 1993). A high score suggests that a respondent is feeling excited because of some stimulus.

MAJOR FINDINGS:

Mano and Oliver (1993) examined the dimensionality and causal structure of product evaluation, affect, and satisfaction. Among the many findings involving the **elation** emotion was that it was significantly greater for subjects in a high-involvement manipulation.

REFERENCES:

Mano, Haim (1991), ''The Structure and Intensity of Emotional Experiences: Method and Context Convergence,'' *Multivariate Behavioral Research*, 26 (3), 389-411.

_____ and Richard L. Oliver (1993), ''Assessing the Dimensionality and

Structure of the Consumption Experience: Evaluation, Feeling, and Satisfaction,'' *JCR*, 20 (December), 451-66.

Watson, David, Lee Anna Clark, and Auke Tellegen (1988), ''Development and Validation of Brief Measures of Positive and Negative Affect: The PANAS Scales,'' *Journal of Personality and Social Psychology*, 54 (6), 1063-70.

SCALE ITEMS: ELATION

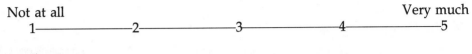

Not at all   Very much
1————————2————————3————————4————————5

1. elated
2. active
3. excited

SCALE NAME: Emotional Valence (Mellow)

SCALE DESCRIPTION:

A three-item, seven-point scale purporting to measure the extent to which a stimulus triggers ''mellow'' sorts of emotions due to the experiences it is associated with in memory. MacInnis and Park (1991) refer to the scale variously as the valence of ''sad'' emotions and ''negative'' emotions.

SCALE ORIGIN:

Although the origin was not identified by MacInnis and Park (1991), all the items can be found in the Reaction Profile for TV Commercials developed by Wells, Leavitt, and McConville (1971). In addition, the scale is composed of items that were used by Edell and Burke (1987; Burke and Edell 1989) to measure two different dimensions of attitude toward the ad feelings: negative and warm.

SAMPLES:

The scale was used by MacInnis and Park (1991) in a pretest stage of a study before the experiment stage. The pretest sample was composed of **20** subjects. Although not described, they were likely to have been similar to those used in the final experiment (college students).

RELIABILITY:

MacInnis and Park (1991) reported an alpha of **.71.**

VALIDITY:

MacInnis and Park (1991) do not indicate using a factor analysis to examine the dimensionality of these items, probably because the sample was too small. However, when the same items were used in the experiment stage of the study and factor analyzed along with some other items, two of the items (1 and 3) loaded on a positive factor, and the remaining item loaded by itself.

ADMINISTRATION:

MacInnis and Park (1991) administered this scale in a pretest as a manipulation check. High scores on the scale indicate that very mellow emotional memories are triggered by a stimulus, whereas low scores suggest that a stimulus evokes little if any such mellow feelings.

MAJOR FINDINGS:

MacInnis and Park (1991) examined the influence of two dimensions of music on low- and high-involvement ad processing: the music's fit with the ad message and the music's links to past emotion-laden experiences (indexicality). The scale was used in the pretest stage of the study to confirm that two selected songs were no different in their levels of indexicality.

COMMENTS:

The questionable face validity and the lack of evidence regarding the scale's unidimensionality suggest that further developmental work is necessary before the scale can be used further.

REFERENCES:

Burke, Marian C. and Julie A. Edell (1989), ''The Impact of Feelings on Ad-Based Affect and Cognitions,'' *JMR*, 26 (February), 69-83.

Edell, Julie E. and Marian C. Burke (1987), ''The Power of Feelings in Understanding Advertising Effects,'' *JCR*, 14 (December), 421-33.

MacInnis, Deborah J. and C. Whan Park (1991), ''The Differential Role of Characteristics of Music on High- and Low-Involvement Consumers' Processing of Ads,'' *JCR*, 18 (Sept.), 161-73.

Wells, William D., Clark Leavitt, and Maureen McConville (1971), ''A Reaction Profile for TV Commercials,'' *JAR*, 11 (December), 11-17.

SCALE ITEMS: EMOTIONAL VALENCE (MELLOW)

If this song is associated with past experiences/memories, are they:

Not at all   ___ : ___ : ___ : ___ : ___ : ___ : ___   Very

             1   2   3   4   5   6   7

1. peaceful
2. sad
3. sentimental

SCALE NAME: Emotional Valence (Positive)

SCALE DESCRIPTION:

A seven-point scale composed of multiple descriptors purporting to measure the extent to which a stimulus triggers positive emotions due to the experiences it is associated with in memory. MacInnis and Park (1991) used a six-item version in a pretest and an eight-item version in an experiment.

SCALE ORIGIN:

Although the origin was not identified by MacInnis and Park (1991), all the items except one (item 7) can be found in the Reaction Profile for TV Commercials developed by Wells, Leavitt, and McConville (1971). In addition, the scale is composed of items that were used by Edell and Burke (1987; Burke and Edell 1989) to measure two different dimensions of attitude toward the ad feelings: upbeat and warm.

SAMPLES:

As noted previously, two slightly different versions of the scale were used by MacInnis and Park (1991): one in a pretest and another in an experiment. The pretest sample was composed of **20** subjects. Although undescribed, they were likely to have been similar to those used in the final experiment (college students). **One hundred seventy-eight** college females composed the sample used in the experiment phase of the study. Subjects were given course credit for participating in the experiment and were assigned randomly to conditions.

RELIABILITY:

MacInnis and Park (1991) reported alphas of **.84** and **.93** for the versions of the scale used in the pretest and experiment phases of their study, respectively.

VALIDITY:

A factor analysis by MacInnis and Park (1991) of nine items used in the experiment stage resulted in all but one of the items loading on a factor that explained 67.9% of the variation. One item (sad) loaded on another factor.

ADMINISTRATION:

MacInnis and Park (1991) administered this scale in both a pretest and an experiment as a manipulation check. High scores on the scale indicate that very positive emotional memories are triggered by a stimulus, whereas low scores suggest that a stimulus evokes little if any positive feelings.

MAJOR FINDINGS:

MacInnis and Park (1991) examined the influence of two dimensions of music on low- and high-involvement ad processing: the music's fit with the ad message and the music's links to past emotion-laden experiences (indexicality). The scale was used in both the pretest and experimental stages of the study to confirm that two selected songs were no different in their levels of indexicality.

COMMENTS:

Although a factor analysis indicated that these items loaded on one factor, their unidimensionality and content validity are suspect given the results of the several studies conducted by Edell and Burke (1987; Burke and Edell 1989). The items composing this scale are a subset of the many items they analyzed and come from two of the three dimensions they found: upbeat and warm.

REFERENCES:

Burke, Marian C. and Julie A. Edell (1989), ''The Impact of Feelings on Ad-Based Affect and Cognitions,'' *JMR*, 26 (February), 69-83.

Edell, Julie E. and Marian C. Burke (1987), ''The Power of Feelings in Understanding Advertising Effects,'' *JCR*, 14 (December), 421-33.

MacInnis, Deborah J. and C. Whan Park (1991), ''The Differential Role of Characteristics of Music on High- and Low-Involvement Consumers' Processing of Ads,'' *JCR*, 18 (Sept.), 161-73.

Wells, William D., Clark Leavitt, and Maureen McConville (1971), ''A Reaction Profile for TV Commercials,'' *JAR*, 11 (December), 11-17.

SCALE ITEMS: EMOTIONAL VALENCE (POSITIVE)*

If this song is associated with past experiences/memories, are they:

Not at all ___ : ___ : ___ : ___ : ___ : ___ : ___ Very

      1   2   3   4   5   6   7

1. lighthearted
2. peaceful
3. playful
4. pleasant
5. positive
6. sentimental
7. upbeat
8. warmhearted
9. warm

* Items 1-8 composed the final version of the scale used by MacInnis and Park (1991), and items 1, 3-5, 7, and 9 composed the shorter version used in their pretest.

SCALE NAME: Envy

SCALE DESCRIPTION:

An eight-item, five-point Likert-type summated ratings scale measuring the degree to which a person desires another person's possessions and resents others with the desired possessions. A shorter version of the scale was used by O'Guinn and Faber (1989; Faber and O'Guinn 1992).

SCALE ORIGIN:

The origin of the scale is reported in Belk (1984). The measure of envy was one of three scales constructed for examining aspects of materialism. Initial pools of 30 or more items were tested for each of the three measures with 237 business school students. Using factor analysis, item-total correlations, and measures of internal consistency, seven or more items were chosen from each pool to measure the three materialism-related constructs. The eight items retained for measuring envy were reported to have an alpha of .80.

SAMPLES:

Belk (1984, 1985) examined the scale in various ways with three more samples. One was composed of 48 business students. Another sample had 338 subjects, 213 of whom were business students. (These two samples were reported to be about two-thirds male.) A third sample was composed of 33 families representing 99 people who ranged in age from 13 to 92 years.

Two samples were employed by O'Guinn and Faber (1989). One was of 386 completed responses (out of 808 questionnaires sent) from people who previously had written an organization that aided compulsive buyers. A second group was used for comparison purposes and was intended to represent the general population. Eight hundred questionnaires were mailed to people in three Illinois areas: Chicago, Springfield, and Bloomington-Normal. Two mailings produced a total of 250 completed survey forms. The database used in Faber and O'Guinn (1992) is basically the same except that sample 1 had a few more responses (n = 388) and the second survey benefited from a third mailing (n = 292).

Studies with four samples were described in the article by Richins and Dawson (1992) but the envy scale was used only in survey 2. Little is said about the sample except that the data came from a mail survey of people in a large western U.S. city. The households were chosen randomly and sent a survey form, followed by a reminder letter and a second copy of the questionnaire two weeks later. The response rate was exactly one-third, resulting in 250 usable questionnaires.

RELIABILITY:

An alpha of .64 was reported for one of the Belk (1984) samples (n = 338). A two-week interval, test-retest correlation of .70 (n = 48) was reported for another Belk (1984, 1985) sample. O'Guinn and Faber (1989; Faber and O'Guinn) and Richins and Dawson (1992) reported alphas of .72 and .52, respectively.

VALIDITY:

Belk (1984) compared scale scores with other measures in a multitrait-multimethod matrix. As evidence of convergent validity, scores on the envy scale were correlated significantly with two other measures used to assess the same construct. Only partial support for discriminant validity was found. Evidence of criterion validity was found by noting that two known groups had significantly different mean scores on the scale and the differences were in the hypothesized directions.

No examination of scale validity was made by O'Guinn and Faber (1989) beyond factor analysis. Items regarding envy and two other materialism-related constructs were factor analyzed, and three factors clearly emerged. The authors did indicate that the scales were slightly modified on the basis of the factor analysis, however.

The validity of the envy scale was not addressed by Richins and Dawson (1992) except in the sense that it was used to assess the nomological validity of the materialism scale being developed (see "Findings").

ADMINISTRATION:

The scale was one of several measures in each of the studies, which were self-administered. High scores on the scale indicate that respondents have a tendency to desire others' possessions and hold resentment toward those owning the possessions, whereas those with low scores do not tend to be as envious.

MAJOR FINDINGS:

The purpose of Belk (1984) was to discuss the construction and characteristics of three materialism-related constructs: **envy**, possessiveness, and nongenerosity. Many of the findings are reported previously. In addition, there was evidence that females were significantly less **envious** than males, that older people were less **envious** than younger people, and that the most envious individuals tended to be the least happy. Belk (1985) examined further aspects of the three subscales and also the psychometric characteristics of the materialism scale as a whole. In particular, he studied generational differences in materialism. Among the many findings was that the youngest and middle generations were similar in their **envy** but were both significantly more **envious** than the oldest generation.

O'Guinn and Faber (1989) studied compulsive shopping. Their results showed that a sample of compulsive shoppers were significantly more **envious**. Although using the same general database, Faber and O'Guinn (1992) reported on the development and testing of a scale to identify compulsive buyers.

The purpose of the several surveys conducted by Richins and Dawson (1992) was to construct a new measure of materialism. To examine the scale's nomological validity, it was proposed that materialists would be less satisfied with their lives than others. Part of testing that hypothesis came from the association between materialism and **envy**. A significant correlation between the two constructs was found (r = .47), suggesting that more materialistic people are more likely to be **envious** of what others have as well.

COMMENTS:

The three materialism-related measures mentioned previously have been used not only summed separately but together as well. Two alphas for the combined scale were reported by Belk (1985): .66 (n = 338) and .73 (n = 48). Belk (1985) also reported a test-retest correlation of .68 (n = 48). O'Guinn and Faber (1989; Faber and O'Guinn 1992) calculated an alpha of .71 for the combined scale.

REFERENCES:

Belk, Russell W. (1984), "Three Scales to Measure Constructs Related to Materialism: Reliability, Validity, and Relationships to Measures of Happiness," in *Advances in Consumer Research*, Vol. 11, Thomas Kinnear, ed. Provo, UT: Association for Consumer Research, 291-97.

_____ (1985), "Materialism: Trait Aspects of Living in the Material World," *JCR*, 12 (December), 265-80.

Faber, Ronald J. and Thomas C. O'Guinn (1992), "A Clinical Screener for Compulsive Buying," *JCR*, 19 (December), 459-69.

O'Guinn, Thomas C. and Ronald J. Faber (1989), "Compulsive Buying: A Phenomenological Exploration," *JCR*, 16 (September), 147-57.

Richins, Marsha L. and Scott Dawson (1992), "A Consumer Values Orientation for Materialism and Its Measurement: Scale Development and Validation," *JCR*, 19 (December), 303-16.

SCALE ITEMS: ENVY*

Strongly disagree	Disagree	Neutral	Agree	Strongly agree
1	2	3	4	5

1. I am bothered when I see people who buy anything they want.
2. I don't know anyone whose spouse or steady date I would like to have as my own. **(r)**
3. When friends do better than me in competition it usually makes me feel happy for them. **(r)**
4. People who are very wealthy often feel they are too good to talk to average people.
5. There are certain people I would like to trade places with.
6. When friends have things I cannot afford it bothers me.
7. I don't seem to get what is coming to me.
8. When Hollywood stars or prominent politicians have things stolen I really feel sorry for them. **(r)**

* The short version of the scale used by O'Guinn and Faber (1989; Faber and O'Guinn 1992) employed only items 1, 5, 6, and 7.

SCALE NAME: Ethnocentrism (CETSCALE)

SCALE DESCRIPTION:

A 17-item, seven-point Likert-type summated ratings scale measuring a respondent's attitude regarding the appropriateness of purchasing American-made products versus those manufactured in other countries. its originators (Shimp and Sharma 1987) called the scale CETSCALE (consumers' ethnocentric tendencies). A revised version of the scale was used by Herche (1992).

SCALE ORIGIN:

The scale is original to the studies reported by Shimp and Sharma (1987). Development of the scale passed through several stages and employed numerous different samples. The information provided here is based primarily on the final 17-item version of the scale rather than larger preliminary sets.

Four separate samples were used to assess the psychometric properties of the CETSCALE. One sample was made up of names and addresses obtained from a list broker. One thousand questionnaires were mailed to each of three deliberately chosen cities: Detroit, Denver, and Los Angeles. The response rate was just less than a third for each area. At the same time, 950 questionnaires were sent to former panel members in the Carolinas. The response rate was nearly 60%. The total sample size in this "four-areas study" was **1535**. The "Carolinas study" was composed of a group of **417** people who were a part of the "four-areas study." Data for the former study was collected two years prior to the latter. A smaller, ten-item version of the scale was tested in a national consumer goods study. A total of more than **2000** completed responses were received. A fourth study examined data from **145** college students. Although having varying proportions, each of the samples except the student group had respondents representing most age and income groups.

SAMPLES:

Herche (1992) collected data in a nationwide mail survey of 1000 car owners and 1000 PC owners. Eight hundred six people returned questionnaires, but only **520** were complete enough to be used in the analysis. Of these, 320 were from car buyers and 200 were from PC buyers. Most regions of the country and many occupational groups were represented in both of the samples. In addition, a majority of each sample were college graduates, were males, earned more than $35,000 a year, and were married. The mean age of respondents in both samples was in the low to mid-forties. The sample compositions were different in that the car group had many more retirees and the PC group seemed to have more professionals. The PC group also seemed to be better educated and have greater income.

Netemeyer, Durvasula, and Lichtenstein (1991) used undergraduate students studying business in four different countries. The sample consisted of **76** subjects from two universities in Japan, **70** subjects from a college in France,

73 subjects from a college in Germany; and **71** subjects from a major state university in the United States.

RELIABILITY:

The alpha for the revised version of the scale used by Herche (1992) was **.93**. Netemeyer, Durvasula, and Lichtenstein (1991) reported alphas of **.91**, **.92**, **.94**, and **.95** for the Japanese, French, German, and American samples, respectively. Alphas of between **.94** and **.96** were found for the scale in the four samples used by Shimp and Sharma (1987). Test-retest reliability was estimated with the student sample only. With a five-week interval between administrations, a correlation of **.77** was reported.

VALIDITY:

Although bearing somewhat on the scale's predictive validity, Herche (1992) did not directly assess the scale's construct validity. However, the revised version of the scale he used was discussed in a previous paper (Herche 1990) as being a superior measure to the original CETSCALE. In that previous paper, Herche argued that the absence of negatively stated items in the scale made it vulnerable to response bias. He developed a version of the scale with seven of the original items stated in the opposite direction, which were reverse coded during summation. The evidence indicated that the revised version of the scale explained substantially more variance than the original and had a better factor structure. He since has modified his recommendations still further (Herche and Engelland 1994).

Using the original version of the scale and confirmatory factor analysis, Netemeyer, Durvasula, and Lichtenstein (1991) found evidence that it was unidimensional and had adequate discriminant validity. Moderate support also was found for the scale's nomological validity. Convergent, discriminant, and nomological validity were addressed by Shimp and Sharma (1987) and provided evidence of the scale's quality. Some of the specific evidence is discussed in "Major Findings."

ADMINISTRATION:

The version of the scale used by Herche (1992) was part of a larger mail survey instrument. Netemeyer, Durvasula, and Lichtenstein (1991) administered the scale as part of a larger questionnaire during class time. The survey instrument went through a series of translations, back-translations, pretests, and retranslations to ensure that the four different language versions were as similar in meaning as possible. The scale was self-administered by Shimp and Sharma (1987) along with other measures as part of a larger survey instrument in each of their four studies. All except the student sample received questionnaires in the mail.

Scores on the scale can range from 17 to 119. High scores imply that respondents strongly believe in buying American-made products, whereas low scores suggest that respondents do not think buying domestically produced goods is particularly important.

MAJOR FINDINGS:

Herche (1992) explored the predictive validity of the revised version of the CETSCALE. It was found that the CETSCALE is better than demographic variables in understanding import buying behavior. However, the findings also suggested that the predictive validity of the scale could be product specific; that is, there was a much higher negative correlation between **ethnocentrism** and ownership of goods perceived as being foreign-made for cars than for PCs.

Netemeyer, Durvasula, and Lichtenstein (1991) examined the psychometric properties of the **CETSCALE** using homogeneous samples from four countries that actively trade with each other. The scale was found to be translatable and showed strong evidence of internal consistency and unidimensionality as well as some evidence of discriminant and nomological validities.

The purpose of the Shimp and Sharma's (1987) study was to describe the construction and validation of the CETSCALE. In one or more samples **ethnocentrism** was found to have a significant positive correlation with the following variables: patriotism, politicoeconomic conservatism, dogmatism, domestic car ownership, intent to purchase a domestic car, and country-of-origin importance. **Ethnocentrism** had a significant negative correlation with attitude toward foreign made products.

REFERENCES:

Herche, Joel (1990), ''The Measurement of Consumer Ethnocentrism: Revisiting the CETSCALE,'' *Proceedings of the Thirteenth Annual Conference of the Academy of Marketing Science*, B. J. Dunlap, ed. Western Carolina University, 371-75.

_____ (1992), ''A Note on the Predictive Validity of the CETSCALE,'' *JAMS*, 20 (Summer), 261-64.

_____ and Brian Engelland (1994), ''Reversed-Polarity Items, Attribution Effects and Scale Dimensionality,'' *Office of Scale Research Technical Report #9401*. Carbondale, IL: Marketing Department, Southern Illinois University.

Netemeyer, Richard G. Srinvas Durvasula, and Donald R. Lichtenstein (1991), ''A Cross-National Assessment of the Reliability and Validity of the CETSCALE,'' *JMR*, 28 (August), 320-27.

Shimp, Terence A. and Subhash Sharma (1987), ''Consumer Ethnocentrism: Construction and Validation of the CETSCALE,'' *JMR*, 24 (August), 280-89.

SCALE ITEMS: ETHNOCENTRISM (CETSCALE)*

Strongly agree	Moderately agree	Slightly agree	Neither agree nor disagree	Slightly disagree	Moderately disagree	Strongly disagree
7	6	5	4	3	2	1

1. American people should always buy American-made products instead of imports.

2. Only those products that are unavailable in the U.S. should be imported.
3. Buy American-made products. Keep America working.
4. American products first, last, and foremost.
5. Purchasing foreign-made products is un-American.
6. It is not right to purchase foreign products, because it puts Americans out of jobs.
7. A real American should always buy American-made products.
8. We should purchase products manufactured in America instead of letting other countries get rich off us.
9. It is always best to purchase American products.
10. There should be very little trading or purchasing of goods from other countries unless out of necessity.
11. Americans should not buy foreign products, because this hurts American business and causes unemployment.
12. Curbs should be put on all imports.
13. It may cost me in the long-run but I prefer to support American products.
14. Foreigners should not be allowed to put their products on our markets.
15. Foreign products should be taxed heavily to reduce their entry into the U.S.
16. We should buy from foreign countries only those products that we cannot obtain within our own country.
17. American consumers who purchase products made in other countries are responsible for putting their fellow Americans out of work.

* The seven items altered by Herche (1990, 1992) were 1, 5, 7, 9, 12, 14, and 17. The alterations in each case essentially amounted to the addition of the word "not" in the sentence. The ten items used in the national consumer good study by Shimp and Sharma (1987) were 2, 4-8, 11, 13, 16, and 17.

SCALE NAME: Evaluation (Appeal)

SCALE DESCRIPTION:

A three-item, seven-point semantic differential scale measuring the degree to which one evaluates a stimulus (such as a product) as being desirable and appealing.

SCALE ORIGIN:

Although all of the items have been used previously, Mano and Oliver (1993) appear to have been the first to use them as a summated scale. They took all 20 items of Zaichkowsky's (1985) involvement scale and factor analyzed them along with five nonoverlapping items from Batra and Ahtola's (1990) hedonic and utilitarian scales.

SAMPLES:

Data were collected by Mano and Oliver (1993) from **118** undergraduate business students attending a midwestern U.S. university.

RELIABILITY:

Mano and Oliver (1993) reported an alpha of **.71** for the scale.

VALIDITY:

Mano and Oliver (1993) did not specifically address the scale's validity, but a factor analysis of the 25 items described in ''Scale Origin'' indicated that the 7 items composing this scale had moderate loadings (43 to .66) on the same factor.

ADMINISTRATION:

The scale was part of a longer questionnaire self-administered by students in a classroom (Mano and Oliver 1993). A high score suggests that a respondent considers a stimulus to be desirable and appealing.

MAJOR FINDINGS:

Mano and Oliver (1993) examined the dimensionality and causal structure of product evaluation, affect, and satisfaction. Among the many findings was that subjects in a high-involvement manipulation considered the product to have greater **appeal** than those in a low-involvement condition.

COMMENTS:

Mano and Oliver (1993) also combined the items in this scale with two others related to product evaluation (#104 and #105) and described the outcome as a measure of the hedonic component of product evaluation. Its reliability (alpha) was reported to be .91.

REFERENCES:

Batra, Rajeev and Olli T. Ahtola (1990), "Measuring the Hedonic and Utilitarian Sources of Consumer Attitudes," *Marketing Letters*, 2 (April), 159-70.

Mano, Haim and Richard L. Oliver (1993), "Assessing the Dimensionality and Structure of the Consumption Experience: Evaluation, Feeling, and Satisfaction," *JCR*, 20 (December), 451-66.

Zaichkowsky, Judith L. (1985), "Measuring the Involvement Construct," *JCR*, 12 (December), 341-52.

SCALE ITEMS: EVALUATION (APPEAL)

(name of object)

Unappealing	___ : ___ : ___ : ___ : ___ : ___ : ___ 1 2 3 4 5 6 7	Appealing
Undesirable	___ : ___ : ___ : ___ : ___ : ___ : ___ 1 2 3 4 5 6 7	Desirable
Unwanted	___ : ___ : ___ : ___ : ___ : ___ : ___ 1 2 3 4 5 6 7	Wanted

SCALE NAME: Evaluation (Interest)

SCALE DESCRIPTION:

A five-item, seven-point semantic differential scale measuring the degree to which one evaluates a stimulus (such as a product) as being exciting and interesting.

SCALE ORIGIN:

Although all of the items have been used previously, Mano and Oliver (1993) appear to have been the first to use them as a summated scale. They took all 20 items of Zaichkowsky's (1985) involvement scale (#148) and factor analyzed them along with five nonoverlapping items from Batra and Ahtola's (1990) hedonic and utilitarian scales.

SAMPLES:

Data were collected by Mano and Oliver (1993) from **118** undergraduate business students attending a midwestern U.S. university.

RELIABILITY:

Mano and Oliver (1993) reported an alpha of **.90** for the scale.

VALIDITY:

Mano and Oliver (1993) did not specifically address the scale's validity, but a factor analysis of the 25 items described in "Scale Origin" indicated that the five items composing this scale had high loadings (r.60) on the same factor. One item (intelligent) also had a high loading on another evaluation factor (positivity; see #106).

Some concern might be expressed about the scale's face validity given that several of the items described the stimulus (e.g., exciting) but one or two others appear to describe the respondent (e.g., interested).

ADMINISTRATION:

The scale was part of a longer questionnaire self-administered by students in a classroom (Mano and Oliver 1993). A high score suggests that a respondent considers a stimulus to be exciting and interesting.

MAJOR FINDINGS:

Mano and Oliver (1993) examined the dimensionality and causal structure of product evaluation, affect, and satisfaction. Among the many findings was that subjects in a high-involvement manipulation evaluated the product as being significantly more **interesting** to them than those in the low-involvement condition.

COMMENTS:

Mano and Oliver (1993) also combined the items in this scale with two others related to product evaluation (#103 and #105) and described the outcome as a measure of the hedonic component of product evaluation. Its reliability (alpha) was reported to be .91.

REFERENCES:

Batra, Rajeev and Olli T. Ahtola (1990), "Measuring the Hedonic and Utilitarian Sources of Consumer Attitudes," *Marketing Letters*, 2 (April), 159-70.

Mano, Haim and Richard L. Oliver (1993), "Assessing the Dimensionality and Structure of the Consumption Experience: Evaluation, Feeling, and Satisfaction," *JCR*, 20 (December), 451-66.

Zaichkowsky, Judith L. (1985), "Measuring the Involvement Construct," *JCR*, 12 (December), 341-52.

SCALE ITEMS: EVALUATION (INTEREST)

(name of object)

| Uninterested | __ : __ : __ : __ : __ : __ : __ | Interested |
| | 1   2   3   4   5   6   7 | |

| Boring | __ : __ : __ : __ : __ : __ : __ | Interesting |
| | 1   2   3   4   5   6   7 | |

| Unexciting | __ : __ : __ : __ : __ : __ : __ | Exciting |
| | 1   2   3   4   5   6   7 | |

| Mundane | __ : __ : __ : __ : __ : __ : __ | Fascinating |
| | 1   2   3   4   5   6   7 | |

| Unintelligent | __ : __ : __ : __ : __ : __ : __ | Intelligent |
| | 1   2   3   4   5   6   7 | |

SCALE NAME: Evaluation (Need)

SCALE DESCRIPTION:

A seven-item, seven-point semantic differential scale measuring the degree to which one evaluates a stimulus (such as a product) as being vital and necessary.

SCALE ORIGIN:

Although all of the items have been used previously, Mano and Oliver (1993) appear to have been the first to use them as a summated scale. They took all 20 items of Zaichkowsky's (1985) involvement scale (#148) and factor analyzed them along with five nonoverlapping items from Batra and Ahtola's (1990) hedonic and utilitarian scales.

SAMPLES:

Data were collected by Mano and Oliver (1993) from **118** undergraduate business students attending a midwestern U.S. university.

RELIABILITY:

Mano and Oliver (1993) reported an alpha of **.91** for the scale.

VALIDITY:

Mano and Oliver (1993) did not specifically address the scale's validity, but a factor analysis of the 25 items described in "Scale Origin" indicated that the seven items composing this scale had high loadings (r.56) on the same factor. One item (important) also had a high loading on another factor (value; see #107).

ADMINISTRATION:

The scale was part of a longer questionnaire self-administered by students in a classroom (Mano and Oliver 1993). A high score suggests that a respondent considers a stimulus to be vital and necessary.

MAJOR FINDINGS:

Mano and Oliver (1993) examined the dimensionality and causal structure of product evaluation, affect, and satisfaction. Among the many findings was that subjects in a high-involvement manipulation expressed a marginally higher (p = .08) **need** for the product than those in the low-involvement condition.

COMMENTS:

Mano and Oliver (1993) also combined the items in this scale with one measuring product value (#107) and described it as the utilitarian component of product evaluation. Its reliability (alpha) was reported to be .91.

REFERENCES:

Batra, Rajeev and Olli T. Ahtola (1990), ''Measuring the Hedonic and Utilitarian Sources of Consumer Attitudes,'' *Marketing Letters*, 2 (April), 159-70.

Mano, Haim and Richard L. Oliver (1993), ''Assessing the Dimensionality and Structure of the Consumption Experience: Evaluation, Feeling, and Satisfaction,'' *JCR*, 20 (December), 451-66.

Zaichkowsky, Judith L. (1985), ''Measuring the Involvement Construct,'' *JCR*, 12 (December), 341-52.

SCALE ITEMS: EVALUATION (NEED)

(name of object)

Unimportant	___ : ___ : ___ : ___ : ___ : ___ : ___ 1 2 3 4 5 6 7	Important
Useless	___ : ___ : ___ : ___ : ___ : ___ : ___ 1 2 3 4 5 6 7	Useful
Trivial	___ : ___ : ___ : ___ : ___ : ___ : ___ 1 2 3 4 5 6 7	Fundamental
Not beneficial	___ : ___ : ___ : ___ : ___ : ___ : ___ 1 2 3 4 5 6 7	Beneficial
Superfluous	___ : ___ : ___ : ___ : ___ : ___ : ___ 1 2 3 4 5 6 7	Vital
Nonessential	___ : ___ : ___ : ___ : ___ : ___ : ___ 1 2 3 4 5 6 7	Essential
Not needed	___ : ___ : ___ : ___ : ___ : ___ : ___ 1 2 3 4 5 6 7	Needed

SCALE NAME: Evaluation (Positivity)

SCALE DESCRIPTION:

A five-item, seven-point semantic differential scale measuring the degree to which one evaluates a stimulus (such as a product) as being positive and agreeable.

SCALE ORIGIN:

Although all the items have been used previously, Mano and Oliver (1993) appear to have been the first to use them as a summated scale. They took all 20 items of Zaichkowsky's (1985) involvement scale (#148) and factor analyzed them along with five nonoverlapping items from Batra and Ahtola's (1990) hedonic and utilitarian scales. As it turns out, the five items composing the measure of **positive evaluation** were the ones from the study by Batra and Ahtola (1990). In their study these items along with others loaded highest on the same hedonic factor except for ''intelligent'' which had its higher loading on a utilitarian factor.

SAMPLES:

Data were collected by Mano and Oliver (1993) from **118** undergraduate business students attending a midwestern U.S. university.

RELIABILITY:

Mano and Oliver (1993) reported an alpha of **.84** for the scale.

VALIDITY:

Mano and Oliver (1993) did not specifically address the scale's validity but a factor analysis of the 25 items described in ''Scale Origin'' indicated that the seven items composing this scale had high loadings (r.51) on the same factor. One item (intelligent) also had a high loading on another evaluation factor (interest; see #104).

ADMINISTRATION:

The scale was part of a longer questionnaire self-administered by students in a classroom (Mano and Oliver 1993). A high score suggests that a respondent considers a stimulus to be positive and agreeable.

MAJOR FINDINGS:

Mano and Oliver (1993) examined the dimensionality and causal structure of product evaluation, affect, and satisfaction. Among the many findings was that subjects in a high-involvement manipulation evaluated the product as being significantly more **positive** than those in the low-involvement condition.

COMMENTS:

Mano and Oliver (1993) also combined the items in this scale with two others related to product evaluation (#103 and #104) and described the outcome as a measure of the hedonic component of product evaluation. Its reliability (alpha) was reported to be .91.

REFERENCES:

Batra, Rajeev and Olli T. Ahtola (1990), ''Measuring the Hedonic and Utilitarian Sources of Consumer Attitudes,'' *Marketing Letters*, 2 (April), 159-70.
Mano, Haim and Richard L. Oliver (1993), ''Assessing the Dimensionality and Structure of the Consumption Experience: Evaluation, Feeling, and Satisfaction,'' *JCR*, 20 (December), 451-66.
Zaichkowsky, Judith L. (1985), ''Measuring the Involvement Construct,'' *JCR*, 12 (December), 341-52.

SCALE ITEMS: EVALUATION (POSITIVITY)

(name of object)

Unpleasant ___ : ___ : ___ : ___ : ___ : ___ : ___ Pleasant
　　　　　　　1　　2　　3　　4　　5　　6　　7

Negative ___ : ___ : ___ : ___ : ___ : ___ : ___ Positive
　　　　　　1　　2　　3　　4　　5　　6　　7

Disagreeable ___ : ___ : ___ : ___ : ___ : ___ : ___ Agreeable
　　　　　　　　1　　2　　3　　4　　5　　6　　7

Awful ___ : ___ : ___ : ___ : ___ : ___ : ___ Nice
　　　　1　　2　　3　　4　　5　　6　　7

Unintelligent ___ : ___ : ___ : ___ : ___ : ___ : ___ Intelligent
　　　　　　　　1　　2　　3　　4　　5　　6　　7

SCALE NAME: Evaluation (Value)

SCALE DESCRIPTION:

A seven-item, seven-point semantic differential scale measuring the degree to which one evaluates a stimulus (such as a product) as being relevant and meaningful to oneself.

SCALE ORIGIN:

Although all of the items have been used previously, Mano and Oliver (1993) appear to have been the first to use them as a summated scale. They took all 20 items of Zaichkowsky's (1985) involvement scale (#148) and factor analyzed them along with five nonoverlapping items from Batra and Ahtola's (1990) hedonic and utilitarian scales.

SAMPLES:

Data were collected by Mano and Oliver (1993) from **118** undergraduate business students attending a midwestern U.S. university.

RELIABILITY:

Mano and Oliver (1993) reported an alpha of **.89** for the scale.

VALIDITY:

Mano and Oliver (1993) did not specifically address the scale's validity, but a factor analysis of the 25 items described in "Scale Origin" indicated that the seven items composing this scale had high loadings (r.50) on the same factor. One item (important) also had a high loading on another factor (need; see #105).

ADMINISTRATION:

The scale was part of a longer questionnaire self-administered by students in a classroom (Mano and Oliver 1993). A high score suggests that a stimulus is very meaningful to a respondent.

MAJOR FINDINGS:

Mano and Oliver (1993) examined the dimensionality and causal structure of product evaluation, affect, and satisfaction. Among the many findings was that subjects in a high-involvement manipulation evaluated the product as being significantly more **valuable** to them than those in the low-involvement condition.

COMMENTS:

Mano and Oliver (1993) also combined the items in this scale with one measuring product value (#107) and described it as the utilitarian component of product evaluation. Its reliability (alpha) was reported to be .91.

REFERENCES:

Batra, Rajeev and Olli T. Ahtola (1990), "Measuring the Hedonic and Utilitarian Sources of Consumer Attitudes," *Marketing Letters*, 2 (April), 159-70.

Mano, Haim and Richard L. Oliver (1993), "Assessing the Dimensionality and Structure of the Consumption Experience: Evaluation, Feeling, and Satisfaction," *JCR*, 20 (December), 451-66.

Zaichkowsky, Judith L. (1985), "Measuring the Involvement Construct," *JCR*, 12 (December), 341-52.

SCALE ITEMS: EVALUATION (VALUE)

(name of object)

	1	2	3	4	5	6	7	
Unimportant	_ :	_ :	_ :	_ :	_ :	_ :	_	Important
Of no concern	_ :	_ :	_ :	_ :	_ :	_ :	_	Of concern to me
Irrelevant	_ :	_ :	_ :	_ :	_ :	_ :	_	Relevant
Means nothing to me	_ :	_ :	_ :	_ :	_ :	_ :	_	Means a lot to me
Worthless	_ :	_ :	_ :	_ :	_ :	_ :	_	Valuable
Doesn't matter	_ :	_ :	_ :	_ :	_ :	_ :	_	Matters to me
Insignificant	_ :	_ :	_ :	_ :	_ :	_ :	_	Significant

SCALE NAME: Expected Picture Quality (Camera)

SCALE DESCRIPTION:

A three-item, seven-point summated ratings scale measuring the level of picture quality a consumer expects in a particular camera. *Expectations* is supposed to be distinct from *desires* because whereas the latter relates to beliefs about "ideal" product performance that led to achievement of higher-level values, the former are beliefs about performance benefits that will occur with a specified focal brand but may be short of what is "ideal" (Spreng and Olshavsky 1993, p. 172). Thus, *desires* implies a higher standard than does *expectations*.

SCALE ORIGIN:

The origin of the scale was not specified by Spreng and Olshavsky (1993) but it appears to have been developed for that study.

SAMPLES:

The subjects (n = **128**) used by Spreng and Olshavsky (1993) were graduate and undergraduate students attending a major university. They were from both the business school and journalism. Cash prizes were offered as incentives to volunteer.

RELIABILITY:

Spreng and Olshavsky (1993) reported an alpha of **.97** for the scale.

VALIDITY:

Spreng and Olshavsky (1993) performed confirmatory factor analysis and other tests, and the evidence was sufficient for them to conclude that this and their other scales showed convergent and discriminant validity.

ADMINISTRATION:

The scale was administered *after* subjects were exposed to the camera but *before* they saw a picture supposedly taken with it (Spreng and Olshavsky 1993). A high score on the scale suggests that a respondent expects a particular camera to produce professional quality pictures, whereas a low score indicates that he/she thinks it simply will make "average" quality photos.

MAJOR FINDINGS:

Spreng and Olshavsky (1993) investigated the relative strengths of two models of satisfaction: *expectancy disconfirmation* and *desires congruency*. The results supported the latter model. **Expected picture quality** was not found to have a significant impact on overall satisfaction.

#108 *Expected Picture Quality (Camera)*

REFERENCE:

Spreng, Richard A. and Richard W. Olshavsky (1993), ''A Desires Congruency Model of Satisfaction,'' *JAMS*, 21 (Summer), 169-77.

SCALE ITEMS: EXPECTED PICTURE QUALITY (CAMERA)

What would be the level of picture quality you would expect from this camera?*

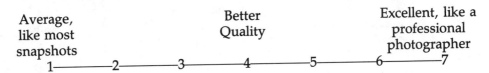

| Average, like most snapshots | | | Better Quality | | | Excellent, like a professional photographer |
| 1 | 2 | 3 | 4 | 5 | 6 | 7 |

1. clarity of the picture
2. sharpness of the picture
3. color of the picture

* This statement was not provided in the article but appears to be consistent with descriptions of the manner in which the measure was made.

SCALE NAME: Expertise (Information Source)

SCALE DESCRIPTION:

A five-item, seven-point semantic differential measuring a consumer's assessment of a specified person's knowledge and competency as a source of information about a particular product.

SCALE ORIGIN:

There is no information to indicate that the scale is anything other than original to Netemeyer and Bearden (1992).

SAMPLES:

The experiment conducted by Netemeyer and Bearden (1992) was based on data from a sample of 372 undergraduate students. They were assigned randomly to a 2 (informational influence) × 2 (normative influence) design. The sample was split approximately in half to test two different models of Behavioral Intention. Therefore, there were four cells per model tested, with each cell having between 46 and 49 subjects.

RELIABILITY:

Netemeyer and Bearden (1992) reported the scale to have alphas of .94 and .91 for the two models of Behavioral Intention that were tested.

VALIDITY:

Netemeyer and Bearden (1992) reported no specific examination of the scale's validity.

ADMINISTRATION:

The scale was self-administered along with other measures after the experimental manipulation (Netemeyer and Bearden 1992). High scores on the scale indicate that a person who is the information source for a product is perceived to have great deal of knowledge and competency.

MAJOR FINDINGS:

Netemeyer and Bearden (1992) conducted an experiment to compare the causal structure and predictive ability of the models of Behavioral Intentions by Ajzen and Fishbein (1980) and Miniard and Cohen (1983). **Expertise** of an information source (audio store employee) was manipulated as part of the experiment. The **expertise** scale was used to provide evidence that a successful manipulation had been made.

REFERENCES:

Ajzen, Icek and Martin Fishbein (1980), *Understanding Attitudes and Predicting Social Behavior*. Englewood Cliffs, NJ: Prentice-Hall.

Miniard, Paul W. and Joel B. Cohen (1983), ''Modeling Personal and Normative Influences on Behavior,'' *JCR*, 10 (September), 169-80.

Netemeyer, Richard G. and William O. Bearden (1992), ''A Comparative Analysis of Two Models of Behavioral Intention,'' *JAMS*, 20 (Winter), 49-59.

SCALE ITEMS: EXPERTISE (INFORMATION SOURCE)

Knowledgeable	___ :	___ :	___ :	___ :	___ :	___ :	___	Not knowledgeable
	7	6	5	4	3	2	1	
Competent	___ :	___ :	___ :	___ :	___ :	___ :	___	Not competent
	7	6	5	4	3	2	1	
Expert	___ :	___ :	___ :	___ :	___ :	___ :	___	Not expert
	7	6	5	4	3	2	1	
Trained	___ :	___ :	___ :	___ :	___ :	___ :	___	Not trained
	7	6	5	4	3	2	1	
Experienced	___ :	___ :	___ :	___ :	___ :	___ :	___	Not experienced
	7	6	5	4	3	2	1	

SCALE NAME: Expertise (Product Development)

SCALE DESCRIPTION:

A four-item, eight-point semantic differential measuring a consumer's assessment of a new product inventor's intelligence and competency.

SCALE ORIGIN:

The scale is original to Ratneshwar and Chaiken (1991).

SAMPLES:

The scale was used in two experiments reported by Ratneshwar and Chaiken (1991). Complete and useable information for the first experiment came from **105** male and female undergraduate college students. They were assigned randomly to small groups in a 2 (source expertise) × 2 (comprehensibility) between-subjects design. Similarly, the subjects for the second experiment were **125** college students, and three levels of comprehensibility were used.

RELIABILITY:

Alphas of **.89** and **.86** were reported for the scale for its use in Experiments 1 and 2, respectively (Ratneshwar and Chaiken 1991).

VALIDITY:

Ratneshwar and Chaiken (1991) reported no direct examination of the scale's validity.

ADMINISTRATION:

The scale was self-administered by subjects after they were exposed to the experimental stimuli (Ratneshwar and Chaiken 1991). A high score on the scale indicates that the supposed inventor of a product is perceived to have great deal of knowledge and competency.

MAJOR FINDINGS:

Ratneshwar and Chaiken (1991) examined the roles of message comprehension and source expertise on persuasion. Findings among the two experiments led the authors to conclude that subjects who received information difficult to comprehend expressed more favorable new product attitudes when the source of the information was perceived to be an **expert** compared with when it was attributed to a **novice**.

REFERENCE:

Ratneshwar, S. and Shelly Chaiken (1991), "Comprehension's Role in Persuasion: The Case of Its Moderating Effect on the Persuasive Impact of Source Cues," *JCR*, 18 (June), 52-62.

SCALE ITEMS: EXPERTISE (PRODUCT DEVELOPMENT)

Directions: We would like you to give us your impression of the *person* who has invented this new product on the following opinion scales. In each case please circle the number on the scale that best represents the way you feel about this person. Would you say that this person is:

Not at all competent ___ : ___ : ___ : ___ : ___ : ___ : ___ : ___ : ___ Very competent
-4 -3 -2 -1 0 $+1$ $+2$ $+3$ $+4$

Not at all expert ___ : ___ : ___ : ___ : ___ : ___ : ___ : ___ : ___ Very expert
-4 -3 -2 -1 0 $+1$ $+2$ $+3$ $+4$

Not at all intelligent ___ : ___ : ___ : ___ : ___ : ___ : ___ : ___ : ___ Very intelligent
-4 -3 -2 -1 0 $+1$ $+2$ $+3$ $+4$

Not at all knowledge-able ___ : ___ : ___ : ___ : ___ : ___ : ___ : ___ : ___ Very knowledge-able
-4 -3 -2 -1 0 $+1$ $+2$ $+3$ $+4$

SCALE NAME: Family Brand Belief

SCALE DESCRIPTION:

A three-item, seven-point summated rating scale measuring one's belief that a specified product attribute is possessed by the products sharing the same brand name (family). The attributes studied by Loken and John (1993) were *gentleness* and *quality*.

SCALE ORIGIN:

The origin of the scale was not specified by Loken and John (1993) but appears to have been developed by them for their study.

SAMPLES:

Data were gathered in the study by Loken and John (1993) from women recruited by a research firm in a Minneapolis mall. The subjects were the principal shoppers for their families, had at least high school education levels, had incomes of at least $10,000 a year, and were between 18 and 49 years of age. Screening questions were used to eliminate some women (or their data) from the study and the final sample size was not specified. However, **196** women appear to have completed the experiment.

RELIABILITY:

Loken and John (1993) reported alphas of **.92** and **.97** for the scale when measuring *gentleness* and *quality* attributes, respectively.

VALIDITY:

Loken and John (1993) reported no evidence regarding the validity of the scale.

ADMINISTRATION:

In Loken and John (1993) the scale was part of a self-administered questionnaire subjects completed in a research facility of a shopping mall. High scores on the scale indicate that respondents perceive a particular product attribute to be characteristic of a group of products bearing the same brand name.

MAJOR FINDINGS:

Loken and John (1993) studies the situations in which brand extension failures affect specific attribute beliefs associated with family brand image. **Beliefs** were significantly lower when brand extensions had one or two inconsistent attributes. This was found when **beliefs** were measured before *typicality*. More complicated results were found when the measures were taken in the opposite order.

REFERENCE:

Loken, Barbara and Deborah Roedder John (1993), ''Diluting Brand Beliefs: When Do Brand Extensions Have a Negative Impact?'' *JM*, 57 (July), 71-84.

SCALE ITEMS: FAMILY BRAND BELIEF

Brand A products are _____.*

1. Strongly disagree	___ : ___ : ___ : ___ : ___ : ___ : ___ 1 2 3 4 5 6 7	Strongly agree
2. Extremely unlikely	___ : ___ : ___ : ___ : ___ : ___ : ___ 1 2 3 4 5 6 7	Extremely likely
3. Not at all probable	___ : ___ : ___ : ___ : ___ : ___ : ___ 1 2 3 4 5 6 7	Very probable

* The name of the brand as well as the focal attribute should be specified in this phrase to focus the subject's attention. As noted previously, Loken and John (1993) used the scale to measure both *gentleness* and *quality* characteristics of a particular family brand extension.

SCALE NAME: Fantasizing

SCALE DESCRIPTION:

A three-item, five-point, Likert-type summated ratings scale measuring the degree to which a person has a vivid imagination and fantasizes.

SCALE ORIGIN:

The scale was apparently original to O'Guinn and Faber (1989).

SAMPLES:

Two samples were employed by O'Guinn and Faber (1989). One was of **386** completed responses (out of 808 questionnaires sent) from people who previously had written an organization that aided compulsive buyers. A second group was used for comparison purposes and was intended to represent the general population. Eight hundred questionnaires were mailed to people in three Illinois areas: Chicago, Springfield, and Bloomington-Normal. Two mailings produced a total of **250** completed survey forms. The database used in Faber and O'Guinn (1992) is basically the same except that sample 1 had a few more responses (n = 388) and the second survey benefited from a third mailing (n = 292).

RELIABILITY:

An alpha of **.75** was reported for this scale (O'Guinn and Faber 1989; Faber and O'Guinn 1992).

VALIDITY:

O'Guinn and Faber (1989; Faber and O'Guinn 1992) reported no examination of scale validity except as it bears on the findings reported here.

ADMINISTRATION:

The scale was one of several self-administered measures used in mail survey instruments (O'Guinn and Faber 1989; Faber and O'Guinn 1992). High scores on the scale indicate that respondents have a strong tendency to fantasize, whereas low scores indicate respondents do not have vivid imaginations.

MAJOR FINDINGS:

O'Guinn and Faber (1989) studied compulsive shopping. Their results showed that a sample of compulsive shoppers scored significantly higher on the **fantasizing** scale than a general sample of consumers. Although using the same general database, Faber and O'Guinn (1992) reported on the development and testing of a scale to identify compulsive buyers.

REFERENCES:

Faber, Ronald J. and Thomas C. O'Guinn (1992), ''A Clinical Screener for Compulsive Buying,'' *JCR*, 19 (December), 459-69.

O'Guinn, Thomas C. and Ronald J. Faber (1989), ''Compulsive Buying: A Phenomenological Exploration,'' *JCR*, 16 (September), 147-57.

SCALE ITEMS: FANTASIZING

Strongly disagree	Disagree	Neutral	Agree	Strongly agree
1	2	3	4	5

1. I daydream a lot.
2. When I go to the movies I find it easy to lose myself in the film.
3. I often think of what might have been.

SCALE NAME: Fashion Consciousness

SCALE DESCRIPTION:

A scale measuring the importance of being in fashion, particularly with regard to dress. A four-item version was suggested by Wells and Tigert (1971) and apparently used by Darden and Perreault (1976). Two- and four-item versions were used by Lumpkin and Darden (1982) and Wilkes (1992), respectively. See also the scale used by Schnaars and Schiffman (1984).

SCALE ORIGIN:

These items were part of an early classic study of psychographics by Wells and Tigert (1971). One thousand questionnaires were mailed to homemaker members of the Market Facts mail panel. In addition to gathering demographic, product use, and media data, the survey contained 300 statements that have become the basis for the construction of many lifestyle-related scales. Although the four items for this scale are reported in the article, they were not analyzed as a multi-item scale. The purpose of the article was to explain how psychographics could improve on mere demographic description of target audiences and product users. No psychometric information was reported.

One of the first uses of the items as a multi-item scale was in Darden and Perreault (1976). Analysis was based on self-administered questionnaires completed by 278 suburban housewives randomly selected in Athens, Georgia. A split-half reliability of .61 was reported for the scale. Fashion consciousness was significantly lower for "inshoppers" than for any of the four "outshopping" groups. It was highest for the group that primarily outshopped for home entertainment products, not clothing.

SAMPLES:

Lumpkin and Darden (1982) had 145 usable responses gathered from the consumer research panel of the University of Arkansas. Data were collected from the individuals using a mail questionnaire.

Wilkes (1992) collected data from **363** females from three cities in a southwestern state. The ages of respondents ranged from 60 to 79 years of age. Private, religious, and civic groups were contacted followed by identification of additional groups and eventually the individuals who were asked to participate. Questionnaires were apparently delivered to respondents' homes and then retrieved within a week.

RELIABILITY:

Lumpkin and Darden (1982) calculated an alpha of .**71.** Wilkes (1992) reported a composite reliability of .**91.**

VALIDITY:

Exploratory factor analysis (Lumpkin and Darden 1982) and confirmatory factor analysis Wilkes (1992) have indicated that the items load together.

ADMINISTRATION:

Data were gathered through self-administered questionnaires in the studies by Lumpkin and Darden (1982) and Wilkes (1992). A high score indicates that a respondent is very concerned about being in fashion, whereas a low score means a respondent has little interest in his/her fashionability.

MAJOR FINDINGS:

In their study of television program preference groups, Lumpkin and Darden (1982) found **fashion consciousness** to be one of only a few lifestyle variables that were significantly different between the six groups. Specifically, in the most **fashion conscious** group were the youngest, those with the least education, and those who seemed to prefer female-oriented comedies or dramas, *not* football.

Wilkes (1992) studied the measurement characteristics of ''cognitive age'' and its association with demographic antecedent variables as well as lifestyle-related consequential factors. Among the many findings was that cognitively younger women had greater **fashion consciousness**.

COMMENTS:

All of the following items refer to clothes except one (item 4). If one is studying clothing alone, it might be best to drop this item.

REFERENCES:

Darden, William R. and William D. Perreault, Jr. (1976), ''Identifying Interurban Shoppers: Multiproduct Purchase Patterns and Segmentation Profiles,'' *JMR*, 13 (February), 51-60.

Lumpkin, James R. and William R. Darden (1982), ''Relating Television Preference Viewing to Shopping Orientations, Lifestyles, and Demographics,'' *JA*, 11 (4), 56-67.

Schnaars, Steven P. and Leon G. Schiffman (1985), ''An Application of Segmentation Design Based on a Hybrid of Canonical Correlation and Simple Crosstabulation,'' *JAMS*, 12 (Fall), 177-89.

Wells, William D. and Douglas Tigert (1971), ''Activities, Interests, and Opinions,'' *JAR*, 11 (August), 27-35.

Wilkes, Robert E. (1992), ''A Structural Modeling Approach to the Measurement and Meaning of Cognitive Age,'' *JCR*, 19 (September), 292-301.

SCALE ITEMS: FASHION CONSCIOUSNESS*

Strongly disagree	Disagree	Slightly disagree	Slightly agree	Agree	Strongly agree
1	2	3	4	5	6

1. I usually have one or more outfits that are of the very latest style.
2. When I must choose between the two I usually dress for fashion, not for comfort.

3. An important part of my life and activities is dressing smartly.
4. I often try the latest hairdo styles when they change.
5. It is important to me that my clothes be of the latest style.
6. A person should try to dress in style.
7. I like to shop for clothes.

* Items 1-4 were suggested by Wells and Tigert (1971) and apparently used by Darden and Perreault (1976). Items 5 and 6 were used by Lumpkin and Darden (1982). Wilkes (1992) used items 1-3 and 7.

SCALE NAME: Fear

SCALE DESCRIPTION:

A three-item, five-point summated ratings scale assessing a person's experience with the fear-related emotion. The directions and response scale can be worded so as to measure the *intensity* of the emotional state at the present time, or they can be adjusted to measure the *frequency* with which a person has experienced the emotional trait during some specified time period. One-word items were used in the study by Westbrook and Oliver (1991), and phrases based on those same items were used by Allen, Machleit, and Kleine (1992).

SCALE ORIGIN:

The measure was developed by Izard (1977) and is part of the Differential Emotions Scale (DES II). The instrument originally was designed as a measure of a person's emotional "state" at a particular point in time, but adjustments in the instrument's instructions allow the same items to be used in the assessment of emotional experiences as perceived over a longer time period. The latter was viewed by Izard as measure of one's emotional "trait" (1977, p. 125). Test-retest reliability for the fear subscale of DES II was reported to be .68 (n = 63) and item-factor correlations were .88 and more (Izard 1977, p. 126).

The items in DES II were composed solely of one word. In contrast, the items in DES III are phrases describing the target emotion. They were developed by Izard, although the first published validity testing was conducted by Kotsch, Gerbing, and Schwartz (1982). A study by Allen, Machleit, and Marine (1988) provides some insight to the factor structure of both DES II and III. With specific reference to fear items, the items in the DES II version loaded separately and by themselves, whereas the DES III version tended to load with items representing other emotions.

SAMPLES:

The data used by Allen, Machleit, and Kleine (1992) came from a stratified sample of people of diverse experience with blood donation. Nine hundred questionnaires were mailed, and **361** usable forms were returned. Given that all respondents had previously donated blood, limited information was known about them and allowed a comparison with nonrespondents. Respondents were a little older, less likely to be male, and more likely to be heavier donors than nonrespondents.

The data for Westbrook and Oliver's (1991) study came from a judgmental area sample. Convenience samples were taken at four shopping centers in a large northeastern city and were limited to persons who had purchased a new or used car in the past year. Complete and usable questionnaires were obtained from **125** respondents. A majority (74%) of the sample was male. The average respondent had an income in the $25,000-$40,000 range and was 33 years of age. The frequency version of the scale was used in this study.

Two samples were used in the study by Oliver (1993), one examining satisfaction with cars and the other examining course satisfaction. The one involving cars is the same as the one described previously in Westbrook and Oliver (1991). The other sample was composed of students who volunteered from nine sections of a required marketing class. Usable questionnaires were provided by **178** students. The intensity version of the scale was used in this study.

RELIABILITY:

Westbrook and Oliver (1991) reported an alpha of **.90** for the scale. An alpha of **.84** was calculated by Allen, Machleit, and Kleine (1992; Allen 1994). Oliver (1993) reported alphas of **.89** (n = 125) and **.88** (n = 178).

VALIDITY:

No specific examination of the scale's validity was reported in any of the studies.

ADMINISTRATION:

The scale was included with many other measures in the instrument used by Westbrook and Oliver (1991), Oliver (1993), as well as Allen, Machleit, and Kleine (1992). High scores on the frequency version of the scale suggest that a respondent perceives him/herself as having experienced the fear-related emotional trait very often in some specified time period. A high score on the intensity version of the scale indicates that he/she is feeling very scared at the time of measurement.

MAJOR FINDINGS:

The study by Allen, Machleit, Kleine (1992) examined whether emotions affect behavior through attitudes or are better viewed as having a separate and distinct impact. Among the many findings was that **fear** (DES III) plays a key role with behavior, at least with regard to donating blood. Specifically, a strong relationship was found between **fear** involving the act of donating blood and the act of donating for those making three to seven donations in a year's time. The relationship was negative, which means that these donors had a positive emotion linked with the behavior.

The separate roles of positive and negative affect, attribute performance, and disconfirmation were examined by Oliver (1993) for their impact on satisfaction. Negative affect was viewed as a function of several emotions, **fear** being one of them. For both samples, negative affect was found to have direct influence on satisfaction.

Westbrook and Oliver (1991) studied the correspondence of the consumption emotional responses and satisfaction judgments that occur in the postpurchase period of the consumer decision process. **Fear** had its highest correlation with contempt (r = .83) and its lowest correlation with joy (r = -.07). **Fear** was also found to be a primary emotional trait linked to the cluster of consumers who had the lowest satisfaction in their car-buying experiences.

REFERENCES:

Allen, Chris T. (1994), personal correspondence.

_____, Karen A. Machleit, and Susan Schultz Kleine (1992), "A Comparison of Attitudes and Emotions as Predictors of Behavior at Diverse Levels of Behavioral Experience," *JCR*, 18 (March), 493-504.

_____, _____, and Susan S. Marine (1988), "On Assessing the Emotionality of Advertising Via Izard's Differential Emotions Scale," in *Advances in Consumer Research*, Vol. 15, Michael J. Houston, ed. Provo, UT: Association for Consumer Research, 226-31.

Izard, Carroll E. (1977), *Human Emotions*. New York: Plenum Press.

Kotsch, William E., Davis W. Gerbing, and Lynne E. Schwartz (1982), "The Construct Validity of the Differential Emotions Scale as Adapted for Children and Adolescents," in *Measuring Emotions in Infants and Children*, Carroll E. Izard, ed. New York: Cambridge University Press, 251-78.

Oliver, Richard L. (1993), "Cognitive, Affective, and Attribute Bases of the Satisfaction Response," *JCR*, 20 (December), 418-30.

Westbrook, Robert A. and Richard L. Oliver (1991), "The Dimensionality of Consumption Emotion Patterns and Consumer Satisfaction," *JCR*, 18 (June), 84-91.

SCALE ITEMS: FEAR

POSSIBLE DIRECTIONS FOR FREQUENCY VERSION OF SCALE: Below is a list of words that you can use to show how you feel. We want you to tell us how often you felt each of these feelings _____.* You can tell us how often you felt each of these feelings on the list by marking one of the numbers next to each question.

Almost never	___ : ___ : ___ : ___ : ___	Very often
	1 2 3 4 5	

POSSIBLE DIRECTIONS FOR INTENSITY VERSION OF SCALE: Below is a list of words that you can use to show how you feel. We want you to tell us how strongly you feel. You can tell us how strongly you feel each of these feelings on the list by marking one of the numbers next to each question.

Very weak	___ : ___ : ___ : ___ : ___	Very strong
	1 2 3 4 5	

DES II
1. scared
2. fearful
3. afraid

DES III
1. feel scared, uneasy, like something might harm you
2. feel fearful, like you're in danger, very tense
3. feel afraid

* The blank should be used to specify the time period of interest such as "during the last week."

SCALE NAME: Fearfulness

SCALE DESCRIPTION:

A scale to assess the fear and tension a person reports feeling with respect to some stimulus. The measure is composed of seven items with seven-point response scales.

SCALE ORIGIN:

The article by Maheswaran and Meyers-Levy (1990) did not specify the origin of the scale, but it is likely to have been developed for use in their study.

SAMPLES:

The study conducted by Maheswaran and Meyers-Levy (1990) used a sample of 98 undergraduate students who received extra course credit for participating. The data were gathered from small groups of students (5–7 at a time) and then analyzed as a 2 × 2 factorial design.

RELIABILITY:

Maheswaran and Meyers-Levy (1990) reported the scale to have an alpha of .86.

VALIDITY:

Maheswaran and Meyers-Levy (1990) provided no evidence of the scale's validity.

ADMINISTRATION:

The scale was administered by Maheswaran and Meyers-Levy (1990) along with several other measures in an experiment after subjects had read some test material. A high score on the scale indicates that a respondent reports a strong response in reaction to some stimulus, whereas a low score suggests that he/she has not felt fearful at all.

MAJOR FINDINGS:

Maheswaran and Meyers-Levy (1990) examined the persuasiveness of different ways to frame a message and the role played by issue involvement. A check was made among the treatments to determine if significantly different levels of **fear** had been unintentionally induced in the subjects. This helped to rule out **fear** as a cause for changes in attitudes and purchase intentions.

REFERENCE:

Maheswaran, Durairja and Joan Meyers-Levy (1990), ''The Influence of Message Framing and Issue Involvement,'' *JMR*, 27 (August), 361-67.

SCALE ITEMS: FEARFULNESS

DIRECTIONS: When you read the previous materials about . . ., to what extent did you experience the following feelings?

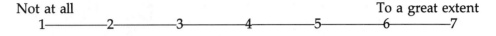

Not at all   To a great extent

1————2————3————4————5————6————7

1. Fearful
2. Tense
3. Nervous
4. Anxious
5. Reassured
6. Relaxed **(r)**
7. Comforted **(r)**

SCALE NAME: Femininity

SCALE DESCRIPTION:

A seven-point, summated ratings scale measuring the degree to which a person indicates having feminine personality characteristics. Barak and Stern (1985/86) used a ten-item version of the scale.

SCALE ORIGIN:

The items for the scale were taken from the Bem Sex-Role Inventory (BSRI; 1974). The inventory went through several rounds of development and testing. The initial development involved 40 undergraduate students judging 400 personality characteristics for their appropriateness for each sex. The list was narrowed to the 20 characteristics for each sex which were considered to be the most desirable for them to have in American society. Once finished, the measure asked respondents to rate themselves on all of the characteristics so that both masculinity and femininity scale scores could be computed. (An androgyny score also could be calculated by determining the difference between the other two scores.)

Internal consistency was estimated using two samples: 444 male and 279 female students in introductory psychology at Stanford University, and an additional 117 male and 77 female paid volunteers at Foothill Junior College. From the two samples, an alpha of .86 was calculated both times for the masculinity scale, and alphas of .8 and .82 were calculated for the femininity scale. Using 28 males and 28 females, test-retest stability was estimated. The students took the BSRI once and then four weeks later. For both scales the correlation of the scores was reported to be .90. Scores on the scales were correlated with two other measures of sex roles. The low correlations led the author to conclude that her scales were tapping into constructs not directly measured by the others.

SAMPLES:

The survey form used by Barak and Stern (1985/86) was distributed personally to and collected from an age-quota sample of women living in the greater New York metropolitan area. The study focused on the 567 responding women who categorized themselves as either "young" or "middle-aged" and stated an age between 25 and 69 years.

Data were collected through multistage cluster sampling by Fischer and Arnold (1990). The study was based on data from the 299 people who completed the questionnaire. Compared with the population from which the data were collected, the sample had fewer males but was more upscale. A $1 lottery ticket was given to respondents for participating.

RELIABILITY:

Barak and Stern (1985/86) say only that the scale's alpha was more than .85. Fischer and Arnold (1990) reported an alpha of .76.

VALIDITY:

Factor analysis was performed on the BSRI inventory offered by Bem (1974). Though not expressly stated, the ten items used by Barak and Stern (1985/86) were probably the ones that loaded highest on the factor related to masculinity. Fischer and Arnold (1990) did not report any examination of the scale's validity.

ADMINISTRATION:

The scale used by Barak and Stern (1985/1986) was self-administered by respondents in their homes as part of a larger survey form. The scale was administered by Fischer and Arnold (1990) as part of a structured survey instrument during in-home personal interviews with respondents. High scores indicate greater femininity, whereas low scores suggest little femininity though not necessarily strong masculinity.

MAJOR FINDINGS:

Barak and Stern (1985/86) examined the differences in profiles between the baby-boomer and pre-boomer generations as well as between those who characterized themselves as young versus middle-aged. No significant difference was found in **femininity** between either pair of groups.

Fischer and Arnold (1990) studied the impact of several gender-related variables on Christmas gift shopping patterns. The authors concluded that, in general, there was a significant though moderate positive relationship between feminine gender identities and involvement in Christmas gift shopping.

COMMENTS:

Although presented here by itself, the scale is used most properly with the masculinity scale of the BSRI (see #167). The lack of stronger evidence regarding scale validity should cause scores to be viewed cautiously. See also Qualls (1987) for another use of the scale.

REFERENCES:

Barak, Benny and Barbara Stern (1985/1986), "Women's Age in Advertising: An Examination of Two Consumer Age Profiles," *JAR*, 25 (Dec./Jan.), 38-47.

Bem, Sandra L. (1974), "The Measurement of Psychological Androgyny," *Journal of Consulting and Clinical Psychology*, 42 (2), 155-62.

Fischer, Eileen and Stephen J. Arnold (1990), "More Than a Labor of Love: Gender Roles and Christmas Gift Shopping," *JCR*, 17 (December), 333-45.

Qualls, William J. (1987), "Household Decision Behavior: The Impact of Husbands' and Wives' Sex Role Orientation," *JCR*, 14 (September), 264-79.

SCALE ITEMS: FEMININITY*

Indicate on the following scale how well each of the following traits describes you:

Never or almost never true   ___ : ___ : ___ : ___ : ___ : ___ : ___   Always or almost always true

    1   2   3   4   5   6   7

1. Affectionate
2. Cheerful
3. Childlike
4. Compassionate
5. Does not use harsh language
6. Eager to soothe hurt feelings
7. Feminine
8. Flatterable
9. Gentle
10. Gullible
11. Loves Children
12. Loyal
13. Sensitive to the needs of others
14. Shy
15. Soft spoken
16. Sympathetic
17. Tender
18. Understanding
19. Warm
20. Yielding

* Barak and Stern (1985/86) calculated scale scores on just ten of these items on the basis of the results of a factor analysis. Those ten items were not specified in their article.

SCALE NAME: Fit (Brand/Company)

SCALE DESCRIPTION:

A three-item, seven-point semantic differential measuring a person's attitude about the appropriateness that a certain product/brand be marketed by a certain company. As used by Keller and Aaker (1992), the scenario focused the respondent's attention on a *proposed* brand extension apparently being considered by the company. The scale seems to be amenable for use in a variety of situations in which the fit between the product and the marketer (manufacturer, retailer, or other channel member) is of interest.

SCALE ORIGIN:

No information is provided by Keller and Aaker (1992) regarding the scales' origin, but it is assumed to have been developed for use in their study.

SAMPLES:

The sample employed by Keller and Aaker (1992) was composed of **430** university employees, most of whom were female (90%). About half had a college degree, and the average age was 28 years of age. Respondents were paid $5 for their participation and given a chance to win cash prizes in a lottery.

RELIABILITY:

Keller and Aaker (1992) say only that the reliabilities of their multi-item scales were all in excess of .70.

VALIDITY:

Keller and Aaker (1992) reported no specific examination of the scale's validity.

ADMINISTRATION:

The scale was self-administered by subjects along with other measures after exposure to experimental manipulation information (Keller and Aaker 1992). A high score on the scale indicates that a respondent considers a product to be appropriate for a marketer to be associated with.

MAJOR FINDINGS:

The experiment by Keller and Aaker (1992) examined the factors influencing evaluation of proposed extensions of a core brand. The findings appeared to support the conclusion that perceived **product/company fit** along with company credibility mediate the impact of previous brand extensions on evaluations of a proposed extension.

REFERENCE:

Keller, Kevin Lane and David A. Aaker (1992), ''The Effects of Sequential Introduction of Brand Extensions,'' *JMR*, 29 (February), 35-50.

SCALE ITEMS: FIT (BRAND/COMPANY)

Bad fit between company and product	__ : __ : __ : __ : __ : __ : __ 1 2 3 4 5 6 7	Good fit between company and product
Not at all logical for company	__ : __ : __ : __ : __ : __ : __ 1 2 3 4 5 6 7	Very logical for company
Not at all appropriate for company	__ : __ : __ : __ : __ : __ : __ 1 2 3 4 5 6 7	Very appropriate for company

SCALE NAME: Generosity

SCALE DESCRIPTION:

A seven-item, five-point Likert-type summated ratings scale measuring the degree to which a person likes to share one's possessions. As used by Belk (1985), O'Guinn and Faber (1989), and Richins and Dawson (1992) the scoring of the items was done in such a way as to measure *nongenerosity*. A five-item version of the scale was used by O'Guinn and Faber (1989).

SCALE ORIGIN:

The origin of the scale is reported in Belk (1984). The measure of generosity was one of three scales constructed for examining aspects of materialism. Initial pools of 30 or more items were tested for each of the three measures with **237** business school students. Using factor analysis, item-total correlations, and measures of internal consistency, seven or more items were chosen from each pool to measure the three materialism-related constructs. The eight items retained for measuring generosity were reported to have an alpha of **.72**.

SAMPLES:

Belk (1984, 1985) examined the scale in various ways with three more samples. One was composed of **48** business students. Another sample had **338** subjects, 213 of whom were business students. (These two samples were reported to be about two-thirds male.) A third sample was composed of 33 families representing **99** people who ranged in age from 13 to 92 years.

Two samples were employed by O'Guinn and Faber (1989). One was of **386** completed responses (out of 808 questionnaires sent) from people who previously had written an organization that aided compulsive buyers. A second group was used for comparison purposes and was intended to represent the general population. Eight hundred questionnaires were mailed to people in three Illinois areas: Chicago, Springfield, and Bloomington-Normal. Two mailings produced a total of **250** completed survey forms.

Studies with four samples were described in the article by Richins and Dawson (1992) but the generosity scale was used only in survey 2. Little is said about the sample except that the data came from a mail survey of people in a large western U.S. city. The households were chosen randomly and sent a survey form, followed by a reminder letter and a second copy of the questionnaire two weeks later. The response rate was exactly one-third, resulting in **250** usable questionnaires.

RELIABILITY:

An alpha of **.58** was reported for one of the Belk (1984) samples (n = 338). A two-week interval, test-retest correlation of **.64** (n = 48) was reported for another Belk (1984, 1985) sample. Alphas of **.63** were reported by both O'Guinn and Faber (1989) as well as Richins and Dawson (1992).

VALIDITY:

Belk (1984) compared scale scores with other measures in a multitrait-multimethod matrix. As evidence of convergent validity, scores on the generosity scale were correlated significantly with two other measures used to assess the same construct. Only partial support for discriminant validity was found. Evidence of criterion validity was found by noting that two known groups had significantly different mean scores on the scale, and the differences were in the hypothesized directions.

No examination of scale validity was made by O'Guinn and Faber (1989) beyond factor analysis. Items regarding generosity and two other materialism-related constructs were factor analyzed, and three factors clearly emerged. The authors did indicate that the scales were slightly modified on the basis of the factor analysis, however.

The validity of the generosity scale was not addressed by Richins and Dawson (1992) except in the sense that it was used to assess the nomological validity of the materialism scale being developed (see ''Findings'').

ADMINISTRATION:

The scale was one of several measures in each of the studies, which were self-administered. High scores on the scale indicate that respondents do not want to share their possessions with others, whereas low scores indicate respondents who are more generous.

MAJOR FINDINGS:

The purpose of Belk (1984) was to discuss the construction and characteristics of three materialism-related constructs: envy, possessiveness, and **nongenerosity**. Many of the findings are reported previously. In addition, there was evidence that older people were less **generous** than younger people and that the most **generous** individuals tended to be the happiest with their lives. Belk (1985) examined further aspects of the three subscales but also the psychometric characteristics of the materialism scale as a whole. In particular, he studied generational differences in materialism. Among the many findings was that each of three generational groups were significantly different from one another in terms of their **generosity**. Specifically, the oldest generation was the most **generous** while the middle generation was the least **generous**.

O'Guinn and Faber (1989) studied compulsive shopping. Their results showed that a sample of compulsive shoppers were significantly less **generous** than a general sample of consumers.

The purpose of the several surveys conducted by Richins and Dawson (1992) was to construct a new measure of materialism. To examine the scale's nomological validity, it was proposed that materialists would be more self-centered and unconcerned about others. Part of testing that hypothesis came from the association between materialism and **generosity**. A significant though low correlation between the two constructs was found, suggesting that more materialistic people are somewhat more likely to be less **generous** with their possessions and nonmonetary resources as well.

COMMENTS:

The three materialism-related measures mentioned here have been used summed not only separately but together as well. Two alphas for the combined scale were reported by Belk (1985): .66 (n = 338) and .73 (n = 48). Belk (1985) also reported a test-retest correlation of .68 (n = 48). O'Guinn and Faber (1989; Faber and O'Guinn 1992) calculated an alpha of .71 for the combined scale. Given the low reliability of the combined scale and the generosity subscale, further work is called for before they can be used extensively.

REFERENCES:

Belk, Russell W. (1984), "Three Scales to Measure Constructs Related to Materialism: Reliability, Validity, and Relationships to Measures of Happiness," in *Advances in Consumer Research*, Vol. 11, Thomas Kinnear, ed. Provo, UT: Association for Consumer Research, 291-97.

——— (1985), "Materialism: Trait Aspects of Living in the Material World," *JCR*, 12 (December), 265-80.

Faber, Ronald J. and Thomas C. O'Guinn (1992), "A Clinical Screener for Compulsive Buying," *JCR*, 19 (December), 459-69.

O'Guinn, Thomas C. and Ronald J. Faber (1989), "Compulsive Buying: A Phenomenological Exploration," *JCR*, 16 (September), 147-57.

Richins, Marsha L. and Scott Dawson (1992), "A Consumer Values Orientation for Materialism and Its Measurement: Scale Development and Validation," *JCR*, 19 (December), 303-16.

SCALE ITEMS: GENEROSITY*

Strongly disagree	Disagree	Neutral	Agree	Strongly agree
1————	——2————	———3————	——4————	——5

1. I enjoy having guests stay at my home. **(r)**
2. I enjoy sharing what I have. **(r)**
3. I don't like to lend things, even to good friends.
4. It makes sense to buy a lawnmower with a neighbor and share it. **(r)**
5. I don't mind giving rides to those who don't have a car. **(r)**
6. I don't like to have anyone in my home when I'm not there.
7. I enjoy donating things to charities. **(r)**

* Items similar to or exactly the same as the following were used by O'Guinn and Faber (1989): 1, 2, 3, 5, and 7.

SCALE NAME: Guilt

SCALE DESCRIPTION:

A three-item, five-point summated ratings scale assessing the experience a person has had with guilt-related emotions. The directions and response scale can be worded so as to measure the *intensity* of the emotional state at the present time, or they can be adjusted to measure the *frequency* with which a person has experienced the emotional trait during some specified time period. One-word items were used in the study by Westbrook and Oliver (1991), and phrases based on those same items were used by Allen, Machleit, and Kleine (1992).

SCALE ORIGIN:

The measure was developed by Izard (1977) and is part of the Differential Emotions Scale (DES II). The instrument originally was designed as a measure of a person's emotional "state" at a particular point in time, but adjustments in the instrument's instructions allow the same items to be used in the assessment of emotional experiences as perceived over a longer time period. The latter was viewed by Izard as measure of one's emotional "trait" (1977, p. 125). Test-retest reliability for the guilt subscale of DES II was reported to be .77 (n = 63) and item-factor correlations were .78 and more (Izard 1977, p. 126).

The items in DES II were composed solely of one word. In contrast, the items in DES III are phrases describing the target emotion. They were developed by Izard, although the first published validity testing was conducted by Kotsch, Gerbing, and Schwartz (1982). A study by Allen, Machleit, and Marine (1988) provides some insight to the factor structure of both DES II and III. With specific reference to guilt items, they tended to load on the same factor except in the DES III version when the items were mixed on a questionnaire with the items representing other emotions rather than being grouped together.

SAMPLES:

The data used by Allen, Machleit, and Kleine (1992) came from a stratified sample of people of diverse experience with blood donation. Nine hundred questionnaires were mailed and **361** usable forms were returned. Given that all respondents had previously donated blood, limited information was known about them and allowed a comparison with nonrespondents. Respondents were a little older, less likely to be male, and more likely to be heavier donors than nonrespondents.

The data for the study conducted by Westbrook and Oliver (1991) came from a judgmental area sample. Convenience samples were taken at four shopping centers in a large northeastern city and were limited to persons who had purchased a new or used car in the past year. Complete and usable questionnaires were obtained from **125** respondents. A majority (74%) of the sample was male. The average respondent had an income in the $25,000–

$40,000 range and was 33 years of age. The frequency version of the scale was used in this study.

Two samples were used in the study by Oliver (1993), one examining satisfaction with cars and the other examining course satisfaction. The one involving cars is the same as the one described previously in Westbrook and Oliver (1991). The other sample was composed of students who volunteered from nine sections of a required marketing class. Usable questionnaires were provided by **178** students. The intensity version of the scale was used in this study.

RELIABILITY:

Westbrook and Oliver (1991) reported an alpha of **.84** for the scale . Allen, Machleit, and Kleine (1992; Allen 1994) calculated an alpha of **.83.** Oliver (1993) reported alphas of **.86** (n = 125) and **.80** (n = 178).

VALIDITY:

No specific examination of the scale's validity was reported in any of the studies.

ADMINISTRATION:

The scale was included with many other measures in the instrument used by Westbrook and Oliver (1991), Oliver (1993), and Allen, Machleit, and Kleine (1992). High scores on the frequency version of the scale suggest that a respondent perceives him/herself as having experienced the guilt-related emotional trait very often in some specified time period. A high score on the intensity version of the scale indicates that he/she is feeling very guilty at the time of measurement.

MAJOR FINDINGS:

Allen, Machleit, Kleine (1992) examined whether emotions effect behavior via attitudes or are better viewed as having a separate and distinct impact. Although several emotions were found to play a key role in predicting behavior, **guilt** (DES III) was not found to have a significant relationship, at least with regard to donating blood.

The separate roles of positive and negative affect, attribute performance, and disconfirmation were examined by Oliver (1993) for their impact on satisfaction. Negative affect was viewed as a function of several emotions, **guilt** being one of them. For both samples, negative affect was found to have direct influence on satisfaction.

Westbrook and Oliver (1991) studied the correspondence of the consumption emotional responses and satisfaction judgments that occur in the postpurchase period of the consumer decision process. **Guilt** had its highest correlations with disgust and contempt (r = .78 for both) and its lowest correlation with joy (r = -.21). **Guilt** was also found to be a primary emotional trait linked to low satisfaction in the car buying experience.

REFERENCES:

Allen, Chris T. (1994), personal correspondence.

———, Karen A. Machleit, and Susan Schultz Kleine (1992), ''A Comparison of Attitudes and Emotions as Predictors of Behavior at Diverse Levels of Behavioral Experience,'' *JCR*, 18 (March), 493-504.

———, ———, and Susan S. Marine (1988), ''On Assessing the Emotionality of Advertising Via Izard's Differential Emotions Scale,'' in *Advances in Consumer Research*, 226-31.

Izard, Carroll E. (1977), *Human Emotions*. New York: Plenum Press.

Kotsch, William E., Davis W. Gerbing, and Lynne E. Schwartz (1982), ''The Construct Validity of the Differential Emotions Scale as Adapted for Children and Adolescents,'' in *Measuring Emotions in Infants and Children*, Carroll E. Izard, ed. New York: Cambridge University Press, 251-78.

Oliver, Richard L. (1993), ''Cognitive, Affective, and Attribute Bases of the Satisfaction Response,'' *JCR*, 20 (December), 418-30.

Westbrook, Robert A. and Richard L. Oliver (1991), ''The Dimensionality of Consumption Emotion Patterns and Consumer Satisfaction,'' *JCR*, 18 (June), 84-91.

SCALE ITEMS: GUILT

POSSIBLE DIRECTIONS FOR FREQUENCY VERSION OF SCALE: Below is a list of words that you can use to show how you feel. We want you to tell us how often you felt each of these feelings _____.* You can tell us how often you felt each of these feelings on the list by marking one of the numbers next to each question.

Almost never ____ : ____ : ____ : ____ : ____ Very often
  1   2   3   4   5

POSSIBLE DIRECTIONS FOR INTENSITY VERSION OF SCALE: Below is a list of words that you can use to show how you feel. We want you to tell us how strongly you feel. You can tell us how strongly you feel each of these feelings on the list by marking one of the numbers next to each question.

Very weak ____ : ____ : ____ : ____ : ____ Very strong
  1   2   3   4   5

DES II
1. repentant
2. guilty
3. blameworthy

DES III
1. feel regret, sorry about something you did
2. feel like you did something wrong
3. feel like you ought to be blamed for something

* The blank should be used to specify the time period of interest such as ''during the last week.''

SCALE NAME: Health Behavioral Control

SCALE DESCRIPTION:

A 12-item, seven-point Likert-type scale measuring the degree of control one believes he/she has over his/her health-related behaviors. The emphasis is on *engaging in* the behaviors rather than the *outcome* of those behaviors.

SCALE ORIGIN:

The scale was developed by Moorman and Matulich (1993). Development and refinement of the many scales used in their study generally followed the Churchill (1979) paradigm. Measures were pretested on 67 undergraduate students. Then in the main test, the scales were purified further using alpha, item-total correlations, and LISREL.

SAMPLES:

Moorman and Matulich (1993) used two sampling techniques to obtain respondents who differed on the variables under examination. First, a stratified sample with low and high income as well as young and elderly strata was taken. Respondents from the two income strata were obtained by randomly selecting from lower- and higher-income neighborhoods in Milwaukee and Madison, Wisconsin. Respondents representing the elderly segment were selected randomly from adult centers and retirement communities. Data for young consumers was retained from the pretest (students in an introductory marketing class). In the second sample, survey forms were mailed to addresses of those randomly selected from the phone books of the two previously mentioned cities. The total number of usable questionnaires was **404**, indicating about a 51% overall response rate. A dollar was enclosed with the questionnaires received by all respondents as a token of appreciation and incentive to return the form.

RELIABILITY:

Moorman and Matulich (1993) reported an alpha of **.73** for the scale.

VALIDITY:

Although specific details about this scale were not provided in the article, Moorman and Matulich (1993) engaged in various purification activities in both the pretest and the main study for all their scales. At the least, then, it would appear that evidence was collected that indicated the scale was unidimensional and internally consistent.

ADMINISTRATION:

The scale was self-administered along with many other measures in a questionnaire (Moorman and Matulich 1993). A high score on the scale suggests that a respondent believes he/she has great control over and engages in such health-related activities as nutrition, rest, and check-ups.

MAJOR FINDINGS:

Moorman and Matulich (1993) presented and tested a model of the impact various consumer characteristics have on some health-related behaviors. **Health behavioral control** was found to have a significant positive impact on several behaviors, such as contact with health professionals, diet restriction, and tobacco restriction.

COMMENTS:

Moorman and Matulich (1993) reported the mean score of the sample on the scale to be 4.69, with a standard deviation of .89.

REFERENCES:

Churchill, Gilbert A., Jr. (1979), "A Paradigm for Developing Better Measures of Marketing Constructs," *JMR*, 16 (February), 64-73.

Moorman, Christine and Erika Matulich (1993), "A Model of Consumers' Preventive Health Motivation and Health Ability," *JCR*, 20 (September), 208-28.

SCALE ITEMS: HEALTH BEHAVIORAL CONTROL

Disagree ___ : ___ : ___ : ___ : ___ : ___ : ___ Agree
         1   2   3   4   5   6   7

1. It's difficult to reduce my sodium intake. **(r)**
2. It's too hard for me to exercise three days a week. **(r)**
3. It's not easy to cut back on snacks and treats. **(r)**
4. It's too hard to eat fresh fruits and vegetables regularly. **(r)**
5. I find it easy to moderate my red meat consumption
6. I find it hard to get enough rest and sleep. **(r)**
7. It's difficult to minimize the additives I consume. **(r)**
8. Going for an annual physical exam is easy for me.
9. It's easy to see my dentist on a regular basis
10. As hard as I try, I can't reduce the stress in my life. **(r)**
11. It's hard to go for an eye examination. **(r)**
12. I find it easy to maintain a balance between work and play.

SCALE NAME: Health Information Sources (Nonpersonal)

SCALE DESCRIPTION:

A five-item, seven-point summated rating scale measuring the frequency with which one uses media and other nonpersonal sources for gathering information about health-related issues.

SCALE ORIGIN:

The scale was developed by Moorman and Matulich (1993). Development and refinement of the many scales used in their study generally followed the Churchill (1979) paradigm. Measures were pretested on 67 undergraduate students. Then in the main test, the scales were purified further using alpha, item-total correlations, and LISREL.

SAMPLES:

Moorman and Matulich (1993) used two sampling techniques to obtain respondents who differed on the variables under examination. First, a stratified sample with low and high income as well as young and elderly strata was taken. Respondents from the two income strata were obtained by randomly selecting from lower- and higher-income neighborhoods in Milwaukee and Madison, Wisconsin. Respondents representing the elderly segment were selected randomly from adult centers and retirement communities. Data for young consumers was retained from the pretest (students in an introductory marketing class). In the second sample, survey forms were mailed to addresses of those randomly selected from the phone books of the two previously mentioned cities. The total number of usable questionnaires was **404**, indicating about a 51% overall response rate. A dollar was enclosed with the questionnaires received by all respondents as a token of appreciation and incentive to return the form.

RELIABILITY:

Moorman and Matulich (1993) reported an alpha of **.72** for the scale.

VALIDITY:

Although specific details about this scale were not provided in the article, Moorman and Matulich (1993) engaged in various purification activities in both the pretest and the main study for all of their scales. At the least then, it would appear that evidence was collected that indicated the scale was unidimensional and internally consistent.

ADMINISTRATION:

The scale was self-administered along with many other measures in a questionnaire (Moorman and Matulich 1993). A high score on the scale indicates

that a respondent reports frequently using nonpersonal sources for gathering health-related information.

MAJOR FINDINGS:

The study by Moorman and Matulich (1993) presented and tested a model of the impact various consumer characteristics have on some health-related behaviors. Among the findings was that people with high health motivation had significantly greater use of **nonpersonal sources of health information**.

COMMENTS:

Moorman and Matulich (1993) reported the mean score of the sample on the scale to be 2.84 with a standard deviation of .99.

REFERENCES:

Churchill, Gilbert A., Jr. (1979), ''A Paradigm for Developing Better Measures of Marketing Constructs,'' *JMR*, 16 (February), 64-73.

Moorman, Christine and Erika Matulich (1993), ''A Model of Consumers' Preventive Health Motivation and Health Ability,'' *JCR*, 20 (September), 208-28.

SCALE ITEMS: HEALTH INFORMATION SOURCES (NONPERSONAL)

On the scale below please indicate how much you utilize the following sources of health information.*

None of the time   ___ : ___ : ___ : ___ : ___ : ___ : ___   All of the time

         1   2   3   4   5   6   7

1. Ads
2. Books, magazines, or pamphlets about health
3. Newspaper
4. Television and radio programming
5. Product labels

* The instructional statement was not provided in the article but is recreated on the basis of the description provided there.

SCALE NAME: Health Motivation

SCALE DESCRIPTION:

A multi-item, seven-point Likert-type scale measuring the degree to which people say they are concerned about health hazards and try to take actions to protect themselves before the problems occur. As noted subsequently, several versions of the scale have been used, each with a slightly different emphasis. Moorman (1990) used a subset of the scale that emphasized actions taken to protect oneself before health problems occur. In the same study, she also had a six-item scale that focused on the motivation to *not* take action to protect one's health unless a problem has occurred. Moorman and Matulich (1993) used an eight-item combination of those previous two scales.

SCALE ORIGIN:

The scale was developed by Moorman (1993). The work reported in Moorman (1990) led to the use of two scales but further examination led to a combination of those items in the subsequent study (Moorman 1994). Development and refinement of the many scales used in Moorman and Matulich (1993) generally followed the Churchill (1979) paradigm. Measures were pretested on 67 undergraduate students. Then in the main study the scales were purified further using alpha, item-total correlations, and LISREL.

SAMPLES:

The sample used by Moorman (1990) came from the staff at a northeastern U.S. university. Using a list of staff, a systematic sample of people were contacted by mail. (Due to the nature of the research, those staff employed in health-related areas were dropped from the list.) Of the 274 employees sent a letter, **180** completed the experiment. Incentives to participate were in the form of dollar bills in each of the initial letters of contact and eligibility to win more money if they cooperated fully.

Moorman and Matulich (1993) used two sampling techniques to obtain respondents who differed on the variables under examination. First, a stratified sample with low and high income as well as young and elderly strata was taken. Respondents from the two income strata were obtained by randomly selecting from lower- and higher-income neighborhoods Milwaukee and Madison, Wisconsin. Respondents representing the elderly segment were selected randomly from adult centers and retirement communities. Data for young consumers were retained from the pretest (students in an introductory marketing class). In the second sample, survey forms were mailed to addresses of those randomly selected from the telephone books of the two previously mentioned cities. The total number of usable questionnaires was **404**, indicating about a 51% overall response rate. A dollar was enclosed with the questionnaires received by all respondents as a token of appreciation and incentive to return the form.

RELIABILITY:

Moorman (1990) reported alphas of **.76** and **.80** for the three- and six-item versions of the scale, respectively. An alpha of **.82** was reported for the eight-item scale used by Moorman and Matulich (1993).

VALIDITY:

Limited analysis by Moorman (1990) led her to treat the set of items as two scales. Although specific details were not provided in the article, Moorman and Matulich (1993) engaged in more rigorous purification activities in both the pretest and the main study, which led them to view the items as unidimensional and internally consistent.

ADMINISTRATION:

Moorman (1990) included the scale along with several other measures on a pre-experiment questionnaire sent to subjects along with the initial letter of contact. In Moorman and Matulich (1993), the scale was self-administered along with many other measures in a mail questionnaire. High scores on the scale appear to indicate that respondents are very interested in being healthy and they engage in protective behaviors to prevent problems from occurring.

MAJOR FINDINGS:

Moorman's (1990) study examined the influence of consumer and stimulus characteristics on the use of nutrition information. In general, both types of characteristics were found to affect information processing and decision quality. **Preventive and curative health orientations** were not variables of primary interest in the investigation and were not found to have significant effects on several variables related to the use of nutritional information.

Moorman and Matulich (1993) presented and tested a model of the impact various consumer characteristics have on some health-related behaviors. Among the findings was that people with high **health motivation** had significantly more interaction with health care professionals, gathered more health-related information from the media, and engaged in more healthy diet-related behaviors.

COMMENTS:

Moorman and Matulich (1993) reported the mean score of the sample on the scale to be 4.01 with a standard deviation of 1.11. It is worth noting that Moorman (1994) prefers that the **health motivation** measure be viewed as one scale rather than two.

REFERENCES:

Churchill, Gilbert A., Jr. (1979), ''A Paradigm for Developing Better Measures of Marketing Constructs,'' *JMR*, 16 (February), 64-73.

Moorman, Christine (1990), ''The Effects of Stimulus and Consumer Characteristics on the Utilization of Nutrition Information,'' *JCR*, 17 (December), 362-74.

_____ (1993), personal correspondence.

_____ (1994), personal correspondence.

_____ and Erika Matulich (1993), ''A Model of Consumers' Preventive Health Motivation and Health Ability,'' *JCR*, 20 (September), 208-28.

SCALE ITEMS: HEALTH MOTIVATION*

Strongly disagree ___ : ___ : ___ : ___ : ___ : ___ : ___ Strongly agree

1   2   3   4   5   6   7

1. I try to prevent health problems before I feel any symptoms.
2. I am concerned about health hazards and try to take action to prevent them.
3. I try to protect myself against health hazards I hear about.
4. I don't worry about health hazards until they become a problem for me or someone close to me. **(r)**
5. There are so many things that can hurt you these days. I'm not going to worry about them. **(r)**
6. I often worry about the health hazards I hear about, but don't do anything about them. **(r)**
7. I don't take any action against health hazards I hear about until I know I have a problem. **(r)**
8. I'd rather enjoy life than try to make sure I'm not exposing myself to a health hazard. **(r)**
9. I don't think health hazards I hear about will happen to me. **(r)**

* Items 1-3 were used by Moorman (1990) to measure a *preventative health orientation* and items 4-9 were used to measure a *curative health orientation*. Moorman and Matulich (1993) used items 1-8.

SCALE NAME: Imagery Quality/Quantity

SCALE DESCRIPTION:

A 17-item, seven-point summated ratings scale that measures the degree and ease with which a person reports images coming to mind while processing some specific stimulus as well as the intensity of those images. Burns, Biwas, and Bibin (1993) referred to the measure as **vividness**.

SCALE ORIGIN:

The 17 items used by Burns, Biwas, and Bibin (1993) were from scales created by Ellen and Bone (1991). Using two different samples, the latter were led to conclude that the items composed three scales measuring imagery vividness (#125), imagery quantity/ease (#124), and paleness.

SAMPLES:

Burns, Biwas, and Bibin (1993) gathered data from **377** undergraduate business students. Students were assigned randomly to one of eight treatment groups, and the experiment was conducted in a classroom setting.

RELIABILITY:

Burns, Biwas, and Bibin (1993) reported a reliability coefficient for the scale of **.94**.

VALIDITY:

Burns, Biwas, and Bibin (1993) did not directly address the validity of the scale. However, they did conduct confirmatory factor analysis of the 17 items mentioned in "Scale Origin" as well as two more from Ellen and Bone (1991) related to the memories triggered by an ad. Two-, three-, and four-factor solutions were compared, and each had significant chi-squares. For various reasons the authors chose the two-factor solution.

ADMINISTRATION:

Burns, Biwas, and Bibin (1993) had subjects complete the scale along with other measures after exposure to experimental stimuli. A high score on the scale indicates that the quantity, ease, and quality (vividness) of images that have been evoked by a stimulus are high.

MAJOR FINDINGS:

Burns, Biwas, and Bibin (1993) examined the influence of visual imagery as well as verbal/visual processing style on several typical attitude-related consequences of advertising. One of the major conclusions drawn by the authors was that **imagery quality/quantity** is an important mediator of the effect of advertising tactics (e.g., use of concrete terms) on consumer attitudes of interest (e.g., A_{ad}).

COMMENTS:

The dimensionality of this scale is far from clear given that the originators (Ellen and Bone 1991) used confirmatory factor analysis to justify treating the items as three different scales whereas Burns, Biwas, and Bibin (1993) used the same routine and other information to argue for treating the items as one scale. Further testing is strongly advised before these items are all used as a one summated scale.

REFERENCES:

Bone, Paula Fitzgerald and Pam Scholder Ellen (1992), "The Generation and Consequences of Communication-Evoked Imagery," *JCR*, 19 (June), 93-104.

Burns, Alvin C., Abhijit Biwas, and Lauren A. Babin (1993), "The Operation of Visual Imagery as a Mediator of Advertising Effects," *JA*, 22 (June), 71-85.

Ellen, Pam Scholder and Paula Fitzgerald Bone (1991), "Measuring Communication-Evoked Imagery Processing," in *Advances in Consumer Research*, Vol. 18, Rebecca H. Holman and Michael R. Soloman, eds. Provo, UT: Association of Consumer Research, 806-12.

SCALE ITEMS: IMAGERY QUALITY/QUANTITY

Does not describe at all								Describes perfectly
	__ :	__ :	__ :	__ :	__ :	__ :	__	
	1	2	3	4	5	6	7	

Vividness
1. clear
2. vivid
3. intense
4. lifelike
5. sharp
6. defined the images
7. detailed

Paleness
1. Pale
2. Fuzzy
3. Weak
4. Vague

Imagery Ease

1. How difficult or easy were the images to create?

Extremely
difficult   ___ : ___ : ___ : ___ : ___ : ___ : ___ : ___ : ___   Extremely
           1   2   3   4   5   6   7   8   9   easy

2. How quickly were the images aroused:

Not
quickly
at all   ___ : ___ : ___ : ___ : ___ : ___ : ___ : ___ : ___   Very
quickly
           1   2   3   4   5   6   7   8   9

3. I had no difficulty imagining the scene in my head.

Strongly
disagree   ___ : ___ : ___ : ___ : ___ : ___ : ___ : ___ : ___   Strongly
agree
           1   2   3   4   5   6   7   8   9

Imagery Quantity

1. As you listened to the ad, to what extent did any images come to mind?

To a
very
small
extent   ___ : ___ : ___ : ___ : ___ : ___ : ___ : ___ : ___   To a very
great
extent
           1   2   3   4   5   6   7   8   9

2. While listening to the ad, I experienced:

Few or
no
images   ___ : ___ : ___ : ___ : ___ : ___ : ___ : ___ : ___   Lots of
images
           1   2   3   4   5   6   7   8   9

3. All sorts of pictures, sounds, tastes and/or smells came to mind while I listened to
   the ad.

Strongly
disagree   ___ : ___ : ___ : ___ : ___ : ___ : ___ : ___ : ___   Strongly
agree
           1   2   3   4   5   6   7   8   9

SCALE NAME: Imagery Quantity/Ease

SCALE DESCRIPTION:

A six-item, nine-point, Likert-like scale that measures the degree and ease with which a person reports images coming to mind while processing some specific stimulus. In the experiments by Bone and Ellen (1992) as well as Miller and Marks (1992), the stimuli were mock radio commercials. (See also the 17-item scale used by Burns, Biwas, and Bibin (1993), which combines the items from this scale as well as those from two others.)

SCALE ORIGIN:

The origin of the scale was not specified by Bone and Ellen (1992), but it is clear from Ellen and Bone (1991) that it is original. **Imagery ease** and *imagery quantity* were measured using three items each, as indicated subsequently. Exploratory and confirmatory factor analysis led the authors to combine the items of these two subscales. The six-item scale was reported to have alphas of .88 (n = 179) and .91 (n = 144). (It appears that the sample referred to as study 1 in Ellen and Bone (1991) is the same as the one referred to as study 2 in Bone and Ellen 1992). Some evidence of the scale's discriminant validity was found given that it appeared to be related to but distinct from a measure of a person's innate ability to imagine.

SAMPLES:

Two experiments were discussed in the article by Bone and Ellen (1992). The sample for the first experiment was composed of **127** college students, and the second one had **179**. The experiments were similar in their collection of data. They took place in an audiovisual lab with students randomly assigned to treatments.

The data gathered by Miller and Marks (1992) came from **124** undergraduate marketing students attending a large midwestern U.S. university. Volunteers were compensated for their participation with extra credit points.

RELIABILITY:

Bone and Ellen (1992) reported an alpha of **.88** (n = 179) for the six-item combined scale. Alphas for the *imagery ease* subscale were reported by Bone and Ellen (1992) to be **.89** (study 1) and **.83** (study 2). Similar figures for the *imagery quantity* subscale were **.84** (study 1) and **.80** (study 2). Miller and Marks (1992; Marks 1994) calculated an alpha of **.91** for the full scale.

VALIDITY:

The validity of the scale was not directly addressed by Bone and Ellen (1992) or Miller and Marks (1992). However, a factor analysis of several scales used in the research by Bone and Ellen (1992) indicated that the items for this scale loaded together on a factor that was distinct from another somewhat similar factor, *imagery vividness*. The *imagery ease* items loaded on the same factor as those intended to measure the *quantity of imagery evoked* and were subsequently combined to form one measure of the degree of imagery evoked by the subject in response to the stimulus. A factor analysis by Miller and Marks (1992) confirmed that the *imagery ease* and *quantity* items loaded together but were distinct from the *imagery vividness* factor.

ADMINISTRATION:

The scale was administered in the experiments by both Bone and Ellen (1992) and Miller and Marks (1992) to subjects along with other measures after exposure to mock radio commercials. A high score on the scale indicates that a respondent reports a high number of images coming to mind very easily while listening to an ad, whereas a low score suggests that it was difficult for the respondent to arouse images.

MAJOR FINDINGS:

Bone and Ellen (1992) investigated the influence that imagery has on recall, brand attitudes, and purchase intentions. Two experiments were conducted, and both showed that **imagery quantity/ease** had a significant positive impact on Attitude Toward the Ad but not on Brand Attitudes or Purchase Intentions.

Miller and Marks (1992) investigated the impact of sound effects on processing and reactions to advertisements. For two different products it was found that **imagery quantity/ease** was significantly greater in commercials with sound effects than in those with just a verbal message.

COMMENTS:

Although retesting would be necessary, the scale items appear to be amenable for modification and use with stimuli other than radio ads.

REFERENCES:

Bone, Paula Fitzgerald and Pam Scholder Ellen (1992), ''The Generation and Consequences of Communication-Evoked Imagery,'' *JCR*, 19 (June), 93-104.

Burns, Alvin C., Abhijit Biwas, and Laurie A. Bibin (1993), ''The Operation of Visual Imagery as a Mediator of Advertising Effects,'' *JA*, 22 (June), 71- 85.

Ellen, Pam Scholder and Paula Fitzgerald Bone (1991), ''Measuring Communication-Evoked Imagery Processing,'' in *Advances in Consumer Research*, Vol. 18, Rebecca H. Holman and Michael R. Soloman, eds. Provo, UT: Association of Consumer Research, 806-12.

Marks, Lawrence J. (1994), personal correspondence.

Miller, Darryl W. and Lawrence J. Marks (1992), ''Mental Imagery and Sound Effects in Radio Commercials,'' *JA*, 21 (4), 83-93.

SCALE ITEMS: IMAGERY QUANTITY/EASE

Imagery Ease
1. How difficult or easy were the images to create?

Extremely   ___ : ___ : ___ : ___ : ___ : ___ : ___ : ___ : ___   Extremely
difficult   1   2   3   4   5   6   7   8   9   easy

2. How quickly were the images aroused:

Not
quickly   ___ : ___ : ___ : ___ : ___ : ___ : ___ : ___ : ___   Very
at all   1   2   3   4   5   6   7   8   9   quickly

3. I had no difficulty imagining the scene in my head.

Strongly   ___ : ___ : ___ : ___ : ___ : ___ : ___ : ___ : ___   Strongly
disagree   1   2   3   4   5   6   7   8   9   agree

Imagery Quantity
1. As you listened to the ad, to what extent did any images come to mind?

To a
very   ___ : ___ : ___ : ___ : ___ : ___ : ___ : ___ : ___   To a very
small   1   2   3   4   5   6   7   8   9   great
extent   extent

2. While listening to the ad, I experienced:

Few or
no   ___ : ___ : ___ : ___ : ___ : ___ : ___ : ___ : ___   Lots of
images   1   2   3   4   5   6   7   8   9   images

3. All sorts of pictures, sounds, tastes and/or smells came to mind while I listened to
   the ad.

Strongly   ___ : ___ : ___ : ___ : ___ : ___ : ___ : ___ : ___   Strongly
disagree   1   2   3   4   5   6   7   8   9   agree

SCALE NAME: Imagery Vividness (General)

SCALE DESCRIPTION:

A six-item, five-point summated ratings scale that measures the degree to which a specific stimulus image is described as being intense and lifelike. A Staple scale was used by Bone and Ellen (1992), whereas Miller and Marks (1992) used a modified Likert format. (See ''Comments'' regarding the nature of the construct measured; see also the 17-item scale used by Burns, Biwas, and Bibin (1993), which combines the items from this scale as well as those from two others.)

SCALE ORIGIN:

The origin of the scale was not specified by Bone and Ellen (1992), but it is clear from Ellen and Bone (1991) that it is original. Vividness was measured initially using 11 items. Exploratory and confirmatory factor analysis led the authors to define the vividness scale with seven items, six of which are indicated subsequently. In two different samples, the seven-item scale was reported to have alphas of .88 (n = 179) and .87 (n = 144). (It appears that the sample referred to as study 1 in Ellen and Bone 1991 is the same as the one referred to as study 2 in Bone and Ellen 1992). Some evidence of the scale's discriminant validity was found given that it appeared to be related to but distinct from a measure of a person's innate ability to imagine.

SAMPLES:

Two experiments were discussed in the article by Bone and Ellen (1992). The sample for the first experiment was composed of **127** college students, and the second one had **179**. The experiments were similar in their collection of data. They took place in an audiovisual lab with students randomly assigned to treatments.

The data gathered by Miller and Marks (1992) came from **124** undergraduate marketing students attending a large midwestern U.S. university. Volunteers were compensated for their participation with extra credit points.

RELIABILITY:

Bone and Ellen (1992) reported alphas for the scale to be **.86** (study 1) and **.88** (study 2). The alpha for the scale used by Miller and Marks (1992) was **.90** (Marks 1994).

VALIDITY:

The validity of the scale was not directly addressed by Bone and Ellen (1992) or Miller and Marks (1992). However, in both studies the results of factor analyses indicated that the items loaded together on the same factor and not on a somewhat similar factor, *imagery quantity/ease*.

ADMINISTRATION:

The scale was administered in the experiments by both Bone and Ellen (1992) and Miller and Marks (1992) to subjects along with other measures after exposure to mock radio commercials. Subjects were asked to indicate how vivid an image they formed while listening to a radio commercial. A high score on the scale indicates that a respondent has experienced an image that is very clear and lifelike, whereas a low score suggests that an image was not conceived well.

MAJOR FINDINGS:

Bone and Ellen (1992) investigated the influence that imagery has on recall, brand attitudes, and purchase intentions. Two experiments were conducted and both showed that **vividness** of imagination had a significant positive impact on Attitude Toward the Ad but not on Brand Attitudes or Purchase Intentions.

Miller and Marks (1992) investigated the impact of sound effects on processing and reactions to advertisements. For only one of the two products tested was it found that **imagery vividness** was significantly greater in commercials with sound effects than in those with just a verbal message.

COMMENTS:

In the experiments by Bone and Ellen (1992) as well as Miller and Marks (1992), subjects were not shown any visual stimuli but had to imagine it on the basis of the audio stimuli. Therefore, it may be more appropriate to describe the construct measured as the *vividness of conceiving* (rather than perceiving) *an image*. Perception implies than one is exposed to a physical stimulus and has the opportunity to attend to it rather than having to create it in the mind.

REFERENCES:

Bone, Paula Fitzgerald and Pam Scholder Ellen (1992), ''The Generation and Consequences of Communication-Evoked Imagery,'' *JCR*, 19 (June), 93-104.

Burns, Alvin C., Abhijit Biwas, and Laurie A. Bibin (1993), ''The Operation of Visual Imagery as a Mediator of Advertising Effects,'' *JA*, 22 (June), 7-85.

Ellen, Pam Scholder and Paula Fitzgerald Bone (1991), ''Measuring Communication-Evoked Imagery Processing,'' in *Advances in Consumer Research*, Vol. 18, Rebecca H. Holman and Michael R. Soloman, ed. Provo, UT: Association of Consumer Research, 806-12.

Marks, Lawrence J. (1994), personal correspondence.

Miller, Darryl W. and Lawrence J. Marks (1992), ''Mental Imagery and Sound Effects in Radio Commercials,'' *JA*, 21 (4), 83-93.

SCALE ITEMS: IMAGERY VIVIDNESS*

```
            +2
            +1
1. clear    0
           −1
           −2
```

2. vivid
3. intense
4. lifelike
5. sharp
6. defined the images

* Bone and Ellen (1992) used a Staple scale to record the responses to each of the items. It is likely that the items were positioned somewhere next to the 0 level of their respective response scales, such as shown in item 1. Miller and Marks (1992) used a more typical Likert-like response scale with endpoints labeled ''Does not describe at all'' and ''Describes perfectly.''

SCALE NAME: Imagery Vividness (Visual)

SCALE DESCRIPTION:

A 16-item, five-point Likert-type summated ratings scale measuring the clarity of mental images a person evokes. It measures a person's general visual imagery ability rather than the clarity of a particular stimulus under investigation. Referred to by several users as the Vividness of Visual Imagery Questionnaire (e.g., Childers 1984, 1985; Marks 1973).

SCALE ORIGIN:

The origin of this particular scale is Marks (1973). Eleven of the items in the scale are original, but five items were taken from a 35-item measure reported by Sheehan (1967), which was itself a shortened form of the 150-item measure of mental imagery developed by Betts (1909). Marks (1973) reported that his scale had a test-retest correlation of .74 (n = 68) and a split-half reliability coefficient of .85 (n = 150). The results of three experiments indicated that visual image vividness was an accurate predictor of the recall of information contained in pictures. Unexpectedly, it was also found in two of the three experiments that females were more accurate in their recall

SAMPLES:

The scale was administered in two studies reported by Childers and colleagues (1985). The first study involved **263** undergraduate college student volunteers. The second study collected data from 106 subjects who were described as being undergraduate students at a major midwestern U.S. university. The subjects in the second study were divided into two groups, one with **54** subjects and the other with **52**.

RELIABILITY:

An alpha of **.85** was reported for the scale in the first study, and alphas of **.84** and **.85** were found in the second study. With respect to item-total correlations, the authors reported that "each item was relatively equivalent in tapping the domain of interest" (Childers et al. 1985, p. 127).

VALIDITY:

A factor analysis in the first study by Childers and colleagues (1985) indicated that the items all loaded together. All of the loadings were more than .30 but six were less than .50. Evidence of the scale's discriminant validity came from its insignificant correlation with a measure of social desirability.

ADMINISTRATION:

The scale was self-administered by students along with other measures in both studies reported in the article (Childers et al. 1985). Low scores on the scale indicate that respondents are able to evoke clear mental images, whereas high scores suggest that they do not have vivid imagery.

MAJOR FINDINGS:

Childers and colleagues (1985) compared several measures of visual/verbal mental imagery. The measure of **imagery vividness** was *not* found to be significantly correlated with measures of imagery control, imagery style, aided recall, or recognition.

COMMENTS:

See also Hirschman (1986) for another apparent use of this or a similar scale.

REFERENCES:

Betts, G. H. (1909), ''The Distributions and Functions of Mental Imagery,'' *Columbia University Contributions to Education*, 26, 1-99.

Childers, Terry L. and Michael J. Houston (1984), ''Conditions for a Picture-Superiority Effect on Consumer Memory,'' *JCR*, 11 (September), 643-54.

———, ———, and Susan E. Heckler (1985), ''Measurement of Individual Differences in Visual Versus Verbal Information Processing,'' *JCR*, 12 (September), 125-34.

Hirschman, Elizabeth C. (1986), ''The Effect of Verbal and Pictorial Advertising Stimuli on Aesthetic, Utilitarian and Familiarity Perceptions,'' *JA*, 15 (2), 27-34.

Marks, David F. (1973), ''Visual Imagery Differences in the Recall of Pictures,'' *British Journal of Psychology*, 64 (1), 17-24.

Sheehan, Peter Winston (1967), ''A Shortened Form of Betts Questionnaire Upon Mental Imagery,'' *Journal of Clinical Psychology*, 23 (3), 386-89.

SCALE ITEMS: IMAGERY VIVIDNESS (VISUAL)

Rating	Description
1	Perfectly clear and as vivid as normal vision
2	Clear and reasonably vivid
3	Moderately clear and vivid
4	Vague and dim
5	No image at all, you only ''know'' that you are thinking of the object

INSTRUCTIONS:
For items 1-4, think of some relative or friend whom you frequently see (but who is not with you at present) and consider carefully the picture that comes before your mind's eye.

1. The exact contour of face, head, shoulders, and body.
2. Characteristic poses of head, attitudes of body, etc.

3. The precise carriage, length of step, etc., in walking.
4. The different colors worn in some familiar clothes. Visualize a rising sun.

Visualize a rising sun. Consider carefully the picture that comes before your mind's eye.

5. The sun is rising above the horizon into a hazy sky.
6. The sky clears and surrounds the sun with blueness.
7. Clouds. A storm blows up, with flashes of lightning.
8. A rainbow appears.

Think of the front of a shop which you often go to. Consider the picture that comes before your mind's eye.

9. The overall appearance of the shop from the opposite side of the road.
10. A window display, including colors, shapes and details of individual items for sale.
11. You are near the entrance. The color, shape and details of the door.
12. You enter the shop and go to the counter. The counter assistant serves you. Money changes hands.

Finally, think of a country scene which involves trees, mountains, and a lake. Consider the picture that comes before your mind's eye.

13. The contours of the landscape.
14. The color and shape of the trees.
15. The color and shape of the lake.
16. A strong wind blows on the trees and on the lake causing waves.

SCALE NAME: Imagery Vividness (Multiple Senses)

SCALE DESCRIPTION:

A 35-item, seven-point, Likert-like summated ratings scale measuring the clarity of mental images a person is able to evoke. This measures a person's general ability to imagine several types of sensations and is not limited to a particular sense or stimulus. It has been referred to by various names, but most of them include the original creator's names, Betts (see ''Origin'').

SCALE ORIGIN:

The items were constructed originally by Betts (1909). The 35-item condensed version was developed by Sheehan (1967a). He has reported correlations between the short and long versions as being more than .90 and the short version as having a test-retest reliability of .78 using an interval of seven months (Richardson 1969; Sheehan 1967b).

SAMPLES:

The data gathered by Miller and Marks (1992) came from **124** undergraduate marketing students attending a large midwestern U.S. university. Volunteers were compensated for their participation with extra credit points.

RELIABILITY:

Miller and Marks (1992; Marks 1994) calculated an alpha of **.92** for the scale.

VALIDITY:

Miller and Marks (1992) reported no examination of the scale's validity.

ADMINISTRATION:

The scale was administered by Miller and Marks (1992) to subjects along with other measures after exposure to a mock radio commercial. A low score on the scale indicates that a respondent can evoke clear mental images easily, whereas a high score suggests he/she does not have a vivid imagination.

MAJOR FINDINGS:

Miller and Marks (1992) investigated the impact of sound effects on processing and reactions to advertisements. The Betts measure of **imagery vividness** was used solely as a confound check. It was reported that there was no significant difference between treatment groups on the basis of their natural ability to evoke vivid images.

COMMENTS:

The 35-item test has separate sections devoted to the five senses. Validity testing is sorely needed to indicate, among other things, whether scoring would be more appropriate on the subscales rather than on the overall instrument.

See also Bone and Ellen (1992; Ellen and Bone 1991) for another apparent use of this scale.

REFERENCES:

Betts, G. H. (1909), "The Distributions and Functions of Mental Imagery," *Columbia University Contributions to Education*, 26, 1-99.

Bone, Paula Fitzgerald and Pam Scholder Ellen (1992), "The Generation and Consequences of Communication-Evoked Imagery," *JCR*, 19 (June), 93-104.

Ellen, Pam Scholder and Paula Fitzgerald Bone (1991), "Measuring Communication-Evoked Imagery Processing," in *Advances in Consumer Research*, Vol. 18, Rebecca H. Holman and Michael R. Soloman, eds. Provo, UT: Association of Consumer Research, 806-12.

Marks, Lawrence J. (1994), personal correspondence.

Miller, Darryl W. and Lawrence J. Marks (1992), "Mental Imagery and Sound Effects in Radio Commercials," *JA*, 21 (4), 83-93.

Richardson, Alan (1969), *Mental Imagery*. New York: Springer Publishing Co.

Sheehan, Peter Winston (1967a), "A Shortened Form of Betts Questionnaire Upon Mental Imagery," *Journal of Clinical Psychology*, 23 (3), 386-89.

_____ (1967b), "Reliability of a Short Test of Imagery," *Perceptual & Motor Skills*, 25 (3), 744.

SCALE ITEMS: IMAGERY VIVIDNESS (MULTIPLE SENSES)

Directions: The aim of this test is to determine the vividness of your imagery. The items of the test will bring certain images to your mind. You are to rate the vividness of each image by reference to the accompanying rating scale, which is shown below. For example, if your image is 'vague and dim' you give it a rating of 5. Refer to the rating scale when judging the vividness of each image. Try to do each item separately independent of how you may have done other items.

An image aroused by an item of this test may be:

Rating	Description
1	Perfectly clear and as vivid as the actual experience
2	Very clear and as vivid as the actual experience
3	Moderately clear and vivid
4	Not clear or vivid, but recognizable
5	Vague and dim
6	So vague and dim as to be hardly discernible
7	No image present at all, you only "know" that you are thinking of the object

For items 1-4, think of some relative or friend whom you frequently **see**, considering carefully the picture that comes before your mind's eye. Classify the images suggested by each of the following questions as indicated by the degrees of clearness and vividness specified on the rating scale.

1. the exact contour of face, head, shoulders, and body.
2. characteristic poses of head, attitudes of body, etc.
3. the precise carriage, length of step, etc., in walking.
4. the different colors worn in some familiar clothes.

Think of **seeing** the following, considering carefully the picture which comes before your mind's eye; and classify the image suggested by the following question as indicated by the degree of clearness and vividness specified on the rating scale.

5. the sun as it is sinking below the horizon

Think of each of the following **sounds** and classify the images on the rating scale.

6. the whistle of a locomotive
7. the honk of an automobile
8. the mewing of a cat
9. the sound of escaping steam
10. the clapping of hands in applause

Think of ''feeling'' or **touching** each of the following and classify the images on the rating scale.

11. sand
12. linen
13. fur
14. the prick of a pin
15. the warmth of a tepid bath

Think of **performing** each of the following acts, considering carefully the image which comes to your mind's arms, legs, lips, etc., and classify the images on the rating scale.

16. running upstairs
17. springing across a gutter
18. drawing a circle on paper
19. reaching up to a high shelf
20. kicking something out of your way

Think of **tasting** each of the following and classify the images on the rating scale.

21. salt
22. granulated (white) sugar
23. oranges
24. jelly
25. your favorite soup

Think of **smelling** each of the following and classify the images on the rating scale.

26. an ill-ventilated room
27. cooking cabbage
28. roast beef
29. fresh paint
30. new leather

Think of each of the following **sensations** and classify the images on the rating scale.

31. fatigue
32. hunger
33. a sore throat
34. drowsiness
35. repletion as from a very full meal

SCALE NAME: Importance of Social Approval (From Best Friend)

SCALE DESCRIPTION:

A five-item, seven-point Likert-type scale measuring the importance placed on the influence of one best friend in the consumption of certain expressive products.

SCALE ORIGIN:

Although not specifically stated by Fisher (1993), the scale(s) are original (Fisher 1994). Data were collected in a pretest to help identify consumption decisions that had a high probability of being considered by students (the relevant population of interest) as greatly influenced by others. The top 5 of 25 consumption decisions were ultimately developed into the items composing the scale.

SAMPLES:

Three studies are reported on in the article by Fisher (1993), although only the third one made use of the **social approval** scales. Little is known about the sample used in that study except that it was composed of 75 male and female undergraduate students who were assigned to one of three groups. The group in which one's *best friend* was identified as the source of influence had **24** respondents.

RELIABILITY:

Fisher (1993) used three versions of the scale. They differed by who was identified as the object of the influence: *self, the respondent's best friend,* or the *typical student*. Alphas of **.78, .82,** and **.73** were reported for the *self, best friend,* and *typical student* versions of the scale, respectively.

VALIDITY:

Fisher (1993) reported no examination of the scale's validity.

ADMINISTRATION:

The various versions of the scale as well as other measures were self-administered by respondents (Fisher 1993). A high score on the scale suggests that a respondent believes it is important to him/herself, to his/her best friend, or to the typical student that one's best friend approves of certain specified products and activities.

MAJOR FINDINGS:

Fisher (1993) examined the extent to which indirect questioning could be used to reduce social desirability bias on self-report measures. As noted previously, only the third study used the **social approval** scales. The author concluded that respondents were indicating that *the typical student* is more motivated by **social approval** than he/she was him/herself.

COMMENTS:

This scale was specifically designed for use with a student sample. Modification and retesting is called for if used with other groups.

REFERENCES:

Fisher, Robert J. (1994), personal correspondence.
_____ (1993), "Social Desirability Bias and the Validity of Indirect Questioning," *JCR*, 20 (September), 303-15.

SCALE ITEMS: IMPORTANCE OF SOCIAL APPROVAL (FROM BEST FRIEND)*

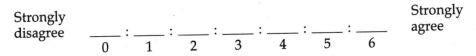

Strongly
disagree ____ : ____ : ____ : ____ : ____ : ____ : ____ Strongly
                 0   1   2   3   4   5   6   agree

It's very important to me that my best friend approve of . . .
1. the kind of athletic shoes I wear.
2. where I go for Spring Break.
3. my hairstyle.
4. the music I listen to.
5. the kind of cologne (perfume) I wear.

It's very important to _____ that his/her best friend approve of . . .+
1. the kind of athletic shoes s/he wears.
2. where s/he goes for Spring Break.
3. his/her hairstyle.
4. the music s/he listens to.
5. the kind of cologne (perfume) s/he wears.

* The items were supplied by Fisher (1994).
+ The blank in the scale stem was filled in by either *my best friend* or *the typical student*.

SCALE NAME: Importance of Social Approval (From Friends)

SCALE DESCRIPTION:

A five-item, seven-point, Likert-type scale measuring the importance placed on the influence of friends in the consumption of certain expressive products.

SCALE ORIGIN:

Although not specifically stated by Fisher (1993), the scale(s) are original (Fisher 1994). Data were collected in a pretest to help identify consumption decisions that had a high probability of being considered by students (the relevant population of interest) as greatly influenced by others. The top 5 of 25 consumption decisions were ultimately developed into the items composing the scale.

SAMPLES:

Three studies are reported on in the article by Fisher (1993), although only the third one made use of the **social approval** scales. Little is known about the sample used in that study except that it was composed of 75 male and female undergraduate students who were assigned to one of three groups. The group in which *friends* were identified as the source of influence had **26** respondents.

RELIABILITY:

Three versions of the scale were used by Fisher (1993). They differed by who was identified as the object of the influence: *self, the respondent's best friend,* or the *typical student*. Alphas of **.78**, **.82**, and **.73** were reported for the *self, best friend,* and *typical student* versions of the scale, respectively.

VALIDITY:

Fisher (1993) reported no examination of the scale's validity.

ADMINISTRATION:

The various versions of the scale as well as other measures were self-administered by respondents (Fisher 1993). A high score on the scale suggests that a respondent believes it is important to him/herself, to his/her best friend, or to the typical student that friends approve of certain specified products and activities.

MAJOR FINDINGS:

Fisher (1993) examined the extent to which indirect questioning could be used to reduce social desirability bias on self-report measures. As noted previously, only the third study used the **social approval** scales. The author concluded that respondents were indicating that the typical student is more motivated by **social approval** than he/she was him/herself.

COMMENTS:

This scale was specifically designed for use with a student sample. Modification and retesting is called for if used with other groups.

REFERENCES:

Fisher, Robert J. (1994), personal correspondence.
_____ (1993), ''Social Desirability Bias and the Validity of Indirect Questioning,'' JCR, 20 (September), 303-15.

SCALE ITEMS: IMPORTANCE OF SOCIAL APPROVAL (FROM FRIENDS)*

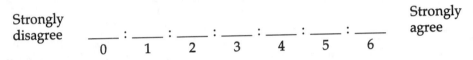

Strongly disagree ___ : ___ : ___ : ___ : ___ : ___ : ___ Strongly agree

$$0 \quad 1 \quad 2 \quad 3 \quad 4 \quad 5 \quad 6$$

It's very important to me that my friends approve of . . .
1. the kind of athletic shoes I wear.
2. where I go for Spring Break.
3. my hairstyle.
4. the music I listen to.
5. the kind of cologne (perfume) I wear.

It's very important to _____ that friends approve of . . .+
1. the kind of athletic shoes s/he wears.
2. where s/he goes for Spring Break.
3. his/her hairstyle.
4. the music s/he listens to.
5. the kind of cologne (perfume) s/he wears.

* The items were supplied by Fisher (1994).
\+ The blank in the scale stem was filled in by either *my best friend* or *the typical student*.

SCALE NAME: Importance of Social Approval (From Others)

SCALE DESCRIPTION:

A five-item, seven-point, Likert-type scale measuring the importance placed on the influence of others in the consumption of certain expressive products.

SCALE ORIGIN:

Although not specifically stated by Fisher (1993), the scale(s) are original (Fisher 1994). Data were collected in a pretest to help identify consumption decisions that had a high probability of being considered by students (the relevant population of interest) as greatly influenced by others. The top 5 of 25 consumption decisions were ultimately developed into the items composing the scale.

SAMPLES:

Three studies are reported on in the article by Fisher (1993), although only the third one made use of the **social approval** scales. Little is known about the sample used in that study except that it was composed of 75 male and female undergraduate students who were assigned to one of three groups. The group in which *others* were identified as the source of influence had **25** respondents.

RELIABILITY:

Fisher (1993) used three versions of the scale. They differed by who was identified as the object of the influence: *self, the respondent's best friend,* or the *typical student*. Alphas of **.67, .72,** and **.85** were reported for the *self, best friend,* and *typical student* versions of the scale, respectively.

VALIDITY:

Fisher (1993) reported no examination of the scale's validity.

ADMINISTRATION:

The various versions of the scale as well as other measures were self-administered by respondents (Fisher 1993). A high score on the scale suggests that a respondent believes it is important to him/herself, to his/her best friend, or to the typical student that others approve of certain specified products and activities.

MAJOR FINDINGS:

The studies conducted by Fisher (1993) examined the extent to which indirect questioning could be used to reduce social desirability bias on self-report measures. As noted previously, only the third study used the **social approval** scales. The author concluded that respondents were indicating that the typical student is more motivated by **social approval** than he/she was him/herself.

COMMENTS:

This scale was specifically designed for use with a student sample. Modification and retesting is called for if used with other groups.

REFERENCES:

Fisher, Robert J. (1994), personal correspondence.
_____ (1993), ''Social Desirability Bias and the Validity of Indirect Questioning,'' *JCR*, 20 (September), 303-15.

SCALE ITEMS: IMPORTANCE OF SOCIAL APPROVAL (FROM OTHERS)*

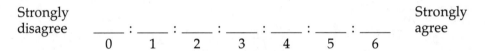

It's very important to me that others approve of . . .
1. the kind of athletic shoes I wear.
2. where I go for Spring Break.
3. my hairstyle.
4. the music I listen to.
5. the kind of cologne (perfume) I wear.

It's very important to _____ that others approve of . . .+
1. the kind of athletic shoes s/he wears.
2. where s/he goes for Spring Break.
3. his/her hairstyle.
4. the music s/he listens to.
5. the kind of cologne (perfume) s/he wears.

* The items were supplied by Fisher (1994).
+ The blank in the scale stem was filled in by either *my best friend* or *the typical student*.

SCALE NAME: Indexicality (Music)

SCALE DESCRIPTION:

> An eight-item, seven-point summated ratings scale measuring the degree to which a piece of music has evoked emotion-laden memories.

SCALE ORIGIN:

> Although not stated explicitly, it appears that the scale was original to the work of MacInnis and Park (1991). In a pretest stage of the study the alpha was reported to be .95 (n = 20).

SAMPLES:

> Data were gathered in the experiment by MacInnis and Park (1991) from **178** female undergraduates. Subjects received course credit for their participation and were assigned randomly to treatments.

RELIABILITY:

> MacInnis and Park (1991) reported an alpha of **.93** for the scale.

VALIDITY:

> MacInnis and Park (1991) reported no examination of scale validity. However, evidence from a factor analysis indicated that the scale was unidimensional.

ADMINISTRATION:

> The scale was administered to students along with other measures after they had been exposed to experimental stimuli (MacInnis and Park 1991). A high score on the scale indicates that a person believes a particular piece of music is familiar and brought back personal and emotional memories.

MAJOR FINDINGS:

> MacInnis and Park (1991) examined the influence of two dimensions of music on low- and high-involvement ad processing: the music's fit with the ad message and the music's links to past emotion-laden experiences (**indexicality**). **Indexicality** had a very strong and positive effect on attention to music despite the level of one's involvement.

REFERENCE:

> MacInnis, Deborah J. and C. Whan Park (1991), ''The Differential Role of Characteristics of Music on High- and Low-Involvement Consumers' Processing of Ads,'' *JCR*, 18 (Sept.), 161-73.

SCALE ITEMS: INDEXICALITY*

1. The music was

Not familiar ___ : ___ : ___ : ___ : ___ : ___ : ___ Familiar
  1   2   3   4   5   6   7

Use the following scale for items 2–6:

Disagree ___ : ___ : ___ : ___ : ___ : ___ : ___ Agree
  1   2   3   4   5   6   7

2. The music made me think about my past.
3. The music made me think about a person, place, or time in my life.
4. The music aroused memories.
5. The music was associated with people I have known or experiences I have had.
6. The music was relevant to me personally.

7. To what extent did the music evoke an emotional response?

Not at all ___ : ___ : ___ : ___ : ___ : ___ : ___ A lot
  1   2   3   4   5   6   7

8. To what extent did the music bring back emotions?

Not at all ___ : ___ : ___ : ___ : ___ : ___ : ___ A lot
  1   2   3   4   5   6   7

* The items and response scales are reconstructed here on the basis of descriptions provided in the article but may not be phrased exactly as MacInnis and Park (1991) used them.

SCALE NAME: Influence on Family Decision Making

SCALE DESCRIPTION:

A five-item scale measuring the degree to which a person describes him/herself as having more influence over family decision- making than the spouse. It is a global measure because it is not specific to any one type of decision. Responses were recorded on a 100-point constant sum scale for each item. The 100 points are to be divided between oneself and one's spouse to represent relative influence in the relationship over family decisions.

SCALE ORIGIN:

The items used by Corfman (1991) to measure this construct are apparently original to that study (Corfman 1994).

SAMPLES:

Data for the survey and experiment conducted by Corfman (1991) came from **61** couples from various church, school, and community groups in a major metro area. The couples received compensation for their participation. A broad range of education, age, and income groups were represented. For the survey portion of the study, two copies of the questionnaire were delivered to each couple's home, and they were told to complete the forms independently without discussing their answers during or after. The experimental sessions were conducted in the couples' homes about 19 days after filling out the questionnaire.

RELIABILITY:

Corfman (1991) reported the scale to have an alpha of **.89**.

VALIDITY:

The items in the scale were factor analyzed along with many others used to measure other constructs. The items for all of the scales were described as loading at .69 or more on their respective factors.

ADMINISTRATION:

The scale was self-administered by subjects along with many other measures in a questionnaire format during the survey phase of the study and before the experiment by Corfman (1991). Only the points out of 100 that are assigned by a respondent to him/herself (not to the spouse) are used to calculate that person's score. High scores on the scale indicate that a respondent perceives him/herself to be the head of the family, whereas low scores suggest a respondent does not perceive he/she has much influence over family decision-making.

MAJOR FINDINGS:

The purpose of the study by Corfman (1991) was to identify sources of inaccuracy in measuring perceived influence of spouses in their decision making. Desire to win, empathy, and traditionalism were the most significant predictors of the inaccuracy of a spouse's **influence** such that those with a greater desire to win, who were more traditional, and who were less empathetic were less accurate in describing their general level of relative influence in decision making.

COMMENTS:

See also Corfman and Lehmann (1987) for further analysis of this same data set.

REFERENCES:

Corfman, Kim P. (1994), personal correspondence.
_____ (1991), ''Perceptions of Relative Influence: Formation and Measurement,'' *JMR*, 28 (May), 125-36.
_____ and Donald R. Lehmann (1987), ''Models of Cooperative Group Decision-Making and Relative Influence: An Experimental Investigation of Family Purchase Decisions,'' *JCR*, 14 (June), 1-13.

SCALE ITEMS: INFLUENCE ON FAMILY DECISION MAKING

Directions: Please show how much more or less each scale applies to you than to your husband or wife by *dividing 100 points between you*.

YOU   YOUR SPOUSE   TOTAL
____ + _____ =   100

1. makes the important decisions in our home
2. has influence over decisions made with spouse
3. has control over things spouse wants or values
4. has authority in relationship
5. head of household

SCALE NAME: Information Relevance

SCALE DESCRIPTION:

A five-item, seven-point summated ratings scale measuring the level of usefulness a person reports some piece of information to have. In Mishra, Umesh, and Stem (1993), the scale was used with regard to the relevance of some information in distinguishing between alternative brands as part of a decision task.

SCALE ORIGIN:

There is nothing to indicate that the scale is anything other than original to the research reported by Mishra, Umesh, and Stem (1993).

SAMPLES:

The sample used by Mishra, Umesh, and Stem (1993) was composed of undergraduate and graduate students attending a large university. The mean age of the subjects was 22 years and ranged from 19 to 45 years. Credit was given for participation in the study. The final sample sizes used in the analyses were **359** for beer and television sets and **330** for cars.

RELIABILITY:

Alphas for the products studied by Mishra, Umesh, and Stem (1993) were **.94**, **.94**, and **.96** for beer, cars, and television sets, respectively.

VALIDITY:

Mishra, Umesh, and Stem (1993) did not specifically examine the validity of the scale.

ADMINISTRATION:

The scale was self-administered along with other measures after subjects had been exposed to stimulus information (Mishra, Umesh, and Stem 1993). A high score on the scale means that a respondent describes some information as being very relevant to an activity.

MAJOR FINDINGS:

Mishra, Umesh, and Stem (1993) performed a causal analysis of the attraction effect that occurs when the introduction of a relatively inferior "decoy" brand increases (rather than decreases) choice probability of an existing target brand. The results showed that for three different products, the attraction effect decreased as the perceived **information relevance** increased.

REFERENCE:

Mishra, Sanjay, U. N. Umesh, and Donald E. Stem, Jr. (1993), ''Antecedents of the Attraction Effect: An Information-Processing Approach,'' *JMR*, 30 (August), 331-49.

SCALE ITEMS: INFORMATION RELEVANCE

Not at all ___ : ___ : ___ : ___ : ___ : ___ : ___ Very much
      1   2   3   4   5   6   7

1. How relevant was the information?
2. How meaningful was the information?
3. How important was the information?
4. How useful was the information?
5. How helpful was the information?

SCALE NAME: Innovativeness (Product Specific)

SCALE DESCRIPTION:

A six-item, five-point, Likert-type scale measuring the tendency to learn about and adopt innovations (new products) within a specific domain of interest. The scale is intended to be distinct from a generalized personality trait on one extreme and a highly specific single-product purchase at the other.

SCALE ORIGIN:

The scale was constructed by Goldsmith and Hofacker (1991). Their desire was to develop a short, flexible measure of consumer innovativeness modeled after the King and Summers (1970) measure of opinion leadership.

SAMPLES:

Goldsmith and Hofacker (1991) described six different studies as being used to examine various aspects of the scale's reliability and validity. Study 1 was composed of **309** complete questionnaires from 151 men and 157 women with a mean age of 21.6 years. The data were collected by 31 college students in a marketing research class who were each asked to conduct personal interviews with five males and five females. In Study 2, researchers asked 28 marketing research students to have five men and five women self-administer the scale. This produced **275** usable questionnaires from 146 males and 129 females with a mean age of 21.5 years. Study 3 was based on **97** completed questionnaires collected by two male interviewers. The all-female sample had a mean age of 22.1 years. A mall intercept approach was used in Study 4 to collect data. Highly trained interviewers gathered usable information from **462** adults. The sample had the following characteristics: 44% had at least a college degree, 48.7% were under 30 years of age, 40% were married, 64.1% were white, and a little more than half (51.3%) were female. In Study 5, the scale's stability was assessed by administering a questionnaire to **75** students in a marketing research class. Fifteen weeks later, **70** of the same students filled out the scale again. Finally, Study 6 was composed of completed questionnaires from **306** respondents. The data were collected by students in two marketing research classes from 152 males and 154 females with a mean age of 21.3 years.

RELIABILITY:

Due to the multiple studies described previously, Goldsmith and Hofacker (1991) reported several examinations of the scale's internal consistency. The following alphas were calculated: **.83** (Study 2, records); **.82** (Study 3, records); **.79** (Study 4, fashion); **.81** (Study 4, electronics); **.88** (Study 5, records, n = 75) and **.90** (Study 4, records, n = 70); and **.85**, **.83**, and **.83** for records, fashion, and scent, respectively, in Study 6. The stability of the scale as measured in Study 5 was .86.

VALIDITY:

Goldsmith and Hofacker (1991) examined validity of the scale in detail. Data from Study 2 were subjected to both exploratory and confirmatory factor analysis with similar results: the items loaded on the same factor and were unidimensional. Also in Study 2, a pattern of significant positive correlations with seven criterion measures provided evidence of the scale's criterion validity. Studies 3, 4, and 5 had results very similar to Study 2 in that the evidence supported the notion that the scale was unidimensional and had criterion validity. In addition, Study 5 provided evidence of discriminant validity in that the scale was not significantly correlated with yea-saying or social desirability bias. Study 6 measured innovativeness in three product categories (music, fashion, scent). Using a multitrait-multimethod approach, the authors concluded that there was strong evidence of convergent and discriminant validity.

ADMINISTRATION:

As noted previously, the six studies conducted by Goldsmith and Hofacker (1991) involved two main types of administration: in most studies, the scale was administered as part of a personal interview, but in the others it was included in a self-administered questionnaire. High scores on the scale indicate that consumers not only have knowledge and interest about new products in a specified category but perceive themselves to be among the first to purchase those new items.

MAJOR FINDINGS:

The purpose of the studies by Goldsmith and Hofacker (1991) was to provide evidence of the **innovativeness** scale's psychometric quality. This appears to have been accomplished. They further showed that, although the items are Likert-type statements, they seem to be amenable for use in several product categories. Among the interesting findings not described here were that for both records and fashion, high correlations were found between innovativeness and opinion leadership. Also, though record **innovativeness** was not related to **innovativeness** for fashion or scent, the latter two were significantly associated.

COMMENTS:

The authors say that the scale is most appropriate for studying products in categories that are purchased rather frequently. Products that are bought often may not be measured as well with this scale because there are fewer attitudes and behavior for consumers to draw on in making their responses.

For other uses of the scale see Goldsmith and Flynn (1992) as well as Flynn and Goldsmith (1993).

REFERENCES:

Flynn, Leise R. and Ronald E. Goldsmith (1993), "Identifying Innovators in Consumer Service Markets," *The Service Industries Journal*, 13 (July), 9-109.

Goldsmith, Ronald E. and Leise Reinecke Flynn (1992), ''Identifying Innovators in Consumer Markets,'' *European Journal of Marketing*, 26 (12), 42-55.

———— and Charles F. Hofacker (1991), ''Measuring Consumer Innovativeness,'' *JAMS*, 19 (Summer), 209-21.

King, Charles W. and John O. Summers (1970), ''Overlap of Opinion Leadership Across Consumer Product Categories,'' *JMR*, 7 (February), 43-50.

SCALE ITEMS: INNOVATIVENESS (PRODUCT SPECIFIC)

Disagree ____ : ____ : ____ : ____ : ____ Agree
         1   2   3   4   5

1. In general, I am among the last in my circle of friends to buy a new rock album when it appears. **(r)**
2. If I heard that a new rock album was available in the store, I would not be interested enough to buy it. **(r)**
3. Compared to my friends I own few rock albums. **(r)**
4. In general, I am the last in my circle of friends to know the titles of the latest rock albums. **(r)**
5. I will buy a new rock album, even if I haven't heard it yet.
6. I know the names of new rock acts before other people do.

SCALE NAME: Intention to Choose Best Alternative

SCALE DESCRIPTION:

A three-item, Likert-type summated ratings scale measuring a person's description of his/her intention in a recently completed consumption-related choice activity to select the best product alternative among those available.

SCALE ORIGIN:

The scale is original to the work of Cooper-Martin (1993, 1994).

SAMPLES:

A convenience sample of **36** women was used by Cooper-Martin (1993). The women were from the New York City area and were paid $25 for participating. The mean age was 34 years and ranged from 18 to 70 years.

RELIABILITY:

Cooper-Martin (1993) reported an alpha of **.63** for the scale.

VALIDITY:

Cooper-Martin (1993) did not specifically address the validity of the scale, though it was said that a factor analysis indicated that this scale and another scale (*cognitive effort*) were independent. In work not reported in the article, a factor analysis was performed on six items and indicated that the three listed here loaded on the same factor (Cooper-Martin 1994).

ADMINISTRATION:

The scale was administered along with other measures after subjects had been exposed to experimental stimuli. A high score on the scale indicates that a respondent believes that in some particular choice activity in which he/she had engaged, his/her intention was to select the best alternative available.

MAJOR FINDINGS:

Cooper-Martin (1993) examined how the degree of similarity among product alternatives may affect cognitive effort and **intention to choose the best alternative**. Among the findings was that **intention to choose the best alternative** was lower for a similar set of alternatives than for a dissimilar set. However, this appears to be sensitive to the product category involved because it held for one (mugs) but not the other (sweaters).

REFERENCES:

Cooper-Martin, Elizabeth (1993), "Effects of Information Format and Similarity Among Alternatives on Consumer Choice Processes," *JAMS*, 21 (Summer), 239-46.

_____ (1994), personal correspondence.

SCALE ITEMS: INTENTION TO CHOOSE BEST ALTERNATIVE*

1. When I was making this choice, any _____ that seemed satisfactory was OK. I didn't need to find the absolute best _____. **(r)**

Strongly disagree	___ :	___ :	___ :	___ :	___ :	___ :	___	Strongly agree
	1	2	3	4	5	6	7	

2. It was not very important to me to choose the best _____. **(r)**

Strongly disagree	___ :	___ :	___ :	___ :	___ :	___ :	___	Strongly agree
	1	2	3	4	5	6	7	

3. Please check the one phrase that best describes this particular choice. I was looking for:

- _____ any _____.
- _____ a _____ that was good enough but not necessarily the best for me, of the ones on the table.
- _____ the best _____ for me, of the ones on the table.

* Items were supplied by Cooper-Martin (1994a). The name of the product category should be placed in the blanks. In item 3, the first answer is coded as a 1, the second answer as a 4, and the last answer as a 7. Moreover, the wording of item 3 may have to be modified slightly to accommodate the particular research conditions in which it is used.

SCALE NAME: Intention to Recommend School

SCALE DESCRIPTION:

A six-item summated rating measuring the degree to which a person indicates an inclination to recommend a business school to others. The scale appears to be intended for a current student of a MBA program. Five of the items have seven-point Likert-type response scales and one has a yes/no format.

SCALE ORIGIN:

Although not explicitly stated, the scale appears to be original to Boulding and colleagues (1993) and is fully described in Boulding and colleagues (1992).

SAMPLES:

Boulding and colleagues (1993) collected data from **177** students of a business education institution. Participation was voluntary but was apparently stimulated to some extent by a lottery and cash prizes.

RELIABILITY:

An alpha of **.80** was reported for the scale (Boulding et al. 1993).

VALIDITY:

Neither study reported examination of the scale's validity.

ADMINISTRATION:

The scale was apparently self-administered by students, but the details were not provided by Boulding and colleagues (1993). A high score on the scale suggests a respondent plans on recommending an educational institution to others as well as donating money.

MAJOR FINDINGS:

Boulding and colleagues (1993) describe two studies bearing on a behavioral process model. Among the many findings was that perceptions of an educational institution's quality have a significant positive relationship with a student's **intention to recommend** the school to others.

REFERENCES:

Boulding, William, Ajay Kalra, Richard Staelin, and Valerie A. Zeithaml (1993), ''A Dynamic Process Model of Service Quality: From Expectations to Behavioral Intentions,'' *JMR*, 30 (February), 7-27.

_____, Richard Staelin, Ajay Kalra, and Valerie A. Zeithaml (1992), *Conceptu-*

alizing and Testing a Dynamic Process Model of Service Quality, Working paper No. 92-121. Cambridge, MA: Marketing Science Institute.

SCALE ITEMS: INTENTION TO RECOMMEND SCHOOL*

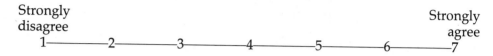

Strongly
disagree
1————2————3————4————5————6————7
Strongly
agree

1. I would recommend this organization to my employer as a place to recruit MBA students.
2. I would recommend this organization as a place to get an MBA.
3. I plan to contribute to the class pledge upon graduation.
4. I plan to contribute money to this organization after graduation.
5. When talking to people about this organization outside the school, I say positive things.
6. Would you recommend this organization to a friend applying to business schools? No (0) Yes (7)

* The first five items use the Likert-type response scales, and item 6 has only yes/no response alternatives.

SCALE NAME: Interaction With Health Care Professionals

SCALE DESCRIPTION:

A six-item, seven-point summated rating scale measuring the frequency with which one contacts professionals in the health care industry for information about health-related issues.

SCALE ORIGIN:

The scale was developed by Moorman and Matulich (1993). Development and refinement of the many scales used in their study generally followed the Churchill (1979) paradigm. Measures were pretested on 67 undergraduate students. Then in the main test, the scales were purified further using alpha, item-total correlations, and LISREL.

SAMPLES:

Moorman and Matulich (1993) used two sampling techniques to obtain respondents who differed on the variables under examination. First, a stratified sample with low and high income as well as young and elderly strata was taken. Respondents from the two income strata were obtained by randomly selecting from lower- and higher-income neighborhoods in Milwaukee and Madison, Wisconsin. Respondents representing the elderly segment were selected randomly from adult centers and retirement communities. Data for young consumers was retained from the pretest (students in an introductory marketing class). In the second sample, survey forms were mailed to addresses of those randomly selected from the telephone books of the two previously mentioned cities. The total number of usable questionnaires was 404, indicating about a 51% overall response rate. A dollar was enclosed with the questionnaires received by all respondents as a token of appreciation and incentive to return the form.

RELIABILITY:

Moorman and Matulich (1993) reported an alpha of .72 for the scale.

VALIDITY:

Although specific details about this scale were not provided in the article, Moorman and Matulich (1993) engaged in various purification activities in both the pretest and the main study for all of their scales. At the least then, it would appear that evidence was collected that indicated the scale was unidimensional and internally consistent.

ADMINISTRATION:

The scale was self-administered along with many other measures in a questionnaire (Moorman and Matulich 1993). A high score on the scale indicates

that a person reports very frequent contact with health professionals for the purpose of gathering health-related information.

MAJOR FINDINGS:

Moorman and Matulich (1993) presented and tested a model of the impact various consumer characteristics have on some health-related behaviors. Among the findings was that people with high health motivation as well as control had significantly more **interaction with health care professionals**.

COMMENTS:

Moorman and Matulich (1993) reported the mean score of the sample on the scale to be 4.01 with a standard deviation of 1.11.

REFERENCES:

Churchill, Gilbert A., Jr. (1979), "A Paradigm for Developing Better Measures of Marketing Constructs," *JMR*, 16 (February), 64-73.
Moorman, Christine and Erika Matulich (1993), "A Model of Consumers' Preventive Health Motivation and Health Ability," *JCR*, 20 (September), 208-28.

SCALE ITEMS: INTERACTION WITH HEALTH PROFESSIONALS

On the scale below please indicate how much you utilize the following sources of health information.*

None of the time	__ : __ : __ : __ : __ : __ : __	All of the time
	1 2 3 4 5 6 7	

1. Doctors
2. Other health care professionals (e.g., physical therapist)
3. Pharmacist
4. Obtain a physical exam
5. See my dentist for a checkup
6. Visit my eye doctor

* The instructional statement was not provided in the article but is recreated on the basis of the description provided there.

SCALE NAME: Interest

SCALE DESCRIPTION:

A three-item, five-point summated ratings scale assessing a person's experience of the interest-related emotion. The directions and response scale can be worded so as to measure the *intensity* of the emotional state at the present time, or they can be adjusted to measure the *frequency* with which a person has experienced the emotional trait during some specified time period. One-word items were used in the study by Westbrook and Oliver (1991), and phrases based on those same items were used by Allen, Machleit, and Kleine (1992).

SCALE ORIGIN:

The measure was developed by Izard (1977) and is part of the Differential Emotions Scale (DES II). The instrument was designed originally as a measure of a person's emotional "state" at a particular point in time, but adjustments in the instrument's instructions enable the same items to be used in the assessment of emotional experiences as perceived over a longer time period. The latter was viewed by Izard as measure of one's emotional "trait" (1977, p. 125). Test-retest reliability for the interest subscale of DES II was reported to be .76 (n = 63) and item-factor correlations were .79 and more (Izard 1977, p. 126). Beyond this evidence, several other studies have provided support for the validity of the scale, even in consumption settings (e.g., Westbrook 1987).

The items in DES II were composed solely of one word. In contrast, the items in DES III are phrases describing the target emotion. They were developed by Izard, although the first published validity testing was conducted by Kotsch, Gerbing, and Schwartz (1982). A study by Allen, Machleit, and Marine (1988) provides some insight to the factor structure of both DES II and III. The results indicate that when presented with the other DES items, the interest items typically load together and not with items supposed to measure other emotions.

SAMPLES:

The data used by Allen, Machleit, and Kleine (1992) came from a stratified sample of people of diverse experience with blood donation. Nine hundred questionnaires were mailed and 361 usable forms were returned. Given that all respondents had previously donated blood, limited information was known about them and allowed a comparison with nonrespondents. Respondents were a little older, less likely to be male, and more likely to be heavier donors than nonrespondents.

The data for the study conducted by Westbrook and Oliver (1991) came from a judgmental area sample. Convenience samples were taken at four shopping centers in a large northeastern city and were limited to persons who had purchased a new or used car in the past year. Complete and usable questionnaires were obtained from 125 respondents. A majority (74%) of the sample was male. The average respondent had an income in the $25,000–$40,000 range and was 33 years of age. The frequency version of the scale was used in this study.

Two samples were used in the study by Oliver (1993), one examining satisfaction with cars and the other examining course satisfaction. The one involving cars is the same as the one described previously in Westbrook and Oliver (1991). The other sample was composed of students who volunteered from nine sections of a required marketing class. Usable questionnaires were provided by **178** students. The intensity version of the scale was used in this study.

RELIABILITY:

Allen, Machleit, and Kleine (1992; Allen 1994) and Westbrook and Oliver (1991) calculated alphas of **.82** and **.77**, respectively, for the scale. Oliver (1993) reported alphas of **.82** (n = 125) and **.77** (n = 178).

VALIDITY:

No specific examination of the scale's validity was reported in any of the studies.

ADMINISTRATION:

The scale was included with many other measures in the instrument used by Westbrook and Oliver (1991), Oliver (1993), and Allen, Machleit, and Kleine (1992). High scores on the frequency version of the scale suggest that a respondent perceives him/herself as having experienced the interest-related emotional trait very often in some specified time period. A high score on the intensity version of the scale indicates that one is feeling very attentive at the time of measurement.

MAJOR FINDINGS:

The study by Allen, Machleit, Kleine (1992) examined whether emotions affect behavior through attitudes or are better viewed as having a separate and distinct impact. Although several emotions were found to play a key role in predicting behavior, **interest** (DES III) was not found to have a significant relationship, at least with regard to donating blood.

The separate roles of positive and negative affect, attribute performance, and disconfirmation were examined by Oliver (1993) for their impact on satisfaction. Positive affect was viewed as a function of two emotions, joy and **interest**. For both samples, positive affect was found to have direct influence on satisfaction, but **interest** by itself only had a significant effect on satisfaction with one sample (college course evaluation).

Westbrook and Oliver (1991) studied the correspondence of the consumption emotional responses and satisfaction judgments that occur in the postpurchase period of the consumer decision process. **Interest** had its highest correlation with fear (r = .33) and its lowest correlation with surprise (r = .08). **Interest** also was found to be a primary emotional trait linked to a high-satisfaction experience.

REFERENCES:

Allen, Chris T. (1994), personal correspondence.

_____, Karen A. Machleit, and Susan Schultz Kleine (1992), "A Comparison of Attitudes and Emotions as Predictors of Behavior at Diverse Levels of Behavioral Experience," *JCR*, 18 (March), 493-504.

_____, _____, and Susan S. Marine (1988), "On Assessing the Emotionality of Advertising Via Izard's Differential Emotions Scale," in *Advances in Consumer Research*, 226-31.

Izard, Carroll E. (1977), *Human Emotions*. New York: Plenum Press.

Kotsch, William E., Davis W. Gerbing, and Lynne E. Schwartz (1982), "The Construct Validity of the Differential Emotions Scale as Adapted for Children and Adolescents," in *Measuring Emotions in Infants and Children*, Carroll E. Izard, ed. New York: Cambridge University Press, 251-78.

Oliver, Richard L. (1993), "Cognitive, Affective, and Attribute Bases of the Satisfaction Response," *JCR*, 20 (December), 418-30.

Westbrook, Robert A. (1987), "Product/Consumption-Based Affective Responses and Postpurchase Processes," *JMR*, 24 (August), 258-70.

_____ and Richard L. Oliver (1991), "The Dimensionality of Consumption Emotion Patterns and Consumer Satisfaction," *JCR*, 18 (June), 84-91.

SCALE ITEMS: INTEREST

POSSIBLE DIRECTIONS FOR FREQUENCY VERSION OF SCALE: Below is a list of words that you can use to show how you feel. We want you to tell us how often you felt each of these feelings _____.* You can tell us how often you felt each of these feelings on the list by marking one of the numbers next to each question.

Almost never   ____ : ____ : ____ : ____ : ____   Very often
                  1   2   3   4   5

POSSIBLE DIRECTIONS FOR INTENSITY VERSION OF SCALE: Below is a list of words that you can use to show how you feel. We want you to tell us how strongly you feel. You can tell us how strongly you feel each of these feelings on the list by marking one of the numbers next to each question.

Very weak   ____ : ____ : ____ : ____ : ____   Very strong
                  1   2   3   4   5

DES II
1. attentive
2. concentrating
3. alert

DES III
1. feel like what you're doing or watching is interesting
2. feel so interested in what you're doing, caught up in it
3. feel alert, kind of curious about something

* The blank should be used to specify the time period of interest such as "during the last week."

SCALE NAME: Interest (Object)

SCALE DESCRIPTION:

A four-item, seven-point Likert-type scale measuring the degree to which a person reports desiring to know more about a some specified object. The scale was referred to by Machleit, Allen, and Madden (1993) as *Brand Interest*.

SCALE ORIGIN:

The scale was constructed by Machleit, Madden, and Allen (1990). Beginning with 11 items, their refinement process ended up with a 4-item scale that showed unidimensionality and discriminant validity for two very different products. Alphas for the scale were more than .80.

SAMPLES:

Machleit, Allen, and Madden (1993) gathered data from students in two sections of a college marketing course. **Eighty** students completed both the pre- and post-exposure questionnaires. Forty-two watched a Pepsi ad, and 38 were exposed to a Levi's ad.

RELIABILITY:

Machleit, Allen, and Madden (1993) reported alphas of **.90** and **.88** for pre-and post-exposure measures, respectively, regarding Levi's. Likewise, alphas of **.91** and **.89** were reported for pre- and post-measures, respectively, involving Pepsi.

VALIDITY:

Using confirmatory factor analysis, Machleit, Allen, and Madden (1993) found strong evidence that the scale was unidimensional and that it showed discriminant validity in comparison with several related measures such as brand attitude.

ADMINISTRATION:

In Machleit, Allen, and Madden (1993), subjects filled out the measure both before and after being exposed to an ad. High scores on the scale indicate greater interest, curiosity, and desire to know more about some specified object such as a brand.

MAJOR FINDINGS:

Machleit, Allen, and Madden (1993) proposed and examined a new model of advertising effects that introduced **brand interest** as a key component of the hierarchy of effects for mature brands. Indeed, the findings indicated that ad-evoked affect affected **brand interest** (but not brand attitude) and further that **brand interest** influenced contact intention (but not purchase intention).

REFERENCES:

Machleit, Karen A., Chris T. Allen, and Thomas J. Madden (1993), ''The Mature Brand and Brand Interest: An Alternative Consequence of Ad-Evoked Affect,'' *JM*, 57 (October), 72-82.

_____, Thomas J. Madden, and Chris T. Allen (1990), ''Measuring and Modeling Brand Interest as an Alternative AINF/ad Effect With Familiar Brands,'' in *Advances in Consumer Research*, Vol. 17, Marvin E. Goldberg, Gerald Gorn, and Richard W. Pollay, eds. Provo, UT: Association for Consumer Research, 223-30.

SCALE ITEMS: INTEREST (OBJECT)*

Strongly disagree	___ : ___ : ___ : ___ : ___ : ___ : ___	Strongly agree
	1 2 3 4 5 6 7	

1. I am intrigued by _____.
2. I'd like to know more about _____.
3. Learning more about _____ would be useless. **(r)**
4. I'm a little curious about _____.

* The name of the object being examined should put in the blanks.

SCALE NAME: Internal Search Tendency

SCALE DESCRIPTION:

A three-item, seven-point, Likert-like scale measuring the probability that a consumer would base his/her decision on the purchase of a product on his/her memories of relevant past experiences. The measure was referred to by Murray (1985) as *past personal experience*.

SCALE ORIGIN:

The scale was developed by Murray (1985) in his dissertation research. The same data are used for Murray (1991).

SAMPLES:

The sample was composed of **256** students attending Arizona State University. Nearly 53% of the sample was female and the mean age was nearly 24 years of age. Students were assigned randomly to one of 15 different treatments systematically varied in terms of the "serviceness" of the three products to which they responded.

RELIABILITY:

A mean alpha of **.836** was reported for the scale averaged over 15 different products systematically varied in their service attributes. For products with high, moderate, and low service attributes, mean alphas of .751, .724, and .738, respectively, were reported. Because the reliability of the scale was calculated across 15 products, it was not based on responses to any one product.

VALIDITY:

No information regarding the scale's validity was reported.

ADMINISTRATION:

The scale was administered as part of a larger questionnaire to students in a classroom setting. Low scores on the scale suggest that respondents would base a purchase decision on what has been learned from past experiences, whereas high scores imply that respondents would gather information before making a purchase.

MAJOR FINDINGS:

The purpose of the study by Murray (1991) was to determine if consumers use information sources in a distinctive way for products varying in their "serviceness." The results indicated that the self-reported tendency to rely on **internal search** is greater for products high in service attributes.

COMMENTS:

The items in this scale are part of a 25-item battery, which can be administered together to measure several aspects of a consumer's pre-purchase search activity.

REFERENCES:

Murray, Keith B. (1985), "Risk Perception and Information Source Use For Products Differing in Service Attributes," doctoral dissertation, Arizona State University: Tempe, Arizona.

_____ (1991), "A Test of Services Marketing Theory: Consumer Information Acquisition Activities," *JM*, 55 (January), 10-25.

SCALE ITEMS: INTERNAL SEARCH TENDENCY

Circle the number that best describes your reaction to each statement if you were considering the purchase of a _____.

Definitely would	= 1
Generally would	= 2
Would be inclined to	= 3
May or may not	= 4
Would not be inclined to	= 5
Generally would not	= 6
Definitely would not	= 7

1. . . . think about my previous involvement with this type of product or service.
2. . . . rely on past personal experience.
3. . . . try to recall relevant events which I can associate with this product or service.

SCALE NAME: Interpersonal Influence Susceptibility (Media-Normative)

SCALE DESCRIPTION:

A three-item, five-point, Likert-type summated ratings scale measuring the degree to which a teenager describes the media as having a major influence on what he/she buys.

SCALE ORIGIN:

This scale is original to Mascarenhas and Higby (1993).

SAMPLES:

Mascarenhas and Higby (1993) collected data in 1990 from **234** teenagers. Convenience samples of teens were taken from two comparable high schools, one a private school in suburban Philadelphia and the other a public school in suburban Detroit. Students completed the scale for both an ordinary purchase situation (inexpensive, everyday apparel items) and a special shopping situation (expensive, occasionally worn items).

RELIABILITY:

Mascarenhas and Higby (1993; Higby 1994) calculated alphas of **.510** and **.575** for the scale as applied to the ordinary and special purchase situations, respectively.

VALIDITY:

Mascarenhas and Higby (1993) reported that, in general, the loadings on the scales composing the TII were significant (.31) and that there were no significant cross loadings. Other information is provided which bears on the issue of nomological validity.

ADMINISTRATION:

The scale was self-administered by students in Mascarenhas and Higby (1993). High scores on the scale indicate that the respondents (teenagers) are very sensitive to media influences on their purchase decisions.

MAJOR FINDINGS:

Mascarenhas and Higby (1993) examined the interpersonal influences that affect teen decision making in apparel shopping. All the other sources of information measured were more significantly influential than **media-normative** sources.

COMMENTS:

Mascarenhas and Higby (1993) reported the mean scores on the ordinary and special applications of the scale to be 1.95 (SD = .799) and 1.93 (SD = .883), respectively. As a word of caution, the level of internal consistency is low enough to indicate that the scale lacks strong reliability and therefore is in need of further development.

REFERENCES:

Higby, Mary A. (1994), personal correspondence.
Mascarenhas, Oswald A. J. and Mary A. Higby (1993), ''Peer, Parent, and Media Influences in Teen Apparel Shopping,'' *JAMS*, 21 (Winter), 53-58.

SCALE ITEMS: INTERPERSONAL INFLUENCE (MEDIA-NORMATIVE)

Strongly disagree ___ : ___ : ___ : ___ : ___ Strongly agree
1 2 3 4 5

1. I buy only those products/brands that are advertised on TV, radio & teen magazines.
2. Radio & TV ads determine my brand loyalties.
3. I continue buying the same brands as long as my favorite rock stars endorse them.

SCALE NAME: Interpersonal Influence Susceptibility (Parent-Informative)

SCALE DESCRIPTION:

A three-item, five-point, Likert-type summated ratings scale measuring the degree to which a person (child, teenager) describes seeking information and advice from his/her parents before making purchase decisions.

SCALE ORIGIN:

This scale is original to Mascarenhas and Higby (1993).

SAMPLES:

Mascarenhas and Higby (1993) collected data in 1990 from **234** teenagers. Convenience samples of teens were taken from two comparable high schools, one a private school in suburban Philadelphia and the other a public school in suburban Detroit. Students completed the scale for both an ordinary purchase situation (inexpensive, everyday apparel items) and a special shopping situation (expensive, occasionally worn items).

RELIABILITY:

Mascarenhas and Higby (1993; Higby 1994) calculated alphas of **.534** and **.616** for the scale as applied to the ordinary and special purchase situations, respectively.

VALIDITY:

Mascarenhas and Higby (1993) reported that, in general, the loadings on the scales composing the TII were significant (.31) and that there were no significant cross loadings. Other information is provided which bears on the issue of nomological validity.

ADMINISTRATION:

The scale was self-administered by students in Mascarenhas and Higby (1993). High scores on the scale indicate that respondents (probably teenagers) often seek advice from their parents before making purchase decisions.

MAJOR FINDINGS:

Mascarenhas and Higby (1993) examined the interpersonal influences that affect teen decision making in apparel shopping. **Parent-informative** information sources were significantly more influential than all the other sources studied.

COMMENTS:

Mascarenhas and Higby (1993) reported the mean scores on the ordinary and special applications of the scale to be 2.73 (SD = .894) and 3.16 (SD = .994), respectively. As a word of caution, the level of internal consistency is low enough to indicate that the scale lacks strong reliability and therefore is in need of further development.

REFERENCES:

Higby, Mary A. (1994), personal correspondence.

Mascarenhas, Oswald A.J. and Mary A. Higby (1993), ''Peer, Parent, and Media Influences in Teen Apparel Shopping,'' *JAMS*, 21 (Winter), 53-58.

SCALE ITEMS: INTERPERSONAL INFLUENCE (PARENT-INFORMATIVE)

Strongly disagree   ___ : ___ : ___ : ___ : ___   Strongly agree
                        1   2   3   4   5

1. I never buy any new product until my parents and I have discussed it.
2. When I do not understand prices and quality I consult my parents.
3. I often discuss my purchase plans with my parents.

SCALE NAME: Interpersonal Influence Susceptibility (Parent-Normative)

SCALE DESCRIPTION:

A five-item, five-point, Likert-type summated ratings scale measuring the degree to which a child describes parents as determining where, when, and what he/she buys.

SCALE ORIGIN:

This scale is original to Mascarenhas and Higby (1993), but they appear to have drawn inspiration from the measures developed by Bearden, Netemeyer, and Teel (1989). This is just one of the six Teen Interpersonal Influence (TII) scales the former team developed and used.

SAMPLES:

Mascarenhas and Higby (1993) collected data in 1990 from **234** teenagers. Convenience samples of teens were taken from two comparable high schools, one a private school in suburban Philadelphia and the other a public school in suburban Detroit. Students completed the scale for both an ordinary purchase situation (inexpensive, everyday apparel items) and a special shopping situation (expensive, occasionally worn items).

RELIABILITY:

Mascarenhas and Higby (1993; Higby 1994) calculated alphas of **.715** and **.721** for the scale as applied to the ordinary and special purchase situations, respectively.

VALIDITY:

Mascarenhas and Higby (1993) reported that, in general, the loadings on the scales composing the TII were significant (.31) and that there were no significant cross loadings. Other information is provided which bears on the issue of nomological validity.

ADMINISTRATION:

The scale was self-administered by students in Mascarenhas and Higby (1993). High scores on the scale indicate that purchases made by and for the respondents are heavily influenced if not controlled by parents.

MAJOR FINDINGS:

Mascarenhas and Higby (1993) examined the interpersonal influences that affect teen decision making in apparel shopping. **Parent- normative** information sources were one of the least influential of all of the types of sources measured.

COMMENTS:

Mascarenhas and Higby (1993) reported the mean scores on the ordinary and special applications of the scale to be 1.95 (SD = .732) and 2.38 (SD = .877), respectively.

REFERENCES:

Bearden, William O., Richard G. Netemeyer, and Jesse E. Teel (1989), "Measurement of Consumer Susceptibility to Interpersonal Influence," *JCR*, 15 (March), 473-81.

Higby, Mary A. (1994), personal correspondence.

Mascarenhas, Oswald A. J. and Mary A. Higby (1993), "Peer, Parent, and Media Influences in Teen Apparel Shopping," *JAMS*, 21 (Winter), 53-58.

SCALE ITEMS: INTERPERSONAL INFLUENCE (PARENT-NORMATIVE)

Strongly disagree   ___ : ___ : ___ : ___ : ___   Strongly agree
                                1   2   3   4   5

1. I always follow my parents' decisions by buying the same products & brands
2. My parents accompany me when I purchase.
3. What, where, and which brand I buy are very much determined by my parents.
4. I always shop with my parents.
5. My parents decide all my shopping needs.

SCALE NAME: Interpersonal Influence Susceptibility (Peer-Informative)

SCALE DESCRIPTION:

A four-item, five-point, Likert-type summated ratings scale measuring the degree to which a person communicates with friends before deciding what to buy. The scale was developed for use with teenagers but appears to be amenable for use with other age groups, though some testing may be necessary.

SCALE ORIGIN:

This scale is original to Mascarenhas and Higby (1993), but they built on a scale used previously by Bearden, Netemeyer, and Teel (1989). This is just one of the six Teen Interpersonal Influence (TII) scales the former team developed and used.

SAMPLES:

Mascarenhas and Higby (1993) collected data in 1990 from **234** teenagers. Convenience samples of teens were taken from two comparable high schools, one a private school in suburban Philadelphia and the other a public school in suburban Detroit. Students completed the scale for both an ordinary purchase situation (inexpensive, everyday apparel items) and a special shopping situation (expensive, occasionally worn items).

RELIABILITY:

Mascarenhas and Higby (1993; Higby 1994) calculated alphas of **.564** and **.510** for the scale as applied to the ordinary and special purchase situations, respectively.

VALIDITY:

Mascarenhas and Higby (1993) reported that, in general, the loadings on the scales composing the TII were significant (.31) and that there were no significant cross loadings. Other information is provided which bears on the issue of nomological validity.

ADMINISTRATION:

The scale was self-administered by students in Mascarenhas and Higby (1993). High scores on the scale indicate that respondents are very interested in what their peers think regarding products, fads, and fashions and they seek information from them before buying things.

MAJOR FINDINGS:

Mascarenhas and Higby (1993) examined the interpersonal influences that affect teen decision-making in apparel shopping. **Peer-informative** sources of information were significantly more influential than all other normative sources but were the least influential of the informative sources.

COMMENTS:

Mascarenhas and Higby (1993) reported the mean scores on the ordinary and special applications of the scale to be 2.33 (SD = .798) and 2.40 (SD = .789), respectively. As a word of caution, the level of internal consistency is low enough to indicate that the scale lacks strong reliability and therefore is in need of further development.

REFERENCES:

Bearden, William O., Richard G. Netemeyer, and Jesse E. Teel (1989), ''Measurement of Consumer Susceptibility to Interpersonal Influence,'' *JCR*, 15 (March), 473-81.

Higby, Mary A. (1994), personal correspondence.

Mascarenhas, Oswald A. J. and Mary A. Higby (1993), ''Peer, Parent, and Media Influences in Teen Apparel Shopping,'' *JAMS*, 21 (Winter), 53-58.

SCALE ITEMS: INTERPERSONAL INFLUENCE (PEER-INFORMATIVE)

Strongly disagree ___ : ___ : ___ : ___ : ___ Strongly agree

  1   2   3   4   5

1. I regularly ask my friends regarding the latest fads and fashions.
2. I always talk to friends about prices and quality before I buy.
3. To make sure I buy the right product, I often watch my friends buy.
4. My siblings always talk to me about the ads before I buy anything.

SCALE NAME: Interpersonal Influence Susceptibility (Peer-Normative)

SCALE DESCRIPTION:

A seven-item, five-point, Likert-type summated ratings scale measuring the degree to which a person expresses the need to have friends' approval of where and what he/she buys. The scale was developed for use with teenagers but appears to be amenable for use with other age groups, though some testing may be necessary.

SCALE ORIGIN:

This scale is original to Mascarenhas and Higby (1993), but they built on a scale used previously by Bearden, Netemeyer, and Teel (1989). This is just one of the six Teen Interpersonal Influence (TII) scales the former team developed and used.

SAMPLES:

Mascarenhas and Higby (1993) collected data in 1990 from **234** teenagers. Convenience samples of teens were taken from two comparable high schools, one a private school in suburban Philadelphia and the other a public school in suburban Detroit. Students completed the scale for both an ordinary purchase situation (inexpensive, everyday apparel items) and a special shopping situation (expensive, occasionally worn items).

RELIABILITY:

Mascarenhas and Higby (1993; Higby 1994) calculated alphas of **.687** and **.672** for the scale as applied to the ordinary and special purchase situations, respectively.

VALIDITY:

Mascarenhas and Higby (1993) reported that, in general, the loadings on the scales composing the TII were significant (.31) and that there were no significant cross loadings. Other information is provided which bears on the issue of nomological validity.

ADMINISTRATION:

The scale was self-administered by students in Mascarenhas and Higby (1993). High scores on the scale indicate that respondents are very sensitive to what others think regarding purchase decisions and want to conform to group norms.

MAJOR FINDINGS:

Mascarenhas and Higby (1993) examined the interpersonal influences that affect teen decision making in apparel shopping. All the other sources of information measured were more significantly influential than **peer-normative** sources except for parent- and media-normative.

COMMENTS:

Mascarenhas and Higby (1993) reported the mean scores on the ordinary and special applications of the scale to be 2.05 (SD = .660) and 2.10 (SD = .660), respectively.

REFERENCES:

Bearden, William O., Richard G. Netemeyer, and Jesse E. Teel (1989), "Measurement of Consumer Susceptibility to Interpersonal Influence," *JCR*, 15 (March), 473-81.

Higby, Mary A. (1994), personal correspondence.

Mascarenhas, Oswald A. J. and Mary A. Higby (1993), "Peer, Parent, and Media Influences in Teen Apparel Shopping," *JAMS*, 21 (Winter), 53-58.

SCALE ITEMS: INTERPERSONAL INFLUENCE (PEER-NORMATIVE)

Strongly disagree ___ : ___ : ___ : ___ : ___ Strongly agree
                   1   2   3   4   5

1. I rarely purchase the latest products until I am sure my peers approve of them.
2. It is important that my peers approve of the store where I buy.
3. Am very loyal to stores where my peers shop.
4. If I want to be like my peers, I always buy the brands they buy.
5. I work long hours and save to afford the things my friends buy.
6. I achieve a sense of belonging by buying the same brands my peers buy.
7. My peers very much influence the choice of my shopping friends.

SCALE NAME: Involvement (Choice Task)

SCALE DESCRIPTION:

A four-item, seven-point summated ratings scale measuring the degree of involvement a person reports having with a particular decision-making activity.

SCALE ORIGIN:

There is nothing to indicate that the scale is anything other than original to the research reported by Mishra, Umesh, and Stem (1993).

SAMPLES:

The sample used by Mishra, Umesh, and Stem (1993) was composed of undergraduate and graduate students attending a large university. The mean age of the subjects was 22 years and ranged from 19 to 45 years. Credit was given for participation in the study. The final sample sizes used in the analyses were **359** for beer and television sets and **330** for cars.

RELIABILITY:

Alphas for the products studied by Mishra, Umesh, and Stem (1993) were **.93**, **.89**, and **.95** for beer, cars, and television sets, respectively.

VALIDITY:

Mishra, Umesh, and Stem (1993) did not specifically examine the validity of the scale.

ADMINISTRATION:

The scale was self-administered along with other measures after subjects had been exposed to stimulus information (Mishra, Umesh, and Stem 1993). A high score on the scale means that a respondent reports being very involved in the specified choice activity.

MAJOR FINDINGS:

Mishra, Umesh, and Stem (1993) performed a causal analysis of the attraction effect that occurs when the introduction of a relatively inferior ''decoy'' brand increases (rather than decreases) choice probability of an existing target brand. The results showed that for three different products, the attraction effect decreased as the **task involvement** increased.

REFERENCE:

Mishra, Sanjay, U.N. Umesh, and Donald E. Stem, Jr. (1993), "Antecedents of the Attraction Effect: An Information-Processing Approach," *JMR*, 30 (August), 331-49.

SCALE ITEMS: INVOLVEMENT (CHOICE TASK)

Not at all ____ : ____ : ____ : ____ : ____ : ____ : ____ Very much
          1   2   3   4   5   6   7

1. How stimulating was the choice task?
2. How enjoyable was the choice task?
3. How interesting was the choice task?
4. How exciting was the choice task?

SCALE NAME: Involvement (Coupons)

SCALE DESCRIPTION:

An eight-item, seven-point, Likert-type scale measuring the increased probability of a consumer to purchase a product if the purchase offer is in coupon form. A shorter four-item version was used by Lichtenstein, Ridgway, and Netemeyer (1993). In both studies by Lichtenstein and colleagues (1990, 1993) the scale was referred to as *Coupon Proneness*.

SCALE ORIGIN:

The scale is original to Lichtenstein, Netemeyer, and Burton (1990). Five marketing academicians judged the appropriateness of 33 items generated to represent the construct. Twenty-five items remained after this procedure. On the basis of a second round of five additional judges assessing the face validity of the items, all items were retained.

The items were then interspersed throughout a questionnaire given to 263 undergraduate and graduate business students. The eight items composing the final version of the scale were those that had corrected item-total correlations equal to or greater than .40. Confirmatory factor analysis provided evidence that the items were unidimensional and had discriminant validity. The construct reliability was calculated to be .88.

SAMPLES:

The data for the main study by Lichtenstein, Netemeyer, and Burton (1990) came from a convenience sample of **350** nonstudent adults from a medium-size SMSA. The majority of the sample was female (57%) and married (69%). College graduates composed 40% of the sample. The median age of respondents was between 35 and 44 years old and household income was between $30,000 and $39,999.

Lichtenstein, Ridgway, and Netemeyer (1993) collected data from shoppers who had received questionnaires in one of two grocery stores in a western SMSA (Boulder, Colorado). One thousand questionnaires were handed out at the stores, and **582** usable ones were returned by mail. A majority of the sample was female (75.9%) and married (58.6%). The median annual income range was $35,000–$49,999 and the median age range was 35 to 44 years.

RELIABILITY:

Lichtenstein, Netemeyer, and Burton (1990) calculated the internal consistency of the scale to be **.88** and item-total correlations were more than .40. The main study by Lichtenstein, Ridgway, and Netemeyer (1993) also showed an alpha for the scale of **.88**.

VALIDITY:

Confirmatory factor analysis was used by Lichtenstein and colleagues (1990, 1993) in both studies to conclude that the scale was unidimensional and showed evidence of discriminant validity. In the latter study it was stated that after using CFA, items with low standardized factor loadings were dropped. This is likely to be the reason that fewer items composed the scale in the later study.

ADMINISTRATION:

Lichtenstein, Netemeyer, and Burton (1990) did not describe the manner in which the scale was administered to the subjects in their study. However, it was clear that the scale was just one of many measures that composed the survey instrument. In the study by Lichtenstein, Ridgway, and Netemeyer (1993), the scale was part of a survey instrument self-administered by shoppers after leaving the grocery store. High scores on the scale indicate that respondents get a lot of enjoyment out of using coupons, whereas low scores suggest little or no involvement with coupons.

MAJOR FINDINGS:

Lichtenstein, Netemeyer, and Burton (1990) examined the effect of both value consciousness and **coupon involvement** on coupon redemption behavior. One of the major findings was that value consciousness explained a significant amount of variance in redemption behavior after accounting for **coupon involvement**.

Lichtenstein, Ridgway, and Netemeyer (1993) identified and measured seven related but distinct price perception constructs. The dependent variable that **coupon involvement** predicted most strongly was coupon redemption frequency (self-reported).

REFERENCES:

Lichtenstein, Donald R., Richard D. Netemeyer, and Scot Burton (1990), "Distinguishing Coupon Proneness From Value Consciousness: An Acquisition-Transaction Utility Theory Perspective," *JM*, 54 (July), 54-67.

_____, Nancy M. Ridgway, and Richard G. Netemeyer (1993), "Price Perceptions and Consumer Shopping Behavior: A Field Study," *JMR*, 30 (May), 234-45.

SCALE ITEMS: INVOLVEMENT (COUPONS)*

Strongly disagree ___ : ___ : ___ : ___ : ___ : ___ : ___ Strongly agree

          1   2   3   4   5   6   7

1. Redeeming coupons makes me feel good.
2. I enjoy clipping coupons out of the newspapers.
3. When I use coupons, I feel that I am getting a good deal.
4. I enjoy using coupons, regardless of the amount I save by doing so.

5. I have favorite brands, but most of the time I buy the brand I have a coupon for.
6. I am more likely to buy brands for which I have a coupon.
7. Coupons have caused me to buy products I normally would not buy.
8. Beyond the money I save, redeeming coupons gives me a sense of joy.

* All the items were used by Lichtenstein, Netemeyer, and Burton (1990), but only items 1-4, and 8 were used by Lichtenstein, Ridgway, and Netemeyer (1993).

SCALE NAME: Involvement (Enduring)

SCALE DESCRIPTION:

A 20-item, seven-point semantic differential scale measuring the enduring and intrinsic (rather than situational) relevance of an object to a person. The scale is easily customized to measure involvement with a product category, a particular brand, an ad for a particular brand, or a particular purchase decision. Its originator (Zaichkowsky 1985) referred to he scale as *Personal Involvement Inventory* (PII). A 16-item version has been used by Mick (1992); 9- and 11-item versions of the scale were used by Lichtenstein and colleagues (1988; 1990); a 4-item version has been used by Mittal (1990) as well as Singh and Cole (1993); and a 3-item variation of the scale was used by Maheswaran and Meyers-Levy (1990). (For a greatly modified version of the scale, see Steenkamp and Wedel 1991, where store involvement was measured in Holland. Also see McQuarrie and Munson 1987 for another modified version of the scale [RPII].)

SCALE ORIGIN:

Although previous research was reviewed and may have provided ideas for scale items, the scale as a unit was generated and tested first by Zaichkowsky (1985). Construction of the scale used four data sets of 286 undergraduate psychology students, two data sets with 49 MBA students, and two data sets with 57 clerical and administrative staff members. The stability of the measure was checked over two subject groups for four products producing test-retest correlations from .88 to .93. Internal consistency was calculated with the same data as ranging from .95 to .97 (Cronbach's alpha). Content validity was demonstrated by the scale through use of expert judges at two points: first, by reducing the list of word pairs to those most appropriate for measuring the construct; and second, by successful classification of open-ended statements from subjects. Criterion validity was examined by demonstrating the similarity between subjects' average involvement levels with four products and the expected degree of involvement on the basis of previous studies. Construct validity was checked for three products by noting the association between subjects' scale scores and their statements of behavior expected to reflect involvement. For each of the three products, there was a positive relationship between scale scores and responses to statements.

The scale used by Maheswaran and Meyers-Levy (1990) may not have been directly derived from the Zaichkowsky measure and is very short but is similar enough to be viewed here as measuring the same thing.

SAMPLES:

Subjects for the experiment by Celsi and Olson (1988) were **91** undergraduate students, **10** graduate students, **20** adult residents of the local community, and **15** present or former members of university tennis teams. Subjects ages ranged from 17 to 79 years, with a mean of 23 years. Fifty-one percent of the sample were female.

Survey instruments were completed by **148** subjects in the experiment conducted by Gotlieb and Sarel (1991). The subjects were all selected from a pool of upperclasspersons attending a large urban university and were assigned randomly to treatments in a 2 × 2 × 2 factorial experimental design.

Very little description was provided about the sample used by Gotlieb and Swan (1990). The study was a 2 × 2 × 2 factorial experiment with **126** college students. Fifty-nine percent of the students had visited a lawyer in the last five years.

Data were gathered by Laczniak and Muehling (1993) from **280** students in introductory marketing classes. The experiment took place in an college auditorium and students were assigned randomly to one of 12 treatment conditions.

Lichtenstein and colleagues (1988) mailed questionnaires to 1800 participants in a regional running event. Analysis was based on the **452** persons who responded within five weeks. Compared with the area's general population, the respondents were more likely to be younger and male and have higher education and income. The data for the main study by Lichtenstein, Netemeyer, and Burton (1990) came from a convenience sample of **350** nonstudent adults from a medium-size SMSA. The majority of the sample was female (57%) and married (69%). College graduates composed 40% of the sample. The median age of respondents was between 35 to 44 years and household income was between $30,000 and $39,999.

Machleit, Allen, and Madden (1993) gathered data from students in two sections of a college marketing course. **Eighty** students completed both the pre- and post-exposure questionnaires. Forty-two watched a Pepsi ad, and 38 were exposed to a Levi's ad.

The study conducted by Maheswaran and Meyers-Levy (1990) used a sample of **98** undergraduate students who received extra course credit for participating. The data were gathered from small groups of students (5–7 at a time) and then analyzed as a 2 × 2 factorial design.

The experiment conducted by Mick (1992) was based on data collected from **161** (53% female) undergraduates attending a large U.S. university. Students received extra credit for their participation and were also eligible for participation in a drawing for a new CD player.

The data gathered by Miller and Marks (1992) came from **124** undergraduate marketing students attending a large midwestern U.S. university. Volunteers were compensated for their participation with extra credit points.

The sample used by Mishra, Umesh, and Stem (1993) was composed of undergraduate and graduate students attending a large university. The mean age of the subjects was 22 years and ranged from 19 to 45 years. Credit was given for participation in the study. The final sample sizes used in the analyses were **359** for beer and television sets and **330** for cars.

Mittal (1990) reported on two studies. In the first he collected data from **83** undergraduate students meeting in a large auditorium. Students saw two ads of research interest, one for wine and the other for shampoo. In the second study, data were gathered from **60** more students, but in this case only half saw the wine ad and the other half saw the shampoo ad.

Data related to the **involvement** scale were collected by Singh and Cole (1993) separately from that gathered for their main experiment. Information came from two groups of 23 undergraduate students (n = **46**).

RELIABILITY:

Alphas of **.97** and **.95** were reported by Gotlieb and Swan (1990) and Gotlieb and Sarel (1991), respectively. An alpha of **.97** was calculated for the scale by Laczniak and Muehling (1993; Muehling 1994). The reliabilities (LISREL estimates) of the condensed versions of the scale used by Lichtenstein and colleagues (1988; 1990) were calculated to be **.93** and **.90**, respectively. The short scales used by Maheswaran and Meyers-Levy (1990), Mick (1992), and Singh and Cole (1993) were reported to have alphas of **.89**, **.96**, and **.81**, respectively. An alpha of **.94** was calculated for the scale as used by Miller and Marks (1992; Marks 1994). Alphas of **.966** and **.969** were calculated by Machleit, Allen, and Madden (1993; Allen 1994) for involvement with blue jeans and soft drinks, respectively. Alphas of **.98**, **.94**, and **.97** were calculated in the study by Mishra, Umesh, and Stem (1993) for beer, car, and television involvement, respectively (Mishra 1994). No test of reliability was reported by Celsi and Olson (1988) or Mittal (1990).

VALIDITY:

No test of validity was reported by Celsi and Olson (1988), Gotlieb and Sarel (1991), Gotlieb and Swan (1990), Laczniak and Muehling (1993), Lichtenstein and colleagues (1988; 1990), Machleit, Allen, and Madden (1993), Maheswaran and Meyers-Levy (1990), Miller and Marks (1992), Mishra, Umesh, and Stem (1993), Mittal (1990), or Singh and Cole (1993).

A factor analysis of the 20-item scale performed by Mick (1992) produced a two-factor solution. Only the 16 items loading strongly on the first factor were retained for calculating scale scores.

ADMINISTRATION:

The scale was given by Celsi and Olson (1988) as a screening instrument to 400 college students and adults in unspecified settings; Lichtenstein and colleagues (1988) administered it in a mail survey along with many other measures. Lichtenstein and colleagues (1990) did not describe the manner in which the scale was administered in their study, but the scale was just one of many measures that composed the survey instrument. The scale was administered by Maheswaran and Meyers-Levy (1990) along with several other measures in an experiment after subjects had read some test material. Gotlieb and Sarel (1991), Laczniak and Muehling (1993), Miller and Marks (1992), and Singh and Cole (1993) had subjects complete the scale along with other measures after exposure to experimental stimuli. In the study by Mick (1992), the scale was self-administered by subjects in a phase four weeks prior to the exposure to experimental stimuli. Gotlieb and Swan (1990) say little about the setting in which they administered the scale.

Scores are calculated by summing numerical responses to items, reverse coding when necessary. A low scores suggests that a respondent has little involvement with the object. A high score implies that people are very interested and personally involved with the object. The objects examined in the studies were playing tennis (Celsi and Olson 1988); VCRs (Gotlieb and Sarel

1991); legal services (Gotlieb and Swan 1990); 35mm cameras (Laczniak and Muehling 1993) running shoes (Lichtenstein et al. 1988); regularly purchased grocery products (Lichtenstein et al. 1990); diagnostic blood tests (Maheswaran and Meyers-Levy 1990); and lawnmowers and tires (Miller and Marks 1992).

MAJOR FINDINGS:

The purpose of the Celsi and Olson (1988) study was to examine the effects of enduring and situational involvement on felt involvement as well as on information processing of print advertising. It was found that subjects' knowledge of tennis was correlated significantly with their enduring involvement with the sport. Both enduring and situational involvement affected felt involvement, the former having a substantially larger impact. Enduring **involvement** was also significantly related to time spent processing ads and cognitive effort exerted during the processing of ads.

The role of **involvement** and source credibility on the influence of comparative advertising was studied by Gotlieb and Sarel (1991). The findings indicated that when there is high **involvement** with a product and high credibility of the message's source, comparative advertising for a new brand has a greater positive impact than noncomparative ads on purchase intentions.

Gotlieb and Swan (1990) investigated the influence of price savings on motivation to process a message. As hypothesized, ads featuring price savings were associated with higher levels of **involvement** than ads without price savings.

Several manipulations of advertising message involvement were tested by Laczniak and Muehling (1993). They were compared for their ability to place people into high- and low-involvement groups. The **involvement** scale was not used to test a hypothesis but merely to determine whether product **involvement** was significantly different between the manipulation groups.

Lichtenstein and colleagues (1988) examined the cognitive tradeoffs consumers make between price and product quality. The findings indicated that there was a positive relationship between product **involvement** and price-quality inferences as well as price acceptability level but that it was inversely correlated with price consciousness. The study by Lichtenstein and colleagues (1990) examined the effect of both value consciousness and coupon involvement on coupon redemption behavior. One of the major findings was that value consciousness had a much greater positive relationship with **enduring involvement** (grocery products) than did coupon involvement.

Machleit, Allen, and Madden (1993) proposed and examined a new model of advertising effects that introduced brand interest as a key component of the hierarchy of effects for mature brands. Very little was said in the article about **involvement** except that it was significantly higher for blue jeans than for soft drinks given the sample used.

Maheswaran and Meyers-Levy (1990) examined the persuasiveness of different ways to frame a message and the role played by issue **involvement**. A manipulation check was made among the treatments and determined that significantly different levels of **involvement** had been induced in the subjects.

Mick (1992) studied the levels of subjective comprehension in terms of its effect on various attitudes and memory. **Involvement** was measured merely to provide evidence that the product chosen for study (CD players) was associated with high **involvement** for the study group.

Miller and Marks (1992) investigated the impact of sound effects on processing and reactions to advertisements. The **product involvement** scale was not used to test any hypotheses but to determine if there was a significant difference between treatment groups on that factor. No significant difference was detected.

Mishra, Umesh, and Stem (1993) performed a causal analysis of the attraction effect that occurs when the introduction of a relatively inferior ''decoy'' brand increases (rather than decreases) choice probability of an existing target brand. The measure of product **involvement** was used merely as a manipulation check. Involvement was highest for cars, and lowest for beer, and involvement with television sets was in between. (No test for statistical significance was reported.)

The two studies reported on by Mittal (1990) examined the effect of image-related brand beliefs on brand attitudes. Involvement was not an experimental variable of interest and was reported merely for purposes of comparison with further studies. In both studies product **involvement** appeared to be substantially higher for shampoo than for wine. (A test for statistical significance was not reported.)

Singh and Cole (1993) evaluated the relative effectiveness of 15-second and 30-second commercials. The **involvement** scale was used as a manipulation check with a sample independent of the main study. The findings indicated that there was no significant variation in **involvement** across the four product categories under study.

COMMENTS:

Zaichkowsky (1985) admitted that a smaller number of items composing the scale might be almost as reliable as the 20-item version but warned against haphazardly reducing the number of items. She also pointed out that although the scale could be used for various purposes, her work had focused mainly on demonstrating its quality regarding product involvement. More research was called for to verify its quality for other objects such as ads and purchase decisions.

Lichtenstein and colleagues (1988) do not say how they determined which items of the full scale to use in their condensed version. See also Lord and Burnkrandt (1993), Machleit, Allen, and Madden (1993) and Mano and Oliver (1993) for other uses of the scale.

REFERENCES:

Allen, Chris T. (1994), personal correspondence.

Celsi, Richard L. and Jerry C. Olson (1988), ''The Role of Involvement in Attention and Comprehension Processes,'' *JCR*, 15 (September), 210-24.

Gotlieb, Jerry B. and Dan Sarel (1991), ''Comparative Advertising Effectiveness: The Role of Involvement and Source Credibility,'' *JA*, 20 (1), 38-45.

———— and John E. Swan (1990), ''An Application of the Elaboration Likelihood Model,'' *JAMS*, 18 (Summer), 221-28.

Laczniak, Russell N. and Darrel D. Muehling (1993), ''The Relationship Between Experimental Manipulations and Tests of Theory in an Advertising Message Involvement Context,'' *JA*, 22 (September), 59-74.

Lichtenstein, Donald R., Peter H. Bloch, and William C. Black (1988), ''Correlates of Price Acceptability,'' *JCR*, 15 (September), 243-52.

————, Richard D. Netemeyer, and Scot Burton (1990), ''Distinguishing Coupon Proneness From Value Consciousness: An Acquisition-Transaction Utility Theory Perspective,'' *JM*, 54 (July), 54-67.

Lord, Kenneth R. and Robert E. Burnkrant (1993), ''Attention Versus Distraction: The Interactive Effect of Program Involvement and Attentional Devices on Commercial Processing,'' *JA*, 22 (March), 47-60.

Maheswaran, Durairja and Joan Meyers-Levy (1990), ''The Influence of Message Framing and Issue Involvement,'' *JMR*, 27 (August), 361-67.

Machleit, Karen A., Chris T. Allen, and Thomas J. Madden (1993), ''The Mature Brand and Brand Interest: An Alternative Consequence of Ad-Evoked Affect,'' *JM*, 57 (October), 72-82.

Mano, Haim and Richard L. Oliver (1993), ''Assessing the Dimensionality and Structure of the Consumption Experience: Evaluation, Feeling, and Satisfaction,'' *JCR*, 20 (December), 451-66.

Marks, Lawrence J. (1994), personal correspondence.

McQuarrie, Edward F. and J. Michael Munson (1987), ''The Zaichkowsky Personal Inventory: Modification and Extension,'' in *Advances in Consumer Research*, Vol. 14, Melanie Wallendorf and Paul Anderson, eds. Provo, UT: Association for Consumer Research, 36-40.

Mick, David Glen (1992), ''Levels of Subjective Comprehension in Advertising Processing and Their Relations to Ad Perceptions, Attitudes, and Memory,'' *JCR*, 18 (March), 411-24.

Miller, Darryl W. and Lawrence J. Marks (1992), ''Mental Imagery and Sound Effects in Radio Commercials,'' *JA*, 21 (4), 83-93.

Mishra, Sanjay (1994), personal correspondence.

————, U.N. Umesh, and Donald E. Stem, Jr. (1993), ''Antecedents of the Attraction Effect: An Information-Processing Approach,'' *JMR*, 30 (August), 331-49.

Mittal, Banwari (1990), ''The Relative Roles of Brand Beliefs and Attitude Toward the Ad as Mediators of Brand Attitude: A Second Look,'' *JMR*, 27 (May), 209-19.

Muehling, Darrel D. (1994), personal correspondence.

Singh, Surendra N. and Catherine Cole (1993), ''The Effects of Length, Content, and Repetition on Television Commercial Effectiveness,'' *JMR*, 30 (February), 91-104.

Steenkamp, Jan-Benedict E.M. and Michel Wedel (1991), ''Segmenting Retail Markets on Store Image Using a Consumer-Based Methodology,'' *JR*, 67 (Fall), 300-320.

Zaichkowsky, Judith L. (1985), ''Measuring the Involvement Construct,'' *JCR*, 12 (December), 341-52.

SCALE ITEMS: INVOLVEMENT (ENDURING)*

(name of object)

1. Important ___:___:___:___:___:___:___ Unimportant (r)
   1 2 3 4 5 6 7

2. Of no concern ___:___:___:___:___:___:___ Of concern to me
   1 2 3 4 5 6 7

3. Irrelevant ___:___:___:___:___:___:___ Relevant
   1 2 3 4 5 6 7

4. Means a lot to me ___:___:___:___:___:___:___ Means nothing to me (r)
   1 2 3 4 5 6 7

5. Useless ___:___:___:___:___:___:___ Useful
   1 2 3 4 5 6 7

6. Valuable ___:___:___:___:___:___:___ Worthless (r)
   1 2 3 4 5 6 7

7. Trivial ___:___:___:___:___:___:___ Fundamental
   1 2 3 4 5 6 7

8. Beneficial ___:___:___:___:___:___:___ Not beneficial (r)
   1 2 3 4 5 6 7

9. Matters to me ___:___:___:___:___:___:___ Doesn't matter (r)
   1 2 3 4 5 6 7

10. Uninterested ___:___:___:___:___:___:___ Interested
    1 2 3 4 5 6 7

11. Significant ___:___:___:___:___:___:___ Insignificant (r)
    1 2 3 4 5 6 7

12. Vital ___:___:___:___:___:___:___ Superfluous (r)
    1 2 3 4 5 6 7

13. Boring ___:___:___:___:___:___:___ Interesting
    1 2 3 4 5 6 7

14. Unexciting ___:___:___:___:___:___:___ Exciting
    1 2 3 4 5 6 7

15. Appealing ___:___:___:___:___:___:___ Unappealing (r)
    1 2 3 4 5 6 7

16. Mundane ___:___:___:___:___:___:___ Fascinating
    1 2 3 4 5 6 7

17. Essential ___:___:___:___:___:___:___ Nonessential (r)
    1 2 3 4 5 6 7

18. Undesirable ___ : ___ : ___ : ___ : ___ : ___ : ___ Desirable
            1   2   3   4   5   6   7

19. Wanted ___ : ___ : ___ : ___ : ___ : ___ : ___ Unwanted (r)
            1   2   3   4   5   6   7

20. Not needed ___ : ___ : ___ : ___ : ___ : ___ : ___ Needed
            1   2   3   4   5   6   7

21. Not involved ___ : ___ : ___ : ___ : ___ : ___ : ___ Highly involved
            1   2   3   4   5   6   7

* Items are numerically coded from 1 (left) to 7 (right). The first 20 items are those used by Zaichkowsky (1985) as well as Miller and Marks (1992; Marks 1994). The 9 items used by Lichtenstein and colleagues (1988) were 1-6, 8, 17, and 20. The 11 items used by Lichtenstein and colleagues (1990) were 1-4, 6, 8, 9, 13 to 15, and 17. Maheswaran and Joan Meyers-Levy (1990) used short phrases based on items 3, 10, 21. It is not clear which four items were used by Mittal (1990) and Singh and Cole (1993). The four items *not* used by Mick (1992) were 7, 12, 17, and 20.

SCALE NAME: Involvement (Experiment)

SCALE DESCRIPTION:

A four-item, seven-point semantic differential scale measuring the level of involvement a subject reports with regard to an experimental exercise that he/she has just engaged in. The exercise studied by Swinyard (1993) was a retail shopping experience.

SCALE ORIGIN:

The origin of the scale was not described by Swinyard (1993), but it appears to be original.

SAMPLES:

Little description was provided about the sample used by Swinyard (1993) in his experiment except to say that it was composed of **109** undergraduate business students. Another person besides the class instructor conducted the experiment, and students were monitored to ensure that they worked quietly and independently on their randomly assigned exercises.

RELIABILITY:

Swinyard (1993) reported an alpha of **.82** for the scale.

VALIDITY:

Swinyard (1993) reported no examination of the scale's validity.

ADMINISTRATION:

The scale was self-administered by subjects as part of a questionnaire after exposure to experimental stimuli (Swinyard 1993). A high score on the scale indicates that a respondent in an study feels that the research exercise he/she participated in was involving and personally relevant.

MAJOR FINDINGS:

Swinyard (1993) investigated the impact of mood and other factors on shopping intentions. The **involvement** scale used a manipulation check, which was considered to be successful. Among the findings was that mood effects are greater in a more **involving** shopping experience.

REFERENCE:

Swinyard, William R. (1993), ''The Effects of Mood, Involvement, and Quality of Store Experience on Shopping Intentions,'' *JCR*, 20 (September), 271-80.

SCALE ITEMS: INVOLVEMENT (EXPERIMENT)

During the store exchange experience with the slacks did you feel:*

Uninvolved	___ : ___ : ___ : ___ : ___ : ___ : ___ 1 2 3 4 5 6 7	Involved
Not absorbed	___ : ___ : ___ : ___ : ___ : ___ : ___ 1 2 3 4 5 6 7	Absorbed
Not stimulated	___ : ___ : ___ : ___ : ___ : ___ : ___ 1 2 3 4 5 6 7	Stimulated
It was not personally relevant	___ : ___ : ___ : ___ : ___ : ___ : ___ 1 2 3 4 5 6 7	It was personally relevant

* This is the lead-in phrase used by Swinyard (1993), but it may be adjusted depending on the study and the exercise in which subjects engage.

SCALE NAME: Involvement (Processing Nutritional Information)

SCALE DESCRIPTION:

A three-item, summated ratings scale measuring the degree to which people say they are interested and exhibit behaviors that indicate concern about nutritional information on food packaging. The scale was referred to as *Enduring Motivation To Process* by Moorman (1990).

SCALE ORIGIN:

As specified in personal correspondence, the scale was developed by Moorman (1990).

SAMPLES:

The sample used by Moorman (1990) came from the staff at a northeastern U.S. university. On the basis of a list of staff, a systematic sample of people was contacted by mail. (Because of the nature of the research, those staff employed in health-related areas were dropped from the list.) Of the 274 employees sent a letter, **180** completed the experiment. Incentives to participate were in the form of dollar bills in each of the initial letters of contact and eligibility to win more money if subjects cooperated fully.

RELIABILITY:

Moorman (1990) reported an alpha of **.92** for the scale.

VALIDITY:

On the basis of personal correspondence, the only validation of the scale came from using principal components analysis with Varimax rotation. The items composing the scale loaded high on a single factor and not on factors used to compose other scales.

ADMINISTRATION:

The scale was included along with several other measures on a pre-experimental questionnaire sent to subjects along with the initial letter of contact. High scores on the scale appear to indicate that respondents have an ongoing involvement in reading nutrition-related information on products while in a grocery store.

MAJOR FINDINGS:

Moorman (1990) examined the influence of consumer and stimulus characteristics on the use of nutrition information. In general, both types of characteristics were found to affect information processing and decision quality. **Involve-**

ment was not one of the main variables of interest in the investigation but was found to have a positive effect on ability to process nutritional information.

REFERENCE:

Moorman, Christine (1990), ''The Effects of Stimulus and Consumer Characteristics on the Utilization of Nutrition Information,'' *JCR*, 17 (December), 362-74.

SCALE ITEMS: INVOLVEMENT (PROCESSING NUTRITIONAL INFORMATION)

None of
the time
All of
the time
1————2————3————4————5————6————7

1. How often do you read nutritional labels?
2. How interested are you in reading nutrition and health-related information at the grocery store?
3. How often do you read nutrition labels at the grocery store?

SCALE NAME: Involvement (Product)

SCALE DESCRIPTION:

A six-item, seven-point Likert-type measure of the interest a person reports having in some specified product category. The measure was referred to as *interest in cars* by Srinivasan and Ratchford (1991).

SCALE ORIGIN:

Although not expressly stated in the article, the scale appears to have been used first in published research by Srinivasan and Ratchford (1991), which was based on the dissertation of Srinivasan (1987). Some initial assessment of scale reliability and face validity was made in pre-test stage of the study.

SAMPLES:

A sample of new car buyers was obtained by Srinivasan and Ratchford (1991) through a mail survey of new car registrants in the Buffalo, New York area. More than three thousand people were sent three mailings of the questionnaire and, ultimately **1401** usable responses were received. No demographic description is provided of the respondents.

RELIABILITY:

Srinivasan and Ratchford (1991) reported an alpha of **.86** for the scale.

VALIDITY:

Srinivasan and Ratchford (1991) provided no discussion of this scale's validity.

ADMINISTRATION:

The scale was used by Srinivasan and Ratchford (1991) along with other measures in a mail survey instrument. A low score on the scale indicates that a respondent is very interested in some specified product, whereas a high score suggests that a respondent cares very little about the product.

MAJOR FINDINGS:

Srinivasan and Ratchford (1991) examined a model of the determinants of external search for new car purchases. As hypothesized, product involvement had a positive impact on both perceived search benefits and search effort. With the former, the effect was large relative to the other variables tested, whereas with the latter the effect was relatively small.

COMMENTS:

The purchase decision focused on in Srinivasan and Ratchford (1991) was for new cars. Except for item 5, the scale appears to be adaptable to other products, although its reliability and validity would need to be reexamined.

REFERENCES:

Srinivasan, Narasimhan (1987), ''A Causal Model of External Search for Information for Durables: A Particular Investigation in the Case of New Automobiles,'' doctoral dissertation, State University of New York at Buffalo.

_____ and Brian T. Ratchford (1991), ''An Empirical Test of a External Search for Automobiles,'' *JCR*, 18 (September), 233-42.

SCALE ITEMS: INVOLVEMENT (PRODUCT)

DIRECTIONS: There are no right or wrong answers to the following statements and a large number of people agree and disagree. Kindly indicate *your* personal opinion by circling any one number for each statement.

```
Strongly                                                    Strongly
agree                                                       disagree
   1———————2———————3———————4———————5———————6———————7
```

1. I have a great interest in _____.
2. _____ are fascinating.
3. I have a compulsive need to know more about _____.
4. I'm crazy about _____.
5. I like _____ races.
6. I like to engage in conversation about _____.

SCALE NAME: Involvement (Product Class)

SCALE DESCRIPTION:

A five-item, seven-point summated ratings scale measuring various aspects (knowledge, use, importance) of a consumer's involvement with a specified product category.

SCALE ORIGIN:

The origin of the scale is not specified by Keller (1991a, 1991b), but it is apparently the same or similar to the scale he used previously (1987) and was original to that use. Keller drew on earlier work by Batra and Ray (1986) as well as Lutz, MacKenzie, and Belch (1983), who used multiple items to examine constructs such as knowledge, importance, and motivation (although the items they used were not summated).

SAMPLES:

The study by Keller (1991a) was based on data collected from **103** adults who were either members of a local PTA or employees of a large private university. A majority of the sample was female (89%), half had at least a college degree, and half were 40 years of age or older. For their participation, either subjects received a small fee and participated in a lottery or a contribution was made to their organization. Subjects were assigned randomly to experimental conditions.

Keller (1991b) conducted an experiment using data collected from **145** undergraduate students attending a large west coast U.S. university. Involvement was required for credit in a basic marketing course.

RELIABILITY:

Keller (1991a, 1991b) reported alphas of **.71** and **.74** for the scale.

VALIDITY:

Keller (1991a, 1991b) reported no information regarding the scale's validity.

ADMINISTRATION:

The scale was included with other measures in the questionnaires used by Keller (1991a, 1991b) and was given to subjects after they were exposed to experimental stimuli. High scores on the scale indicate that respondents are very involved with some particular product category, whereas low scores suggest that respondents have little interest in and usage of the product.

MAJOR FINDINGS:

Keller (1991a) tested three propositions regarding conditions under which retrieval cues should work. **Product class involvement** was incorporated in the study only as a covariate. It produced no main effects and did not interact with any of the experimental variables.

In a similar study, Keller (1991b) examined how competitive advertising and retrieval cues influence memory and brand judgments. As with the previous study, **product class involvement** was tested only as a covariate. The only experimental factor with which involvement was significantly related was correct claims recall. This suggests that higher levels of claims recall were produced by greater **class involvement**.

REFERENCES:

Batra, Rajeev and Michael L. Ray (1986), "Situational Effects of Advertising Repetition: The Moderating Influence of Motivation, Ability, and Opportunity to Respond," *JCR*, 12 (March), 432-45.

Keller, Kevin Lane (1987), "Memory Factors in Advertising: The Effect of Advertising Retrieval Cues on Brand Evaluations," *JCR*, 14 (December), 316-33.

———— (1991a), "Cue Compatibility and Framing in Advertising," *JMR*, 28 (February), 42-57.

———— (1991b), "Memory and Evaluation Effects in Competitive Advertising Environments," *JCR*, 17 (March), 463-76.

Lutz, Richard J., Scott B. MacKenzie, and George E. Belch (1983), "Attitude Toward the AD as a Mediator of Advertising Effectiveness: Determinants and Consequences," in *Advances in Consumer Research*, Vol. 10, Richard P. Bagozzi and Alice M. Tybout, eds. Provo, UT: Association for Consumer Research, 532-39.

SCALE ITEMS: INVOLVEMENT (PRODUCT CLASS)

1. How frequently do you make a purchase in each of the following product categories?

Very
infrequently
___ : ___ : ___ : ___ : ___ : ___ : ___
 1   2   3   4   5   6   7
Very
frequently

2. How frequently do you use a brand in each of the following product categories?

Very
infrequently
___ : ___ : ___ : ___ : ___ : ___ : ___
 1   2   3   4   5   6   7
Very
frequently

3. How knowledgeable do you feel you are in each of the following product categories in terms of knowing which features are important in choosing among brands?

Not at all
knowledgeable
___ : ___ : ___ : ___ : ___ : ___ : ___
 1   2   3   4   5   6   7
Very
knowledgeable

4. Please indicate for each product category how important the brand decision is to you. In other words, how much does it matter to you which brand you use in the product category?

Very unimportant   ___ : ___ : ___ : ___ : ___ : ___ : ___   Very important

                     1   2   3   4   5   6   7

5. How much difference in quality do you think exists among the brands available in supermarkets in the following product categories? That is, to what extent do you think the brands in these categories vary in quality?

Very little difference   ___ : ___ : ___ : ___ : ___ : ___ : ___   Very great difference

                     1   2   3   4   5   6   7

SCALE NAME: Involvement (Product Class)

SCALE DESCRIPTION:

A nine-item, seven-point, Likert-type measure of the interest a person reports having in some specified product category.

SCALE ORIGIN:

Although not used as a summated scale, the items originally were developed and analyzed in a study by Lastovicka and Gardner (1979). They proposed that involvement was a multidimensional construct and performed a study using 22 items, 14 products, and 40 subjects (college students). A factor analysis of the items yielded three factors, one of which they referred to as *normative importance*.

SAMPLES:

Muehling, Stoltman, and Grossbart (1990) collected data from **197** male and female undergraduate students who were exposed to either a comparative or a noncomparative advertisement. The sample of **105** used by Muehling, Laczniak, and Stoltman (1991) was the subset of students from the previous sample who were exposed to the noncomparative ad.

RELIABILITY:

Muehling, Laczniak, and Stoltman (1991) and Muehling, Stoltman, and Grossbart (1990) reported alphas of **.86** for the scale.

VALIDITY:

No examination for the scale's validity was reported by Muehling, Laczniak, and Stoltman (1991) or Muehling, Stoltman, and Grossbart (1990). The latter did report that the scale had a beta of .77, which provides some evidence of its unidimensionality.

ADMINISTRATION:

The scale was administered to students as part of a larger survey instrument after they read a booklet that contained the test ad (Muehling, Stoltman, and Grossbart 1990; Muehling, Laczniak, and Stoltman 1991). A high score on the scale indicates that a respondent has a strong involvement with the product class and feels it *should* be important to him/her.

MAJOR FINDINGS:

Muehling, Laczniak, and Stoltman (1991) examined the moderating effect of ad message involvement (AMI) in the context of brand attitude formation. **Product involvement** was not directly examined in the study but along with a measure of product class knowledge was used to form an AMI measure. Those scoring high on AMI were more likely to own, use, and consider buying the item advertised compared with those who scored low.

The purpose of the Muehling, Stoltman, and Grossbart (1990) study was to determine if comparative ads with references to well known competitors were more involving than noncomparative ads. No significant differences in **product involvement** were found between the groups who were exposed to a comparative and those exposed to a noncomparative ad.

COMMENTS:

A database and analysis similar to what is described in Muehling, Laczniak, and Stoltman (1991) and Muehling, Stoltman, and Grossbart (1990) was examined by Muehling and Laczniak (1988), and more discussion of the product involvement scale can be found there.

REFERENCES:

Lastovicka, John L. and David M. Gardner (1979), *Attitude Research Plays for High Stakes*, John C. Maloney and Bernard Silverman, eds. Chicago: American Marketing Association.

Muehling, Darrel D. (1994), personal correspondence.

_____ and Russell N. Laczniak (1988), ''Advertising's Immediate and Delayed Influence on Brand Attitudes: Considerations Across Message-Involvement Levels,'' *JA*, 17 (4), 23-34.

_____, _____, and Jeffrey J. Stoltman (1991), ''The Moderating Effects of Ad Message Involvement: A Reassessment,'' *JA*, 20 (June), 29-38.

_____, Jeffrey J. Stoltman, and Sanford Grossbart (1990), ''The Impact of Comparative Advertising on Levels of Message Involvement,'' *JA*, 19 (4), 4-50.

SCALE ITEMS: INVOLVEMENT (PRODUCT CLASS)

Directions: Indicate your general feelings about _____ by responding to the following statements. Please try to answer in terms of all _____ rather than any particular brand. Please place an ''X'' along each scale to indicate your response.*

				Neither				
Strongly disagree	___ :	___ :	___ :	___ :	___ :	___ :	___	Strongly agree
	1	2	3	4	5	6	7	

1. My use of this product allows others to see me as I would ideally like them to see me.
2. This product helps me to attain the type of life I strive for.
3. I can make many connections or associations between experiences in my life and this product.
4. I definitely have a ''wanting'' for this product.

5. I use this product to help define and express the ''I'' and ''me'' within myself.
6. I rate this product as being of the highest importance to me personally.
7. Because of my personal values, I feel that this is a product that *ought* to be important to me.
8. Use of this product helps me behave in the manner that I would like to behave.
9. Because of what others think, I feel that this is a product that should be important to me.

* These directions and items were provided by Muehling (1994).

SCALE NAME: Involvement (Situational)

SCALE DESCRIPTION:

An 11-item, seven-point semantic differential scale measuring the temporary (rather than enduring and/or intrinsic) relevance of an object to a person. Whereas enduring involvement is ongoing and probably related to a product class, situational involvement is a passing motivation given that it is related to a certain product-related situation. The scale is customized easily to measure involvement with a product category, a particular brand, an ad for a particular brand, or a particular purchase decision.

SCALE ORIGIN:

The items for the scale come from the Personal Involvement Inventory (PII) by its originator (Zaichkowsky 1985). However, that scale was constructed to assess enduring involvement. In contrast, Lichtenstein, Netemeyer, and Burton (1990) have used half of the PII items and specifically modified instructions to measure a distinct though related construct: **situational involvement.**

SAMPLES:

The data for the main study by Lichtenstein, Netemeyer, and Burton (1990) came from a convenience sample of **350** nonstudent adults from a medium-size SMSA. The majority of the sample was female (57%) and married (69%). College graduates composed 40% of the sample. The median age of respondents was between 35 to 44 years and household income was between $30,000 and $39,999.

RELIABILITY:

Lichtenstein, Netemeyer, and Burton (1990) reported the reliability (LISREL estimate) of the scale to be **.96.**

VALIDITY:

Although the scale may have been used to help validate another scale or two developed in the study, no explicit test of the situational involvement scale's validity was reported by Lichtenstein, Netemeyer, and Burton (1990).

ADMINISTRATION:

Lichtenstein, Netemeyer, and Burton (1990) did not describe the manner in which the scale was administered to the subjects in their study. However, it was clear that the scale was just one of many measures that composed the survey instrument. Responses were coded such that more positive answers received higher numbers. These numbers were then summated. A high score indicates that a respondent is highly interested in price-related deals, whereas a low score suggests that a respondent has little or no concern with such things as coupons and rebates.

MAJOR FINDINGS:

The study by Lichtenstein, Netemeyer, and Burton (1990) examined the effect of both value consciousness and coupon involvement on coupon redemption behavior. One of the major findings was that value consciousness had a much lower positive relationship with **situational involvement** (grocery products) than did coupon involvement.

REFERENCES:

Lichtenstein, Donald R., Richard D. Netemeyer, and Scot Burton (1990), "Distinguishing Coupon Proneness From Value Consciousness: An Acquisition-Transaction Utility Theory Perspective," *JM*, 54 (July), 54-67.

Zaichkowsky, Judith L. (1985), "Measuring the Involvement Construct," *JCR*, 12 (December), 341-52.

SCALE ITEMS: INVOLVEMENT (SITUATIONAL)*

Directions: Using coupons, getting rebates, and taking advantage of price deals is:

1. Important ___ : ___ : ___ : ___ : ___ : ___ : ___ Unimportant **(r)**
   1 2 3 4 5 6 7

2. Of no concern ___ : ___ : ___ : ___ : ___ : ___ : ___ Of concern to me
   1 2 3 4 5 6 7

3. Irrelevant ___ : ___ : ___ : ___ : ___ : ___ : ___ Relevant
   1 2 3 4 5 6 7

4. Means a lot to me ___ : ___ : ___ : ___ : ___ : ___ : ___ Means nothing to me **(r)**
   1 2 3 4 5 6 7

5. Valuable ___ : ___ : ___ : ___ : ___ : ___ : ___ Worthless **(r)**
   1 2 3 4 5 6 7

6. Not beneficial ___ : ___ : ___ : ___ : ___ : ___ : ___ Beneficial
   1 2 3 4 5 6 7

7. Matters to me ___ : ___ : ___ : ___ : ___ : ___ : ___ Doesn't matter **(r)**
   1 2 3 4 5 6 7

8. Boring ___ : ___ : ___ : ___ : ___ : ___ : ___ Interesting
   1 2 3 4 5 6 7

9. Unexciting ___ : ___ : ___ : ___ : ___ : ___ : ___ Exciting
   1 2 3 4 5 6 7

10. Unappealing ___ : ___ : ___ : ___ : ___ : ___ : ___ Appealing
                               1   2   3   4   5   6   7

11. Essential ___ : ___ : ___ : ___ : ___ : ___ : ___ Nonessential **(r)**
                            1   2   3   4   5   6   7

* The directions shown here are those as used by Lichtenstein, Netemeyer, and Burton (1990) but would obviously need to change on the basis of the object toward which situational involvement is being measured.

SCALE NAME: Involvement (Social)

SCALE DESCRIPTION:

A three-item, seven-point, Likert-type scale measuring the degree to which a person reports enjoyment of community activities and being around other people.

SCALE ORIGIN:

Wilkes (1992) suggests that the items came from the AIO Item Library (Wells 1971). However, they were not apparent in that list, although they bear some similarity to items found there.

SAMPLES:

Data were collected by Wilkes (1992) from **363** females from three cities in a southwestern state. The ages of respondents ranged from 60 to 79 years. Private, religious, and civic groups were contacted followed by identification of additional groups, and eventually the individuals who were asked to participate. Questionnaires were apparently delivered to respondents' homes and then picked up within a week.

RELIABILITY:

Wilkes (1992) reported a composite reliability of **.88**.

VALIDITY:

A confirmatory factor analysis by Wilkes (1992) indicated that the items had high loadings on a single factor.

ADMINISTRATION:

Data were gathered through self-administered questionnaires in Wilkes (1992). A high score indicates that a respondent likes to be socially involved, whereas a low score suggests that a respondent does not enjoy such interaction and activity.

MAJOR FINDINGS:

Wilkes (1992) studied the measurement characteristics of "cognitive age" and its association with demographic antecedent variables as well as lifestyle-related consequential factors. No significant relationship was found between the cognitive age of women and their **social involvement**. However, among other significant effects that were found, self-confidence had a strong positive impact on **social involvement**.

REFERENCES:

Wells, William D. (1971), "AIO Item Library," unpublished paper, Graduate School of Business, University of Chicago.

Wilkes, Robert E. (1992), "A Structural Modeling Approach to the Measurement and Meaning of Cognitive Age," *JCR*, 19 (September), 292-301.

SCALE ITEMS: INVOLVEMENT (SOCIAL)

Strongly disagree	Disagree	Slightly disagree	Neutral	Slightly agree	Agree	Strongly agree
1	2	3	4	5	6	7

1. I like to be around and involve myself with other people.
2. Taking part in social and community activities is not very important to me. **(r)**
3. I enjoy having people around.

SCALE NAME: Involvement (Study Task)

SCALE DESCRIPTION:

A five-item, seven-point summated rating scale assessing a research subject's interest in and concern about the task he/she is performing as part of the study.

SCALE ORIGIN:

The origin of the scale was not specified by Ozanne, Brucks, and Grewal (1992) but there was nothing to indicate that it was anything other than developed by them for that particular study.

SAMPLES:

Ozanne, Brucks, and Grewal (1992) used a sample composed of 43 undergraduate business majors. The study took place at a major state university, and students agreed to participate in the study as one way to meet a course requirement.

RELIABILITY:

Ozanne, Brucks, and Grewal (1992) reported an alpha for the scale of .72.

VALIDITY:

Ozanne, Brucks, and Grewal (1992) discussed no examination of the scale's validity.

ADMINISTRATION:

The scale was employed by Ozanne, Brucks, and Grewal (1992) as a check on the similarity of subjects in different treatments in their involvement with the experimental task (see "Major Findings"). The scale was scored such that a low score meant that a respondent perceived him/herself to be very involved in the task being performed as part of some study.

MAJOR FINDINGS:

Ozanne, Brucks, and Grewal (1992) examined the information search behavior of consumers with particular regard for the process of categorizing products that differ from previously familiar categories. The **involvement** of subjects in the experimental task was checked to ensure that it was reasonably similar. No differences were found between those people randomly assigned to the luxury car and the economy car conditions.

REFERENCE:

> Ozanne, Julie L., Merrie Brucks, and Dhruv Grewal (1992), "A Study of Information Search Behavior During the Categorization of New Products," *JCR*, 18 (March), 452-63.

SCALE ITEMS: INVOLVEMENT (STUDY TASK)

1. I _____ to do a good job.

Wanted ____ : ____ : ____ : ____ : ____ : ____ : ____ Did not want
      7   6   5   4   3   2   1

2. I _____ care about performance.

Did ____ : ____ : ____ : ____ : ____ : ____ : ____ Did not
    7   6   5   4   3   2   1

3. The study was _____.

Enjoyable ____ : ____ : ____ : ____ : ____ : ____ : ____ Unenjoyable
      7   6   5   4   3   2   1

4. The study was _____. **(r)**

Boring ____ : ____ : ____ : ____ : ____ : ____ : ____ Interesting
     7   6   5   4   3   2   1

5. I _____ participation.

Recommend ____ : ____ : ____ : ____ : ____ : ____ : ____ Do not recommend
      7   6   5   4   3   2   1

SCALE NAME: Joy

SCALE DESCRIPTION:

A three-item, five-point summated ratings scale assessing a person's experience of the joy-related emotion. The directions and response scale can be worded so as to measure the *intensity* of the emotional state at the present time, or they can be adjusted to measure the *frequency* with which a person has experienced the emotional trait during some specified time period. One-word items were used in the study by Westbrook and Oliver (1991), and phrases based on those same items were used by Allen, Machleit, and Kleine (1992).

SCALE ORIGIN:

The measure was developed by Izard (1977) and is part of the Differential Emotions Scale (DES II). The instrument originally was designed as a measure of a person's emotional "state" at a particular point in time, but adjustments in the instrument's instructions enable the same items to be used in the assessment of emotional experiences as perceived over a longer time period. The latter was viewed by Izard as measure of one's emotional "trait" (1977, p. 125). Test-retest reliability for the joy subscale of DES II was reported to be .87 (n = 63) and item-factor correlations were .81 and more (Izard 1977, p. 126). Beyond this evidence, several other studies have provided support for the validity of the scale, even in consumption settings (e.g., Westbrook 1987).

The items in DES II were composed of only one word. In contrast, the items in DES III are phrases describing the target emotion. They were developed by Izard, although the first published validity testing was conducted by Kotsch, Gerbing, and Schwartz (1982). A study by Allen, Machleit, and Marine (1988) provides some insight to the factor structure of both DES II and III. The results indicate that when presented with the other DES items, the joy items typically load together and not with items purported to measure other emotions.

SAMPLES:

The data used by Allen, Machleit, and Kleine (1992) came from a stratified sample of people of diverse experience with blood donation. Nine hundred questionnaires were mailed, and **361** usable forms were returned. Given that all respondents previously had donated blood, limited information was known about them and allowed a comparison with nonrespondents. Respondents were a little older, less likely to be male, and more likely to be heavier donors than nonrespondents.

The data for the study conducted by Westbrook and Oliver (1991) came from a judgmental area sample. Convenience samples were taken at four shopping centers in a large northeastern city and were limited to persons who had purchased a new or used car in the past year. Complete and usable questionnaires were obtained from **125** respondents. A majority (74%) of the sample was male. The average respondent had an income in the $25,000–

$40,000 range and was 33 years of age. The frequency version of the scale was used in this study.

Two samples were used in the study by Oliver (1993) with one examining satisfaction with cars and the other examining course satisfaction. The one involving cars is the same as the one described previously in Westbrook and Oliver (1991). The other sample was composed of students who volunteered from nine sections of a required marketing class. Usable questionnaires were provided by **178** students. The intensity version of the scale was used in this study.

RELIABILITY:

Allen, Machleit, and Kleine (1992; Allen 1994) and Westbrook and Oliver (1991) calculated alphas of **.90** and **.73,** respectively, for the scale. Oliver (1993) reported alphas of **.70** (n = 125) and **.84** (n = 178).

VALIDITY:

No specific examination of the scale's validity was reported in any of the studies.

ADMINISTRATION:

The scale was included with many other measures in the instrument used by Westbrook and Oliver (1991), Oliver (1993) and Allen, Machleit, and Kleine (1992). High scores on the frequency version of the scale suggest that a respondent perceives him/herself as having experienced the joy-related emotional trait very often in some specified time period. A high score on the intensity version of the scale indicates that he/she is feeling very joyous at the time of measurement.

MAJOR FINDINGS:

The study by Allen, Machleit, Kleine (1992) examined whether emotions affect behavior through attitudes or are better viewed as having a separate and distinct impact. Among the many findings was that **joy** (DES III) plays a key role with the act of donating blood for the least experienced donors.

The separate roles of positive and negative affect, attribute performance, and disconfirmation were examined by Oliver (1993) for their impact on satisfaction. Positive affect was viewed as a function of two emotions, **joy** and interest. For both samples, positive affect was found to have direct influence on satisfaction and, of all the emotions measured, **joy** appeared to have the greatest effect on satisfaction.

Westbrook and Oliver (1991) studied the correspondence of the consumption emotional responses and satisfaction judgments that occur in the postpurchase period of the consumer decision process. **Joy** had its highest correlations with surprise (r = .30) and sadness (r = -.30) and its lowest correlation with fear (r = -.07). **Joy** was also found to be a primary emotional trait linked to a high satisfaction experience by being combined with either surprise or with interest.

REFERENCES:

Allen, Chris T. (1994), personal correspondence.

———, Karen A. Machleit, and Susan Schultz Kleine (1992), "A Comparison of Attitudes and Emotions as Predictors of Behavior at Diverse Levels of Behavioral Experience," *JCR*, 18 (March), 493-504.

———, ———, and Susan S. Marine (1988), "On Assessing the Emotionality of Advertising Via Izard's Differential Emotions Scale," in *Advances in Consumer Research*, Vol. 14, Michael J. Houston, ed. Provo, UT: Association for Consumer Research, 226-31.

Izard, Carroll E. (1977), *Human Emotions*. New York: Plenum Press.

Kotsch, William E., Davis W. Gerbing, and Lynne E. Schwartz (1982), "The Construct Validity of the Differential Emotions Scale as Adapted for Children and Adolescents," in *Measuring Emotions in Infants and Children*, Carroll E. Izard, ed. New York: Cambridge University Press, 251-78.

Oliver, Richard L. (1993), "Cognitive, Affective, and Attribute Bases of the Satisfaction Response," *JCR*, 20 (December), 418-30.

Westbrook, Robert A. (1987), "Product/Consumption-Based Affective Responses and Postpurchase Processes," *JMR*, 24 (August), 258-70.

——— and Richard L. Oliver (1991), "The Dimensionality of Consumption Emotion Patterns and Consumer Satisfaction," *JCR*, 18 (June), 84-91.

SCALE ITEMS: JOY

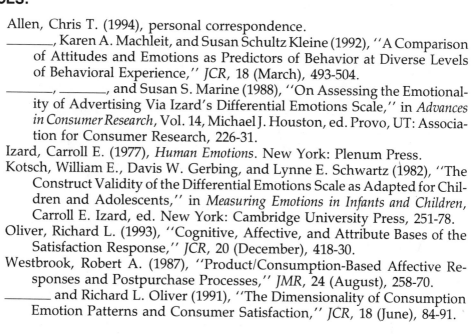

POSSIBLE DIRECTIONS FOR FREQUENCY VERSION OF SCALE: Below is a list of words that you can use to show how you feel. We want you to tell us how often you felt each of these feelings _____.* You can tell us how often you felt each of these feelings on the list by marking one of the numbers next to each question.

Almost
never ____ : ____ : ____ : ____ : ____   Very
         1   2   3   4   5   often

POSSIBLE DIRECTIONS FOR INTENSITY VERSION OF SCALE: Below is a list of words that you can use to show how you feel. We want you to tell us how strongly you feel. You can tell us how strongly you feel each of these feelings on the list by marking one of the numbers next to each question.

Very
weak ____ : ____ : ____ : ____ : ____   Very
        1   2   3   4   5   strong

DES II
1. delighted
2. happy
3. joyful

DES III
1. feel glad about something
2. feel happy
3. feel joyful, like everything is going your way, everything is rosy

* The blank should be used to specify the time period of interest, such as ''during the last week.''

SCALE NAME: Knowledge (Cars)

DESCRIPTION:

A seven-item, seven-point, Likert-type measure of the relative knowledge a person reports having about cars and their operation compared with the "average" buyer.

SCALE ORIGIN:

Although not expressly stated in the article, the scale appears to be have been used first in published research by Srinivasan and Ratchford (1991), which was based on the dissertation of Srinivasan (1987). Some initial assessment of scale reliability and face validity was made in the pretest stage of the study.

SAMPLES:

Srinivasan and Ratchford (1991) obtained a sample of new car buyers through a mail survey of new car registrants in the Buffalo, New York area. More than 3000 people were sent three mailings of the questionnaire, and ultimately **1401** usable responses were received. No demographic description is provided of the respondents.

RELIABILITY:

Srinivasan and Ratchford (1991) reported an alpha of **.87** for the scale.

VALIDITY:

Srinivasan and Ratchford (1991) provided no discussion of this scale's validity.

ADMINISTRATION:

The scale was used by Srinivasan and Ratchford (1991) along with other measures in a mail survey instrument. A low score on the scale indicates that a respondent reports having a lot of familiarity with cars and their workings compared with other people.

MAJOR FINDINGS:

Srinivasan and Ratchford (1991) examined a model of the determinants of external search for new car purchases. As hypothesized, product **knowledge** had a negative effect on perceived risk and positive effects on both evoked-set size and perceived search benefits.

REFERENCES:

Srinivasan, Narasimhan (1987), ''A Causal Model of External Search for Information for Durables: A Particular Investigation in the Case of New Automobiles,'' doctoral dissertation, State University of New York at Buffalo.

———— and Brian T. Ratchford (1991), ''An Empirical Test of an External Search for Automobiles,'' *JCR*, 18 (September), 233-42.

SCALE ITEMS: KNOWLEDGE (CARS)

DIRECTIONS: There are no right or wrong answers to the following statements and a large number of people agree and disagree. Kindly indicate *your* personal opinion by circling any one number for each statement.

```
Strongly                                               Strongly
agree                                                  disagree
  1————————2————————3————————4————————5————————6————————7
```

1. Compared to the average person, I know a lot about cars.
2. I like to work on cars myself.
3. I don't understand a lot of my car's workings. **(r)**
4. I know how an internal combustion engine works.
5. My friends consider me an expert on cars.

6. Please rate you knowledge of cars compared to the average buyer by circling one number:

```
One of the most                                  One of the least
knowledgeable                                       knowledgeable
  1————————2————————3————————4————————5————————6————————7
```

7. Please circle one of the numbers below to describe *your* familiarity with cars:

```
Extremely                                             Not at all
familiar                                                familiar
  1————————2————————3————————4————————5————————6————————7
```

SCALE NAME: Knowledge (Food Product)

SCALE DESCRIPTION:

A three-item, seven-point, Likert-type scale measuring the self-reported familiarity with and interest in a specified food product category. Cole and Balasubramanian (1993) studied breakfast cereal.

SCALE ORIGIN:

The scale is original to the study by Cole and Balasubramanian (1993).

SAMPLES:

Cole and Balasubramanian (1993) conducted two studies, but the scale apparently was used in only the first. Data were gathered in three grocery stores located in a small midwestern town, and interviews were conducted in those stores with **79** shoppers. Subjects ranged in age from 20 to 89 years.

RELIABILITY:

Cole and Balasubramanian (1993) reported an alpha of **.71** for the scale.

VALIDITY:

Cole and Balasubramanian (1993) reported no examination of scale validity for the scale.

ADMINISTRATION:

The scale was completed along with other measures after shoppers had engaged in a brand selection exercise (Cole and Balasubramanian 1993). A high score on the scale indicates that a respondent believes that he/she has a lot of knowledge about the specified product category, whereas a low score suggests that he/she is unfamiliar with the category.

MAJOR FINDINGS:

The purpose of the studies reported by Cole and Balasubramanian (1993) was to examine the effect that age might have on the ability to search for and use information to make a better decision. The scale was not part of hypothesis testing, but in the field study it was used to show that there was no significant difference between young adults (mean = 36) and the elderly (mean = 68) in their self-reported **product knowledge**.

REFERENCE:

Cole, Catherine A. and Siva K. Balasubramanian (1993), ''Age Differences in Consumers' Search for Information: Public Policy Implications,'' *JCR*, 20 (June), 157-69.

SCALE ITEMS: KNOWLEDGE (FOOD PRODUCT)*

Strongly ___ : ___ : ___ : ___ : ___ : ___ : ___ Strongly
disagree   1   2   3   4   5   6   7   agree

1. I am knowledgeable about the nutritional aspects of _____.
2. In general, I know a lot about _____.
3. I am very interested in the _____ product category.

* The name of the product category should go in the blanks.

SCALE NAME: Knowledge (Product)

SCALE DESCRIPTION:

A four-item, seven-point, Likert-type measure assessing a consumer's perceived knowledge of brands in a specified product category as well as the important evaluative criteria.

SCALE ORIGIN:

Although Lichtenstein, Netemeyer, and Burton (1990) may have drawn inspiration from previous research, this scale appears to be original to their study.

SAMPLES:

The data for the main study by Lichtenstein, Netemeyer, and Burton (1990) came from a convenience sample of **350** nonstudent adults from a medium-size SMSA. The majority of the sample was female (57%) and married (69%). College graduates composed 40% of the sample. The median age of respondents was between 35 to 44 years, and household income was between $30,000 and $39,999.

RELIABILITY:

Lichtenstein, Netemeyer, and Burton (1990) reported the reliability (LISREL estimate) of the scale to be **.77**.

VALIDITY:

Lichtenstein, Netemeyer, and Burton (1990) reported no test of validity.

ADMINISTRATION:

Lichtenstein, Netemeyer, and Burton (1990) did not describe the manner in which the scale was administered to the subjects in their study. However, it was clear that the scale was just one of many measures that composed the survey instrument. High scores on the scale indicate that consumers perceive having a lot of knowledge to aid them in their choice of brands within a product class, whereas low scores suggest that they feel they have little or no such knowledge to guide their selections.

MAJOR FINDINGS:

Lichtenstein, Netemeyer, and Burton (1990) examined the effect of both value consciousness and coupon involvement on coupon redemption behavior. One of the major findings was that value consciousness had a much greater positive relationship with **product knowledge** (grocery products) than did coupon involvement.

REFERENCE:

Lichtenstein, Donald R., Richard D. Netemeyer, and Scot Burton (1990), ''Distinguishing Coupon Proneness From Value Consciousness: An Acquisition-Transaction Utility Theory Perspective,'' *JM*, 54 (July), 54-67.

SCALE ITEMS: KNOWLEDGE (PRODUCT)

Strongly disagree	___ : ___ : ___ : ___ : ___ : ___ : ___	Strongly agree
	1 2 3 4 5 6 7	

1. I have a lot of knowledge about how to select the best brand within a product class.
2. I have a clear idea about which product characteristics are really important ones in providing me with maximum usage satisfaction.
3. I do not have a clear idea about which product characteristics are really important ones in providing me with maximum usage satisfaction. **(r)**
4. Please rate your level of knowledge of the products you buy.

Not knowlegeable	___ : ___ : ___ : ___ : ___ : ___ : ___	Very knowledgeable
	1 2 3 4 5 6 7	

SCALE NAME: Knowledge (Product Class)

SCALE DESCRIPTION:

A four-item, seven-point, Likert-type measure assessing a consumer's perceived knowledge of brands in a specified product category as well as the confidence to make purchase decisions and give advice to others about the product class.

SCALE ORIGIN:

The origin of the scale was not specified by Smith and Park (1992).

SAMPLES:

Smith and Park (1992) reported on findings based on analysis of data gathered from product managers and consumers. The **product class knowledge** scale was used only in a survey of the latter group. Data were collected in that survey by door-to-door interviews in suburban neighborhoods of a large midwestern city. The sample was ultimately composed of **1383** respondents. Each respondent was asked questions regarding two products, 35 consumers were interviewed for each product, and there was a total of 79 products examined. The interviews were conducted by students who received some training before going into the field.

RELIABILITY:

Smith and Park (1992) reported an alpha of **.80** for the scale.

VALIDITY:

Smith and Park (1992) did not address the validity of the scale.

ADMINISTRATION:

The scale was administered along with other measures by trained student interviewers in door-to-door settings (Smith and Park 1992). A high score on the scale indicates that a respondent perceives that he/she has a great deal of familiarity with the product class and would be confident enough with that knowledge to make a purchase decision.

MAJOR FINDINGS:

Smith and Park (1992) examined several issues related to brand strategy. One hypothesis was that the impact of brand extensions on market share and advertising efficiency is greater when consumer **knowledge** of a extension product class is low rather than high. The evidence supported the hypothesis, with the strongest effect involving advertising efficiency.

REFERENCE:

Smith, Daniel C. and C. Whan Park (1992), "The Effects of Brand Extensions on Market Share and Advertising Efficiency," *JMR*, 29 (August), 296-313.

SCALE ITEMS: KNOWLEDGE (PRODUCT CLASS)

Strongly disagree	___ : ___ : ___ : ___ : ___ : ___ : ___	Strongly agree
	1 2 3 4 5 6 7	

1. I feel very knowledgeable about this product.
2. If a friend asked me about this product, I could give them advice about different brands.
3. If I had to purchase this product today, I would need to gather very little information in order to make a wise decision.
4. I feel very confident about my ability to tell the difference in quality among different brands of this product.

SCALE NAME: Knowledge (Automotive)

SCALE DESCRIPTION:

A seven-item, seven-point summated rating scale assessing a person's perceived understanding of cars, with particular emphasis on knowledge of the purchase process.

SCALE ORIGIN:

The origin of the scale was not specified by Ozanne, Brucks, and Grewal (1992), but there was nothing to indicate that it was anything other than developed by them for that particular study.

SAMPLES:

Ozanne, Brucks, and Grewal (1992) used a sample composed of 43 undergraduate business majors. The study took place at a major state university, and students agreed to participate in the study as one way to meet a course requirement.

RELIABILITY:

Ozanne, Brucks, and Grewal (1992) reported an alpha for the scale of **.82**.

VALIDITY:

Ozanne, Brucks, and Grewal (1992) discussed no examination of the scale's validity.

ADMINISTRATION:

The scale was employed by Ozanne, Brucks, and Grewal (1992) as a check on the success of subject randomization in their experiment (see ''Major Findings''). The scale was scored such that a low score meant that a respondent perceived him/herself to be very knowledgeable about cars.

MAJOR FINDINGS:

Ozanne, Brucks, and Grewal (1992) examined the information search behavior of consumers with particular regard for the process of categorizing products that differ from previously familiar categories. The **knowledge** of subjects in the treatments was checked to ensure that they were reasonably similar in their understanding of the general product category (cars). No differences were found between those people randomly assigned to the luxury car and economy car conditions.

REFERENCE:

> Ozanne, Julie L., Merrie Brucks, and Dhruv Grewal (1992), ''A Study of Information Search Behavior During the Categorization of New Products,'' *JCR*, 18 (March), 452-63.

SCALE ITEMS: KNOWLEDGE (AUTOMOTIVE)

1. I _____ the necessary information to buy a car.

Have   ___ : ___ : ___ : ___ : ___ : ___ : ___   Do not have
        7   6   5   4   3   2   1

2. I_____ the important automotive characteristics for buying a car.

Know   ___ : ___ : ___ : ___ : ___ : ___ : ___   Do not know
        7   6   5   4   3   2   1

3. I _____ the steps in purchasing a car.

Understand   ___ : ___ : ___ : ___ : ___ : ___ : ___   Do not
          7   6   5   4   3   2   1   understand

4. I am _____ knowledgeable about buying a car.

Most   ___ : ___ : ___ : ___ : ___ : ___ : ___   Least
        7   6   5   4   3   2   1

5. I am _____ knowledgeable about automotive terminology.

Most   ___ : ___ : ___ : ___ : ___ : ___ : ___   Least
        7   6   5   4   3   2   1

6. I _____ purchasing procedures.

Understand   ___ : ___ : ___ : ___ : ___ : ___ : ___   Do not
          7   6   5   4   3   2   1   understand

7. I _____ the automotive characteristics to compare when buying a car.

Know   ___ : ___ : ___ : ___ : ___ : ___ : ___   Do not know
        7   6   5   4   3   2   1

SCALE NAME: Life Balance

SCALE DESCRIPTION:

A three-item, seven-point, summated ratings scale measuring the relative amount of time a person believes a healthy balance is achieved between stress and work on the one hand and rest and relaxation on the other.

SCALE ORIGIN:

The scale was developed by Moorman and Matulich (1993). Development and refinement of the many scales used in their study generally followed the Churchill (1979) paradigm. Measures were pretested on 67 undergraduate students. Then in the main test, the scales were purified further using alpha, item-total correlations, and LISREL.

SAMPLES:

Moorman and Matulich (1993) used two sampling techniques to obtain respondents who differed on the variables under examination. First, a stratified sample with low and high income as well as young and elderly strata was taken. Respondents from the two income strata were obtained by randomly selecting from lower- and higher-income neighborhoods in Milwaukee and Madison, Wisconsin. Respondents representing the elderly segment were selected randomly from adult centers and retirement communities. Data for young consumers was retained from the pretest (students in an introductory marketing class). In the second sample, survey forms were mailed to addresses of those randomly selected from the telephone books of the two previously mentioned cities. The total number of usable questionnaires was **404**, indicating about a 51% overall response rate. A dollar was enclosed with the questionnaires received by all respondents as a token of appreciation and incentive to return the form.

RELIABILITY:

Moorman and Matulich (1993) reported an alpha of **.74** for the scale.

VALIDITY:

Although specific details about this scale were not provided in the article, Moorman and Matulich (1993) engaged in various purification activities in both the pretest and the main study for all their scales. At the least then, it would appear that evidence was collected that indicated the scale was unidimensional and internally consistent.

ADMINISTRATION:

The scale was self-administered along with many other measures in a questionnaire (Moorman and Matulich 1993). A high score on the scale indicates

that a respondent reports frequently being able to maintain a balance between the stress and rest in his/her life.

MAJOR FINDINGS:

Moorman and Matulich (1993) presented and tested a model of the impact various consumer characteristics have on some health-related behaviors. Among the findings was that people with high health control achieved a healthy **life balance** significantly more frequently.

COMMENTS:

Moorman and Matulich (1993) reported the mean score of the sample on the scale to be 4.75 with a standard deviation of 1.31.

REFERENCES:

Churchill, Gilbert A., Jr. (1979), "A Paradigm for Developing Better Measures of Marketing Constructs," *JMR*, 16 (February), 64-73.

Moorman, Christine and Erika Matulich (1993), "A Model of Consumers' Preventive Health Motivation and Health Ability," *JCR*, 20 (September), 208-28.

SCALE ITEMS: LIFE BALANCE

On the scale below please indicate how much you engage in the following activities.*

None of the time	____ : ____ : ____ : ____ : ____ : ____ : ____	All of the time
	1 2 3 4 5 6 7	

1. Get enough rest and sleep
2. Reduce stress and anxiety
3. Maintain a balance between "work" and "play"

* The instructional statement was not provided in the article but was probably something similar to this.

SCALE NAME: Locus of Control (Health)

SCALE DESCRIPTION:

A 27-item, seven-point, Likert-type scale measuring the degree to which one believes that heath outcomes are controllable. *Internals* are those who believe outcomes are based upon their own behavior, whereas *externals* think that outcomes depend more on luck, fate, or others.

SCALE ORIGIN:

The scale derives from work by Lau and Ware (1981), who developed four multi-item scales related to a health-specific locus of control. The scales had a total of 27 items, and a factor analysis generally supported a four-factor solution. In contrast, Moorman and Matulich (1993) treated the items as a single scale and seem to have dropped a few of the original items and replaced them with others of their own creation.

SAMPLES:

Moorman and Matulich (1993) used two sampling techniques to obtain re-spondents who differed on the variables under examination. First, a stratified sample with low and high income as well as young and elderly strata was taken. Respondents from the two income strata were obtained by randomly selecting from lower- and higher-income neighborhoods in Milwaukee and Madison, Wisconsin. Respondents representing the elderly segment were selected randomly from adult centers and retirement communities. Data for young consumers was retained from the pretest (students in an introductory marketing class). In the second sample, survey forms were mailed to ad-dresses of those randomly selected from the telephone books of the two previously mentioned cities. The total number of usable questionnaires was **404**, indicating about a 51% overall response rate. A dollar was enclosed with the questionnaires received by all respondents as a token of appreciation and incentive to return the form.

RELIABILITY:

Moorman and Matulich (1993) reported an alpha of **.79** for the scale.

VALIDITY:

Although the originators of the items provided evidence of the sets' multidi-mensional structure (Lau and Ware 1981), the results of the confirmatory factor analysis performed by Moorman and Matulich (1993) led them to treat the items as a composite measure.

ADMINISTRATION:

The scale was self-administered along with many other measures in a ques-tionnaire (Moorman and Matulich 1993). A high score on the scale suggests that a respondent believes that people can have a great deal of control over health-related outcomes (internal locus of control), whereas a low score indicates that a respondent thinks that other factors such as people or luck control health (external locus of control).

MAJOR FINDINGS:

Moorman and Matulich (1993) presented and tested a model of the impact various consumer characteristics have on some health- related behaviors. Among the findings was that **health-related locus of control** had a significant positive impact on achieving a balance between stress and relaxation.

COMMENTS:

Moorman and Matulich (1993) reported the mean score of the sample on the scale to be 4.74 with a standard deviation of .58.

REFERENCES:

Lau, Richard R. and John F. Ware (1981), ''Refinements in the Measurement of Health-Specific Locus-of-Control Beliefs,'' *Medical Care*, 19 (November), 1147-57.

Moorman, Christine and Erika Matulich (1993), ''A Model of Consumers' Preventive Health Motivation and Health Ability,'' *JCR*, 20 (September), 208-28.

SCALE ITEMS: LOCUS OF CONTROL

Disagree ____ : ____ : ____ : ____ : ____ : ____ : ____ Agree

1   2   3   4   5   6   7

1. Anyone can learn a few basic health principles that can go a long way in preventing illnesses.
2. I have a lot of confidence in my ability to cure myself once I get sick.
3. ''Taking care of yourself'' has little or no relation to whether you get sick. **(r)**
4. In the long run, people who take care of themselves stay healthy and get well quickly.
5. There is little one can do to prevent illness. **(r)**
6. People's ill health results from their own carelessness.
7. Doctors can rarely do very much for people who are sick. **(r)**
8. Many times doctors do not help their patients to get well. **(r)**
9. Recovery from illness requires good medical care more than anything else.
10. Doctors can do very little to prevent illness. **(r)**
11. Doctors relieve or cure only a few of the medical problems their patients have. **(r)**
12. Most sick people are helped a great deal when they go to a doctor.

13. Seeing a doctor for regular checkups is a key factor in staying healthy.
14. I only do what my doctor tells me to do.
15. Medical technology can handle health problems
16. Doctors can almost always help their patients feel better.
17. Whether or not people get well is often a matter of chance. **(r)**
18. When it comes to health, there is no such thing as "bad luck."
19. People who never get sick are just plain lucky. **(r)**
20. Good health is largely a matter of good fortune. **(r)**
21. Staying well has little or nothing to do with chance.
22. Recovery from illness has nothing to do with luck.
23. Healthwise, there isn't much you can do for yourself when you get sick. **(r)**
24. Some kinds of illnesses are so bad that nothing can be done about them. **(r)**
25. In today's world, few diseases are totally debilitating (crippling).
26. No matter what anybody does, there are many diseases that can just wipe you out. **(r)**
27. There are a lot of medical problems that can be very serious or even can kill you. **(r)**

SCALE NAME: Loneliness

SCALE DESCRIPTION:

A four-item, four-point, Likert-type scale measuring the deficiency one perceives in his/her social relationships. Referring to an unpleasant subjective experience, this is not necessarily the same as social isolation. Therefore, a person could feel lonely in a crowd or could be alone and not feel lonely.

SCALE ORIGIN:

The scale was constructed by Russell, Peplau, and Cutrona (1980) and is an abridged version of a larger instrument called the Revised UCLA Loneliness scale. Two administrations of the 20-item instrument provided strong support for its internal consistency and validity. The four-item version was recommended specifically by the authors because the four were the subset of items that best predicted scores on a six-item, self-labeled loneliness index. The Cronbach's alpha for the short version was reported to be .75 compared with the long version's .94.

SAMPLES:

A convenience sample of **327** adults in a large, northeastern U.S. metropolitan area was used by Forman and Sriram (1991). Respondents were asked to return questionnaires by mail to ensure anonymity. Fifty-nine percent of the sample was female and the median age was 44 years. About 43% of the sample was married, and 32% had completed some college.

RELIABILITY:

An alpha of **.74** was reported for the scale by Forman and Sriram (1991). Item-total correlations ranged from .46 to .57.

VALIDITY:

Forman and Sriram (1991) conducted a factor analysis of the items composing the scale and examined the intercorrelations of several scales used in their study. The findings provided some evidence of the scale's unidimensionality as well as its convergent and discriminant validities.

ADMINISTRATION:

The scale was administered as part of a larger questionnaire apparently through personal interviews (Forman and Sriram 1991). High scores on the scale indicate that respondents feel lonely, whereas low scores suggest that they have no such major deficiency in their social relationships.

MAJOR FINDINGS:

Forman and Sriram (1991) examined the affect of automated retailing systems on **lonely** consumers. There were no significant differences on any demographic variables between those scoring high on **loneliness** and those scoring low. Moreover, **lonely** consumers were found to perceive greater depersonalization of the shopping experience than were the **nonlonely**.

REFERENCES:

Forman, Andrew M. and Ven Sriram (1991), ''The Depersonalization of Retailing: Its Impact on the 'Lonely' Consumer,'' *JR*, 67 (Summer), 226-43.
Russell, D., L.A. Peplau, and C.E. Cutrona (1980), ''The Revised UCLA Loneliness Scale: Concurrent and Discriminant Validity Evidence,'' *Journal of Personality and Social Psychology*, 39 (3), 472-80.

SCALE ITEMS: LONELINESS

Directions: Indicate how often you feel the way described in each of the following statements.

Never	Rarely	Sometimes	Often
1	2	3	4

1. I feel in tune with the people around me. **(r)**
2. No one really knows me well.
3. I can find companionship when I want it. **(r)**
4. People are around me, but not with me.

SCALE NAME: Loyalty Proneness (Product)

SCALE DESCRIPTION:

A five-item, seven-point, Likert-type measure assessing a consumer's general tendency to buy the same brands over time rather than switching around to try other brands. The measure is not as specific as normally considered of "brand loyalty," in which the tendency to purchase a particular brand is assessed rather than the propensity to be loyal in all sorts of purchases.

SCALE ORIGIN:

The scale used by Lichtenstein, Netemeyer, and Burton (1990) appears to be original, although they drew on Raju (1980) for two of their items.

SAMPLES:

The data for Lichtenstein, Netemeyer, and Burton's (1990 main study) came from a convenience sample of **350** nonstudent adults from a medium-size SMSA. The majority of the sample was female (57%) and married (69%). College graduates composed 40% of the sample. The median age of respondents was between 35 to 44 years, and household income was between $30,000 and $39,999.

RELIABILITY:

Lichtenstein, Netemeyer, and Burton (1990) reported the reliability (LISREL estimate) of the scale to be **.88.**

VALIDITY:

Lichtenstein, Netemeyer, and Burton (1990) reported no test of validity.

ADMINISTRATION:

Lichtenstein, Netemeyer, and Burton (1990) did not described the manner in which the scale was administered to the subjects in their study. However, it was clear that the scale was just one of many measures that composed the survey instrument. High scores on the scale indicate that respondents have a tendency to purchase the same brands, whereas low scores suggest that they are not generally brand loyal.

MAJOR FINDINGS:

Lichtenstein, Netemeyer, and Burton (1990) examined the effect of both value consciousness and coupon involvement on coupon redemption behavior. Both value consciousness and coupon involvement had low, negative correlations with **loyalty proneness,** and the levels of those correlations were not significantly different.

REFERENCES:

Lichtenstein, Donald R., Richard D. Netemeyer, and Scot Burton (1990), ''Distinguishing Coupon Proneness From Value Consciousness: An Acquisition-Transaction Utility Theory Perspective,'' *JM*, 54 (July), 54-67.

Raju, P. S. (1980), ''Optimum Stimulation Level: Its Relationship to Personality, Demographics, and Exploratory Behavior,'' *JCR*, 7 (December), 272-82.

SCALE ITEMS: LOYALTY PRONENESS

Strongly disagree	___ :	___ :	___ :	___ :	___ :	___ :	___	Strongly agree
	1	2	3	4	5	6	7	

1. I generally buy the same brands I have always bought.
2. Once I have made a choice on which brand to purchase, I am likely to continue to buy it without considering other brands.
3. Once I get used to a brand, I hate to switch.
4. If I like a brand, I rarely switch from it just to try something different.
5. Even though certain products are available in a number of different brands, I always tend to buy the same brand.

SCALE NAME: Masculinity

SCALE DESCRIPTION:

A 20-item, seven-point, summated ratings scale measuring the degree to which a person indicates having male-like personality characteristics. Barak and Stern (1985/86) used a ten-item version of the scale.

SCALE ORIGIN:

The items for the scale were taken from the Bem Sex-Role Inventory (BSRI; 1974). The inventory went through several rounds of development and testing. The initial development involved 40 undergraduate students judging 400 personality characteristics for their appropriateness for a each sex. The list was narrowed to the 20 characteristics for each sex which were considered to be most the most desirable for them to have in American society. Once finished, the measure asked respondents to rate themselves on all the characteristics so that both masculinity and femininity scale scores could be computed. (An androgyny score also could be calculated by determining the difference between the other two scores.)

Internal consistency was estimated using two samples: 444 male and 279 female students in introductory psychology at Stanford University and an additional 117 male and 77 female paid volunteers at Foothill Junior College. From the two samples, an alpha of .86 was calculated both times for the masculinity scale and alphas of .8 and .82 were calculated for the femininity scale. Using 28 males and 28 females, test-retest stability was estimated. The students took the BSRI once and then four weeks later. For both scales, the correlation of the scores was reported to be .90. Scores on the scales were correlated with two other measures of sex roles. The low correlations led the author to conclude that her scales were tapping into constructs not directly measured by the others.

SAMPLES:

The survey form used by Barak and Stern (1985/86) was personally distributed to and collected from an age-quota sample of women living in the greater New York metropolitan area. The study focused on the 567 responding women who categorized themselves as either "young" or "middle-aged" and stated an age between 25 and 69 years.

Data were collected through multistage cluster sampling by Fischer and Arnold (1990). The study was based on data from the 299 people who completed the questionnaire. Compared with the population from which the data were collected, the sample had fewer males but was more upscale. A $1 lottery ticket was given to respondents for participating.

RELIABILITY:

Barak and Stern (1985/86) say only that the scale's alpha was more than .85. Fischer and Arnold (1990) reported an alpha of .84.

VALIDITY:

Factor analysis was performed on the BSRI inventory offered by Bem (1974). Though not expressly stated, the ten items used by Barak and Stern (1985/86) were probably the ones that loaded highest on the factor related to masculinity. Fischer and Arnold (1990) did not report any examination of the scale's validity.

ADMINISTRATION:

The scale used by Barak and Stern (1985/1986) was self-administered by respondents in their homes as part of a larger survey form. The scale was administered by Fischer and Arnold (1990) as part of a structured survey instrument during in-home personal interviews with respondents. High scores indicate greater masculinity, whereas low scores suggest little masculinity though not necessarily strong femininity.

MAJOR FINDINGS:

Barak and Stern (1985/86) examined the differences in profiles between the baby-boomer and pre-boomer generations as well as between those who characterized themselves as young versus middle-aged. The only significant difference found in **masculinity** was between those who identified themselves as either young or middle-aged. Specifically, those identifying themselves as young expressed more masculine characteristics than those identifying themselves as middle-aged.

Fischer and Arnold (1990) studied the impact of several gender-related variables on Christmas gift shopping patterns. The theory being tested in the study involved only feminine traits, so though the **masculinity** scale was administered to respondents, no results relating to its use were discussed in the article.

COMMENTS:

Although presented here by itself, the scale is used most properly along with the femininity scale of the BSRI (see #116). The lack of stronger evidence regarding scale validity should cause scores to be viewed cautiously. See also Qualls (1987) for another use of the scale.

REFERENCES:

Barak, Benny and Barbara Stern (1985/1986), ''Women's Age in Advertising: An Examination of Two Consumer Age Profiles,'' *JAR*, 25 (Dec./Jan.), 38-47.

Bem, Sandra L. (1974), ''The Measurement of Psychological Androgyny,'' *Journal of Consulting and Clinical Psychology*, 42 (2), 155-62.

Fischer, Eileen and Stephen J. Arnold (1990), ''More Than a Labor of Love: Gender Roles and Christmas Gift Shopping,'' *JCR*, 17 (December), 333-45.

Qualls, William J. (1987), "Household Decision Behavior: The Impact of Husbands' and Wives' Sex Role Orientation," *JCR*, 14 (September), 264-79.

SCALE ITEMS: MASCULINITY*

Indicate on the following scale how well each of the following traits describes you:

```
                                                                Always or
Never or almost   ___ : ___ : ___ : ___ : ___ : ___ : ___      almost
never true          1     2     3     4     5     6     7      always true
```

1. Acts as a leader
2. Aggressive
3. Ambitious
4. Analytical
5. Assertive
6. Athletic
7. Competitive
8. Defends own beliefs
9. Dominant
10. Forceful
11. Has leadership abilities
12. Independent
13. Individualistic
14. Makes decisions easily
15. Masculine
16. Self-reliant
17. Self-sufficient
18. Strong personality
19. Willing to take a stand
20. Willing to take risks

* Barak and Stern (1985/86) calculated scale scores on just ten of these items on the basis of the results of a factor analysis. Those ten items were not specified in their article.

SCALE NAME: Materialism

SCALE DESCRIPTION:

A six-item, five-point, Likert-type summated ratings scale measuring the degree to which a person is oriented toward possessing goods and money as a means of personal happiness and social progress.

SCALE ORIGIN:

The measure originates from a dissertation published by Moschis in 1978. His study, reported subsequently, is from that same dissertation research. Some of the items for the scale were apparently derived from items used by Ward and Wackman (1971). The psychometric properties of the latter are unknown. In the Ward and Wackman (1971) study, it was found that there was no significant difference between the mean score of 537 for eighth and ninth graders on the materialism scale compared with the mean score of 557 for tenth, eleventh, and twelfth graders.

SAMPLES:

The data in Moschis (1981) came from **806** middle or senior high school students. There were 365 "older" adolescents (15 years of age and older) and 441 "younger" adolescents (younger than 15 years of age). The students came from 13 schools and seven towns in Wisconsin representing a wide variety of urban to rural situations. The author indicates that the sample was well balanced in terms of most demographic characteristics except for sex—nearly two-thirds of the respondents were female.

The same data set is reported on in two articles by Carlson and Grossbart (1988; Grossbart, Carlson, and Walsh 1991). The survey instrument was distributed to mothers through students at three elementary schools of an unidentified U.S. city. The schools were chosen on a convenience basis but appeared to represent a variety of socioeconomic areas of the city. A $1 contribution to the PTO was made for each completed questionnaire returned by the children. Analysis was based on **451** completed questionnaires. Ninety-three percent of the responding mothers indicated that they were the primary person in the child's socialization.

RELIABILITY:

Moschis (1981) and Carlson and Grossbart (1988; Grossbart, Carlson, and Walsh 1991) reported alphas of **.60** and **.68,** respectively, for the scale.

VALIDITY:

No examination of scale validity has been reported, although Grossbart, Carlson, and Walsh (1991) report a beta coefficient for the scale of .51. Also, their findings showed that social desirability was a significant covariate with the scale.

ADMINISTRATION:

The scale was self-administered along with other measures in the studies reported by Moschis (1981) as well as Carlson and Grossbart (1988; Grossbart, Carlson, and Walsh 1991). High scores on the scale indicate that respondents do not tend to be materialistic, whereas low scores suggest that they are very oriented toward accumulating material things as a means of achieving happiness.

MAJOR FINDINGS:

Moschis (1981) investigated the validity of the cognitive development approach to socialization (e.g., Piaget) to predict a wide variety of consumer-related cognitions learned during adolescence. In general, the findings indicated that the cognitive developmental model did not explain consumer socialization during adolescence very well. Older adolescents had significantly less favorable attitudes toward advertising, brands, and prices compared with younger children but used prepurchase information source to a significantly greater extent. No significant difference was found between the two groups of adolescents with regard to **materialism.**

Carlson and Grossbart (1988; Grossbart, Carlson, and Walsh 1991) investigated the relationship between general parental socialization styles and children's consumer socialization. "Neglecting" mothers exhibited more **materialism** than any of the other four parental socialization styles examined. However, the difference was only significant in comparison to "Authoritative" mothers, who scored lowest on **materialism.**

COMMENTS:

The available evidence indicates that the scale may not be reliable or valid. This could be because several different factors are represented in the scale. Redevelopment and testing should be conducted before the scale is used further.

REFERENCES:

Carlson, Les and Sanford Grossbart (1988), "Parental Style and Consumer Socialization of Children," **JCR**, 15 (June), 77-94.

Grossbart, Sanford, Les Carlson, and Ann Walsh (1991), "Consumer Socialization and Frequency of Shopping with Children," *JAMS*, 19 (Summer), 155-63.

Moschis, George P. (1978), *Acquisition of the Consumer Role By Adolescents*, Research Monograph No. 82. Atlanta, GA: Publishing Services Division, College of Business Administration, Georgia State University.

_____ (1981), "Patterns of Consumer Learning," *JAMS*, 9 (2), 110-26.

Ward, Scott and Daniel Wackman (1971), "Family and Media Influences on

Adolescent Consumer Learning,'' *American Behavioral Scientist*, 14 (January/February), 415-27.

SCALE ITEMS: MATERIALISM

Strongly agree	Agree	Neutral	Disagree	Strongly disagree
1—————	—2—————	—3—————	—4—————	—5

1. It is really true that money can buy happiness.
2. My dream in life is to be able to own expensive things.
3. People judge others by the things they own.
4. I buy some things that I secretly hope will impress other people.
5. Money is the most important thing to consider in choosing a job.
6. I think others judge me as a person by the kinds of products and brands I use.

SCALE NAME: Materialism (Centrality)

SCALE DESCRIPTION:

A seven-item, five-point, Likert-type summated ratings scale measuring the degree to which a person believes that buying and owning things are important in his/her life.

SCALE ORIGIN:

The scale is original to Richins and Dawson (1990, 1992a). The former paper describes the preliminary work in constructing the scale. Items were generated through open-ended discussions with consumers, noting how materialistic people were described in the literature, and by adapting a few items used in past studies. Using three studies with student samples, the 100+ original items were condensed to 29 items representing about four factors. The items relating to the centrality factor either loaded on different factors or had low commonalties. At least two of the items shown subsequently, however, were part of an asceticism scale tested in the earlier studies.

SAMPLES:

Four surveys were described in Richins and Dawson (1992a) as being used to refine and test the materialism scale. Little is said about the samples except that the data were collected in each case by a mail survey. The households were chosen randomly and sent a survey form, followed by a reminder letter and a second copy of the questionnaire two weeks later. Survey 1 was made in a medium-sized northeastern city and was composed of **144** people. There were **250** people in the second sample who were living in a large western city. A large western city was also the site of the third survey, which ultimately had **235** usable questionnaires. Finally, the fourth survey was composed of **86** people from a northeastern college town and **119** people from a northeastern rural area.

RELIABILITY:

Richins and Dawson (1992a) reported alphas ranging between .71 and .75 for the scale. The stability of the scale was estimated using 58 students at an urban university. The test-retest correlation (three-week interval) was .82.

VALIDITY:

Richins and Dawson (1992a) addressed the validity of the scale in a variety of ways. For example, the results of an exploratory factor analysis of the 6 success items as well as 12 items composing two other components of materialism (centrality and happiness) showed that the success items had their highest loadings (3r.493) on the same factor. Some evidence of discriminant validity came from the fact that the scale had a very low correlation ($r = -.12$) with a measure of social desirability. The rest of the evidence provided generally positive support for nomological validity but was reported just for the overall scale, with items for the three components combined.

ADMINISTRATION:

The scale was one of several measures in each of the studies, which were self-administered (Richins and Dawson 1992a). High scores on the scale indicate that respondents have a tendency to believe that the acquisition and possession of material objects is important in life.

MAJOR FINDINGS:

The purpose of the multiple surveys conducted by Richins and Dawson (1992a) was to construct a new measure of materialism. Except for some basic psychometric qualities, no relationship between the scale and other constructs was made in the article. However, among the most significant of the many findings shown in supplementary material (Richins and Dawson 1992b) was that those high in **material centrality** spent two and a half times less than those low in **material centrality** on contributions to church/charities.

COMMENTS:

Although reported separately here, Richins and Dawson (1992a) argued for combining scores of the three components of materialism. Much of the article's information is about the overall instrument's psychometric quality. For example, in the same studies described previously it was reported to have alphas between .80 and .88 and a test-retest reliability of .87.

REFERENCES:

Richins, Marsha L. and Scott Dawson (1990), ''A Preliminary Report of Scale Development,'' in *Advances in Consumer Research*, Vol. 17, Marvin E. Goldberg, Gerald Gorn, and Richard W. Pollay, eds. Provo, UT: Association for Consumer Research, 169-75.

_____ and _____ (1992a), ''A Consumer Values Orientation for Materialism and Its Measurement: Scale Development and Validation,'' *JCR*, 19 (December), 303-16.

_____ and _____ (1992b), ''A Consumer Values Orientation for Materialism and Its Measurement: Scale Development and Validation,'' unpublished results of hypothesis tests by subscale, available from the authors.

SCALE ITEMS: MATERIALISM (CENTRALITY)

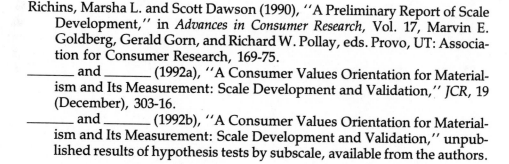

1. I usually buy only the things I need. **(r)**

2. I try to keep my life simple, as far as possessions are concerned. **(r)**
3. The things I own aren't all that important to me. **(r)**
4. I enjoy spending money on things that aren't that practical.
5. Buying things gives me a lot of pleasure.
6. I like a lot of luxury in my life.
7. I put less emphasis on material things than most people I know. **(r)**

SCALE NAME: Materialism (Happiness)

SCALE DESCRIPTION:

A five-item, five-point, Likert-type summated ratings scale measuring the degree to which a person believes that the number and quality of a person's possessions are necessary to achieve happiness in life.

SCALE ORIGIN:

The scale is original to Richins and Dawson (1990, 1992a). The former paper describes the preliminary work in constructing the scale. Items were generated through open-ended discussions with consumers, noting how materialistic people were described in the literature, and by adapting a few items used in past studies. Using three studies with student samples, the 100+ original items were condensed to 29 items representing about four factors. The factor related to the final scale shown subsequently always had the highest reliabilities (.75–.80).

SAMPLES:

Four surveys were described in Richins and Dawson (1992a) as being used to refine and test the materialism scale. Little is said about the samples except that the data were collected in each case by a mail survey. The households were chosen randomly and sent a survey form, followed by a reminder letter and a second copy of the questionnaire two weeks later. Survey 1 was made in a medium-sized northeastern city and was composed of **144** people. There were **250** people in the second sample who were living in a large western city. A large western city was also the site of the third survey, which ultimately had **235** usable questionnaires. Finally, the fourth survey was composed of **86** people from a northeastern college town and **119** people from a northeastern rural area.

RELIABILITY:

Richins and Dawson (1992a). reported alphas ranging between .73 and .83 for the scale. The stability of the scale was estimated using 58 students at an urban university. The test-retest correlation (three-week interval) was .86.

VALIDITY:

Richins and Dawson (1992a) addressed the validity of the scale in a variety of ways. For example, the results of an exploratory factor analysis of the 5 happiness items as well as 13 items composing two other components of materialism (centrality and success) showed that the happiness items had their highest loadings (3r.553) on the same factor. Some evidence of discriminant validity came from the fact that the scale had practically no correlation ($r = -.03$) with a measure of social desirability. The rest of the evidence provided generally positive support for nomological validity but was reported just for the overall scale, with items for the three components combined.

ADMINISTRATION:

The scale was one of several measures in each of the studies, which were self-administered Richins and Dawson (1992a). High scores on the scale indicate that respondents have a tendency to believe that one's possessions are needed for happiness in life.

MAJOR FINDINGS:

The purpose of the multiple surveys conducted by Richins and Dawson (1992a) was to construct a new measure of materialism. Except for some basic psychometric qualities, no relationship between the scale and other constructs was made in the article. However, among the many findings shown in supplementary material (Richins and Dawson 1992b) was that those high in **material happiness** stated that they spent more than twice as much as those low in **material happiness** on buying the things they wanted but spent less than half as much on contributions to church/charities and gifts/loans to friends/relatives.

COMMENTS:

Although reported separately here, Richins and Dawson (1992a) argued for combining scores of the three components of materialism. Much of the article's information is about the overall instrument's psychometric quality. For example, in the same studies described previously, it was reported to have alphas between .80 and .88 and a test-retest reliability of .87.

REFERENCES:

Richins, Marsha L. and Scott Dawson (1990), ''A Preliminary Report of Scale Development,'' in *Advances in Consumer Research*, Vol. 17, Marvin E. Goldberg, Gerald Gorn, and Richard W. Pollay, eds. Provo, UT: Association for Consumer Research, 169-75.

_____ and _____ (1992a), ''A Consumer Values Orientation for Materialism and Its Measurement: Scale Development and Validation,'' *JCR*, 19 (December), 303-16.

_____ and _____ (1992b), ''A Consumer Values Orientation for Materialism and Its Measurement: Scale Development and Validation,'' unpublished results of hypothesis tests by subscale, available from the authors.

SCALE ITEMS: MATERIALISM (HAPPINESS)

Strongly disagree	Disagree	Neutral	Agree	Strongly agree
1	2	3	4	5

1. I have all the things I really need to enjoy life. **(r)**
2. My life would be better if I owned certain things I don't have.
3. I wouldn't be any happier if I owned nicer things. **(r)**
4. I'd be happier if I could afford to buy more things.
5. It sometimes bothers me quite a bit that I can't afford to buy all the things I'd like.

SCALE NAME: Materialism (Success)

SCALE DESCRIPTION:

A six-item, five-point, Likert-type summated ratings scale measuring the degree to which a person believes that the number and quality of a person's possessions are an indicator of his/her success in life.

SCALE ORIGIN:

The scale is original to Richins and Dawson (1990, 1992a). The former paper describes the preliminary work in constructing the scale. Items were generated through open-ended discussions with consumers, noting how materialistic people were described in the literature, and by adapting a few items used in past studies. Using three studies with student samples, the 100+ original items were condensed to 29 items representing about four factors. The factor related to the final scale shown subsequently always had the highest reliabilities (.80–.85).

SAMPLES:

Four surveys were described in Richins and Dawson (1992a) as being used to refine and test the materialism scale. Little is said about the samples except that the data were collected in each case by a mail survey. The households were chosen randomly and sent a survey form, followed by a reminder letter and a second copy of the questionnaire two weeks later. Survey 1 was made in a medium-sized northeastern city and was composed of **144** people. There were **250** people in the second sample who were living in a large western city. A large western city was also the site of the third survey, which ultimately had **235** usable questionnaires. Finally, the fourth survey was composed of **86** people from a northeastern college town and **119** people from a northeastern rural area.

RELIABILITY:

Richins and Dawson (1992a) reported alphas ranging between .74 and .78 for the scale. The stability of the scale was estimated using 58 students at an urban university. The test-retest correlation (three week interval) was .82.

VALIDITY:

Richins and Dawson (1992a) addressed the validity of the scale in a variety of ways. For example, the results of an exploratory factor analysis of the 6 success items as well as 12 items composing two other components of materialism (centrality and happiness) showed that the success items had their highest loadings (3r.433) on the same factor. Some evidence of discriminant validity came from the fact that the scale had practically no correlation (r = −.06) with a measure of social desirability. The rest of the evidence provided generally positive support for nomological validity but was reported only for the overall scale, with items for the three components combined.

ADMINISTRATION:

The scale was one of several measures in each of the studies, which were self-administered (Richins and Dawson 1992a). High scores on the scale indicate that respondents have a tendency to believe that one's possessions are an important symbol of success in life.

MAJOR FINDINGS:

The purpose of the multiple surveys conducted by Richins and Dawson (1992a) was to construct a new measure of materialism. Except for some basic psychometric qualities, no relationship between the scale and other constructs was made in the article. However, among the many findings shown in supplementary material (Richins and Dawson 1992b) was that those high in **material success** stated that they spent more than twice as much as those low in **material success** on buying the things they wanted but spent less than half as much on contributions to church/charities.

COMMENTS:

Although reported separately here, Richins and Dawson (1992a) argued for combining scores of the three components of materialism. Much of the article's information is about the overall instrument's psychometric quality. For example, in the same studies described previously, it was reported to have alphas between .80 and .88 and a test-retest reliability of .87.

REFERENCES:

Richins, Marsha L. and Scott Dawson (1990), ''A Preliminary Report of Scale Development,'' in Advances in Consumer Research, Vol. 17, Marvin E. Goldberg, Gerald Gorn, and Richard W. Pollay, eds. Provo, UT: Association for Consumer Research, 169-75.

_____ and _____ (1992a), ''A Consumer Values Orientation for Materialism and Its Measurement: Scale Development and Validation,'' JCR, 19 (December), 303-16.

_____ and _____ (1992b), ''A Consumer Values Orientation for Materialism and Its Measurement: Scale Development and Validation,'' unpublished results of hypothesis tests by subscale, available from the authors.

SCALE ITEMS: MATERIALISM (SUCCESS)

Strongly disagree	Disagree	Neutral	Agree	Strongly agree
1	2	3	4	5

1. I admire people who own expensive homes, cars, and clothes.
2. Some of the most important achievements in life include acquiring material possessions.
3. I don't place much emphasis on the amount of material objects people own as a sign of success. **(r)**
4. The things I own say a lot about how well I'm doing in life.
5. I like to own things that impress people.
6. I don't pay much attention to the material objects other people own. **(r)**

SCALE NAME: Mood

SCALE DESCRIPTION:

A four-item, seven-point semantic differential purporting to measure the feeling that has been induced by an object in a person. The measure was called *affect* by Yi (1990) but it is more similar to *mood* scales than to measures of *affect*.

SCALE ORIGIN:

Although not specifically stated, it would appear that the scale is original to Yi (1990).

SAMPLES:

Yi (1990) gathered data from **72** undergraduate students who were recruited from introductory business courses. Little more was said about the subjects except that they were assigned randomly to one of four treatment groups.

RELIABILITY:

Yi (1990) reported an alpha of **.90** for the scale.

VALIDITY:

Yi (1990) reported no examination of the scale's validity.

ADMINISTRATION:

Administration of the scale appears to have occurred as part of a larger questionnaire after subjects had viewed test stimuli (Yi 1990). A high score on the scale would indicate that after exposure to some particular stimulus, a respondent experiences a positive feeling (e.g., happy), whereas a low score suggests that a respondent is feeling bad.

MAJOR FINDINGS:

Yi (1990) examined how exposure to magazine articles can effect processing of ads in the magazine. The **mood** scale was used as a manipulation check to determine if affective priming of the ad context had occurred. Indeed, subjects in the positive condition had more positive **moods**.

REFERENCES:

Yi, Youjae (1990), ''Cognitive and Affective Priming Effects of the Context for Print Advertisements,'' *JA*, 19 (2), 40-48.

SCALE ITEMS: MOOD

How did the _____ make you feel?*

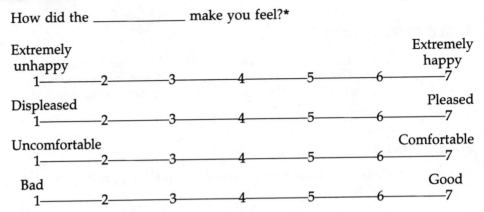

Extremely unhappy						Extremely happy
1——————2——————3——————4——————5——————6——————7

Displeased						Pleased
1——————2——————3——————4——————5——————6——————7

Uncomfortable						Comfortable
1——————2——————3——————4——————5——————6——————7

Bad						Good
1——————2——————3——————4——————5——————6——————7

* This lead-in sentence was not provided in the article but something like it appears to be necessary to use with the items.

SCALE NAME: Mood (Global)

SCALE DESCRIPTION:

A four-item, five-point, Likert-type scale measuring a particular state of feeling of transient duration. Mood is conceptualized as being a milder form of feeling than emotions that nonetheless is not sudden and lasts hours or days. The scale measures mood at a particular point in time on a simple good/bad continuum rather than attempting to assess various dimensions of mood.

SCALE ORIGIN:

Most of the developmental work on the scale is reported by Peterson and Sauber (1983), with previous work reported by Peterson (1981) and Peterson and Kerin (1983). Mood was viewed as a "nuisance factor" that introduces nonsampling error into response data. The scale was constructed for the purpose of being able to assess its influence statistically on responses by using it as a covariate during data analysis.

With a series of tests employing several samples, Peterson and Sauber (1983) examined the scale's psychometric qualities. In general, the final version of the scale was found to have satisfactory internal consistency (r.74) and examination of its validity indicated that it was not strongly or consistently related to demographic characteristics or item nonresponse. As expected, the stability of the test was found to be low ($r = .18$), given the transitory nature of the construct.

SAMPLES:

The sample used by Boles and Burton (1992) was composed of **213** undergraduate students enrolled in an introductory marketing course. A little more than half of the subjects were male.

Kamins, Marks, and Skinner (1991) used the four-item scale in a pretest and two items (items 1 and 2, unsummed) in the main experiment. The pretest had **50** undergraduate student subjects, and the main study had 124.

Peterson and Wilson (1992) used the scale in a study whose sample was composed of adults living in a major southern city. Telephone surveys were conducted with **186** randomly selected adults.

RELIABILITY:

Alphas of **.84, .814,** and **.74** were reported for the scale by Boles and Burton (1992), Kamins, Marks, and Skinner (1991), and Peterson and Wilson (1992), respectively.

VALIDITY:

None of the studies reported examination of the scale's validity.

ADMINISTRATION:

In Boles and Burton (1992), the scale was self-administered by subjects *before* exposure to a test ad stimulus, whereas Kamins, Marks, and Skinner (1991) administered it *after* subjects had viewed test stimuli. In the Peterson and Wilson (1992) study, the scale was administered along with other questions as part of a telephone survey. A high score on the scale indicates that a respondent is feeling irritable and uncomfortable, whereas a low score suggests that a respondent is in a good mood.

MAJOR FINDINGS:

The study by Boles and Burton (1992) compared scaled measures of ad-related feelings and judgments to free elicitation of same. Subjects' pre-exposure **mood** was not found to be a significant predictor of subsequent attitude toward the ad.

Kamins, Marks, and Skinner (1991) studied the influence of **mood** as evoked by television programming on evaluation of ads. In a pretest, the scale was used to confirm that a program segment expected to make viewers happy and a segment expected to make viewers sad were indeed significantly different in the **moods** they induced.

Peterson and Wilson (1992) reported on the various artifacts that can affect the measurement and interpretation of customer satisfaction. The authors suspected that **mood** was a nuisance variable in satisfaction measurement and provided data in support of that notion.

COMMENTS:

See also Hill and Ward (1989) for another use of the scale.

REFERENCES:

Boles, James and Scot Burton (1992), ''An Examination of Free Elicitation and Response Scale Measures of Feelings and Judgments Evoked by Television Advertisements,'' *JAMS*, 20 (Winter), 225-33.

Hill, Ronald P. and James C. Ward (1989), ''Mood Manipulation in Marketing Research: An Examination of Confounding Effects,'' *JMR*, 26 (February), 97-104.

Kamins, Michael A., Lawrence J. Marks, and Deborah Skinner (1991), ''Television Commercial Evaluation in the Context of Program Induced Mood: Congruency Versus Consistency Effects,'' *JA*, 20 (June), 1-14.

Peterson, Robert A. (1981), ''An Exploratory Investigation of Mediating Factors in Retail Store Image Responses,'' in *Advances in Consumer Research*, Vol. 8, Kent Monroe, ed. Ann Arbor, MI: Association for Consumer Research, 662-64.

_____ and Roger A. Kerin (1983), ''Store Image Measurement in Patronage Research: Fact and Artifact,'' in *Patronage Behavior and Retail Management*, William R. Darden and Robert F. Lusch, eds. New York: North-Holland, 293-306.

_____ and Matthew Sauber (1983), ''A Mood Scale For Survey Research,'' in *Proceedings of the American Marketing Association's Educators' Conference.* Chicago: American Marketing Association, 409-14.

_____ and William R. Wilson (1992), ''Measuring Customer Satisfaction: Fact and Artifact,'' *JAMS*, 20 (Winter), 61-71.

SCALE ITEMS: MOOD (GLOBAL)

Strongly agree	Agree	Neutral	Disagree	Strongly disagree
1—————	—2—————	—3—————	—4—————	—5

1. Currently, I am in a good mood.
2. As I answer these questions I feel very cheerful.
3. For some reason I am not very comfortable right now. **(r)**
4. At this moment I feel ''edgy'' or irritable. **(r)**

SCALE NAME: Mood (Global)

SCALE DESCRIPTION:

A four-item, seven-point semantic differential measuring a particular state of feeling of transient duration. The scale measures mood at a particular point in time on a simple good/bad continuum rather than attempting to assess various dimensions of mood.

SCALE ORIGIN:

Although Swinyard (1993) says that the scale is adapted from a scale developed by Peterson and Sauber (1983), the scales are different enough to be treated separately here. It does appear that both scales measure the same construct, but the items are very different.

SAMPLES:

Little description was provided about the sample used by Swinyard (1993) in his experiment, except to say that it was composed of **109** undergraduate business students. Another person besides the class instructor conducted the experiment, and students were monitored to ensure that they worked quietly and independently on their randomly assigned exercises.

RELIABILITY:

Swinyard (1993) reported an alpha of **.85** for the scale. The author also indicated that data were collected for another item, but it was not used in the final version of the scale because of its unacceptably low item-total correlation.

VALIDITY:

Swinyard (1993) reported no examination of the scale's validity.

ADMINISTRATION:

The scale was self-administered by subjects as part of a questionnaire after exposure to experimental stimuli (Swinyard 1993). A high score on the scale indicates that a respondent is in a good mood, whereas a low score suggests that a respondent is sad, irritable, or upset in some way.

MAJOR FINDINGS:

Swinyard (1993) investigated the impact of **mood** and other factors on shopping intentions. The **mood** scale used a manipulation check, which was considered to be successful. Although **mood** was not found to have a significant main effect on shopping intentions, it did appear to play important roles in several interaction effects.

REFERENCES:

Peterson, Robert and Matthew Sauber (1983), ''A Mood Scale For Survey Research,'' in *Proceedings of the American Marketing Association's Educators' Conference*. Chicago: American Marketing Association, 409-14.

Swinyard, William R. (1993), ''The Effects of Mood, Involvement, and Quality of Store Experience on Shopping Intentions,'' *JCR*, 20 (September), 71-280.

SCALE ITEMS: MOOD (GLOBAL)*

Sad   ___ : ___ : ___ : ___ : ___ : ___ : ___   Happy
               1   2   3   4   5   6   7

Bad mood   ___ : ___ : ___ : ___ : ___ : ___ : ___   Good mood
               1   2   3   4   5   6   7

Irritable   ___ : ___ : ___ : ___ : ___ : ___ : ___   Pleased
               1   2   3   4   5   6   7

Depressed   ___ : ___ : ___ : ___ : ___ : ___ : ___   Cheerful
               1   2   3   4   5   6   7

* The lead-in sentence used by Swinyard (1993) was not provided in the article, but it likely asked subjects to describe how they felt at that moment.

SCALE NAME: Need for Cognition

SCALE DESCRIPTION:

An 18-item, summated ratings scale measuring a person's tendency to engage in and enjoy effortful information processing.

SCALE ORIGIN:

The scale was developed by Cacioppo, Petty, and Kao (1984) as a short form of a 34-item version (Cacioppo and Petty 1982). The short version was reported to have a theta coefficient (maximized Cronbach's alpha) of .90 compared with the long version's .91. Also, the two versions of the scale had a correlation of .95. Finally, factor analysis indicated that all items except one had substantial and higher loadings on the first factor than subsequent factors. It is unclear why the weak item was not suggested for elimination in further use, and because factor loadings were not presented in the article, it is unknown which particular item it is.

SAMPLES:

The sample used by Batra and Stayman (1990) was composed of **251** undergraduate business students attending the University of Texas and recruited from student organizations. The organizations as well as the students were given $3 each for their participation.

Darley and Smith (1993) used the mall intercept method of recruiting respondents. The final number of subjects was not directly specified, but it was said that "thirty subjects were randomly assigned to each treatment" of the 3 × 2 factorial design. Given this, it is assumed that analysis was based on data from about 180 subjects. All respondents were 18 years of age or older, with 27% being more than 45 years of age. The sample was split almost evenly on gender (51% male) and marital status (56% married).

RELIABILITY:

Both Batra and Stayman (1990) and Darley and Smith (1993) reported an alpha of **.88** for the scale.

VALIDITY:

No information regarding the scale's validity was reported by either Batra and Stayman (1990) or Darley and Smith (1993).

ADMINISTRATION:

Batra and Stayman (1990) administered the scale to subjects at the beginning of an experiment *before* a mood manipulation stimulus was presented, and the subjects in the Darley and Smith (1993) experiment filled out the scale along with other measures *after* exposure to the experimental stimulus. High scores on the scale indicate that respondents engage in and enjoy effortful cognitive activities.

MAJOR FINDINGS:

Batra and Stayman (1990) investigated the influence of mood on brand attitudes. Although no main effect of **need for cognition** on brand attitude was found, there were several significant interaction effects. Specifically, the attitudinal effect of mood was greater for those with low **need for cognition**. In contrast, the attitudinal effect of argument quality was greater for those with high **need for cognition**.

Darley and Smith (1993) examined the objectivity of claims made in advertising as well as media type (print or radio). **Need for cognition** was examined solely as a covariate. The only dependent measure on which it had an effect was brand beliefs.

COMMENTS:

Also see Inman, McAlister, and Hoyer (1990), MacKenzie (1986), and Meyers-Levy and Tybout (1989) for other uses of the scale.

REFERENCES:

Batra, Rajeev and Stayman (1990), "The Role of Mood in Advertising Effectiveness," *JCR*, 17 (September), 203-14.

Cacioppo, John T. and Richard E. Petty (1982), "The Need for Cognition," *Journal of Personality and Social Psychology*, 42 (1), 116-31.

———, ———, and Chuan Feng Kao (1984), "The Efficient Assessment of Need for Cognition," *Journal of Personality Assessment*, 48 (3), 306, 307.

Darley, William K. and Robert E. Smith (1993), "Advertising Claim Objectivity: Antecedents and Effects," *JM*, 57 (October), 100-113.

Inman, J. Jeffrey, Leigh McAlister, and Wayne D. Hoyer (1990), "Promotion Signal: Proxy for a Price Cut?" *JCR*, 17 (June), 74-81.

MacKenzie, Scott B. (1986), "The Role of Attention in Mediating the Effect of Advertising on Attribute Importance," *JCR*, 13 (September), 174-95.

Meyers-Levy, Joan and Alice M. Tybout (1989), "Schema Congruity as a Basis for Product Evaluation," *JCR*, 16 (June), 39-54.

SCALE ITEMS: NEED FOR COGNITION

1. I would prefer complex to simple problems.
2. I like to have the responsibility of handling a situation that requires a lot of thinking.
3. Thinking is not my idea of fun. **(r)**
4. I would rather do something that requires little thought than something that is sure to challenge my thinking abilities. **(r)**
5. I try to anticipate and avoid situations where there is a likely chance I will have to think in depth about something. **(r)**
6. I find satisfaction in deliberating hard and for long hours.

7. I only think as hard as I have to. **(r)**
8. I prefer to think about small, daily projects to long-term ones. **(r)**
9. I like tasks that require little thought once I have learned them. **(r)**
10. The idea of relying on thought to make my way to the top appeals to me.
11. I really enjoy a task that involves coming up with new solutions to problems.
12. Learning new ways to think doesn't excite me very much. **(r)**
13. I prefer my life to be filled with puzzles that I must solve.
14. The notion of thinking abstractly is appealing to me.
15. I would prefer a task that is intellectual, difficult, and important to one that is somewhat important but does not require much thought.
16. I feel relief rather than satisfaction after completing a task that required a lot of mental effort. **(r)**
17. It's enough for me that something gets the job done: I don't care how or why it works. **(r)**
18. I usually end up deliberating about issues even when they do not affect me personally.

SCALE NAME: Non-Search Purchase Tendency

SCALE DESCRIPTION:

A three-item, seven-point, Likert-like scale measuring the probability that a consumer would forego much if not all methodical prepurchase information search activity and instead make a rather immediate product selection. The measure was referred to by Murray (1985, 1991) as *Buy*.

SCALE ORIGIN:

The scale was developed by Murray (1985) in his dissertation research. The same data are used for the article described subsequently (Murray 1991).

SAMPLES:

The sample was composed of **256** students attending Arizona State University. Nearly 53% of the sample was female and the mean age was nearly 24 years. Students were assigned randomly to one of 15 different treatments systematically varied in terms of the "serviceness" of the three products they responded to.

RELIABILITY:

A mean alpha of **.871** was reported for the scale averaged over 15 different products systematically varied in their service attributes. For products with high, moderate, and low service attributes, mean alphas of .867, .856, and .857, respectively, were reported. Because the reliability of the scale was calculated across 15 products, it was not based on responses to any one product.

VALIDITY:

No information regarding the scale's validity was reported.

ADMINISTRATION:

The scale was administered as part of a larger questionnaire to students in a classroom setting. Low scores on the scale suggest that respondents do little or no prechoice external search, whereas high scores imply that consumers gather information before making a purchase.

MAJOR FINDINGS:

The purpose of the study by Murray (1991) was to determine if consumers use information sources in a distinctive way for products varying in their "serviceness." The results indicated that the self-reported tendency to engage in outright buy (**non-search purchase**) is greater for products low in service attributes (goods).

COMMENTS:

The items in this scale are part of a 25-item battery that can be administered together to measure several aspects of a consumer's prepurchase search activity.

REFERENCES:

Murray, Keith B. (1985), "Risk Perception and Information Source Use For Products Differing in Service Attributes," doctoral dissertation, Arizona State University: Tempe, Arizona.

_____ (1991), "A Test of Services Marketing Theory: Consumer Information Acquisition Activities," *JM*, 55 (January), 10-25.

SCALE ITEMS: NON-SEARCH PURCHASE TENDENCY

Circle the number that best describes your reaction to each statement if you were considering the purchase of a _____.

definitely would	= 1
generally would	= 2
would be inclined to	= 3
may or may not	= 4
would not be inclined to	= 5
generally would not	= 6
definitely would not	= 7

1. . . . simply go ahead and make a selection of the product or service without additional information or further prepurchase deliberation.
2. . . . buy the first purchase alternative I found.
3. . . . be ready to make a purchase selection and not worry about acquiring more information prior to buying.

SCALE NAME: Normative Outcomes

SCALE DESCRIPTION:

A four-item, seven-point, summated ratings scale focusing on the extent to which the motivation to own a product is viewed as instrumental to achieving a social purpose. The *beliefs* version of the scale measures the perceived probability that certain desirable consequences will occur. The *evaluation* version measures the personal importance of these consequences. There are also *direct* and *indirect* versions of the scale. As shown in "Scale Items," the difference between the two has to do with whether the items are responded to in the first person (direct version) or the third person (indirect version).

SCALE ORIGIN:

Although not specifically stated by Fisher (1993), the scale(s) are original (Fisher 1994). They were refined during a pretest phase using 90 students.

SAMPLES:

Fisher (1993) reported on three studies, though the scale(s) were only used in the first two. Both these studies were two group experiments: one group in each study received a *direct* version of the scale and the other received an *indirect* version. The sample in study 1 was composed of male and female undergraduate students, with **92** subjects being assigned to each group. Similarly, the convenience sample used in study 2 was composed of mixed-gender undergraduate students. The direct group had **170** students and the indirect group had **182**.

RELIABILITY:

As noted previously, there were several versions of the scale. The author reported separate alphas for the different versions. For the *direct* version of the scale, alphas were **.91** and **.92** for the *beliefs* and *evaluations* versions, respectively. For the *indirect* version, alphas were **.82** and **.88** for the *beliefs* and *evaluations* versions, respectively. No alphas were reported for the scale(s) as used in study 2.

VALIDITY:

Fisher (1993) did not specifically address the validity of the scale(s), though the results of the confirmatory factor analysis provided some evidence of unidimensionality.

ADMINISTRATION:

The scale(s) were administered to the subjects after they had been exposed to experimental stimuli (Fisher 1993). High scores on the *beliefs* version of the scale indicate that a respondent considers it very likely that a product will have certain desirable social consequences, whereas high scores on the *evaluation* version suggest that a respondent thinks the specified outcomes are very important. As used by Fisher, normative outcomes were calculated as the sum of the product of belief and evaluation item scores.

MAJOR FINDINGS:

Using three studies, Fisher (1993) examined the ability of indirect questioning to reduce the influence of social desirability bias on self-report measures. Among the many findings reported was that the association between adoption intentions and **normative outcomes** was significantly higher for the group receiving the indirect version of the scale than it was for the group receiving the direct version.

COMMENTS:

Fisher (1993) used the scale to measure students' perceptions regarding a fictional new product idea: cordless headphones. If a group other than students is studied then the term *student* should be replaced with a word/phrase that describes an important reference group that the respondents are members of (e.g., professors, employees, housewives). If a general term such as *persons* is used, it changes the meaning of the scale somewhat.

REFERENCES:

Fisher, Robert J. (1994), personal correspondence.
_____ (1993), ''Social Desirability Bias and the Validity of Indirect Questioning,'' *JCR*, 20 (September), 303-15.

SCALE ITEMS: NORMATIVE OUTCOMES*

Directions for all versions of scale: The following statements are outcomes that might result from buying the new headphones. For each statement please indicate the likelihood and importance of each outcome.
General question and response scale accompanying *direct belief* version of scale:

How **likely** is this to occur?

Not very likely	___ : ___ : ___ : ___ : ___ : ___ : ___	Likely
	0 1 2 3 4 5 6	

General question and response scale accompanying *direct evaluation* version of scale:

How **important** is this outcome as a reason for purchase?

Not very important	___ : ___ : ___ : ___ : ___ : ___ : ___	Important
	0 1 2 3 4 5 6	

Items for *direct* version of scale:
1. Others I know would like the idea that I bought one of the new products.
2. Students I know would have a favorable reaction to my buying one of the new products.
3. Students I know would be interested that I owned one of the new products.
4. People I know would be pleased that I had one of the new products.

General question and response scale accompanying *indirect belief* version of scale:

How **likely** is the typical student to expect this outcome?

Not very   ___ : ___ : ___ : ___ : ___ : ___ : ___   Likely
likely   0   1   2   3   4   5   6

General question and response scale accompanying *indirect evaluation* version of scale:

How **important** is this outcome to the typical student as a reason a for purchase?

Not very   ___ : ___ : ___ : ___ : ___ : ___ : ___   Important
important   0   1   2   3   4   5   6

Items for *indirect* version of scale:

THE TYPICAL STUDENT WILL THINK THAT . . .
1. . . . others s/he knows will like the idea that s/he bought one of the new products.
2. . . . students s/he knows will have a favorable reaction to his/her buying one of the new products.
3. . . . students s/he knows would be interested that s/he owned one of the new products.
4. . . . people s/he knows would be pleased that s/he has one of the new products.

* The items were supplied by Fisher (1994).

SCALE NAME: Nostalgia Proneness

SCALE DESCRIPTION:

An eight-item, nine-point, Likert-type scale measuring the degree of preference one has toward objects that were more common in the past.

SCALE ORIGIN:

A 20-item scale was developed and refined by Holbrook (1993), as detailed subsequently.

SAMPLES:

Holbrook (1993) reported using the scale in two studies. The sample in the first study was composed of **167** students (57% male) from two introductory marketing classes at a large graduate school of business. Analysis was limited to those who were between the ages of 21 and 34 years and indicated that they were from the United States.

Data in the second study were collected **by but not from** students in the same classes as in the first study during a subsequent semester. They were asked to have questionnaires filled out by Americans of at least 18 years of age but who were not present or former students of the school. This led to there being **156** usable survey forms. The sample was 60% female, and ages ranged from 21 to 85 years.

RELIABILITY:

Holbrook (1993) reported the construct reliability and alpha for the scale to be **.78** in study 1 and **.73** in study 2.

VALIDITY:

In study 1 a confirmatory factor analysis was performed on the original version of the scale, and it did not appear to be unidimensional (Holbrook 1993). After eliminating some items, the eight items shown subsequently were found to fit a one-factor model. A confirmatory factor analysis in study 2 also provided some evidence of the eight items' unidimensionality.

ADMINISTRATION:

The scale was self-administered in both studies as part of a larger survey instrument (Holbrook 1993). A high score on the scale suggests that a respondent has a great longing for things that were more popular in days gone by, whereas a low score indicates that a respondent prefers things that are relatively recent and new.

MAJOR FINDINGS:

The purpose of the study by Holbrook (1993) was to examine the independent influences of age and **nostalgia proneness** on consumer preferences. Indeed, the evidence led the author to conclude that both variables are connected to nostalgia-related preferences but that age and **nostalgia proneness** represent different constructs, with only trivial variance being shared between them.

REFERENCE:

Holbrook, Morris B. (1993), ''Nostalgia and Consumption Preferences: Some Emerging Patterns of Consumer Tastes,'' *JCR*, 20 (September), 245-56.

SCALE ITEMS: NOSTALGIA PRONENESS

Strongly disagree ___ : ___ : ___ : ___ : ___ : ___ : ___ : ___ : ___ Strongly agree
         1   2   3   4   5   6   7   8   9

1. They don't make 'em like they used to.
2. Things used to be better in the good old days.
3. Products are getting shoddier and shoddier.
4. Technological change will insure a brighter future. **(r)**
5. History involves a steady improvement in human welfare. **(r)**
6. We are experiencing a decline in the quality of life.
7. Steady growth in GNP has brought increased human happiness. **(r)**
8. Modern business constantly builds a better tomorrow. **(r)**

SCALE NAME: Novelty Experience Seeking

SCALE DESCRIPTION:

An 80-item, five-point, Likert-type response scale. The scale is intended to capture a person's tendency to approach rather than avoid varied and novel experiences. The originator of the scale has said that the "degree of novelty in any experience is a function of the discrepancy between an individual's past experience and the present one" (Pearson 1970, p. 199). An abridged version of the instrument measured two dimensions of innovativeness with eight items each using a dichotomous response scale (Venkatraman 1991; Venkatraman and Price 1990).

SCALE ORIGIN:

The scale used by Steenkamp and Baumgartner (1992) was adapted from a scale constructed by Pearson (1970). The former used a Likert-type response format, and the latter used a dichotomous format (like/dislike).

Pearson developed the scale because she thought that previous measures of novelty seeking did not provide full coverage of the construct's domain. She constructed the following four types of statements differing on the source of stimulation and the type of subjective experience: external sensation, internal sensation, external cognition, and internal cognition. Internal consistencies (KR-20) for the four subscales ranged from .76 to .87, and the internal consistency for the scale as a whole was .87. The correlation among the subscales was low to moderate, with the highest correlation being .50 between external cognition and internal cognition. The highest correlation (.38) between the Novelty Experience Seeking scale and a global measure of novelty was with a 34-item version of the Sensation Seeking scale (Zuckerman et al. 1964).

SAMPLES:

The sample used by Steenkamp and Baumgartner (1992) was composed of 223 volunteers from undergraduate marketing courses at a university. A lottery with cash prizes was used to help motivate students to participate.

Venkatraman (1991) collected data from a household list compiled by Dunhill International. A systematic sampling plan was used so that households were selected from each state in the same proportions that they were represented in the country's population. Of the 450 surveys mailed out, 18 245 usable forms were returned. Respondents tended to be male (59.4%), have white collar type jobs ((57.1%), and be college graduates (68.7%). More than half (53.5%) were between 30 and 44 years of age, and the average annual income was $41,440. This same sample was referred to in Venkatraman and Price (1990) as "study 3."

RELIABILITY:

Steenkamp and Baumgartner (1992) reported a reliability (LISREL) of **.913** for the total scale. Reliabilities of .89, .84, .81, and .88 were found for the external sensation, internal sensation, external cognitive, and internal cognitive subscales, respectively.

Venkatraman and Price (1990) reported an alpha of **.64** for this scale.

VALIDITY:

Steenkamp and Baumgartner (1992) concluded that principal components factor analysis did not provide strong evidence of a unidimensional or a four-dimensional structure. Scores on the scale had correlations of between .41 and .46 with three other measures of optimum stimulation level, which provides some evidence of convergent validity. A confirmatory factor analysis of all four scales also provided some evidence of convergent validity because the Novelty Experience Seeking scale loaded significantly on the underlying construct, although it had the lowest loading of the four measures tested.

Confirmatory factor analysis was used by Venkatraman and Price (1990) to examine the structure of 16 items taken from the full version of the Novelty Experience Seeking scale. The results indicated that the best fit came from a hierarchical second-order model. Specifically, cognitive and sensory innovativeness dimensions formed the higher-order factors, and they in turn were each composed of internal and external dimensions.

ADMINISTRATION:

The scale was administered by Steenkamp and Baumgartner (1992) as part of a larger questionnaire composed primarily of four scales that measured optimum stimulation level in various ways. The questionnaire was handed out to students in class, and they were asked to bring the completed form back to the next class period. The abridged version of the scale as used by Venkatraman (1991; Venkatraman and Price 1990) was included with many other measures in a self-administered mail questionnaire. High scores on the scale indicate that respondents desire novel sensations and cognitions, whereas low scores indicate respondents have a tendency to avoid such experiences.

MAJOR FINDINGS:

Steenkamp and Baumgartner (1992) studied the role of optimum stimulation level in exploratory consumer behavior. A weighted composite of the **Novelty Experience Seeking** scale and three other well-known measures were used to examine people's desire for stimulation. Beyond the information provided previously regarding reliability and validity, the authors did not discuss the findings of any one scale (however, they can be obtained from the authors).

The purpose of the study by Venkatraman (1991; Venkatraman and Price 1990) was to examine the impact of innovativeness on two different types of adoption decisions: the cognitive innovators and the sensory innovators. The results showed within-segment consistencies in innovation-related characteristics for two different product types but also that there were within-segment differences as well between the two products.

COMMENTS:

Because the full scale is so long and all the items are stated in the positive direction, some caution regarding response styles is advised. Moreover, although a score on the full scale provides a general idea of one's desire for novelty seeking, it is composed of multiple dimensions, and scores on those separate dimensions should have greater meaning and validity.

REFERENCES:

Pearson, Pamela H. (1970), "Relationships Between Global and Specified Measures of Novelty Seeking," *Journal of Consulting and Clinical Psychology*, 34 (2), 199-204.

Steenkamp, Jan-Benedict E.M. and Hans Baumgartner (1992), "The Role of Optimum Stimulation Level in Exploratory Consumer Behavior," *JCR*, 19 (December), 434-48.

Venkatraman, Meera P. (1991), "The Impact of Innovativeness and Innovation Type on Adoption," *JR*, 67 (Spring), 51-67.

_____ and Linda L. Price (1990), "Differentiating Between Cognitive and Sensory Innovativeness: Concepts, Measurement, and Implications," *Journal of Business Research*, 20 (June), 293-315.

Zuckerman, Marvin, E.A. Kolin, L. Price, and I. Zoob (1964), "Development of a Sensation-Seeking Scale," *Journal of Consulting Psychology*, 28, 477-82.

SCALE ITEMS: NOVELTY EXPERIENCE SEEKING*

Directions: Listed below are a series of statements that describe things you might do or experiences you might have. Please use the following scale to indicate your degree of liking or disliking with each of the statements. Circle the number that best represents your opinion. Work rapidly and give your first impression.

Strongly disagree	Disagree	Neither agree nor disagree	Agree	Strongly agree
—2——————	—1——————	—0——————	—1——————	—2

External Sensation

1. Exploring the ruins of an old city in Mexico.
2. Being on a raft in the middle of the Colorado River. #
3. Riding on a sled in Alaska pulled by huskies.
4. Scuba diving in the Bahamas.
5. Being at the top of a roller coaster ready to go down.
6. Sleeping out under pine trees and stars.
7. Watching a colorful bullfight in Spain.
8. Going on a safari in Africa to hunt lions.
9. Orbiting the Earth in a spaceship.
10. Skiing down a high slope in the Alps.
11. Climbing to the top of a high rugged mountain.

12. Riding the rapids in a swift moving stream. #
13. Walking into an old deserted house at midnight.
14. Driving a sports car in the Indianapolis 500.
15. Diving from a board 50 feet above the water.
16. Riding a wild horse in a rodeo.
17. Steering a sled down a steep hill covered with trees. #
18. Walking across a swinging bridge over a deep canyon. #
19. Swinging on a vine across a river filled with snakes.
20. Camping out in a wilderness location.

Internal Sensation
1. Letting myself go in fantasy before I go to sleep.
2. Losing myself in daydreams when I am bored with what is going on.
3. Letting myself experience new and unusual feelings.
4. Watching a red rose turn blue before my eyes.
5. Looking through a blue bottle and seeing people in a dark restaurant.
6. Having an unusual dream in which I swam underwater for hours.
7. Having a vivid dream with strange colors and sounds. #
8. Having a dream in which I lived in England in an old, haunted castle.
9. Seeing a duck with the head of a cat.
10. Having a dream in which I seemed to be flying.
11. Dreaming that I was lying on the beach with the waves washing over me.
12. Letting my body totally relax and seeing what I feel.
13. Feeling chills run all over my body.
14. Having my feelings change from moment to moment.
15. Having a strange new feeling as I awake in the morning.#
16. Experiencing abrupt changes in my moods.
17. Experiencing my feelings intensely.
18. Suddenly feeling happy for no reason at all.
19. Focusing inside on the flow of my feelings.
20. Having a vivid and unusual daydream as I am riding along. #

External Cognitive
1. Finding out how a carburetor on a car works.
2. Finding out the meanings of words I don't know. +
3. Learning about a subject I don't know much about.
4. Learning new facts about World War II.
5. Understanding how a computer works.
6. Visiting a factory to see how paper is made.
7. Figuring out how a light meter works.
8. Seeing a glass blowing exhibition and listening to an explanation.
9. Reading the World Almanac.
10. Planning moves in checkers or chess.
11. Discovering a difficult word in a crossword puzzle.
12. Solving a problem involving numbers or figures.
13. Figuring out how much it would cost to construct a building.
14. Finding out how to unlock the two pieces of a wire puzzle.
15. Discovering the villain in a detective story before he is revealed.

16. Learning how to put a watch together.
17. Putting together a complicated picture puzzle.
18. Reading a book entitled How Things Work.
19. Figuring out how many bricks it would take to construct a fireplace. +
20. Learning how to make pottery.

Internal Cognitive
1. Thinking about why people behave the way they do.
2. Knowing why politicians act the way they do.
3. Trying to figure out the meaning of unusual statements. +
4. Thinking a lot about a new idea.
5. Thinking of different ways to explain the same thing. +
6. Thinking about unusual events or happenings.
7. Figuring out the shortest distance from one city to another. +
8. Analyzing my own dreams.
9. Figuring out why I did something.
10. Analyzing my own feelings and reactions. +
11. Thinking about ideas that contradict each other.
12. Listening to a lecture or talk that makes me think afterwards.
13. Reading books on subjects that stimulate me to think.
14. Seeing movies after which I think about something differently.
15. Discussing unusual ideas. +
16. Reading articles in the newspaper that provoke my thought.
17. Thinking about why the world is in the shape it is. +
18. Analyzing a theory to see if it is a good one.
19. Figuring out why some event happened the way it did.
20. Starting off with a new idea and seeing the new ones suggested by the original one.

* Venkatraman (1991; Venkatraman and Price 1990) used a dichotomous rating scale such that Like = 1 and Dislike = 0. Moreover, instead of having four subscales and four separate scores, there were two scales for which separate scores were calculated. Items composing the **cognitive innovativeness** scale are indicated by a + symbol, and those used in the **sensory innovativeness** scale are identified with the # symbol.

SCALE NAME: Opinion Leadership (Price)

SCALE DESCRIPTION:

A six-item, seven-point, Likert-type scale measuring a consumer's self-reported tendency to be used by others as a good source of price information for a variety of products. This measures a general tendency rather than the likelihood that the behavior occurs for any particular product category. Lichtenstein, Ridgway, and Netemeyer (1993) referred to the scale as *Price Mavenism*.

SCALE ORIGIN:

The scale is a revision of the Market Maven scale by Feick and Price (1987). Lichtenstein, Ridgway, and Netemeyer (1993) modified the six items in that scale and generated eight more. These 14 items were tested along with many others in a pretest. The sample was composed of 341 nonstudent adult consumers who had the grocery-shopping responsibility for their households. Factor analysis and coefficient alpha were used to eliminate weaker items. The ten items remaining were reported to have an alpha of .90. These items were used in the main study, though the next round of analysis eliminated four of them, leaving the final version of the scale with six items. Of these six, four were very similar to items used by Feick and Price (1987).

SAMPLES:

Lichtenstein, Ridgway, and Netemeyer (1993) collected data from shoppers who had received questionnaires in one of two grocery stores in a western SMSA (Boulder, Colorado). One thousand questionnaires were handed out at the stores, and **582** usable ones were returned by mail. A majority of the sample was female (75.9%) and married (58.6%). The median annual income range was $35,000–$49,999, and the median age was range was 35 to 44 years.

RELIABILITY:

The main study by Lichtenstein, Ridgway, and Netemeyer (1993) showed an alpha for the scale of **.90**.

VALIDITY:

Lichtenstein, Ridgway, and Netemeyer (1993) used confirmatory factor analysis to conclude that the scale was unidimensional and showed evidence of discriminant validity.

ADMINISTRATION:

In the study by Lichtenstein, Ridgway, and Netemeyer (1993), the scale was part of a survey instrument self-administered by shoppers after leaving the grocery store. A high score on the scale indicates that a respondent is likely to be a diffuser of information about product prices to others, whereas a low score suggests that he/she is not sought out by others for such information.

MAJOR FINDINGS:

Lichtenstein, Ridgway, and Netemeyer (1993) identified and measured seven related but distinct price perception constructs. **Price opinion leadership** was a significant predictor of only one of the dependent variables examined in the study, intention to redeem a coupon for free bread. Specifically, there was a slightly negative relationship with a person having some **price opinion leadership** and intending to use a particular coupon given in the study redeemable for free bread at a nearby bakery.

REFERENCES:

Feick, Lawrence F. and Linda L. Price (1987), ''The Market Maven: A Diffuser of Marketplace Information,'' *JM*, 51 (January), 83-97.
Lichtenstein, Donald R., Nancy M. Ridgway, and Richard G. Netemeyer (1993), ''Price Perceptions and Consumer Shopping Behavior: A Field Study,'' *JMR*, 30 (May), 234-45.

SCALE ITEMS: OPINION LEADERSHIP (PRICE)

Strongly disagree ___ : ___ : ___ : ___ : ___ : ___ : ___ Strongly agree
               1   2   3   4   5   6   7

1. People ask me for information about prices for different types of products.
2. I'm considered somewhat of an expert when it comes to knowing the prices of products.
3. For many kinds of products, I would be better able than most people to tell someone where to shop to get the best buy.
4. I like helping people by providing them with price information about many kinds of products.
5. My friends think of me as a good source of price information.
6. I enjoy telling people how much they might expect to pay for different kinds of products.

SCALE NAME: Parental Style (Concept-Orientation)

SCALE DESCRIPTION:

A seven-item, five-point, Likert-type summated ratings scale measuring the degree to which a parent reports taking an interest in his/her kids' ideas regarding the use of money and purchasing products. The tone suggested in the items is of positive communication in which the child's role, assistance, and opinion is respected rather than their purchases being dictated to them.

SCALE ORIGIN:

Some of the items in this scale are similar to those used in a scale by Moschis (1978, p. 45). However, items in that measure were written from the child's point of view.

SAMPLES:

The same data set is reported on in two articles by Carlson and Grossbart (1988; Grossbart, Carlson, and Walsh 1991). The survey instrument was distributed to mothers through students at three elementary schools of an unidentified U.S. city. The schools were chosen on a convenience basis but appeared to represent a variety of socioeconomic areas of the city. A $1 contribution was made to the PTO for each completed questionnaire returned by the children. Analysis was based on **451** completed questionnaires. Ninety-three percent of the responding mothers indicated that they were the primary person in the child's socialization.

RELIABILITY:

Carlson and Grossbart (1988; Grossbart, Carlson, and Walsh 1991) reported an alpha of **.71** and a beta of **.61** for the scale.

VALIDITY:

Carlson and Grossbart (1988; Grossbart, Carlson, and Walsh 1991) reported no examination of scale validity.

ADMINISTRATION:

The scale was self-administered along with many other measures in the questionnaire used by Carlson and Grossbart (1988; Grossbart, Carlson, and Walsh 1991). High scores on the scale mean that respondents report a high frequency of positive communication with their children, whereas low scores imply that there is either a dictatorial mode of communication from the parents or that there is little communication of any kind at all.

MAJOR FINDINGS:

The authors (Carlson and Grossbart (1988; Grossbart, Carlson, and Walsh 1991). investigated the relationship between general parental socialization styles and children's consumer socialization. In a factor analysis of scale scores, scores on the **Concept-Orientation** scale loaded on a factor described as the "parent-child communication about consumption." On the basis of this, a significant difference was found in the degree of parent-child communication among several of the parental socialization styles examined.

REFERENCES:

Carlson, Les and Sanford Grossbart (1988), "Parental Style and Consumer Socialization of Children," *JCR*, 15 (June), 77-94.

Grossbart, Sanford, Les Carlson, and Ann Walsh (1991), "Consumer Socialization and Frequency of Shopping with Children," *JAMS*, 19 (Summer), 155-63.

Moschis, George P. (1978), *Acquisition of the Consumer Role By Adolescents*, Research Monograph No. 82. Atlanta, GA: Publishing Services Division, College of Business Administration, Georgia State University.

SCALE ITEMS: PARENTAL STYLE (CONCEPT ORIENTATION)

Very seldom	Seldom	Sometimes	Often	Very often
1	2	3	4	5

1. I ask my child to help me buy things for the family.
2. I tell my child to decide how to spend his/her money.
3. I tell my child to decide about things he/she should or shouldn't buy.
4. I tell my child buying things he/she likes is important even if others don't like them.
5. I ask my child what he/she thinks about things he/she buys for him/herself.
6. I ask my child for advice about buying things.
7. To teach my child to become a consumer I allow my child to learn from his/her own experience.

SCALE NAME: Personal Growth

SCALE DESCRIPTION:

A six-item, seven-point, Likert-type scale measuring the degree to which a person who has just had an extraordinary experience views it as being personally challenging and instructive.

SCALE ORIGIN:

The origin of the scale was not specified by Arnould and Price (1993), but it appears that it was developed in a series of stages described in their article. A previous use of the scale had an alpha of .84 and a correlation of .65 with a measure of trip satisfaction.

SAMPLES:

Very little information was provided by Arnould and Price (1993) regarding their sample. The respondents are described simply as a stratified random sample of people taking multi-day river trips with one of three clients' rafting companies. A total of **137** clients filled out post-trip questionnaires, but only 97 of those had completed pre-trip surveys.

RELIABILITY:

Arnould and Price (1993) reported an alpha of **.91** for the scale.

VALIDITY:

A considerable amount of research in the form of participant observation and focus groups was conducted by Arnould and Price (1993) in preparation for development of the scale and probably improved the scale's content validity. A factor analysis of the items in this scale and two others showed that the items for this scale had loadings of at least .72 on the same factor and no greater than .29 on either of the other two factors.

ADMINISTRATION:

The scale was self-administered by respondents as part of a larger survey after they had finished the rafting trip (Arnould and Price 1993). High scores on the scale suggest that respondents have experienced something unusual that has led to a sense of personal renewal and growth.

MAJOR FINDINGS:

Arnould and Price (1993) explored the impact of several experiential variables on satisfaction with an extraordinary hedonic experience. There was a strong and significant correlation (r = .62) between one's feeling that the experience had produced **personal growth** and overall satisfaction with the trip.

REFERENCE:

Arnould, Eric J. and Linda L. Price (1993), ''River Magic: Extraordinary Experience and the Extended Service Encounter,'' *JCR*, 20 (June), 24-45.

SCALE ITEMS: PERSONAL GROWTH*

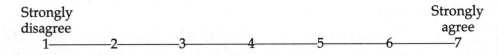

Strongly
disagree

1————2————3————4————5————6————7

Strongly
agree

1. I felt a sense of adventure or risk.
2. I felt personally challenged.
3. I felt an adrenaline rush.
4. I learned new things.
5. I mastered new skills.
6. I tested my limits.

SCALE NAME: Personal Outcomes

SCALE DESCRIPTION:

A four-item, seven point summated ratings scale focusing on thoughts about the features of a product that would be intrinsically valuable. The *beliefs* version of the scale measures the perceived probability that the product has certain characteristics. The *evaluation* version measures the personal importance of these features. There are also *direct* and *indirect* versions of the scale. As shown in "Scale Items," the difference between the two has to do with whether the items are responded to in the first person (direct version) or the third person (indirect version).

SCALE ORIGIN:

Although not specifically stated by Fisher (1993), the scale(s) are original (Fisher 1994). They were refined during a pretest phase using 90 students.

SAMPLES:

Fisher (1993) reported on three studies, though the scale(s) were only used in the first two. Both of these studies were two-group experiments: one group in each study received a *direct* version of the scale, and the other received an *indirect* version. The sample in study 1 was composed of male and female undergraduate students, with **92** subjects being assigned to each group. Similarly, the convenience sample used in study 2 was composed of mixed-gender undergraduate students. The direct group had **170** students and the indirect group had **182**.

RELIABILITY:

As noted previously, there were several versions of the scale. The author reported separate alphas for the different versions. For the *direct* version of the scale, alphas were **.68** and **.73** for the *beliefs* and *evaluations* versions, respectively. For the *indirect* version, alphas were **.75** and **.79** for the *beliefs* and *evaluations* versions, respectively. No alphas were reported for the scale(s) as used in study 2.

VALIDITY:

Fisher (1993) did not specifically address the validity of the scale(s), though the results of the confirmatory factor analysis provided some evidence of unidimensionality.

ADMINISTRATION:

The scale(s) were administered to the subjects after they had been exposed to experimental stimuli (Fisher 1993). High scores on the *beliefs* version of the scale indicate that a respondent considers it very likely that a product will have certain desirable attributes, whereas high scores on the *evaluation* version suggest that a respondent thinks the specified features are very important. As used by Fisher, personal outcomes was calculated as the sum of the product of belief and evaluation item scores.

MAJOR FINDINGS:

Using three studies, Fisher (1993) examined the ability of indirect questioning to reduce the influence of social desirability bias on self-report measures. Among the many findings reported was that there was no significant difference between the direct and indirect groups in the association between adoption intentions and **personal outcomes**.

COMMENTS:

Fisher (1993) used the scale to measure students' perceptions regarding a fictional new product idea: cordless headphones. If a group other than students is studied then the term *student* should be replaced in the indirect version with a word/phrase that describes an important reference group that the respondents are members of (e.g., professors, employees, housewives). If a general term such as *persons* is used, it changes the meaning of the scale somewhat. Much more work would be necessarily to prepare the scale for use with other products.

REFERENCES:

Fisher, Robert J. (1994), personal correspondence.
_____ (1993), "Social Desirability Bias and the Validity of Indirect Questioning," *JCR*, 20 (September), 303-15.

SCALE ITEMS: PERSONAL OUTCOMES*

Directions for all versions of scale: The following statements are outcomes that might result from buying the new headphones. For each statement please indicate the likelihood and importance of each outcome.

General question and response scale accompanying *direct belief* version of scale:

How **likely** is this to occur?

Not likely	___ : ___ : ___ : ___ : ___ : ___ : ___	Very likely
	0 1 2 3 4 5 6	

General question and response scale accompanying *direct evaluation* version of scale:

How **important** is this outcome as a reason for purchase?

Not important	___ : ___ : ___ : ___ : ___ : ___ : ___	Very important
	0 1 2 3 4 5 6	

Items for *direct* version of scale:
1. The new headphones are convenient to use.
2. The new headphones place fewer restrictions on movement than other headphones.
3. The new headphones won't limit my movements.
4. The new headphones provide more freedom of movement than other headphones.

General question and response scale accompanying *indirect belief* version of scale:

How **likely** is the typical student to expect this outcome?

Not   ____ : ____ : ____ : ____ : ____ : ____ : ____   Very
likely   0   1   2   3   4   5   6   likely

General question and response scale accompanying *indirect evaluation* version of scale:

How **important** is this outcome to the typical student as a reason a for purchase?

Not   ____ : ____ : ____ : ____ : ____ : ____ : ____   Very
important   0   1   2   3   4   5   6   important

Items for *indirect* version of scale:
THE TYPICAL STUDENT WILL THINK THAT . . .
1. . . . the new headphones are convenient to use.
2. . . . the new headphones place fewer restrictions on movement than other headphones.
3. . . . the new headphones won't limit his/her movements.
4. . . . the new headphones provide more freedom of movement than other headphones.

* The items were supplied by Fisher (1994).

SCALE NAME: Personal Source Confidence

SCALE DESCRIPTION:

> A seven-item, seven-point, summated ratings scale measuring the amount of confidence a consumer has in personal independent sources (relative or friend) as well as personal advocate sources (store manager or employee).

SCALE ORIGIN:

> The items were developed and used by Murray (1985) in his dissertation research. The same data are used for the article described subsequently (Murray 1991). However, in the dissertation the items composing the personal source usage scale were used to measure two distinct though related measures of information source confidence: personal independent and personal advocate. Items for the two scales were combined in Murray (1991) to form a single measure of personal source confidence.

SAMPLES:

> The sample used by Murray (1991) was composed of **256** students attending Arizona State University. Nearly 53% of the sample was female and the mean age was nearly 24 years. Students were assigned randomly to one of 15 different treatments systematically varied in terms of the "serviceness" of the three products to which they responded.

RELIABILITY:

> Murray (1991) reported no alpha for the nine-item scale. However, a mean alpha of **.897** was reported for the first three items (personal advocate) averaged over 15 different products that were systematically varied in their service attributes (Murray 1985, p. 100). Likewise, a mean alpha of **.901** was reported for the last four items (personal independent).

VALIDITY:

> No information regarding the scale's validity was reported.

ADMINISTRATION:

> The scale was administered as part of a larger questionnaire to students in a classroom setting. Low scores on the scale suggest that respondents have a lot of confidence in using information from personal sources such as friends, family, and store employees.

MAJOR FINDINGS:

> The purpose of the study by Murray (1991) was to determine if consumers use information sources in a distinctive way for products varying in their

"serviceness." The results indicated that respondents have a greater confidence in using **personal sources of information** for service purchases rather than goods.

COMMENTS:

Caution is urged in the use of this scale given that no direct evidence has been presented that the seven items form a scale that is reliable and valid.

REFERENCES:

Murray, Keith B. (1985), "Risk Perception and Information Source Use For Products Differing in Service Attributes," doctoral dissertation, Arizona State University: Tempe, Arizona.

_____ (1991), "A Test of Services Marketing Theory: Consumer Information Acquisition Activities," *JM*, 55 (January), 10-25.

SCALE ITEMS: PERSONAL SOURCE CONFIDENCE

Indicate the confidence you have in each of the following information sources when considering the purchase of a _____.

extreme confidence	= 1
moderate confidence	= 2
slight confidence	= 3
neutral in terms of confidence	= 4
slight lack of confidence	= 5
moderate lack of confidence	= 6
extreme lack of confidence	= 7

1. The opinion of an employee of the store, retail outlet, or office (e.g., receptionist, delivery person, etc.)
2. Salesperson
3. Owner or manager of the store, office, or retail outlet
4. Recommendations of a neighbor or a friend
5. Family members or relatives
6. What previous customers had to say about the product
7. Friends or acquaintances

SCALE NAME: Personal Source Usage

SCALE DESCRIPTION:

A seven-item, seven-point, Likert-like scale measuring the probability that a consumer would base his/her purchase decision on information gathered from personal independent sources (relative or friend) as well as personal advocate sources (store manager or employee).

SCALE ORIGIN:

The items were developed and used by Murray (1985) in his dissertation research. The same data are used for the article described subsequently (Murray 1991). However, in the dissertation the items composing the personal source usage scale were used to measure two distinct though related measures of information source usage: personal independent and personal advocate. Items for the two scales were combined in Murray (1991) to form a single measure of personal source usage.

SAMPLES:

The sample used by Murray (1991) was composed of **256** students attending Arizona State University. Nearly 53% of the sample was female and the mean age was nearly 24 years. Students were assigned randomly to one of 15 different treatments systematically varied in terms of the ''serviceness'' of the three products to which they responded.

RELIABILITY:

Murray (1991) reported no alpha for the seven-item scale. However, a mean alpha of **.821** was reported for the first four items (personal independent) averaged over 15 different products that were systematically varied in their service attributes (Murray 1985, p. 100). Likewise, a mean alpha of **.72** was reported for the last three items (personal advocate).

VALIDITY:

No information regarding the scale's validity was reported.

ADMINISTRATION:

The scale was administered as part of a larger questionnaire to students in a classroom setting. Low scores on the scale suggest that respondents would base a purchase decision on information gained from personal sources of information such as friends, family, and store employees.

MAJOR FINDINGS:

The purpose of the study by Murray (1991) was to determine if consumers use information sources in a distinctive way for products varying in their ''serviceness.'' The results indicated that respondents have a greater preference to use **personal sources of information** for service purchases rather than goods.

COMMENTS:

The items in this scale are part of a 25-item battery that can be administered together to measure several aspects of a consumer's pre-purchase search activity. As indicated previously, no direct evidence has been presented that the seven items form a scale that is reliable and valid.

REFERENCES:

Murray, Keith B. (1985), ''Risk Perception and Information Source Use For Products Differing in Service Attributes,'' doctoral dissertation, Arizona State University: Tempe, Arizona.

———— (1991), ''A Test of Services Marketing Theory: Consumer Information Acquisition Activities,'' *JM*, 55 (January), 10-25.

SCALE ITEMS: PERSONAL SOURCE USAGE

Circle the number that best describes your reaction to each statement if you were considering the purchase of a _____.

definitely would	= 1
generally would	= 2
would be inclined to	= 3
may or may not	= 4
would not be inclined to	= 5
generally would not	= 6
definitely would not	= 7

1. . . . try to remember what alternative my friends use.
2. . . . ask members of my family or a relative for their opinion.
3. . . . ask the opinion of a friend or someone I know.
4. . . . pay attention to what previous customers had to say about the product or service.
5. . . . ask the opinion of the salesperson.
6. . . . ask the opinion of the owner or manager of the store, office, or retail outlet.
7. . . . ask the opinion of an employee of the firm offering the product such as a receptionist, delivery person, etc.

SCALE NAME: Personalizing Shopper

SCALE DESCRIPTION:

A four-item, five-point, Likert-type scale measuring the degree to which a consumer enjoys shopping where store employees know his/her name and will converse with him/her about topics other than products. The scale was referred to by Forman and Sriram (1991) as *Shopping as a Social Experience* (SSE).

SCALE ORIGIN:

The scale is original to the study by Forman and Sriram (1991).

SAMPLES:

A convenience sample of **327** adults in a large northeastern U.S. metropolitan area was used by Forman and Sriram (1991). Respondents were asked to return questionnaires by mail to ensure anonymity. Fifty-nine percent of the sample was female and the median age was 44 years of age. About 43% of the sample was married, and 32% had completed some college.

RELIABILITY:

Forman and Sriram (1991) reported an alpha of **.70** for the scale. Item-total correlations ranged from .42 to .58.

VALIDITY:

Forman and Sriram (1991) conducted a factor analysis of the items composing the scale and examined the intercorrelations of several scales used in their study. The findings provided some evidence of the scale's unidimensionality as well as its convergent and discriminant validities.

ADMINISTRATION:

The scale was administered as part of a larger questionnaire apparently through personal interviews (Forman and Sriram 1991). High scores on the scale indicate that respondents like to shop where they are known and spoken to by store employees, whereas low scores suggest that they prefer to be left alone when shopping.

MAJOR FINDINGS:

Forman and Sriram (1991) examined the affect of automated retailing systems on lonely consumers. Although there was some mixed evidence, the authors ultimately concluded that lonely and nonlonely consumers were probably not too much different in their tendencies to be **personalizing shoppers**.

REFERENCE:

Forman, Andrew M. and Ven Sriram (1991), ''The Depersonalization of Retailing: Its Impact on the 'Lonely' Consumer,'' *JR*, 67 (Summer), 226-43.

SCALE ITEMS: PERSONALIZING SHOPPERS

Strongly disagree	Disagree	Neutral	Agree	Strongly agree
1	2	3	4	5

1. I like when salespeople know my name.
2. In a store, I would prefer to be left alone. **(r)**
3. I talk to salespeople other than about the purchase.
4. I enjoy talking to store personnel.

SCALE NAME: Pleasure

SCALE DESCRIPTION:

A multi-item, summated ratings scale measuring one's pleasure-related emotional reaction to an environmental stimulus. Holbrook and colleagues (1984) used a six-item, seven-point semantic differential version of the scale. Four of the positive anchors were used by themselves in a different version of the scale by Dawson, Bloch, and Ridgway (1990). Mano and Oliver (1993) used four positive items and a five-point response scale.

SCALE ORIGIN:

This scale is taken from the work of Mehrabian and Russell (1974). Given previous work by others as well as their own research, they proposed that there are three factors that compose all emotional reactions to environmental stimuli. They referred to these factors as *pleasure, arousal,* and *dominance.* A series of studies were used to develop measures of each factor. A study of the "final" set of items used 214 University of California undergraduates, each of whom used the scales to evaluate a different subset of six situations. (The analysis was based, therefore, on 1284 observations.) A principal components factor analysis with oblique rotation was used, and the expected three factors emerged. Pleasure, arousal, and dominance explained 27%, 23%, and 14% of the available evidence, respectively. Scores on the pleasure scale had correlations of -.07 and .03 with arousal and dominance, respectively. Dominance had a correlation of .18 with arousal.

The set of items used by Mano and Oliver (1993) appear to have been used first as a summated scale by Mano (1991). With 224 college students the scale was reported to have an alpha of .82. A factor analysis indicated that three of the four items had strong loadings on the same factor, and a cluster analysis grouped all four items together.

SAMPLES:

Bateson and Hui (1992) conducted two separate studies, one described as a laboratory experiment and the other a field quasi-experiment. The subjects were recruited from the streets of a southern England coastal town and randomly assigned to either a slide or video setting. Complete data were received from 119 persons (60 with slides and 59 videos). In the second study, passengers in a major train station in London were asked to fill out a questionnaire regarding their experience at the train ticket office. Usable surveys were received back from 92 people.

The sample collected by Dawson, Bloch, and Ridgway (1990) came from a large arts and crafts market in a major West Coast city. Shoppers were approached over four summer days by trained survey administrators and asked to participate. Those who did participate were paid $1. The analysis was based on data from 278 respondents. The only significant difference noted between the sample and that of the surrounding SMSA was that the former contained more females.

All that is known about the sample used by Holbrook and colleagues (1984) is that it was composed of **60** MBA students with a mean age of 25.6 years.

Data were collected by Mano and Oliver (1993) from **118** undergraduate business students attending a midwestern U.S. university.

RELIABILITY:

Alphas of **.86**, **.72**, **.89**, and **.81** were reported for the versions of the scale used by Bateson and Hui (1992), Dawson, Bloch, and Ridgway (1990), Holbrook and colleagues (1984), and Mano and Oliver (1993), respectively.

VALIDITY:

Some idea of the scale's convergent validity can be taken from correlations between it and another scale used to measure the same construct (Bateson and Hui 1992, p. 278). In three different situations the correlations were .65 or more, providing evidence that the two measures were tapping into the same construct.

Dawson, Bloch, and Ridgway (1990) performed an exploratory factor analysis on the items composing this scale as well as three other items composing an *Arousal* scale. Although the items loaded highest on their respective factors, it was mentioned that one item (happy) had split loadings.

The validity of the scale was not specifically addressed by Holbrook and colleagues (1984) or Mano and Oliver (1993).

ADMINISTRATION:

The scale was self-administered as part of a larger survey instrument in the field study conducted by Dawson, Bloch, and Ridgway (1990). In the study by Holbrook and colleagues (1984), the scale was self-administered along with several other measures in the middle of individual experimental sessions. The scale was part of a longer questionnaire self-administered by students in a classroom study (Mano and Oliver 1993). The scale was self-administered by subjects along with other measures after being exposed to experimental stimuli in the studies conducted by Bateson and Hui 1992.

High scores on the scale suggest that respondents were happy with some specified stimulus, whereas low scores imply that they are displeased with the stimulus. Holbrook and colleagues (1984) noted that scores were normalized for each individual by subtracting the scale mean from the response to each item and then summing the corrected numeric responses.

MAJOR FINDINGS:

Bateson and Hui (1992) investigated the ecological validity of slide and video presentations in controlled (laboratory) settings. The illustration of ecological validity made use of most of the same variables used in the study by Hui and Bateson (1991) and produced similar findings. In particular, perceived crowding and control both seemed to have been significant effects on **pleasure**.

Dawson, Bloch, and Ridgway (1990) investigated the role played by shopping motives in shaping the emotions triggered during a retail shopping experienced. The clearest finding involving the construct measured by this scale was that the **pleasure** experienced by shoppers at the market had a significant positive relationship with their product-related shopping motives and to a lesser extent their experience-related motives.

Holbrook and colleagues (1984) examined the role played by emotions, performance, and personality in the enjoyment of games. In general, it was found that emotions depend on personality-game congruity, perceived complexity, and prior performance. Specifically, **pleasure** expressed with playing a video game was most significantly predicted by a match between cognitive style (visualizing/verbalizing) and game format (visual/verbal), perceived complexity of the game, and number of successful performances out of four immediately preceding plays.

Mano and Oliver (1993) examined the dimensionality and causal structure of product evaluation, affect, and satisfaction. Among the many findings involving the **pleasure** emotion was that it was significantly greater for subjects in a high-involvement manipulation.

COMMENTS:

As noted previously, this scale originally was developed along with two other scales, arousal and dominance. Although scored separately, they are typically used together in a study.

See also Havlena and Holbrook (1986) as well as Hui and Bateson (1991).

REFERENCES:

Dawson, Scott, Peter H. Bloch, and Nancy M. Ridgway (1990), ''Shopping Motives, Emotional States, and Retail Outcomes,'' *JR*, 66 (Winter), 408-27.

Havlena, William J. and Morris B. Holbrook (1986), ''The Varieties of Consumption Experience: Comparing Two Typologies of Emotion in Consumer Behavior,'' *JCR*, 13 (December), 394-404.

Holbrook, Morris B., Robert W. Chestnut, Terence A. Oliva, and Eric A. Greenleaf (1984), ''Play as a Consumption Experience: The Roles of Emotions, Performance, and Personality in the Enjoyment of Games,'' *JCR*, 11 (September), 728-39.

Hui, Michael K. and John E. G. Bateson (1991), ''Perceived Control and the Effects of Crowding and Consumer Choice on the Service Experience,'' *JCR*, 18 (September), 174-84.

Mano, Haim (1991), ''The Structure and Intensity of Emotional Experiences: Method and Context Convergence,'' *Multivariate Behavioral Research*, 26 (3), 389-411.

_____ and Richard L. Oliver (1993), ''Assessing the Dimensionality and Structure of the Consumption Experience: Evaluation, Feeling, and Satisfaction,'' *JCR*, 20 (December), 451-66.

Mehrabian, Albert and James A. Russell (1974), *An Approach to Environmental Psychology*. Cambridge, MA: The MIT Press.

SCALE ITEMS: PLEASURE*

Happy	___ : ___ : ___ : ___ : ___ : ___ : ___	Unhappy
	7 6 5 4 3 2 1	
Pleased	___ : ___ : ___ : ___ : ___ : ___ : ___	Annoyed
	7 6 5 4 3 2 1	
Satisfied	___ : ___ : ___ : ___ : ___ : ___ : ___	Unsatisfied
	7 6 5 4 3 2 1	
Contented	___ : ___ : ___ : ___ : ___ : ___ : ___	Melancholic
	7 6 5 4 3 2 1	
Hopeful	___ : ___ : ___ : ___ : ___ : ___ : ___	Despairing
	7 6 5 4 3 2 1	
Relaxed	___ : ___ : ___ : ___ : ___ : ___ : ___	Bored
	7 6 5 4 3 2 1	

* This is the version of the scale used by Holbrook and colleagues (1984). The version used by Dawson, Bloch, and Ridgway (1990) used just the positive anchors of items 1, 3, 4, and 6 and a five-point response scale ranging from "does not describe at all" to "describes a great deal." Likewise, Mano and Oliver (1993) used just the positive anchors to items the items 1-3 as well as the item "in a good mood." The actual items used by Bateson and Hui (1992) were not explicitly provided.

SCALE NAME: Pleasure

SCALE DESCRIPTION:

A six-item, six-point summated ratings scale measuring the pleasure-related emotional reaction one has to an environmental stimulus. The scale focuses on the person's feelings rather than being a direct description of the stimulus.

SCALE ORIGIN:

The scale used by Baker, Levy, and Grewal (1992) is a modified version of one developed by Russell and Pratt (1980). Specifically, the latter constructed a five-item measure of the "unpleasant" quality of a place. This scale was reported to have an alpha of .87 (n = 241). Baker, Levy, and Grewal (1992) used those items plus one from the "pleasant" quality scale also developed by Russell and Pratt (1980). Therefore, the scale could be more accurately described as measuring the "unpleasant" quality of places except that by reversing scores on five of the items it appears instead to measure the pleasant dimension.

SAMPLES:

The data analyzed by Baker, Levy, and Grewal (1992) came from an experiment using **147** undergraduate students. The study used a 2 (store ambient levels) × 2 (store social levels) between-subjects factorial design with between 35 and 39 subjects per cell.

RELIABILITY:

Baker, Levy, and Grewal (1992) reported an alpha of **.84** for the scale.

VALIDITY:

Baker, Levy, and Grewal (1992) reported that the intra-item correlations within the scale were higher than the intercorrelations with items from a related scale (arousal). Moreover, confirmatory factor analysis indicated that a two-factor model (pleasure and arousal) fit the data better than a one factor model.

ADMINISTRATION:

The scale was self-administered by subjects as part of a questionnaire after exposure to experimental stimuli (Baker, Levy, and Grewal 1992). High scores on the scale suggest that respondents consider some specified stimulus to make them feel comfortable and satisfied, whereas low scores imply that they feel unpleasant.

MAJOR FINDINGS:

Baker, Levy, and Grewal (1992) examined the effects of two retail atmospheric factors, ambient and social cues, on respondents' **pleasure**, arousal, and shopping intentions. Overall, the results led the authors to conclude that store environment influences consumers' **pleasure** emotion, which enhances shopping intentions.

REFERENCES:

Baker, Julie, Michael Levy, and Dhruv Grewal (1992), ''An Experimental Approach to Making Retail Store Environmental Decisions,'' *JR*, 68 (Winter), 445-60.

Russell, James A. and Geraldine Pratt (1980), ''A Description of Affective Quality Attributed to Environments,'' *Journal of Personality and Social Psychology*, 38 (February), 311-22.

SCALE ITEMS: PLEASURE

Directions: Below is a list of words that can be used to describe places. We would like you to rate how accurately each word below described this place. Use the following rating scale for your answer.*

Extremely ____ : ____ : ____ : ____ : ____ : ____ Extremely
inaccurate   1   2   3   4   5   6   accurate

1. nice
2. dissatisfying **(r)**
3. displeasing **(r)**
4. repulsive **(r)**
5. unpleasant **(r)**
6. uncomfortable **(r)**

* This are the directions as reported by Russell and Pratt (1980).

#189 *Possessiveness*

SCALE NAME: Possessiveness

SCALE DESCRIPTION:

A nine-item, five-point, Likert-type summated ratings scale measuring the degree to which a person desires to maintain control over one's possessions. A four-item version of the scale was used by O'Guinn and Faber (1989).

SCALE ORIGIN:

The origin of the scale is reported in Belk (1984). The measure of possessiveness was one of three scales constructed for examining aspects of Materialism. Initial pools of 30 or more items were tested for each of the three measures with 237 business school students. Using factor analysis, item-total correlations, and measures of internal consistency, seven or more items were chosen from each pool to measure the three materialism-related constructs. The eight items retained for measuring possessiveness were reported to have an alpha of .68.

SAMPLES:

Belk (1984, 1985) examined the scale in various ways with three more samples. One was composed of 48 business students. Another sample had 338 subjects, 213 of whom were business students. (These two samples were reported to be about two-thirds male.) A third sample was composed of 33 families representing 99 people who ranged in age from 13 to 92 years.

O'Guinn and Faber (1989) used two samples. One was composed of 386 completed responses (out of 808 questionnaires sent) from people who previously had written an organization that aided compulsive buyers. A second group was used for comparison purposes and was intended to represent the general population. Eight hundred questionnaires were mailed to people in three Illinois areas: Chicago, Springfield, and Bloomington-Normal. Two mailings produced a total of 250 completed survey forms.

RELIABILITY:

An alpha of .57 was reported for one of the Belk (1984) samples (n = 338). A two-week interval, test-retest correlation of .87 (n = 48) was reported for another Belk (1984, 1985) sample. O'Guinn and Faber (1989) calculated an alpha of .61.

VALIDITY:

Belk (1984) compared scale scores with other measures in a multitrait-multimethod matrix. As evidence of convergent validity, scores on the possessiveness scale were correlated significantly with two other measures used to assess the same construct. Only partial support for discriminant validity was found. Evidence of criterion validity was found by noting that two known groups had significantly different mean scores on the scale and the differences were in the hypothesized directions.

O'Guinn and Faber (1989) made no examination of scale validity beyond factor analysis. Items regarding possessiveness and two other materialism-related constructs were factor analyzed, and three factors clearly emerged. The authors did indicate that the scales were slightly modified on the basis of the factor analysis, however.

ADMINISTRATION:

The scale was one of several measures in each of the studies, which were self-administered. High scores on the scale indicate that respondents have a strong tendency to buy and save objects, whereas low scores indicate respondents are more willing to rent, borrow, and discard items.

MAJOR FINDINGS:

The purpose of Belk (1984) was to discuss the construction and characteristics of three materialism-related constructs: envy, **possessiveness**, and nongenerosity. Many of the findings are reported previously. In addition, possessiveness had a low but significant negative correlation with life satisfaction. Belk (1985) examined further aspects of the three subscales and also the psychometric characteristics of the materialism scale as a whole. In particular, he studied generational differences in materialism. Among the many findings was that the youngest and middle generations were similar in their **possessiveness** but were both significantly more **possessive** than the oldest generation.

O'Guinn and Faber (1989) studied compulsive shopping. Their results showed that a sample of compulsive shoppers were more, but not significantly more, **possessive** than a general sample of consumers.

COMMENTS:

The three materialism-related measures mentioned here have been used summed not only separately but together as well. Two alphas for the combined scale were reported by Belk (1985): .66 (n = 338) and .73 (n = 48). Belk (1985) also reported a test-retest correlation of .68 (n = 48). O'Guinn and Faber (1989; Faber and O'Guinn 1992) calculated an alpha of .71 for the combined scale.

REFERENCES:

Belk, Russell W. (1984), ''Three Scales to Measure Constructs Related to Materialism: Reliability, Validity, and Relationships to Measures of Happiness,'' in *Advances in Consumer Research*, Vol. 11. Thomas Kinnear, ed. Provo, UT: Association for Consumer Research, 291-97.

———— (1985), ''Materialism: Trait Aspects of Living in the Material World,'' *JCR*, 12 (December), 265-80.

Faber, Ronald J. and Thomas C. O'Guinn (1992), ''A Clinical Screener for Compulsive Buying,'' *JCR*, 19 (December), 459-69.

O'Guinn, Thomas C. and Ronald J. Faber (1989), ''Compulsive Buying: A Phenomenological Exploration,'' *JCR*, 16 (September), 147-57.

SCALE ITEMS: POSSESSIVENESS*

Strongly disagree	Disagree	Neutral	Agree	Strongly agree
1————	—2————	——3————	—4————	——5

1. Renting or leasing a car is more appealing to me than owning one. **(r)**
2. I tend to hang on to things I should probably throw out.
3. I get very upset if something is stolen from me even if it has little monetary value.
4. I don't get particularly upset when I lose things. **(r)**
5. I am less likely than most people to lock things up. **(r)**
6. I would rather buy something I need than borrow it from someone else.
7. I worry about people taking my possessions.
8. When I travel I like to take a lot of photographs.
9. I never discard old pictures or snapshots.

* Items similar to or exactly the same as the following were used by O'Guinn and Faber (1989): items 2, 3, 7, and 9.

SCALE NAME: Power (Reward)

SCALE DESCRIPTION:

A three-item, seven-point summated ratings scale measuring a consumer's perception that a store employee has reward power such that the consumer will be given a reward (discount) for buying a product.

SCALE ORIGIN:

There is no information to indicate that the scale is anything other than original to Netemeyer and Bearden (1992).

SAMPLES:

The experiment conducted by Netemeyer and Bearden (1992) was based on data from a sample of **372** undergraduate students. They were assigned randomly to a 2 (informational influence) × 2 (normative influence) design. The sample was split approximately in half to test two different models of Behavioral Intention. Therefore, there were four cells per model tested, with each cell having between 46 and 49 subjects.

RELIABILITY:

Netemeyer and Bearden (1992) reported the scale to have internal consistency estimates of **.95** and **.94** for the two models of Behavioral Intention that were tested.

VALIDITY:

Netemeyer and Bearden (1992) reported no specific examination of the scale's.

ADMINISTRATION:

The scale was self-administered along with other measures after the experimental manipulation (Netemeyer and Bearden 1992). High scores on the scale indicate that a respondent considers a store employee to have reward power at least with regard to a specific product purchase.

MAJOR FINDINGS:

Netemeyer and Bearden (1992) conducted an experiment to compare the causal structure and predictive ability of the models of Behavioral Intentions by Ajzen and Fishbein (1980) and Miniard and Cohen (1983). The **reward power** of an information source (audio store employee) was manipulated as part of the experimental. The **reward power** scale was used to provide evidence that a successful manipulation had been made.

REFERENCES:

Ajzen, Icek and Martin Fishbein (1980), *Understanding Attitudes and Predicting Social Behavior*. Englewood Cliffs, NJ: Prentice-Hall.

Miniard, Paul W. and Joel B. Cohen (1983), "Modeling Personal and Normative Influences on Behavior," *JCR*, 10 (September), 169-80.

Netemeyer, Richard G. and William O. Bearden (1992), "A Comparative Analysis of Two Models of Behavioral Intention," *JAMS*, 20 (Winter), 49-59.

SCALE ITEMS: POWER (REWARD)

1. If I buy the CD player, the audio store employee will . . .

Not get me the discount	___ :	___ :	___ :	___ :	___ :	___ :	___	Get me the discount
	1	2	3	4	5	6	7	
Not reward me	___ :	___ :	___ :	___ :	___ :	___ :	___	Reward me by getting me the discount
	1	2	3	4	5	6	7	

2. If I buy the CD player, the audio store employee can get me a discount.

strongly disagree	___ :	___ :	___ :	___ :	___ :	___ :	___	strongly agree
	1	2	3	4	5	6	7	

SCALE NAME: Preference Heterogeneity

SCALE DESCRIPTION:

A three-item, seven-point, summated ratings scale measuring the degree to which personal tastes and partiality for a product varies across consumers. According to Feick and Higie (1992), this variance in preference may be due to "different attribute weightings across consumers or to different ideal levels of particular attributes" (p. 10).

SCALE ORIGIN:

The origin of the scale was not specified by Feick and Higie (1992), but it would appear to have been developed for use in their study.

SAMPLES:

Feick and Higie (1992) used the scale in two experiments. The samples were alike in that both had samples composed of students enrolled at a northeastern U.S. university. The first one was a 2 × 2 × 2 between-subjects design with 20 subjects per cell. The sample was composed of **92** male and **68** female MBA students who were required to participate in the experiment for a course credit. The sample in the second experiment was composed of **58** males and **62** females who were either junior or seniors. No students more than 29 years of age were included in the analysis to control for age effects.

RELIABILITY:

Feick and Higie (1992) reported alphas of **.61** and **.84** for the scale in the first and second experiments, respectively.

VALIDITY:

Feick and Higie (1992) provided no information regarding the scale's validity.

ADMINISTRATION:

Feick and Higie (1992) administered the scale after subjects had been exposed to experimental stimuli. A high score on the scale indicates that a respondent perceives that for some specified product there is substantial variation among consumers in what they want, whereas a low score suggests that the respondent thinks there is little variation in tastes and preferences.

MAJOR FINDINGS:

Feick and Higie (1992) investigated the effect of experienced and similar sources of information on attitudes and intentions for services that differ on **preference heterogeneity**. The scale was used as a manipulation check to be sure that the services being examined were significantly different in terms of their perceived **preference heterogeneity**. In the first experiment, respondents said that an auto mechanic had a significantly lower **preference heterogeneity** than a night club. In the second experiment, rug cleaners, plumbers, and accountants were found to have significantly lower scores than restaurants, hair stylists, and interior decorators.

COMMENTS:

The scale was used by Feick and Higie (1992) to measure services, but with a slight change to item 3, the scale could also be used to measure preference heterogeneity for goods.

REFERENCE:

Feick, Lawrence and Robin A. Higie (1992), "The Effects of Preference Heterogeneity and Source Characteristics on Ad Processing and Judgments About Endorsers," JA, 21 (June), 9-24.

SCALE ITEMS: PREFERENCE HETEROGENEITY*

strongly   ___ : ___ : ___ : ___ : ___ : ___ : ___   strongly
disagree   1   2   3   4   5   6   7   agree

1. Most people want the same things from a _____. **(r)**
2. Tastes and preferences are not important in how people choose a _____. **(r)**
3. _____ are a service in which people look for different things.

* The verbal anchors used in the scale were not specified by Feick and Higie (1992) but were likely to have been something like this.

SCALE NAME: Prepurchase Trial Tendency

SCALE DESCRIPTION:

A three-item, seven-point, Likert-like scale measuring the probability that a consumer would base his/her decision on the purchase of a product on his/her first-hand experiences with the product. The measure was referred to by Murray (1985) as ''direct observation/trial.''

SCALE ORIGIN:

A four-item version of the scale was developed by Murray (1985) in his dissertation research. The same data are used for the article described subsequently (Murray 1991), but the scale has only three items.

SAMPLES:

The sample was composed of **256** students attending Arizona State University. Nearly 53% of the sample was female and the mean age was nearly 24 years. Students were assigned randomly to one of 15 different treatments systematically varied in terms of the ''serviceness'' of the three products they responded to.

RELIABILITY:

A mean alpha of **.749** was reported for the scale averaged over 15 different products systematically varied in their service attributes. For products with high, moderate, and low service attributes, mean alphas of .768, .789, and .734, respectively, were reported. Because the reliability of the scale was calculated across 15 products, it was not based on responses to any one product.

VALIDITY:

No information regarding the scale's validity was reported.

ADMINISTRATION:

The scale was administered as part of a larger questionnaire to students in a classroom setting. Low scores on the scale suggest that respondents would base a purchase decision on information gained from trial or observation of the product, whereas high scores imply that respondents make decisions without such information.

MAJOR FINDINGS:

The purpose of Murray's (1991) study was to determine if consumers use information sources in a distinctive way for products varying in their ''serviceness.'' The results indicated that the self-reported tendency to rely on **prepurchase trial** is greater for products low in service attributes (goods).

COMMENTS:

The items in this scale are part of a 25-item battery, which can be administered together to measure several aspects of a consumer's pre-purchase search activity. As noted previously, the four-item scale was used in Murray's (1985) dissertation, but a three-item version was reported in the article (1991). Item 4 appears to be the statement that was dropped given its difference from the others. Certainly, the unidimensionality of the four-item version should be examined before it is used further.

REFERENCES:

Murray, Keith B. (1985), ''Risk Perception and Information Source Use For Products Differing in Service Attributes,'' doctoral dissertation, Arizona State University: Tempe, Arizona.

_____ (1991), ''A Test of Services Marketing Theory: Consumer Information Acquisition Activities,'' *JM*, 55 (January), 10-25.

SCALE ITEMS: PREPURCHASE TRIAL TENDENCY

Circle the number that best describes your reaction to each statement if you were considering the purchase of a _____.

definitely would	= 1
generally would	= 2
would be inclined to	= 3
may or may not	= 4
would not be inclined to	= 5
generally would not	= 6
definitely would not	= 7

1. . . . ask for a demonstration of the product or service.
2. . . . ask to try or sample the product before purchasing.
3. . . . experience first-hand all I could about the product or service.

SCALE NAME: Price Consciousness

SCALE DESCRIPTION:

A five-item, seven-point, Likert-type scale measuring a consumer's willingness to expend the time and energy necessary to shop around if need be to purchase grocery products at the lowest prices.

SCALE ORIGIN:

The scale is original to Lichtenstein, Ridgway, and Netemeyer (1993). Although a few items were found in previous research, many were generated specifically for this study. A total of 18 items for this scale were tested along with many others in a pretest. The sample was composed of **341** nonstudent adult consumers who had the grocery-shopping responsibility for their households. Factor analysis and coefficient alpha were used to eliminate weaker items. The 13 items remaining were reported to have an alpha of .84. These items were used in the main study, although the next round of analysis eliminated eight of them, leaving the final version of the scale with five items.

SAMPLES:

Lichtenstein, Ridgway, and Netemeyer (1993) collected data from shoppers who had received questionnaires in one of two grocery stores in a western SMSA (Boulder, Colorado). One thousand questionnaires were handed out at the stores, and **582** usable ones were returned by mail. A majority of the sample was female (75.9%) and married (58.6%). The median annual income range was $35,000–$49,999, and the median age was range was 35 to 44 years.

RELIABILITY:

The main study by Lichtenstein, Ridgway, and Netemeyer (1993) showed an alpha for the scale of **.85**.

VALIDITY:

Confirmatory factor analysis was used by Lichtenstein, Ridgway, and Netemeyer (1993) to conclude that the scale was unidimensional and showed evidence of discriminant validity.

ADMINISTRATION:

In the study by Lichtenstein, Ridgway, and Netemeyer (1993), the scale was part of a survey instrument self-administered by shoppers after leaving the grocery store. High scores on the scale indicate that respondents are willing to shop around to find lower prices for grocery items, whereas low scores suggest that they feel the money saved by such shopping around is not worth the time and effort.

MAJOR FINDINGS:

Lichtenstein, Ridgway, and Netemeyer (1993) identified and measured seven related but distinct price perception constructs. The dependent variable that **price consciousness** predicted most strongly was examination of store ads before making purchases.

REFERENCE:

Lichtenstein, Donald R., Nancy M. Ridgway, and Richard G. Netemeyer (1993), ''Price Perceptions and Consumer Shopping Behavior: A Field Study,'' *JMR*, 30 (May), 234-45.

SCALE ITEMS: PRICE CONSCIOUSNESS

Strongly   ____ : ____ : ____ : ____ : ____ : ____ : ____   Strongly
disagree   1   2   3   4   5   6   7   agree

1. I am not willing to go to extra effort to find lower prices. **(r)**
2. I will grocery shop at more than one store to take advantage of low prices.
3. The money saved by finding low prices is usually not worth the time and effort. **(r)**
4. I would never shop at more than one store to find low prices. **(r)**
5. The time it takes to find low prices is usually not worth the effort. **(r)**

SCALE NAME: Price Reduction Believability

SCALE DESCRIPTION:

A three-item, Likert-type scale assessing the degree to which a consumer believes that a sale price is a true decrease in the price of a product rather than being the price typically charged by a retailer. The scale was referred to by Lichtenstein, Burton, and Karson (1991) as *cue consistency*.

SCALE ORIGIN:

The scale is apparently original to Lichtenstein, Burton, and Karson (1991).

SAMPLES:

The scale was used in a pretest stage of a study reported by Lichtenstein, Burton, and Karson (1991). The sample was composed of **86** undergraduate business majors.

RELIABILITY:

The scale was used to assess the consistency of six semantic cues under examination in the experimental phase of the study by Lichtenstein, Burton, and Karson (1991). Alphas for these cues ranged from **.28** to **.82** with a mean of .69.

VALIDITY:

Lichtenstein, Burton, and Karson (1991) reported no examination of the scale's validity.

ADMINISTRATION:

The scale was self-administered by students along with a few other measures in a pretest. High scores on the scale imply that respondents agree that the sale price for a product is different from its normal selling price, whereas low scores suggest that respondents believe the sale price is not much different from the price that is usually charged for the product.

MAJOR FINDINGS:

Lichtenstein, Burton, and Karson (1991) studied the way reference price ads are phrased (semantic cues) and consumer's price-related responses. High distinctiveness semantic cues indicate the difference between the advertised price and what is charged by competitors, whereas low consistency cues compare prices charged at other times by the same retailer. As part of the pretest, six different pricing cues were tested for their **price reduction believability** and distinctiveness. Four phrasings of the pricing cues thought to connote low consistency (e.g., "Was $__, Now Only $__") were indeed viewed by subjects as more **believable price reductions** than two other phrasings that emphasized comparisons with other retailers' prices (e.g., ''Seen Elsewhere for $__, Our Price $__'').

REFERENCE:

Lichtenstein, Donald R. Scot Burton, and Eric J. Karson (1991), ''The Effect of Semantic Cues on Consumer Perceptions of Reference Price Ads,'' *JCR*, 18 (December), 380-91.

SCALE ITEMS: PRICE REDUCTION BELIEVABILITY

Disagree   ___ : ___ : ___ : ___ : ___ : ___ : ___   Agree
             1   2   3   4   5   6   7

1. The lower price is a temporary price.
2. The higher price is a price previously charged by the particular merchant running this advertisement.
3. After the sale is over, the advertising merchant will sell the product at a price similar to the higher price.

SCALE NAME: Price-Prestige Relationship

SCALE DESCRIPTION:

A nine-item, seven-point, Likert-type scale measuring a consumer's belief that buying the most expensive brands is a positive experience for oneself and it impresses others. Lichtenstein, Ridgway, and Netemeyer (1993) referred to the scale as *Prestige Sensitivity*.

SCALE ORIGIN:

The scale is original to Lichtenstein, Ridgway, and Netemeyer (1993). Most of the items were generated specifically for this study. A total of 19 items were tested for this scale along with many others in a pretest. The sample was composed of 341 nonstudent adult consumers who had the grocery-shopping responsibility for their households. Factor analysis and coefficient alpha were used to eliminate weaker items. The 11 items remaining were reported to have an alpha of .89. These items were used in the main study, although the next round of analysis eliminated two of them, leaving the final version of the scale with nine items.

SAMPLES:

Lichtenstein, Ridgway, and Netemeyer (1993) collected data from shoppers who had received questionnaires in one of two grocery stores in a western SMSA (Boulder, Colorado). One thousand questionnaires were handed out at the stores, and 582 usable ones were returned by mail. A majority of the sample was female (75.9%) and married (58.6%). The median annual income range was $35,000–$49,999 and the median age was range was 35 to 44 years.

RELIABILITY:

The main study by Lichtenstein, Ridgway, and Netemeyer (1993) showed an alpha for the scale of .87.

VALIDITY:

Confirmatory factor analysis was used by Lichtenstein, Ridgway, and Netemeyer (1993) to conclude that the scale was unidimensional and showed evidence of discriminant validity.

ADMINISTRATION:

In Lichtenstein, Ridgway, and Netemeyer (1993), the scale was part of a survey instrument self-administered by shoppers after leaving the grocery store. A high score on the scale indicates that a respondent generally believes that purchasing high-priced brands leads to greater enjoyment and better impressions, whereas a low score suggests that he/she does not think there is any such general association between price and prestige.

MAJOR FINDINGS:

Lichtenstein, Ridgway, and Netemeyer (1993) identified and measured seven related but distinct price perception constructs. **Prestige sensitivity** was a significant predictor of coupon redemption frequency (self-reported). Specifically, there was a slightly negative relationship between the two variables.

REFERENCE:

Lichtenstein, Donald R., Nancy M. Ridgway, and Richard G. Netemeyer (1993), ''Price Perceptions and Consumer Shopping Behavior: A Field Study,'' *JMR*, 30 (May), 234-45.

SCALE ITEMS: PRICE-PRESTIGE RELATIONSHIP

Strongly ____ : ____ : ____ : ____ : ____ : ____ : ____ Strongly
disagree   1   2   3   4   5   6   7   agree

1. People notice when you buy the most expensive brand of a product.
2. Buying a high priced brand makes me feel good about myself.
3. Buying the most expensive brand of a product makes me feel classy.
4. I enjoy the prestige of buying a high priced brand.
5. It says something to people when you buy the high priced version of a product.
6. Your friends will think your are cheap if you consistently buy the lowest priced version of a product.
7. I have purchased the most expensive brand of a product just because I knew other people would notice.
8. I think others make judgments about me by the kinds of products and brands I buy.
9. Even for a relatively inexpensive product, I think that buying a costly brand is impressive.

SCALE NAME: Price-Quality Relationship

SCALE DESCRIPTION:

A four-item, seven-point, Likert-type scale measuring a consumer's belief that there is a positive relationship between product price and quality.

SCALE ORIGIN:

Gotlieb and Sarel (1991) provided no information regarding the origin of the scale. It appears to have been developed by them for their study, although item 1 is similar to the one-item measure used by Peterson and Wilson (1985).

SAMPLES:

Survey instruments were completed by **148** subjects in the experiment conducted by Gotlieb and Sarel (1991). The subjects were all selected from a pool of upperclasspersons attending a large urban university and were assigned randomly to treatments in a 2 × 2 × 2 factorial experimental design.

RELIABILITY:

Gotlieb and Sarel (1991) reported an alpha of **.90** for the scale.

VALIDITY:

Gotlieb and Sarel (1991) reported no examination of the scale's validity.

ADMINISTRATION:

In Gotlieb and Sarel (1991), the scale was part of a survey instrument self-administered by subjects after being exposed to the experimental stimuli. A high score on the scale indicates that a respondent believes that there is a positive relationship between a product's price and its quality, whereas a low score suggests that he/she does not think there is any such general association between price and quality.

MAJOR FINDINGS:

Gotlieb and Sarel (1991) studied the role of involvement and source credibility on the influence of comparative advertising. The **price-quality relationship** was used in the study as a covariate and was found to have a statistically significant effect on purchase intentions.

REFERENCES:

Gotlieb, Jerry B. and Dan Sarel (1991), ''Comparative Advertising Effectiveness: The Role of Involvement and Source Credibility,'' *JA*, 20 (1), 38-45.
Peterson, Robert A. and William R. Wilson (1985), ''Perceived Risk and Price-

Reliance Schema as Price-Perceived-Quality Mediators," in *Perceived Quality: How Consumers View Stores and Merchandise*, Jacob Jacoby and Jerry C. Olson, eds. Lexington, MA: D.C. Heath and Company, 247-67.

SCALE ITEMS: PRICE-QUALITY RELATIONSHIP

Strongly disagree	___ : ___ : ___ : ___ : ___ : ___ : ___	Strongly agree
	1 2 3 4 5 6 7	

1. The higher the price of the product, the better the quality of the product.
2. The more one pays for the product, the better the quality of the product.
3. A product that costs more will give you better service.
4. Products which are low priced are also low quality.

SCALE NAME: Price-Quality Relationship

SCALE DESCRIPTION:

A four-item, seven-point, Likert-type scale measuring a consumer's belief that there is a positive relationship between product price and quality.

SCALE ORIGIN:

This multi-item summated scale is original to Lichtenstein, Ridgway, and Netemeyer (1993). Inspiration for the scale came from several previous studies of the topic. In particular, item 1 is very similar to the one-item measure used by Peterson and Wilson (1985).

SAMPLES:

Lichtenstein, Ridgway, and Netemeyer (1993) collected data from shoppers who had received questionnaires in one of two grocery stores in a western SMSA (Boulder, Colorado). One thousand questionnaires were handed out at the stores, and **582** usable ones were returned by mail. A majority of the sample was female (75.9%) and married (58.6%). The median annual income range was $35,000–$49,999, and the median age was range was 35 to 44 years.

RELIABILITY:

The main study by Lichtenstein, Ridgway, and Netemeyer (1993) showed an alpha for the scale of **.78**.

VALIDITY:

Lichtenstein, Ridgway, and Netemeyer (1993) used confirmatory factor analysis to conclude that the scale was unidimensional and showed evidence of discriminant validity.

ADMINISTRATION:

In Lichtenstein, Ridgway, and Netemeyer (1993), the scale was part of a survey instrument self-administered by shoppers after leaving the grocery store. A high score on the scale indicates that a respondent believes that there is a positive relationship between a product's price and its quality, whereas a low score suggests that he/she does not think there is any such general association between price and quality.

MAJOR FINDINGS:

Lichtenstein, Ridgway, and Netemeyer (1993) identified and measured seven related but distinct price perception constructs. Belief in a **price-quality relationship** was a significant predictor of only one of the many dependent variables examined in the study, price recall accuracy. Specifically, there was a slightly negative relationship between a person believing in a **price-quality relationship** and their accuracy of recalling prices paid for grocery items.

REFERENCES:

Lichtenstein, Donald R., Nancy M. Ridgway, and Richard G. Netemeyer (1993), "Price Perceptions and Consumer Shopping Behavior: A Field Study," *JMR*, 30 (May), 234-45.

Peterson, Robert A. and William R. Wilson (1985), "Perceived Risk and Price-Reliance Schema as Price-Perceived-Quality Mediators," in *Perceived Quality: How Consumers View Stores and Merchandise*, Jacob Jacoby and Jerry C. Olson, eds. Lexington, MA: D.C. Heath and Company, 247-67.

SCALE ITEMS: PRICE-QUALITY RELATIONSHIP

Strongly disagree ___ : ___ : ___ : ___ : ___ : ___ : ___ Strongly agree

     1 2 3 4 5 6 7

1. Generally speaking, the higher the price of a product, the higher the quality.
2. The old saying "you get what you pay for" is generally true.
3. The price of a product is a good indicator of its quality.
4. You always have to pay a bit more for the best.

SCALE NAME: Product Attribute Correlation

SCALE DESCRIPTION:

It is a three item, seven point summated ratings scale measuring the extent to which a person perceives a relationship between two specific product attributes.

SCALE ORIGIN:

The scale is original to the study by Dick, Chakravarti, and Biehal (1990).

SAMPLES:

The study by Dick, Chakravarti, and Biehal (1990) was based on data supplied by **68** undergraduate business students. A little more than half (53%) were female and the average age was 22 years. The students received extra credit for participating.

RELIABILITY:

Dick, Chakravarti, and Biehal (1990) reported an alpha of **.84** for the scale.

VALIDITY:

Dick, Chakravarti, and Biehal (1990) did not address the scale's validity in the article.

ADMINISTRATION:

The scale was administered by Dick, Chakravarti, and Biehal (1990) along with other measures after subjects had been exposed to experimental procedures. A high score on the scale suggests that a respondent perceives there to be a strong positive association between two specified product attributes such that if a product is known to perform well on one characteristic, it is assumed to perform well on the other one as well.

MAJOR FINDINGS:

Dick, Chakravarti, and Biehal (1990) examined the inferences made by consumers in a choice task involving memory, external information, and missing information. Among the many findings was that subjects who had been manipulated to have highly accessible brand attribute information in memory perceived significantly stronger correlations between two product characteristics, one for which the necessary information had been provided to them and the other for which it had to be inferred.

COMMENTS:

The product category studied by Dick, Chakravarti, and Biehal (1990) was cameras. The items listed here are specific to a study of cameras, and some modification and retesting will be necessary if a similar scale is desired for use in a study of a different product class.

REFERENCE:

Dick, Alan, Dipankar Chakravarti, and Gabriel Biehal (1990), ''Memory-Based Inferences During Consumer Choice,'' *JCR*, 17 (June), 82-93.

SCALE ITEMS: PRODUCT ATTRIBUTE CORRELATION*

1. Using the scale below, please indicate your belief about how related each of the pair of attributes was FOR THE INFORMATION YOU WERE GIVEN IN THE STUDY.

Strong negative relation		Not related at all		Strong positive relation
−3————−2————−1————0————1————2————3				

Based on the information about the cameras THAT YOU WERE GIVEN IN THE EXPERIMENT, indicate the extent to which you agree or disagree with the following statements.

2. Cameras that had low scores on the lens sharpness index usually had high scores on maximum shutter speed. **(r)**
3. Cameras with high scores on the lens sharpness index usually had high scores on maximum shutter speed.

* The instructions before these items appeared on the questionnaire specified the two attributes of interest, e.g., lens sharpness and shutter speed.

SCALE NAME: Product Experience

SCALE DESCRIPTION:

A five-item, seven-point, Likert-type scale measuring the degree of familiarity a consumer has with shopping for some specified product.

SCALE ORIGIN:

The scale was developed by Murray (1985) in his dissertation research. The same data is used for the article described subsequently (Murray and Schlacter (1990)).

SAMPLES:

The sample was composed of **256** students attending Arizona State University. Nearly 53% of the sample was female and the mean age was nearly 24 years. Students were assigned randomly to one of 15 different treatments systematically varied in terms of the "serviceness" of the three products to which they responded.

RELIABILITY:

A mean alpha of **.82** was reported for the scale averaged over 15 different products. For products with high, moderate, and low service attributes, mean alphas of .924, .895, and .905, respectively, were reported.

VALIDITY:

No information regarding the scale's validity was reported.

ADMINISTRATION:

The scale was administered as part of a larger questionnaire to students in a classroom setting. Low scores on the scale suggest that respondents have shopped frequently for the specified product, whereas high scores indicate that they are not familiar with shopping for the product.

MAJOR FINDINGS:

The purpose of the study by Murray and Schlacter (1990) was to examine how products placed along a goods-services continuum vary in the kind and amount of prechoice risk perceived. **Product experience** was included as a covariate in post hoc analysis. Respondents with much **product experience** perceived no significant difference for performance and financial risk across all levels of goods-services. However, performance and financial risk were significantly higher for services rather than goods among respondents with low **product experience**.

COMMENTS:

The overall reliability of the scale reported here appears to have been calculated across 15 products systematically varied in their service attributes and therefore is not based on responses to any one product.

REFERENCES:

Murray, Keith B. (1985), ''Risk Perception and Information Source Use For Products Differing in Service Attributes,'' doctoral dissertation, Arizona State University: Tempe, Arizona.

_____ and John L. Schlacter (1990), ''The Impact of Services Versus Goods on Consumers' Assessment of Perceived Risk and Variability,'' *JAMS*, 18 (Winter), 51-65.

SCALE ITEMS: PRODUCT EXPERIENCE*

Directions: In this part of the questionnaire we are interested in your EXPERIENCE as a consumer with products like _____.

Definitely agree	= 1	Moderately disagree	= 5
Generally agree	= 2	Generally disagree	= 6
Moderately agree	= 3	Definitely disagree	= 7
Neither agree nor disagree	= 4		

1. I have a great deal of experience in buying a product like a _____.
2. I have used or been exposed to this type of product in the past.
3. I am familiar with many brands of this product or service.
4. I frequently shop for this type or similar types of goods and services.
5. I am very confident in buying a _____.

* The name of the generic product being examined should be placed in the blanks.

SCALE NAME: Product Expertise

SCALE DESCRIPTION:

A four-item, seven-point semantic differential measuring the degree of knowledge and experience a person reports having about a specified product class.

SCALE ORIGIN:

There is nothing to indicate that the scale is anything other than original to the research reported by Mishra, Umesh, and Stem (1993).

SAMPLES:

The sample used by Mishra, Umesh, and Stem (1993) was composed of undergraduate and graduate students attending a large university. The mean age of the subjects was 22 years and ranged from 19 to 45 years. Credit was given for participation in the study. The final sample sizes used in the analyses were **359** for beer and television sets and **330** for cars.

RELIABILITY:

Alphas for all three product classes studied by Mishra, Umesh, and Stem (1993) were **.90**.

VALIDITY:

Mishra, Umesh, and Stem (1993) did not specifically examine the validity of the scale.

ADMINISTRATION:

The scale was self-administered along with other measures after subjects had been exposed to stimulus information (Mishra, Umesh, and Stem 1993). A high score on the scale suggests that a respondent views him/ herself as being an expert on a specified product class.

MAJOR FINDINGS:

Mishra, Umesh, and Stem (1993) performed a causal analysis of the attraction effect that occurs when the introduction of a relatively inferior ''decoy'' brand increases (rather than decreases) choice probability of an existing target brand. Product knowledge was treated as a two-dimensional (**expertise** and familiarity) latent construct. The results showed that only for beer was there a significant relationship such that the attraction effect decreases as the knowledge of the product class increases.

REFERENCE:

Mishra, Sanjay, U.N. Umesh, and Donald E. Stem, Jr. (1993), ''Antecedents of the Attraction Effect: An Information-Processing Approach,'' *JMR*, 30 (August), 331-49.

SCALE ITEMS: PRODUCT EXPERTISE

Know very little about	__ :	__ :	__ :	__ :	__ :	__ :	__	Know very much about
	1	2	3	4	5	6	7	
Inexperienced	__ :	__ :	__ :	__ :	__ :	__ :	__	Experienced
	1	2	3	4	5	6	7	
Uninformed	__ :	__ :	__ :	__ :	__ :	__ :	__	Informed
	1	2	3	4	5	6	7	
Novice buyer	__ :	__ :	__ :	__ :	__ :	__ :	__	Expert buyer
	1	2	3	4	5	6	7	

SCALE NAME: Purchase Intention

SCALE DESCRIPTION:

A three-item, summated ratings scale purporting to measure the likelihood that a consumer will buy a product he/she is knowledgeable of. In Bone and Ellen (1992), the product was a fictitious brand of popcorn and respondents were made aware of the product through mock radio ads.

SCALE ORIGIN:

The origin of the scale used by Bone and Ellen (1992) was not specified, but the measure appears to have been developed for use in their study.

SAMPLES:

Two experiments were discussed in the article by Bone and Ellen (1992). The sample for the first experiment was composed of **127** college students, and the second one had **179**. Both experiments were very similar in their collection of data. They took place in an audiovisual lab with students randomly assigned to treatments.

RELIABILITY:

Bone and Ellen (1992) reported alphas for the scale to be **.90** (study 1) and **.92** (study 2).

VALIDITY:

Bone and Ellen (1992). did not directly address the validity of the scale. A correlation matrix did indicate that the scale was associated strongly with Attitude Toward the Brand, as might be expected.

ADMINISTRATION:

The scale was administered by Bone and Ellen (1992) to subjects along with other measures after exposure to an experimental radio advertisement. The individual item scores must be standardized in some way before determining summated scale scores because they do not all share the same number of response alternatives. A high score on the scale indicates that a respondent reports a strong inclination to purchase the advertised product, whereas a low score suggests that the respondent feels little or no compulsion to buy the product.

MAJOR FINDINGS:

Bone and Ellen (1992) investigated the influence that imagery has on recall, brand attitudes, and purchase intentions. Two experiments were conducted, and both showed that imagery-related variables had significant positive impacts on Attitude toward the Ad but not on Brand Attitudes or **Purchase Intentions**.

COMMENTS:

Although retesting would be necessary, the scale items appear to be amenable for modification and use with stimuli other than popcorn.

REFERENCE:

Bone, Paula Fitzgerald and Pam Scholder Ellen (1992), ''The Generation and Consequences of Communication-Evoked Imagery,'' *JCR*, 19 (June), 93-104.

SCALE ITEMS: PURCHASE INTENTION*

1. What is the probability that you will purchase the advertised brand?
   1 = no chance (0 in 100 chances)
   2 =
   3 =
   4 =
   5 =
   6 =
   7 =
   8 =
   9 =
   10 =
   11 = virtually certain (99 in 100 chances)

2. What's the likelihood of you purchasing the advertised brand the next time you buy popcorn?

Extremely unlikely	___ :	___ :	___ :	___ :	___ :	___ :	___ :	___ :	___	Extremely likely
	1	2	3	4	5	6	7	8	9	

3. The next time I purchase popcorn, I will buy the brand in the advertisement.

Strongly disagree	___ :	___ :	___ :	___ :	___ :	___ :	___ :	___ :	___	Strongly agree
	1	2	3	4	5	6	7	8	9	

* These items were reconstructed on the basis of descriptions provided in the article by Bone and Ellen (1992).

SCALE NAME: Purchase Intention

SCALE DESCRIPTION:

A five-item, summated ratings scale purporting to measure the likelihood that a consumer will buy a product he/she is knowledgeable of. The measure was referred to as "willingness to buy" by Dodds, Monroe, and Grewal (1991).

SCALE ORIGIN:

Dodds, Monroe, and Grewal (1991) state that the items for this and two other scales were "developed from previous research" (p. 312), although the source of the items and the extent of the borrowing were not specified.

SAMPLES:

The sample used in Dodds, Monroe, and Grewal (1991) was composed of **585** undergraduate marketing students in a marketing class at a large state university. The study used a 5 × 3 × 3 factorial design with 13 students per cell. The experiment was run a second time, apparently identical to the first one except for the product being studied.

RELIABILITY:

Dodds, Monroe, and Grewal (1991) reported the scale to have alphas of **.97** and **.96** for the two similar experiments in which they were used. Average interitem correlations were .97 and .96.

VALIDITY:

Quantitative results were not provided, but Dodds, Monroe, and Grewal (1991) stated that the results of an exploratory factor analysis indicated a three-factor solution was found using items from this scale and two others. The suggestion was that the items in this scale loaded on one factor.

ADMINISTRATION:

The scale was administered by Dodds, Monroe, and Grewal (1991) to subjects two times, once after each of the two experiments they participated in. A high score on the scale indicates that a respondent expresses a strong inclination to purchase the specified product, whereas a low score suggests that the respondent has a very low willingness to buy the product.

MAJOR FINDINGS:

Dodds, Monroe, and Grewal (1991) conducted a study of the impact of price, brand, and store information on consumers' perceptions of product quality, value, and **purchase intention**. Favorable store and brand information had positive effects on **purchase intentions,** but price had a negative impact.

REFERENCE:

Dodds, William B., Kent B. Monroe, and Dhruv Grewal (1991), ''The Effects of Price, Brand, and Store Information on Buyers' Product Evaluations,'' *JMR*, 28 (August), 307-19.

SCALE ITEMS: PURCHASE INTENTION

1. The likelihood of purchasing this product is:

Very low   ___ : ___ : ___ : ___ : ___ : ___ : ___   Very high
       1   2   3   4   5   6   7

2. If I were going to buy this product, I would consider buying the model at the price shown.

Strongly   ___ : ___ : ___ : ___ : ___ : ___ : ___   Strongly
disagree   1   2   3   4   5   6   7   agree

3. At the price shown, I would consider buying the product.

Strongly   ___ : ___ : ___ : ___ : ___ : ___ : ___   Strongly
disagree   1   2   3   4   5   6   7   agree

4. The probability that I would consider buying the product is:

Very low   ___ : ___ : ___ : ___ : ___ : ___ : ___   Very high
       1   2   3   4   5   6   7

5. My willingness to buy the product is:

Very low   ___ : ___ : ___ : ___ : ___ : ___ : ___   Very high
       1   2   3   4   5   6   7

SCALE NAME: Purchase Intention

SCALE DESCRIPTION:

Multiple Likert-like items used to measure the inclination of a consumer to buy a specified product. The various versions of the scale discussed here have between two and four items. Most of the studies appear to have used seven-point response scales, with the exception of Okechuku and Wang (1988), who used a nine-point format. The uses of the scale are similar in that they have at least one item in common with every other version and all share two items with two of the other three versions.

SCALE ORIGIN:

The source of this scale is a study of the physical attractiveness of models in advertisements (Baker and Churchill 1977). Consistent with the tripartite theory of attitudes, scales were developed to measure the cognitive, affective, and conative components of one's evaluation of an ad. Item-total correlations indicated that the three items expected to capture the conative component (items 1, 2, and 3) were homogeneous. It should be noted that though the scale was developed to measure the conative dimension of one's attitude toward an ad, the statements instead measured the conative dimension of attitude toward the brand. This scale, therefore, does not measure behavioral intention toward an ad but rather behavioral intention toward the product described in an ad.

SAMPLES:

Kilbourne (1986) used a convenience sample of **49** males and **52** females residing in several communities around a large metropolitan area. Median age was 30 years, median income was $20,700, and 79% were either college graduates or attending college. The sample used by Kilbourne, Painton and Ridley (1985) was composed of **238** male and **186** female undergraduate students from a southwestern university. The students were recruited from either marketing, management, or psychology classes but were not required to participate in the experiment.

Okechuku and Wang (1988) used subjects recruited at shopping malls and other public places in Detroit and surrounding suburbs in Michigan and in Windsor, London, Sarnia, Toronto, and Hamilton, Ontario. Sample sizes were: 27, 27, and 26 for three Chinese ads for clothes and 29, 30, and 26 for three North American ads for clothes; 26, 26, and 30 for three Chinese ads for shoes and 25, 24, and 26 for three North American ads for shoes.

The study of Perrien, Dussart, and Paul (1985) was based on **186** questionnaires returned by advertising industry professionals who were members of the Montreal Advertising Club. This represented a 26% response rate. Because French was the official language of the club, the questionnaires were in French. The authors admitted that what little was known about the representativeness of their sample indicated that it was different from the population at least in terms of the proportions of different professional groups. However, their results indicated that the respondents' professional categories did not affect the evaluation of ads.

RELIABILITY:

Kilbourne (1986), Kilbourne, Painton and Ridley (1985), and Perrien, Dussart, and Paul (1985) reported alphas of **.73**, **.91**, and **.8115**, respectively. Okechuku and Wang (1988) reported two alphas: **.82** and **.77** for clothing and shoe ads, respectively. The item-total correlations reported in their study also provide some evidence of scale item homogeneity.

VALIDITY:

The item-total correlations reported by Okechuku and Wang (1988) indicated that items composing this scale had much higher correlations with scores on this scale than with correlations with total scores on two other scales (cognitive and affective dimensions of attitude). This provides some evidence of convergent and discriminate validities, though at the *item* level rather than the *scale* level.

As some evidence of content validity, Perrien, Dussart and Paul (1985) used items taken from the literature and tested them with 15 marketing experts. All were unanimous in connecting the expected items with the proper dimensions of attitude (affective, cognitive, and conative).

ADMINISTRATION:

The studies by Kilbourne (1986) and Okechuku and Wang (1988) administered their questionnaires to respondents in various field settings after they had read some test ads. The student subjects in the study by Kilbourne, Painton, and Ridley (1985) completed the experiment along with the questionnaire in groups. Administration of this scale in the Perrien, Dussart and Paul (1985) study was in a mail survey instrument, and scale items were randomized with those for two other scales. High scores on the scale indicate that respondents are expressing a strong inclination to purchase the specified product, whereas low scores suggest that they do not plan on buying the product.

MAJOR FINDINGS:

Kilbourne (1986) found **purchase intentions** were significantly higher for those who had viewed an ad for the product in which the female model in the ad was portrayed as a professional than when she was portrayed as a housewife. Kilbourne, Painton and Ridley (1985) found significantly higher **purchase intentions** toward Scotch whiskey when the print ad contained a sexual embed than when it did not. A significant difference was not found for another product (a brand of cigarettes) that was tested as well.

Okechuku and Wang (1988) compared North American subjects' attitudes toward ads from China and North America. They found a significant difference in **purchase intentions** for two different product categories such that respondents (North Americans) expressed a greater likelihood of purchasing products presented in ads prepared by North American advertisers than those presented in ads by Chinese advertisers.

Perrien, Dussart and Paul (1985) examined those in the advertising trade and their perceptions of advertising effectiveness. Their findings indicated that the more factual information contained in an ad, the more positively advertisers evaluated it. Specifically, advertisers thought that consumers' **purchase intentions** would be higher for products advertised with much factual content. This finding was not affected by the amount of perceived risk associated with the product or respondents' professional category in the advertising industry.

COMMENTS:

All the users of this scale referred to it as a semantic differential. However, it is described here as a Likert-type because it *does not use a series of bipolar adjectives* but is instead composed of a series of different statements responded to on a scale with *the same verbal anchors.*

REFERENCES:

Baker, Michael J. and Gilbert A. Churchill, Jr. (1977), ''The Impact of Physically Attractive Models on Advertising Evaluations,'' *JMR*, 14 (November), 538-55.

Kilbourne, William E. (1986), ''An Exploratory Study of Sex Role Stereotyping on Attitudes Toward Magazine Advertisements,'' *JAMS*, 14 (4) 43-46.

_____, Scott Painton, and Danny Ridley (1985), ''The Effect of Sexual Embedding on Responses to Magazine Advertisements,'' *JA*, 14 (2) 48-56.

Okechuku, Chike and Gongrong Wang (1988), ''The Effectiveness of Chinese Print Advertisements in North America,'' *JAR*, 28 (October/ November) 25-34.

Perrien, Jean, Christian Dussart and Francoise Paul (1985), ''Advertisers and the Factual Content of Advertising,'' *JA*, 14 (1), 30-35, 53.

SCALE ITEMS: PURCHASE INTENTION*

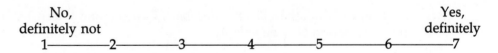

```
    No,                                                    Yes,
definitely not                                         definitely
    1————————2————————3————————4————————5————————6————————7
```

1. Would you like to try this product?
2. Would you buy this product if you happened to see it in a store?
3. Would you actively seek out this product in a store in order to purchase it?

* This is the version of the scale reported by Baker and Churchill (1977). Both Kilbourne, Painton, and Ridley (1985) and Kilbourne (1986) used phrases based on items 1, 2, and 3. Okechuku and Wang (1988) used items 2 and 3. Perrien, Dussart, and Paul (1985) used items similar to those above but phrased them such that they asked the respondents' opinions about how consumers would react to the product. Their scale also incorporated one bipolar adjective item (influential/not influential) used to measure one's evaluation of an ad.

SCALE NAME: Purchase Influence (Child's)

SCALE DESCRIPTION:

A seven-item, five-point, Likert-type summated ratings scale that measures the degree to which a parent reports a child's opinion should be included when purchase decisions are made for a variety of goods and services.

SCALE ORIGIN:

The idea for the scale comes from a study reported by Jenkins (1979). However, he does not appear to have used the items in summated scale form, so that aspect seems to be original to Carlson and Grossbart (1988; Grossbart, Carlson, and Walsh 1991).

SAMPLES:

The same data set is reported on in two articles by Carlson and Grossbart (1988; Grossbart, Carlson, and Walsh 1991). The survey instrument was distributed to mothers through students at three elementary schools of an unidentified U.S. city. The schools were chosen on a convenience basis but appeared to represent a variety of socioeconomic areas of the city. A $1 contribution was made to the PTO for each completed questionnaire returned by the children. Analysis was based on 451 completed questionnaires. Ninety-three percent of the responding mothers indicated that they were the primary person in the child's socialization.

RELIABILITY:

Carlson and Grossbart (1988; Grossbart, Carlson, and Walsh 1991) reported an alpha of .84 and a beta of .63 for the scale.

VALIDITY:

Carlson and Grossbart (1988; Grossbart, Carlson, and Walsh 1991) reported no examination of scale validity.

ADMINISTRATION:

The scale was self-administered along with many other measures in the questionnaire used by Carlson and Grossbart (1988; Grossbart, Carlson, and Walsh 1991). High scores on the scale suggest that parents believe that their children's opinions should be considered when making purchase decisions, whereas low scores imply that they do not think that their children's opinions should be included.

MAJOR FINDINGS:

The authors (Carlson and Grossbart 1988; Grossbart, Carlson, and Walsh 1991) investigated the relationship between general parental socialization styles and children's consumer socialization. In a factor analysis of scale scores, scores on the **Child's Influence** scale loaded on a factor described as the *parent-child communication about consumption*. On the basis of this, a significant difference was found in the degree of parent-child communication between several of the parental socialization styles examined.

REFERENCES:

Carlson, Les and Sanford Grossbart (1988), "Parental Style and Consumer Socialization of Children," *JCR*, 15 (June), 77-94.

Grossbart, Sanford, Les Carlson, and Ann Walsh (1991), "Consumer Socialization and Frequency of Shopping with Children," *JAMS*, 19 (Summer), 155-63.

Jenkins, Roger L. (1979), "The Influence of Children in Family Decision Making: Parents' Perceptions," in *Advances in Consumer Research*, Vol. 6, William L. Wilkie, ed. Ann Arbor, MI: Association for Consumer Research, 413-18.

SCALE ITEMS: PURCHASE INFLUENCE (CHILD'S)

Strongly disagree	Disagree	Neither	Agree	Strongly agree
1	2	3	4	5

My child's opinions should be included when we make purchase decisions for:
1. Major appliances
2. Automobiles
3. Furniture
4. Groceries
5. Life Insurance
6. Vacations
7. General Purchases

SCALE NAME: Quality (Audio/Video Product)

SCALE DESCRIPTION:

A three-item, seven-point bipolar adjective scale measuring the perceived quality of an audio/video product. The specific product used in the experiment by Gotlieb and Sarel (1992) was a VCR, but the items would appear to be very appropriate for examining televisions and possibly such kindred products as laser disk and video game players.

SCALE ORIGIN:

The origin is not specified by Gotlieb and Sarel (1992), but there is nothing to indicate that it is anything other than original to their work in this study.

SAMPLES:

Gotlieb and Sarel (1992) gathered data from 113 upperclasspersons and graduate students attending a large urban university. Students were assigned randomly to treatments in the $2 \times 2 \times 2$ factorial experimental design.

RELIABILITY:

Gotlieb and Sarel (1992) reported an alpha of **.92** for the scale.

VALIDITY:

Gotlieb and Sarel (1992) reported no specific examination of the scale.

ADMINISTRATION:

The scale was self-administered by students along with several other measures after exposure to experimental stimuli. A high score on the scale implies that a respondent perceives the quality of some audio/video product to be very high, whereas a low score suggests that he/she believes the quality to be poor.

MAJOR FINDINGS:

Gotlieb and Sarel (1992) examined the impact of comparative advertising, price, and source credibility on perceived quality of a new brand. Among the findings was that a direct comparative ad had a significantly greater positive influence on perceived **quality** than did a noncomparative ad.

REFERENCE:

Gotlieb, Jerry B. and Dan Sarel (1992), "The Influence of Type of Advertisement, Price, and Source Credibility on Perceived Quality," *JAMS*, 20 (Summer), 253-60.

SCALE ITEMS: QUALITY (AUDIO/VIDEO)

Low quality picture	___ : ___ : ___ : ___ : ___ : ___ : ___	High quality picture
	1 2 3 4 5 6 7	

Low quality
picture   ___ : ___ : ___ : ___ : ___ : ___ : ___   High quality
picture
                1   2   3   4   5   6   7

Low sound
quality   ___ : ___ : ___ : ___ : ___ : ___ : ___   High sound
quality
                1   2   3   4   5   6   7

Overall low
quality   ___ : ___ : ___ : ___ : ___ : ___ : ___   Overall high
quality
                1   2   3   4   5   6   7

SCALE NAME: Quality (Brand)

SCALE DESCRIPTION:

A three-item, seven-point semantic differential measuring a person's attitude toward some specific brand. The scale was used in two slightly different ways by Keller and Aaker (1992): One version focused on the *core* brand and the other measured a person's evaluation of a *proposed* brand extension. (In the experimental scenario, the company was considering only the introduction of the new product.)

SCALE ORIGIN:

Keller and Aaker (1992) provided no information regarding the scales' origin, but it is assumed to have been used first in their study.

SAMPLES:

The sample employed by Keller and Aaker (1992) was composed of **430** university employees, most of whom were female (90%). About half had a college degree, and the average age was 28 years. Respondents were paid $5 for their participation and given a chance to win cash prizes in a lottery.

RELIABILITY:

All Keller and Aaker (1992) say about the reliability of their multi-item scales is that they were all in excess of .70.

VALIDITY:

Keller and Aaker (1992) reported no specific examination of the scale's validity. However, core brand quality was one of the experimental manipulations and, indeed, the high-quality core brand was evaluated significantly higher than the average-quality core brand.

ADMINISTRATION:

The scale was self-administered by subjects along with other measures after exposure to experimental manipulation information (Keller and Aaker 1992). A high score on the scale indicates that a respondent considers a brand (core or proposed extension) to be of high quality, whereas a low score suggests the brand is evaluated poorly and is unlikely to be tried.

MAJOR FINDINGS:

The experiment by Keller and Aaker (1992) examined the factors influencing evaluation of proposed extensions of a core brand. Among the many findings was that a successful previous brand extension by a company (compared with no previous extension) leads to better evaluations of a proposed brand extension's **quality** for an average-quality core brand but not a high-quality one.

REFERENCE:

Keller, Kevin Lane and David A. Aaker (1992), ''The Effects of Sequential Introduction of Brand Extensions,'' *JMR*, 29 (February), 35-50.

SCALE ITEMS: QUALITY (BRAND)

Low quality	__ :	__ :	__ :	__ :	__ :	__ :	__	High quality
	1	2	3	4	5	6	7	
Not at all likely to try	__ :	__ :	__ :	__ :	__ :	__ :	__	Very likely to try
	1	2	3	4	5	6	7	
Inferior product	__ :	__ :	__ :	__ :	__ :	__ :	__	Superior product
	1	2	3	4	5	6	7	

SCALE NAME: Quality (Product)

SCALE DESCRIPTION:

A five-item, summated ratings scale purporting to measure the perceptions of quality that a consumer has about a product he/she is knowledgeable of. The measure was referred to as *perceived quality indicators* by Dodds, Monroe, and Grewal (1991).

SCALE ORIGIN:

Dodds, Monroe, and Grewal (1991) state that the items for this and two other scales were "developed from previous research" (p. 312), though the source of the items and the extent of the borrowing were not specified.

SAMPLES:

The sample used in study conducted by Dodds, Monroe, and Grewal (1991) was composed of **585** undergraduate marketing students in a marketing class at a large state university. The study used a 5 × 3 × 3 factorial design with 13 students per cell. The experiment was run a second time, apparently identical to the first one except for the product being studied.

RELIABILITY:

Dodds, Monroe, and Grewal (1991) reported the scale to have an alpha of **.95** for both of the experiments in which it was used. Average interitem correlations were .78 and .80.

VALIDITY:

Quantitative results were not provided, but Dodds, Monroe, and Grewal (1991) stated that the results of an exploratory factor analysis indicated a three-factor solution was found using items from this scale and two others. The suggestion was that the items in this scale loaded on one factor.

ADMINISTRATION:

The scale was administered by Dodds, Monroe, and Grewal (1991) to subjects two times, once after each of the two experiments they participated in. A high score on the scale indicates that a respondent perceives a specified product to be of very high quality.

MAJOR FINDINGS:

Dodds, Monroe, and Grewal (1991) conducted a study of the impact of price, brand, and store information on consumers' perceptions of **product quality**, value, and purchase intention. Favorable store and brand information and price had positive effects on **product quality.**

REFERENCE:

> Dodds, William B., Kent B. Monroe, and Dhruv Grewal (1991), ''The Effects of Price, Brand, and Store Information on Buyers' Product Evaluations,'' *JMR*, 28 (August), 307-19.

SCALE ITEMS: QUALITY (PRODUCT)

1. The likelihood that the product would be reliable is:

Very low ___ : ___ : ___ : ___ : ___ : ___ : ___ Very high
       1   2   3   4   5   6   7

2. The workmanship of the product would be:

Very low ___ : ___ : ___ : ___ : ___ : ___ : ___ Very high
       1   2   3   4   5   6   7

3. This product would seem to be durable.

Strongly ___ : ___ : ___ : ___ : ___ : ___ : ___ Strongly
disagree 1   2   3   4   5   6   7   agree

4. The likelihood that this product is dependable is:

Very low ___ : ___ : ___ : ___ : ___ : ___ : ___ Very high
       1   2   3   4   5   6   7

5. This product should be of:

Very low ___ : ___ : ___ : ___ : ___ : ___ : ___ Very high
quality 1   2   3   4   5   6   7   quality

SCALE NAME: Quality (Relative Product Performance)

SCALE DESCRIPTION:

A four-item, seven-point summated ratings scale measuring a person's perception of the performance quality of a product compared with other brands in its product class. The authors viewed *performance* as having two dimensions: breakdown and non-breakdown related (Boulding and Kirmani 1993). This scale was used to measure the latter dimension.

SCALE ORIGIN:

The origin of the scale was not described by Boulding and Kirmani (1993), but it appears to have been developed for their study.

SAMPLES:

Little description was provided about the sample used by Boulding and Kirmani (1993) except that it was composed of **150** MBA students. They were assigned randomly to one of eight treatment in a $2 \times 2 \times 2$ between-subjects design, and cell sizes were 18 or 19.

RELIABILITY:

Boulding and Kirmani (1993) reported an alpha of **.77** for the scale.

VALIDITY:

Boulding and Kirmani (1993) reported no examination of the scale's validity.

ADMINISTRATION:

Subjects completed the scale along with other measures after being exposed to experimental stimuli (Boulding and Kirmani 1993). A high score on the scale indicates that a respondent believes that a specified brand performs better than the average brand in a particular product category.

MAJOR FINDINGS:

Boulding and Kirmani (1993) explored consumer perceptions of warranties as quality cues within the framework of economic signaling theory. Among the many findings was that an unconditional warranty by a high-credibility firm was associated with significantly better **product quality** perceptions than for a low-credibility firm.

REFERENCE:

Boulding, William and Amna Kirmani (1993), ''A Consumer-Side Experimental Examination of Signaling Theory: Do Consumers Perceive Warranties as Signals of Quality?'' *JCR*, 20 (June), 111-23.

SCALE ITEMS: QUALITY (RELATIVE PRODUCT PERFORMANCE)

Much less   ____ : ____ : ____ : ____ : ____ : ____ : ____   Much more
than average   1   2   3   4   5   6   7   than average

1. Compared to other _____, how many features does the _____ offer?
2. Compared to other _____, how flexible is the _____?
3. Compared to other _____, how much storage space does the _____ have?
4. Compared to other _____, how powerful is the _____?

* The name of the generic product goes in the first blank, and the name of the brand being evaluated should be placed in the second blank.

SCALE NAME: Quality Evaluation Mode

SCALE DESCRIPTION:

A three-item, seven-point, Likert-type scale measuring the degree to which a consumer believes that the quality of brands in a particular product category can be judged adequately by visual inspection rather than actual trial.

SCALE ORIGIN:

Smith and Park (1992) did not specify the origin of the scale.

SAMPLES:

Smith and Park (1992) reported on findings based on analysis of data gathered from product managers and consumers. The **quality evaluation mode** scale was used only in a survey of the latter group. Data were collected in that survey by door-to-door interviews in suburban neighborhoods of a large midwestern city. The sample ultimately was composed of **1383** respondents. Each respondent was asked questions regarding two products, 35 consumers were interviewed for each product, and there was a total of 79 products examined. The interviews were conducted by students who received some training before going into the field.

RELIABILITY:

Smith and Park (1992) reported an alpha of **.84** for the scale.

VALIDITY:

Smith and Park (1992) did not address the validity of the scale.

ADMINISTRATION:

The scale was administered along with other measures by trained student interviewers in door-to-door settings (Smith and Park 1992). A high score on the scale indicates that a respondent perceives that the quality of brands in a specified product class can be assessed accurately through visual examination rather than actual usage.

MAJOR FINDINGS:

Smith and Park (1992) examined several issues related to brand strategy. One hypothesis was that the impact of brand extensions on market share and advertising efficiency is greater when the **quality evaluation mode** of a extension product class is actual trial rather than visual. The evidence supported the hypothesis with the strongest effect involving market share.

REFERENCE:

Smith, Daniel C. and C. Whan Park (1992), ''The Effects of Brand Extensions on Market Share and Advertising Efficiency,'' *JMR*, 29 (August), 296-313.

SCALE ITEMS: QUALITY EVALUATION MODE

Strongly ____ : ____ : ____ : ____ : ____ : ____ : ____ Strongly
disagree   1   2   3   4   5   6   7   agree

1. First time buyers of this product would find it difficult to judge its quality through visual inspection alone. **(r)**
2. The only way you can tell the quality of this product is to actually try it. **(r)**
3. You can easily tell the quality of different brands by simply looking at them.

SCALE NAME: Quietness

SCALE DESCRIPTION:

> A three-item, five-point scale measuring one's stillness-related emotional reaction to some specified stimulus.

SCALE ORIGIN:

> Although not expressly indicated, the items used by Mano and Oliver (1993) appear to have been used first as a summated scale by Mano (1991). With 224 college students, the scale was reported to have an alpha of .64. A cluster analysis grouped these three items together, but in a factor analysis the items loaded along with three more related to *calmness*.

SAMPLES:

> Data were collected by Mano and Oliver (1993) from **118** undergraduate business students attending a midwestern U.S. university.

RELIABILITY:

> Mano and Oliver (1993) reported an alpha of **.65** for the scale.

VALIDITY:

> Mano and Oliver (1993) did not specifically address the validity of the scale.

ADMINISTRATION:

> The scale was part of a longer questionnaire self-administered by students in a classroom (Mano and Oliver 1993). A high score suggests that some stimulus has evoked a quiet, still feeling.

MAJOR FINDINGS:

> Mano and Oliver (1993) examined the dimensionality and causal structure of product evaluation, affect, and satisfaction. The **quietness** emotion was not found to be significantly different for subjects in the high- and low-involvement manipulations.

REFERENCES:

> Mano, Haim (1991), "The Structure and Intensity of Emotional Experiences: Method and Context Convergence," *Multivariate Behavioral Research*, 26 (3), 389-411.
> _____ and Richard L. Oliver (1993), "Assessing the Dimensionality and Structure of the Consumption Experience: Evaluation, Feeling, and Satisfaction," *JCR*, 20 (December), 451-66.

SCALE ITEMS: QUIETNESS

Not at all   Very much
1————————2————————3————————4————————5

1. quiet
2. still
3. quiescent

SCALE NAME: Refusal of Child's Purchase Requests (With Explanation)

SCALE DESCRIPTION:

A five-item, five-point, Likert-type summated ratings scale measuring the degree to which a parent reports refusing to buy any of several products for his/her child when the latter asks for it but provides an explanation of why the request is denied.

SCALE ORIGIN:

The use of these items as a multi-item measure appears to be original to Carlson and Grossbart (1988; Grossbart, Carlson, and Walsh 1991). They got ideas for some of the items, however, from the research of Ward and colleagues (1977).

SAMPLES:

The same data set is reported on in two articles by Carlson and Grossbart (1988; Grossbart, Carlson, and Walsh 1991). The survey instrument was distributed to mothers through students at three elementary schools of an unidentified U.S. city. The schools were chosen on a convenience basis but appeared to represent a variety of socioeconomic areas of the city. A $1 contribution was made to the PTO for each completed questionnaire returned by the children. Analysis was based on **451** completed questionnaires. Ninety-three percent of the responding mothers indicated that they were the primary person in the child's socialization.

RELIABILITY:

Carlson and Grossbart (1988; Grossbart, Carlson, and Walsh 1991) reported an alpha of **.84** and a beta of **.77** for the scale.

VALIDITY:

Carlson and Grossbart (1988; Grossbart, Carlson, and Walsh 1991) reported no examination of scale validity.

ADMINISTRATION:

The scale was self-administered along with many other measures in the questionnaire used by Carlson and Grossbart (1988; Grossbart, Carlson, and Walsh 1991). High scores on the scale mean that respondents report that they, the parents, tend to refuse to buy their children any of several products when asked but do give them a reason why their requests are denied. Low scores could imply either that parents are more likely to yield to their children's' requests or that they deny requests and do not provide explanations.

MAJOR FINDINGS:

The authors (Carlson and Grossbart 1988; Grossbart, Carlson, and Walsh 1991) investigated the relationship between general parental socialization styles and children's consumer socialization. In a factor analysis of scale scores, scores on the **Refusal** scale loaded on a factor described as *restriction of consumption*. On the basis of this, there were some but not many significant differences found in the degree of consumption restriction between the five parental socialization styles examined.

REFERENCES:

Carlson, Les and Sanford Grossbart (1988), ''Parental Style and Consumer Socialization of Children,'' *JCR*, 15 (June), 77-94.

Grossbart, Sanford, Les Carlson, and Ann Walsh (1991), ''Consumer Socialization and Frequency of Shopping with Children,'' *JAMS*, 19 (Summer), 155-63.

Ward, Scott, Daniel B. Wackman, and Ellen Wartella (1977), *How Children Learn to Buy* Beverly Hills, CA: Sage Publications.

SCALE ITEMS: REFUSAL OF CHILD'S PURCHASE REQUESTS (WITH EXPLANATION)

Very seldom	Seldom	Sometimes	Often	Very often
1	2	3	4	5

1. If my child asks for candy I refuse to buy it but give an explanation why.
2. If my child asks for a game or toy I refuse to buy it but give an explanation why.
3. If my child asks for a magazine/comic book I refuse to buy it but give an explanation why.
4. If my child asks for a snack food I refuse to buy it but give an explanation why.
5. If my child asks for sports equipment I refuse to buy it but give an explanation why.

SCALE NAME: Response Care

SCALE DESCRIPTION:

A four-item, seven-point, Likert-type scale measuring the degree of care used by a person in completing a questionnaire to provide answers that accurately reflected his/her feelings.

SCALE ORIGIN:

Although not specifically stated by Fisher (1993), the scale is assumed to be original to his study.

SAMPLES:

Fisher (1993) reported on three studies, though the scale was only used in the first one. The study was a two-group experiment: one group received a *direct* version of the scale and the other received an *indirect* version. The sample was composed of male and female undergraduate students, with 92 subjects being assigned to each group.

RELIABILITY:

An alpha of .76 was calculated for the scale (Fisher 1994).

VALIDITY:

Fisher (1993) reported no direct examination of the scale's validity.

ADMINISTRATION:

The scale(s) was administered to the subjects after they had been exposed to experimental stimuli (Fisher 1993). High scores on the scale suggest that respondents believe that the information they have provided on a survey is an honest indication of their true opinions.

MAJOR FINDINGS:

Fisher (1993) examined the ability of indirect questioning to reduce the influence of social desirability bias on self-report measures. The measure of **response care** was used as a manipulation check, and all he says about the findings is that there were no significant associations between **response care** and any of the major variables under examination.

REFERENCES:

Fisher, Robert J. (1994), personal correspondence.

_____ (1993), "Social Desirability Bias and the Validity of Indirect Questioning," *JCR*, 20 (September), 303-15.

SCALE ITEMS: RESPONSE CARE

Strongly   ___ : ___ : ___ : ___ : ___ : ___ : ___   Strongly
disagree   0   1   2   3   4   5   6   agree

1. I tried to fill out this survey as accurately as possible.
2. My responses closely reflect my feelings.
3. I was careful when I answered the questions on this survey.
4. It was important to me to answer this survey honestly.

SCALE NAME: Risk (Enjoyment)

SCALE DESCRIPTION:

A three-item, five-point summated ratings scale measuring the importance of the prepurchase role played by the perception that a specified product will not be enjoyed after its purchase.

SCALE ORIGIN:

The scale was developed by Venkatraman (1993; and Price 1990).

SAMPLES:

Venkatraman (1991) collected data from a household list compiled by Dunhill International. A systematic sampling plan was used so that households were selected from each state in the same proportions that were represented in the country's population. Of the 450 surveys mailed out, **245** usable forms were returned. Respondents tended to be male (59.4%), have white-collar jobs (57.1%), and be college graduates (68.7%). More than half (53.5%) were between 30 and 44 years of age, and the average annual income was $41,440. This same sample was referred to in Venkatraman and Price (1990) as "study 3."

RELIABILITY:

The scale was calculated to have an alpha of **.82** (Venkatraman 1993).

VALIDITY:

Venkatraman (1991) reported no evidence of the scale's validity.

ADMINISTRATION:

The scale was included with many other measures in a self-administered mail questionnaire (Venkatraman (1991; Venkatraman and Price 1990). A high score on the scale suggests that a respondent perceives that enjoyment risk is an important consideration when purchasing some specified product.

MAJOR FINDINGS:

The purpose of Venkatraman (1991; Venkatraman and Price 1990) was to examine the impact of innovativeness on two different types of adoption decisions. Two different types of innovators were identified: the cognitive innovators and the sensory innovators. The results showed that for cognitive innovators, there was a significant negative relationship between **enjoyment risk** and the adoption of two different products.

REFERENCES:

Venkatraman, Meera P. (1991), ''The Impact of Innovativeness and Innovation Type on Adoption,'' *JR*, 67 (Spring), 51-67.

———— (1993), personal correspondence.

———— and Linda L. Price (1990), ''Differentiating Between Cognitive and Sensory Innovativeness: Concepts, Measurement, and Implications,'' *Journal of Business Research*, 20 (June), 293-315.

SCALE ITEMS: RISK (ENJOYMENT)*

Directions: For the statements listed below, please indicate the importance each has when making a purchase decision.

Very   ___ : ___ : ___ : ___ : ___   Very
unimportant   1   2   3   4   5   important

1. Getting bored with the product after the purchase.
2. Do not like it as much as I expected.
3. Not using it as much as I expected.

* The directions, response scale, and full items are reconstructed here on the basis of descriptions in Venkatraman (1991; 1993; Venkatraman and Price 1990) but may not be exactly as used by the author.

SCALE NAME: Risk (Performance/Financial)

SCALE DESCRIPTION:

A four-item, five-point summated ratings scale measuring the importance of several risk attributes related primarily to the performance of some specified product or economic aspects of its purchase.

SCALE ORIGIN:

Venkatraman (1993; Venkatraman and Price 1990) developed the scale.

SAMPLES:

Venkatraman (1991) collected data from a household list compiled by Dunhill International. A systematic sampling plan was used so that households were selected from each state in the same proportions that were represented in the country's population. Of the 450 surveys mailed out, **245** usable forms were returned. Respondents tended to be male (59.4%), have white collar jobs (57.1%), and be college graduates (68.7%). More than half (53.5%) were between 30 and 44 years of age, and the average annual income was $41,440. This same sample was referred to in Venkatraman and Price (1990) as "study 3."

RELIABILITY:

The scale was calculated to have an alpha of **.65** (Venkatraman 1993).

VALIDITY:

Venkatraman (1991).reported no evidence of the scale's validity.

ADMINISTRATION:

The scale was included with many other measures in a self-administered mail questionnaire (Venkatraman 1991; Venkatraman and Price 1990). A high score on the scale suggests that a respondent perceives that performance and financial aspects of risk are important considerations when purchasing some specified product.

MAJOR FINDINGS:

The purpose of the study by Venkatraman (1991; Venkatraman and Price 1990) was to examine the impact of innovativeness on two different types of adoption decisions. Two different types of innovators were identified: the cognitive innovators and the sensory innovators. The results showed for sensory innovators (but not for cognitive innovators) that there was a significant negative relationship between **performance/financial risk** and adoption for two different products.

COMMENTS:

An examination of the item content of the scale as well as the lower level of alpha suggest that the scale is not unidimensional. Further development and testing appear to be required.

REFERENCES:

Venkatraman, Meera P. (1991), "The Impact of Innovativeness and Innovation Type on Adoption," *JR*, 67 (Spring), 51-67.

_____ (1993), personal correspondence.

_____ and Linda L. Price (1990), "Differentiating Between Cognitive and Sensory Innovativeness: Concepts, Measurement, and Implications," *Journal of Business Research*, 20 (June), 293-315.

SCALE ITEMS: RISK (PERFORMANCE/FINANCIAL)*

Directions: For the statements listed below, please indicate the importance each has when making a purchase decision.

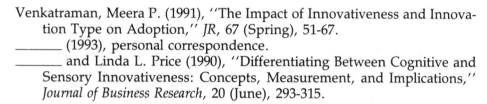

Very   ___ : ___ : ___ : ___ : ___   Very
unimportant   1   2   3   4   5   important

1. The purchase affects the financial ability to buy other products.
2. There is a fall in prices soon after buying the product.
3. There are unanticipated performance problems after the purchase.
4. The product does not do the things I expected it to do.

* The directions, response scale, and full items are reconstructed here on the basis of descriptions in Venkatraman (1991; 1993; Venkatraman and Price 1990) but may not be exactly as used by the author.

SCALE NAME: Risk (Purchase)

SCALE DESCRIPTION:

A four-item, Likert-type scale purported to measure a consumer's level of perceived risk associated with the purchase of some specified product.

SCALE ORIGIN:

There is no information to indicate that the scale reported by Eroglu and Machleit (1990) was anything other than original.

SAMPLES:

Subjects used by Eroglu and Machleit (1990) were recruited from professional, nonprofit, and church organizations. The sample was composed of **112** adults and had the following characteristics: 58% were female, 70% were married, and 63% were between the ages of 20 and 49 years.

RELIABILITY:

Eroglu and Machleit (1990) reported an alpha of .86 for the scale.

VALIDITY:

Eroglu and Machleit (1990) reported no information regarding the scale's validity.

ADMINISTRATION:

The scale was administered along with other measures as part of a experiment in a laboratory setting. A high score on the scale indicates that a respondent perceives a lot of risk with the purchase of a specified product, whereas a low score would imply that a respondent sees little risk in the purchase of a product.

MAJOR FINDINGS:

Eroglu and Machleit (1990) examined some of the determinants and outcomes of retail crowding. Only under the high retail density conditions was **purchase risk** found to be significantly related to perceived crowding.

COMMENTS:

Until some evidence of the scale's unidimensionality and validity are provided, the scale should be used cautiously.

REFERENCE:

> Eroglu, Segin A. and Karen A. Machleit (1990), ''An Empirical Study of Retail Crowding: Antecedents and Consequences,'' *JR*, 66 (Summer), 201-21.

SCALE ITEMS: RISK (PURCHASE)*

Strongly disagree	Disagree	Neutral	Agree	Strongly agree
1—————————	2—————————	3—————————	4—————————	5

1. The product I was shopping for is an expensive product.
2. I don't have much experience in purchasing this product.
3. The decision to purchase this product involved high risk.
4. This is a technologically complex product.

* Eroglu and Machleit (1990) did not specify the number of points on their scale or the anchors used, but they were likely similar to the one shown.

SCALE NAME: Risk Perception (Composite)

SCALE DESCRIPTION:

A six-item, seven-point, summated ratings scale measuring the probability that a consumer perceives the purchase of some specified product to be associated with six types of losses.

SCALE ORIGIN:

The scale was developed by Murray (1985) in his dissertation research. The same data are used for the article described subsequently (Murray and Schlacter 1990). The six items used by Murray (1985, and Schlacter 1990) are adaptations of six items developed by Peter and Tarpey (1975).

SAMPLES:

The sample was composed of **256** students attending Arizona State University. Nearly 53% of the sample was female and the mean age was nearly 24 years. Students were assigned randomly to one of 15 different treatments systematically varied in terms of the "serviceness" of the three products they responded to.

RELIABILITY:

A mean alpha of **.877** was reported for the scale averaged over 15 different products. For products with high, moderate, and low service attributes, mean alphas of .861, .797, and .802, respectively, were reported.

VALIDITY:

No information regarding the scale's validity was reported.

ADMINISTRATION:

The scale was administered as part of a larger questionnaire to students in a classroom setting. High scores on the scale suggest that respondents perceive most, if not all, of the types of losses to be associated with the purchase of some specified product, whereas low scores indicate that expectations of negative consequences are low.

MAJOR FINDINGS:

The purpose of the study by Murray and Schlacter (1990) was to examine how products placed along a goods-services continuum vary in the kind and amount of prechoice **risk** perceived. Their findings indicated that that there are differences in the **risk** perceived in the purchase of goods and services such that products high in service attributes have more **risk** associated with them than products low in serviceness.

COMMENTS:

See also Srinivasan and Ratchford (1991) for use of similar items in a multiplicative measure of risk perception.

REFERENCES:

Murray, Keith B. (1985), "Risk Perception and Information Source Use For Products Differing in Service Attributes," doctoral dissertation, Arizona State University: Tempe, Arizona.

_____ and John L. Schlacter (1990), "The Impact of Services Versus Goods on Consumers' Assessment of Perceived Risk and Variability," *JAMS*, 18 (Winter), 51-65.

Peter, J. Paul and Lawrence X. Tarpey, Sr. (1975), "A Comparative Analysis of Three Consumer Decision Strategies," *JCR*, 2 (June), 29-37.

Srinivasan, Narasimhan and Brian T. Ratchford (1991), "An Empirical Test of a External Search for Automobiles," *JCR*, 18 (September), 233-42.

SCALE ITEMS: RISK PERCEPTION (COMPOSITE)

Circle the number that best describes your reaction to each statement if you were considering the purchase of a _____.

Extremely	= 1	Slightly	= 5
Moderately	= 2	Moderately	= 6
Slightly	= 3	Extremely	= 7
Neither	= 4		

Improbable ____ : ____ : ____ : ____ : ____ : ____ : ____ Probable

          1   2   3   4   5   6   7

1. What is the probability that a purchase of an unfamiliar alternative for a _____ will lead to a FINANCIAL LOSS for you because it would function poorly or would not meet your expectations based on the amount of money required to pay for it?
2. What is the probability that a purchase of an unfamiliar alternative for a _____ will lead to a PERFORMANCE LOSS for you because it would function poorly or would not meet your needs, desires, or expectations very well?
3. What is the probability that a purchase of an unfamiliar alternative for a _____ will lead to a PHYSICAL LOSS for you because it would not be very safe, would become unsafe, or would be dangerous or harmful?
4. What is the probability that a purchase of an unfamiliar alternative for a _____ will lead to a PSYCHOLOGICAL LOSS for you because it would not fit well with your self image or self-concept?
5. What is the probability that a purchase of an unfamiliar alternative for a _____ will lead to a SOCIAL LOSS for you because others would think less highly of you?

6. What is the probability that a purchase of an unfamiliar alternative for a _____ will lead to a LOSS OF CONVENIENCE for you because you would have to waste a lot of time and effort before having your needs satisfied?

SCALE NAME: Role Overload

SCALE DESCRIPTION:

A 13-item, five-point, Likert-type summated ratings scale measuring the degree to which a person perceives him/herself to be under time pressure because of the number of commitments and responsibilities one has in life.

SCALE ORIGIN:

The scale was constructed and tested by Reilly (1982). After reviewing scales previously developed for organizational settings, the author and doctoral candidates wrote items more appropriate for female consumers. Several items were tested on a convenience sample of **106** married women. Those items with weak item-total correlations were removed from the scale, leaving 13 items. Other properties of the scale are provided subsequently.

SAMPLES:

Data used by Reilly (1982) were collected by ten experienced interviewers working for a marketing research organization in Milwaukee. The interviewers were told to use the first ten dwellings in each of two random starting points in the SMSA. The procedure produced **186** completed survey forms from women.

The study conducted by Kaufman, Lane, and Lindquist (1991) was based on a sample of 310 respondents. The data were collected by student interviewers who were assigned locations in an urban residential area and asked to select every fifth residence as an initial sample. The sample was 58% female, and 63.3% worked 40 hours or more a week. The range of ages and incomes was quite wide, but the medians were 26 to 35 years if age and $45,000–$49,000, respectively.

RELIABILITY:

Reilly (1982) reports an alpha of **.88** and item-total correlations from .544 to .797. Kaufman, Lane, and Lindquist (1991) reported an alpha of .86.

VALIDITY:

The validity of the scale was not specifically addressed in either article.

ADMINISTRATION:

Although the data collection reported in both studies involved information from interviews and interviewers' judgments, the scale itself was self-administered along with several other measures in a survey instrument. High scores on the scale imply that respondents are experiencing the stress and pressures of having too much to do, whereas low scores indicate respondents either do not play as many roles or are not reacting negatively to the demands on their time.

MAJOR FINDINGS:

Reilly (1982) used causal modeling to examine the relationship between wife's employment status, **role overload**, and the purchase of time-saving durables and convenience foods. Although it was found that **role overload** was causally related to working and time-saving purchases, the relationships were rather weak.

Kaufman, Lane, and Lindquist (1991) examined the degree to which consumers were conscious of polychronic time use (engaging in multiple activities simultaneously). **Role Overload** had a weak but significant correlation with the polychronic attitude scale developed in the study. Education was the only demographic variable with which **Role Overload** was related.

COMMENTS:

Until validity is assessed, there is some question whether the scale measures role overload, as purported, or rather time pressure. The two constructs indeed may be related, but they are not the same thing. For example, there are likely to be some who are quite busy just playing one role, just as there are others who handle multiple roles without expressing much conflict. Therefore, care must be exercised in assuming too much about what this scale can say in terms of the quantity of roles played; however, it does appear to indicate the degree of perceived stress regardless of the amount of role conflict.

For another use of the scale see Bellizzi and Hite (1986).

REFERENCES:

Bellizzi, Joseph A. and Robert E. Hite (1986), ''Convenience Consumption and Role Overload,'' *JAMS*, 14 (Winter), 1-9.

Kaufman, Carol Felker, Paul M. Lane, and Jay D. Lindquist (1991), ''Exploring More than 24 Hours a Day: A Preliminary Investigation of Polychronic Time Use,'' *JCR*, 18 (December), 392-401.

Reilly, Michael D. (1982), ''Working Wives and Convenience Consumption,'' *JCR*, 8 (March), 407-18.

SCALE ITEMS: ROLE OVERLOAD

Strongly disagree	Disagree	Neutral	Agree	Strongly agree
1	2	3	4	5

1. I have to do things I don't really have the time and energy for.
2. There are too many demands on my time.
3. I need more hours in the day to do all the things which are expected of me.

4. I can't ever seem to get caught up.
5. I don't ever seem to have any time for myself.
6. There are times when I can't meet everyone's expectations.
7. Sometimes I feel as if there are not enough hours in the day.
8. Many times I have to cancel commitments.
9. I seem to have to overextend myself in order to be able to finish everything I have to do.
10. I seem to have more commitments to overcome than some of the other wives I know. *
11. I find myself having to prepare priority lists (lists which tell me which things I should do first) to get done all the things I have to do. Otherwise I forget because I have so much to do.
12. I feel I have to do things hastily and maybe less carefully in order to get everything done.
13. I just can't find the energy in me to do all the things expected of me.

* The word *wives* in item 10 must be changed when using the scale with men and those who are not married.

SCALE NAME: Rule-Breaking Behavior

SCALE DESCRIPTION:

A ten-item, five-point, summated rating scale measuring the frequency with which an adolescent reports engaging in behaviors that would be considered by most adults as improper if not immoral.

SCALE ORIGIN:

Although not specified in the article, the scale appears to be original to the study of Cox, Cox, and Moschis (1990).

SAMPLES:

The sample for Cox, Cox, and Moschis (1990) came from middle and high school students in Georgia. Several schools were selected to represent a variety of socioeconomic and community types. The survey forms were administered only in classes that were required of all students. Usable data were received from **1692** students. The sample was 51.5% male, 58% in grades 7 or 8, and 58.9% white.

RELIABILITY:

Cox, Cox, and Moschis (1990) reported an alpha for this scale of **.70.**

VALIDITY:

Cox, Cox, and Moschis (1990) provided no information regarding the scale's validity.

ADMINISTRATION:

The scale was part of a larger survey instrument apparently administered to students in classroom settings (Cox, Cox, and Moschis 1990). High scores on the scale would indicate that respondents frequently engage in behaviors that are improper for an adolescent, whereas low scores indicate respondents who do not typically "break the rules."

MAJOR FINDINGS:

Cox, Cox, and Moschis (1990) investigated the reasons for adolescent shoplifting. Those adolescents who were identified as shoplifters reported a significantly greater frequency of **rule-breaking** than nonshoplifting teens.

REFERENCES:

Cox, Dena, Anthony D. Cox, and George P. Moschis (1990), "When Consumer Behavior Goes Bad: An Investigation of Adolescent Shoplifting," *JCR*, 17 (September), 149-59.

SCALE ITEMS: RULE-BREAKING BEHAVIOR*

```
        Very                                              Very
    infrequently                                      frequently
        1————————2————————3————————4————————5
```

1. smoking where not allowed
2. lying to teacher
3. copying homework from a friend
4. disobeying parents
5. swearing and cursing

* Only part of the items were supplied in the article. Contact the authors
  for the rest.

SCALE NAME: Sadness

SCALE DESCRIPTION:

A three-item, five-point summated ratings scale assessing a person's experience with the sadness-related emotion. The directions and response scale can be worded so as to measure the *intensity* of the emotional state at the present time, or they can be adjusted to measure the *frequency* with which a person has experienced the emotional trait during some specified time period. One-word items were used by Westbrook and Oliver (1991), whereas phrases based on those same items were used by Allen, Machleit, and Kleine (1992).

SCALE ORIGIN:

The measure was developed by Izard (1977) and is part of the Differential Emotions Scale (DES II). The instrument was originally designed as a measure of a person's emotional "state" at a particular point in time, but adjustments in the instrument's instructions enable the same items to be used in the assessment of emotional experiences as perceived over a longer time period. The latter was viewed by Izard as measure of one's emotional "trait" (1977, p. 125). Test-retest reliability for the sadness subscale of DES II was reported to be .85 (n = 63) and item-factor correlations were .79 and more (Izard 1977, p. 126).

The items in DES II were composed solely of one word. In contrast, the items in DES III are phrases describing the target emotion. They were developed by Izard, although the first published validity testing was conducted by Kotsch, Gerbing, and Schwartz (1982). A study by Allen, Machleit, and Marine (1988) provides some insight to the factor structure of both DES II and III. With specific reference to sadness items, although they tended to load on the same factor, items representing other emotions loaded with them as well. Thus, evidence exists to indicate that these three items by themselves are unidimensional, but there is also evidence that they lack strong discriminant validity with respect to other emotions such as anger, guilt, and disgust.

SAMPLES:

The data used by Allen, Machleit, and Kleine (1992) came from a stratified sample of people of diverse experience with blood donation. Nine hundred questionnaires were mailed and **361** usable forms were returned. Given that all respondents previously had donated blood, limited information was known about them and allowed a comparison with nonrespondents. Respondents were a little older, less likely to be male, and more likely to be heavier donors than nonrespondents.

The data for the study conducted by Westbrook and Oliver (1991) came from a judgmental area sample. Convenience samples were taken at four shopping centers in a large northeastern city and were limited to persons who had purchased a new or used car in the past year. Complete and usable questionnaires were obtained from **125** respondents. A majority (74%) of the

sample was male. The average respondent had an income in the $25,000–$40,000 range and was 33 years of age. The frequency version of the scale was used in this study.

Two samples were used in the study by Oliver (1993), one examining satisfaction with cars and the other examining course satisfaction. The one involving cars is the same as the one described previously in Westbrook and Oliver (1991). The other sample was composed of students who volunteered from nine sections of a required marketing class. Usable questionnaires were provided by **178** students. The intensity version of the scale was used in this study.

RELIABILITY:

Westbrook and Oliver (1991) reported an alpha of **.88** for the scale. Allen, Machleit, and Kleine (1992; Allen 1994) calculated an alpha of **.88.** Oliver (1993) reported alphas of **.90** (n = 125) and **.81** (n = 178).

VALIDITY:

No specific examination of the scale's validity was reported in any of the studies.

ADMINISTRATION:

The scale was included with many other measures in the instruments used by Westbrook and Oliver (1991), Oliver (1993), and Allen, Machleit, Kleine (1992). High scores on the frequency version of the scale suggest that a respondent perceives him/herself as having experienced the sadness-related emotional trait very often in some specified time period. A high score on the intensity version of the scale indicates that a respondent is feeling very sad at the time of measurement.

MAJOR FINDINGS:

The study by Allen, Machleit, Kleine (1992) examined whether emotions effect behavior via attitudes or are better viewed as having a separate and distinct impact. Among the many findings was that **sadness** (DES III) plays a key role with behavior, at least with regard to donating blood. Specifically, a strong positive relationship was found between **sadness** involving the act of donating blood and the act of donating but only for the least experienced blood donors.

Oliver (1993) examined the separate roles of positive and negative affect, attribute performance, and disconfirmation for their impact on satisfaction. Negative affect was viewed as a function of several emotions, **sadness** being one of them. For both samples, negative affect was found to have direct influence on satisfaction.

Westbrook and Oliver (1991) studied the correspondence of the consumption emotional responses and satisfaction judgments that occur in the postpurchase period of the consumer decision process. **Sadness** (DES II) had its highest correlation with disgust (r = .84) and its lowest correlation with interest (r = .13). **Sadness** also was found to be a primary emotional trait linked to a cluster of consumers who had low satisfaction in their car buying experiences.

REFERENCES:

Allen, Chris T. (1994), personal correspondence.

_____, Karen A. Machleit, and Susan Schultz Kleine (1992), ''A Comparison of Attitudes and Emotions as Predictors of Behavior at Diverse Levels of Behavioral Experience,'' *JCR*, 18 (March), 493-504.

_____, _____, and Susan S. Marine (1988), ''On Assessing the Emotionality of Advertising Via Izard's Differential Emotions Scale,'' in *Advances in Consumer Research*, Vol. ??, ??, ed. Provo, UT: Association for Consumer Research, 226-31.

Izard, Carroll E. (1977), *Human Emotions*. New York: Plenum Press.

Kotsch, William E., Davis W. Gerbing, and Lynne E. Schwartz (1982), ''The Construct Validity of the Differential Emotions Scale as Adapted for Children and Adolescents,'' in *Measuring Emotions in Infants and Children*, Carroll E. Izard, ed. New York: Cambridge University Press, 251-78.

Oliver, Richard L. (1993), ''Cognitive, Affective, and Attribute Bases of the Satisfaction Response,'' *JCR*, 20 (December), 418-30.

Westbrook, Robert A. and Richard L. Oliver (1991), ''The Dimensionality of Consumption Emotion Patterns and Consumer Satisfaction,'' *JCR*, 18 (June), 84-91.

SCALE ITEMS: SADNESS

POSSIBLE DIRECTIONS FOR FREQUENCY VERSION OF SCALE: Below is a list of words that you can use to show how you feel. We want you to tell us how often you felt each of these feelings _____.* You can tell us how often you felt each of these feelings on the list by marking one of the numbers next to each question.

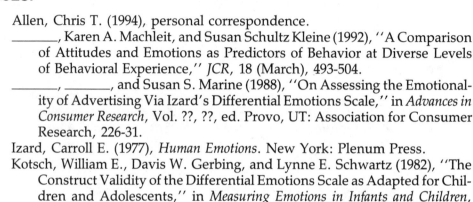

Almost
never   ____ : ____ : ____ : ____ : ____   Very
             1   2   3   4   5   often

POSSIBLE DIRECTIONS FOR INTENSITY VERSION OF SCALE: Below is a list of words that you can use to show how you feel. We want you to tell us how strongly you feel. You can tell us how strongly you feel each of these feelings on the list by marking one of the numbers next to each question.

Very
weak   ____ : ____ : ____ : ____ : ____   Very
           1   2   3   4   5   strong

DES II
1. downhearted
2. sad
3. discouraged

DES III
1. feel unhappy, blue, downhearted
2. feel sad and gloomy, almost like crying
3. feel discouraged, like you can't make it, nothing is going right

* The blank should be used to specify the time period of interest such as ''during the last week.''

SCALE NAME: Sadness

SCALE DESCRIPTION:

A four-item, five-point scale measuring a sadness-related emotional reaction to some specified stimulus. Mano and Oliver (1993) referred to the scale as *Unpleasantness*.

SCALE ORIGIN:

Although not expressly indicated, the items used by Mano and Oliver (1993) appear to have been used first as a summated scale by Mano (1991). With 224 college students, the scale was reported to have an alpha of .87. A cluster analysis grouped these three items together by themselves, but in a factor analysis, the items loaded along with two items (with negative loadings), three more related to *happiness*.

SAMPLES:

Data were collected by Mano and Oliver (1993) from **118** undergraduate business students attending a midwestern U.S. university.

RELIABILITY:

Mano and Oliver (1993) reported an alpha of **.79** for the scale.

VALIDITY:

Mano and Oliver (1993) did not specifically address the validity of the scale.

ADMINISTRATION:

The scale was part of a longer questionnaire self-administered by students in a classroom (Mano and Oliver 1993). A high score suggests that some stimulus has evoked a sad feeling.

MAJOR FINDINGS:

Mano and Oliver (1993) examined the dimensionality and causal structure of product evaluation, affect, and satisfaction. Among the many findings involving the **sadness** emotion was that it was slightly higher for subjects in a high-involvement manipulation.

REFERENCES:

Mano, Haim (1991), ''The Structure and Intensity of Emotional Experiences: Method and Context Convergence,'' *Multivariate Behavioral Research*, 26 (3), 389-411.

_____ and Richard L. Oliver (1993), ''Assessing the Dimensionality and

Structure of the Consumption Experience: Evaluation, Feeling, and Satisfaction," *JCR*, 20 (December), 451-66.

SCALE ITEMS: SADNESS

Not at all   Very much

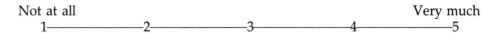

1. unhappy
2. sad
3. blue
4. in a bad mood

SCALE NAME: Sale Proneness

SCALE DESCRIPTION:

A six-item, seven-point, Likert-type scale measuring a consumer's tendency to buy the brands that are on sale. This measures a general tendency rather than the likelihood that the behavior occurs for any particular product category.

SCALE ORIGIN:

The scale is original to Lichtenstein, Ridgway, and Netemeyer (1993). Eight items in Lichtenstein, Netemeyer, and Burton's (1990) coupon proneness scale were modified and more were generated specifically for this study. A total of 18 items were tested along with many others in a pretest. The sample was composed of **341** nonstudent adult consumers who had the grocery-shopping responsibility for their households. Factor analysis and coefficient alpha were used to eliminate weaker items. The 16 items remaining for this scale were reported to have an alpha of .90. These items were used in the main study, although the next round of analysis eliminated ten of them. Of the remaining six items in the final version of the scale, three were very similar to items used by Lichtenstein, Netemeyer, and Burton (1990).

SAMPLES:

Lichtenstein, Ridgway, and Netemeyer (1993) collected data from shoppers who had received questionnaires in one of two grocery stores in a western SMSA (Boulder, Colorado). One thousand questionnaires were handed out at the stores, and **582** usable ones were returned by mail. A majority of the sample was female (75.9%) and married (58.6%). The median annual income range was $35,000–$49,999, and the median age was range was 35 to 44 years.

RELIABILITY:

The main study by Lichtenstein, Ridgway, and Netemeyer (1993) showed an alpha for the scale of **.88**.

VALIDITY:

Lichtenstein, Ridgway, and Netemeyer (1993) used confirmatory factor analysis to conclude that the scale was unidimensional and showed evidence of discriminant validity.

ADMINISTRATION:

In Lichtenstein, Ridgway, and Netemeyer (1993), the scale was part of a survey instrument self-administered by shoppers after leaving the grocery store. High scores on the scale indicate that respondents like to buy the brands that are on sale, whereas low scores suggest that they are more likely to be motivated by something like brand loyalty than by price.

MAJOR FINDINGS:

Lichtenstein, Ridgway, and Netemeyer (1993) identified and measured seven related but distinct price perception constructs. The dependent variable that **sale proneness** predicted most strongly was actual number of items purchased in a grocery store that were on sale.

REFERENCES:

Lichtenstein, Donald R., Richard D. Netemeyer, and Scot Burton (1990), ''Distinguishing Coupon Proneness From Value Consciousness: An Acquisition-Transaction Utility Theory Perspective,'' *JM*, 54 (July), 54-67.

_____, Nancy M. Ridgway, and Richard G. Netemeyer (1993), ''Price Perceptions and Consumer Shopping Behavior: A Field Study,'' *JMR*, 30 (May), 234-45.

SCALE ITEMS: SALE PRONENESS

Strongly   ___ : ___ : ___ : ___ : ___ : ___ : ___   Strongly
disagree   1   2   3   4   5   6   7   agree

1. If a product is on sale, that can be a reason for me to buy it.
2. When I buy a brand that's on sale, I feel that I am getting a good deal.
3. I have favorite brands, but most of the time I buy the brand that's on sale.
4. One should try to buy the brand that's on sale.
5. I am more likely to buy brands that are on sale.
6. Compared to most people, I am more likely to buy brands that are on special.

SCALE NAME: Satisfaction (Generalized)

SCALE DESCRIPTION:

A multi-item, seven-point semantic differential summated ratings scale measuring a consumer's degree of satisfaction with some stimulus. Crosby and Stephens (1987) used it with regard to insurance agents, the service policy, and the insurance agency, and Eroglu and Machleit (1990) used it with reference to shopping.

SCALE ORIGIN:

Neither the Crosby and Stephens (1987) study nor the Eroglu and Machleit (1990) study indicates the origin of the sets of items that were used.

SAMPLES:

The sample was selected from a nationally representative consumer panel and screened for ownership of life insurance. The first wave of the survey was based on **2311** returned and usable questionnaires. The sample was slightly better educated and more upscale than the population at large, but the authors considered the differences to be minor and unrelated to the studied relationships. A year later, **983** respondents to the first wave of the survey (or from a holdout sample) responded to the second wave. Comparison of main sample and holdout sample data did not indicate any bias due to wave 1 premeasurement.

Subjects used by Eroglu and Machleit (1990) were recruited from professional, nonprofit, and church organizations. The sample was composed of **112** adults and had the following characteristics: 58% were female, 70% were married, and 63% were between the ages of 20 and 49 years.

RELIABILITY:

Crosby and Stephens (1987) reported the alphas for the scales in both waves to be more than **.96**. The scale was completed for five slides representing different levels of retail density in the study by Eroglu and Machleit (1990). Alphas of **.94**, **.91**, **.90**, **.93**, and **.87** were reported for the slides from least to most dense retail conditions, respectively.

VALIDITY:

Crosby and Stephens (1987) provided some evidence of their scale's predictive validity by comparing the satisfaction level of four known groups that varied on their policy status: those who paid the premium and stayed with the same company, those for whom the policy was still in effect but had not yet paid the next year's premium, those who switched to a different company, and those whose policy lapsed and had not replaced it with another. The means for each of those groups in wave 1 on the overall satisfaction scale were 5.94,

5.29, 4.99, and 4.79, respectively. This shows that the scale gave an accurate indication of the policy owners' actual behavior.

Eroglu and Machleit (1990) did not address the validity of the version of the scale they used.

ADMINISTRATION:

The scales were self-administered by Crosby and Stephens (1987) as part of a larger mail questionnaire. In the Eroglu and Machleit (1990) study, the scale was filled out by subjects after viewing each of five experimental slides. High scores indicate greater satisfaction with the object, whereas low scores imply that respondents are not pleased.

MAJOR FINDINGS:

The purpose of Crosby and Stephens (1987) was to compare two proposed models of buyer satisfaction with life insurance: the relationship generalization model (RGM) and a rational evaluation model (REM). The RGM assumes that consumers generalize positive feelings about the provider to the core service, and the REM views consumers as most concerned about core service quality with the relationship merely adding value to it. In general, the results supported the REM over the RGM. This means that though the agent's performance affects satisfaction, it is balanced against the perceived performance of the core service.

Eroglu and Machleit (1990) examined some of the determinants and outcomes of retail crowding. Under conditions of low retail density (crowding), there were positive relationships between time pressure and **shopping satisfaction**. In contrast, under conditions of high retail density, there were negative relationships with **satisfaction**.

REFERENCES:

Crosby, Lawrence A. and Nancy Stephens (1987), ''Effects of Relationship Marketing on Satisfaction, Retention, and Prices in the Life Insurance Industry,'' *JMR*, 24 (November), 404-11.

Eroglu, Segin A. and Karen A. Machleit (1990), ''An Empirical Study of Retail Crowding: Antecedents and Consequences,'' *JR*, 66 (Summer), 201-21.

SCALE ITEMS: SATISFACTION (GENERALIZED)*

1. Satisfied ____ : ____ : ____ : ____ : ____ : ____ : ____ Dissatisfied
           7   6   5   4   3   2   1

2. Pleased ____ : ____ : ____ : ____ : ____ : ____ : ____ Displeased
           7   6   5   4   3   2   1

3. Favorable   ___ : ___ : ___ : ___ : ___ : ___ : ___   Unfavorable
               7   6   5   4   3   2   1

4. Pleasant   ___ : ___ : ___ : ___ : ___ : ___ : ___   Unpleasant
               7   6   5   4   3   2   1

5. I like it   ___ : ___ : ___ : ___ : ___ : ___ : ___   I didn't like
   very much   7   6   5   4   3   2   1   it at all

* Crosby and Stephens (1987) used items 1-3, and Eroglu and Machleit (1990) used items 1, 2, 4, and 5. Also, the latter used the term ''unsatisfied'' as the negative anchor for item 1.

SCALE NAME: Satisfaction (Generalized)

SCALE DESCRIPTION:

A 12-item, Likert-type summated ratings scale measuring a consumer's degree of satisfaction with a product he/she recently has purchased. Most of its uses have been in reference to the purchase of cars, but Mano and Oliver (1993) appear to have adapted it to be general enough to apply to whatever product a respondent was thinking about.

SCALE ORIGIN:

The scale originally was generated and used by Westbrook and Oliver (1981) measure consumer satisfaction with cars and calculators. Four other satisfaction measures were used as well, and their results compared in a multitrait-multimethod matrix. Convenience samples of students were used from two different universities (n = **68** + **107**). In terms of internal consistency, the alphas were **.93** and **.96** as measured for cars in the two samples. For both samples, the scale showed strong evidence of construct validity by converging with like constructs and discriminating between unlike constructs. Compared with the other measures of satisfaction, this Likert version produced the greatest dispersion of individual scores while maintaining a symmetrical distribution.

SAMPLES:

Data were collected by Mano and Oliver (1993) from **118** undergraduate business students attending a midwestern U.S. university.

Two samples were used in the study by Oliver (1993) with only one examining **satisfaction with cars**. The sample is the same as the one described in Westbrook and Oliver (1991). The data for the study came from a judgmental area sample. Convenience samples were taken at four shopping centers in a large northeastern city and were limited to persons who had purchased a new or used car in the past year. Complete and usable questionnaires were obtained from **125** respondents. A majority (74%) of the sample was male. The average respondent had an income in the $25,000–$40,000 range and was 33 years of age.

Findings in Oliver and Swan (1989) were based on **184** completed questionnaires from people who had bought new cars within six months prior to the survey. The average respondent was male (67%), college educated (32%), had an income between $20,000 and $29,999, was 43 years of age, had owned 7.8 cars in his lifetime, and had purchased his latest car 4.5 months previously.

RELIABILITY:

Mano and Oliver (1993), Oliver (1993), and Westbrook and Oliver (1991) reported alphas of **.95, .98,** and **.94,** respectively, for the scale.

VALIDITY:

No specific examination of scale validity was reported in any of the studies. However, Mano and Oliver (1993) performed a factor analysis that provided evidence that the scale was unidimensional.

ADMINISTRATION:

The name of the product can be put in the blanks to focus the respondent's attention on a specific product, for example, car. Alternatively, a phrase such as *the product* can be used if, similar to Mano and Oliver (1993), respondents have been asked to think of a recently purchased product and the wording of the items must be more general to allow for the differences that will occur.

The scale was one of many other measures that were self-administered (Mano and Oliver 1993; Oliver 1993; Oliver and Swan 1989). High scores on the scale suggest that respondents are very satisfied with their cars (or products), whereas low scores imply that respondents are not pleased with their cars (or products).

MAJOR FINDINGS:

Mano and Oliver (1993) examined the dimensionality and causal structure of product evaluation, affect, and satisfaction. As hypothesized, **satisfaction** was found to have a significant positive relationship with pleasantness, a significant negative relationship with unpleasantness, and no significant relationship with arousal and quietness.

The separate roles of positive and negative affect, attribute performance, and disconfirmation were examined by Oliver (1993) for their impact on satisfaction. Disconfirmation was found to have direct and very significant influence on **satisfaction**.

The general purpose of Oliver and Swan (1989) was to examine customer perceptions of satisfaction in the context of new car purchases. The results indicated that **car satisfaction** was positively influenced by satisfaction with the dealer and with car disconfirmation but was negatively influenced by complaint frequency.

COMMENTS:

The scale has exhibited repeatedly such high internal consistency that it appears some items might be judiciously eliminated if need be without seriously affecting reliability.

REFERENCES:

Mano, Haim and Richard L. Oliver (1993), "Assessing the Dimensionality and Structure of the Consumption Experience: Evaluation, Feeling, and Satisfaction," *JCR*, 20 (December), 451-66.

Oliver, Richard L. (1993), "Cognitive, Affective, and Attribute Bases of the Satisfaction Response," *JCR*, 20 (December), 418-30.

_____ and John E. Swan (1989), ''Equity and Disconfirmation Perceptions as Influences on Merchant and Product Satisfaction,'' *JCR*, 16 (December), 372-83.

Westbrook, Robert A. and Richard L. Oliver (1981), ''Developing Better Measures of Consumer Satisfaction: Some Preliminary Results,'' in *Advances in Consumer Research*, Vol. 8, Kent B. Monroe, ed. Ann Arbor, MI: Association for Consumer Research, 94-99.

_____ and _____ (1991), ''The Dimensionality of Consumption Emotion Patterns and Consumer Satisfaction,'' *JCR*, 18 (June), 84-91.

SCALE ITEMS: SATISFACTION (CAR)*

Strongly
disagree   Neither   Strongly
                                                           agree
1————2————3————4————5————6————7

1. This is one of the best _____ I could have bought.
2. This _____ is exactly what I need.
3. This _____ hasn't worked out as well as I thought it would. **(r)**
4. I am satisfied with my decision to buy this _____.
5. Sometimes I have mixed feelings about keeping it. **(r)**
6. My choice to buy this _____ was a wise one.
7. If I could do it over again, I'd buy a different make/model. **(r)**
8. I have truly enjoyed this _____.
9. feel bad about my decision to buy this _____. **(r)**
10. I am *not* happy that I bought this _____. **(r)**
11. Owning this _____ has been a good experience.
12. I'm sure it was the right thing to buy this _____.

* Mano and Oliver (1993), Oliver (1993), and Westbrook and Oliver (1981) used five-point scales whereas Oliver and Swan (1989) used one with seven points.

SCALE NAME: Satisfaction (With Activity)

SCALE DESCRIPTION:

>A six-item, seven-point, Likert-type summated ratings scale measuring the degree to which a person who has just been involved in an activity such as a river rafting trip thinks that it was a good experience and worth the price.

SCALE ORIGIN:

>The scale was developed for the research reported by Fisher and Price (1991; Price 1994).

SAMPLES:

>Very little information was provided by Arnould and Price (1993) regarding their sample. The respondents are described simply as a stratified random sample of people taking multiday river trips with one of three clients' rafting companies. A total of **137** persons filled out post-trip questionnaires but only 97 of those had completed pre-trip surveys.

RELIABILITY:

>Arnould and Price (1993) reported an alpha of **.90** for the scale.

VALIDITY:

>Arnould and Price (1993) reported no specific examination of the scale's validity.

ADMINISTRATION:

>The scale was self-administered by respondents as part of a larger survey after they had finished a rafting trip (Arnould and Price 1993). High scores on the scale suggest that respondents have experienced something quite satisfying, whereas low scores imply that they did not have a good experience.

MAJOR FINDINGS:

>Arnould and Price (1993) explored the impact of several experiential variables on satisfaction with an extraordinary hedonic experience. There were strong positive correlations between overall **satisfaction** with the river rafting trip and several other variables: one's feeling that the experience had produced a communion with others, communion with nature, and personal growth.

COMMENTS:

See also MacInnis and Price (1990) for another use of the scale.

REFERENCES:

Arnould, Eric J. and Linda L. Price (1993), "River Magic: Extraordinary Experience and the Extended Service Encounter," *JCR*, 20 (June), 24-45.

Fisher, Robert J. and Linda L. Price (1991), "The Relationship Between International Travel Motivations and Cultural Receptivity," *Journal of Leisure Research*, 23 (3), 193-208.

MacInnis, Deborah J. and Linda L. Price (1990), "An Exploratory Study of the Effect of Imagery Processing and Consumer Experience on Expectations and Satisfaction," in *Advances in Consumer Research*, Vol. 17, Marvin E. Goldberg, Gerald Gorn, and Richard W. Pollay, eds. Provo, UT: Association for Consumer Research, 41-47.

Price, Linda L. (1994), personal correspondence.

SCALE ITEMS: SATISFACTION (WITH ACTIVITY)

```
Strongly                                                    Strongly
disagree                                                      agree
    1————————2————————3————————4————————5————————6————————7
```

This _____:
1. had many unique or special moments.
2. had special meaning to me.
3. was as good as I expected.
4. was satisfying to me.
5. stands out as one of my best experiences.
6. was worth the price I paid for it.

SCALE NAME: Satisfaction (With Brand Selection)

SCALE DESCRIPTION:

A six-item, six-point, Likert-type scale measuring the certainty with which a person indicates he/she has made the best selection from among the brands available. The category studied by Cole and Balasubramanian (1993) was breakfast cereal.

SCALE ORIGIN:

The scale is original to the study by Cole and Balasubramanian (1993).

SAMPLES:

Cole and Balasubramanian (1993) conducted two studies; the scale was used only in the second one, a laboratory experiment. Though not stated explicitly, there appear to have been **82** participants and they were recruited from university staff, churches, and a senior citizen center. Subjects ranged in age from 22 to 88 years.

RELIABILITY:

Cole and Balasubramanian (1993) reported an alpha of **.75** for the scale.

VALIDITY:

Cole and Balasubramanian (1993) reported no examination of scale validity for the scale.

ADMINISTRATION:

The scale was self-administered by subjects after they had engaged in a computerized brand selection exercise (Cole and Balasubramanian 1993). A high score on the scale indicates that a respondent is certain that he/she made the best decision, whereas a low score suggests that he/she is dissatisfied with the decision made.

MAJOR FINDINGS:

The purpose of the studies reported by Cole and Balasubramanian (1993) was to examine the effect that age could have on the ability to search for and use information to make a better choice decision. In both the field and laboratory studies, it was found that young adults (mean = 36) were significantly more **satisfied** with their choices than the elderly (mean = 75) were.

COMMENTS:

The scale was developed for use in a laboratory constrained choice situation. For use in the field, some minor adjustment in phrasing appears to be called for (e.g., item 5).

REFERENCE:

Cole, Catherine A. and Siva K. Balasubramanian (1993), ''Age Differences in Consumers' Search for Information: Public Policy Implications,'' *JCR*, 20 (June), 157-69.

SCALE ITEMS: SATISFACTION (WITH BRAND SELECTION)*

Strongly
disagree   ____ : ____ : ____ : ____ : ____ : ____   Strongly
agree
 1 2 3 4 5 6

1. I am pretty satisfied with the _____ I chose.
2. I am pretty certain that I made the best decision about which _____ to select.
3. I felt confused while shopping for _____. **(r)**
4. I am pretty sure that one of the other brands of _____ that I did not choose would have been equal to or better than the brand I chose to satisfy my desires and expectations. **(r)**
5. I really would not like any more information about the various brands of _____ in the study.
6. It is likely that the brand of _____ I chose is better than the brands of _____ I am currently familiar with.

* The name of the product category should go in the blanks.

SCALE NAME: Satisfaction (With Course)

SCALE DESCRIPTION:

A six-item, five-point, Likert-type summated ratings scale measuring a student's degree of satisfaction with a class he/she recently took.

SCALE ORIGIN:

The scale is a modification of one originally generated and used by Westbrook and Oliver (1981) to measure consumer satisfaction with cars and calculators. Not only was the focal item changed (course versus car) but items suggesting that there was a choice were eliminated given that the sample was taken from marketing majors who were required to take the course. (See #223 for more information.)

SAMPLES:

Two samples were used in Oliver (1993), only one examining **course satisfaction**. That sample was composed of students who volunteered from nine sections of a required marketing class. Usable questionnaires were provided by **178** students.

RELIABILITY:

Oliver (1993) reported an alpha of **.92** for the scale.

VALIDITY:

No specific examination of scale validity was reported by either Oliver (1993) or Oliver and Swan (1989).

ADMINISTRATION:

The scale was one of many measures that were self-administered (Oliver 1993). High scores on the scale suggest that respondents are very satisfied with a particular course they took, whereas low scores imply that respondents are very displeased with the class.

MAJOR FINDINGS:

The separate roles of positive and negative affect, attribute performance, and disconfirmation were examined by Oliver (1993) for their impact on satisfaction. Disconfirmation was found to have direct and very significant influence on **satisfaction**.

COMMENTS:

Oliver (1993) reported the mean score of the sample to be 3.49 on the scale, with a standard deviation of .91.

REFERENCES:

Oliver, Richard L. (1993), ''Cognitive, Affective, and Attribute Bases of the Satisfaction Response,'' *JCR*, 20 (December), 418-30.

_____ (1994), personal correspondence.

Westbrook, Robert A. and Richard L. Oliver (1981), ''Developing Better Measures of Consumer Satisfaction: Some Preliminary Results,'' in *Advances in Consumer Research*, Vol. 8, Kent B. Monroe, ed. Ann Arbor, MI: Association for Consumer Research, 94-99.

SCALE ITEMS: SATISFACTION (WITH COURSE)*

Strongly disagree	Disagree	Neither agree nor disagree	Agree	Strongly agree
1	2	3	4	5

1. This is one of the best courses I could have taken.
2. This course has worked out as well as I thought it would.
3. I am satisfied with my decision to take this course.
4. I have truly enjoyed this course.
5. I am happy that I took this course.
6. Taking this course has been a good experience.

* Items were supplied by Oliver (1994).

SCALE NAME: Satisfaction (With Facility)

SCALE DESCRIPTION:

A four-item, seven-point scale measuring the degree to which a consumer is satisfied with the nonproduct, facility-related aspects of a shopping area. As described subsequently, the shopping area studied by Dawson, Bloch, and Ridgway (1990) was a crafts market.

SCALE ORIGIN:

This scale is original to Dawson, Bloch, and Ridgway (1990).

SAMPLES:

The sample collected by Dawson, Bloch, and Ridgway (1990) came from a large outdoor arts and crafts market in a major west coast city. Shoppers were approached over four summer days by trained survey administrators and asked to participate. Those who did participate were paid $1. The analysis was based on data from **278** respondents. The only significant difference noted between the sample and that of the surrounding SMSA was that the former contained more females.

RELIABILITY:

Dawson, Bloch, and Ridgway (1990) reported an alpha of **.70** for the scale.

VALIDITY:

Dawson, Bloch, and Ridgway (1990) performed an exploratory factor analysis on 12 items that related to satisfaction in a shopping experience. The four items composing this scale loaded high on the same factor and low on the other factor (satisfaction with the product), providing some evidence of unidimensionality for the scale and convergent and discriminant validity for the items.

ADMINISTRATION:

The scale was self-administered as part of a larger survey instrument in the field study conducted by Dawson, Bloch, and Ridgway (1990). High scores on the scale suggest that respondents are very satisfied with the facility-related aspects of a store, mall, or market, whereas low scores imply that they are very displeased with several aspects of the facility.

MAJOR FINDINGS:

Dawson, Bloch, and Ridgway (1990) investigated the role played by shopping motives in shaping the emotions triggered during a retail shopping experienced. Among the many findings was that those shoppers with strong experience-related shopping motives experienced greater **satisfaction with the market** than those shoppers with weak experience motives.

COMMENTS:

Except for item 3, the items in the scale would appear to be appropriate for many different types of retail facilities. When not appropriate, the item could be dropped from the scale or consideration could be given to its replacement with other relevant items such as "helpfulness of employees," "lighting," or "security." In fact, the internal consistency and content validity of the scale probably could be improved by adding several more appropriate items.

REFERENCE:

Dawson, Scott, Peter H. Bloch, and Nancy M. Ridgway (1990), "Shopping Motives, Emotional States, and Retail Outcomes," *JR*, 66 (Winter), 408-27.

SCALE ITEMS: SATISFACTION (WITH FACILITY)

Directions: How satisfied are you with each of the following aspects of _____.

Not at all ____ : ____ : ____ : ____ : ____ : ____ : ____ Very satisfied
satisfied   1   2   3   4   5   6   7

1. parking
2. crowds
3. seating
4. cleanliness

SCALE NAME: Satisfaction (With Hospital)

SCALE DESCRIPTION:

A five-item, six-point, Likert-like scale measuring the degree to which a person expresses satisfaction with several aspects of his/her hospital.

SCALE ORIGIN:

The idea for the satisfaction scales used by Singh (1991) came from work by Ware and Snyder (1975). The items themselves and the response format were modified greatly to measure three dimensions of satisfaction (instrumental, expressive, access/cost) of three medically related objects of satisfaction (physicians, hospitals, insurance).

SAMPLES:

In collecting data for the study, Singh (1991) tried to select four areas in the United States that varied geographically and in the number of physicians per capita. Randomly selected households in one major city for each of four states were sent questionnaires. This amounted to 375 households per city. After accounting for about 10% of the surveys returned for nondelivery, the following responses were received per city: 154 (Cleveland), 103 (Jacksonville), 133 (Omaha), and 140 (Salt Lake City). Because it was critical that respondents have medical insurance coverage, some returned questionnaires were not used in addition to those that were not deemed complete enough to analyze. Data from **367** households, therefore, composed the final sample used in the analyses. Although the sample was dominated by white married women, it had a wide range of respondents from different age, education, and income groups.

RELIABILITY:

Singh (1991) reported an alpha of **.85** for the scale.

VALIDITY:

Although Singh (1991) did not go into great detail about this scale's validity, some evidence was provided. Apparently, the exploratory factor analysis of all of scale items used in the study showed that the five final items composing this scale loaded high and together on a single factor. LISREL was used to test a larger multiconstruct model, and its findings appear to confirm those of the exploratory factor analysis.

ADMINISTRATION:

The scale was administered by Singh (1991) as part of a larger mail survey instrument. High scores on the scale indicate that respondents are very satisfied with several different aspects of their hospitals, whereas low scores suggest that they are very dissatisfied with the service with which they have been provided.

MAJOR FINDINGS:

The purpose of Singh (1991) was to test and compare several competing models of patient's satisfaction with medical care. **Satisfaction with the hospital** was one of the three "objects" examined in the study. The findings supported a multi-object, multidimensional model of satisfaction, with the former explaining about 61% of total variance.

REFERENCES:

Singh, Jagdip (1991), "Understanding the Structure of Consumers' Satisfaction Evaluations of Service Delivery," *JAMS*, 19 (Summer), 223-44.

Ware, John E. and Mary K. Snyder (1975), "Dimensions of Patient Attitudes Regarding Doctors and Medical Care Services," *Medical Care*, 13 (August), 669-82.

SCALE ITEMS: SATISFACTION (WITH HOSPITAL)

1 = Very dissatisfied   4 = Somewhat satisfied
2 = Dissatisfied   5 = Satisfied
3 = Somewhat dissatisfied   6 = Very satisfied

Use the possible alternatives above to complete the phrases below.
1. With my hospital's personal concern for me, I felt . . .
2. With my hospital's willingness to explain its procedures, I felt . . .
3. With my hospital's medical capabilities, I felt . . .
4. With my hospital's physical appearance, I felt . . .
5. With my hospital's costs, I felt . . .

SCALE NAME: Satisfaction (With Insurance)

SCALE DESCRIPTION:

A five-item, six-point, Likert-like scale measuring the degree to which a person expresses satisfaction with several aspects of his/her insurance.

SCALE ORIGIN:

The idea for the satisfaction scales used by Singh (1991) came from work by Ware and Snyder (1975). The items themselves and the response format were modified greatly to measure three dimensions of satisfaction (instrumental, expressive, access/cost) of three medically related objects of satisfaction (physicians, hospitals, insurance).

SAMPLES:

In collecting data for the study, Singh (1991) tried to select four areas in the United States that varied geographically and in the number of physicians per capita. Randomly selected households in one major city for each of four states were sent questionnaires. This amounted to 375 households per city. After accounting for about 10% of the surveys returned for nondelivery, the following responses were received per city: 154 (Cleveland); 103 (Jacksonville); 133 (Omaha); and, 140 (Salt Lake City). Because it was critical that respondents have medical insurance coverage, some returned questionnaires, in addition to those that were not deemed complete enough to analyze, were not used. Data from **367** households, therefore, composed the final sample used in the analyses. Although the sample was dominated by white married women, it had a wide range of respondents from different age, education, and income groups.

RELIABILITY:

Singh (1991) reported an alpha of **.92** for the scale.

VALIDITY:

Although Singh (1991) did not go into great detail about this scale's validity, some evidence was provided. Apparently, the exploratory factor analysis of all of scale items used in the study showed that the five final items composing this scale loaded high and together on a single factor. LISREL was used to test a larger multiconstruct model, and its findings appear to confirm those of the exploratory factor analysis.

ADMINISTRATION:

The scale was administered by Singh (1991) as part of a larger mail survey instrument. High scores on the scale indicate that respondents are very satisfied with several different aspects of their insurance providers, whereas low scores suggest that they are very dissatisfied with the service with which they have been provided.

MAJOR FINDINGS:

The purpose of Singh (1991) was to test and compare several competing models of patient's satisfaction with medical care. **Satisfaction with the insurance provider** was one of the three "objects" examined in the study. The findings supported a multi-object, multidimensional model of satisfaction, with the former explaining about 61% of total variance.

REFERENCES:

Singh, Jagdip (1991), "Understanding the Structure of Consumers' Satisfaction Evaluations of Service Delivery," *JAMS*, 19 (Summer), 223-44.

Ware, John E. and Mary K. Snyder (1975), "Dimensions of Patient Attitudes Regarding Doctors and Medical Care Services," *Medical Care*, 13 (August), 669-82.

SCALE ITEMS: SATISFACTION (WITH INSURANCE)

1 = Very dissatisfied	4 = Somewhat satisfied
2 = Dissatisfied	5 = Satisfied
3 = Somewhat dissatisfied	6 = Very satisfied

Use the possible alternatives above to complete the phrases below.

1. With my insurance provider's personal concern for me, I felt . . .
2. With my insurance provider's willingness to explain its procedures, I felt
. . .
3. With my insurance provider's benefits, I felt . . .
4. With my insurance provider's speed when responding to concerns/claims, I felt . . .
5. With my insurance provider's expectation of the cost I should pay, I felt
. . .

SCALE NAME: Satisfaction (With Marketer)

SCALE DESCRIPTION:

A four-item, seven-point, Likert-type scale measuring the degree to which a consumer has had a positive experience with the manufacturer and dealer in the purchase of some specified product. Srinivasan and Ratchford (1991) referred to the scale as *experience with previous manufacturer or dealer*.

SCALE ORIGIN:

Although not expressly stated in the article, the scale appears to be have been used first in published research by Srinivasan and Ratchford (1991), which was based on the dissertation of Srinivasan (1987). Some initial assessment of scale reliability and face validity was made in the pretest stage of the study.

SAMPLES:

Srinivasan and Ratchford (1991) obtained a sample of new car buyers through a mail survey of new car registrants in the Buffalo, New York area. More than three thousand people were sent three mailings of the questionnaire, and ultimately, **1401** usable responses were received. No demographic description is provided of the respondents.

RELIABILITY:

Srinivasan and Ratchford (1991) reported an alpha of **.77** for the scale.

VALIDITY:

Srinivasan and Ratchford (1991) provided no detailed discussion of this scale's validity.

ADMINISTRATION:

Srinivasan and Ratchford (1991) used the scale along with other measures in a mail survey instrument. A low score on the scale means that a respondent reports having a positive experience with a manufacturer and dealer for some specified product, whereas a high score suggests that a respondent did not have a satisfying experience.

MAJOR FINDINGS:

Srinivasan and Ratchford (1991) examined a model of the determinants of external search for new car purchases. **Satisfaction with the marketer** was not tested by itself but in combination with a measure of product satisfaction. As hypothesized, **satisfaction** had negative effects on perceived risk, evoked-set size, and perceived search benefits. For risk and evoked-set size, **satisfac-**

tion was the variable with largest effect. It had a relatively small impact on search benefits.

COMMENTS:

The purchase decision focused on in Srinivasan and Ratchford (1991) was for new cars. The scale may be adaptable to other purchase decisions, although its reliability and validity will need to be reexamined.

REFERENCES:

Srinivasan, Narasimhan (1987), "A Causal Model of External Search for Information for Durables: A Particular Investigation in the Case of New Automobiles," doctoral dissertation, State University of New York at Buffalo.
_____ and Brian T. Ratchford (1991), "An Empirical Test of an External Search for Automobiles," *JCR*, 18 (September), 233-42.

SCALE ITEMS: SATISFACTION (WITH MARKETER)

DIRECTIONS: There are no right or wrong answers to the following statements and a large number of people agree and disagree. Kindly indicate *your* personal opinion by circling any one number for each statement.

Strongly   Strongly
agree   disagree
1————2————3————4————5————6————7

1. My old dealer provided me with very good advice.
2. I would like to own another model of my previous _____.
3. I would never buy another _____ from the same manufacturer as my previous _____. **(r)**
4. All the guarantees I got on my old _____ from the dealer were honored.

SCALE NAME: Satisfaction (With Physician)

SCALE DESCRIPTION:

A five-item, six-point, Likert-like scale measuring the degree to which a person expresses satisfaction with several aspects of interaction with his/her physician.

SCALE ORIGIN:

The idea for the satisfaction scales used by Singh (1991) came from work by Ware and Snyder (1975). The items themselves and the response format were modified greatly to measure three dimensions of satisfaction (instrumental, expressive, access/cost) of three medically related objects of satisfaction (physicians, hospitals, insurance).

SAMPLES:

In collecting data for the study, Singh (1991) tried to select four areas in the United States that varied geographically and in the number of physicians per capita. Randomly selected households in one major city for each of four states were sent questionnaires. This amounted to 375 households per city. After accounting for about 10% of the surveys returned for nondelivery, the following responses were received per city: 154 (Cleveland); 103 (Jacksonville); 133 (Omaha); and, 140 (Salt Lake City). Because it was critical that respondents have medical insurance coverage, some returned questionnaires, in addition to those that were not deemed complete enough to analyze, were not used. Data from **367** households, therefore, composed the final sample used in the analyses. Although the sample was dominated by white married women, it had a wide range of respondents from different age, education, and income groups.

RELIABILITY:

Singh (1991) reported an alpha of **.83** for the scale.

VALIDITY:

Although Singh (1991) did not go into great detail about this scale's validity, some evidence was provided. Apparently, the exploratory factor analysis of all of scale items used in the study showed that the five final items composing this scale loaded high and together on a single factor. LISREL was used to test a larger multiconstruct model, and its findings appear to confirm those of the exploratory factor analysis.

ADMINISTRATION:

Singh (1991) administered the scale as part of a larger mail survey instrument. High scores on the scale indicate that respondents are very satisfied with several different aspects of interaction with their physicians, whereas low scores suggest that they are very dissatisfied with the service with which they have been provided.

MAJOR FINDINGS:

The purpose of Singh (1991) was to test and compare several competing models of patient's satisfaction with medical care. **Satisfaction with the physician** was one of the three "objects" examined in the study. The findings supported a multi-object, multidimensional model of satisfaction, with the former explaining about 61% of total variance.

REFERENCES:

Singh, Jagdip (1991), "Understanding the Structure of Consumers' Satisfaction Evaluations of Service Delivery," *JAMS*, 19 (Summer), 223-44.

Ware, John E. and Mary K. Snyder (1975), "Dimensions of Patient Attitudes Regarding Doctors and Medical Care Services," *Medical Care*, 13 (August), 669-82.

SCALE ITEMS: SATISFACTION (WITH PHYSICIAN)

1 = Very dissatisfied   4 = Somewhat satisfied
2 = Dissatisfied   5 = Satisfied
3 = Somewhat dissatisfied   6 = Very satisfied

Use the possible alternatives above to complete the phrases below.
1. With my doctor's personal concern for me, I feel . . .
2. With my doctor's willingness to explain reasons for medical treatment, I feel . . .
3. With my doctor's medical abilities, I feel . . .
4. With my doctor's ability to see me on time, I feel . . .
5. With my doctor's costs of medical visits, I feel . . .

SCALE NAME: Satisfaction (With Product)

SCALE DESCRIPTION:

A seven-item, seven-point, Likert-type scale measuring the degree to which a consumer recalls having a positive experience with some specified product. The scale was referred to as *experience with previous car* by Srinivasan and Ratchford (1991).

SCALE ORIGIN:

Although not expressly stated in the article, the scale appears to be have been used first in published research by Srinivasan and Ratchford (1991), which was based on the dissertation of Srinivasan (1987). Some initial assessment of scale reliability and face validity was made in pretest stage of the study.

SAMPLES:

A sample of new car buyers was obtained by Srinivasan and Ratchford (1991) through a mail survey of new car registrants in the Buffalo, New York area. More than three thousand people were sent three mailings of the questionnaire, and ultimately, **1401** usable responses were received. No demographic description is provided of the respondents.

RELIABILITY:

Srinivasan and Ratchford (1991) reported an alpha of **.91** for the scale.

VALIDITY:

Srinivasan and Ratchford (1991) provided no detailed discussion of this scale's validity.

ADMINISTRATION:

Srinivasan and Ratchford (1991) used the scale along with other measures in a mail survey instrument. A low score on the scale means that a respondents reports having a positive experience with some specified product, whereas a high score suggests that a respondent did not have a satisfying experience with the product.

MAJOR FINDINGS:

Srinivasan and Ratchford (1991) examined a model of the determinants of external search for new car purchases. **Satisfaction with the product** was not tested by itself but in combination with a measure of satisfaction with the dealer/manufacturer. As hypothesized, **satisfaction** had negative effects on perceived risk, evoked-set size, and perceived search benefits. For risk and evoked-set size, **satisfaction** was the variable with largest effect. It had a relatively small impact on search benefits.

COMMENTS:

The purchase decision focused on in Srinivasan and Ratchford (1991) was for new cars. The scale may be adaptable to other products, though its reliability and validity will need to be reexamined.

REFERENCES:

Srinivasan, Narasimhan (1987), ''A Causal Model of External Search for Information for Durables: A Particular Investigation in the Case of New Automobiles,'' doctoral dissertation, State University of New York at Buffalo.

_____ and Brian T. Ratchford (1991), ''An Empirical Test of an External Search for Automobiles,'' *JCR*, 18 (September), 233-42.

SCALE ITEMS: SATISFACTION (WITH PRODUCT)

DIRECTIONS: There are no right or wrong answers to the following statements and a large number of people agree and disagree. Kindly indicate *your* personal opinion by circling any one number for each statement.

Strongly agree						Strongly disagree
1————	2————	3————	4————	5————	6————	7

1. My previous _____ gave me a lot of headaches. **(r)**
2. Repairs on my previous _____ were becoming expensive. **(r)**
3. My previous _____ gave me very satisfactory performance.
4. My old _____ was very reliable.
5. Overall, my experience with my previous _____ was positive.
6. Overall, my experience with my previous _____ was negative. **(r)**
7. The performance of my previous _____ lived up to expectations.

SCALE NAME: Satisfaction (With Products)

SCALE DESCRIPTION:

A three-item, seven-point scale measuring the degree to which a consumer is satisfied with the product-related aspects of a shopping area. As described subsequently, the shopping area studied by Dawson, Bloch, and Ridgway (1990) was a crafts market.

SCALE ORIGIN:

This scale is original to Dawson, Bloch, and Ridgway (1990).

SAMPLES:

The sample collected by Dawson, Bloch, and Ridgway (1990) came from a large outdoor arts and crafts market in a major west coast city. Shoppers were approached over four summer days by trained survey administrators and asked to participate. Those who did participate were paid $1. The analysis was based on data from **278** respondents. The only significant difference noted between the sample and that of the surrounding SMSA was that the former contained more females.

RELIABILITY:

Dawson, Bloch, and Ridgway (1990) reported an alpha of **.76** for the scale.

VALIDITY:

Dawson, Bloch, and Ridgway (1990) performed an exploratory factor analysis on 12 items that related to satisfaction in a shopping experience. The three items composing this scale loaded high on the same factor and low on the other factor (satisfaction with the facility), providing some evidence of unidimensionality for the scale and convergent and discriminant validity for the items.

ADMINISTRATION:

The scale was self-administered as part of a larger survey instrument in the field study conducted by Dawson, Bloch, and Ridgway (1990). High scores on the scale suggest that respondents are very satisfied with the product-related aspects of a store, mall, or market, whereas low scores imply that they are dissatisfied with the products.

MAJOR FINDINGS:

Dawson, Bloch, and Ridgway (1990) investigated the role played by shopping motives in shaping the emotions triggered during a retail shopping experienced. Among the many findings was that those shoppers with strong product-related motives experienced greater **satisfaction with the market's crafts** than those shoppers with weak product motives.

COMMENTS:

The items in the scale may have to be modified somewhat depending on the particular retail situation being examined. As it is, the items are most appropriate for a store or market with crafts and would not be appropriate if studying many other types of products (e.g., electronics, clothing, food).

REFERENCE:

Dawson, Scott, Peter H. Bloch, and Nancy M. Ridgway (1990), "Shopping Motives, Emotional States, and Retail Outcomes," *JR*, 66 (Winter), 408-27.

SCALE ITEMS: SATISFACTION (PRODUCTS)*

Directions: How satisfied are you with each of the following aspects of _____.

Not at all   _____ : _____ : _____ : _____ : _____ : _____ : _____   Very satisfied
satisfied   1   2   3   4   5   6   7

1. quality of _____
2. selection of _____
3. prices of _____

* Dawson, Bloch, and Ridgway (1990) used the word *crafts* in the items shown here because they were studying a crafts market. The scale could be used easily to measure satisfaction of other goods by either using the word *products* in the blanks or a more specific and relevant descriptor (e.g., *suits, stereos, furniture*).

SCALE NAME: Search Benefits

SCALE DESCRIPTION:

A seven-item, seven-point, Likert-type scale measuring the perceived benefits of gathering information from external sources before making a purchase decision.

SCALE ORIGIN:

Although not expressly stated in the article, the scale appears to be have been used first in published research by Srinivasan and Ratchford (1991), which was based on the dissertation of Srinivasan (1987). Some initial assessment of scale reliability and face validity was made in pretest stage of the study.

SAMPLES:

A sample of new car buyers was obtained by Srinivasan and Ratchford (1991) through a mail survey of new car registrants in the Buffalo, New York area. More than three thousand people were sent three mailings of the questionnaire, and ultimately, **1401** usable responses were received. No demographic description of the respondents is provided.

RELIABILITY:

Srinivasan and Ratchford (1991) reported the LISREL estimate of reliability for the items to be **.93**.

VALIDITY:

Srinivasan and Ratchford (1991) provided no detailed discussion of this scale's validity. However, it was suggested that generally the measures used in the study showed evidence of convergent and discriminant validity.

ADMINISTRATION:

The scale was used by Srinivasan and Ratchford (1991) along with other measures in a mail survey instrument. A low score on the scale indicates that a respondent thinks it is beneficial to shop around before buying some new product (specified), whereas a high score suggests that a respondent does not think it is important to engage in prepurchase external search.

MAJOR FINDINGS:

Srinivasan and Ratchford (1991) examined a model of the determinants of external search for new car purchases. Among the variables tested, evoked-set size and interest in cars had the greatest impact on perceived **search benefits**. In turn, **search benefits** had the largest effect on search effort.

COMMENTS:

The purchase decision focused on in Srinivasan and Ratchford (1991) was for new cars. As noted subsequently, the scale is easily adaptable to other purchase decisions, although its reliability and validity will need to be reexamined.

REFERENCES:

Srinivasan, Narasimhan (1987), ''A Causal Model of External Search for Information for Durables: A Particular Investigation in the Case of New Automobiles,'' doctoral dissertation, State University of New York at Buffalo.
_____ and Brian T. Ratchford (1991), ''An Empirical Test of a External Search for Automobiles,'' *JCR*, 18 (September), 233-42.

SCALE ITEMS: SEARCH BENEFITS

DIRECTIONS: There are no right or wrong answers to the following statements and a large number of people agree and disagree. Kindly indicate *your* personal opinion by circling any one number for each statement.

```
Strongly                                              Strongly
agree                                                 disagree
    1———————2———————3———————4———————5———————6———————7
```

1. It pays to shop around before buying a _____.
2. By searching for more information, I am certain of making the best buy.
3. I learned which _____ are suitable for me by shopping around.
4. Shopping around at various dealers helped me to find the lowest price when I bought my new _____.
5. I got exactly what I wanted by searching enough before I bought my new _____.
6. There is too much to lose by being ignorant about _____ when one has to buy one.
7. By rushing into a purchase of a new _____, one is bound to miss a good deal.

SCALE NAME: Search Effort

SCALE DESCRIPTION:

A six-item, seven-point, Likert-type measure of the time, energy, and effort a person reports having spent on the information search process before buying some new specified product.

SCALE ORIGIN:

Although not expressly stated in the article, the scale appears to be have been used first in published research by Srinivasan and Ratchford (1991), which was based on the dissertation of Srinivasan (1987). Some initial assessment of scale reliability and face validity was made in pretest stage of the study.

SAMPLES:

A sample of new car buyers was obtained by Srinivasan and Ratchford (1991) through a mail survey of new car registrants in the Buffalo, New York area. More than three thousand people were sent three mailings of the questionnaire, and ultimately, **1401** usable responses were received. No demographic description of the respondents is provided.

RELIABILITY:

Srinivasan and Ratchford (1991) reported an alpha of **.83** for the scale.

VALIDITY:

Srinivasan and Ratchford (1991) provided no discussion of this scale's validity.

ADMINISTRATION:

The scale was used by Srinivasan and Ratchford (1991) along with other measures in a mail survey instrument. A low score on the scale indicates that a respondent reports spending a lot of time in search-related activities before some previous specified purchase, whereas a high score suggests that a respondent did not put much effort into prepurchase information gathering.

MAJOR FINDINGS:

Srinivasan and Ratchford (1991) examined a model of the determinants of external search for new car purchases. Among the variables included in the study, evoked-set size and perceived search benefits had the largest effects on **search effort**.

COMMENTS:

The purchase decision focused on in Srinivasan and Ratchford (1991) was for new cars. As noted subsequently, the scale is easily adaptable to other purchase decisions, although its reliability and validity will need to be reexamined.

REFERENCES:

Srinivasan, Narasimhan (1987), ''A Causal Model of External Search for Information for Durables: A Particular Investigation in the Case of New Automobiles,'' doctoral dissertation, State University of New York at Buffalo.
_____ and Brian T. Ratchford (1991), ''An Empirical Test of an External Search for Automobiles,'' *JCR*, 18 (September), 233-42.

SCALE ITEMS: SEARCH EFFORT

DIRECTIONS: There are no right or wrong answers to the following statements and a large number of people agree and disagree. Kindly indicate *your* personal opinion by circling any one number for each statement.

```
Strongly                                                    Strongly
agree                                                       disagree
  1————————2————————3————————4————————5————————6————————7
```

1. I spent a lot of time talking with sales people when I was deciding on my new _____.
2. At the time I bought my new _____, I thought I had gathered sufficient information to make my best purchase.
3. Before I bought my new _____, I thought a great deal about it.
4. I referred to newspaper, magazines, and brochures a lot before I bought my new _____.
5. I visited all the conveniently located dealers before I decided which _____ to buy.
6. I spent adequate time searching for information before I bought my new _____.

SCALE NAME: Search Intention (Lower Price)

SCALE DESCRIPTION:

A three-item, summated ratings scale measuring a person's expectation of the likelihood that he/she would shop around for a lower price than that stated in an ad if he/she was in the market for a product like that mentioned in the ad.

SCALE ORIGIN:

Although it is not specifically stated, the scale was apparently developed by Biswas and Burton (1993). The one-item scale used by Lichtenstein, Burton, and Karson (1991) appears to have been used as inspiration for Biswas and Burton's (1993) multi-item version.

SAMPLES:

Biswas and Burton (1993) reported on two studies in their article. In the first, data were collected from **392** undergraduate business students. Little more is said about the sample except there was a nearly equal portion of each gender and they were assigned randomly to one of the 12 treatments. The second sample was composed of **303** nonstudents who were recruited by students in a marketing course. All those in the sample were 18 years of age and older, with a median of 40 years. A little more than half were female (56%), and the median household income was $35,000.

RELIABILITY:

Biswas and Burton (1993) reported alphas of **.91** and **.85** in their first and second studies, respectively.

VALIDITY:

Biswas and Burton (1993) reported no specific examination of the scale's validity.

ADMINISTRATION:

The scale was self-administered by subjects along with several other measures after exposure to experimental stimuli (Biswas and Burton 1993). High scores on the scale imply that respondents perceive that if they were going to buy a product like that shown in an ad, they first would engage in more external search activity to see if a lower price could be found.

MAJOR FINDINGS:

Biswas and Burton (1993) investigated the impact of three different price claims on various perceptions and intentions. Among the many findings was that **intentions to search for a lower price** at other stores were lower when claims were made in the form of maximum savings versus minimum savings or a range of possible savings. This finding was significant only for the student sample, although the means were in the right direction.

REFERENCES:

Biswas, Abhijit and Scot Burton (1993), ''Consumer Perceptions of Tensile Price Claims in Advertisements: An Assessment of Claim Types Across Different Discount Levels,'' JAMS, 21 (Summer), 217-29.

Lichtenstein, Donald R., Scot Burton, and Eric J. Karson (1991), ''The Effect of Semantic Cues on Consumer Perceptions of Reference Price Ads,'' JCR, 18 (December), 380-91.

SCALE ITEMS: SEARCH INTENTION (LOWER PRICE)*

1. If you were going to purchase a _____, how likely is it that you would search at other stores for a lower price than what you would find at the store running this ad?

Very unlikely	____ : ____ : ____ : ____ : ____ : ____ : ____	Very likely
	1 2 3 4 5 6 7	

2. How probable is it that you would shop around town looking for a lower price if you had decided to buy a _____?

Not probable at all	____ : ____ : ____ : ____ : ____ : ____ : ____	Very probable
	1 2 3 4 5 6 7	

3. If you were going to buy a _____ similar to the one advertised, would you check the prices at other stores in search of a price lower than that you would find at the store in the ad?

Definitely would not check prices at other stores	____ : ____ : ____ : ____ : ____ : ____ : ____	Definitely would check prices at other stores
	1 2 3 4 5 6 7	

* The name of the product category on sale goes in the blanks. Biswas and Burton (1993) used *35mm cameras*. Also, even though the number of response alternatives was not specified, it was likely a seven-point scale.

SCALE NAME: Self-Confidence (Generalized)

SCALE DESCRIPTION:

The scale measures the perception of oneself as a leader and having confidence. A four-item version of this scale was used by Davis and Rubin (1983) and referred to as *Self-Confidence/Leadership*. A shorter, three-item version was utilized by Lumpkin and Hunt (1989).

SCALE ORIGIN:

These items were part of an early classic study of psychographics by Wells and Tigert (1971). One thousand questionnaires were mailed to homemaker members of the Market Facts mail panel. In addition to gathering demographic, product use, and media data, the survey contained 300 statements that have served as the basis for the construction of many lifestyle-related scales ever since. Although the four items for this scale are reported in the article, they were not analyzed as a multi-item scale. The purpose of the article was to explain how psychographics could improve on mere demographic description of target audiences and product users. No psychometric information was reported.

One of the first uses of the items as a multi-item scale was in Darden and Ashton (1974-1975). Analysis was based on self-administered questionnaires completed by 116 middle-class suburban housewives selected from the directory of a medium-sized southern city. A split-half reliability of .65 was reported for the scale. Respondents were grouped on the basis of their supermarket attribute preferences. Self-confidence was significantly different between groups and was highest for the group distinguished by their desire for clean stores with a wide variety of brands.

SAMPLES:

Davis and Rubin (1983) mailed questionnaires to a sample of two groups in Florida: known adopters of solar energy devices and the general population 18 years of age and older. Analysis was based on 817 usable questionnaires, of which **488** were solar energy adopters.

Two mailing lists were used to collect data in the Dickerson and Gentry study (1983): a list of *Psychology Today* subscribers and a list of members in computer clubs. The former was used to reach non-adopters of computers and the latter was used to reach PC adopters. Analysis was based on a total of **639** questionnaires. Results from a second mailing to nonrespondents indicated that their demographic makeup was not significantly different from respondents. Compared with 1980 Census data, the sample was younger and more upscale than the general population.

A large sample from the Market Facts Consumer Mail Panel was utilized in Lumpkin and Hunt (1989). The article focused on a subset of all respondents who indicated they were 65 years of age or older, (n = **789**).

RELIABILITY:

Davis and Rubin (1983), Dickerson and Gentry (1983), and Lumpkin and Hunt (1989), reported alphas of **.69**, **.61**, and **.728**, respectively.

VALIDITY:

Assessment generally was made through factor analysis. More effort was used by Davis and Rubin (1983), who randomly split their data in half and factor analyzed the two. Identical factor solutions were found in the two subsamples. The factors found within the full data set were consistent with the subsample solutions.

ADMINISTRATION:

Data were gathered in all the studies through self-administered mail questionnaires. Scale scores are calculated by averaging numerical responses to individual items. A score of 6 indicates that a respondent strongly expresses confidence in his/her abilities, whereas a score of 1 means the respondent does not see him/herself as the confident/leader type.

MAJOR FINDINGS:

Davis and Rubin (1983) determined that persons who expressed a high degree of energy conservation opinion leadership were significantly more confident in their abilities and were more financially optimistic than those with less leadership.

Dickerson and Gentry (1983) expected to find a positive relationship between adoption of home computers and self-confidence but it was *not* among the lifestyle variables that significantly discriminated between adopters and non-adopters.

Lumpkin and Hunt (1989) broke the elderly down into two groups: those who were self-reliant in terms of transportation and those who were dependent on others. The self-reliant were significantly more self-confident than those who were dependent.

COMMENTS:

The reliability and validity of this measure might be improved by using items that tapped into either the confidence trait or the leadership issue but not both.

See also a variation on the scale by Hawes and Lumpkin (1984) as well as a two-item version of the scale by Wilkes (1992). This could be the scale used by Burnett and Bush (1986).

REFERENCES:

Burnett, John J. and Alan J. Bush (1986), "Profiling the Yuppies," *JAR*, 26 (April/May), 27-35.

Darden, William R. and Dub Ashton (1974-1975), ''Psychographic Profiles of Patronage Preference Groups,'' *JR*, 50 (Winter), 99-112.

Davis, Duane L. and Ronald S. Rubin (1983), ''Identifying the Energy Conscious Consumer: The Case of the Opinion Leader,'' *JAMS*, 11 (Spring), 169-90.

Dickerson, Mary D. and James W. Gentry (1983), ''Characteristics of Adopters and Non-Adopters of Home Computers,'' *JCR*, 10 (Sept.), 225-35.

Hawes, Jon M. and James R. Lumpkin (1984), ''Understanding the Outshopper,'' *JAMS*, 12 (Fall), 200-218.

Lumpkin, James R. and James B. Hunt (1989), ''Mobility as an Influence on Retail Patronage Behavior of the Elderly: Testing Conventional Wisdom,'' *JAMS*, 17 (Winter), 1-12.

Tigert, Douglas J. (1974), ''Life Style Analysis as a Basis for Media Selection,'' in *Life Style and Psychographics*, William D. Wells, ed. Chicago: American Marketing Association.

Wells, William D. and Douglas Tigert (1971), ''Activities, Interests, and Opinions,'' *JAR*, 11 (August), 27-35.

Wilkes, Robert E. (1992), ''A Structural Modeling Approach to the Measurement and Meaning of Cognitive Age,'' *JCR*, 19 (September), 292-301.

SCALE ITEMS: SELF-CONFIDENCE (GENERALIZED)

Strongly disagree	Disagree	Slightly disagree	Slightly agree	Agree	Strongly agree
1	2	3	4	5	6

1. I think I have more self-confidence than most people.
2. I am more independent than most people.
3. I think I have a lot of personal ability.
4. I like to be considered a leader.
5. I have never been really outstanding at anything. **(r)**
6. I often can talk others into doing something.

* The first four items are those offered by Wells and Tigert (1971) and were probably the set used by Dickerson and Gentry (1983). Items 3-6 are given by Tigert (1974, p. 181) and were apparently the ones used by Davis and Rubin (1983). Lumpkin and Hunt (1989) used items 1-3.

SCALE NAME: Self-Consciousness (Public)

SCALE DESCRIPTION:

A seven-item, seven-point, Likert-type scale measuring the degree to which a person expresses an awareness of self as a social object with an effect on others. Feningstein, Scheier, and Buss (1975) used a five-point response scale ranging from 0 (extremely uncharacteristic) to 4 (extremely characteristic). Bearden and Rose (1990) used a seven-point disagree-agree response format.

SCALE ORIGIN:

The scale was constructed by Feningstein, Scheier, and Buss (1975). Preliminary work involved identifying behaviors contained in the domain of the construct. Then 38 items were created and tested. Factor analysis indicated that there were three main factors: private self-consciousness, public self-consciousness, and social anxiety. The items were modified and retested several times, and the same three factors consistently were found. The final versions of the scales were tested using 432 college students. The 23 items retained from the pilot studies had loadings higher than .40 on their three appropriate factors as expected. The items then were administered to a new sample of 84 subjects at two-week intervals as a measure of stability. The seven items composing the public self-consciousness scale had a test-retest correlation of .84.

SAMPLES:

Bearden and Rose (1990) reported using the scale in three of four different studies/samples. Each sample apparently was composed of undergraduate business students with the following sizes for studies 1, 2, and 4, respectively: **62**, **99**, and **85**.

RELIABILITY:

Bearden and Rose (1990) reported alphas of **.83**, **.74**, and **.79** for the scale in studies 1, 2, and 4, respectively.

VALIDITY:

Bearden and Rose (1990) did not directly examine the validity of the scale. However, some idea of its nomological validity can be found in the findings discussed here.

ADMINISTRATION:

The scale was administered to students in the three studies by Bearden and Rose (1990) in larger survey instruments. High scores on the scale indicate that respondents are quite concerned about making a good impression with others, whereas low scores suggest that respondents are not socially self-conscious.

MAJOR FINDINGS:

Bearden and Rose (1990) conducted a series of studies to investigate the reliability and validity of a measure of attention to social comparison information (ATSCI) and the extent to which this construct is a moderator of interpersonal influence. As noted previously, **public self-consciousness** was included in three of the studies. In each case, the scale was found to have a significant positive relationship with ATSCI. In one study, it was also found to be positively correlated with a measure of social anxiety.

REFERENCE:

Bearden, William O. and Randall L. Rose (1990), ''Attention to Social Comparison Information: An Individual Difference Factor Affecting Consumer Conformity,'' *JCR*, 16 (March), 461-71.

SCALE ITEMS: SELF-CONSCIOUSNESS (PUBLIC)*

Strongly disagree ____ : ____ : ____ : ____ : ____ : ____ : ____ Strongly agree
1 2 3 4 5 6 7

1. I'm concerned about my style of doing things.
2. I'm concerned about the way I present myself.
3. I'm self-conscious about the way I look.
4. I usually worry about making a good impression.
5. One of the last things I do before leaving my house is look in the mirror.
6. I'm concerned about what other people think of me.
7. I'm usually aware of my appearance.

SCALE NAME: Self-Esteem

SCALE DESCRIPTION:

A five-item, five-point, Likert-type summated ratings scale measuring the degree of confidence a person has in his/her own abilities.

SCALE ORIGIN:

The scale was apparently original to O'Guinn and Faber (1989).

SAMPLES:

Two samples were employed by O'Guinn and Faber (1989). One was of **386** completed responses (out of 808 questionnaires sent) from people who previously had written an organization that aided compulsive buyers. A second group was used for comparison purposes and was intended to represent the general population. Eight hundred questionnaires were mailed to people in three Illinois areas: Chicago, Springfield, and Bloomington-Normal. Two mailings produced a total of **250** completed survey forms. The database used in Faber and O'Guinn (1992) is basically the same except that sample 1 had a few more responses (n = 388) and the second survey benefited from a third mailing (n = 292).

RELIABILITY:

O'Guinn and Faber (1989; Faber and O'Guinn 1992) reported an alpha of .**84** for the scale.

VALIDITY:

No examination of scale validity was reported (O'Guinn and Faber 1989; Faber and O'Guinn 1992).

ADMINISTRATION:

The scale was one of several self-administered measures used in mail survey instruments (O'Guinn and Faber 1989; Faber and O'Guinn 1992). High scores on the scale indicate that respondents have low self-esteem, whereas low scores indicates that respondents are likely to have greater confidence in their abilities.

MAJOR FINDINGS:

O'Guinn and Faber (1989) studied compulsive shopping. Their results showed that a sample of compulsive shoppers had significantly lower **self-esteem** than a general sample of consumers. Although using the same general database, Faber and O'Guinn (1992) reported on the development and testing of a scale to identify compulsive buyers.

REFERENCES:

Faber, Ronald J. and Thomas C. O'Guinn (1992), ''A Clinical Screener for Compulsive Buying,'' *JCR*, 19 (December), 459-69.

O'Guinn, Thomas C. and Ronald J. Faber (1989), ''Compulsive Buying: A Phenomenological Exploration,'' *JCR*, 16 (September), 147-57.

SCALE ITEMS: SELF-ESTEEM

Strongly disagree	Disagree	Neutral	Agree	Strongly agree
1————	——2————	——3————	——4————	——5

1. I certainly feel useless at times.
2. Life is a strain for me much of the time.
3. I have several times given up doing a thing because I thought too little of my ability.
4. Much of the time I feel as if I have done something wrong or evil.
5. I am certainly lacking in self confidence.

SCALE NAME: Self-Esteem

SCALE DESCRIPTION:

A ten-item, Likert-type scale measuring the degree to which one approves of oneself. It does not necessarily imply that a person scoring high on the scale considers him/herself to be perfect or superior to others. A four-point agree-disagree response scale was used by the originator (Rosenberg 1965), and a five-point scale was used by Richins (1991). A four-point scale with various "like me" anchors was used by Richins and Dawson (1992; Richins 1994). The nature of the response scale used by Bearden and Rose (1990) was not reported.

SCALE ORIGIN:

The scale was constructed by Rosenberg (1965) for use in a study of high school students. It was developed with at least four practical and theoretical considerations strongly in mind: that it be easy to administer, that respondents could complete it quickly, that it be unidimensional, and that it have face validity. The Guttman scale reproducibility was reported as .92 and its scalability was .72. The book provides considerable data that bear on the validity of the scale.

SAMPLES:

Bearden and Rose (1990) reported the use of several studies and samples. The only study in which the self-esteem scale was used involved data collected from **85** undergraduate business students. They were urged to volunteer for the study with the chance of winning a random drawing as an incentive.

The scale was used in all but the first of four studies reported by Richins (1991). Study 2 was composed of **80** female college students; study 3 had **73** female students enrolled in a beginning marketing course; and study 4 was composed of **125** female undergraduate students apparently recruited from a principles of marketing class.

Studies with four samples were described in the article by Richins and Dawson (1992), but the self-esteem scale was used only in survey 3. Little is said about the sample except that the data came from a mail survey of people in a large western U.S. city. The households were randomly chosen and sent a survey form, followed by a reminder letter and a second copy of the questionnaire two weeks later. The response rate was 31.3%, resulting in **235** usable questionnaires.

RELIABILITY:

Bearden and Rose (1990) and Richins and Dawson (1992) reported alphas of **.80** and **.81,** respectively, for the scale. Richins (1991) reported alphas of **.86** and **.87** for the scale as used in studies 2 and 3, respectively, and the alpha for the scale's use in study 4 was not reported.

VALIDITY:

The validity of the scale was not directly examined by Bearden and Rose (1990) or Richins (1991; Richins and Dawson 1992). However, some idea of its nomological validity can be found in the findings discussed subsequently.

ADMINISTRATION:

The scale was administered by Bearden and Rose (1990) as well as Richins and Dawson (1992) in a larger survey instrument. Richins (1991) used the scale in her study 2 as part of a survey; in studies 3 and 4 it was used as part of an experiment. High scores on the scale indicate that respondents are quite content with themselves, whereas low scores suggest that respondents lack respect for themselves.

MAJOR FINDINGS:

Bearden and Rose (1990) conducted a series of studies to investigate the reliability and validity of a measure of attention to social comparison information (ATSCI) and the extent to which this construct is a moderator of interpersonal influence. **Self-esteem** was only measured in one study and was little discussed. However, it was reported that **self-esteem** was found, as expected, to have a significant inverse relationship with ATSCI.

Richins (1991) conducted four studies in an effort to better understand how advertising can lead to dissatisfaction with the self. **Self-esteem** was used in the analyses mainly as a covariate related to self-ratings of attractiveness. Because of this there were no separate results from the studies involving **self-esteem**.

The purpose of the multiple surveys conducted by Richins and Dawson (1992) was to construct a new measure of materialism. To examine the scale's nomological validity, it was proposed that materialists would be less satisfied with their lives than others. Part of testing that hypothesis came from the association between materialism and **self-esteem**. A significant though very low negative correlation between the two constructs was found ($r = -0.12$) suggesting that more materialistic people are somewhat more likely to have less **self-esteem** than others have.

REFERENCES

Bearden, William O. and Randall L. Rose (1990), ''Attention to Social Comparison Information: An Individual Difference Factor Affecting Consumer Conformity,'' *JCR*, 16 (March), 461-71.

Richins, Marsha L. (1991), ''Social Comparison and the Idealized Images of Advertising,'' *JCR*, 18 (June), 71-83.

_____ and Scott Dawson (1992), ''A Consumer Values Orientation for Materialism and Its Measurement: Scale Development and Validation,'' *JCR*, 19 (December), 303-16.

_____ (1994), personal correspondence.

Rosenberg, Morris (1965), **Society** *and the Adolescent Self-Image*. Princeton, NJ: Princeton University Press.

SCALE ITEMS: SELF-ESTEEM*

Strongly agree	Agree	Disagree	Strongly disagree
1	2	3	4

1. On the whole, I am satisfied with myself. **(r)**
2. At times I think I am no good at all.
3. I feel that I have a number of good qualities. **(r)**
4. I am able to do things as well as most other people. **(r)**
5. I feel I do not have much to be proud of.
6. I certainly feel useless at times.
7. I feel that I am a person of worth, at least on a equal plane with others. **(r)**
8. I wish I could have more respect for myself.
9. All in all, I am inclined to feel that I am a failure.
10. I take a positive attitude toward myself. **(r)**

* The four-point response scale was used by Rosenberg (1965) and a five-point scale was used by Richins (1991) but it is not known how many points were on the scales as used by Bearden and Rose (1990). The anchors used by Richins and Dawson (1992) were as follows: 0 = *not at all like me*, 1 = *a little like me*, 2 = *somewhat like me*, and 3 = *a lot like me* (Richins 1994).

SCALE NAME: Self-Oriented Values

SCALE DESCRIPTION:

A three-item, six-point summated ratings scale measuring the degree to which a person places importance on values related directly to self such as self-respect, self-fulfillment, and a sense of accomplishment.

SCALE ORIGIN:

The summated scale is apparently original to Corfman, Lehmann, and Narayanan (1991), but the items themselves come from the List of Values (LOV) developed by Kahle (1983). Nine values composed LOV, but the analysis conducted by Corfman, Lehmann, and Narayanan (1991) indicated that the three values specified here were tapping into the same factor.

SAMPLES:

Corfman, Lehmann, and Narayanan (1991) collected data using a self-administered questionnaire. Subjects were described as being initially contacted in person or by mail on an ''intercept basis.'' Completed surveys were received from **735** respondents, mostly from the northeastern part of the United States. A range of values for several demographic characteristics were represented in the sample such that the authors said ''. . . the aggregate distribution closely matched that of the U.S. population . . . .'' (p. 191).

RELIABILITY:

Corfman, Lehmann, and Narayanan (1991) reported an alpha of **.74** for the scale.

VALIDITY:

Corfman, Lehmann, and Narayanan (1991) factor analyzed the items composing LOV and settled on a three-factor solution that accounted for 64% of the variance. The items composing this scale all had high loadings on the second factor, providing some evidence of the scale's unidimensionality.

ADMINISTRATION:

The scale was part of a larger self-administered survey instrument used by Corfman, Lehmann, and Narayanan (1991). High scores on the scale indicate that self-oriented values are very important to a respondent, whereas low scores suggest that such values are not very important, at least not as important as other values, to the respondent.

MAJOR FINDINGS:

Corfman, Lehmann, and Narayanan (1991) examined the relationships among consumer utility, values, and ownership of durable products. Ownership was viewed as a function of a product's utility as well as a consumer's income and age. Utility was viewed as a function of a consumer's values and ownership of a product. The findings showed that **self-oriented values** had a significant effect only on the utility of convenience products.

COMMENTS:

A more rigorous analysis of this scale's psychometric quality is presented by Homer and Kahle (1988).

REFERENCES

Corfman, Kim P., Donald R. Lehmann, and Sunder Narayanan (1991), ''Values, Utility, and Ownership: Modeling the Relationships for Consumer Durables,'' *JR*, 67 (Summer), 184-204.

Homer, Pamela M. and Lynn R. Kahle (1988), ''A Structural Equation Test of the Value-Attitude-Behavior Hierarchy,'' *Journal of Personality and Social Psychology*, 54 (4), 638-46.

Kahle, Lynn R.,ed. (1983), *Social Values and Social Change*. New York: Praeger Publishers.

SCALE ITEMS: SELF-ORIENTED VALUES*

Not very   Very
important ____ : ____ : ____ : ____ : ____ : ____ important
        1   2   3   4   5   6

1. self-respect
2. sense of accomplishment
3. self-fulfillment

* The anchors used for the scale were not specified in the article but would appear to have been something like those used here.

SCALE NAME: Sensation Seeking

SCALE DESCRIPTION:

A 40-item, five-point, Likert-type response scale, as used by Steenkamp and Baumgartner (1992). The scale is intended to capture a person's need for varied and novel sensations as well as one's willingness to take the risks necessary to achieve those sensations. This is a measure of a personality *trait* rather than a situation-specific *state*.

SCALE ORIGIN:

The scale used by Steenkamp and Baumgartner (1992) was adapted from a scale constructed by Zuckerman (1979). The latter has been working on sensation seeking measures since the early 1960s, and Form V is the version adapted by Steenkamp and Baumgartner (1992). That version was composed of 40 forced-choice pairs of items. Steenkamp and Baumgartner (1992) used 19 of the negative statements and 21 of the positive statements in a Likert-type format. Form V has four subscales: thrill and adventure seeking, experience seeking, disinhibition, and boredom susceptibility.

Much information about the psychometric qualities of Form V can be found in Zuckerman (1979, Ch. 4). Briefly, the scale was found to be quite stable, with test-retest of .94. Analyzed separately for both sexes and for two cultures (English and Americans), internal consistency was more than .80 for each of the four samples. Factor loadings and internal consistencies of the subscales were generally best for thrill and adventure seeking and worst for boredom susceptibility.

SAMPLES:

The sample used by Steenkamp and Baumgartner (1992) was composed of 223 volunteers from undergraduate marketing courses at a university. A lottery with cash prizes was used to help motivate students to participate.

RELIABILITY:

Steenkamp and Baumgartner (1992) reported a reliability (LISREL) of **.806** for the total scale. Reliabilities of .79, .50, .72, and .50 were found for the thrill seeking, experience seeking, disinhibition, and boredom susceptibility subscales, respectively.

VALIDITY:

Steenkamp and Baumgartner (1992) concluded that principal components factor analysis did not provide strong evidence of a unidimensional or four-dimensional structure. Scores on the scale had correlations of between .43 and .60 with three other measures of optimum stimulation level, which provides some evidence of convergent validity. A confirmatory factor analysis of all four scales also provided some evidence of convergent validity because the sensation seeking scale loaded significantly on the underlying construct, though not nearly as well as some of the other scales.

ADMINISTRATION:

The scale was administered by Steenkamp and Baumgartner (1992) as part of a larger questionnaire composed primarily of four scales measuring optimum stimulation level in various ways. The questionnaire was handed out to students in class, and they were asked to bring the completed form back at the next class period. High scores on the scale indicate that respondents desire thrills and adventures, whereas low scores indicate that respondents have a tendency to seek safe and familiar sensations.

MAJOR FINDINGS:

Steenkamp and Baumgartner (1992) studied the role of optimum stimulation level in exploratory consumer behavior. A weighted composite of the **Sensation Seeking** scale and three other well-known measures were used to examine people's desire for stimulation. Beyond the information provided here regarding reliability and validity, the article did not discuss the findings of any one scale (however, they can be obtained from the authors).

COMMENTS:

As noted previously, Steenkamp and Baumgartner (1992) modified Zuckerman's (1979) SSS-V by not using all of the available items. A total of 40 more items were part of the scale. (Zuckerman must be contacted if those items are desired.)

REFERENCES;

Steenkamp, Jan-Benedict E.M. and Hans Baumgartner (1992), ''The Role of Optimum Stimulation Level in Exploratory Consumer Behavior,'' *JCR*, 19 (December), 434-48.

Zuckerman, Marvin (1979), *Sensation Seeking: Beyond the Optimum Level of Arousal*. Hillsdale, NJ: Lawrence Erlbaum Associates.

SCALE ITEMS: SENSATION SEEKING

Directions: Please use the following scale to indicate your degree of agreement or disagreement with each of the statements below. Circle the number that best represents your opinion.

Strongly disagree	Disagree	Neither agree nor disagree	Agree	Strongly agree
−2	−1	0	1	2

1. I prefer quiet parties with good conversation. **(r)**
2. I can't stand watching a movie that I've seen before.

3. I can't understand people who risk their necks climbing mountains. (r)
4. I dislike all body odors. (r)
5. I like the comfortable familiarity of everyday friends. (r)
6. I like to explore a strange city or section of town by myself, even if it means getting lost.
7. I dislike people who do or say things just to shock or upset others. (r)
8. I usually don't enjoy a movie or play where I can predict what will happen in advance.
9. I have tried marijuana or would like to.
10. I would not like to try any drug which might product strange and dangerous effects on me. (r)
11. A sensible person avoids activities that are dangerous. (r)
12. I dislike "swingers." (r)
13. I often like to get high (drinking liquor or smoking marijuana).
14. I like to try new foods that I have never tasted before.
15. Looking at someone's home movies or travel slides bores me tremendously.
16. I would like to take up the sport of water-skiing.
17. I would like to try surf-board riding.
18. When I go on a trip, I like to plan my route and timetable fairly carefully. (r)
19. I prefer the "down-to-earth" kinds of people as friends. (r)
20. I would like to learn to fly an airplane.
21. I prefer the surface of the water to the depths.
22. I would like to meet some persons who are homosexuals (men or women).
23. I would like to try parachute jumping.
24. I prefer friends who are excitingly unpredictable.
25. I like to have new and exciting experiences and sensations even if they are a little frightening, unconventional or illegal.
26. The essence of good art is in its clarity, symmetry of form and harmony of colors. (r)
27. I enjoy spending time in the familiar surroundings of home. (r)
28. I like to dive off the high board.
29. I like to date members of the opposite sex who share my values. (r)
30. Keeping the drinks full is the key to a good party.
31. The worst social sin is to be a bore.
32. A person should have considerable sexual experience before marriage.
33. Even if I had the money, I would not care to associate with flighty persons like those in the "jet set." (r)
34. I dislike people who have their fun at the expense of hurting the feelings of others. (r)
35. I enjoy watching many of the "sexy" scenes in movies.
36. I feel best after taking a couple of drinks.
37. People should dress in individual ways even if the effects are sometimes strange.
38. Sailing long distances in small sailing crafts is foolhardy. (r)
39. I have no patience with dull or boring persons.
40. I think I would enjoy the sensations of skiing very fast down a high mountain slope.

SCALE NAME: Service Quality (Access)

SCALE DESCRIPTION:

A seven-point, Likert-type scale with a variable number of items measuring the degree to which a person thinks access to the employees, facilities, and services of an organization is convenient.

SCALE ORIGIN:

Although inspiration for the scale definitely came from the SERVQUAL instrument developed by Parasuraman, Zeithaml, and Berry (1988), all the items except for the first one were developed by Carman (1990).

SAMPLES:

Carman (1990) adjusted and tested the SERVQUAL instrument in four different service settings. The two samples relevant to this scale were a tire store (n = **74**) and a business school placement center (n = **82**).

RELIABILITY:

Carman (1990) reported alphas of **.66** and **.85** for use of the scale in the tire store and placement center settings, respectively.

VALIDITY:

Carman (1990) factor analyzed the SERVQUAL data from each setting. In the placement center study, the items loaded on two different factors. Similarly, all the items except one used in the tire store study had split loadings among two or more factors. Given this, it is clear that the scale has not shown evidence of unidimensionality.

ADMINISTRATION:

The SERVQUAL instrument was self-administered by respondents after they received service (Carman 1990). High scores on the perception version of the scale show that respondents think that employees of a service firm are very attentive and understanding of customer needs.

MAJOR FINDINGS:

The purpose of Carman's (1990) studies was to test the SERVQUAL instrument in a variety of service settings. Some modifications in wording were always found to be necessary. An **access**-related dimension was found in both the placement center and tire store settings.

REFERENCES

Carman, James M. (1990), "Consumer Perceptions of Service Quality: An Assessment of the SERVQUAL Dimensions," *JR*, 66 (Spring), 33-55.

———— (1994), personal correspondence.

Parasuraman, A., Valerie A. Zeithaml, and Leonard L. Berry (1988), "SERV-QUAL: A Multiple-Item Scale for Measuring Customer Perceptions of Service Quality," *JR*, 64 (Spring), 12-40.

SCALE ITEMS: SERVICE QUALITY (ACCESS)*

Strongly disagree						Strongly agree
1———	—2———	—3———	—4———	—5———	—6———	—7

1. _____ does not have operating hours convenient to all their customers. **(r)**
2. You never have trouble getting through to the person or information you need on the telephone.
3. If you need to talk to the manager, you can do so without difficulty.
4. Service is available daily at the placement center.
5. You have to wait as long as five days for an appointment at the placement center. **(r)**
6. The service there is prompt.
7. It often takes longer than ten minutes to receive service at the front desk of the center. **(r)**

* The name of the specific service company being studied should be placed in the blanks. Statements similar to items 1-3 and 6 were used in the tire store study conducted by Carman (1990, 1994). In the placement center study he used all of the items except 2.

SCALE NAME: Service Quality (Assurance)

SCALE DESCRIPTION:

A four-item, seven-point, Likert-type scale measuring the degree to which a person thinks the knowledge and courtesy of a service company's employees instill trust and confidence in customers. As described here, the scale relates to the Assurance dimension of the SERVQUAL instrument (Parasuraman, Zeithaml, and Berry 1988, 1991) but is not equivalent to it. Each dimension of the SERVQUAL measure is composed of the summated differences between expectation items and perceptual items, not just the latter as the scale described here is.

SCALE ORIGIN:

The scale is a part of the larger SERVQUAL instrument described by Parasuraman, Berry, and Zeithaml (1991), which measures five separate dimensions of service quality. That version of the instrument is a revision of a previous version described in detail by Parasuraman, Zeithaml, and Berry (1988), and considerable information is provided in that article about the scale's conceptualization, development, and validation. As far as the assurance dimension is concerned, the authors kept only one item intact in the revised version and changed the other three.

SAMPLES:

A questionnaire was sent by Parasuraman, Berry, and Zeithaml (1991) to randomly chosen customers of five nationally known companies: one telephone company, two banks, and two insurance companies. A reminder postcard was sent two weeks after the initial mailing. The number of usable questionnaires ranged from 290 to 487 for the five companies. The total number of completed returns was **1936,** a 21% overall response rate. Managers in the companies reviewed the demographic profiles of the respondents and considered them to be representative of their customer populations.

RELIABILITY:

The alphas reported by Parasuraman, Berry, and Zeithaml (1991) for the five companies ranged from .87 to .91. These alphas relate to the summated differences between expectation items and perceptual items. The alpha for only the perceptions items was **.92** using the combined sample (Parasuraman 1993).

VALIDITY:

Parasuraman, Berry, and Zeithaml (1991) reported the results of several factor analyses using oblique rotations. With regard to the perception version of the scale using the combined samples, all the items had their highest loadings on the same factor. However, items from another dimension (responsiveness) also loaded highest on this factor. Therefore, the two scales do not have discriminate validity relative to each other.

ADMINISTRATION:

The scale was administered to customers in a mail-survey format by Parasuraman, Berry, and Zeithaml (1991). High scores on the perception version of the scale to show that respondents think that employees of a specific service firm are very knowledgeable and courteous, which helps customers to feel more confident about their transactions.

MAJOR FINDINGS:

Parasuraman, Berry, and Zeithaml (1991) conducted a study to refine their SERVQUAL scales and to examine the revised scales in five different customer samples. They also compared their results with those of others who had used the scales. When respondents were asked to divide 100 points among the five service quality dimensions on the basis of importance, for each of the five samples the result was the same: the **assurance** dimension was always was the third most important dimension.

COMMENTS:

Although this scale can be used by itself, it was designed to be used along with its companion perceptions version. For example, the expectations version of item 1 would be something like ''The behavior of employees of excellent _____ companies will instill confidence in customers.'' The authors also encourage researchers to measure all the dimensions to capture the domain of service quality fully.

For further discussion of theoretical and psychometric properties of the SERVQUAL instrument, see Parasuraman, Zeithaml, and Berry (1994), Cronin and Taylor (1994), and Teas (1994).

See also Teas (1993) for use of a two-item version of the scale.

REFERENCES:

Cronin, J. Joseph, Jr. and Steven A. Taylor (1994), ''SERVPERF Versus SERVQUAL: Reconciling Performance-Based and Perceptions-Minus-Expectations Measurement of Service Quality,'' *JM*, 58 (January), 124-31.

Parasuraman, A. (1993), personal correspondence.

_____, Leonard L. Berry, and Valarie A. Zeithaml (1991), ''Refinement and Reassessment of the SERVQUAL Scale,'' *JR*, 67 (Winter), 420-50.

_____, Valerie A. Zeithaml, and Leonard L. Berry (1988), ''SERVQUAL: A Multiple-Item Scale for Measuring Customer Perceptions of Service Quality,'' *JR*, 64 (Spring), 12-40.

_____, _____, and _____ (1994), ''Reassessment of Expectations as a Comparison Standard in Measuring Service Quality: Implications for Further Research,'' *JM*, 58 (January), 111-24.

Teas, R. Kenneth (1993), "Expectations, Performance Evaluation, and Consumers' Perceptions of Quality," *JM*, 57 (October), 18-34.

———— (1994), "Expectations as a Comparison Standard in Measuring Service Quality: An Assessment of a Reassessment," *JM*, 58 (January), 132-39.

SCALE ITEMS: SERVICE QUALITY (ASSURANCE)*

Directions: The following set of statements relate to your feelings about _____'s service. For each statement, please show the extent to which you believe _____ has the feature described by the statement. Circling a "1" means that you strongly disagree that _____ has that feature, and circling a "7" means that you strongly agree. You may circle any of the numbers in the middle that show how strong your feelings are. There are no right or wrong answers—all we are interested in is a number that best shows your perceptions about _____'s service.

Strongly   Strongly
disagree   agree
   1————2————3————4————5————6————7

1. The behavior of employees of _____ instills confidence in customers.
2. You feel safe in your transactions with _____.
3. Employees of _____ are consistently courteous with you.
4. Employees of _____ have the knowledge to answer your questions.

* The name of the specific service firm studied should be placed in the blanks.

SCALE NAME: Service Quality (Assurance)

SCALE DESCRIPTION:

A five-item, seven-point, Likert-type scale that is purported to measure the degree to which a person thinks a service company's employees are courteous and give customers a sense of security about doing business with them.

SCALE ORIGIN:

The version of the scale described here is original to Carman (1990), although three of the items come from the SERVQUAL instrument constructed by Parasuraman, Zeithaml, and Berry (1988) to measure service quality. Items 3 and 4 are original to Carman (1990).

SAMPLES:

Carman (1990) adjusted and tested the SERVQUAL instrument in four different service settings. This version of the scale was used only in the tire store setting, in which there were **74** respondents.

RELIABILITY:

Carman (1990) reported an alpha of **.74** for the scale.

VALIDITY:

Carman factor analyzed the SERVQUAL data from each setting. Only items with loadings greater than .30 on the same factor in at least one setting were used to compose scales (Carman 1994). However, the sets of items used to compose the summated scales for each of the settings were ultimately different on the basis of several factors. These variable results led him to conclude that it had problems with construct validity. For the tire store data, all the items except item 2 had loadings of .58 or greater on the same factor.

ADMINISTRATION:

The SERVQUAL instrument was self-administered by respondents after they received service in the study by Carman (1990). High scores on the perception version of the scale show that respondents think that employees of a service firm are very attentive and understanding of customer needs.

MAJOR FINDINGS:

The purpose of Carman's (1990) studies was to test the SERVQUAL instrument in a variety of service settings. Some modifications in wording were always found to be necessary. An **assurance**-related dimension was found in at least three of the settings, including the tire store. However, the items composing the scales in the various settings were very different.

REFERENCES:

Carman, James M. (1990), "Consumer Perceptions of Service Quality: An Assessment of the SERVQUAL Dimensions," *JR*, 66 (Spring), 33-55.
———— (1994), personal correspondence.
Parasuraman, A., Valerie A. Zeithaml, and Leonard L. Berry (1988), "SERV-QUAL: A Multiple-Item Scale for Measuring Customer Perceptions of Service Quality," *JR*, 64 (Spring), 12-40.

SCALE ITEMS: SERVICE QUALITY (ASSURANCE)*

Strongly   Strongly
disagree   agree
1————2————3————4————5————6————7

1. You feel safe in your transactions with _____.
2. Employees get adequate support from _____ to do their jobs well.
3. It is easy to make an appointment there.
4. The telephone manners of the staff are not very good. **(r)**
5. _____ has up-to-date equipment.

* The name of the specific service company being studied should be placed in the blanks.

SCALE NAME: Service Quality (Assurance of Professors)

SCALE DESCRIPTION:

An 11-item, seven-point, Likert-type scale measuring the degree to which a person thinks the professors working for an educational institution engage in various specified activities that help ensure a high-quality education to students.

SCALE ORIGIN:

The scale is original to Boulding and colleagues (1993) and is more fully described in Boulding and colleagues (1992). However, it is modeled on the SERVQUAL instrument (Parasuraman, Zeithaml, and Berry 1988), which measures five separate dimensions of service quality. The scale described here relates to the Assurance dimension of the SERVQUAL instrument but is not equivalent to it. Each dimension of the SERVQUAL measure is composed of the summated differences between expectation items and perceptual items, not just the latter as the scale described here is.

SAMPLES:

Boulding and colleagues (1993) collected data from **177** students of a business education institution. Participation was voluntary but was apparently stimulated to some extent by a lottery and cash prizes.

RELIABILITY:

An alpha of **.63** was reported for the scale (Boulding et al. 1992).

VALIDITY:

Boulding and colleagues (1993) performed no examination of scale validity. A factor analysis of all 36 items in this version of the SERVQUAL instrument was performed, but managerial judgment was used to form the individual subscales and no quantitative data were provided.

ADMINISTRATION:

The scale was apparently self-administered by students but the details were not provided by Boulding and colleagues (1993). A high score on the scale suggests a respondent believes that professors and the institution are doing things involved in the delivery of a high-quality education.

MAJOR FINDINGS:

Boulding and colleagues (1993) describe two studies bearing on a behavioral process model. The second study involved the service quality scales. Among the many findings was that the **assurance** of the professors and institution providing the education was *not* a primary influence on overall quality perceptions.

COMMENTS:

It is difficult to find commonality among the scale items. The low alpha as well as this lack of strong face validity suggest that the scale may not be unidimensional. Further testing and development is required.

REFERENCES:

Boulding, William, Ajay Kalra, Richard Staelin, and Valerie A. Zeithaml (1993), "A Dynamic Process Model of Service Quality: From Expectations to Behavioral Intentions," JMR, 30 (February), 7-27.

———, Richard Staelin, Ajay Kalra, and Valerie A. Zeithaml (1992), "Conceptualizing and Testing a Dynamic Process Model of Service Quality," Working paper No. 92-121. Cambridge, MA: Marketing Science Institute.

Parasuraman, A., Valerie A. Zeithaml, and Leonard L. Berry (1988), "SERVQUAL: A Multiple-Item Scale for Measuring Customer Perceptions of Service Quality," JR, 64 (Spring), 12-40.

SCALE ITEMS: SERVICE QUALITY (ASSURANCE OF PROFESSORS)*

Directions: The following set of statements relate to your feelings about _____'s service. For each statement, please show the extent to which you believe _____ has the feature described by the statement. Circling a "1" means that you strongly disagree that _____ has that feature, and circling a "7" means that you strongly agree. You may circle any of the numbers in the middle that show how strong your feelings are. There are no right or wrong answers—all we are interested in is a number that best shows your perceptions about _____'s service.

Strongly   Strongly
disagree   agree
1———2———3———4———5———6———7

1. Professors structure their classes to encourage interaction among students.
2. Professors deliver lectures aimed at the upper third of the class.
3. Professors communicate ideas clearly and effectively.
4. Professors do not tolerate dishonesty.
5. The organization provides students exposure to business executives.
6. Professors have at least one guest lecturer.
7. Professors set high expectations for students.
8. Professors show respect for students.
9. Full professors teach core courses.
10. Professors balance theory and real world application in class.
11. Students are admitted to elective courses for which they register.

* These directions were not provided in the article but are assumed to be similar to what was actually used.

SCALE NAME: Service Quality (Education Tangibles)

SCALE DESCRIPTION:

A seven-item, seven-point, Likert-type scale measuring the degree to which a person thinks an educational institution has grounds, buildings, equipment, and professors that are neat and clean.

SCALE ORIGIN:

The scale is original to Boulding and colleagues (1993) and is more fully described in Boulding and colleagues (1992). However, it is modeled on the SERVQUAL instrument (Parasuraman, Zeithaml, and Berry 1988), which measures five separate dimensions of service quality. The scale described here relates to the Tangibles dimension of the SERVQUAL instrument but is not equivalent to it. Each dimension of the SERVQUAL measure is composed of the summated differences between expectation items and perceptual items, not just the latter as the scale described here is.

SAMPLES:

Boulding and colleagues (1993) collected data from 177 students of a business education institution. Participation was voluntary but was apparently stimulated to some extent by a lottery and cash prizes.

RELIABILITY:

An alpha of **.63** was reported for the scale (Boulding et al. 1992).

VALIDITY:

No examination of scale validity was performed by Boulding and colleagues (1993). A factor analysis of all 36 items in this version of the SERVQUAL instrument was performed, but managerial judgment was used to form the individual subscales and no quantitative data were provided.

ADMINISTRATION:

The scale was apparently self-administered by students, but Boulding and colleagues (1993) did not provide the details .A high score on the scale suggests a respondent thinks that an educational institution is visually appealing in both its personnel (professors) and facilities.

MAJOR FINDINGS:

Boulding and colleagues (1993) describe two studies bearing on a behavioral process model. The second study involved the service quality scales. Among the many findings was that the **tangible** aspect of education was *not* a primary influence on overall quality perceptions.

REFERENCES:

Boulding, William, Ajay Kalra, Richard Staelin, and Valerie A. Zeithaml (1993), ''A Dynamic Process Model of Service Quality: From Expectations to Behavioral Intentions,'' *JMR*, 30 (February), 7-27.

_____, Richard Staelin, Ajay Kalra, and Valerie A. Zeithaml (1992), ''Conceptualizing and Testing a Dynamic Process Model of Service Quality,'' Working paper No. 92-121. Cambridge, MA: Marketing Science Institute.

Parasuraman, A., Valerie A. Zeithaml, and Leonard L. Berry (1988), ''SERVQUAL: A Multiple-Item Scale for Measuring Customer Perceptions of Service Quality,'' *JR*, 64 (Spring), 12-40.

SCALE ITEMS: SERVICE QUALITY (EDUCATION TANGIBLES)*

Directions: The following set of statements relate to your feelings about _____'s service. For each statement, please show the extent to which you believe _____ has the feature described by the statement. Circling a ''1'' means that you strongly disagree that _____ has that feature, and circling a ''7'' means that you strongly agree. You may circle any of the numbers in the middle that show how strong your feelings are. There are no right or wrong answers—all we are interested in is a number that best shows your perceptions about _____'s service.

Strongly disagree
1————2————3————4————5————6————7
Strongly agree

1. The building and grounds are clean.
2. Professors wear business attire.
3. Classroom equipment is in working order.
4. Professors are appropriately dressed and appear neat.
5. The facilities are visually appealing.
6. The temperature is uniformly comfortable throughout the building.
7. Overheads used in teaching are clear and error free.

* These directions were not provided in the article but are assumed to be similar to what was actually used.

SCALE NAME: Service Quality (Empathy)

SCALE DESCRIPTION:

A five-item, seven-point, Likert-type scale measuring the degree to which a person thinks a service company's employees give attention to customers and understand their needs. As described here, the scale relates to the Empathy dimension of the SERVQUAL instrument (Parasuraman, Zeithaml, and Berry 1988, 1991) but is not equivalent to it. Each dimension of the SERVQUAL measure is composed of the summated differences between expectation items and perceptual items, not just the latter as the scale described here is. Carman (1990) used a few variations on the scale describing, one as a *Personal Attention* factor and the other as a *Courtesy* factor.

SCALE ORIGIN:

The scale is a part of the larger SERVQUAL instrument described by Parasuraman, Zeithaml, and Berry (1988, 1991), which measures five separate dimensions of service quality. Considerable information is provided in those articles about the scale's conceptualization, development, and validation.

The version of the scale discussed by Parasuraman, Zeithaml, and Berry (1988) is the one followed to a great extent by Carman (1990). In the former's 1991 article some suggestions for changes to the scale were made. As far as the empathy dimension is concerned, the revised version modified all the items by making them positive rather than negative in wording. Items 6 and 7 were developed by Carman (1990) for use in his tire store study.

SAMPLES:

Carman (1990) adjusted and tested the SERVQUAL instrument in four different service settings. However, one set of items assessed an empathy factor in a business school placement center (n = **82**). Another set of items was used to assess a courtesy factor in a tire store setting (n = **74**). Very little description of the samples was provided.

A questionnaire was sent by Parasuraman, Berry, and Zeithaml (1991) to randomly chosen customers of five nationally known companies: one telephone company, two banks, and two insurance companies. A reminder postcard was sent two weeks after the initial mailing. The number of usable questionnaires ranged from 290 to 487 for the five companies. The total number of completed returns was **1936,** a 21% overall response rate. Managers in the companies reviewed the demographic profiles of the respondents and considered them to be representative of their customer populations.

RELIABILITY:

Carman (1990) reported alphas of **.82** and **.84** for use of the scale in the placement center and tire store settings, respectively. The alphas reported by Parasuraman, Berry, and Zeithaml (1991) for the five companies ranged from .85 to .89. These alphas relate to the summated differences between

expectation items and perceptual items. The alpha for just the perceptions items was **.90** using the combined sample (Parasuraman 1993).

VALIDITY:

Carman factor analyzed the SERVQUAL data from each setting. Only items with loadings greater than .30 on the same factor in at least one setting were used to compose scales (Carman 1994). However, the sets of items used to compose the summated scales for each of the settings were ultimately different on the basis of several factors. These variable results led him to conclude that it had problems with construct validity.

Parasuraman, Berry, and Zeithaml (1991) reported the results of several factor analyses using oblique rotations. With regard to the perception version of the scale using the combined samples, all the items had their highest loadings on the same factor.

ADMINISTRATION:

The SERVQUAL instrument was self-administered by respondents after they received service in the study by Carman (1990). The scale was administered to customers in a mail survey format by Parasuraman, Berry, and Zeithaml (1991). High scores on the perception version of the scale show that respondents think that employees of a service firm are very attentive and understanding of customer needs.

MAJOR FINDINGS:

The purpose of Carman's (1990) studies was to test the SERVQUAL instrument in a variety of service settings. Some modifications in wording were always found to be necessary. An **empathy**-related dimension was found in both the placement center and tire store settings, however, as noted elsewhere, their item compositions were not identical. In fact, Carman called the set of items in the tire study a *Courtesy* factor and the items in the placement center study a *Personal Attention* factor.

Parasuraman, Berry, and Zeithaml (1991) conducted a study to refine their SERVQUAL scales and to examine the revised scales in five different customer samples. They also compared their results with those of others who had used the scales. When respondents were asked to divide 100 points among the five service quality dimensions on the basis of importance, for each of the five samples the result was the same: the **empathy** dimension was always was the next to least most important dimension.

COMMENTS:

Although this scale can be used by itself, it was designed to be used along with its companion expectations version. For example, the expectations version of item 1 would be something like ''Excellent companies will give customers individual attention.'' The authors also encourage researchers to measure all of the dimensions to capture the domain of service quality fully.

For further discussion of theoretical and psychometric properties of the SERVQUAL instrument see Parasuraman, Zeithaml, and Berry (1994), Cronin and Taylor (1994), and Teas (1994).

See also Teas (1993) for use of a two-item version of the scale.

REFERENCES:

Carman, James M. (1990), "Consumer Perceptions of Service Quality: An Assessment of the SERVQUAL Dimensions," *JR*, 66 (Spring), 33-55.

_____ (1994), personal correspondence.

Cronin, J. Joseph, Jr. and Steven A. Taylor (1994), "SERVPERF Versus SERV-QUAL: Reconciling Performance-Based and Perceptions-Minus-Expectations Measurement of Service Quality," *JM*, 58 (January), 124-31.

Parasuraman, A. (1993), personal correspondence.

_____, Leonard L. Berry, and Valarie A. Zeithaml (1991), "Refinement and Reassessment of the SERVQUAL Scale," *JR*, 67 (Winter), 420-50.

_____, Valerie A. Zeithaml, and Leonard L. Berry (1988), "SERVQUAL: A Multiple-Item Scale for Measuring Customer Perceptions of Service Quality," *JR*, 64 (Spring), 12-40.

_____, _____, and _____ (1994), "Reassessment of Expectations as a Comparison Standard in Measuring Service Quality: Implications for Further Research," *JM*, 58 (January), 111-24.

Teas, R. Kenneth (1993), "Expectations, Performance Evaluation, and Consumers' Perceptions of Quality," *JM*, 57 (October), 18-34.

_____ (1994), "Expectations as a Comparison Standard in Measuring Service Quality: An Assessment of a Reassessment," *JM*, 58 (January), 132-39.

SCALE ITEMS: SERVICE QUALITY (EMPATHY)*

Directions: The following set of statements relate to your feelings about _____'s service. For each statement, please show the extent to which you believe _____ has the feature described by the statement. Circling a "1" means that you strongly disagree that _____ has that feature, and circling a "7" means that you strongly agree. You may circle any of the numbers in the middle that show how strong your feelings are. There are no right or wrong answers—all we are interested in is a number that best shows your perceptions about _____'s service.

```
Strongly                                                      Strongly
disagree                                                        agree
  1————————2————————3————————4————————5————————6————————7
```

1. _____ does not give you individual attention. **(r)**
2. Employees of _____ do not give you personal attention. **(r)**
3. Employees of _____ do not know what your needs are. **(r)**
4. _____ does not have your best interests at heart. **(r)**
5. _____ does not have operating hours convenient to all their customers. **(r)**

6. My dealings here are very pleasant.
7. The employees of this store know what they are doing.
8. Employees of _____ are too busy to respond to customer requests promptly. **(r)**
9. Employees of _____ are polite.
10. _____ gives you individual attention.
11. _____ has operating hours convenient to all of its customers.
12. _____ has employees who give you personal attention.
13. _____ has your best interests at heart.
14. Employees of _____ understand your specific needs.

* The name of the specific service company being studied should be placed in the blanks. Items 1-5 were the form used by Parasuraman, Zeithaml, and Berry (1988), and the revised items (10-14) were recommended in their 1991 article. Statements similar to items 2-4 and 8 were used in the placement center study conducted by Carman (1990, 1994). In the tire store study, he used items 2-4, 6, 7, and 9.

SCALE NAME: Service Quality (Empathy of Professors)

SCALE DESCRIPTION:

A five-item, seven-point, Likert-type scale measuring the degree to which a person thinks the professors working for an educational institution are sensitive and concerned about their students' needs.

SCALE ORIGIN:

The scale is original to Boulding and colleagues (1993) and is described more fully in Boulding and colleagues (1992). However, it is modeled on the SERV-QUAL instrument (Parasuraman, Zeithaml, and Berry 1988), which measures five separate dimensions of service quality. The scale described here relates to the Empathy dimension of the SERVQUAL instrument but is not equivalent to it. Each dimension of the SERVQUAL measure is composed of the summated differences between expectation items and perceptual items, not just the latter, as the scale described here is.

SAMPLES:

Boulding and colleagues (1993) collected data from **177** students of a business education institution. Participation was voluntary but was apparently stimulated to some extent by a lottery and cash prizes.

RELIABILITY:

An alpha of **.74** was reported for the scale (Boulding et al. 1992).

VALIDITY:

Boulding and colleagues (1993) performed no examination of scale validity. A factor analysis of all 36 items in this version of the SERVQUAL instrument was performed, but managerial judgment was used to form the individual subscales and no quantitative data were provided.

ADMINISTRATION:

The scale was apparently self-administered by students, but Boulding and colleagues (1993) provided no details. A high score on the scale suggests a respondent believes that professors of an institution truly care about their students.

MAJOR FINDINGS:

Boulding and colleagues (1993) describe two studies bearing on a behavioral process model. The second study involved the service quality scales. Among the many findings was that the **empathy** of the professors providing the education was a significant influence on overall quality perceptions.

REFERENCES:

Boulding, William, Ajay Kalra, Richard Staelin, and Valerie A. Zeithaml (1993), ''A Dynamic Process Model of Service Quality: From Expectations to Behavioral Intentions,'' *JMR*, 30 (February), 7-27.

_____, Richard Staelin, Ajay Kalra, and Valerie A. Zeithaml (1992), ''Conceptualizing and Testing a Dynamic Process Model of Service Quality,'' Working paper No. 92-121. Cambridge, MA: Marketing Science Institute.

Parasuraman, A., Valerie A. Zeithaml, and Leonard L. Berry (1988), ''SERVQUAL: A Multiple-Item Scale for Measuring Customer Perceptions of Service Quality,'' *JR*, 64 (Spring), 12-40.

SCALE ITEMS: SERVICE QUALITY (EMPATHY OF PROFESSORS)*

Directions: The following set of statements relate to your feelings about _____'s service. For each statement, please show the extent to which you believe _____ has the feature described by the statement. Circling a ''1'' means that you strongly disagree that _____ has that feature, and circling a ''7'' means that you strongly agree. You may circle any of the numbers in the middle that show how strong your feelings are. There are no right or wrong answers—all we are interested in is a number that best shows your perceptions about _____'s service.

Strongly   Strongly
disagree   agree
1————2————3————4————5————6————7

1. Professors give students individual attention.
2. Professors help students with personal problems and career advice.
3. Students are able to contact a professor at home.
4. Professors know what the needs of their students are.
5. Professors have their students' best interests at heart.

* These directions were not provided in the article but are assumed to be similar to what was actually used.

SCALE NAME: Service Quality (Hospital Admission)

SCALE DESCRIPTION:

A three-item, five-point, Likert-type scale measuring the degree to which a person thinks a hospital's staff provided prompt attention and service during the admissions process.

SCALE ORIGIN:

Although inspiration for the items definitely came from the SERVQUAL instrument developed by Parasuraman, Zeithaml, and Berry (1988), this scale was specifically developed by Carman (1990) for use with hospitals.

SAMPLES:

Carman (1990) adjusted and tested the SERVQUAL instrument in four different service settings. However, the specific items listed here were used only in the hospital study. Little is known about the respondents in that study except that data were collected from **720** patients.

RELIABILITY:

Carman (1990) reported an alpha of **.84**.

VALIDITY:

Carman (1990) factor analyzed the data for many scales related to hospital service quality. The three items composing the admissions quality scale loaded on the same factor at .78 or higher.

ADMINISTRATION:

The scale was part of a larger instrument apparently self-administered by respondents after they received service (Carman 1990). High scores on the scale show that respondents think that the hospital staff provided them with prompt service when they were admitted as patients.

MAJOR FINDINGS:

The purpose of Carman's (1990) studies was to test the SERVQUAL instrument in a variety of service settings. Some modifications in wording were always found to be necessary, to the greatest extent in the hospital study. No findings specifically related to this scale were reported beyond what is noted here regarding some of its psychometric qualities. It was noted in general, however, that the dimensions of service quality described by Parasuraman, Zeithaml, and Berry (1988) may change depending on the context being studied and especially if the instrument must be greatly modified.

REFERENCES:

Carman, James M. (1990), "Consumer Perceptions of Service Quality: An Assessment of the SERVQUAL Dimensions," *JR*, 66 (Spring), 33-55.

_____ (1993), personal correspondence.

Parasuraman, A., Valerie A. Zeithaml, and Leonard L. Berry (1988), "SERV-QUAL: A Multiple-Item Scale for Measuring Customer Perceptions of Service Quality," *JR*, 64 (Spring), 12-40.

SCALE ITEMS: SERVICE QUALITY (HOSPITAL ADMISSION)*

Directions: The following set of statements relate to your feelings about _____'s service. For each statement, please show the extent to which you believe _____ has the feature described by the statement. Circling a "1" means that you strongly disagree that _____ has that feature, and circling a "5" means that you strongly agree. You may circle any of the numbers in the middle that show how strong your feelings are. There are no right or wrong answers—all we are interested in is a number that best shows your perceptions about _____'s service.

Strongly   Strongly
disagree   agree
1————————2————————3————————4————————5

1. My admission to the hospital was prompt.
2. Hospital staff were too busy to respond to patient requests promptly. **(r)**
3. Hospital staff were polite during the admissions process.

* These statements have been constructed on the basis of descriptions in Carman (1990) and from personal correspondence (Carman 1993); statements similar to these were used.

SCALE NAME: Service Quality (Hospital Billing)

SCALE DESCRIPTION:

A three-item, five-point, Likert-type scale measuring the degree to which a person thinks a specified hospital where he/she has been a patient was accurate in its billing process.

SCALE ORIGIN:

Although inspiration for the items definitely came from the SERVQUAL instrument developed by Parasuraman, Zeithaml, and Berry (1988), this scale was specifically developed by Carman (1990) for use with hospitals.

SAMPLES:

Carman (1990) adjusted and tested the SERVQUAL instrument in four different service settings. However, the specific items listed here were used only in the hospital study. Little is known about the respondents in that study except that data were collected from **720** patients.

RELIABILITY:

Carman (1990) reported an alpha of **.82**.

VALIDITY:

Carman (1990) factor analyzed the data for many scales related to hospital service quality. The three items composing this scale loaded on the same factor at .75 and higher.

ADMINISTRATION:

The scale was part of a larger instrument apparently self-administered by respondents after they received service (Carman 1990). High scores on the scale show that respondents think that a specified hospital kept accurate records and charged the correct amounts for the services provided.

MAJOR FINDINGS:

The purpose of Carman's (1990) studies was to test the SERVQUAL instrument in a variety of service settings. Some modifications in wording were always found to be necessary, to the greatest extent in the hospital study. No findings specifically related to this scale were reported beyond what is noted here regarding some of its psychometric qualities. It was noted in general, however, that the dimensions of service quality described by Parasuraman, Zeithaml, and Berry (1988) may change depending on the context being studied and especially if the instrument must be greatly modified.

REFERENCES:

Carman, James M. (1990), "Consumer Perceptions of Service Quality: An Assessment of the SERVQUAL Dimensions," *JR*, 66 (Spring), 33-55.

_____ (1993), personal correspondence.

Parasuraman, A., Valerie A. Zeithaml, and Leonard L. Berry (1988), "SERV-QUAL: A Multiple-Item Scale for Measuring Customer Perceptions of Service Quality," *JR*, 64 (Spring), 12-40.

SCALE ITEMS: SERVICE QUALITY (HOSPITAL BILLING)*

Directions: The following set of statements relate to your feelings about _____'s service. For each statement, please show the extent to which you believe _____ has the feature described by the statement. Circling a "1" means that you strongly disagree that _____ has that feature, and circling a "5" means that you strongly agree. You may circle any of the numbers in the middle that show how strong your feelings are. There are no right or wrong answers—all we are interested in is a number that best shows your perceptions about _____'s service.

Strongly   Strongly
disagree   agree
1————————2————————3————————4————————5

1. The hospital keeps its records accurately.
2. I feel that the charges for my stay were accurate.
3. You can trust the hospital employees when it comes to billing.

* These statements have been constructed on the basis of descriptions in Carman (1990) and from personal correspondence (Carman 1993); statements similar to these were used.

SCALE NAME: Service Quality (Hospital Discharge Procedures)

SCALE DESCRIPTION:

A six-item, five-point, Likert-type scale measuring the degree to which a person thinks the discharge process he/she experienced upon being released from a hospital stay was well handled by the hospital staff.

SCALE ORIGIN:

Although inspiration for the items definitely came from the SERVQUAL instrument developed by Parasuraman, Zeithaml, and Berry (1988), this scale was specifically developed by Carman (1990) for use with hospitals.

SAMPLES:

Carman (1990) adjusted and tested the SERVQUAL instrument in four different service settings. However, the specific items listed here were used only in the hospital study. Little is known about the respondents in that study except that data were collected from **720** patients.

RELIABILITY:

Carman (1990) reported an alpha of **.86**.

VALIDITY:

Carman (1990) factor analyzed the data for many scales related to hospital service quality. The six items composing this scale loaded on the same factor at .44 or higher.

ADMINISTRATION:

The scale was part of a larger instrument apparently self-administered by respondents after they received service (Carman 1990). High scores on the scale show that respondents think that the discharge process provided by a specified hospital is of high quality.

MAJOR FINDINGS:

The purpose of Carman's (1990) studies was to test the SERVQUAL instrument in a variety of service settings. Some modifications in wording were always found to be necessary, to the greatest extent in the hospital study. No findings specifically related to this scale were reported beyond what is noted here regarding some of its psychometric qualities. It was noted in general, however, that the dimensions of service quality described by Parasuraman, Zeithaml, and Berry (1988) may change depending on the context being studied and especially if the instrument must be greatly modified.

REFERENCES:

Carman, James M. (1990), "Consumer Perceptions of Service Quality: An Assessment of the SERVQUAL Dimensions," *JR*, 66 (Spring), 33-55.

_____ (1993), personal correspondence.

Parasuraman, A., Valerie A. Zeithaml, and Leonard L. Berry (1988), "SERV-QUAL: A Multiple-Item Scale for Measuring Customer Perceptions of Service Quality," *JR*, 64 (Spring), 12-40.

SCALE ITEMS: SERVICE QUALITY (HOSPITAL DISCHARGE PROCEDURES)*

Directions: The following set of statements relate to your feelings about _____'s service. For each statement, please show the extent to which you believe _____ has the feature described by the statement. Circling a "1" means that you strongly disagree that _____ has that feature, and circling a "5" means that you strongly agree. You may circle any of the numbers in the middle that show how strong your feelings are. There are no right or wrong answers—all we are interested in is a number that best shows your perceptions about _____'s service.

Strongly   Strongly
disagree   agree
  1————————2————————3————————4————————5

1. My discharge from the hospital was prompt.
2. Hospital staff are not always willing to help patients. **(r)**
3. The nurses explained my discharge instructions.
4. Hospital procedures and routines were clearly explained to me.
5. The nurses explained things to my family so they felt well prepared for my discharge.
6. You can trust the hospital staff as they handle the discharge process.

* These statements have been constructed on the basis of descriptions in Carman (1990) and from personal correspondence (Carman 1993); statements similar to these were used.

SCALE NAME: Service Quality (Hospital Explanations)

SCALE DESCRIPTION:

A three-item, five-point, Likert-type scale measuring the degree to which a person thinks the instructions given by hospital staff during his/her stay regarding various procedures and routines were explained well.

SCALE ORIGIN:

Although inspiration for the items definitely came from the SERVQUAL instrument developed by Parasuraman, Zeithaml, and Berry (1988), this scale was specifically developed by Carman (1990) for use with hospitals.

SAMPLES:

Carman (1990) adjusted and tested the SERVQUAL instrument in four different service settings. However, the specific items listed here were used only in the hospital study. Little is known about the respondents in that study except that data were collected from **720** patients.

RELIABILITY:

Carman (1990) reported an alpha of **.78**.

VALIDITY:

Carman (1990) factor analyzed the data for many scales related to hospital service quality. Only one of the three items composing this particular scale had its highest loading on this factor. The other two items had very low loadings (s.25) on this factor and much higher loadings (r.50) on another factor (discharge planning). Given this, the unidimensionality of the scale as well as its validity is suspect.

ADMINISTRATION:

The scale was part of a larger instrument apparently self-administered by respondents after they received service (Carman 1990). High scores on the scale show that respondents think that the hospital staff provided good explanations for various procedures and activities with which the patient was involved.

MAJOR FINDINGS:

The purpose of Carman's (1990) studies was to test the SERVQUAL instrument in a variety of service settings. Some modifications in wording were always found to be necessary, to the greatest extent in the hospital study. No findings specifically related to this scale were reported beyond what is noted here regarding some of its psychometric qualities. It was noted in general, however, that the dimensions of service quality described by Parasuraman, Zeithaml, and Berry (1988) may change depending on the context being studied and especially if the instrument must be greatly modified.

REFERENCES:

Carman, James M. (1990), "Consumer Perceptions of Service Quality: An Assessment of the SERVQUAL Dimensions," *JR*, 66 (Spring), 33-55.

_____ (1993), personal correspondence.

Parasuraman, A., Valerie A. Zeithaml, and Leonard L. Berry (1988), "SERVQUAL: A Multiple-Item Scale for Measuring Customer Perceptions of Service Quality," *JR*, 64 (Spring), 12-40.

SCALE ITEMS: SERVICE QUALITY (HOSPITAL EXPLANATIONS)*

Directions: The following set of statements relate to your feelings about _____'s service. For each statement, please show the extent to which you believe _____ has the feature described by the statement. Circling a "1" means that you strongly disagree that _____ has that feature, and circling a "5" means that you strongly agree. You may circle any of the numbers in the middle that show how strong your feelings are. There are no right or wrong answers—all we are interested in is a number that best shows your perceptions about _____'s service.

```
Strongly                                                        Strongly
disagree                                                           agree
   1———————————2———————————3———————————4———————————5
```

1. Hospital procedures and routines were clearly explained to me.
2. The nurses explained things to me. I knew what was being done and why I was receiving the treatment.
3. The nurses explained things to my family so they felt well prepared for my discharge.

* Statements are constructed on the basis of descriptions in Carman (1990) and from personal correspondence (Carman 1993); statements similar to these were used.

SCALE NAME: Service Quality (Hospital Food)

SCALE DESCRIPTION:

A three-item, five-point, Likert-type scale measuring the degree to which a person thinks the food served in the hospital was delivered when expected and was appetizing.

SCALE ORIGIN:

Although inspiration for the items definitely came from the SERVQUAL instrument developed by Parasuraman, Zeithaml, and Berry (1988), this scale was specifically developed by Carman (1990) for use with hospitals.

SAMPLES:

Carman (1990) adjusted and tested the SERVQUAL instrument in four different service settings. However, the specific items listed here were used only in the hospital study. Little is known about the respondents in that study except that data were collected from **720** patients.

RELIABILITY:

Carman (1990) reported an alpha of **.82**.

VALIDITY:

Carman (1990) factor analyzed the data for many scales related to hospital service quality. The three items composing the food quality scale loaded on the same factor at .64 or higher.

ADMINISTRATION:

The scale was part of a larger instrument apparently self-administered by respondents after they received service in the study by Carman (1990). High scores on the scale show that respondents think that the hospital food and its delivery were satisfying.

MAJOR FINDINGS:

The purpose of Carman's (1990) studies was to test the SERVQUAL instrument in a variety of service settings. Some modifications in wording were always found to be necessary, to the greatest extent in the hospital study. No findings specifically related to this scale were reported beyond what is noted here regarding some of its psychometric qualities. It was noted in general, however, that the dimensions of service quality described by Parasuraman, Zeithaml, and Berry (1988) may change depending on the context being studied and especially if the instrument must be greatly modified.

REFERENCES:

Carman, James M. (1990), "Consumer Perceptions of Service Quality: An Assessment of the SERVQUAL Dimensions," *JR*, 66 (Spring), 33-55.

_____ (1993), personal correspondence.

Parasuraman, A., Valerie A. Zeithaml, and Leonard L. Berry (1988), "SERV-QUAL: A Multiple-Item Scale for Measuring Customer Perceptions of Service Quality," *JR*, 64 (Spring), 12-40.

SCALE ITEMS: SERVICE QUALITY (HOSPITAL FOOD)*

Directions: The following set of statements relate to your feelings about _____'s service. For each statement, please show the extent to which you believe _____ has the feature described by the statement. Circling a "1" means that you strongly disagree that _____ has that feature, and circling a "5" means that you strongly agree. You may circle any of the numbers in the middle that show how strong your feelings are. There are no right or wrong answers—all we are interested in is a number that best shows your perceptions about _____'s service.

Strongly disagree | Strongly agree
1————2————3————4————5

1. My meals were attractive and appetizing.
2. Meals were served at the right temperature.
3. When the staff promised to deliver meals at a certain time, they did so.

* Statements are constructed on the basis of descriptions in Carman (1990) and from personal correspondence (Carman 1993); statements similar to these were used.

SCALE NAME: Service Quality (Hospital Nurses)

SCALE DESCRIPTION:

A nine-item, five-point, Likert-type scale measuring the degree to which a person thinks the nursing staff at a specified hospital provided high-quality attention and service during his/her stay as a patient.

SCALE ORIGIN:

Although inspiration for the items definitely came from the SERVQUAL instrument developed by Parasuraman, Zeithaml, and Berry (1988), this scale was specifically developed by Carman (1990) for use with hospitals.

SAMPLES:

Carman (1990) adjusted and tested the SERVQUAL instrument in four different service settings. However, the specific items listed here were used only in the hospital study. Little is known about the respondents in that study except that data were collected from **720** patients.

RELIABILITY:

Carman (1990) reported an alpha of **.94**.

VALIDITY:

Carman (1990) factor analyzed the data for many scales related to hospital service quality. The nine items composing this scale loaded on the same factor at .47 or higher.

ADMINISTRATION:

The scale was part of a larger instrument apparently self-administered by respondents after they received service in the study by Carman (1990). High scores on the scale show that respondents think that the nursing staff at a hospital provide high-quality service.

MAJOR FINDINGS:

The purpose of Carman's (1990) studies was to test the SERVQUAL instrument in a variety of service settings. Some modifications in wording were always found to be necessary, to the greatest extent in the hospital study. No findings specifically related to this scale were reported beyond what is noted here regarding some of its psychometric qualities. It was noted in general, however, that the dimensions of service quality described by Parasuraman, Zeithaml, and Berry (1988) may change depending on the context being studied and especially if the instrument must be greatly modified.

REFERENCES:

Carman, James M. (1990), "Consumer Perceptions of Service Quality: An Assessment of the SERVQUAL Dimensions," *JR*, 66 (Spring), 33-55.

_____ (1993), personal correspondence.

Parasuraman, A., Valerie A. Zeithaml, and Leonard L. Berry (1988), "SERV-QUAL: A Multiple-Item Scale for Measuring Customer Perceptions of Service Quality," *JR*, 64 (Spring), 12-40.

SCALE ITEMS: SERVICE QUALITY (HOSPITAL NURSES)*

Directions: The following set of statements relate to your feelings about _____'s service. For each statement, please show the extent to which you believe _____ has the feature described by the statement. Circling a "1" means that you strongly disagree that _____ has that feature, and circling a "5" means that you strongly agree. You may circle any of the numbers in the middle that show how strong your feelings are. There are no right or wrong answers—all we are interested in is a number that best shows your perceptions about _____'s service.

```
Strongly                                                    Strongly
disagree                                                       agree
   1——————————2——————————3——————————4——————————5
```

1. When the staff promised to do something by a certain time, they did so.
2. Nurses responded promptly when I called.
3. You can trust the nurses at that hospital.
4. You feel safe in your transactions with the hospital's employees.
5. The nurses were knowledgeable about my illness and treatment.
6. The nurses at the hospital are polite.
7. The nurses were cheerful.
8. My family and friends were treated well by the hospital personnel.
9. Nurses at that hospital do not know what your needs are. **(r)**

* Statements are constructed on the basis of descriptions in Carman (1990) and from personal correspondence (Carman 1993); statements similar to these were used.

SCALE NAME: Service Quality (Overall)

SCALE DESCRIPTION:

A 21-item, seven-point, Likert-type performance-based measure of service quality. It is viewed as a measure of a consumer's long-term overall attitude toward an organization rather than his/her transaction-specific satisfaction.

SCALE ORIGIN:

The items for this scale are taken directly from the performance portion of the SERVQUAL instrument described by Parasuraman, Zeithaml, and Berry (1988), which measures five separate dimensions of service quality. Considerable information is provided in their article about the scale's conceptualization, development, and validation. The chief difference between their instrument and that of Cronin and Taylor (1992) is that the latter treated all of the items as one summated scale, whereas the former used the items to compose five different subscales.

SAMPLES:

The sample used by Cronin and Taylor (1992) was composed of completed questionnaires from **660** respondents. The survey took place in a southeastern U.S. city over a two-week period. Trained interviewers were assigned parts of the town and approached residences randomly. Although data were gathered on two firms for each of four industries, respondents evaluated just one firm each. Screening ensured that respondents were familiar with the organization they were asked about. The sample sizes for the four industries were: **188** (banking), **175** (pest control), **178** (dry cleaning), and **189** (fast food).

RELIABILITY:

The alphas for the scale calculated by industry were **.925** (banks), **.964** (pest control), **.932** (dry cleaning), and **.884** (fast food) (Cronin and Taylor 1992).

VALIDITY:

Cronin and Taylor (1992) used an oblique factor rotation procedure to analyze the data for each of the four industries. Although the full item-factor matrix was not reported, the authors described the results as providing evidence of unidimensionality. Very low loadings ($< .40$) were evident, however, for several items in three of the industries.

ADMINISTRATION:

The scale was administered by trained interviewers as part of a larger personal interview to consumers at their residences (Cronin and Taylor 1992). A high score on the scale indicates that a respondent perceives a specified organization to have high service quality.

MAJOR FINDINGS:

Cronin and Taylor (1992) examined the conceptualization and measurement of service quality using the model and instruments created by Parasuraman, Zeithaml, and Berry (1988). The findings of the study suggested that service quality should be measured as an attitude rather than satisfaction. Moreover, the scale that used a summation of Parasuraman, Zeithaml, and Berry's (1988) *performance* items (not *expectations*) was considered to be the superior measure.

COMMENTS:

Despite the statement of Cronin and Taylor that the items "can be treated as unidimensional" (1992, p. 61), the conclusion has been seriously questioned (Parasuraman, Zeithaml, and Berry 1994, p. 113). The findings in other studies (e.g., Carman 1990; Parasuraman, Zeithaml, and Berry 1988) consistently support a multidimensional structure. Moreover, the variability of factor loadings across industries indicate that, as found by Carman (1990), some items do not work well in most settings. These weaknesses of using these items as a summated scale were acknowledged to some extent by Cronin and Taylor more recently (1994, pp. 128, 130).

REFERENCES:

Carman, James M. (1990), "Consumer Perceptions of Service Quality: An Assessment of the SERVQUAL Dimensions," *JR*, 66 (Spring), 33-55.

Cronin, J. Joseph, Jr., and Stephen A. Taylor (1992), "Measuring Service Quality: A Reexamination and Extension," *JM*, 56 (July), 55-68.

_____ and _____ (1994), "SERVPERF Versus SERVQUAL: Reconciling Performance-Based and Perceptions-Minus-Expectations Measurement of Service Quality," *JM*, 58 (January), 124-31.

Parasuraman, A., Valerie A. Zeithaml, and Leonard L. Berry (1988), "SERVQUAL: A Multiple-Item Scale for Measuring Customer Perceptions of Service Quality," *JR*, 64 (Spring), 12-40.

_____, _____, and _____ (1994), "Reassessment of Expectations as a Comparison Standard in Measuring Service Quality: Implications for Further Research," *JM*, 58 (January), 111-24.

SCALE ITEMS: SERVICE QUALITY (OVERALL)*

Strongly   Strongly
disagree   agree

1————2————3————4————5————6————7

1. _____ has up-to-date equipment.
2. _____'s physical facilities are visually appealing.
3. _____'s employees are well dressed and appear neat.
4. The appearance of the physical facilities of _____ is in keeping with the type of services provided.

5. When _____ promises to do something by a certain time, it does so.
6. When you have problems, _____ is sympathetic and reassuring.
7. _____ is dependable.
8. _____ provides its services at the time it promises to do so.
9. _____ keeps its records accurately.
10. _____ does not tell customers exactly when services will be performed. **(r)**
11. You do not receive prompt service from _____. **(r)**
12. Employees of _____ are not always willing to help customers. **(r)**
13. Employees of _____ are too busy to respond to customer requests promptly. **(r)**
14. You can trust employees of _____.
15. You feel safe in your transactions with _____.
16. Employees of _____ are polite.
17. mployees get adequate support from _____ to do their jobs well.
18. _____ does not give you individual attention. **(r)**
19. Employees of _____ do not know what your needs are. **(r)**
20. _____ does not have your best interests at heart. **(r)**
21. _____ does not have operating hours convenient to all their customers. **(r)**

* The name of the specific service company being studied should be placed in the blanks.

SCALE NAME: Service Quality (Reliability)

SCALE DESCRIPTION:

A five-item, seven-point, Likert-type scale measuring the degree to which a person thinks a service company is responsible and can be depended on to do what it promises to do. As described here, the scale relates to the Reliability dimension of the SERVQUAL instrument (Parasuraman, Zeithaml, and Berry 1988, 1991) but is not equivalent to it. Each dimension of the SERVQUAL measure is composed of the summated differences between expectation items and perceptual items, not just the latter as the scale described here is. Carman (1990) used several variations on the scale, as described subsequently.

SCALE ORIGIN:

The scale is a part of the larger SERVQUAL instrument described by Parasuraman, Zeithaml, and Berry (1988, 1991), which measures five separate dimensions of service quality. Considerable information is provided in those articles about the scale's conceptualization, development, and validation.

The version of the scale discussed by Parasuraman, Zeithaml, and Berry (1988) is the one followed to a great extent by Carman (1990). In the former's 1991 article, some suggestions for changes to the scale were made. As far as the Reliability dimension is concerned, only two items were kept intact from the original version, and the other three items were changed. Item 6 is original to Carman (1990).

SAMPLES:

Carman (1990) adjusted and tested the SERVQUAL instrument in four different service settings: a dental school patient clinic (n = 612), a business school placement center (n = 82), a tire store (n = 74), and an acute care hospital (n = 720). The scale used in the hospital setting warranted treatment as a different scale and therefore is written up separately (see #250, #251, #252, #253, #254, #255, and #263).

Parasuraman, Berry, and Zeithaml (1991) sent questionnaires to randomly chosen customers of five nationally known companies: one telephone company, two banks, and two insurance companies. A reminder postcard was sent two weeks after the initial mailing. The number of usable questionnaires ranged from 290 to 487 for the five companies. The total number of completed returns was **1936,** a 21% overall response rate. Managers in the companies reviewed the demographic profiles of the respondents and considered them to be representative of their customer populations.

RELIABILITY:

The following alphas were reported by Carman (1990) for the scale: **.51** (tire store), **.52** (placement center), and **.79** (dental clinic). The alphas reported by Parasuraman, Berry, and Zeithaml (1991) for the five companies ranged from .88 to .92. These alphas relate to the summated differences between

expectation items and perceptual items. The alpha for just the perceptions items was **.92** using the combined sample (Parasuraman 1993).

VALIDITY:

Carman factor analyzed the SERVQUAL data from each setting. In general, only items with loadings greater than .30 on the same factor in at least one setting were used to compose scales (Carman 1994). However, the sets of items used to compose the summated scales for each of the three settings were ultimately different on the basis of several factors. These variable results led Carman to conclude that the scale had problems with construct validity.

Parasuraman, Berry, and Zeithaml (1991) reported the results of several factor analyses using oblique rotations. With regard to the perception version of the scale using the combined samples, all the items except item 2 had their highest loadings on the same factor. The item apparently was left in the scale because its loading was greater than .50 in factor analysis of the expectation scores.

ADMINISTRATION:

In Carman (1990), the SERVQUAL instrument was self-administered by respondents after they received service. The scale was administered to customers in a mail-survey format by Parasuraman, Berry, and Zeithaml (1991). High scores on the perception version of the scale show that respondents think a specific service firm can be depended on to do what it says it will do.

MAJOR FINDINGS:

The purpose of Carman's (1990) studies was to test the SERVQUAL instrument in a variety of service settings. Some modifications in wording were always found to be necessary. Moreover, testing of the data indicated that though a **reliability**-related dimension was found across settings, the items loading on that dimension were not stable.

Parasuraman, Berry, and Zeithaml (1991) conducted a study to refine their SERVQUAL scales and to examine the revised scales in five different customer samples. They also compared their results with those of others who had used the scales. When respondents were asked to divide 100 points among the five service quality dimensions on the basis of importance, for each of the five samples the result was the same: the **reliability** dimension was by far the most important.

COMMENTS:

Although this scale can be used by itself, it was designed to be used along with its companion expectations version. For example, the expectations version of item 1 would be something like "When excellent _____ companies promise to do something by a certain time, they will do so." The authors also encourage researchers to measure all the dimensions to capture the domain of service quality fully.

For further discussion of theoretical and psychometric properties of the SERVQUAL instrument, see Parasuraman, Zeithaml, and Berry (1994), Cronin and Taylor (1994), and Teas (1994).

See also Teas (1993) for use of a two-item version of the scale.

REFERENCES:

Carman, James M. (1990), ''Consumer Perceptions of Service Quality: An Assessment of the SERVQUAL Dimensions,'' *JR*, 66 (Spring), 33-55.

_____ (1994), personal correspondence.

Cronin, J. Joseph, Jr. and Steven A. Taylor (1994), ''SERVPERF Versus SERV-QUAL: Reconciling Performance-Based and Perceptions-Minus-Expectations Measurement of Service Quality,'' *JM*, 58 (January), 124-31.

Parasuraman, A. (1993), personal correspondence.

_____, Leonard L. Berry, and Valarie A. Zeithaml (1991), ''Refinement and Reassessment of the SERVQUAL Scale,'' *JR*, 67 (Winter), 420-50.

_____, Valerie A. Zeithaml, and Leonard L. Berry (1988), ''SERVQUAL: A Multiple-Item Scale for Measuring Customer Perceptions of Service Quality,'' *JR*, 64 (Spring), 12-40.

_____, _____, and _____ (1994), ''Reassessment of Expectations as a Comparison Standard in Measuring Service Quality: Implications for Further Research,'' *JM*, 58 (January), 111-24.

Teas, R. Kenneth (1993), ''Expectations, Performance Evaluation, and Consumers' Perceptions of Quality,'' *JM*, 57 (October), 18-34.

_____ (1994), ''Expectations as a Comparison Standard in Measuring Service Quality: An Assessment of a Reassessment,'' *JM*, 58 (January), 132-39.

SCALE ITEMS: SERVICE QUALITY (RELIABILITY)*

Directions: The following set of statements relate to your feelings about _____'s service. For each statement, please show the extent to which you believe _____ has the feature described by the statement. Circling a ''1'' means that you strongly disagree that _____ has that feature, and circling a ''7'' means that you strongly agree. You may circle any of the numbers in the middle that show how strong your feelings are. There are no right or wrong answers—all we are interested in is a number that best shows your perceptions about _____'s service.

Strongly   Strongly
disagree   agree
    1————————2————————3————————4————————5————————6————————7

1. When _____ promises to do something by a certain time, it does so.
2. When you have problems, _____ is sympathetic and reassuring.
3. _____ is dependable.
4. _____ provides its services at the time it promises to do so.
5. _____ keeps its records accurately.

6. It is easy to make an appointment there.
7. When you have a problem, _____ shows a sincere interest in following it.
8. _____ performs the service right the first time.
9. _____ insists on error-free records.

* The name of the specific service firm studied should be placed in the blanks. Items 1-5 were the form used by Parasuraman, Zeithaml, and Berry (1988), and items 1, 4, and 7-9 were recommended in their 1991 article. Although not completely clear, it appears that statements similar to the following items were used in the three studies conducted by Carman (1990, 1994): 1, 3, and 5 (tire store); 3-5 (placement center); and 1, 4, and 6 (dental clinic).

SCALE NAME: Service Quality (Reliability of Professors)

SCALE DESCRIPTION:
A six-item, seven-point, Likert-type scale measuring the degree to which a person thinks the professors working for an educational institution are responsible and can be depended on to do what they promise to do.

SCALE ORIGIN:
The scale is original to Boulding and colleagues (1993) and is more fully described in Boulding and colleagues (1992). However, it is modeled on the SERVQUAL instrument (Parasuraman, Zeithaml, and Berry 1988), which measures five separate dimensions of service quality. The scale described here relates to the Reliability dimension of the SERVQUAL instrument but is not equivalent to it. Each dimension of the SERVQUAL measure is composed of the summated differences between expectation items and perceptual items, not just the latter as the scale described here is.

SAMPLES:
Boulding and colleagues (1993) collected data from 177 students of a business education institution. Participation was voluntary but was apparently stimulated to some extent by a lottery and cash prizes.

RELIABILITY:
An alpha of **.73** was reported for the scale (Boulding et al. 1992).

VALIDITY:
Boulding and colleagues (1993) performed no examination of scale validity. A factor analysis of all 36 items in this version of the SERVQUAL instrument was performed, but managerial judgment was used to form the individual subscales and no quantitative data were provided.

ADMINISTRATION:
The scale was apparently self-administered by students but Boulding and colleagues (1993) provided no details. A high score on the scale suggests a respondent believes that professors of an institution are providing reliable instruction and assistance to the students.

MAJOR FINDINGS:
Boulding and colleagues (1993) describe two studies bearing on a behavioral process model. The second study involved the service quality scales. Among the many findings was that the **reliability** of the professors providing the education was the primary influence on overall quality perceptions.

REFERENCES:

Boulding, William, Ajay Kalra, Richard Staelin, and Valerie A. Zeithaml (1993), ''A Dynamic Process Model of Service Quality: From Expectations to Behavioral Intentions,'' *JMR*, 30 (February), 7-27.

———, Richard Staelin, Ajay Kalra, and Valerie A. Zeithaml (1992), ''Conceptualizing and Testing a Dynamic Process Model of Service Quality,'' Working paper No. 92-121. Cambridge, MA: Marketing Science Institute.

Parasuraman, A., Valerie A. Zeithaml, and Leonard L. Berry (1988), ''SERVQUAL: A Multiple-Item Scale for Measuring Customer Perceptions of Service Quality,'' *JR*, 64 (Spring), 12-40.

SCALE ITEMS: SERVICE QUALITY (RELIABILITY OF PROFESSORS)*

Directions: The following set of statements relate to your feelings about _____'s service. For each statement, please show the extent to which you believe _____ has the feature described by the statement. Circling a ''1'' means that you strongly disagree that _____ has that feature, and circling a ''7'' means that you strongly agree. You may circle any of the numbers in the middle that show how strong your feelings are. There are no right or wrong answers—all we are interested in is a number that best shows your perceptions about _____'s service.

Strongly disagree						Strongly agree
1	2	3	4	5	6	7

1. Professors and teaching assistants grade fairly and accurately.
2. Courses are taught well.
3. The staff ensure that the MBA program runs smoothly.
4. Professors are organized and prepared for class.
5. When professors promise to be available during office hours, they are there to see students.
6. Professors have prior teaching experience before coming to this organization.

* These directions were not provided in the article but are assumed to be similar to what was actually used.

SCALE NAME: Service Quality (Responsiveness)

SCALE DESCRIPTION:

A four-item, seven-point, Likert-type scale measuring the degree to which a person thinks a service company's employees are helpful and responsive to customer needs. As described here, the scale relates to the Responsiveness dimension of the SERVQUAL instrument (Parasuraman, Zeithaml, and Berry 1988, 1991) but is not equivalent to it. Each dimension of the SERVQUAL measure is composed of the summated differences between expectation items and perceptual items, not just the latter as the scale described here is. Carman (1990) used several variations on the scale, as described subsequently.

SCALE ORIGIN:

The scale is a part of the larger SERVQUAL instrument described by Parasuraman, Zeithaml, and Berry (1988, 1991), which measures five separate dimensions of service quality. Considerable information is provided in those articles about the scale's conceptualization, development, and validation.

The version of the scale discussed by Parasuraman, Zeithaml, and Berry (1988) is the one followed to a great extent by Carman (1990). In the former's 1991 article some suggestions for changes to the scale were made. As far as the Responsiveness dimension is concerned, the revised version modified all the items by making them positive rather than negative in wording. Items 5 and 6 are original to Carman (1990).

SAMPLES:

Carman (1990) adjusted and tested the SERVQUAL instrument in four different service settings: a dental school patient clinic (n = 612), a business school placement center (n = 82), a tire store (n = 74), and an acute care hospital (n = 720). The scale used in the hospital setting warranted treatment as a different scale and therefore is written up separately (see #250, #251, #252, #253, #254, #255, and #263).

Parasuraman, Berry, and Zeithaml (1991) sent questionnaires to randomly chosen customers of five nationally known companies: one telephone company, two banks, and two insurance companies. A reminder postcard was sent two weeks after the initial mailing. The number of usable questionnaires ranged from 290 to 487 for the five companies. The total number of completed returns was **1936,** a 21% overall response rate. Managers in the companies reviewed the demographic profiles of the respondents and considered them to be representative of their customer populations.

RELIABILITY:

The following alphas were reported by Carman (1990) for the scale: **.64** (tire store), **.75** (placement center), and **.55** (dental clinic). The alphas reported by Parasuraman, Berry, and Zeithaml (1991) for the five companies ranged from .88 to .93. These alphas relate to the summated differences between

expectation items and perceptual items. The alpha for just the perceptions items was **.94** using the combined sample (Parasuraman 1993).

VALIDITY:

Carman factor analyzed the SERVQUAL data from each setting. In general, only items with loadings greater than .30 on the same factor in at least one setting were used to compose scales (Carman 1994). However, the sets of items used to compose the summated scales for each of the three settings were ultimately different on the basis of several factors. These variable results led Carman to conclude that the scale had problems with construct validity.

Parasuraman, Berry, and Zeithaml (1991) reported the results of several factor analyses using oblique rotations. With regard to the perception version of the scale using the combined samples, the items did *not* load on a single factor. As it is, the perception version of the scale is not unidimensional. The five items were apparently left as a group because their loadings were all greater than .50 in a factor analysis of the expectation scores.

ADMINISTRATION:

In Carman (1990), the instrument was self-administered by respondents after they received service. The scale was administered to customers in a mail-survey format by Parasuraman, Berry, and Zeithaml (1991). High scores on the perception version of the scale show that respondents think that employees of a specific service firm are very responsive to customer requests.

MAJOR FINDINGS:

The purpose of Carman's (1990) studies was to test the SERVQUAL instrument in a variety of service settings. Some modifications in wording were always found to be necessary. Moreover, testing of the data indicated that though a **responsiveness**-related dimension was found across settings, the items loading on that dimension were not stable.

Parasuraman, Berry, and Zeithaml (1991) conducted a study to refine their SERVQUAL scales and to examine the revised scales in five different customer samples. They also compared their results with those of others who had used the scales. When respondents were asked to divide 100 points among the five service quality dimensions on the basis of importance, for each of the five samples the result was the same: the **responsiveness** dimension was always was the second most important dimension.

COMMENTS:

Although this scale can be used by itself, it was designed to be used along with its companion perceptions version. For example, the perceptions version of item 1 would be something like ''Employees of excellent _____ companies will tell customers exactly when services will be performed.'' The developers also encourage researchers to measure all the dimensions to capture the domain of service quality fully.

For further discussion of theoretical and psychometric properties of the SERVQUAL instrument, see Parasuraman, Zeithaml, and Berry (1994), Cronin and Taylor (1994), and Teas (1994).

See also Teas (1993) for use of a two item version of the scale.

REFERENCES:

Carman, James M. (1990), "Consumer Perceptions of Service Quality: An Assessment of the SERVQUAL Dimensions," *JR*, 66 (Spring), 33-55.

_____ (1994), personal correspondence.

Cronin, J. Joseph, Jr. and Steven A. Taylor (1994), "SERVPERF Versus SERVQUAL: Reconciling Performance-Based and Perceptions-Minus-Expectations Measurement of Service Quality," *JM*, 58 (January), 124-31.

Parasuraman, A. (1993), personal correspondence.

_____, Leonard L. Berry, and Valarie A. Zeithaml (1991), "Refinement and Reassessment of the SERVQUAL Scale," *JR*, 67 (Winter), 420-50.

_____, Valerie A. Zeithaml, and Leonard L. Berry (1988), "SERVQUAL: A Multiple-Item Scale for Measuring Customer Perceptions of Service Quality," *JR*, 64 (Spring), 12-40.

_____, _____, and _____ (1994), "Reassessment of Expectations as a Comparison Standard in Measuring Service Quality: Implications for Further Research," *JM*, 58 (January), 111-24.

Teas, R. Kenneth (1993), "Expectations, Performance Evaluation, and Consumers' Perceptions of Quality," *JM*, 57 (October), 18-34.

_____ (1994), "Expectations as a Comparison Standard in Measuring Service Quality: An Assessment of a Reassessment," *JM*, 58 (January), 132-39.

SCALE ITEMS: SERVICE QUALITY (RESPONSIVENESS)*

Directions: The following set of statements relate to your feelings about _____'s service. For each statement, please show the extent to which you believe _____ has the feature described by the statement. Circling a "1" means that you strongly disagree that _____ has that feature, and circling a "7" means that you strongly agree. You may circle any of the numbers in the middle that show how strong your feelings are. There are no right or wrong answers—all we are interested in is a number that best shows your perceptions about _____'s service.

Strongly   Strongly
disagree   agree
1————2————3————4————5————6————7

1. _____ does not tell customers exactly when services will be performed. **(r)**
2. You do not receive prompt service from _____. **(r)**
3. Employees of _____ are not always willing to help customers. **(r)**

4. Employees of _____ are too busy to respond to customer requests promptly. **(r)**
5. The manual provided by the placement office is informative.
6. There is an adequate choice of interviews at the placement office.
7. Employees of _____ tell you exactly when services will be performed.
8. Employees of _____ give you prompt service.
9. Employees of _____ are always willing to help you.
10. Employees of _____ are never too busy to respond to your requests.

* The name of the specific service firm studied should be placed in the blanks. Items 1-4 were the form used by Parasuraman, Zeithaml, and Berry (1988), and the revised version of those items (7-10) were recommended in their 1991 article. Although not completely clear, it appears that statements similar to the following items were used in the three studies conducted by Carman (1990, 1994): 1 and 2 (tire store); 1, 2, 5, and 6 (placement center); and 2 and 4 (dental clinic).

SCALE NAME: Service Quality (Responsiveness of Professors)

SCALE DESCRIPTION:

A six-item, seven-point, Likert-type scale measuring the degree to which a person thinks the professors working for an educational institution are helpful to students.

SCALE ORIGIN:

The scale is original to Boulding and colleagues (1993) and is more fully described in Boulding and colleagues (1992). However, it is modeled on the SERVQUAL instrument (Parasuraman, Zeithaml, and Berry 1988), which measures five separate dimensions of service quality. The scale described here relates to the Responsiveness dimension of the SERVQUAL instrument but is not equivalent to it. Each dimension of the SERVQUAL measure is composed of the summated differences between expectation items and perceptual items, not just the latter as the scale described here is.

SAMPLES:

Boulding and colleagues (1993) collected data from **177** students of a business education institution. Participation was voluntary but was apparently stimulated to some extent by a lottery and cash prizes.

RELIABILITY:

An alpha of **.60** was reported for the scale (Boulding et al. 1992).

VALIDITY:

Boulding and colleagues (1993) performed no examination of scale validity. A factor analysis of all 36 items in this version of the SERVQUAL instrument was performed, but managerial judgment was used to form the individual subscales and no quantitative data were provided.

ADMINISTRATION:

The scale was apparently self-administered by students, but Boulding and colleagues (1993) provided no the details. A high score on the scale suggests a respondent believes that professors of an institution are helpful in providing assistance to the students.

MAJOR FINDINGS:

Boulding and colleagues (1993) describe two studies bearing on a behavioral process model. The second study involved the service quality scales. Among the many findings was that the **responsiveness** of the professors providing the education was *not* a primary influence on overall quality perceptions.

REFERENCES:

Boulding, William, Ajay Kalra, Richard Staelin, and Valerie A. Zeithaml (1993), "A Dynamic Process Model of Service Quality: From Expectations to Behavioral Intentions," *JMR*, 30 (February), 7-27.

_____, Richard Staelin, Ajay Kalra, and Valerie A. Zeithaml (1992), "Conceptualizing and Testing a Dynamic Process Model of Service Quality," Working paper No. 92-121. Cambridge, MA: Marketing Science Institute.

Parasuraman, A., Valerie A. Zeithaml, and Leonard L. Berry (1988), "SERVQUAL: A Multiple-Item Scale for Measuring Customer Perceptions of Service Quality," *JR*, 64 (Spring), 12-40.

SCALE ITEMS: SERVICE QUALITY (RESPONSIVENESS OF PROFESSORS)*

Directions: The following set of statements relate to your feelings about _____'s service. For each statement, please show the extent to which you believe _____ has the feature described by the statement. Circling a "1" means that you strongly disagree that _____ has that feature, and circling a "7" means that you strongly agree. You may circle any of the numbers in the middle that show how strong your feelings are. There are no right or wrong answers—all we are interested in is a number that best shows your perceptions about _____'s service.

```
Strongly                                                    Strongly
disagree                                                      agree
   1————————2————————3————————4————————5————————6————————7
```

1. Professors help students with course work.
2. Professors hand out lecture notes each class session.
3. Professors provide individual advice if students are interested in exploring areas of further interest.
4. Professors require that students attend class.
5. Professors respond to students requests promptly.
6. Professors answer student questions completely and accurately during the same class session.

* These directions were not provided in the article but are assumed to be similar to what was actually used.

SCALE NAME: Service Quality (Security)

SCALE DESCRIPTION:

A seven-point, Likert-type scale that has been used with a variable number of items and is purported to measure the degree to which a person feels secure in doing business with an organization and its employees.

SCALE ORIGIN:

The version of the scale described here is original to Carman (1990), though two of the items come from scale constructed by Parasuraman, Zeithaml, and Berry (1988) to measure the assurance dimension of service quality. Items 3-5 are original to Carman (1990).

SAMPLES:

Carman (1990) adjusted and tested the SERVQUAL instrument in four different service settings. The two samples relevant to this scale were a dental school patient clinic (n = **612**) and a business school placement center (n = 82).

RELIABILITY:

Carman (1990) reported alphas of **.71** and **.87** for use of the scale in the placement center and dental clinic settings, respectively.

VALIDITY:

Carman factor analyzed the SERVQUAL data from each setting. Only items with loadings greater than .30 on the same factor in at least one setting were used to compose scales (Carman 1994). However, the sets of items used to compose the summated scales for each of the settings were ultimately different on the basis of several factors. These variable results led him to conclude that it had problems with construct validity.

ADMINISTRATION:

The SERVQUAL instrument was self-administered by respondents after they received service (Carman 1990). High scores on the perception version of the scale show that respondents think that employees of a service firm are very attentive and understanding of customer needs.

MAJOR FINDINGS:

The purpose of Carman's (1990) studies was to test the SERVQUAL instrument in a variety of service settings. Some modifications in wording were always found to be necessary. A **security**-related dimension was found in at least three of the settings; however, the items composing the scales in the various settings were very different.

REFERENCES:

Carman, James M. (1990), ''Consumer Perceptions of Service Quality: An Assessment of the SERVQUAL Dimensions,'' *JR*, 66 (Spring), 33-55.

—————— (1994), personal correspondence.

Parasuraman, A., Valerie A. Zeithaml, and Leonard L. Berry (1988), ''SERV-QUAL: A Multiple-Item Scale for Measuring Customer Perceptions of Service Quality,'' *JR*, 64 (Spring), 12-40.

SCALE ITEMS: SERVICE QUALITY (SECURITY)*

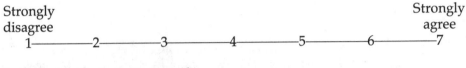

Strongly
disagree

Strongly
agree

1————2————3————4————5————6————7

1. You can trust employees of _____.
2. You feel safe in your transactions with _____.
3. The dental clinic is available for emergencies.
4. The dental clinic is responsive to complaints.
5. The dental clinic has good infection control practices.

* The name of the specific service company being studied should be placed in the blanks. Statements similar to these were used in the dental clinic study by Carman (1990, 1994), and in the placement center study, he used only items 1 and 2.

SCALE NAME: Service Quality (Tangibles)

SCALE DESCRIPTION:

A four-item, seven-point, Likert-type scale measuring the degree to which a person thinks the material and human aspects of a service company are visually appealing. As described here, the scale relates to the Tangibles dimension of the SERVQUAL instrument (Parasuraman, Zeithaml, and Berry 1988, 1991) but is not equivalent to it. Each dimension of the SERVQUAL measure is composed of the summated differences between expectation items and perceptual items, not just the latter as the scale described here is. Carman (1990) used several variations on the scale, as described subsequently.

SCALE ORIGIN:

The scale is a part of the larger SERVQUAL instrument described by Parasuraman, Zeithaml, and Berry (1988, 1991), which measures five separate dimensions of service quality. Considerable information is provided in those articles about the scale's conceptualization, development, and validation.

The version of the scale discussed by Parasuraman, Zeithaml, and Berry (1988) was followed to a great extent by Carman (1990). In the former's 1991 article some suggestions for changes to the scale were made. As far as the Tangibles dimension is concerned, the revised version replaced one item with another item and made slight modifications in wording of two other items.

SAMPLES:

Carman (1990) adjusted and tested the SERVQUAL instrument in four different service settings: a dental school patient clinic (n = 612), a business school placement center (n = 82), a tire store (n = 74), and an acute care hospital (n = 720). The scale used in the hospital setting warranted treatment as a different scale and therefore is written up separately (see #250, #251, #252, #253, #254, #255, and #263).

Parasuraman, Berry, and Zeithaml (1991) sent questionnaires to randomly chosen customers of five nationally known companies: one telephone company, two banks, and two insurance companies. A reminder postcard was sent two weeks after the initial mailing. The number of usable questionnaires ranged from 290 to 487 for the five companies. The total number of completed returns was **1936,** a 21% overall response rate. Managers in the companies reviewed the demographic profiles of the respondents and considered them to be representative of their customer populations.

RELIABILITY:

Carman (1990) reported the following alphas for the scale: **.70** (tire store), **.79** (placement center), and **.78** (dental clinic). The alphas reported by Parasuraman, Berry, and Zeithaml (1991) for the five companies ranged from .80 for one of the insurance companies to .86 for one of the banks. These alphas relate to the summated differences between expectation items and perceptual items. The alpha for just the perceptions items was **.86** using the combined sample (Parasuraman 1993).

VALIDITY:

Carman factor analyzed the SERVQUAL data from each setting. Only items with loadings greater than .30 on the same factor in at least one setting were used to compose scales (Carman 1994). However, the sets of items used to compose the summated scales for each of the three settings were ultimately different on the basis of several factors. These variable results led Carman to conclude that the scale had problems with construct validity.

Parasuraman, Berry, and Zeithaml (1991) reported the results of several factor analyses using oblique rotations. With regard to the perception version of the scale using the combined samples, items 1 and 2 had high loadings on one factor, whereas items 3 and 4 were split between that factor and another. The four items were apparently left in the scale because their loadings were all greater than .50 in a factor analysis of the expectation scores.

ADMINISTRATION:

In Carman (1990), the SERVQUAL instrument was self-administered by respondents after they received service. The scale was administered to customers in a mail-survey format by Parasuraman, Berry, and Zeithaml (1991). High scores on the perception version of the scale show that respondents think that a specific service firm has attractive-looking material assets associated with it.

MAJOR FINDINGS:

The purpose of Carman's (1990) studies was to test the SERVQUAL instrument in a variety of service settings. Some modifications in wording were always found to be necessary. Moreover, testing of the data indicated that though a **tangibles**-related dimension was found across settings, the items loading on that dimension were not stable.

Parasuraman, Berry, and Zeithaml (1991) conducted a study to refine their SERVQUAL scales and to examine the revised scales in five different customer samples. They also compared their results with those of others who had used the scales. With regard to **tangible aspects of service quality** the authors found that the gap scores were splitting into two subdimensions: one relating to employees/communication materials and the other facilities/equipment. The split seemed to be caused by differences in the structure of perceptions and not expectations.

COMMENTS:

Although this scale can be used by itself, it was designed to be used along with its companion expectations version. For example, the expectations version of item 1 would be something like ''Excellent _____ companies will have modern-looking equipment.'' The authors also encourage researchers to measure all the dimensions to capture the domain of service quality fully.

For further discussion of theoretical and psychometric properties of the SERVQUAL instrument, see Parasuraman, Zeithaml, and Berry (1994), Cronin and Taylor (1994), and Teas (1994).

See also Teas (1993) for use of a two item version of the scale.

REFERENCES:

Carman, James M. (1990), "Consumer Perceptions of Service Quality: An Assessment of the SERVQUAL Dimensions," *JR*, 66 (Spring), 33-55.

_____ (1994), personal correspondence.

Cronin, J. Joseph, Jr. and Steven A. Taylor (1994), "SERVPERF Versus SERVQUAL: Reconciling Performance-Based and Perceptions-Minus-Expectations Measurement of Service Quality," *JM*, 58 (January), 124-31.

Parasuraman, A. (1993), personal correspondence.

_____, Valerie A. Zeithaml, and Leonard L. Berry (1988), "SERVQUAL: A Multiple-Item Scale for Measuring Customer Perceptions of Service Quality," *JR*, 64 (Spring), 12-40.

_____, _____, and _____ (1994), "Reassessment of Expectations as a Comparison Standard in Measuring Service Quality: Implications for Further Research," *JM*, 58 (January), 111-24.

_____, Leonard L. Berry, and Valarie A. Zeithaml (1991), "Refinement and Reassessment of the SERVQUAL Scale," *JR*, 67 (Winter), 420-50.

Teas, R. Kenneth (1993), "Expectations, Performance Evaluation, and Consumers' Perceptions of Quality," *JM*, 57 (October), 18-34.

_____ (1994), "Expectations as a Comparison Standard in Measuring Service Quality: An Assessment of a Reassessment," *JM*, 58 (January), 132-39.

SCALE ITEMS: SERVICE QUALITY (TANGIBLES)*

Directions: The following set of statements relate to your feelings about _____'s service. For each statement, please show the extent to which you believe _____ has the feature described by the statement. Circling a "1" means that you strongly disagree that _____ has that feature, and circling a "7" means that you strongly agree. You may circle any of the numbers in the middle that show how strong your feelings are. There are no right or wrong answers—all we are interested in is a number that best shows your perceptions about _____'s service.

Strongly disagree
1———2———3———4———5———6———7
Strongly agree

1. _____ has up-to-date equipment.
2. _____'s physical facilities are visually appealing.
3. _____'s employees are well dressed and appear neat.
4. The appearance of the physical facilities of _____ is in keeping with the type of services provided.

5. _____ does not give you individual attention. **(r)**
6. Employees of _____ do not give you personal attention. **(r)**
7. _____ has modern-looking equipment.
8. _____ employees are neat-appearing.
9. Materials associated with the service (such as pamphlets or statements) are visually appealing at _____.

* The name of the specific service firm studied should be placed in the blanks. Items 1-4 were the form used by Parasuraman, Zeithaml, and Berry (1988), and items 2 and 7-9 were used in their 1991 article. Although not completely clear, it appears that statements similar to the following items were used in the three studies conducted by Carman (1990): 2-4 (tire store and placement center) and 2-6 (dental clinic).

SCALE NAME: Service Quality (Tangible Hospital Accommodations)

SCALE DESCRIPTION:

A four-item, five-point, Likert-type scale measuring the degree to which a person thinks a hospital and its rooms in particular are appealing and clean.

SCALE ORIGIN:

Although inspiration for the items definitely came from the SERVQUAL instrument developed by Parasuraman, Zeithaml, and Berry (1988), this scale was specifically developed by Carman (1990) for use with hospitals.

SAMPLES:

Carman (1990) adjusted and tested the SERVQUAL instrument in four different service settings. However, the specific items listed here were used only in the hospital study. Little is known about the respondents in that study except that data were collected from **720** patients.

RELIABILITY:

Carman (1990) reported an alpha of **.85**.

VALIDITY:

Carman (1990) factor analyzed the data for many scales related to hospital service quality. The four items composing the tangible accommodations quality scale loaded on the same factor at .55 or higher.

ADMINISTRATION:

The scale was part of a larger instrument apparently self-administered by respondents after they received service in the study by Carman (1990). High scores on the scale show that respondents think that the hospital and its rooms were well kept, whereas low scores would imply that they thought the hospital was dirty and untidy.

MAJOR FINDINGS:

The purpose of Carman's (1990) studies was to test the SERVQUAL instrument in a variety of service settings. Some modifications in wording were always found to be necessary, to the greatest extent in the hospital study. No findings specifically related to this scale were reported beyond what is noted here regarding some of its psychometric qualities. It was noted in general, however, that the dimensions of service quality described by Parasuraman, Zeithaml, and Berry (1988) may change depending on the context being studied and especially if the instrument must be greatly modified.

REFERENCES:

Carman, James M. (1990), ''Consumer Perceptions of Service Quality: An Assessment of the SERVQUAL Dimensions,'' *JR*, 66 (Spring), 33-55.

_____ (1993), personal correspondence.

Parasuraman, A., Valerie A. Zeithaml, and Leonard L. Berry (1988), ''SERV-QUAL: A Multiple-Item Scale for Measuring Customer Perceptions of Service Quality,'' *JR*, 64 (Spring), 12-40.

SCALE ITEMS: SERVICE QUALITY (TANGIBLE HOSPITAL ACCOMMODATIONS)*

Directions: The following set of statements relate to your feelings about _____'s service. For each statement, please show the extent to which you believe _____ has the feature described by the statement. Circling a ''1'' means that you strongly disagree that _____ has that feature, and circling a ''5'' means that you strongly agree. You may circle any of the numbers in the middle that show how strong your feelings are. There are no right or wrong answers—all we are interested in is a number that best shows your perceptions about _____'s service.

Strongly   Strongly
disagree   agree
    1————————2————————3————————4————————5

1. The hospital's physical facilities are visually appealing.
2. My bathroom was kept clean.
3. My room was kept clean.
4. The housekeeping staff were polite.

* These statements are constructed on the basis of descriptions in Carman (1990) and from personal correspondence (Carman 1993); statements similar to these were used.

SCALE NAME: Shop With Children

SCALE DESCRIPTION:

A three-item, five-point, Likert-type summated ratings scale measuring the degree to which a parent reports routinely taking a child along on shopping trips. This was referred to as *Coshopping* by Carlson and Grossbart (1988; Grossbart, Carlson, and Walsh 1991).

SCALE ORIGIN:

The use of these items as a multi-item measure appears to be original to Carlson and Grossbart (1988; Grossbart, Carlson, and Walsh 1991). They got ideas for some of the items, however, from the research of Ward and colleagues (1977).

SAMPLES:

The same data set is reported on in two articles by Carlson and Grossbart (1988; Grossbart, Carlson, and Walsh 1991). The survey instrument was distributed to mothers through students at three elementary schools of an unidentified U.S. city. The schools were chosen on a convenience basis but appeared to represent a variety of socioeconomic areas of the city. A $1 contribution was made to the PTO for each completed questionnaire returned by the children. Analysis was based on **451** completed questionnaires. Ninety-three percent of the responding mothers indicated that they were the primary person in the child's socialization.

RELIABILITY:

Carlson and Grossbart (1988; Grossbart, Carlson, and Walsh 1991) reported an alpha of **.79** and a beta of .62 for the scale.

VALIDITY:

Carlson and Grossbart (1988; Grossbart, Carlson, and Walsh 1991) reported no specific examination of scale validity. However, their findings did indicate that scores on this scale had a unspecified positive correlation with a measure of social desirability bias.

ADMINISTRATION:

The scale was self-administered along with many other measures in the questionnaire used by Carlson and Grossbart (1988; Grossbart, Carlson, and Walsh 1991). High scores on the scale mean that respondents report a high frequency of shopping with their children, whereas low scores imply that they do not shop with their children much at all.

MAJOR FINDINGS:

The authors (Carlson and Grossbart 1988; Grossbart, Carlson, and Walsh 1991) investigated the relationship between general parental socialization styles and children's consumer socialization. In a factor analysis of scale scores, scores on the **Shopping With Child** scale loaded on a factor described as the ''parent-child communication about consumption.'' On the basis of this, a significant difference was found in the degree of parent-child communication among several of the parental socialization styles examined.

REFERENCES:

Carlson, Les and Sanford Grossbart (1988), ''Parental Style and Consumer Socialization of Children,'' *JCR*, 15 (June), 77-94.

Grossbart, Sanford, Les Carlson, and Ann Walsh (1991), ''Consumer Socialization and Frequency of Shopping with Children,'' *JAMS*, 19 (Summer), 155-63.

Ward, Scott, Daniel B. Wackman, and Ellen Wartella (1977), *How Children Learn to Buy*. Beverly Hills, CA: Sage Publications.

SCALE ITEMS: SHOP WITH CHILDREN

Very seldom	Seldom	Sometimes	Often	Very often
1	2	3	4	5

1. When I go grocery shopping, I take my child.
2. When I go general family shopping, I take my child.
3. When I shop for my child, I take him/her along.

SCALE NAME: Shopper (Conservative)

SCALE DESCRIPTION:

A three-item, seven-point, Likert-type measure assessing a consumer's tendency to purchase just what he/she needs regardless of whether products are on sale. The scale was referred to as *marginal utility* by Lichtenstein, Netemeyer, and Burton (1990)

SCALE ORIGIN:

No indication is provided by Lichtenstein, Netemeyer, and Burton (1990) that the scale is anything other than original to their study.

SAMPLES:

The data for the main study by Lichtenstein, Netemeyer, and Burton (1990) came from a convenience sample of **350** nonstudent adults from a medium-size SMSA. The majority of the sample was female (57%) and married (69%). College graduates composed 40% of the sample. The median age of respondents was between 35 and 44 years of age, and household income was between $30,000 and $39,999.

RELIABILITY:

Lichtenstein, Netemeyer, and Burton (1990) reported the reliability (LISREL estimate) of the scale to be **.80.**

VALIDITY:

Lichtenstein, Netemeyer, and Burton (1990) reported no test of validity.

ADMINISTRATION:

Lichtenstein, Netemeyer, and Burton (1990) did not described the manner in which the scale was administered to the subjects in their study. However, it was clear that the scale was just one of many measures that composed the survey instrument. High scores on the scale indicate that respondents only buy the products they "need" regardless of whether there is a deal involved.

MAJOR FINDINGS:

The study by Lichtenstein, Netemeyer, and Burton (1990) examined the effect of both value consciousness and coupon involvement on coupon redemption behavior. One of the major findings was that coupon involvement had a much greater positive relationship with **conservative shopping** behavior (grocery products) than did value consciousness.

REFERENCE:

Lichtenstein, Donald R., Richard D. Netemeyer, and Scot Burton (1990), ''Distinguishing Coupon Proneness From Value Consciousness: An Acquisition-Transaction Utility Theory Perspective,'' *JM*, 54 (July), 54-67.

SCALE ITEMS: SHOPPER (CONSERVATIVE)

Strongly disagree	___ : ___ : ___ : ___ : ___ : ___ : ___	Strongly agree
	1 2 3 4 5 6 7	

1. Even when I find a real good sale on a grocery item, I am careful to buy only as much as I need.
2. When a grocery item is on sale, I often find myself buying more than I really need. **(r)**
3. I rarely buy more of an item than I can use, even if it is on sale.

SCALE NAME: Shopping Competitiveness

SCALE DESCRIPTION:

A five-item, seven-point, Likert-type measure assessing a consumer's perceived adeptness at and enjoyment of bargaining.

SCALE ORIGIN:

Lichtenstein, Netemeyer, and Burton (1990) provided no indication that the scale is anything other than original to their study.

SAMPLES:

The data for the main study by Lichtenstein, Netemeyer, and Burton (1990) came from a convenience sample of **350** nonstudent adults from a medium-size SMSA. The majority of the sample was female (57%) and married (69%). College graduates composed 40% of the sample. The median age of respondents was between 35 and 44 years of age and household income was between $30,000 and $39,999.

RELIABILITY:

Lichtenstein, Netemeyer, and Burton (1990) reported the reliability (LISREL estimate) of the scale to be **.63.**

VALIDITY:

Lichtenstein, Netemeyer, and Burton (1990) reported no test of validity.

ADMINISTRATION:

Lichtenstein, Netemeyer, and Burton (1990) did not describe the manner in which the scale was administered to the subjects in their study. However, it was clear that the scale was just one of many measures that composed the survey instrument. High scores on the scale indicate that respondents enjoy the process of bargaining as well as the result (paying lower prices).

MAJOR FINDINGS:

The study by Lichtenstein, Netemeyer, and Burton (1990) examined the effect of both value consciousness and coupon involvement on coupon redemption behavior. Both value consciousness and coupon involvement had positive correlations with **shopping competitiveness,** but the level of those correlations were not significantly different, as expected.

REFERENCE:

> Lichtenstein, Donald R., Richard D. Netemeyer, and Scot Burton (1990), "Distinguishing Coupon Proneness From Value Consciousness: An Acquisition-Transaction Utility Theory Perspective," *JM*, 54 (July), 54-67.

SCALE ITEMS: SHOPPING COMPETITIVENESS

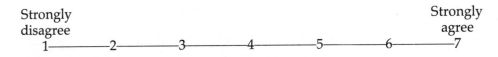

Strongly disagree
1————2————3————4————5————6————7
Strongly agree

1. I am better at shopping for bargains than most people.
2. I do not like to "haggle" with merchants to get lower prices. **(r)**
3. Knowing that I paid less for a product than someone else makes me feel good.
4. I like to bargain and "haggle" with merchants to get lower prices.
5. I would enjoy "haggling" with a car dealer to get a lower price.

SCALE NAME: Shopping Enjoyment

SCALE DESCRIPTION:

A three-item, five-point, Likert-type summated ratings scale measuring the enjoyment a consumer expresses receiving from the shopping experience. The scale was referred to as *emotional lift* by O'Guinn and Faber (1989; Faber and O'Guinn 1992).

SCALE ORIGIN:

The scale was apparently original to O'Guinn and Faber (1989).

SAMPLES:

Two samples were employed by O'Guinn and Faber (1989). One was of **386** completed responses (out of 808 questionnaires sent) from people who previously had written an organization that aided compulsive buyers. A second group was used for comparison purposes and was intended to represent the general population. Eight hundred questionnaires were mailed to people in three Illinois areas: Chicago, Springfield, and Bloomington-Normal. Two mailings produced a total of **250** completed survey forms. The database used in Faber and O'Guinn (1992) is basically the same except that sample 1 had a few more responses (n = 388) and the second survey benefited from a third mailing (n = 292).

RELIABILITY:

An alpha of **.89** was reported for this scale (O'Guinn and Faber 1989; Faber and O'Guinn 1992).

VALIDITY:

Beyond a factor analysis, which indicated that the items loaded together, no specific examination of scale validity was reported (O'Guinn and Faber 1992.)

ADMINISTRATION:

The scale was one of several self-administered measures used in mail survey instruments (O'Guinn and Faber 1989; Faber and O'Guinn 1992). High scores on the scale indicate that respondents believe that shopping is an fun activity, whereas low scores suggest that shopping does not bring them happiness or enjoyment.

MAJOR FINDINGS:

O'Guinn and Faber (1989) studied compulsive shopping. Their results showed that a sample of compulsive shoppers expressed a significantly greater amount of **shopping enjoyment** than did a general sample of consumers. Although using the same general database, Faber and O'Guinn (1992) reported on the development and testing of a scale to identify compulsive buyers.

REFERENCES:

Faber, Ronald J. and Thomas C. O'Guinn (1992), ''A Clinical Screener for Compulsive Buying,'' *JCR*, 19 (December), 459-69.
O'Guinn, Thomas C. and Ronald J. Faber (1989), ''Compulsive Buying: A Phenomenological Exploration,'' *JCR*, 16 (September), 147-57.

SCALE ITEMS: SHOPPING ENJOYMENT

Strongly disagree	Disagree	Neutral	Agree	Strongly agree
1	2	3	4	5

1. I shop because buying things makes me happy.
2. Shopping is fun.
3. I get a real ''high'' from shopping.

SCALE NAME: Shopping Enjoyment

SCALE DESCRIPTION:

A four-item, seven-point, Likert-type scale measuring the degree to which a consumer expresses enjoyment of shopping-related activities. The stated focus in each item is on shopping as part of prepurchase search activity rather than shopping as a recreational activity.

SCALE ORIGIN:

Marmorstein, Grewal, and Fishe (1992) provided no information to indicate that the scale was anything other than original to their study.

SAMPLES:

Marmorstein, Grewal, and Fishe (1992) describe two studies but report the alpha only for the first. The data used in that study were collected by survey forms handed out to customers in 17 retailers' stores during a four-month period in 1987. Customers were offered $5 to motivate them to complete the questionnaire. Usable forms were received from **235** customers, 57.6% of the number that had been distributed. The authors described the sample as ''very similar'' to the local population (a southeastern U.S. city), though no specifics were provided.

RELIABILITY:

Marmorstein, Grewal, and Fishe (1992). reported an alpha of **.82** for the scale.

VALIDITY:

Marmorstein, Grewal, and Fishe (1992) did not address the validity of the scale.

ADMINISTRATION:

The scale was included as part of a larger questionnaire that was distributed to shoppers in several appliance and electronics stores (Marmorstein, Grewal, and Fishe 1992). A high score on the scale indicates that a respondent enjoys doing a lot of shopping before making a purchase, whereas a low score suggests that a respondent dislikes shopping.

MAJOR FINDINGS:

In two studies, Marmorstein, Grewal, and Fishe (1992) examined the role of **shopping enjoyment** in the subjective value placed on time by consumers while they are engaged in price-comparison shopping. The findings in both studies provided strong evidence that consumers who **enjoy shopping** place a lower opportunity cost on such activity.

REFERENCE:

Marmorstein, Howard, Dhruv Grewal, and Raymond P. H. Fishe (1992), ''The Value of Time Spent in Price-Comparison Shopping: Survey and Experimental Evidence,'' *JCR*, 19 (June), 52-61.

SCALE ITEMS: SHOPPING ENJOYMENT

Strongly disagree	___ : ___ : ___ : ___ : ___ : ___ : ___	Strongly agree
	1 2 3 4 5 6 7	

1. I really enjoy gathering information before I make a purchase.
2. I really enjoy visiting stores before I make a purchase.
3. I really enjoy talking to salespeople before I make a purchase.
4. Overall, I really enjoy shopping before I make a purchase.

SCALE NAME: Shopping Enjoyment

SCALE DESCRIPTION:

A five-item, five-point, Likert-type summated ratings scale measuring the enduring tendency of a consumer to derive pleasure from shopping. The scale appears to be tapping into recreational shopping more than focused prepurchase search.

SCALE ORIGIN:

The scale used by Dawson, Bloch, and Ridgway (1990) was original to their study but was described as being based on work by Bellenger and Korgaonkar (1980).

SAMPLES:

The sample collected by Dawson, Bloch, and Ridgway (1990) came from a large arts and crafts market in a major West Coast city. Shoppers were approached over four summer days by trained survey administrators and asked to participate. Those who did participate were paid $1. The analysis was based on data from **278** respondents. The only significant difference noted between the sample and that of the surrounding SMSA was that the former contained more females.

RELIABILITY:

Dawson, Bloch, and Ridgway (1990) reported an alpha of **.81** for the scale.

VALIDITY:

Dawson, Bloch, and Ridgway (1990) provided no evidence of scale validity.

ADMINISTRATION:

The scale was self-administered as part of a larger survey instrument in the field study conducted by Dawson, Bloch, and Ridgway (1990). High scores on the scale suggest that respondents derive a lot of fun and pleasure from shopping, whereas low scores imply that they consider shopping to be unenjoyable and a hassle.

MAJOR FINDINGS:

Dawson, Bloch, and Ridgway (1990) investigated the role played by shopping motives in shaping the emotions triggered during a retail shopping experience. **Shopping enjoyment** was examined merely as a moderating variable given that it was possible for it to moderate the influence of shopping motives on transient emotions experienced during a retail visit. Very little evidence was found to support the potential influence of this variable on the model hypothesized.

REFERENCES:

Bellenger, Danny N. and Pradeep Korgaonkar (1980), ''Profiling the Recreational Shopper,'' *JR*, 56 (Fall), 77-92.

Dawson, Scott, Peter H. Bloch, and Nancy M. Ridgway (1990), ''Shopping Motives, Emotional States, and Retail Outcomes,'' *JR*, 66 (Winter), 408-27.

SCALE ITEMS: SHOPPING ENJOYMENT

Strongly disagree	Disagree	Neither agree nor disagree	Agree	Strongly agree
1	2	3	4	5

1. I consider shopping a big hassle.**(r)**
2. When traveling, I enjoy visiting new and interesting shops.
3. Shopping is generally a lot of fun for me.
4. I enjoy browsing for things even if I cannot buy them yet.
5. I often visit shopping malls or markets just for something to do, rather than to buy something specific.

SCALE NAME: Shopping Guilt

SCALE DESCRIPTION:

A three-item, five-point, Likert-type summated ratings scale measuring the frequency with which a consumer reports experiencing shame or remorse after shopping. The scale was referred to as *remorse* by O'Guinn and Faber (1989).

SCALE ORIGIN:

The scale was apparently original to O'Guinn and Faber (1989).

SAMPLES:

Two samples were employed by O'Guinn and Faber (1989). One was of **386** completed responses (out of 808 questionnaires sent) from people who previously had written an organization that aided compulsive buyers. A second group was used for comparison purposes and was intended to represent the general population. Eight hundred questionnaires were mailed to people in three Illinois areas: Chicago, Springfield, and Bloomington-Normal. Two mailings produced a total of **250** completed survey forms. The database used in Faber and O'Guinn (1992) is basically the same except that sample 1 had a few more responses (n = 388) and the second survey benefited from a third mailing (n = 292).

RELIABILITY:

O'Guinn and Faber (1989; Faber and O'Guinn 1992) reported an alpha of **.71** for the scale.

VALIDITY:

Beyond a factor analysis, which indicated that the items loaded together, no specific examination of scale validity was reported (O'Guinn and Faber 1989).

ADMINISTRATION:

The scale was one of several self-administered measures used in a mail survey instrument (O'Guinn and Faber 1989; Faber and O'Guinn 1992). High scores on the scale indicate that respondents frequently feel shame or remorse after shopping, whereas low scores suggest that shopping rarely makes them feel guilty.

MAJOR FINDINGS:

O'Guinn and Faber (1989) studied compulsive shopping. Their results showed that a sample of compulsive shoppers expressed a significantly greater amount of **shopping guilt** than did a general sample of consumers.

Although using the same general database, Faber and O'Guinn (1992) reported on the development and testing of a scale to identify compulsive buyers.

REFERENCES:

Faber, Ronald J. and Thomas C. O'Guinn (1992), "A Clinical Screener for Compulsive Buying," *JCR*, 19 (December), 459-69.
O'Guinn, Thomas C. and Ronald J. Faber (1989), "Compulsive Buying: A Phenomenological Exploration," *JCR*, 16 (September), 147-57.

SCALE ITEMS: SHOPPING GUILT*

Very infrequent	Infrequent	Sometimes	Frequent	Very frequent
1—————	———2—————	———3—————	———4—————	———5

How frequently have you experienced each of the following?
1. hid new purchases so others wouldn't know about them
2. felt others would be horrified if they knew of my spending habits
3. felt depressed after shopping

* Except for the items themselves, this is the assumed structure of the rest of the scale because it was not described in the article.

SCALE NAME: Shopping Intention

SCALE DESCRIPTION:

A three-item, seven-point, Likert-type scale measuring the self-reported likelihood that a consumer will shop at a specified store. Baker, Levy, and Grewal (1992) called the scale *willingness to buy*.

SCALE ORIGIN:

Although Baker, Levy, and Grewal (1992) state that the scale was developed by Dodds, Monroe, and Grewal (1991), there is only limited similarity between the two. The scale developed by the latter had five items related to the purchase of a product and had only one item similar to the scale used in Baker, Levy, and Grewal (1992). Therefore, it would appear that the scale is original to the study by Baker, Levy, and Grewal (1992), though they drew on the scale by Dodds, Monroe, and Grewal (1991) for inspiration.

SAMPLES:

The data analyzed by Baker, Levy, and Grewal (1992) came from an experiment using **147** undergraduate students. The study used a 2 (store ambient levels) × 2 (store social levels) between-subjects factorial design with 35-39 subjects per cell.

RELIABILITY:

Baker, Levy, and Grewal (1992) reported an alpha of **.86** for the scale.

VALIDITY:

Baker, Levy, and Grewal (1992) reported no examination of the scale's validity.

ADMINISTRATION:

The scale was self-administered by subjects as part of a questionnaire after exposure to experimental stimuli (Baker, Levy, and Grewal 1992). A high score on the scale indicates that a respondent is very willing to shop at a specified store, whereas a low score suggests that he/she has little or no intention of buying there.

MAJOR FINDINGS:

Baker, Levy, and Grewal (1992) examined the effects of two retail atmospheric factors, ambient and social cues, on respondents' pleasure, arousal, and **shopping intentions**. Overall, the results led the authors to conclude that store environment influences consumers' affective states, which in turn affect **shopping intentions**.

REFERENCES:

Baker, Julie, Michael Levy, and Dhruv Grewal (1992), ''An Experimental Approach to Making Retail Store Environmental Decisions,'' *JR*, 68 (Winter), 445-60.

Dodds, William B., Kent B. Monroe, and Dhruv Grewal (1991), ''The Effects of Price, Brand, and Store Information on Buyers' Product Evaluations,'' *JMR*, 28 (August), 307-19.

SCALE ITEMS: SHOPPING INTENTION

Strongly disagree	___ : ___ : ___ : ___ : ___ : ___ : ___	Strongly agree
	1 2 3 4 5 6 7	

1. The likelihood that I would shop in this store is high.
2. I would be willing to buy gifts in this store.
3. I would be willing to recommend this store to my friends.

SCALE NAME: Shopping Intention

SCALE DESCRIPTION:

A three-item, summated ratings scale measuring a person's willingness to shop at the store running an ad for a product (to which he/she has previously been exposed) if he/she was in the market for the advertised product.

SCALE ORIGIN:

Although it is not specifically stated, the scale apparently was developed by Biswas and Burton (1993).

SAMPLES:

Biswas and Burton (1993) reported on two studies in their article. In the first, data were collected from **392** undergraduate business students. Little more is said about the sample except that there was a nearly equal portion of each gender and they were randomly assigned to one of the 12 treatments. The second sample was composed of **303** nonstudents who were recruited by students in a marketing course. All of those in the sample were 18 years of age or older with a median of 40 years. A little more than half were female (56%) and the median household income was $35,000.

RELIABILITY:

Biswas and Burton (1993) reported alphas of **.90** and **.91** in their first and second studies, respectively.

VALIDITY:

Biswas and Burton (1993) reported no specific examination of the scale's validity.

ADMINISTRATION:

The scale was self-administered by subjects along with several other measures after exposure to experimental stimuli (Biswas and Burton 1993). High scores on the scale imply that respondents think it is very likely that they would shop at the store advertising a product if they were in the market for such a product.

MAJOR FINDINGS:

Biswas and Burton (1993) investigated the impact of three different price claims on various perceptions and intentions. Among the many findings was that **intentions to shop** at the store running the ad for the product search were higher when claims were made in the form of maximum savings or a range of possible savings versus a claim of minimum savings.

REFERENCE:

Biswas, Abhijit and Scot Burton (1993), ''Consumer Perceptions of Tensile Price Claims in Advertisements: An Assessment of Claim Types Across Different Discount Levels,'' *JAMS*, 21 (Summer), 217-29.

SCALE ITEMS: SHOPPING INTENTION*

1. If you were considering the purchase of a _____, how willing would you be to shop for a _____ at the store running this advertisement?

Definitely willing to shop	____ : ____ : ____ : ____ : ____ : ____ : ____	Definitely unwilling to shop **(r)**
	1 2 3 4 5 6 7	

2. If you were thinking about buying a _____, would you go to the advertiser's store?

Definitely would go	____ : ____ : ____ : ____ : ____ : ____ : ____	Definitely would not go **(r)**
	1 2 3 4 5 6 7	

3. What is the probability that you would shop for a _____ at the store running this ad if you were considering a _____ purchase?

Not probable at all	____ : ____ : ____ : ____ : ____ : ____ : ____	Very probable
	1 2 3 4 5 6 7	

* The name of the product category on sale goes in the blanks. Biswas and Burton (1993) used *35mm cameras*. Also, though the number of response alternatives was not specified, it was likely a seven-point scale.

SCALE NAME: Shopping Intention

SCALE DESCRIPTION:

A five-item, seven-point, Likert-type scale measuring the self-reported likelihood that a consumer will shop at a specified store with an emphasis on interaction with a particular clerk with which he/she has some familiarity.

SCALE ORIGIN:

The origin of the scale was not described by Swinyard (1993), but it appears to be original.

SAMPLES:

Little description was provided about the sample used by Swinyard (1993) in his experiment except to say that it was composed of **109** undergraduate business students. Another person besides the class instructor conducted the experiment, and students were monitored to ensure that they worked quietly and independently on their randomly assigned exercises.

RELIABILITY:

Swinyard (1993) reported an alpha of **.94** for the scale.

VALIDITY:

Swinyard (1993) reported no examination of the scale's validity.

ADMINISTRATION:

The scale was self-administered by subjects as part of a questionnaire after exposure to experimental stimuli (Swinyard 1993). A high score on the scale indicates that a respondent is very willing to shop at a specified store, whereas a low score suggests that one has little or no intention of spending more time in the store.

MAJOR FINDINGS:

Swinyard (1993) investigated the impact of mood and other factors on **shopping intentions**. Although mood was not found to have a significant main effect on **shopping intentions,** it did appear to play important roles in several interaction effects.

REFERENCE:

Swinyard, William R. (1993), ''The Effects of Mood, Involvement, and Quality of Store Experience on Shopping Intentions,'' *JCR*, 20 (September), 271-80.

SCALE ITEMS: SHOPPING INTENTION

Unlikely   ___ : ___ : ___ : ___ : ___ : ___ : ___   Likely

                     1   2   3   4   5   6   7

How likely or unlikely would you be to:
1. spend more time shopping in that department?
2. buy other items you need in the department?
3. spend more time shopping in the store?
4. let that clerk help with your other shopping?
5. make a purchase from that clerk?

SCALE NAME: Shopping Motivation (Experiential)

SCALE DESCRIPTION:

A six-item, seven-point scale measuring the degree to which the motivation for a consumer's trip to a retail location is related to social or recreational reasons rather than to product and purchase.

SCALE ORIGIN:

Although drawing on the shopping motivation typology proposed by Westbrook and Black (1985), this scale by Dawson, Bloch, and Ridgway (1990) is original.

SAMPLES:

The sample collected by Dawson, Bloch, and Ridgway (1990) came from a large arts and crafts market in a major West Coast city. Shoppers were approached over four summer days by trained survey administrators and asked to participate. Those who did participate were paid $1. The analysis was based on data from **278** respondents. The only significant difference noted between the sample and that of the surrounding SMSA was that the former contained more females.

RELIABILITY:

Dawson, Bloch, and Ridgway (1990) reported an alpha of **.72** for the scale.

VALIDITY:

Dawson, Bloch, and Ridgway (1990) performed an exploratory factor analysis on the items composing this scale as well as five other items composing a Product version of the scale. The items loaded highest on the appropriate factors, providing some evidence of unidimensionality for the scale and convergent and discriminant validity for the items.

ADMINISTRATION:

The scale was self-administered as part of a larger survey instrument in the field study conducted by Dawson, Bloch, and Ridgway (1990). High scores on the scale suggest that respondents' reasons for shopping at a store are very much experience-related, whereas low scores imply that they are motivated to shop for some other reason.

MAJOR FINDINGS:

Dawson, Bloch, and Ridgway (1990) investigated the role played by shopping motives in shaping the emotions triggered during a retail shopping experience. Among the many findings was that those shoppers with strong **experi-**

ence-related motives had higher pleasure and "arousal" during their shopping than did those with weak experiential motives.

REFERENCES:

Dawson, Scott, Peter H. Bloch, and Nancy M. Ridgway (1990), "Shopping Motives, Emotional States, and Retail Outcomes," *JR*, 66 (Winter), 408-27.

Westbrook, Robert A. and William C. Black (1980), "A Motivation-Based Shopper Typology," *JR*, 61 (Spring), 78-103.

SCALE ITEMS: SHOPPING MOTIVATION (EXPERIENTIAL)

DIRECTIONS: People visit [the market] for a variety of reasons. For each item listed below, please indicate how well it describes your reasons for visiting [the market] today.

Not at all _____ : _____ : _____ : _____ : _____ : _____ : _____ Very
descriptive   1   2   3   4   5   6   7   descriptive

1. To watch other people
2. To enjoy the crowds
3. To see and hear entertainment
4. To meet new people
5. To experience interesting sights, sounds, and smells
6. To get out of the house

SCALE NAME: Shopping Motivation (Product)

SCALE DESCRIPTION:

A five-item, seven-point scale measuring the degree to which the reasons a consumer makes a trip to a store are product related.

SCALE ORIGIN:

Although drawing on the shopping motivation typology proposed by Westbrook and Black (1985), this scale by Dawson, Bloch, and Ridgway (1990) is original.

SAMPLES:

The sample collected by Dawson, Bloch, and Ridgway (1990) came from a large arts and crafts market in a major West Coast city. Shoppers were approached over four summer days by trained survey administrators and asked to participate. Those who did participate were paid $1. The analysis was based on data from **278** respondents. The only significant difference noted between the sample and that of the surrounding SMSA was that the former contained more females.

RELIABILITY:

Dawson, Bloch, and Ridgway (1990) reported an alpha of **.69** for the scale.

VALIDITY:

Dawson, Bloch, and Ridgway (1990) performed an exploratory factor analysis on the items composing this scale as well as six other items composing an Experiential version of the scale. The items loaded highest on the appropriate factors, providing some evidence of unidimensionality for the scale and convergent and discriminant validity for the items.

ADMINISTRATION:

The scale was self-administered as part of a larger survey instrument in the field study conducted by Dawson, Bloch, and Ridgway (1990). High scores on the scale suggest that respondents' reasons for shopping at a store are very much product related, whereas low scores imply that they are shopping for some other reason.

MAJOR FINDINGS:

Dawson, Bloch, and Ridgway (1990) investigated the role played by shopping motives in shaping the emotions triggered during a retail shopping experience. Among the many findings was that those shoppers with strong **product-**

related motives experienced higher pleasure and "arousal" during their shopping than those with weak product motives.

COMMENTS:

The items in the scale may have to be modified somewhat depending on the particular retail situation being examined. As it is, the items are most appropriate for a market with arts, crafts, and foods and would not be appropriate if studying many types of shops located in malls (e.g., electronics, clothing, music).

REFERENCES:

Dawson, Scott, Peter H. Bloch, and Nancy M. Ridgway (1990), "Shopping Motives, Emotional States, and Retail Outcomes," *JR*, 66 (Winter), 408-27.
Westbrook, Robert A. and William C. Black (1980), "A Motivation-Based Shopper Typology," *JR*, 61 (Spring), 78-103.

SCALE ITEMS: SHOPPING MOTIVATION (PRODUCT)

DIRECTIONS: People visit [the market] for a variety of reasons. For each item listed below, please indicate how well it describes your reasons for visiting [the market] today.

Not at all   ____ : ____ : ____ : ____ : ____ : ____ : ____   Very
descriptive   1   2   3   4   5   6   7   descriptive

1. To find a variety of products
2. To find unique crafts or foods
3. To see new things
4. To find good prices
5. To keep up with new crafts or foods

SCALE NAME: Shyness

SCALE DESCRIPTION:

A three-item, five-point, summated ratings scale assessing the experience a person has had with shyness-related emotions. The directions and response scale can be worded so as to measure the *intensity* of the emotional state at the present time, or they can be adjusted to measure the *frequency* with which a person has experienced the emotional trait during some specified time period. One-word items were used in the study by Westbrook and Oliver (1991), and phrases based on those same items were used by Allen, Machleit, and Kleine (1992). This scale has also been referred to as *Shame*.

SCALE ORIGIN:

The measure was developed by Izard (1977) and is part of the Differential Emotions Scale (DES II). The instrument originally was designed as a measure of a person's emotional "state" at a particular point in time, but adjustments in the instrument's instructions enable the same items to be used in the assessment of emotional experiences as perceived over a longer time period. The latter was viewed by Izard as measure of one's emotional "trait" (1977, p. 125). Test-retest reliability for the shyness subscale of DES II was reported to be .83 (n = 63) and item-factor correlations were .73 and higher (Izard 1977, p. 126).

The items in DES II were composed of one word; in contrast, the items in DES III are phrases describing the target emotion. They were developed by Izard, although the first published validity testing was conducted by Kotsch, Gerbing, and Schwartz (1982). A study by Allen, Machleit, and Marine (1988) provides some insight to the factor structure of both DES II and III. With specific reference to shyness items, they tended to load on the same factor, especially when the items were grouped together on a questionnaire rather than being mixed with the items representing other emotions.

SAMPLES:

The data used by Allen, Machleit, and Kleine (1992) came from a stratified sample of people of diverse experience with blood donation. Nine hundred questionnaires were mailed, and **361** usable forms were returned. Given that all respondents previously had donated blood, limited information was known about them and allowed a comparison with nonrespondents. Respondents were a little older, less likely to be male, and more likely to be heavier donors than nonrespondents.

The data for the study conducted by Westbrook and Oliver (1991) came from a judgmental area sample. Convenience samples were taken at four shopping centers in a large northeastern city and were limited to persons who had purchased a new or used car in the past year. Complete and usable questionnaires were obtained from **125** respondents. A majority (74%) of the sample was male. The average respondent had an income in the $25,000–

$40,000 range and was 33 years of age. The frequency version of the scale was used in this study.

Two samples were used in the study by Oliver (1993), one examining satisfaction with cars and the other examining course satisfaction. The one involving cars is the same as the one described previously in Westbrook and Oliver (1991). The other sample was composed of students who volunteered from nine sections of a required marketing class. Usable questionnaires were provided by **178** students. The intensity version of the scale was used in this study.

RELIABILITY:

Westbrook and Oliver (1991) reported an alpha of **.82** for the scale. Allen, Machleit, and Kleine (1992; Allen 1994) calculated an alpha of **.81.** Oliver (1993) reported alphas of **.87** (n = 125) and **.81** (n = 178).

VALIDITY:

No specific examination of the scale's validity was reported in any of the studies.

ADMINISTRATION:

The scale was included with many other measures in the instrument used by Westbrook and Oliver (1991), Oliver (1993), and Allen, Machleit, and Kleine (1992). High scores on the frequency version of the scale suggest that a respondent perceives him/herself as having experienced the shyness-related emotional trait very often in some specified time period. A high score on the intensity version of the scale indicates that he/she is feeling very shy/shameful at the time of measurement.

MAJOR FINDINGS:

The study by Allen, Machleit, Kleine (1992) examined whether emotions effect behavior through attitudes or are better viewed as having a separate and distinct impact. Among the many findings was that **shyness** (DES III) plays a key role with behavior, at least with regard to donating blood. Specifically, a strong positive relationship was found between **shyness** involving the act of donating blood and the act of donating but for the most experienced blood donors (16+ donations in one year's time). Given previous findings and theory, the authors speculated that veteran donors may be especially motivated by low self-esteem and the shame aspect of **shyness**.

Oliver (1993) examined the separate roles of positive and negative affect, attribute performance, and disconfirmation for their impact on satisfaction. Negative affect was viewed as a function of several emotions, **shyness** being one of them. For both samples, negative affect as found to have direct influence on satisfaction.

Westbrook and Oliver (1991) studied the correspondence of the consumption emotional responses and satisfaction judgments that occur in the postpurchase period of the consumer decision process. **Shyness** had its highest correlation with contempt (r = .77) and its lowest correlation with joy (r = -.08). **Shyness** also was found to be an emotional trait linked to the cluster of consumers who had the lowest satisfaction in their car buying experiences.

REFERENCES:

Allen, Chris T. (1994), personal correspondence.

———, Karen A. Machleit, and Susan Schultz Kleine (1992), ''A Comparison of Attitudes and Emotions as Predictors of Behavior at Diverse Levels of Behavioral Experience,'' *JCR*, 18 (March), 493-504.

———, ———, and Susan S. Marine (1988), ''On Assessing the Emotionality of Advertising Via Izard's Differential Emotions Scale,'' in *Advances in Consumer Research*, Vol. 15, Michael J. Houston, ed. Provo, UT: Association for Consumer Research, 226-31.

Izard, Carroll E. (1977), *Human Emotions*. New York: Plenum Press.

Kotsch, William E., Davis W. Gerbing, and Lynne E. Schwartz (1982), ''The Construct Validity of the Differential Emotions Scale as Adapted for Children and Adolescents,'' in *Measuring Emotions in Infants and Children*, Carroll E. Izard, ed. New York: Cambridge University Press, 251-78.

Oliver, Richard L. (1993), ''Cognitive, Affective, and Attribute Bases of the Satisfaction Response,'' *JCR*, 20 (December), 418-30.

Westbrook, Robert A. and Richard L. Oliver (1991), ''The Dimensionality of Consumption Emotion Patterns and Consumer Satisfaction,'' *JCR*, 18 (June), 84-91.

SCALE ITEMS: SHYNESS

POSSIBLE DIRECTIONS FOR FREQUENCY VERSION OF SCALE: Below is a list of words that you can use to show how you feel. We want you to tell us how often you felt each of these feelings _____.* You can tell us how often you felt each of these feelings on the list by marking one of the numbers next to each question.

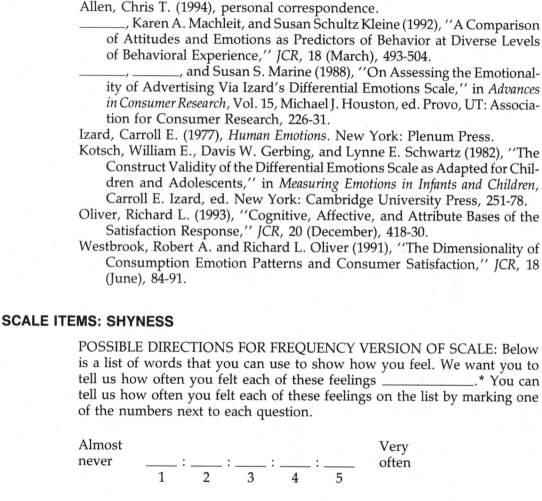

Almost never ____ : ____ : ____ : ____ : ____ Very often
　　　　　　　　 1　　2　　3　　4　　5

POSSIBLE DIRECTIONS FOR INTENSITY VERSION OF SCALE: Below is a list of words that you can use to show how you feel. We want you to tell us how strongly you feel. You can tell us how strongly you feel each of these feelings on the list by marking one of the numbers next to each question.

Very weak ____ : ____ : ____ : ____ : ____ Very strong
　　　　　　 1　　2　　3　　4　　5

DES II
1. sheepish
2. bashful
3. shy

DES III
1. feel ashamed to be seen, like you just want to disappear or get away from people
2. feel bashful, embarrassed
3. feel shy, like you want to hide

* The blank should be used to specify the time period of interest such as ''during the last week.''

SCALE NAME: Sleepiness

SCALE DESCRIPTION:

A three-item, five-point scale measuring the degree to which one reports a stimulus making him/her feel sluggish and drowsy. Mano and Oliver (1993) referred to the scale as *Boredom*.

SCALE ORIGIN:

Although not expressly indicated, the items used by Mano and Oliver (1993) appear to have been used first as a summated scale by Mano (1991). With 224 college students, the scale was reported to have an alpha of .87. Cluster and factor analyses grouped these three items together by themselves.

SAMPLES:

Data were collected by Mano and Oliver (1993) from **118** undergraduate business students attending a midwestern U.S. university.

RELIABILITY:

Mano and Oliver (1993) reported an alpha of **.80** for the scale.

VALIDITY:

Mano and Oliver (1993) did not specifically address the validity of the scale.

ADMINISTRATION:

The scale was part of a longer questionnaire self-administered by students in a classroom (Mano and Oliver 1993). A high score suggests that some stimulus has caused a respondent to feel sleepy.

MAJOR FINDINGS:

Mano and Oliver (1993) examined the dimensionality and causal structure of product evaluation, affect, and satisfaction. The **sleepiness** emotion was not found to be significantly different for subjects in the high- and low-involvement manipulations.

REFERENCES:

Mano, Haim (1991), "The Structure and Intensity of Emotional Experiences: Method and Context Convergence," *Multivariate Behavioral Research*, 26 (3), 389-411.

———— and Richard L. Oliver (1993), "Assessing the Dimensionality and Structure of the Consumption Experience: Evaluation, Feeling, and Satisfaction," *JCR*, 20 (December), 451-66.

SCALE ITEMS: SLEEPINESS

Not at all				Very much
1————————2————————3————————4————————5				

1. sleepiness
2. sluggish
3. drowsy

SCALE NAME: Social Desirability Bias (Marlowe-Crowne)

SCALE DESCRIPTION:

A summated ratings scale purporting to measure the degree to which people describe themselves in socially acceptable terms in order to gain the approval of others. A 19-item, true-false version of the scale was employed by Carlson and Grossbart (1988; Grossbart, Carlson, and Walsh 1991). A ten-item, true-false version was used by Goldsmith and Hofacker (1991). A ten-item, five-point, Likert-type format was used by Richins and Dawson (1992). A 13-item, true-false version was used by Fisher (1993). See other uses of the scale by Raju (1980) and Westbrook (1980, 1987).

SCALE ORIGIN:

The scale was developed by Crowne and Marlowe (1960) by generating items related to behaviors that are culturally sanctioned but are unlikely to occur. Two sets of ten faculty and graduate student judges helped narrow an original inventory of 50 items down to the final set of 33. An internal consistency of .88 (K-R 20) was calculated for the scale using a sample of 10 male and 29 female undergraduates in an abnormal psychology class at Ohio State University. Their mean age was 24.4 years, with a range of 19 to 46 years. Thirty-one of these people completed the instrument a month later, and a test-retest correlation of .89 was calculated. Scores of those 31 students plus 81 others in a course on exceptional children were found to have a correlation of .35 (p < .01) with scores on the Edwards Social Desirability Scale. Considerable work was performed on correlating scale scores with MMPI variables. The authors interpret the findings as being ''more in accord with a definition of social desirability'' than the Edwards scale (1960, p. 354).

Examinations of short versions of the scale can be found in Ballard, Crino, and Reubenfeld (1988), Fraboni and Cooper (1989), Reynolds (1982), as well as Strahan and Gerbasi (1972).

SAMPLES:

Data in the study by Bagozzi and Warshaw (1990) were collected from undergraduate business students at two Canadian universities. Survey forms were filled out on three separate occasions, one week apart, with **240** complete sets being obtained. The **Social Desirability** scale was filled out only on the third occasion. Participation was required as part of the course requirements.

The same data set is reported on in two articles by Carlson and Grossbart (1988; Grossbart, Carlson, and Walsh 1991). The survey instrument was distributed to mothers through students at three elementary schools of an unidentified U.S. city. The schools were chosen on a convenience basis but appeared to represent a variety of socioeconomic areas of the city. A $1 contribution was made to the PTO for each completed questionnaire returned by the children. Analysis was based on **451** completed questionnaires. Ninety-three percent of the responding mothers indicated that they were the primary person in the child's socialization.

The scale was administered in one of two studies reported by Childers and colleagues (1985). The 106 subjects were described as being undergraduate students at a major midwestern university. The subjects were divided into two groups, one with **54** subjects and the other with **52**.

Three studies are reported on in the article by Fisher (1993), although only the third one makes use of the **social desirability bias** scale. Little is known about the sample used in that study except that it was composed of **75** male and female undergraduate students.

In Friedman and Churchill (1987) female graduate students were used as subjects in an experimental setting. A total of **396** students cooperated in the study. Females were used because they were expected to relate better to the female patients on the tape recordings to which they were to listen. Graduate students were used because they were assumed to be experienced enough to make the required judgments about physicians.

Several studies were reported in the article by Goldsmith and Hofacker (1991), and the social desirability scale was only used in Study 5. That study was composed of **70** undergraduate students in a marketing research class.

The study by Moore and colleagues (1985) was based on complete responses received over three time periods from **198** members of the University of South Carolina Consumer Panel. Comparison of the known characteristics of the respondents and the total 360 members of the panel did not indicate any significant response bias.

Several samples were used in the study reported by Richins (1983). All that is reported about the sample in which the Social Desirability Scale was administered was that it was composed of **93** college students.

Studies with four samples were described in the article by Richins and Dawson (1992), but the social desirability scale was used only in survey 1. Little is said about the sample except that the data came from a mail survey of people in a medium-sized northeastern U.S. city. The households were chosen randomly and sent a survey form, followed by a reminder letter and a second copy of the questionnaire two weeks later. The response rate was 36%, resulting in **144** usable questionnaires.

The scale was administered by Saxe and Weitz (1982) to salespeople in 48 firms representing a wide variety of sales positions. Usable responses were received from **191** salespeople.

The Social Desirability Scale was used only in one stage of the overall study reported by Unger and Kernan (1983). The scale was administered by three different people to a total of **169** undergraduate business students at Miami University and the University of Cincinnati (Unger 1981).

RELIABILITY:

The internal consistency of the scale was not reported in many of the studies in which it has been used. An alpha of **.71** was calculated for the scale by Bagozzi and Warshaw (1990; Bagozzi 1994). Childers and colleagues (1985) reported alphas of **.75** and **.77**. Moore and colleagues (1985) calculated a **.83** (Kuder-Richardson 20) for the scale. Alphas of **.71** and **.60** were reported for the modified versions of the scale used by Grossbart, Carlson, and Walsh (1991) and Goldsmith and Hofacker (1991), respectively. The short form used by Fisher (1993) was reported to have an alpha of **.69**. The 13-item version used by Richins and Dawson (1992) had an alpha of .70 (Richins 1994).

VALIDITY:

Grossbart, Carlson, and Walsh (1991) reported a beta of .50 for the modified version of the scale they used. Some evidence of the ten-item version's convergent validity was provided by Goldsmith and Hofacker (1991), who reported a significant positive correlation between the social desirability scale and a lie scale (Eysenck 1958).

No specific examination of the scale's validity was conducted in the other studies. However, as described in "Major Findings," the scale typically has been used to provide evidence of other scales' discriminant validity.

ADMINISTRATION:

The scale was self-administered in all the studies, along with other scales. Scores on the original version of the scale can range between 0 and 33. The higher the score on the scale, the more it appears a respondent tends to respond to questions in a manner he/she deems socially desirable; a low score implies the respondent is less likely to answer questions that way.

MAJOR FINDINGS:

The study by Bagozzi and Warshaw (1990) examined the pursuit of goals, planned behavior, and the role of "trying" in the context of weight-loss planning. **The social desirability bias** of several attitude scales used in the study were tested. None of the correlations were statistically significant (p.05). Thus it was concluded that subjects did not appear to be responding merely on the basis of **social desirability bias**.

Carlson and Grossbart (1988; Grossbart, Carlson, and Walsh 1991) investigated the relationship between general parental socialization styles and children's consumer socialization. **Social desirability bias** was not specifically focused on in the studied but was merely included as a covariate. It was found to be positively related to the Shopping With Child scale and negatively related to the Materialism scale.

Childers and colleagues (1985) examined several measures of visual/verbal mental imagery. The **social desirability** scale was used as one way to test the discriminant validity of the scales. None of them showed any evidence of significant social desirability bias.

The studies conducted by Fisher (1993) examined the extent to which indirect questioning could be used to reduce **social desirability bias** on self-report measures. Only one of his studies measured **social desirability bias** with the Marlowe-Crowne scale. Specifically, a short form suggested by Reynolds (1982) was used. The author concluded that indirect questions can be developed that are not substantially influenced by **social desirability bias**.

The purpose of the studies by Goldsmith and Hofacker (1991) was to provide evidence of an innovativeness scale's psychometric quality. One of the studies provided evidence of discriminant validity for the scale in that it had almost no correlation with the **social desirability** scale.

The purpose of the study by Friedman and Churchill (1987) was to examine how a physician's use of social power behaviors can be used to achieve maximum effectiveness, as judged by patients. Subjects listened to recorded conversations between a physician and a patient and were asked to imagine they were the latter. They then were asked to respond to the physician's behavior on a questionnaire. The **social desirability** scale was used merely to help validate the other scales constructed for the study. As an indication of discriminant validity, the former had low and insignificant correlations with multi-item scales measuring patient satisfaction with physician behavior, patient compliance with physician's recommendations, and potential consequences of poor treatment.

The influence of labeling ("helpful people like yourself") and dependency ("depend upon individual contributions") on potential donor attitudes was examined by Moore and colleagues (1985). The **social desirability** scale did not have significant correlations with any of the covariate or dependent measures used in the study.

The construction of two scales, assertiveness and aggressiveness, was the focus of the study by Richins (1983). The correlation between the **social desirability** scale and assertiveness and aggressiveness scales was **.13** (p > .10) and **−.28** (p < .01), respectively. Although the latter indicates statistical significance, the author downplayed its relevance.

The purpose of the multiple surveys conducted by Richins and Dawson (1992) was to construct a new measure of materialism. To examine the scale's discriminant validity, the association between materialism and **social desirability** was tested. Near-zero correlations were found between the two constructs as well as between **social desirability** and the materialism subscales (success, centrality, and happiness).

The purpose of the Saxe and Weitz (1982) study was to construct a scale for measuring a salesperson's customer orientation. Scores on the scale were not correlated with scores on the Marlowe-Crowne **Social Desirability** Scale. The lack of correlation provided some evidence of discriminant validity of the customer-orientation scale.

Unger and Kernan (1983) examined dimensions of the subjective leisure experience. The **social desirability** scale was used to help construct scales for measuring those dimensions. Six different dimensions were measured in six different situations. Although there was some evidence that **social desirability bias** might be present when using the scales, the bias appeared to be situation specific and not necessarily inherent in the scales themselves.

COMMENTS:

This scale typically is used when constructing scales for measuring particular constructs and not by itself. If the correlation between scores on the **social desirability** scale and another measure is high, it suggests the latter is measuring respondents' desire to answer in socially acceptable ways; if the correlation is low, it is evidence that the scale is relatively free of social desirability bias. Some caution in its use may be called for because it may not be unidimensional, as indicated by its low beta coefficient (Grossbart, Carlson, and Walsh 1991). Further validation is needed.

REFERENCES:

Bagozzi, Richard P. (1994), personal correspondence.

_____ and Paul R. Warshaw (1990), "Trying to Consume," *JCR*, 17 (September), 127-40.

Ballard, Rebecca, Michael D. Crino, and Stephen Rubenfeld (1988), "Social Desirability Response Bias and the Marlowe-Crowne Social Desirability Scale," Psychological Reports, 63 (August), 227-37.

Carlson, Les and Sanford Grossbart (1988), "Parental Style and Consumer Socialization of Children," *JCR*, 15 (June), 77-94.

Childers, Terry L., Michael J. Houston, and Susan E. Heckler (1985), "Measurement of Individual Differences in Visual Versus Verbal Information Processing," *JCR*, 12 (September), 125-34.

Crowne, Douglas P. and David Marlowe (1960), "A New Scale of Social Desirability Independent of Psychopathology," Journal of Consulting Psychology, 24 (August), 349-54.

Eysenck, Hans J. (1958), "A Short Questionnaire for the Measurement of Two Dimensions of Personality," *Journal of Applied Psychology*, 42, 14-17.

Fisher, Robert J. (1993), "Social Desirability Bias and the Validity of Indirect Questioning," *JCR*, 20 (September), 303-15.

Fraboni, Maryann and Douglas Cooper (1989), "Further Validation of Three Short Forms of the Marlowe-Crowne Scale of Social Desirability," *Psychological Reports*, 65 (2), 595-600.

Friedman, Margaret L. and Gilbert A. Churchill, Jr. (1987), "Using Consumer Perceptions and a Contingency Approach to Improve Health Care Delivery," *JCR*, 13 (March), 492-510.

Goldsmith, Ronald E. and Charles F. Hofacker (1991), "Measuring Consumer Innovativeness," *JAMS*, 19 (Summer), 209-221.

Grossbart, Sanford, Les Carlson, and Ann Walsh (1991), "Consumer Socialization and Frequency of Shopping with Children," *JAMS*, 19 (Summer), 155-63.

Moore, Ellen M., William O. Bearden, and Jesse E. Teel (1985), "Use of Labeling and Assertions of Dependency in Appeals for Consumer Support," *JCR*, 12 (June), 90-96.

Raju, P. S. (1980), "Optimum Stimulation Level: Its Relationship to Personality, Demographics, and Exploratory Behavior," *JCR*, 7 (December), 272-82.

Reynolds, William M. (1982), "Development of Reliable and Valid Short Forms of the Marlowe-Crowne Social Desirability Scale," *Journal of Clinical Psychology*, 38 (January), 119-25.

Richins, Marsha L. (1983), "An Analysis of Consumer Interaction Styles in the Marketplace," *JCR*, 10 (June), 73-82.

_____ (1994), personal correspondence.

_____ and Scott Dawson (1992), "A Consumer Values Orientation for Materialism and Its Measurement: Scale Development and Validation," *JCR*, 19 (December), 303-16.

Saxe, Robert and Barton A. Weitz (1982), "The SOCO Scale: A Measure of the Customer Orientation of Salespeople," *JMR*, 19 (August), 343-51.

Strahan, Robert and Kathleen Carrese Gerbasi (1972), "Short, Homogeneous Versions of the Marlowe-Crowne Social Desirability Scale," *Journal of Clinical Psychology*, 28 (April), 191-93.

Unger, Lynette S. (1981), "Measure Validation in the Leisure Domain," doctoral dissertation, University of Cincinnati.

_____ and Jerome B. Kernan (1983), "On the Meaning of Leisure: An Investigation of Some Determinants of the Subjective Experience," *JCR*, 9 (March), 381-91.

Westbrook, Robert A. (1980), "Intrapersonal Affective Influences on Consumer Satisfaction with Products," *JCR*, 7 (June), 49-54.

_____ (1987), "Product/Consumption-Based Affective Responses and Postpurchase Processes," *JMR*, 24 (August), 258-70.

SCALE ITEMS: SOCIAL DESIRABILITY BIAS (MARLOWE-CROWNE)* +

1. Before voting I thoroughly investigate the qualifications of all the candidates. **(T)**
2. I never hesitate to go out of my way to help someone in trouble. **(T)**
3. It is sometimes hard for me to go on with my work if I am not encouraged. **(F)**
4. I have never intensely disliked anyone. **(T)**
5. n occasion I have had doubts about my ability to succeed in life. **(F)**
6. I sometimes feel resentful when I don't get my way. **(F)**
7. I am always careful about my manner of dress. **(T)**
8. My table manners at home are as good as when I eat out in a restaurant. **(T)**
9. If I could get into a movie without paying and be sure I was not seen I would probably do it. **(F)**
10. On a few occasions, I have given up doing something because I thought too little of my ability. **(F)**
11. I like gossip at times. **(F)**
12. There have been times when I felt like rebelling against people in authority even though I knew they were right. **(F)**
13. No matter who I'm talking to, I'm always a good listener. **(T)**
14. I can remember "playing sick" to get out of something. **(F)**
15. There have been occasions when I took advantage of someone. **(F)**
16. I'm always willing to admit it when I've made a mistake. **(T)**
17. I always try to practice what I preach. **(T)**
18. I don't find it particularly difficult to get along with loud mouthed, obnoxious people. **(T)**
19. I sometimes try to get even rather than forgive and forget. **(F)**
20. When I don't know something I don't at all mind admitting it. **(T)**
21. I am always courteous, even to people who are disagreeable. **(T)**
22. At times I have really insisted on having things my way. **(F)**
23. There have been occasions when I felt like smashing things. **(F)**
24. I would never think of letting someone else be punished for my wrongdoings. **(T)**

25. I never resent being asked to return a favor. **(T)**
26. I have never been irked when people expressed ideas very different from my own. **(T)**
27. I never make a long trip without checking the safety of my car. **(T)**
28. There have been times when I was quite jealous of the good fortune of others. **(F)**
29. I have almost never felt the urge to tell someone off. **(T)**
30. I am sometimes irritated by people who ask favors of me. **(F)**
31. I have never felt that I was punished without cause. **(T)**
32. I sometimes think when people have a misfortune they only got what they deserved. **(F)**
33. I have never deliberately said something that hurt someone's feelings. **(T)**

* Respondents should receive a point each time they answer in a socially desirable manner. Social desirability is indicated if respondents answer as indicated at the end of each item. For example, if a respondent answers "True" to item 1, then that is considered to be answering in a socially desirable manner.

+ Carlson and Grossbart (1988; Grossbart, Carlson, and Walsh 1991) used items 1-19. Goldsmith and Hofacker (1991) used the ten-item short form composed of items 11, 15-17, 19, 22, 23, 25, 26, and 33. Although not explicitly described by Richins and Dawson (1992), it appears from other information that they used items 6-8, 12, 16, 19, 21, 26, 30, and 33. Fisher (1993) used the 13-item short form composed of items 3, 6, 10, 12, 13, 15, 16, 19, 21, 26, 28, 30, and 33.

SCALE NAME: Social Position (Personal)

SCALE DESCRIPTION:

A three-item, nine-point, summated ratings scale measuring a person's socio-economic position on the basis of the self-reported "facts": dwelling area, family income, and education.

SCALE ORIGIN:

The scale appears to be original to the study by Dickson and MacLachlan (1990), although inspiration for the scale may have come from Dickson and Albaum (1977).

SAMPLES:

The sample used by Dickson and MacLachlan (1990) came from census tracts surrounding two test stores in Tacoma, Washington. Blocks judged to be composed of either lower or lower-middle class people were put into one group; blocks of upper-middle and upper-class people were assigned to another group. A probability sample was then taken so that those selected generally mirrored the social class makeup of the country. Complete in-home interviews were conducted with **234** people, but the factor analyses were done with data from 161 people.

RELIABILITY:

Using a sample size of 221, Dickson and MacLachlan (1990) reported an alpha of **.596** for the scale.

VALIDITY:

Dickson and MacLachlan (1990) reported no information regarding the scale's validity.

ADMINISTRATION:

The scale was administered along with many other questions by personal interviewers in respondents' homes (Dickson and MacLachlan 1990). The potential range of scores was 4–27, with high scores suggesting that a respondent has high socioeconomic status. The mean score on the scale was 14.4, with a standard deviation of 6.3.

MAJOR FINDINGS:

The purpose of the study by Dickson and MacLachlan (1990) was to determine if the "social distance" between one's own social class and that perceived of those who patronize a particular store would predict store choice. The absolute difference between a respondent's own **social position** and his/her score on a similar measure of a store's clientele produced the "social distance" measure. The data indicated that social distance plays a role in predicting shopping behavior because shoppers avoided stores perceived to attract shoppers of a different social class.

COMMENTS:

Although the scale appeared to have some validity given that the results confirmed expectations, the sensitivity of the scale could be improved if its reliability were increased.

REFERENCES:

Dickson, John P. and Gerald Albaum (1977), "A Method for Developing Tailor-made Semantic Differentials for Specific Marketing Content Areas," *JMR*, 14 (February), 87-91.

_____, Douglas L. MacLachlan (1990), "Social Distance and Shopping Behavior," *JAMS*, 18 (Spring), 153-61.

SCALE ITEMS: SOCIAL POSITION (PERSONAL)

1 = extremely
2 = quite
3 = slightly
4 = neutral
5 = slightly
6 = quite
7 = extremely

Dwelling area lower-class area	___ : ___ : ___ : ___ : ___ : ___ : ___ : ___ : ___ 1 2 3 4 5 6 7 8 9	Higher-class area
Family income under $10,000	___ : ___ : ___ : ___ : ___ : ___ : ___ : ___ : ___ 1 2 3 4 5 6 7 8 9	$50,000 or over
Education 12 or fewer years	___ : ___ : ___ : ___ : ___ : ___ : ___ : ___ : ___ 1 2 3 4 5 6 7 8 9	Graduate work

SCALE NAME: Social Position (Store)

SCALE DESCRIPTION:

A scale composed of four bipolar adjectives in a seven-point response format measuring a consumer's perception of a store's social status on the basis of the occupation, dwelling area, family income, and education of who is thought to shop there.

SCALE ORIGIN:

The scale appears to be original to the study by Dickson and MacLachlan (1990) but drew on work done previously by Dickson and Albaum (1977).

SAMPLES:

The sample used by Dickson and MacLachlan (1990) came from census tracts surrounding two test stores in Tacoma, Washington. Blocks judged to be composed of either lower or lower-middle class people were put into one group; blocks of upper-middle and upper-class people were assigned to another group. A probability sample then was taken so that those selected generally mirrored the social class makeup of the country. Complete in-home interviews were conducted with 234 people, but the factor analyses involving the scale were done with data from 161 people.

RELIABILITY:

Dickson and MacLachlan (1990) reported alphas of .702 (n = 206) and .74 (n = 211) for the scale as used with regard to the Kmart and Nordstrom stores, respectively.

VALIDITY:

The only information regarding the scale's validity reported by Dickson and MacLachlan (1990) came from the factor analyses conducted for both a Kmart store and a Nordstrom store. In both cases the items for this scale loaded most heavily (.50) on one factor and had low loadings (s.20) on the other factors.

ADMINISTRATION:

The scale was administered along with many other questions by personal interviewers in respondents' homes (Dickson and MacLachlan 1990). The potential range of scores was 4–28, with low scores suggesting that a store is patronized by people of high socioeconomic status. The mean score on the scale was 21.7, with a standard deviation of 3.6 for the Kmart store and 10.3 with a standard deviation of 3.8 for the Nordstrom store.

MAJOR FINDINGS:

The purpose of the study by Dickson and MacLachlan (1990) was to determine if the "social distance" between one's own social class and that perceived of those who patronize a particular store would predict store choice. The absolute difference between a person's own socioeconomic status and the **social position** perceived of a store produced the "social distance" measure. The data indicated that social distance plays a role in predicting shopping behavior because shoppers avoided stores perceived to attract shoppers of a different social class.

REFERENCES:

Dickson, John P. and Gerald Albaum (1977), "A Method for Developing Tailor-made Semantic Differentials for Specific Marketing Content Areas," *JMR*, 14 (February), 87-91.

_____, Douglas L. MacLachlan (1990), "Social Distance and Shopping Behavior," *JAMS*, 18 (Spring), 153-61.

SCALE ITEMS: SOCIAL POSITION (STORE)

1 = extremely
2 = quite
3 = slightly
4 = neutral
5 = slightly
6 = quite
7 = extremely

Attracts mostly blue-collar families
___ : ___ : ___ : ___ : ___ : ___ : ___
1   2   3   4   5   6   7
Attracts mostly managerial/ professional families **(r)**

Attracts mostly university educated families
___ : ___ : ___ : ___ : ___ : ___ : ___
1   2   3   4   5   6   7
Attracts mostly high school educated families

Most customers' family incomes are under $10,000
___ : ___ : ___ : ___ : ___ : ___ : ___
1   2   3   4   5   6   7
Most customers' family incomes are over $35,000 **(r)**

Customers live mostly in working-class neighborhoods
___ : ___ : ___ : ___ : ___ : ___ : ___
1   2   3   4   5   6   7
Customers live mostly in wealthy neighborhoods **(r)**

SCALE NAME: Social Values

SCALE DESCRIPTION:

A three-item, six-point, summated ratings scale measuring the degree to which a person places importance on socially related values such as security, belongingness, and respectability in his/her life.

SCALE ORIGIN:

The summated scale is apparently original to Corfman, Lehmann, and Narayanan (1991), but the items themselves come from the List of Values (LOV) developed by Kahle (1983). Nine values composed LOV, but the analysis conducted by Corfman, Lehmann, and Narayanan (1991) indicated that the three values specified here were tapping into the same factor.

SAMPLES:

Corfman, Lehmann, and Narayanan (1991) collected data using a self-administered questionnaire. Subjects were described as being initially contacted in person or by mail on an "intercept basis." Completed surveys were received from **735** respondents, mostly from the northeastern part of the United States. A range of values for several demographic characteristics were represented in the sample such that the authors said "the aggregate distribution closely matched that of the U.S. population" (p. 191).

RELIABILITY:

Corfman, Lehmann, and Narayanan (1991) reported an alpha of **.72** for the scale.

VALIDITY:

Corfman, Lehmann, and Narayanan (1991) factor analyzed the items composing LOV and settled on a three-factor solution that accounted for 64% of the variance. The items composing this scale all had high loadings on the first factor, providing some evidence of the scale's unidimensionality.

ADMINISTRATION:

The scale was part of a larger self-administered survey instrument used by Corfman, Lehmann, and Narayanan (1991). High scores on the scale indicate that social values are very important to a respondent, whereas low scores suggest that such values are not very important, at least not as important as other values.

MAJOR FINDINGS:

Corfman, Lehmann, and Narayanan (1991) examined the relationships among consumer utility, values, and ownership of durable products. Ownership was viewed as a function of a product's utility as well as a consumer's income and age. Utility was viewed as a function of a consumer's values and ownership of a product. The findings showed that **social values** had a negative relationship with the utility of sports, exercise, and luxury products.

COMMENTS:

A more rigorous analysis of this scale's psychometric quality is presented by Homer and Kahle (1988).

REFERENCES:

Corfman, Kim P., Donald R. Lehmann, and Sunder Narayanan (1991), ''Values, Utility, and Ownership: Modeling the Relationships for Consumer Durables,'' *JR*, 67 (Summer), 184-204.

Homer, Pamela M. and Lynn R. Kahle (1988), ''A Structural Equation Test of the Value-Attitude-Behavior Hierarchy,'' *Journal of Personality and Social Psychology*, 54 (4), 638-46.

Kahle, Lynn R.,ed. (1983), *Social Values and Social Change*. New York: Praeger Publishers.

SCALE ITEMS: SOCIAL VALUES*

Not very important	___ : ___ : ___ : ___ : ___ : ___	Very important
	1 2 3 4 5 6	

1. security
2. sense of belonging
3. being well-respected

* The anchors used for the scale were not specified in the article but would appear to have been something like those used here.

SCALE NAME: Store Conveniences (Neatness)

SCALE DESCRIPTION:

A scale composed of three bipolar adjectives in a seven-point response format measuring the degree to which a consumer perceives a store to be organized neatly so that merchandise can be found easily. The scale was referred to by Dickson and MacLachlan (1990) as *Store Environment*.

SCALE ORIGIN:

The items appear to be have been used first as a summated scale by Dickson and MacLachlan (1990), but the items themselves came from the study by Dickson and Albaum (1977). A factor analysis in the latter study indicated for both a discount store and a supermarket that these items loaded on the same factor.

SAMPLES:

The sample used by Dickson and MacLachlan (1990) came from census tracts surrounding two test stores in Tacoma, Washington. Blocks judged to be composed of either lower or lower-middle class people were put into one group; blocks of upper-middle and upper-class people were assigned to another group. A probability sample then was taken so that those selected generally mirrored the social class makeup of the country. Complete in-home interviews were conducted with 234 people, but the factor analyses involving the scale were done with data from 161 people.

RELIABILITY:

Dickson and MacLachlan (1990) reported alphas of .743 (n = 215) and .585 (n = 221) for the scale as used with regard to the Kmart and Nordstrom stores, respectively.

VALIDITY:

The only information regarding the scale's validity reported by Dickson and MacLachlan (1990) came from the factor analyses conducted for both a Kmart store and a Nordstrom store. In both cases the items for this scale loaded most heavily (> .50) on one factor and had low loadings (s.30) on the other factors.

ADMINISTRATION:

The scale was administered along with many other questions by personal interviewers in respondents' homes (Dickson and MacLachlan 1990). The potential range of scores was from 3 to 21, with high scores suggesting that a store is viewed as being messy and having hard-to-find merchandise. The mean score on the scale was 13.1, with a standard deviation of 4.3 for the Kmart store and 7.7 with a standard deviation of 3.2 for the Nordstrom store.

MAJOR FINDINGS:

The purpose of the study by Dickson and MacLachlan (1990) was to determine if the "social distance" between one's own social class and that perceived of those who patronize a particular store would predict store choice. The data indicated that social distance plays a role in predicting shopping behavior because shoppers avoided stores perceived to attract shoppers of a different social class. However, **store conveniences** in the form of the "neatness" scale only was a significant predictor of reported shopping behavior for the Kmart store, not for the Nordstrom store.

REFERENCES:

Dickson, John P. and Gerald Albaum (1977), "A Method for Developing Tailor-made Semantic Differentials for Specific Marketing Content Areas," *JMR*, 14 (February), 87-91.

_____, Douglas L. MacLachlan (1990), "Social Distance and Shopping Behavior," *JAMS*, 18 (Spring), 153-61.

SCALE ITEMS: STORE CONVENIENCES (NEATNESS)

1 = extremely
2 = quite
3 = slightly
4 = neutral
5 = slightly
6 = quite
7 = extremely

Hard to find items you want ___ : ___ : ___ : ___ : ___ : ___ : ___ Easy to find items you want **(r)**
1   2   3   4   5   6   7

Messy ___ : ___ : ___ : ___ : ___ : ___ : ___ Neat **(r)**
1   2   3   4   5   6   7

Crammed merchandise ___ : ___ : ___ : ___ : ___ : ___ : ___ Well-spaced merchandise **(r)**
1   2   3   4   5   6   7

SCALE NAME: Store Conveniences (Personnel & Services)

SCALE DESCRIPTION:

A scale composed of six bipolar adjectives in a seven-point response format measuring the degree to which a consumer perceives a store to have helpful employees and service. The scale was referred to by Dickson and MacLachlan (1990) as *Personnel*.

SCALE ORIGIN:

The items appear to be have been used first as a summated scale by Dickson and MacLachlan (1990), but the items themselves came from the study by Dickson and Albaum (1977). A factor analysis in the latter study indicated for a discount store that most of these items loaded on the same factor. However, for data involving a supermarket, the items did not have a unidimensional structure.

SAMPLES:

The sample used by Dickson and MacLachlan (1990) came from census tracts surrounding two test stores in Tacoma, Washington. Blocks judged to be comprised of either lower or lower-middle class people were put into one group; blocks of upper-middle and upper-class people were assigned to another group. A probability sample was then taken so that those selected generally mirrored the social class makeup of the country. Complete in-home interviews were conducted with **234** people, but the factor analyses involving the scale were done with data from 161 people.

RELIABILITY:

Dickson and MacLachlan (1990) reported alphas of **.78** (n = 208) and **.85** (n = 216) for the scale as used with regard to the Kmart and Nordstrom stores, respectively.

VALIDITY:

The only information regarding the scale's validity reported by Dickson and MacLachlan (1990) came from the factor analyses conducted for both a Kmart store and a Nordstrom store. For the Nordstrom store, items loaded most heavily (r.54) on one factor and had low loadings (s.32) on the other factors. However, for the Kmart store, the items composing this scale had either split loadings or loaded much higher on another factor.

ADMINISTRATION:

The scale was administered along with many other questions by personal interviewers in respondents' homes (Dickson and MacLachlan 1990). The potential range of scores was from 6 to 42, with low scores suggesting that a store is viewed as having good service and friendly personnel. The mean score on the scale was 24.5 with a standard deviation of 6.9 for the Kmart store and 14.7 with a standard deviation of 6.8 for the Nordstrom store.

MAJOR FINDINGS:

The purpose of the study by Dickson and MacLachlan (1990) was to determine if the "social distance" between one's own social class and that perceived of those who patronize a particular store would predict store choice. The data indicated that social distance plays a role in predicting shopping behavior because shoppers avoided stores perceived to attract shoppers of a different social class. However, **store conveniences** in the form of personnel and service did not significantly help to predict reported shopping behavior.

COMMENTS:

The evidence from both Dickson and MacLachlan (1990) as well as Dickson and Albaum (1977) indicate that the items in this scale may not have unidimensional structure. Therefore, caution is advised in its use, particularly for anything other than department stores.

REFERENCES:

Dickson, John P. and Gerald Albaum (1977), "A Method for Developing Tailor-made Semantic Differentials for Specific Marketing Content Areas," *JMR*, 14 (February), 87-91.

_____ and Douglas L. MacLachlan (1990), "Social Distance and Shopping Behavior," *JAMS*, 18 (Spring), 153-61.

SCALE ITEMS: STORE CONVENIENCES (PERSONNEL & SERVICES)

1 = extremely
2 = quite
3 = slightly
4 = neutral
5 = slightly
6 = quite
7 = extremely

Unhelpful salespeople	___ : ___ : ___ : ___ : ___ : ___ : ___	Helpful salespeople **(r)**
	1 2 3 4 5 6 7	
Good service	___ : ___ : ___ : ___ : ___ : ___ : ___	Bad service
	1 2 3 4 5 6 7	
Friendly personnel	___ : ___ : ___ : ___ : ___ : ___ : ___	Unfriendly personnel
	1 2 3 4 5 6 7	

#283 *Store Conveniences (Personnel & Services)*

Easy to return
purchases   ____ : ____ : ____ : ____ : ____ : ____ : ____   Hard to return
purchases
                     1   2   3   4   5   6   7

Fast check-out   ____ : ____ : ____ : ____ : ____ : ____ : ____   Slow check-out
                     1   2   3   4   5   6   7

Good displays   ____ : ____ : ____ : ____ : ____ : ____ : ____   Bad displays
                     1   2   3   4   5   6   7

SCALE NAME: Store Depersonalization

SCALE DESCRIPTION:

A four-item, five-point, Likert-type scale measuring the degree to which a consumer believes that as stores become more self-service oriented, there is less personal interaction between salespeople and customers. The scale was referred to by Forman and Sriram (1991) as *Perceived Depersonalization of the Shopping Experience* (PDS).

SCALE ORIGIN:

The scale is original to the study by Forman and Sriram (1991).

SAMPLES:

A convenience sample of **327** adults in a large, northeastern U.S. metropolitan area was used by Forman and Sriram (1991). Respondents were asked to return questionnaires by mail to ensure anonymity. Fifty-nine percent of the sample was female, and the median age was 44 years. About 43% of the sample was married, and 32% had completed some college.

RELIABILITY:

Forman and Sriram (1991) reported an alpha of **.77** for the scale. Item-total correlations ranged from .42 to .70.

VALIDITY:

Forman and Sriram (1991) conducted a factor analysis of the items composing the scale and examined the intercorrelations of several scales used in their study. The findings provided some evidence of the scale's unidimensionality as well as its convergent and discriminant validities.

ADMINISTRATION:

The scale was administered as part of a larger questionnaire, apparently through personal interviews (Forman and Sriram 1991). High scores on the scale indicate that respondents believe that stores are becoming more self-service oriented and depersonalized, whereas low scores suggest that they believe that stores are just as personal and service oriented as ever.

MAJOR FINDINGS:

Forman and Sriram (1991) examined the affect of automated retailing systems on lonely consumers. Lonely consumers were found to perceive greater **depersonalization of the shopping experience** than were the nonlonely.

REFERENCE:

Forman, Andrew M. and Ven Sriram (1991), ''The Depersonalization of Retailing: Its Impact on the 'Lonely' Consumer,'' *JR*, 67 (Summer), 226-43.

SCALE ITEMS: STORE DEPERSONALIZATION

Strongly disagree	Disagree	Neutral	Agree	Strongly agree
1————————	—2————————	—3————————	—4————————	—5

1. Machines seem to be replacing store personnel.
2. Stores are moving to more self-service.
3. Shopping now involves less social interaction.
4. Salespeople are as available as ever. **(r)**

SCALE NAME: Store Image (Overall)

SCALE DESCRIPTION:

A five-item, five-point, summated ratings scale apparently measuring a shopper's attitude toward a specified store on the basis of a few basic attributes such as cleanliness, variety, friendliness, and check cashing policy. In the study by Kerin, Jain, and Howard (1992), the scale was used with reference to a shopper's most frequently patronized grocery store.

SCALE ORIGIN:

The origin of the scale was not specified by Kerin, Jain, and Howard (1992), but it appears to have been developed in their study after conducting focus interviews and concluding that these sorts of items are essential elements of the grocery shopping experience.

SAMPLES:

The data analyzed by Kerin, Jain, and Howard (1992) came from a telephone survey of **1193** households, randomly selected from the telephone directory of a large city. Interviews were conducted with the person, at least 18 years of age, who was primarily responsible for the household's grocery shopping. The majority of the sample was female (84.8%) and married (69.4%). More than half (54.7%) had reported incomes of more than $30,000 a year, and 46.2% of the household heads had white collar jobs.

RELIABILITY:

Kerin, Jain, and Howard (1992) reported an alpha of **.83** for the scale.

VALIDITY:

A beta coefficient for the scale (.73) as well as the confirmatory factor analysis conducted by Kerin, Jain, and Howard (1992) provide some limited evidence of the scale's unidimensionality and validity.

ADMINISTRATION:

The scale was administered over the telephone to respondents along with several other measures by trained personnel employed by a professional marketing research firm (Kerin, Jain, and Howard 1992). A high score on the scale indicates that a respondent has a good opinion of a store on the basis of a few basic criteria, whereas a low score suggests that a respondent has a poor image of the store.

MAJOR FINDINGS:

Kerin, Jain, and Howard (1992) studied the influence of **store image** on perceptions of store price, quality, and value. Among the findings was that **overall**

store image based on one's store shopping experience not only had a direct impact on consumers' value perceptions but also had indirect effects on value through perceived product prices and quality.

REFERENCE:

Kerin, Roger A., Ambuj Jain, and Daniel J. Howard (1992), "Store Shopping Experience and Consumer Price-Quality-Value Perceptions," *JR*, 68 (Winter), 376-97.

SCALE ITEMS: STORE IMAGE (OVERALL)

Very bad ____ : ____ : ____ : ____ : ____ Very good
          1   2   3   4   5

1. store cleanliness
2. variety and selection
3. employee friendliness
4. check cashing policy
5. checkout waiting time

SCALE NAME: Store Image (Price/Value)

SCALE DESCRIPTION:

A scale composed of four bipolar adjectives in a seven-point response format measuring the degree to which a consumer perceives a store to have good buys on its products. The scale was referred to by Dickson and MacLachlan (1990) as *Price/Value*.

SCALE ORIGIN:

The items appear to be have been used first as a summated scale by Dickson and MacLachlan (1990), but the items themselves came from the study by Dickson and Albaum (1977). A factor analysis in the latter study indicated for both a discount store and a supermarket that these items loaded on the same factor.

SAMPLES:

The sample used by Dickson and MacLachlan (1990) came from census tracts surrounding two test stores in Tacoma, Washington. Blocks judged to be comprised of either lower or lower-middle class people were put into one group; blocks of upper-middle and upper-class people were assigned to another group. A probability sample was then taken so that those selected generally mirrored the social class makeup of the country. Complete in-home interviews were conducted with 234 people, but the factor analyses involving the scale were done with data from 161 people.

RELIABILITY:

Dickson and MacLachlan (1990) reported alphas of .788 (n = 209) and .843 (n = 215) for the scale as used with regard to the Kmart and Nordstrom stores, respectively.

VALIDITY:

The only information regarding the scale's validity reported by Dickson and MacLachlan (1990) came from the factor analyses conducted for both a Kmart store and a Nordstrom store. For the latter, the items for this scale loaded most heavily (> .50) on one factor and had low loadings (s.30) on the other factors. For data from the Kmart store, all of the items loaded heaviest on one factor but one item (item 4) was badly split with another factor.

ADMINISTRATION:

The scale was administered along with many other questions by personal interviewers in respondents' homes (Dickson and MacLachlan 1990). The potential range of scores was 4–28, with high scores suggesting that a store is viewed as having poor sales and buys on its merchandise. The mean score on the scale was 11.4 with a standard deviation of 4.5 for the Kmart store and 12 with a standard deviation of 4.9 for the Nordstrom store.

MAJOR FINDINGS:

The purpose of the study by Dickson and MacLachlan (1990) was to determine if the "social distance" between one's own social class and that perceived of those who patronize a particular store would predict store choice. The data indicated that social distance plays a role in predicting shopping behavior because shoppers avoided stores perceived to attract shoppers of a different social class. **Store image** in terms of price/ value was a significant predictor of reported shopping behavior for both the Kmart and the Nordstrom stores.

REFERENCES:

Dickson, John P. and Gerald Albaum (1977), "A Method for Developing Tailor-made Semantic Differentials for Specific Marketing Content Areas," *JMR*, 14 (February), 87-91.

_____ and Douglas L. MacLachlan (1990), "Social Distance and Shopping Behavior," *JAMS*, 18 (Spring), 153-61.

SCALE ITEMS: STORE IMAGE (PRICE/VALUE)

1 = extremely
2 = quite
3 = slightly
4 = neutral
5 = slightly
6 = quite
7 = extremely

	1	2	3	4	5	6	7	
Bad sales on products								Good sales on products (r)
Bad buys on products								Good buys on products (r)
Unreasonable prices for value								Reasonable prices for value (r)
Bad specials								Good specials (r)

SCALE NAME: Store Image (Product Prices)

SCALE DESCRIPTION:

A three-item, five-point, summated ratings scale apparently measuring a shopper's attitude about the prices associated with a specified store, especially with regard to meat and produce. In the study by Kerin, Jain, and Howard (1992), the scale was used with reference to a shopper's most frequently patronized grocery store.

SCALE ORIGIN:

The origin of the scale was not specified by Kerin, Jain, and Howard (1992), but it appears to have been developed in their study after conducting focus interviews and concluding that these sorts of items are essential elements of the grocery shopping experience.

SAMPLES:

The data analyzed by Kerin, Jain, and Howard (1992) came from a telephone survey of **1193** households, randomly selected from the telephone directory of a large city. Interviews were conducted with the person, at least 18 years of age, who was primarily responsible for the household's grocery shopping. The majority of the sample was female (84.8%) and married (69.4%). More than half (54.7%) had reported incomes of more than $30,000 a year, and 46.2% of the household heads had white collar jobs.

RELIABILITY:

Kerin, Jain, and Howard (1992) reported an alpha of **.85** for the scale.

VALIDITY:

A beta coefficient for the scale (.74) as well as the confirmatory factor analysis conducted by Kerin, Jain, and Howard (1992) provide some limited evidence of the scale's unidimensionality and validity.

ADMINISTRATION:

The scale was administered over the telephone to respondents along with several other measures by trained personnel employed by a professional marketing research firm (Kerin, Jain, and Howard 1992). A high score on the scale indicates that a respondent has a good opinion of the prices charged by a store for its merchandise, whereas a low score suggests that a respondent has a poor image of the store's prices.

MAJOR FINDINGS:

Kerin, Jain, and Howard (1992) studied the influence of store image on **perceptions of store price**, quality, and value. Among the findings was that overall store image based on one's store shopping experience not only had a direct impact on consumers' value perceptions but also had indirect effects on value through **perceived product prices** and quality.

REFERENCE:

Kerin, Roger A., Ambuj Jain, and Daniel J. Howard (1992), "Store Shopping Experience and Consumer Price-Quality-Value Perceptions," *JR*, 68 (Winter), 376-97.

SCALE ITEMS: STORE IMAGE (PRODUCT PRICES)

Very bad   ____ : ____ : ____ : ____ : ____   Very good
                    1   2   3   4   5

1. everyday overall merchandise prices
2. everyday meat prices
3. everyday produce prices

SCALE NAME: Store Image (Product Quality)

SCALE DESCRIPTION:

A three-item, five-point, summated ratings scale apparently measuring a shopper's attitude about the product quality associated with a specified store especially with regard to meat and produce. In the study by Kerin, Jain, and Howard (1992), the scale was used with reference to a shopper's most frequently patronized grocery store.

SCALE ORIGIN:

The origin of the scale was not specified by Kerin, Jain, and Howard (1992), but it appears to have been developed in their study after conducting focus interviews and concluding that these sorts of items are essential elements of the grocery shopping experience.

SAMPLES:

The data analyzed by Kerin, Jain, and Howard (1992) came from a telephone survey of **1193** households, randomly selected from the telephone directory of a large city. Interviews were conducted with the person, at least 18 years of age, who was primarily responsible for the household's grocery shopping. The majority of the sample was female (84.8%) and married (69.4%). More than half (54.7%) had reported incomes of more than $30,000 a year, and 46.2% of the household heads had white collar jobs.

RELIABILITY:

Kerin, Jain, and Howard (1992) reported an alpha of **.87** for the scale.

VALIDITY:

A beta coefficient for the scale (.75) as well as the confirmatory factor analysis conducted by Kerin, Jain, and Howard (1992) provide some limited evidence of the scale's unidimensionality and validity.

ADMINISTRATION:

The scale was administered over the telephone to respondents along with several other measures by trained personnel employed by a professional marketing research firm (Kerin, Jain, and Howard 1992). A high score on the scale indicates that a respondent has a good opinion of the quality of the products carried by a store, whereas a low score suggests that a respondent perceives that a store has poor-quality merchandise.

MAJOR FINDINGS:

Kerin, Jain, and Howard (1992) studied the influence of store image on perceptions of store price, **quality**, and value. Among the findings was that overall store image based on one's store shopping experience not only had a direct impact on consumers' value perceptions but also had indirect effects on value through **perceived product** prices and **quality**.

REFERENCE:

Kerin, Roger A., Ambuj Jain, and Daniel J. Howard (1992), "Store Shopping Experience and Consumer Price-Quality-Value Perceptions," *JR*, 68 (Winter), 376-97.

SCALE ITEMS: STORE IMAGE (PRODUCT QUALITY)

Very bad   ____ : ____ : ____ : ____ : ____   Very good
             1   2   3   4   5

1. everyday overall merchandise quality
2. everyday meat quality
3. everyday produce quality

SCALE NAME: Store Loyalty

SCALE DESCRIPTION:

A three-item, summated rating scale purported to measure the constancy and devotion a consumer expresses in describing his/her shopping at a specified store. As used by Sirgy and colleagues, two of the items employed five-point response scales and one had four-point scaling.

SCALE ORIGIN:

The scale was original to Sirgy and colleagues (1991).

SAMPLES:

The scale was used in study 2 described by Sirgy and colleagues (1991). That study was composed of **110** adults who had just shopped in one of two upscale clothing stores. Every third shopper was approached as he/she exited the store and interviewed if possible. The interviews were conducted at different times during the day and the week.

RELIABILITY:

Sirgy and colleagues (1991) reported an alpha of **.85** for the scale.

VALIDITY:

Sirgy and colleagues (1991) provided no information regarding the scale's validity.

ADMINISTRATION:

The scale was administered by Sirgy and colleagues (1991) as part of a larger survey instrument to shoppers as they left a store. A high score on the scale indicates that a respondent is very loyal to a specified store, whereas a low score suggests that a respondent not only has little devotion to the store but rarely if ever shops there. The scores on item 2 were transformed before the total scale score was calculated. This was done by multiplying each item score by five, then dividing by four.

MAJOR FINDINGS:

Sirgy and colleagues (1991) conducted four studies to test the hypothesis that consumer behavior is more influenced by functional congruity than self-congruity. As a test of this hypothesis, it was found that functional congruity more strongly and significantly predicted **store loyalty** than did self-congruity.

REFERENCE:

Sirgy, M. Joseph, J. S. Johar, A. C. Samli, and C. B. Claiborne (1991), "Self-Congruity Versus Functional Congruity: Predictors of Consumer Behavior," *JAMS*, 19 (Fall), 363-75.

SCALE ITEMS: STORE LOYALTY

1. How often do you buy here?

Twice a week or more	Once a week	Once in 2 weeks	Once a month	Less frequently
5	4	3	2	1

2. How would you characterize your loyalty to this store?

I am very loyal	I am somewhat loyal	I am less loyal than most people	I shop around a lot
4	3	2	1

3. How would you rate this store compared to your ideal store?

Very good	Good	Adequate	Poor	Very poor
5	4	3	2	1

SCALE NAME: Store Personnel (Quantity & Quality)

SCALE DESCRIPTION:

A four-item, seven-point, Likert-type scale measuring a shopper's attitude about the number and quality of the employees working in a store. Although Baker, Levy, and Grewal (1992) described the scale as measuring "the store social factor," it is clear from an examination of the items that only the employee aspect of retail social interaction was assessed.

SCALE ORIGIN:

The scale used by Baker, Levy, and Grewal (1992) was original to their study (Baker 1993).

SAMPLES:

The data analyzed by Baker, Levy, and Grewal (1992) came from an experiment using **147** undergraduate students. The study used a 2 (store ambient levels) × 2 (store social levels) between-subjects factorial design with 35-39 subjects per cell.

RELIABILITY:

Baker, Levy, and Grewal (1992) reported an alpha of **.86** for the scale.

VALIDITY:

Baker, Levy, and Grewal (1992) reported no examination of the scale's validity.

ADMINISTRATION:

The scale was self-administered by subjects as part of a larger questionnaire after exposure to experimental stimuli (Baker, Levy, and Grewal 1992). A high score on the scale indicates that a respondent has a positive opinion about the quantity and quality of employees observed in a store, whereas a low score suggests that a shopper considers several aspects of the personnel to be inadequate.

MAJOR FINDINGS:

Baker, Levy, and Grewal (1992) examined the effects of two retail atmospheric factors, ambient and social cues, on respondents' pleasure, arousal, and shopping intentions. Measurement of attitude about the adequacy of **store personnel** was used only a check on an experimental treatment and, indeed, the results indicated that the manipulation was perceived as intended.

COMMENTS:

Some slight modification in the wording of the items might be necessary if the scale is used with actual shoppers rather than subjects simulating a shopping experience as in the experiment described here.

REFERENCES:

Baker, Julie (1993), personal correspondence.

———, Michael Levy, and Dhruv Grewal (1992), "An Experimental Approach to Making Retail Store Environmental Decisions," *JR*, 68 (Winter), 445-60.

SCALE ITEMS: STORE PERSONNEL (QUANTITY & QUALITY)

Strongly   ____ : ____ : ____ : ____ : ____ : ____ : ____   Strongly
disagree   1   2   3   4   5   6   7   agree

1. There were enough employees in the store to service customers.
2. The employees were dressed and appeared neat.
3. The employees seemed like they would be friendly.
4. The employees seemed like they would be helpful.

SCALE NAME: Store-Price Image

SCALE DESCRIPTION:

A five-item, seven-point, Likert-type scale measuring the extent to which a shopper perceives that a store has high prices and low storewide savings.

SCALE ORIGIN:

The scale was probably developed for use in the study by Cox and Cox (1990), although no specific information about the scale's origin was provided.

SAMPLES:

The sample used by Cox and Cox (1990) was composed of **181** shoppers recruited from a large urban university in the southeastern United States. Most of the respondents (81%) reported making major grocery shopping trips at least once a month. The sample was mostly white (88%), 56% female, and ranged in age from 20 to 42 years (mean = 25).

RELIABILITY:

Cox and Cox (1990) reported an alpha of **.85** for the scale.

VALIDITY:

Cox and Cox (1990) reported no information regarding the scale's validity.

ADMINISTRATION:

The scale was administered to students along with demographic questions in small group after viewing experimental stimuli. High scores on the scale indicate that respondents perceive a store to have low prices and high savings, whereas low scores suggest that respondents think a store has high prices and low savings.

MAJOR FINDINGS:

The purpose of Cox and Cox (1990) was to investigate the effect of retail item-price ads on perceptions of a **store's overall price level**. The only significant main effect involved reference prices: ads presenting selling prices as reductions from previous prices created a greater **impression of low storewide prices** than ads without reference prices. A significant interaction effect was found between brands and product purchase frequency: a store was viewed as having lower **store savings** when ads featured frequently purchased national brands rather than infrequently purchased branded goods.

REFERENCE:

Cox, Anthony and Dena Cox (1990), "Competing on Price: The Role of Retail Price Advertisements in Shaping Store-Price Image," *JR*, 66 (Winter), 428-45.

SCALE ITEMS: STORE-PRICE IMAGE*

This store would probably offer:

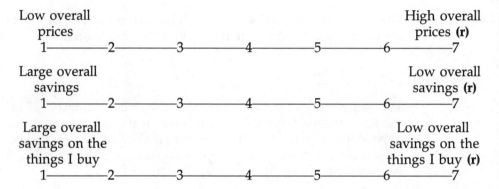

Low overall prices						High overall prices **(r)**
1	2	3	4	5	6	7

Large overall savings						Low overall savings **(r)**
1	2	3	4	5	6	7

Large overall savings on the things I buy						Low overall savings on the things I buy **(r)**
1	2	3	4	5	6	7

* These are the items supplied in the article by Cox and Cox (1990). Contact those authors for the remaining two items.

SCALE NAME: Study Realism

SCALE DESCRIPTION:

A three-item, seven-point summated ratings scale measuring the degree to which a person reports that a situation described in a research study is realistic.

SCALE ORIGIN:

The origin of the scale was not specified by Feick and Higie (1992), but it would appear to have been developed for use in their study.

SAMPLES:

Feick and Higie (1992) describe two experiments they conducted, but the scale was used only in the second experiment. The sample in the second experiment was composed of **58** males and **62** females who were either junior or seniors enrolled at a northeastern U.S. university. No students 29 years of age or older were included in the analysis to control for age effects.

RELIABILITY:

Feick and Higie (1992) reported an alpha of **.73** for the scale.

VALIDITY:

Feick and Higie (1992) provided no information regarding the scale's validity.

ADMINISTRATION:

The scale was administered by Feick and Higie (1992) after subjects had been exposed to experimental stimuli. High scores on the scale indicate the perception that the imaginary situation described in a study is very realistic, whereas low scores indicate that respondents do not see the situation happening to them.

MAJOR FINDINGS:

Feick and Higie (1992) investigated the effect of experienced and similar sources of information on attitudes and intentions for services that differ on preference heterogeneity. The scale was used as a manipulation check to be sure that a simulated word-of-mouth scenario was **realistic**. Those subjects who did not perceive the situation to be **realistic** were eliminated from the analysis.

REFERENCE:

Feick, Lawrence and Robin A. Higie (1992), ''The Effects of Preference Hetero-geneity and Source Characteristics on Ad Processing and Judgments About Endorsers,'' *JA*, 21 (June), 9-24.

SCALE ITEMS: STUDY REALISM*

Strongly ___ : ___ : ___ : ___ : ___ : ___ : ___ Strongly
disagree   1   2   3   4   5   6   7   agree

1. It is hard to imagine being in the situation described in this study. **(r)**
2. The scenario is realistic.
3. Something like this situation will probably happen to me.

* The verbal anchors used in the scale were not specified by Feick and Higie (1992) but were likely to have been something like this.

SCALE NAME: Surprise

SCALE DESCRIPTION:

A three-item, five-point summated ratings scale assessing a person's experience of the surprise-related emotion. The directions and response scale can be worded so as to measure the *intensity* of the emotional state at the present time, or they can be adjusted to measure the *frequency* with which a person has experienced the emotional trait during some specified time period. One-word items were used in the study by Westbrook and Oliver (1991), and phrases based on those same items were used by Allen, Machleit, and Kleine (1992).

SCALE ORIGIN:

The measure was developed by Izard (1977) and is part of the Differential Emotions Scale (DES II). The instrument originally was designed as a measure of a person's emotional "state" at a particular point in time, but adjustments in the instrument's instructions enable the same items to be used in the assessment of emotional experiences as perceived over a longer time period. The latter was viewed by Izard as measure of one's emotional "trait" (1977, p. 125). Test-retest reliability for the surprise subscale of DES II was reported to be .75 (n = 63), and item-factor correlations were .83 and higher (Izard 1977, p. 126). Beyond this evidence, several other studies have provided support for the validity of the scale, even in consumption settings (e.g., Westbrook 1987).

The items in DES II were composed of one word. In contrast, the items in DES III are phrases describing the target emotion. They were developed by Izard, though the first published validity testing was conducted by Kotsch, Gerbing, and Schwartz (1982). A study by Allen, Machleit, and Marine (1988) provides some insight to the factor structure of both DES II and III. The results indicate that when presented with the other DES items, the surprise items typically load together and not with items purported to measure other emotions.

SAMPLES:

The data used by Allen, Machleit, and Kleine (1992) came from a stratified sample of people of diverse experience with blood donation. Nine hundred questionnaires were mailed and **361** usable forms were returned. Given that all respondents had previously donated blood, limited information was known about them and allowed a comparison with nonrespondents. Respondents were a little older, less likely to be male, and more likely to be heavier donors than nonrespondents.

The data for the study conducted by Westbrook and Oliver (1991) came from a judgmental area sample. Convenience samples were taken at four shopping centers in a large northeastern city and were limited to persons who had purchased a new or used car in the past year. Complete and usable questionnaires were obtained from **125** respondents. A majority (74%) of the

sample was male. The average respondent had an income in the $25,000–$40,000 range and was 33 years of age.

RELIABILITY:

Westbrook and Oliver (1991) reported an alpha of **.77** for the scale. Allen, Machleit, and Kleine (1992; Allen 1994) calculated an alpha of **.83**.

VALIDITY:

No specific examination of the scale's validity was reported by either Westbrook and Oliver (1991) or Allen, Machleit, and Kleine (1992).

ADMINISTRATION:

The scale was included with many other measures in the instrument used by Westbrook and Oliver (1991) and Allen, Machleit, and Kleine (1992). High scores on the frequency version of the scale suggest that a respondent perceives him/herself as having experienced the surprise-related emotional trait very often in some specified time period.

MAJOR FINDINGS:

Allen, Machleit, Kleine (1992) examined whether emotions effect behavior through attitudes or are better viewed as having a separate and distinct impact. Although several emotions were found to play a key role in predicting behavior, **surprise** (DES III) was not found to have a significant relationship, at least with regard to donating blood.

Westbrook and Oliver (1991) studied the correspondence of the consumption emotional responses and satisfaction judgments that occur in the postpurchase period of the consumer decision process. **Surprise** had its highest correlation with guilt (r = .48) and its lowest correlation with interest (r = .08). **Surprise** also was found to be a primary emotional trait linked to a high satisfaction experience when combined with joy.

REFERENCES:

Allen, Chris T. (1994), personal correspondence.

_____, Karen A. Machleit, and Susan Schultz Kleine (1992), "A Comparison of Attitudes and Emotions as Predictors of Behavior at Diverse Levels of Behavioral Experience," *JCR*, 18 (March), 493-504.

_____, _____, and Susan S. Marine (1988), "On Assessing the Emotionality of Advertising Via Izard's Differential Emotions Scale," in *Advances in Consumer Research*, Vol. 15, Michael J. Houston, ed. Provo, UT: Association for Consumer Research, 226-31.

Izard, Carroll E. (1977), *Human Emotions*. New York: Plenum Press.

Kotsch, William E., Davis W. Gerbing, and Lynne E. Schwartz (1982), "The Construct Validity of the Differential Emotions Scale as Adapted for Children and Adolescents,'' in *Measuring Emotions in Infants and Children*, Carroll E. Izard, ed. New York: Cambridge University Press, 251-78.

Westbrook, Robert A. (1987), ''Product/Consumption-Based Affective Responses and Postpurchase Processes,'' *JMR*, 24 (August), 258-70.

_____ and Richard L. Oliver (1991), ''The Dimensionality of Consumption Emotion Patterns and Consumer Satisfaction,'' *JCR*, 18 (June), 84-91.

SCALE ITEMS: SURPRISE

DIRECTIONS: Below is a list of words that you can use to show how you feel. We want you to tell us how often you felt each of these feelings _____.* You can tell us how often you felt each of these feelings on the list by marking one of the numbers next to each question.

Almost never	____ : ____ : ____ : ____ : ____	Very often
	1 2 3 4 5	

DES II
1. surprised
2. amazed
3. astonished

DES III
1. feel surprised, like when something suddenly happens you had no idea would happen
2. feel amazed, like you can't believe what's happened, it was so unusual
3. feel like you feel when something unexpected happens

* The blank should be used to specify the time period of interest such as ''during the last week.''

SCALE NAME: Taste Evaluation

SCALE DESCRIPTION:

A seven-item, seven-point semantic differential used to measure a person's affective evaluation of the taste of a beverage such as a soft drink.

SCALE ORIGIN:

Stayman, Alden, and Smith (1992) state that the scale was derived from Meyers-Levy and Tybout (1989). Although not certain, it appears that the scale was developed in the latter study, and no information about the scale's psychometric quality was provided.

SAMPLES:

The scale was used in experiments 2 and 3 reported in the article by Stayman, Alden, and Smith (1992). The samples were similar in that they both were composed of undergraduate business students recruited at a major university. In experiment 2, usable responses were obtained from **103** students who were given class credit for participating. In experiment 3, subjects returned **107** usable responses, and the subjects were given $5 as compensation.

RELIABILITY:

The scale was administered to subjects in both pre-trial and post-trial sessions of experiments 2 and 3 by Stayman, Alden, and Smith (1992). The pre-trial alphas were **.91** and **.80,** and the post-trial alphas were **.97** and **.96** for experiments 2 and 3, respectively.

VALIDITY:

Stayman, Alden, and Smith (1992) reported no information regarding the scale's validity.

ADMINISTRATION:

As noted previously, Stayman, Alden, and Smith (1992) administered the scale in two experiments both before and after actual trial of the beverage. (The pre-trial measure was based on description of the drink to be tasted.) A high score on the scale indicates that a respondent feels a beverage is satisfying, whereas a low score suggests that a respondent does not believe the drink is tasty.

MAJOR FINDINGS:

Stayman, Alden, and Smith (1992) studied how consumer expectations developed before product trial influence judgments made after trial. Among the many findings was that post-trial **evaluations** were significantly lower when subjects tasted a beverage that was substantially different from expectations.

REFERENCES:

Meyers-Levy, Joan and Alice M. Tybout (1989), "Schema Congruity as a Basis for Product Evaluation," *JCR*, 16 (June), 39-54.

Stayman, Douglas, Dana L. Alden, and Karen H. Smith (1992), "Some Effects of Schematic Processing on Consumer Expectations and Disconfirmation Judgments," *JCR*, 19 (September), 240-55.

SCALE ITEMS: TASTE EVALUATION*

Unappealing	___ :	___ :	___ :	___ :	___ :	___ :	___	Appealing
	1	2	3	4	5	6	7	
Tasteless	___ :	___ :	___ :	___ :	___ :	___ :	___	Tasty
	1	2	3	4	5	6	7	
Undesirable	___ :	___ :	___ :	___ :	___ :	___ :	___	Desirable
	1	2	3	4	5	6	7	
Low quality	___ :	___ :	___ :	___ :	___ :	___ :	___	High quality
	1	2	3	4	5	6	7	
Uninterested in trying	___ :	___ :	___ :	___ :	___ :	___ :	___	Interested in trying
	1	2	3	4	5	6	7	
Unsatisfying	___ :	___ :	___ :	___ :	___ :	___ :	___	Satisfying
	1	2	3	4	5	6	7	
Not refreshing	___ :	___ :	___ :	___ :	___ :	___ :	___	Refreshing
	1	2	3	4	5	6	7	

* The semantic differentials shown here are reconstructed from brief descriptions provided by Stayman, Alden, and Smith (1992) as well as Meyers-Levy and Tybout (1989). Given that some guesswork was involved, these reconstructions may not be perfectly representative of the items used in those two studies.

SCALE NAME: Time Pressure

SCALE DESCRIPTION:

A three-item, seven-point, Likert-type measure of the lack of time a person reports having given the things he/she has to do in general. The construct was referred to as *costs of search* by Srinivasan and Ratchford (1991) because of the reasoning that if a person is very busy, time for external search will be in short supply.

SCALE ORIGIN:

Although not expressly stated in the article, the scale appears to be have been used first in published research by Srinivasan and Ratchford (1991), which was based on the dissertation of Srinivasan (1987). Some initial assessment of scale reliability and face validity was made in pre-test stage of the study.

SAMPLES:

A sample of new car buyers was obtained by Srinivasan and Ratchford (1991) through a mail survey of new car registrants in the Buffalo, New York area. More than three thousand people were sent three mailings of the questionnaire, and ultimately, **1401** usable responses were received. No demographic description is provided of the respondents.

RELIABILITY:

Srinivasan and Ratchford (1991) reported the LISREL estimate of reliability for the items to be **.83**.

VALIDITY:

Srinivasan and Ratchford (1991) provided no detailed discussion of this scale's validity. However, it was suggested that generally the measures used in the study showed evidence of convergent and discriminant validity.

ADMINISTRATION:

The scale was used by Srinivasan and Ratchford (1991) along with other measures in a mail survey instrument. A low score on the scale indicates that a respondent thinks he/she is very busy, whereas a high score suggests that a respondent does not perceive much time pressure.

MAJOR FINDINGS:

Srinivasan and Ratchford (1991) examined a model of the determinants of external search for new car purchases. In contrast to expectations, **time pressure** was *not* negatively correlated with search effort.

REFERENCES:

Srinivasan, Narasimhan (1987), INF/"A Causal Model of External Search for Information for Durables: A Particular Investigation in the Case of New Automobiles," doctoral dissertation, State University of New York at Buffalo.

_____ and Brian T. Ratchford (1991), "An Empirical Test of an External Search for Automobiles," *JCR*, 18 (September), 233-42.

SCALE ITEMS: TIME PRESSURE

DIRECTIONS: There are no right or wrong answers to the following statements, and a large number of people agree and disagree. Kindly indicate *your* personal opinion by circling any one number for each statement.

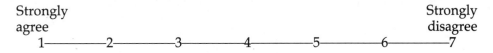

```
Strongly                                                    Strongly
agree                                                       disagree
  1———————2———————3———————4———————5———————6———————7
```

1. I seem to be busier than most people I know.
2. Usually there is so much to do that I wish I had more time.
3. I usually find myself pressed for time.

SCALE NAME: Time Use (Polychronic Behavior)

SCALE DESCRIPTION:

A four-item, five-point, Likert-type summated scale intended to measure the degree to which a person engages in multiple activities simultaneously. This behavior is referred to as *polychronic time use*. The statements in the scale are general and not activity specific.

SCALE ORIGIN:

The scale was developed by Kaufman, Lane, and Lindquist (1981). Several statements were generated that were expected to capture people's attitudes about combining activities through polychronic time use. Ultimately, 15 items were chosen for testing. On the basis of item-total correlations, only four of the items were retained for the testing of unidimensionality, as explained in ''Validity.''

SAMPLES:

The study conducted by Kaufman, Lane, and Lindquist (1991) was based on a sample of 310 respondents. The data were collected by student interviewers who were assigned locations in an urban residential area and asked to select every fifth residence as an initial sample. The sample was 58% female, and 63.3% worked 40 hours or more a week. The range of ages and incomes was quite wide, but the medians were 26–35 years of age and $45,000–$49,000, respectively.

RELIABILITY:

The alpha reported by Kaufman, Lane, and Lindquist (1991) was **.6802**. The item-total correlations of the final four item scale were all higher than .40.

VALIDITY:

Kaufman, Lane, and Lindquist (1991) conducted a principal components factor analysis of the four-item version of the scale and determined that they composed just one factor. As some evidence of convergent and discriminant validities, the scale correlated in the expected directions with several statements of specific behaviors that indicated either polychronic time use or monochronic behavior.

ADMINISTRATION:

Although data collection by Kaufman, Lane, and Lindquist (1991) involved information from interviews and interviewers' judgments, the scale itself was self-administered by respondents in the presence of the interviewer along with several other measures in a survey instrument. High scores on the scale suggest that respondents are comfortable engaging in several activities concurrently, whereas low scores indicate that they prefer to focus on one thing at a time.

MAJOR FINDINGS:

The study by Kaufman, Lane, and Lindquist (1991) examined the degree to which consumers were conscious of **polychronic time use.** Role overload had a weak but significant correlation with the **polychronic time use**. Demographically, those scoring high on the scale were highly educated, worked more than 40 hours a week, and belonged to several social organizations/clubs.

REFERENCE:

Kaufman, Carol Felker, Paul M. Lane, and Jay D. Lindquist (1991), "Exploring More Than 24 Hours a Day: A Preliminary Investigation of Polychronic Time Use," *JCR*, 18 (December), 392-401.

SCALE ITEMS: TIME USE (POLYCHRONIC BEHAVIOR)

Strongly disagree	Disagree	Neutral	Agree	Strongly agree
1	2	3	4	5

1. I do not like to juggle several activities at the same time. **(r)**
2. People should not try to do many things at once. **(r)**
3. When I sit down at my desk, I work on one project at a time. **(r)**
4. I am comfortable doing several things at the same time.

SCALE NAME: Tolerance for Ambiguity

SCALE DESCRIPTION:

A 12-item, seven-point, Likert-type scale measuring the degree of openness one has in general toward stimuli that are less than clear, puzzling, or indefinite.

SCALE ORIGIN:

McQuarrie and Mick (1992) reported that they drew on items that had been used in one or more of three previous studies (Budner 1962; MacDonald 1970; Norton 1975). A 20-item scale was developed and tested. An alpha of .64 resulted, which lead the authors to eliminate all items with item-total correlations less than .15. With another pretest sample, a 12-item version of the scale (same as one reported here) yielded an alpha of .70.

SAMPLES:

Two experiments were reported by McQuarrie and Mick (1992). All that is known about the sample used in the first experiment was that it was composed of **112** undergraduate students. In contrast, the second experiment was composed of a range of age groups but deliberately excluded full-time college students. Usable data were received from **98** subjects. Half of the sample was male and a little more than half (51%) were 35 years of age or younger.

RELIABILITY:

McQuarrie and Mick (1992) provided no information regarding the scale's reliability beyond what is noted here about its development.

VALIDITY:

McQuarrie and Mick (1992) reported no specific testing of the scale's validity.

ADMINISTRATION:

McQuarrie and Mick (1992) administered the scale to subjects in both experiments along with other measures and after they had been exposed to the experimental stimuli. A high score on the scale indicates that a respondent has a high tolerance for ambiguous stimuli, whereas a low score suggests that a respondent prefers for stimuli to be clear and certain in their meaning.

MAJOR FINDINGS:

The purpose of the two experiments reported by McQuarrie and Mick (1992) was to investigate advertising *resonance*, wordplay accompanied by a relevant picture. A significant interaction was found between **tolerance for ambiguity** and resonance in experiment 2 but not experiment 1. The authors speculated that the lack of significant effect in the latter could have occurred because of a high degree of homogeneity among the student sample.

COMMENTS:

McQuarrie (1994) has indicated that this scale is barely adequate in its present form. Potential users are urged to review the larger list of tolerance-for-ambiguity items that can be found in Budner (1962), MacDonald (1970), and Norton (1975) and are encouraged to attempt revisions. Moreover, conceptually similar scales measuring optimal stimulation level and need for cognition should also be considered.

REFERENCES:

Budner, Stanley (1962), "Intolerance of Ambiguity as a Personality Variable," *Journal of Personality*, 30 (March), 29-50.

MacDonald, A. P. (1970), "Revised Scale for Ambiguity Tolerance: Reliability and Validity," *Psychological Reports*, 26 (June), 791-98.

McQuarrie, Edward F. and David Glen Mick (1992), "On Resonance: A Critical Pluralistic Inquiry Into Advertising Rhetoric," *JCR*, 19 (September), 180-97.

———— (1994), personal correspondence.

Norton, Robert W. (1975), "Measurement of Ambiguity Tolerance," *Journal of Personality Assessment*, 39 (6), 607-19.

SCALE ITEMS: TOLERANCE FOR AMBIGUITY

Directions: To help us understand you better we would like to know your opinions about some common objects, situations, and activities. There are no right or wrong answers and therefore your first response is important. Circle a number to indicate your agreement or disagreement.

Strongly disagree	___ :	___ :	___ :	___ :	___ :	___ :	___	Strongly agree
	1	2	3	4	5	6	7	

1. I like movies or stories with definite endings. **(r)**
2. I always want to know what people are laughing at. **(r)**
3. I would like to live in a foreign country for a while.
4. A good job is one where what is to be done and how it is to be done are always clear. **(r)**

5. I tend to like obscure or hidden symbolism.
6. It really disturbs me when I am unable to follow another person's train of thought. **(r)**
7. I am tolerant of ambiguous situations.
8. A poem should never contain contradictions. **(r)**
9. Vague and impressionistic pictures appeal to me more than realistic pictures.
10. I don't like to work on a problem unless there is a possibility of coming out with a clear-cut and unambiguous answer. **(r)**
11. Generally, the more meanings a poem has, the better I like it.
12. I like parties where I know most of the people more than ones where all or most of the people are complete strangers. **(r)**

SCALE NAME: Typicality

SCALE DESCRIPTION:

A multi-item, semantic differential scale developed to measure the degree to which an object is perceived to be representative of a category of objects from which it appears to belong. A three-item, 11-point version of the scale was used by both Loken and Ward (1990) and Ward, Bitner, and Barnes (1992). Loken and John (1993) used a four-item, seven-point version of the scale.

SCALE ORIGIN:

Although not completely clear, it appears that the items composing the scale were used first as a summated measure by Loken and Ward (1990). However, several aspects of the scale were adapted from previous work by others (Barsalou 1985; Hampton and Gardiner 1983; Rosch and Mervis 1975).

SAMPLES:

Data were gathered in the study by Loken and John (1993) from women recruited by a research firm in a Minneapolis mall. The subjects were the principal shoppers for their families, had at least high school education levels, had incomes of at least $10,000 a year, and were between 18 and 49 years of age. Screening questions were used to eliminate some women (or their data) from the study, and the final sample size was not specified. However, **196** women appear to have completed the experiment.

Loken and Ward (1990) indicate that 115 undergraduate marketing students participated in pre-tests and 466 completed the measures in the main study. It is not clear, however, what sample size the analyses involving the scale were based on. The authors do say that 10–12 students completed each individual measure.

The sample employed by Ward, Bitner, and Barnes (1992) was composed of **86** undergraduate students attending a large southwestern U.S. university. In groups of 5–11 the students were taken by a researcher to three fast-food restaurants for "taste tests" and later returned to a laboratory environment to respond to a set of questions regarding the interior and exterior environments they encountered. In total, 15 restaurants were used in the study. Students received credit for their participation in the research.

RELIABILITY:

An alpha of **.98** was reported for the version of the scale used by Loken and John (1993). Loken and Ward (1990) reported an alpha of **.82** for the scale. This appears to have been averaged across 16 product categories with 15 members each (240).

Ward, Bitner, and Barnes (1992) reported an alpha of **.94** for the scale. Keep in mind that each subject visited three restaurants with a total of 15 different restaurants being visited by the 86 students. This alpha appears to be an amalgamation of those experiences and is not linked to a specific restaurant.

VALIDITY:

No evidence regarding the validity of the scale was reported in any of the studies.

ADMINISTRATION:

In the studies by Loken and Ward (1990) as well as Ward, Bitner, and Barnes (1992), the scale was administered to students along with other measures in a "laboratory" environment, most likely on a university campus. In Loken and John (1993), the scale was part of a self-administered questionnaire subjects completed in a research facility of a shopping mall. High scores on the scale indicate that respondents perceive an object, such as a particular brand of product, to be a very typical example of the category of objects it represents.

MAJOR FINDINGS:

The situations in which brand extension failures affect specific attribute beliefs associated with family brand image was studied by Loken and John (1993). Brand extensions with one inconsistent attribute were seen as moderately **typical** of the family brand, and extensions with two inconsistent attributes were considered to be low in **typicality**.

Loken and Ward (1990) examined the determinants of **typicality** as well as the relationship between **typicality** and attitude using eight superordinate and eight subordinate product categories. Several variables tested were found to relate significantly to **typicality**, with family resemblance being a particularly strong predictor. Attitude also was found to correlate with typicality for most product categories and was a significant predictor even when several potentially mediating variables were accounted for.

Ward, Bitner, and Barnes (1992) focused on the influence of external and internal environmental attributes in evaluating the prototypicality of fast food restaurants. They found that though **typicality** was significantly related to several measures of resemblance, exterior environmental resemblance was the most influential. Moreover, **typicality** was correlated highly with two measures of outlet share.

REFERENCES:

Barsalou, Lawrence W. (1985), "Ideals, Central Tendency, and Frequency of Instantiatian as Determinants of Graded Structure in Categories," *Journal of Experimental Psychology: Learning, Memory, and Cognition*, 11 (October), 629-54.

Hampton, John and Margaret Gardiner (1983), "Measures of Internal Category Structure: A Correlational Analysis of Normative Data," *British Journal of Psychology*, 74 (November, Part 4), 491-516.

Loken, Barbara and James Ward (1990), "Alternative Approaches to Understanding the Determinants of Typicality,'' *JCR*, 17 (September), 111-26.

_____ and Deborah Roedder John (1993), ''Diluting Brand Beliefs: When Do Brand Extensions Have a Negative Impact?'' *JM*, 57 (July), 71-84.

Rosch, Eleanor and Carolyn Mervis (1975), ''Family Resemblances: Studies in the Internal Structure of Categories,'' *Cognitive Psychology*, 7 (October), 573- 605.

Ward, James C., Mary Jo Bitner, and John Barnes (1992), ''Measuring the Prototypicality and Meaning of Retail Environments,'' *JR*, 68 (Summer), 194-220.

SCALE ITEMS: TYPICALITY*

1. Very atypical ___ : ___ : ___ : ___ : ___ : ___ : ___ Very typical
     1   2   3   4   5   6   7

2. Very poor example ___ : ___ : ___ : ___ : ___ : ___ : ___ Very good example
     1   2   3   4   5   6   7

3. Very unrepresentative ___ : ___ : ___ : ___ : ___ : ___ : ___ Very representative
     1   2   3   4   5   6   7

4. Dissimilar ___ : ___ : ___ : ___ : ___ : ___ : ___ Similar
     1   2   3   4   5   6   7

5. Inconsistent ___ : ___ : ___ : ___ : ___ : ___ : ___ Consistent
     1   2   3   4   5   6   7

* Loken and John (1993) used items 1, 3-5. Loken and Ward (1990) as well as Ward, Bitner, and Barnes (1992) used items 1-3.

SCALE NAME: Value (Bundle)

SCALE DESCRIPTION:

A four-item, seven-point, summated rating scale measuring the perceived additional value of buying two particular products in a set compared with purchasing them separately. Yadav and Monroe (1993) referred to the measure as *Bundling Transaction Value*.

SCALE ORIGIN:

Although not explicitly stated, the measure appears to have been developed by Yadav and Monroe (1993)

SAMPLES:

Usable data were collected and analyzed by Yadav and Monroe (1993) from **252** undergraduate students at a state university. Extra credit and a chance to win movie tickets were offered for students' cooperation. The average age of the students was 21.4 years, and the sample was 59.8% female.

RELIABILITY:

Yadav and Monroe (1993) reported an alpha of **.95** for the scale.

VALIDITY:

Yadav and Monroe (1993) reported no examination of the scale's validity.

ADMINISTRATION:

The scale used by Yadav and Monroe (1993) was self-administered by subjects along with several other measures after exposure to experimental stimuli. A high score on the scale implies that a respondent perceives the additional savings involved with buying two items as a set versus purchasing them separately as great.

MAJOR FINDINGS:

The purpose of the experiment by Yadav and Monroe (1993) was to study the perceptions of consumers regarding the overall savings when they consider the purchase of multiple products as a set (bundle). The findings appeared to support the notion that the total value of products purchased as a set is a combination of the perceived savings if the products were purchased separately as well as the additional **savings on the products as a bundle**.

REFERENCE:

Yadav, Manjit S. and Kent B. Monroe (1993), "How Buyers Perceive Savings in a Bundle Price: An Examination of a Bundle's Transaction Value," *JMR*, 30 (August), 350-58.

SCALE ITEMS: VALUE (BUNDLE)*

1. Compared to the cost of buying both A and B separately at their sale prices, the additional savings I can get by buying both A and B as a set are:

Very poor ___ : ___ : ___ : ___ : ___ : ___ : ___ Very good
         1   2   3   4   5   6   7

2. Compared to the cost of buying both A and B separately at their sale prices, buying both A and B as a set costs much less.

Strongly ___ : ___ : ___ : ___ : ___ : ___ : ___ Strongly
disagree   1   2   3   4   5   6   7   agree

3. Compared to the cost of buying both A and B separately at their sale prices, buying both A and B as a set saves me a lot of money.

4. Compared to the cost of buying both A and B separately at their sale prices, buying both A and B as a set offers very attractive savings.

* Items 2–4 use Likert-type response scales as shown with item 2, whereas item 1 uses the poor/good format as shown.

SCALE NAME: Value (Items Purchased Separately)

SCALE DESCRIPTION:

A four-item, seven-point, summated ratings scale measuring the perceived level of savings in the purchase of two particular products if purchased separately. Other information provided to respondents indicated that the items could be purchased together as a bundle for a special price. This scale measures their beliefs that savings would be realized even if the items were purchased separately. Yadav and Monroe (1993) referred to the measure as *Items' Transaction Value.*

SCALE ORIGIN:

Although not explicitly stated, the measure appears to have been developed by Yadav and Monroe (1993).

SAMPLES:

Usable data were collected and analyzed by Yadav and Monroe (1993) from **252** undergraduate students at a state university. Extra credit and a chance to win movie tickets were offered for students' cooperation. The average age of the students was 21.4 years, and the sample was 59.8% female.

RELIABILITY:

Yadav and Monroe (1993) reported an alpha of **.84** for the scale.

VALIDITY:

Yadav and Monroe (1993) reported no examination of the scale's validity.

ADMINISTRATION:

The scale used by Yadav and Monroe (1993) was self-administered by subjects along with several other measures after exposure to experimental stimuli. A high score on the scale implies that a respondent perceives there to be great savings on the purchase of two specified products even if they were purchased separately and not as a set

MAJOR FINDINGS:

The purpose of the experiment by Yadav and Monroe (1993) was to study the perceptions of consumers regarding the overall savings when they consider the purchase of multiple products as a set (bundle). The findings appeared to support the notion that the total value of products purchased as a set is a combination of the perceived **savings if the products were purchased separately** as well as the additional savings on the products as a bundle.

REFERENCE:

Yadav, Manjit S. and Kent B. Monroe (1993), "How Buyers Perceive Savings in a Bundle Price: An Examination of a Bundle's Transaction Value," *JMR*, 30 (August), 350-58.

SCALE ITEMS: VALUE (ITEMS PURCHASED SEPARATELY)*

Strongly   ___ : ___ : ___ : ___ : ___ : ___ : ___   Strongly
disagree   1   2   3   4   5   6   7   agree

1. Even if I bought both A and B separately at their sale prices, I would still be saving a lot of money.
2. Even if I bought both A and B separately at their sale prices, I would still be getting a good bargain.
3. Even if I bought both A and B separately at their sale prices, I would still be taking advantage of an attractive price reduction.
4. Even if I bought both A and B separately at their sale prices, the deal I would be getting will be:

Very poor   ___ : ___ : ___ : ___ : ___ : ___ : ___   Very good
         1   2   3   4   5   6   7

* Items 1–3 use the Likert-type response scale, whereas item 4 uses the poor/good format as shown.

SCALE NAME: Value (Offer)

SCALE DESCRIPTION:

A four-item, nine-point, bipolar adjective, summated ratings scale measuring the perceived value of a deal given a certain product offered at a certain price. Lichtenstein, Burton, and Karson (1991) and Biswas and Burton (1993) used the same items with a seven-point response scale. A similar measure employing three Likert-type items and a seven-point response scale was used by Urbany Bearden, and Weilbaker (1988).

SCALE ORIGIN:

The bipolar adjectives employed in most of the studies (Biswas and Burton 1993; Burton and Lichtenstein 1988; Lichtenstein and Bearden 1989; Lichtenstein, Burton, and Karson 1991) were used earlier by Berkowitz and Walton (1980). However, the latter did not sum responses to the items.

SAMPLES:

Biswas and Burton (1993) reported on two studies in their article. In the first one, data were collected from **392** undergraduate business students. Little more is said about the sample except there was a nearly equal portion of each gender and they were assigned randomly to one of the 12 treatments. The second sample was composed of **303** nonstudents who were recruited by students in a marketing course. All those in the sample were 18 years of age or older with a median of 40 years. A little more than half were female (56%) and the median household income was $35,000.

Analysis in Burton and Lichtenstein (1988) as well as Lichtenstein and Bearden (1989) were based on the same data collected from **278** undergraduate business students. The students were assigned randomly to one of 12 treatment conditions in a 2 × 2 × 3 experimental design. There were 21–28 students per cell.

Lichtenstein, Burton, and Karson (1991) used **830** undergraduate business majors and randomly assigned each of them to one of 31 conditions in a 5 × 6 (plus control group) between-subjects experimental design. There were 22–29 subjects per cell.

Urbany, Bearden, and Weilbaker (1988) reported two studies. Both used junior and senior level business majors, one with **150** students and the other with **168**.

RELIABILITY:

Alphas of **.80** and **.90** were reported for the scales used by Burton and Lichtenstein (1988; Lichtenstein and Bearden 1989) and Lichtenstein, Burton, and Karson (1991), respectively. Alphas of **.79** and **.86** were obtained by Urbany, Bearden, and Weilbaker (1988) in the two uses of their scale. Biswas and Burton (1993) reported alphas of **.78** and **.85** in their first and second studies, respectively.

VALIDITY:

No specific examination of scale validity was reported in any of the studies. However, in Biswas and Burton (1993) it was mentioned that though *perceived value of the offer* was highly correlated with a measure of the *attitude toward the offer*, confirmatory factor analysis provided evidence of a two- rather than one-factor model.

ADMINISTRATION:

The scale used by Burton and Lichtenstein (1988; Lichtenstein and Bearden 1989) as well as Lichtenstein, Burton, and Karson (1991) was self-administered by subjects along with several other measures in experimental settings. In the two studies by Urbany, Bearden, and Weilbaker (1988), students responded to questions posed to them on a PC in a university computer lab.

High scores on the scale imply that respondents perceive a deal (price and product) to be a very good value, whereas low scores mean that respondents do not think that the offer is a good buy.

MAJOR FINDINGS:

Biswas and Burton (1993) investigated the impact of three different price claims on various perceptions and intentions. Among the many findings was that **perceptions of the offer's value** were better for larger discount ranges than for smaller.

Burton and Lichtenstein (1988; Lichtenstein and Bearden 1989) examined the influence of merchant-supplied reference prices, ad distinctiveness, and ad message consistency on perception of source credibility, value of the deal, and attitude toward the deal. In Burton and Lichtenstein (1988) the findings indicated that perceptions of the **value of the offer** were strongly related to several measures of attitude toward the ad. Moreover, a price discount was shown to have a significant effect on attitude toward the ad even after covarying out perceptions regarding the **value of the offer.** Among many other findings reported in Lichtenstein and Bearden (1989), perceived **value of the offer** was greatest when the retailers used distinctive ads that did not offer similar deals frequently. Also, the perceived **value of the offer** was greater for plausible-high merchant-supplied prices than for implausible merchant-supplied prices.

Lichtenstein, Burton, and Karson (1991) studied the way reference price ads are phrased (semantic cues) and consumer's price-related responses. High distinctiveness semantic cues indicate the difference between the advertised price and what is charged by competitors, whereas low consistency cues compare prices charged at other times by the same retailer. Among the many findings was that for implausibly high external reference prices, semantic cues that suggest high distinctiveness produced significantly better perceptions of the **offer's value** than low consistency cues.

Urbany, Bearden, and Weilbaker (1988) studied the effect of price claims on consumer perceptions and price search behavior. Their findings from two experiments indicated that ads with high plausible reference prices for products led to greater perceptions of **value** than ads with no reference prices provided.

COMMENTS:

The specific products examined in the studies were a television (Urbany et al. 1988), a desk (Burton and Lichtenstein 1988; Lichtenstein and Bearden 1989), and a calculator (Lichtenstein, Burton, and Karson 1991), but the items in the scale are general enough that they should be amenable for use in studying many other product categories.

REFERENCES:

Berkowitz, Eric N. and John R. Walton (1980), "Contextual Influences on Consumer Price Responses: An Experimental Analysis," *JMR*, 17 (August), 349-58.

Biswas, Abhijit and Scot Burton (1993), "Consumer Perceptions of Tensile Price Claims in Advertisements: An Assessment of Claim Types Across Different Discount Levels," *JAMS*, 21 (Summer), 217-29.

Burton, Scot and Donald R. Lichtenstein (1988), "The Effect of Ad Claims and Ad Context on Attitude Toward the Advertisement," *JA*, 17 (1), 3-11.

Lichtenstein, Donald R. and William O. Bearden (1989), "Contextual Influences on Perceptions of Merchant-Supplied Reference Prices," *JCR*, 16 (June), 55-66.

——, Scot Burton, and Eric J. Karson (1991), "The Effect of Semantic Cues on Consumer Perceptions of Reference Price Ads," *JCR*, 18 (December), 380-91.

Urbany, Joel E., William O. Bearden, and Dan C. Weilbaker (1988), "The Effect of Plausible and Exaggerated Reference Prices on Consumer Perceptions and Price Search," *JCR*, 15 (June), 95-110.

SCALE ITEMS: VALUE (OFFER)

This is the version of the scale as used by Biswas and Burton (1993), Burton and Lichtenstein (1988; Lichtenstein and Bearden 1989), and Lichtenstein, Burton, and Karson (1991).

1. The _____ is: (**r**)

An excellent buy ____ : ____ : ____ : ____ : ____ : ____ : ____ : ____ : ____ A bad buy
       1   2   3   4   5   6   7   8   9

2. The prices represent: an extremely

No savings at all ____ : ____ : ____ : ____ : ____ : ____ : ____ : ____ : ____ Large savings
       1   2   3   4   5   6   7   8   9

3. The price is: **(r)**

An
extremely
fair price ___ : ___ : ___ : ___ : ___ : ___ : ___ : ___ : ___

        1   2   3   4   5   6   7   8   9

An
extremely
unfair
price

4. The _____ is: an extremely

Not a
good value ___ : ___ : ___ : ___ : ___ : ___ : ___ : ___ : ___

        1   2   3   4   5   6   7   8   9

Good
value

This is the version of the scale used by Urbany, Bearden, and Weilbaker (1988) with Likert-type items.

Strongly disagree	Moderately disagree	Slightly disagree	Neither agree nor disagree	Slightly agree	Moderately agree	Strongly agree
1	2	3	4	5	6	7

1. The advertised _____ is an excellent buy for the money.
2. At the sale price, the _____ is not a very good value for the money. **(r)**
3. The advertised offer represents an extremely fair price.

SCALE NAME: Value (Product)

SCALE DESCRIPTION:

A five-item, summated ratings scale purporting to measure the degree to which a consumer perceives that a product is a good value for the money. The measure was referred to as *perceived value indicators* by Dodds, Monroe, and Grewal (1991).

SCALE ORIGIN:

Dodds, Monroe, and Grewal (1991) state that the items for this and two other scales were "developed from previous research" (p. 312), although the source of the items and the extent of the borrowing were not specified.

SAMPLES:

The sample used in study conducted by Dodds, Monroe, and Grewal (1991) was composed of **585** undergraduate marketing students in a marketing class at a large state university. The study used a $5 \times 3 \times 3$ factorial design with 13 students per cell. The experiment was run a second time, apparently identical to the first one except for the product being studied.

RELIABILITY:

The scale was reported to have an alpha of **.93** for both of the experiments in which it was used by Dodds, Monroe, and Grewal (1991). Average interitem correlations were .73 and .72.

VALIDITY:

Quantitative results were not provided, but Dodds, Monroe, and Grewal (1991) stated that the results of an exploratory factor analysis indicated a three-factor solution was found using items from this scale and two others. The suggestion was that the items in this scale loaded on one factor.

ADMINISTRATION:

The scale was administered by Dodds, Monroe, and Grewal (1991) to subjects two times, once after each of the two experiments they participated in. A high score on the scale indicates that a respondent perceives a product to be a very good value for the money, whereas a low score suggests that the respondent thinks purchasing the product at the specified price would be a bad deal.

MAJOR FINDINGS:

Dodds, Monroe, and Grewal (1991) conducted a study of the impact of price, brand, and store information on consumers' perceptions of product quality, **value**, and purchase intention. Favorable store and brand information had positive effects on **product value** but price had a negative impact.

REFERENCE:

> Dodds, William B., Kent B. Monroe, and Dhruv Grewal (1991), ''The Effects of Price, Brand, and Store Information on Buyers' Product Evaluations,'' *JMR*, 28 (August), 307-19.

SCALE ITEMS: VALUE (PRODUCT)

1. The product is a:

Very poor value for the money	___ : ___ : ___ : ___ : ___ : ___ : ___	Very good value for the money
	1 2 3 4 5 6 7	

2. The product is considered to be a good buy.

Strongly disagree	___ : ___ : ___ : ___ : ___ : ___ : ___	Strongly agree
	1 2 3 4 5 6 7	

3. This product appears to be a bargain.

Strongly disagree	___ : ___ : ___ : ___ : ___ : ___ : ___	Strongly agree
	1 2 3 4 5 6 7	

4. At the price shown the product is:

Very uneconomical	___ : ___ : ___ : ___ : ___ : ___ : ___	Very economical
	1 2 3 4 5 6 7	

5. The price shown for the product is:

Very unacceptable	___ : ___ : ___ : ___ : ___ : ___ : ___	Very acceptable
	1 2 3 4 5 6 7	

SCALE NAME: Value (Total Savings)

SCALE DESCRIPTION:

A three-item, seven-point, summated rating scale measuring the perceived value of overall savings in the purchase of two particular products as a set at a certain price. Yadav and Monroe (1993) referred to the measure as *Total Transaction Value.*

SCALE ORIGIN:

Although not explicitly stated, the measure appears to have been developed by Yadav and Monroe (1993)

SAMPLES:

Usable data were collected and analyzed by Yadav and Monroe (1993) from **252** undergraduate students at a state university. Extra credit and a chance to win movie tickets were offered for students' cooperation. The average age of the students was 21.4 years, and the sample was 59.8% female.

RELIABILITY:

Yadav and Monroe (1993) reported an alpha of **.93** for the scale.

VALIDITY:

Yadav and Monroe (1993) reported no examination of the scale's validity.

ADMINISTRATION:

The scale used by Yadav and Monroe (1993) was self-administered by subjects along with several other measures after exposure to experimental stimuli. A high score on the scale implies that a respondent perceives all the savings involved in a two-product bundle to be a very good value, whereas a low score means that a respondent does not think that the offer is a good buy.

MAJOR FINDINGS:

The purpose of the experiment by Yadav and Monroe (1993) was to study the perceptions of consumers regarding the overall savings when they consider the purchase of multiple products as a set (bundle). The findings appeared to support the notion that the **total value of products** purchased as a set is a combination of the perceived savings if the products were purchased separately as well as the additional savings on the products as a bundle.

REFERENCE:

Yadav, Manjit S. and Kent B. Monroe (1993), "How Buyers Perceive Savings in a Bundle Price: An Examination of a Bundle's Transaction Value," *JMR*, 30 (August), 350-58.

SCALE ITEMS: VALUE (TOTAL SAVINGS)

1. Overall, if I bought A and B as a set, the deal I would be getting is

Very poor   ___ : ___ : ___ : ___ : ___ : ___ : ___   Very good
       1   2   3   4   5   6   7

2. Overall, buying both A and B as a set appears to be a good bargain.

Strongly   ___ : ___ : ___ : ___ : ___ : ___ : ___   Strongly
disagree   1   2   3   4   5   6   7   agree

3. Overall, if I bought both A and B as a set, I would be taking advantage of an attractive price reduction.

Strongly   ___ : ___ : ___ : ___ : ___ : ___ : ___   Strongly
disagree   1   2   3   4   5   6   7   agree

SCALE NAME: Value Consciousness

SCALE DESCRIPTION:

A seven-item, seven-point, Likert-type scale measuring the concern a consumer has for paying low prices contingent on some product quality expectations.

SCALE ORIGIN:

The scale is original to Lichtenstein, Netemeyer, and Burton (1990). Five marketing academicians judged the appropriateness of 33 items generated to represent the construct. After this procedure, 18 items remained. On the basis of a second round of five additional judges assessing the face validity of the items, 15 items were retained.

The items were then interspersed throughout a questionnaire given to 263 undergraduate and graduate business students. The seven items composing the final version of the scale were those that had corrected item-total correlations equal to or greater than .40. Confirmatory factor analysis provided evidence that the items were unidimensional and had discriminant validity. The construct reliability was calculated to be .80.

SAMPLES:

The data for the main study by Lichtenstein, Netemeyer, and Burton (1990) came from a convenience sample of **350** nonstudent adults from a medium-size SMSA. The majority of the sample was female (57%) and married (69%). College graduates composed 40% of the sample. The median age of respondents was between 35 and 44 years of age, and household income was between $30,000 and $39,999.

Lichtenstein, Ridgway, and Netemeyer (1993) collected data from shoppers who had received questionnaires in one of two grocery stores in a western SMSA (Boulder, Colorado). One thousand questionnaires were handed out at the stores, and **582** usable ones were returned by mail. A majority of the sample was female (75.9%) and married (58.6%). The median annual income range was $35,000–$49,999, and the median age was range was 35–44 years.

RELIABILITY:

As in the pretest, the internal consistency of the scale was calculated by Lichtenstein, Netemeyer, and Burton (1990) to be **.80** and item-total correlations were greater than .40. The main study by Lichtenstein, Ridgway, and Netemeyer (1993) also showed an alpha for the scale of **.82**.

VALIDITY:

Confirmatory factor analysis was used by Lichtenstein and colleagues (1990, 1993) in both studies to conclude that the scale was unidimensional and showed evidence of discriminant validity.

ADMINISTRATION:

Lichtenstein, Netemeyer, and Burton (1990) did not described the manner in which the scale was administered to the subjects in their study. However, it was clear that the scale was just one of many measures that composed the survey instrument. In Lichtenstein, Ridgway, and Netemeyer (1993), the scale was part of a survey instrument self-administered by shoppers after leaving the grocery store. High scores on the scale indicate that respondents are highly motivated by the desire to get the most for their money, whereas low scores suggest little or no concern with prices, comparative shopping, and/or product quality.

MAJOR FINDINGS:

Lichtenstein, Netemeyer, and Burton (1990) examined the effect of both **value consciousness** and coupon involvement on coupon redemption behavior. One of the major findings was that **value consciousness** explained a significant amount of variance in redemption behavior after accounting for coupon involvement.

Lichtenstein, Ridgway, and Netemeyer (1993) identified and measured seven related but distinct price perception constructs. The dependent variables that **value consciousness** predicted most strongly were ability and accuracy of recalling prices paid for grocery items.

REFERENCES:

Lichtenstein, Donald R., Richard D. Netemeyer, and Scot Burton (1990), "Distinguishing Coupon Proneness From Value Consciousness: An Acquisition-Transaction Utility Theory Perspective," *JM*, 54 (July), 54-67.

_____, Nancy M. Ridgway, and Richard G. Netemeyer (1993), "Price Perceptions and Consumer Shopping Behavior: A Field Study," *JMR*, 30 (May), 234-45.

SCALE ITEMS: VALUE CONSCIOUSNESS

Strongly disagree ___ : ___ : ___ : ___ : ___ : ___ : ___ Strongly agree
           1   2   3   4   5   6   7

1. I am very concerned about low prices, but I am equally concerned about product quality.
2. When grocery shopping, I compare the prices of different brands to be sure I get the best value for the money.
3. When purchasing a product, I always try to maximize the quality I get for the money I spend.
4. When I buy products, I like to be sure that I am getting my money's worth.

5. I generally shop around for lower prices on products, but they still must meet certain quality requirements before I buy them.
6. When I shop, I usually compare the "price per ounce" information for brands I normally buy.
7. I always check the prices at the grocery store to be sure I get the best value for the money I spend.

SCALE NAME: Verbal/Visual Processing Style

SCALE DESCRIPTION:

A 22-item, four-point, Likert-type, summated ratings scale measuring a person's preference for processing information in either a verbal or a visual modality. The measure was referred to as the *Style of Processing* (SOP) scale by Childers, Houston, and Heckler (1985). Burns, Biwas, and Bibin (1993) apparently used a seven-point response scale with the items.

SCALE ORIGIN:

The scale is original to Childers, Houston, and Heckler (1985). The measure was developed after work with another measure, the Verbal Visualizer Questionnaire (VVQ, Richardson 1977), indicated it did not have satisfactory reliability or factor structure. Thirty-six items were generated in addition to six from the VVQ. After administering the 42-item scale to 35 undergraduate students, item-total correlations were used to construct the final 22-item scale. Half of the items tapped the visual component and the other half tapped the verbal component. This final version of the scale included the six items from the VVQ.

SAMPLES:

Burns, Biwas, and Bibin (1993) gathered data from **377** undergraduate business students. Students were assigned randomly to one of eight treatment groups, and the experiment was conducted in a classroom setting.

The scale was administered in two studies reported by Childers, Houston, and Heckler (1985). The first study involved **263** undergraduate college student volunteers. The second study collected data from 106 subjects who were described as being undergraduate students at a major midwestern university. These subjects in the second study were divided into two groups, one with **54** subjects and the other with **52**.

The data gathered by Miller and Marks (1992) came from **124** undergraduate marketing students attending a large midwestern U.S. university. Volunteers were compensated for their participation with extra credit points.

RELIABILITY:

Childers, Houston, and Heckler (1985) reported an alpha of **.88** (n = 54) for the overall scale. The 11 items measuring the verbal component had an alpha of .81, and the 11 items measuring the visual component had an alpha of .86. The overall scale had an alpha of **.73,** and alphas of .72 and .73 were calculated for the verbal and visual subscales, respectively, by Miller and Marks (1992; Marks 1994). Likewise, Burns, Biwas, and Bibin (1993) reported alphas of .75 and .74 for the verbal and visual subscales, respectively.

VALIDITY:

Evidence of the scale's discriminant validity came from the insignificant correlations with two measures of processing ability (not style) by Childers and colleagues (1985). It also had no correlation with a measure of social desirability. Criterion validity was evident from the scale's significant correlations with measures of recall and recognition. Miller and Marks (1992) and Burns, Biwas, and Bibin (1993) did not report any examination of the scale's validity.

ADMINISTRATION:

The scale was self-administered by students along with other measures (Childers, Houston, and Heckler 1985). Miller and Marks (1992) and Burns, Biwas, and Bibin (1993) had subjects complete the scale along with other measures after exposure to experimental stimuli. High scores on the scale indicate that respondents tend to process information visually, whereas low scores suggest that they are more likely to process verbally.

MAJOR FINDINGS:

Burns, Biwas, and Bibin (1993) examined the influence of visual imagery as well as **verbal/visual processing style** on several typical attitude-related consequences of advertising. Among the findings was that **verbal/visual processing style** was found to moderate the effects of instructions to imagine on brand attitude.

Childers, Houston, and Heckler (1985) compared several measures of visual/verbal mental imagery. The measure of **verbal/visual processing style** was found to be significantly correlated with measures of aided recall and recognition. Specifically, retention appeared to be best for the verbally oriented processors.

Miller and Marks (1992) investigated the impact of sound effects on processing and reactions to advertisements. The **processing** scale was not used to test any hypotheses but to determine if there was a significant difference between treatment groups on that factor. No significant difference was detected.

COMMENTS:

Though the authors preferred to compute a single score for the items in this scale, they did point out that some researchers might desire to treat the visual and verbal components as separate dimensions. In that context they noted that the items measuring the verbal and visual components had alphas of .81 and .86, respectively. See also Oliver, Robertson, and Mitchell (1993) for another use of the scale.

REFERENCES:

Burns, Alvin C., Abhijit Biwas, and Laurie A. Bibin (1993), "The Operation of Visual Imagery as a Mediator of Advertising Effects," *JA*, 22 (June), 7-85.

Childers, Terry L., Michael J. Houston, and Susan E. Heckler (1985), "Measurement of Individual Differences in Visual Versus Verbal Information Processing," *JCR*, 12 (September), 125-34.

Marks, Lawrence J. (1994), personal correspondence.

Miller, Darryl W. and Lawrence J. Marks (1992), "Mental Imagery and Sound Effects in Radio Commercials," *JA*, 21 (4), 83-93.

Oliver, Richard L., Thomas S. Robertson, and Deborah J. Mitchell (1993), "Imaging and Analyzing in Response to New Product Advertising," *JA*, 22 (December), 35-50.

Richardson, Alan (1977), "Verbalizer-Visualizer: A Cognitive Style Dimension," *Journal of Mental Imagery*, 1 (1), 109-25.

SCALE ITEMS: VERBAL/VISUAL PROCESSING STYLE

INSTRUCTIONS: The aim of this exercise is to determine the style or manner you use when carrying out different mental tasks. Your answers to the questions should reflect the manner in which you typically engage in each of the tasks mentioned. There are no right or wrong answers, we only ask that you provide honest and accurate answers. Please answer each question by circling one of the four possible responses. For example, if I provided the statement, "I seldom read books," and this was your typical behavior, even though you might read, say, one book a year, you would circle the "ALWAYS TRUE" response.

Possible Responses:

Always true	Usually true	Usually false	Always false
1————————	——2————————	——3————————	——4

Items:
1. I enjoy doing work that requires the use of words. (W)*
2. There are some special times in my life that I like to relive by mentally "picturing" just how everything looked. (P) **(r)**
3. I can never seem to find the right word when I need it. (W) **(r)**
4. I do a lot of reading. (W)
5. When I'm trying to learn something new, I'd rather watch a demonstration than read how to do it. (P) **(r)**
6. I think I often use words in the wrong way. (W) **(r)**
7. I enjoy learning new words. (W)
8. I like to picture how I could fix up my apartment or a room if I could buy anything I wanted. (P) **(r)**
9. I often make written notes to myself. (W)
10. I like to daydream. (P) **(r)**
11. I generally prefer to use a diagram than a written set of instructions. (P) **(r)**
12. I like to "doodle." (P) **(r)**
13. I find it helps to think in terms of mental pictures when doing many things. (P) **(r)**
14. After I meet someone for the first time, I can usually remember what they look like, but not much about them. (P) **(r)**
15. I like to think of synonyms for words. (W)
16. When I have forgotten something, I frequently try to form a mental picture to remember it. (P) **(r)**

17. I like learning new words. (W)
18. I prefer to read instructions about how to do something rather than have someone show me. (W)
19. I prefer activities that don't require a lot of reading. (W) **(r)**
20. I seldom daydream. (P)
21. I spend very little time attempting to increase my vocabulary. (W) **(r)**
22. My thinking often consists of mental "pictures" or images. (P) **(r)**

*(W) = Verbal Items
(P) = Visual Items

SCALE NAME: Visibility (Product Usage)

SCALE DESCRIPTION:

A four-item, seven-point, Likert-type scale measuring the perception that if a new product were purchased it would be noticed by the consumer's reference group.

SCALE ORIGIN:

Although not specifically stated by Fisher and Price (1992), the scale is original (Fisher 1994). Items composing this scale were refined along with items intended to measure four other constructs. No information about this scale in particular was provided. In general, item-to-total correlations had to be more than .50 and items had to load on hypothesized factors. Items that did not fit these criteria were eliminated before use in the main study.

SAMPLES:

The convenience sample analyzed by Fisher and Price (1992) was a mixed-gender group of **172** undergraduate students.

RELIABILITY:

Fisher and Price (1992) reported an alpha of **.86** for the scale.

VALIDITY:

Fisher and Price (1992) did not specifically address the validity of the scale. However, they did state that the variance extracted for the scale was .67, which provides some limited evidence of its unidimensionality.

ADMINISTRATION:

The scale was administered to subjects along with other measures after they had been exposed to experimental stimuli (Fisher and Price 1992). A high score on the scale suggests that a respondent strongly believes that if some specified new product is bought, then its usage will be noticed by others in the reference group.

MAJOR FINDINGS:

The purpose of the study by Fisher and Price (1992) was to investigate the impact of perceived consumption **visibility** and superordinate group influence on the development of new product purchase intentions. Superordinate group influence was found to have a significant positive effect on perceived **visibility of product usage,** which in turn was found to have a significant positive effect on expectations of normative outcomes from early adoption behavior.

COMMENTS:

Fisher and Price (1992) used the scale to measure students' perceptions regarding a new product idea: cordless headphones. As noted subsequently, it seems possible that the statements could be adapted for use with other products and other reference groups.

REFERENCES:

Fisher, Robert J. (1994), personal correspondence.
_____ and Linda L. Price (1992), ''An Investigation Into the Social Context of Early Adoption Behavior,'' *JCR*, 19 (December), 477-86.

SCALE ITEMS: VISIBILITY (PRODUCT USAGE)*

Strongly   Strongly
disagree   ____ : ____ : ____ : ____ : ____ : ____ : ____   agree
                 0   1   2   3   4   5   6

1. If I bought one of the _____, other students would see me using it.
2. If I were to buy a _____, other students would recognize that I owned something that is new to the market.
3. It's likely that other students would notice if I were to buy a   .
4. If I bought a _____, other students would see that I had something that is unusual.

* The items were supplied by Fisher (1994). Also, the generic name of the product should be placed in the blanks. The term *students* should be replaced with a term/phrase that describes an important reference group of which the respondent is a member (e.g., professors, employees, housewives). If a general term such as *persons* is used, it changes the meaning of the scale somewhat.

SCALE NAME: Voluntary Simplicity (Ecological Awareness)

SCALE DESCRIPTION:

A four-item, five-point, summated ratings scale measuring the degree to which a person reports engaging in behaviors that can be interpreted as helping to preserve the environment.

SCALE ORIGIN:

All the items come from the work of Leonard-Barton (1981). Her exploratory factor analysis of an 18-item instrument indicated that there were six factors. A subsequent confirmatory factor analysis by Cowles and Crosby (1986) led to support for a three-factor structure, one of those being a **ecological awareness.** The composition of that factor as well as the phrasing of the items were similar, though not exactly the same, to what is shown here.

SAMPLES:

Four surveys were described in the article by Richins and Dawson (1992), but only the fourth involved the **voluntary simplicity** scales. Little is said about the sample except that the data were collected by a mail survey. The households were chosen randomly and sent a survey form, followed by a reminder letter and a second copy of the questionnaire two weeks later. The sample was composed of **86** people from a northeastern college town and **119** people from a northeastern rural area.

RELIABILITY:

The scale was calculated to have an alpha of **.62** (Richins 1994).

VALIDITY:

Richins and Dawson (1992) did not address the validity of the scale.

ADMINISTRATION:

The scale was one of several measures that were self-administered in the study by Richins and Dawson (1992). High scores on the scale suggest that respondents exhibit a high degree of concern for the environment in their behavior particularly by their recycling activities.

MAJOR FINDINGS:

The purpose of the multiple surveys conducted by Richins and Dawson (1992) was to construct a new measure of materialism. As a means of establishing the nomological validity of the scale, its association with several measures of **voluntary simplicity** were examined. Specifically, materialism was found to have a low though significant ($r = -.24$, $p < .01$) partial correlation with the **ecological awareness** aspect of **voluntary simplicity**. (The correlation was controlled for income.)

COMMENTS:

Richins and Dawson (1992) also used the items composing this scale in a larger measure of voluntary simplicity. That 13-item scale had an alpha of .61 (Richins 1994).

REFERENCES:

Cowles, Deborah and Lawrence A. Crosby (1986), ''Measure Validation in Consumer Research: A Confirmatory Factor Analysis of the Voluntary Simplicity Lifestyle Scale,'' in *Advances in Consumer Research*, Vol. 13, Richard Lutz, ed. Provo, UT: Association for Consumer Research, 392-97.

Leonard-Barton, Dorothy (1981), ''Voluntary Simplicity Lifestyles and Energy Conservation,'' *JCR*, 8 (December), 243-52.

Richins, Marsha L. (1994), personal correspondence.

_____ and Scott Dawson (1990), ''A Preliminary Report of Scale Development,'' in *Advances in Consumer Research*, Vol. 17, Marvin E. Goldbert, Gerald Gorn, and Richard W. Pollay, eds. Provo, UT: Association for Consumer Research, 169-75.

_____ and _____ (1992), ''A Consumer Values Orientation for Materialism and Its Measurement: Scale Development and Validation,'' *JCR*, 19 (December), 303-16.

SCALE ITEMS: VOLUNTARY SIMPLICITY (ECOLOGICAL AWARENESS)

Nearly never	Occasionally	Frequently	Usually	Almost always
1	2	3	4	5

1. Recycle newspapers used at home.
2. Recycle glass jars and bottles used at home.
3. Intentionally eat meatless meals.
4. Contribute to ecological or conservation organizations.

SCALE NAME: Voluntary Simplicity (Material)

SCALE DESCRIPTION:

A four-item, five-point, summated ratings scale measuring the degree of material simplicity in a person's lifestyle with particular emphasis on buying second-hand items and not using a car for transportation.

SCALE ORIGIN:

All the items come from the work of Leonard-Barton (1981). Her exploratory factor analysis of an 18-item instrument indicated that there were six factors. A subsequent confirmatory factor analysis by Cowles and Crosby (1986) led to support for a three-factor structure, one of those being a **material simplicity** component. The composition of that factor as well as the phrasing of the items were similar, though not exactly the same, to what is shown here.

SAMPLES:

Four surveys were described in the article by Richins and Dawson (1992), but only the fourth involved the **voluntary simplicity** scales. Little is said about the sample except that the data were collected by a mail survey. The households were chosen randomly and sent a survey form, followed by a reminder letter and a second copy of the questionnaire two weeks later. The sample was composed of **86** people from a northeastern college town and **119** people from a northeastern rural area.

RELIABILITY:

The scale was calculated to have an alpha of **.60** (Richins 1994).

VALIDITY:

Richins and Dawson (1992) did not address the validity of the scale.

ADMINISTRATION:

The scale was one of several measures that were self-administered in the study by Richins and Dawson (1992). High scores on the scale mean that respondents report a high frequency of buying used goods as well as using bicycles for transportation.

MAJOR FINDINGS:

The purpose of the several surveys conducted by Richins and Dawson (1992) was to construct a new measure of materialism. As a means of establishing the nomological validity of the scale, its association with several measures of **voluntary simplicity** were examined. Specifically, materialism was found to have a very low though significant ($r = -.18$, $p < .01$) partial correlation with the **material** aspect of **voluntary simplicity**. (The correlation was controlled for income.)

COMMENTS:

Richins and Dawson (1992) also used the items composing this scale in a larger measure of voluntary simplicity. That 13-item scale had an alpha of .61 (Richins 1994).

REFERENCES:

Cowles, Deborah and Lawrence A. Crosby (1986), ''Measure Validation in Consumer Research: A Confirmatory Factor Analysis of the Voluntary Simplicity Lifestyle Scale,'' in *Advances in Consumer Research*, Vol. 13, Richard Lutz, ed. Provo, UT: Association for Consumer Research, 392-97.

Leonard-Barton, Dorothy (1981), ''Voluntary Simplicity Lifestyles and Energy Conservation,'' *JCR*, 8 (December), 243-52.

Richins, Marsha L. (1994), personal correspondence.

_____ and Scott Dawson (1990), ''A Preliminary Report of Scale Development,'' in *Advances in Consumer Research*, Vol. 17, Marvin E. Goldberg, Gerald Gorn, and Richard W. Pollay, eds. Provo, UT: Association for Consumer Research, 169-75.

_____ and _____ (1992), ''A Consumer Values Orientation for Materialism and Its Measurement: Scale Development and Validation,'' *JCR*, 19 (December), 303-16.

SCALE ITEMS: VOLUNTARY SIMPLICITY (MATERIAL)

Nearly never	Occasionally	Frequently	Usually	Almost always
1	2	3	4	5

1. Buy the furniture you need at a garage sale or second-hand store.
2. Ride a bicycle or walk for transportation to work.
3. Buy needed clothing at a second-hand store or garage sale.
4. Ride a bicycle on errands close to home.

SCALE NAME: Voluntary Simplicity (Self-Determination)

SCALE DESCRIPTION:

A five-item, five-point, summated ratings scale measuring the degree of simplicity in a person's lifestyle with particular emphasis on making items rather than buying them and doing home repairs rather than hiring someone.

SCALE ORIGIN:

All but one (item 3) of the items come from the work of Leonard-Barton (1981). Her exploratory factor analysis of an 18-item instrument indicated that there were six factors. A subsequent confirmatory factor analysis by Cowles and Crosby (1986) led to support for a three-factor structure, one of those being a **self-determination** component. The composition of that factor as well as the phrasing of the items were similar, though not exactly the same, to what is shown here.

SAMPLES:

Four surveys were described in the article by Richins and Dawson (1992) but only the fourth involved the **voluntary simplicity** scales. Little is said about the sample except that the data were collected by a mail survey. The households were chosen randomly and sent a survey form, followed by a reminder letter and a second copy of the questionnaire two weeks later. The sample was composed of **86** people from a northeastern college town and **119** people from a northeastern rural area.

RELIABILITY:

The scale was calculated to have an alpha of **.48** (Richins 1994).

VALIDITY:

Richins and Dawson (1992) did not address the validity of the scale.

ADMINISTRATION:

The scale was one of several measures that were self-administered in the study by Richins and Dawson (1992). High scores on the scale mean that respondents report a high frequency of self-reliance in making goods (rather than buying them at a store) and performing repairs (rather than hiring someone else to do them).

MAJOR FINDINGS:

The purpose of the several surveys conducted by Richins and Dawson (1992) was to construct a new measure of materialism. As a means of establishing the nomological validity of the scale, its association with several measures of **voluntary simplicity** were examined. Specifically, materialism was found to have a very low though significant (r = −.15, p < .01) partial correlation with the **self-determination** aspect of **voluntary simplicity**. (The correlation was controlled for income.)

COMMENTS:

The reliability of the scale is so low that is unlikely to be reliable or unidimensional. Given that, its validity is suspect. Further development is certainly called for.

Richins and Dawson (1992) also used the items composing this scale in a larger measure of voluntary simplicity. That 13-item scale had an alpha of .61 (Richins 1994).

REFERENCES:

Cowles, Deborah and Lawrence A. Crosby (1986), "Measure Validation in Consumer Research: A Confirmatory Factor Analysis of the Voluntary Simplicity Lifestyle Scale," in *Advances in Consumer Research*, Vol. 13, Richard Lutz, ed. Provo, UT: Association for Consumer Research, 392-97.

Leonard-Barton, Dorothy (1981), "Voluntary Simplicity Lifestyles and Energy Conservation," *JCR*, 8 (December), 243-52.

Richins, Marsha L. (1994), personal correspondence.

_____ and Scott Dawson (1990), "A Preliminary Report of Scale Development," in *Advances in Consumer Research*, Vol. 17, Marvin E. Goldberg, Gerald Gorn, and Richard W. Pollay, eds. Provo, UT: Association for Consumer Research, 169-75.

_____ and _____ (1992), "A Consumer Values Orientation for Materialism and Its Measurement: Scale Development and Validation," *JCR*, 19 (December), 303-16.

SCALE ITEMS: VOLUNTARY SIMPLICITY (SELF-DETERMINATION)

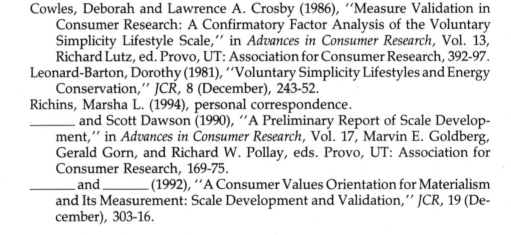

Nearly never	Occasionally	Frequently	Usually	Almost always
1	2	3	4	5

1. Make gifts instead of buying them.
2. Make clothing or furniture for the family.
3. Try to do your own home repairs instead of hiring someone.
4. Grow the vegetables the family uses during the summer season.
5. Family member or friend changes the oil in the family car when it needs changing.

SCALE NAME: Work-Oriented

SCALE DESCRIPTION:

A four-item, seven-point, Likert-type scale measuring the degree to which a person reports enjoyment of work in general and staying busy. This is not necessarily an indication of involvement or interest in a specific job.

SCALE ORIGIN:

Wilkes (1992) suggests that the items came from the AIO Item Library (Wells 1971). However, except for item 4, they were not apparent in that list, though they bear some similarity to items found there.

SAMPLES:

Data were collected by Wilkes (1992) from **363** females from three cities in a southwestern state. The ages of respondents ranged from 60 to 79 years. Private, religious, and civic groups were contacted followed by identification of additional groups and eventually the individuals who were asked to participate. Questionnaires apparently were delivered to respondents' homes and then picked up within a week.

RELIABILITY:

Wilkes (1992) reported a composite reliability of **.90**.

VALIDITY:

A confirmatory factor analysis by Wilkes (1992) indicated that the items had high loadings on a single factor.

ADMINISTRATION:

Data were gathered through self-administered questionnaires in Wilkes (1992). A high score indicates that a respondent likes to work and stay busy, whereas a low score suggests that a respondent would not want to work if he/she did not have to.

MAJOR FINDINGS:

Wilkes (1992) studied the measurement characteristics of "cognitive age" and its association with demographic antecedent variables as well as lifestyle-related consequential factors. Among the many significant findings was that cognitively younger women were more **work-oriented** than "older" females.

REFERENCES:

Wells, William D. (1971), "AIO Item Library," unpublished paper, Graduate School of Business, University of Chicago.

Wilkes, Robert E. (1992), ''A Structural Modeling Approach to the Measurement and Meaning of Cognitive Age,'' *JCR*, 19 (September), 292-301.

SCALE ITEMS: WORK-ORIENTED

Strongly disagree	Disagree	Slightly disagree	Neutral	Slightly agree	Agree	Strongly agree
1	2	3	4	5	6	7

1. I would work even if I did not have to.
2. In a job, satisfaction is more important than money.
3. There are so many things I want to do that I never get them all done.
4. I work very hard most of the time.

Part II

Advertising Scales

SCALE NAME: Ad Impressions

SCALE DESCRIPTION:

A four-item, six-point Likert scale purported to measure the participants' impressions of the ad.

SCALE ORIGIN:

LaTour, Pitts, and Snook-Luther (1990) indicated that this scale has been used previously by Aaker and Bruzzone (1985) and Bello, Pitts, and Etzel (1983).

SAMPLES:

LaTour, Pitts, and Snook-Luther (1990) had a sample of **202** business students who were taking a introductory management course at a southern university. The mean age of the sample was 20.98 years.

RELIABILITY:

LaTour, Pitts, and Snook-Luther (1990) reported a Cronbach's alpha of **.70**.

VALIDITY:

No examination of scale validity was reported.

ADMINISTRATION:

Participants were assigned randomly to one of the three treatment groups (Nude, Semi-nude, Demure). Each group viewed two original ads projected on the screen. The first ad was a perfume ad shown to disguise the nature of the study. The second one was the actual treatment ad shown to the three groups. These ads included the same copy and product image as the first ad, but each was designed to produce different level of arousal. The low-arousal (Demure) ad had a picture containing a fully clothed couple standing apart from each other in a non-suggestive pose, with a perfume bottle superimposed in the corner of the ad. The moderate-stimulus treatment (Semi-nude) had a picture of a nude female model with her breasts and lower abdomen covered with perfume bottle image. The high-stimulus treatment (Nude) had a picture of the same nude female model exposing her breast and lower abdomen without a perfume picture. After viewing the ads subjects administered the questionnaires in paper-and-pencil format. High scores indicate that participants have a positive impression about the ad.

MAJOR FINDINGS:

LaTour, Pitts, and Snook-Luther (1990) found that energy and calmness have a direct and positive effect on ad impressions, but fatigue has a direct negative effect. Gender and gender-by-treatment interactions have a significant total effect on ad impressions. Because of the canceling effect, female nudity will have little net effect on ad cognition if the scores are totaled for an audience made up of almost equal numbers of females and males.

REFERENCE:

Aaker, David A. and Donald E. Bruzzone (1985), "Causes of Irritation in Advertising," *JM*, 49 (2), 47-57.

Bello, Daniel C., Robert E. Pitts, and Michael J. Etzel (1983), "Communication Effects of Controversial Sexual Content in Television Programs and Commercials," *JA*, 12 (3), 32-42.

LaTour, Michael S., Robert E. Pitts, and David C. Snook-Luther (1990), "Female Nudity, Arousal, and Ad Response: An Experimental Investigation," *JA*, 19 (4), 51-62.

SCALE ITEMS: AD IMPRESSIONS

Strongly
disagree

1————————2————————3————————4————————5————————6

Strongly
agree

1. Distinctive
2. Inappropriate (r)
3. Interesting
4. Offensive (r)

SCALE NAME: Attention to Ad (Advertised Product/Message/Visual Aspects of the Ad)

SCALE DESCRIPTION:

A five-item, seven-point Likert scale ranging from ''none/not at all'' to ''very much'' measuring the amount of attention devoted to advertised product or written message in the ad. Muehling, Stoltman, and Grossbart (1990) used two versions of the scale. The first version contained three items and measured the amount of attention paid to the written message. The second version contained the same three items measuring the visual aspects of the ad.

SCALE ORIGIN:

The scales originally were developed by Laczniak, Muehling, and Grossbart (1989). A slightly modified version of the scales were used with broadcast ads by Bucholz and Smith (1991) to measure the amount of attention paid to a computer. Laczniak and Muehling (1993) used the scale to measure the attention paid to the written message in a 35mm camera ad. Muehling, Stoltman, and Grossbart (1990) indicate that the scale had been used previously by Cohen (1983) and Mitchell (1979).

SAMPLES:

Bucholz and Smith (1991) selected a 30-second informational computer commercial for a major national brand from 45 award-winning regional commercials as reviewed by *Advertising Age* (1986). Their test commercial had both strong verbal copy and strong visual elements, making it potentially effective as either a radio or TV spot. The commercial was three years old and had been played only on the west coast markets. None of the subjects reported seeing the commercial previous to the experiment. Bucholz and Smith (1991) selected **80** undergraduate students at a large midwestern university and gave course credit for completing the study. Of the total sample, 82.5% currently used personal computers, and 97.5% planned to use a personal computer in the next year. Laczniak and Muehling (1993) selected **280** students from introductory marketing classes to participate in their study for credit. Because students represent a potential target market for 35mm cameras and most of the studies used the student populations, this sample seems to be very appropriate. A full page for a fictitious brand of 35mm camera was used in the study as a target ad. Muehling, Stoltman, and Grossbart (1990) had **197** undergraduate students in their sample to be exposed to either comparative or noncomparative print ad for personal stereo-cassette players with headphones.

RELIABILITY:

Bucholz and Smith (1991) reported a Cronbach's alpha of **.95**. Laczniak and Muehling (1993) reported a Cronbach's alpha of **.94**. Muehling, Stoltman, and Grossbart (1990) reported a Cronbach's alpha of **.94** for written message and **.86** for visual aspects of the ad.

VALIDITY:

No examination of scale validity was reported.

ADMINISTRATION:

In Bucholz and Smith (1991), study subjects viewed or listened to the program and commercials in groups of ten spaced apart after they arrived at the experiment room. After the media exposure, subjects completed the cognition-listing task and filled out the remaining questionnaire items. The entire procedure took approximately 20 minutes. Laczniak and Muehling (1993) assigned the subjects to one of 12 treatment conditions. Subjects received an ad booklet and were instructed to turn to the inside front cover, read the printed instructions silently in five minutes, and proceed as directed. After the subjects finished reading, the booklets were collected and the questionnaires administered in a paper-and-pencil format. The questionnaires included a cognitive-response elicitation exercise, an unaided message recall measure, several self-report manipulation-check items, as well as measures of beliefs, brand attitudes, and attitude toward the ad. Muehling, Stoltman, and Grossbart (1990) had the subjects complete questionnaires dealing with perceived knowledge about, and product category involvement with, a variety of products. One month later, they randomly assigned the subjects to one of the two treatment conditions in a large group setting and distributed a 12-page booklet containing a test ad for a fictitious brand of personal cassette player. The subjects were allowed seven minutes to read the booklet. Afterward they completed self-administered post-exposure questionnaire.

MAJOR FINDINGS:

Bucholz and Smith (1991) analyzed scale using ANOVA. Their results indicate that the main effect to the scale was significant between the low- and high-involvement groups ($p < .001$). In addition, group means showed that low-involvement subjects were below the midpoint of the scale (3.39). Conversely, high-involvement subjects were above the midpoint of the scale (5.62). Laczniak and Muehling (1993) used this scale as manipulation check items. In their study, one high/low involvement manipulation set (DECIDE) produced the desired levels of discrimination between subjects on all the manipulation check variables. Tests of theoretical relations were not well supported. In fact, the only manipulation set to give consistent results with theory in both high- and low-involvement conditions was the only set that satisfied all the manipulation and confounding check requirements. Their finding emphasizes the need to consider both manipulation and confounding checks in experimental research. Muehling, Stoltman, and Grossbart's (1990) findings indicate that the comparative ad generated higher scores on attention to the written message. In general, they found that the comparative message was perceived as more relevant, received more attention, and was the subject of greater elaboration than the noncomparative message.

REFERENCES:

Bucholz, Laura M. and Robert E. Smith (1991), ''The Role of Consumer Involvement in Determining Cognitive Response to Broadcast Advertising,'' *JA*, 20 (1), 4-17.

Laczniak, Russell N. and Darrel D. Muehling (1993), ''The Relationship Between Experimental Manipulations and Tests of Theory in an Advertising Message Involvement Context,'' *JA*, 22 (3), 59-74.

———, ———, and Sanford Grossbart (1989), ''Manipulating Message Involvement in Advertising Research,'' *JA*, 16 (3), 3-12.

Muehling, Darrel D., Jeffrey J. Stoltman, and Sanford Grossbart (1990), ''The Impact of Comparative Advertising on Levels of Message Involvement,'' *JA*, 19 (4), 41-50.

SCALE ITEMS: ATTENTION TO AD (ADVERTISED PRODUCT/MESSAGE/ VISUAL ASPECTS OF THE AD)

Bucholz and Smith (1991) used the scale to measure the attention paid to the computer ad; therefore, at the end of each item, ''... the computer ad?'' should be appended (e.g., ''How much attention did you pay to the computer ad?'').

Laczniak and Muehling (1993) used the scale to measure the attention paid to the message; consequently, ''... the written message in the 35mm camera ad'' should be appended to each item in the scale (e.g., ''How much attention did you pay to the written message in the 35mm camera ad?'').

Muehling, Stoltman, and Grossbart (1990) used items 1, 2, and 5 to measure the attention paid to the written message; consequently ''... the written message in the ad?'' should be appended to three items in the scale.

Muehling, Stoltman, and Grossbart (1990) used items 1, 2, and 5 with a slight modification to measure the attention paid to visual aspects of the ad; thus ''pictures,'' ''how things looked,'' and ''layout'' should be substituted for ''written message'' accordingly.

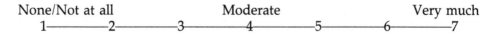

None/Not at all		Moderate				Very much
1———2———3———4———5———6———7						

1. How much attention did you pay to . . .
2. How much did you concentrate on . . .
3. How involved were you with . . .
4. How much thought did you put into evaluating . . .
5. How much did you notice . . .

SCALE NAME: Attention to Ad (Brand Evaluation)

SCALE DESCRIPTION:

A six-item, seven-point Likert-scale measuring how much attention is paid to the advertised brand and its features.

SCALE ORIGIN:

Laczniak and Muehling (1993) indicate that this scale has been used previously by Andrews (1988).

SAMPLES:

Laczniak and Muehling (1993) selected **280** students from introductory marketing classes to participate in their study for credit. Because students represent a potential target market for 35mm cameras and most of the studies used the student populations, this sample seems to be very appropriate. A full page for a fictitious brand of 35mm camera was used in the study as a target ad.

RELIABILITY:

A Cronbach's alpha was reported to be **.83**.

VALIDITY:

No examination of scale validity was reported.

ADMINISTRATION:

Laczniak and Muehling (1993) assigned the subjects to one of 12 treatment conditions. Subjects received an ad booklet and were instructed to turn to the inside front cover, read the printed instructions silently in five minutes, and proceed as directed. After the subjects finished reading, the booklets were collected and the questionnaires administered in a paper-and-pencil format. The questionnaires included a cognitive-response elicitation exercise, an unaided message recall measure, several self-report manipulation-check items, as well as measures of beliefs, brand attitudes, and attitude toward the ad.

MAJOR FINDINGS:

Laczniak and Muehling (1993) used this scale as manipulation check items. In their study, one high-/low-involvement manipulation set (DECIDE) produced the desired levels of discrimination between subjects on all the manipulation check variables. Tests of theoretical relations were not well supported. In fact, the only manipulation set to give consistent results with theory in both high- and low-involvement conditions was the only set that satisfied all the manipulation and confounding check requirements. Their finding emphasizes the need to consider both manipulation and confounding checks in experimental research.

REFERENCE:

Andrews, J. Craig (1988), ''Motivation, Ability and Opportunity to Process Information: Conceptual and Experimental Manipulation Issues,'' in *Advances in Consumer Research*, Vol. 15, Michael J. Houston, ed. Provo, UT: Association for Consumer Research, 219-25.

Laczniak, Russell N. and Darrel D. Muehling (1993), ''The Relationship Between Experimental Manipulations and Tests of Theory in an Advertising Message Involvement Context,'' *JA*, 22 (3), 59-74.

SCALE ITEMS: ATTENTION TO AD (BRAND EVALUATION)

Strongly   ___ : ___ : ___ : ___ : ___ : ___ : ___   Strongly
agree   1   2   3   4   5   6   7   disagree

(I paid attention to what was stated in the 35mm camera ad . . .)

1. . . . so I could evaluate the advertised brand.
2. . . . to help me evaluate the brand featured in it.
3. . . . so that I could determine the attributes of the brand featured in it.
4. . . . so that I could determine the benefits of the brand featured in it.
5. . . . so that I could rate the quality of the brand featured in it.
6. . . . so that I could determine what the brand featured in it had to offer.

SCALE NAME: Attention to Ad (Message Relevance)

SCALE DESCRIPTION:

A ten-item, seven-point Likert scale measuring the relevance of the message or the information in the ad.

SCALE ORIGIN:

Laczniak and Muehling (1993) indicate that this scale has been used previously by Andrews and Durvasula (1991). Muehling, Stoltman, and Grossbart (1990) indicate that this scale has been adapted from Lastovicka (1983), Wells (1986), Wells, Leavitt, and McConville (1971), and Zaichkowsky (1986).

SAMPLES:

Laczniak and Muehling (1993) selected **280** students from introductory marketing classes to participate in their study for credit. Because students represent a potential target market for 35mm cameras and most of the studies used the student populations, this sample seems to be very appropriate. A full page for a fictitious brand of 35mm camera was used in the study as a target ad. Muehling, Stoltman, and Grossbart (1990) had **197** undergraduate students in their sample to be exposed to either comparative or noncomparative print ad for personal stereo-cassette players with headphones.

RELIABILITY:

Laczniak and Muehling reported a Cronbach's alpha of **.96**. Muehling, Stoltman, and Grossbart (1990) reported a Cronbach's alpha of **.96.**

VALIDITY:

No examination of scale validity was reported.

ADMINISTRATION:

Laczniak and Muehling (1993) assigned the subjects to one of 12 treatment conditions. Subjects received an ad booklet and were instructed to turn to the inside front cover, read the printed instructions silently in five minutes, and proceed as directed. After the subjects finished reading, the booklets were collected and the questionnaires administered in a paper-and-pencil format. The questionnaires included a cognitive-response elicitation exercise, an unaided message recall measure, several self-report manipulation-check items, as well as measures of beliefs, brand attitudes, and attitude toward the ad. High scores on this scale indicate that respondents paid attention to the ad, because the message and/or information content of the ad was relevant to them. Muehling, Stoltman, and Grossbart (1990) had the subjects complete questionnaires dealing with perceived knowledge about, and product category involvement with, a variety of products. One month later, they randomly assigned the subjects to one of the two treatment conditions in a large group setting and distributed a 12-page booklet containing a test ad for a fictitious brand of personal cassette player. The subjects were allowed seven minutes to read the booklet. Afterward they completed self-administered post-exposure questionnaire.

MAJOR FINDINGS:

Laczniak and Muehling (1993) used this scale as manipulation check items. In their study, one high-/low-involvement manipulation set (DECIDE) produced the desired levels of discrimination between subjects on all the manipulation check variables. Tests of theoretical relations were not well supported. In fact, the only manipulation set to give consistent results with theory in both high- and low-involvement conditions was the only set that satisfied all the manipulation and confounding check requirements. Their finding emphasizes the need to consider both manipulation and confounding checks in experimental research. Muehling, Stoltman, and Grossbart's (1990) results indicate that comparative ad generated higher scores on perceived message relevance than noncomparative ad. In general, the comparative message was perceived as more relevant, received more attention, and was the subject of greater elaboration than the noncomparative message.

REFERENCES:

Andrews, J. Craig and Srinivas Durvasula (1991), "Suggestions for Manipulating and Measuring Involvement in Advertising Message Content," in *Advances in Consumer Research*, Vol. 18, Rebecca H. Holman and Michael R. Solomon, eds. Provo, UT: Association for Consumer Research, 194-201.

Laczniak, Russell N. and Darrel D. Muehling (1993), "The Relationship Between Experimental Manipulations and Tests of Theory in an Advertising Message Involvement Context," *JA*, 22 (3), 59-74.

Lastovicka, John L. (1983), "Convergent and Discriminant Validity of Television Commercial Rating Scales," *JA*, 12 (2), 14-23, 52.

Muehling, Darrel D., Jeffrey J. Stoltman, and Sanford Grossbart (1990), "The Impact of Comparative Advertising on Levels of Message Involvement," *JA*, 19 (4), 41-50.

Wells, William D., C. Leavitt, and M. McConville (1971), "A Reaction Profile for T.V. Commercials," *JAR*, 11 (6), 11-18.

SCALE ITEMS: ATTENTION TO AD (MESSAGE RELEVANCE)

Strongly disagree ___:___:___:___:___:___:___ Strongly agree
1   2   3   4   5   6   7

Laczniak and Muehling (1993) used the phrase "When I saw the ad for 35mm cameras, I felt the information in it ..."

Muehling, Stoltman, and Grossbart (1990) used the phrase "When I saw the ad for personal cassette player with headphones, I felt the information in it ..."

1. ... might be important to me.
2. ... might be meaningful to me.
3. ... might be "for me."
4. ... might be worth remembering.
5. ... might be of value to me.
6. ... might be relevant to my needs.
7. ... might be useful to me.
8. ... might be worth paying attention.
9. ... might be interesting to me.
10. ... would give me new ideas.

SCALE NAME: Attention to Ad (Task Relevance)

SCALE DESCRIPTION:

A three-item, seven-point Likert-like scale measuring how much attention is paid to the ad because of the purchasing considerations or having a need for the advertised item.

SCALE ORIGIN:

Laczniak and Muehling (1993) indicate that this scale has been used previously by Andrews and Durvasula (1991).

SAMPLES:

Laczniak and Muehling (1993) selected **280** students from introductory marketing classes to participate in their study for credit. Because students represent a potential target market for 35mm cameras and most of the studies used the student populations, this sample seems to be very appropriate. A full page for a fictitious brand of 35mm camera was used in the study as a target ad.

RELIABILITY:

Laczniak and Muehling (1993) reported a Cronbach's alpha of **.83**.

VALIDITY:

No examination of scale validity was reported.

ADMINISTRATION:

Laczniak and Muehling (1993) assigned the subjects to one of 12 treatment conditions. Subjects received an ad booklet and were instructed to turn to the inside front cover, read the printed instructions silently in five minutes, and proceed as directed. After the subjects finished reading, the booklets were collected and the questionnaires administered in a paper-and-pencil format. The questionnaires included a cognitive-response elicitation exercise, an unaided message recall measure, several self-report manipulation-check items, as well as measures of beliefs, brand attitudes, and attitude toward the ad. High scores on this scale indicate that respondents paid attention to the ad because they had a need for the advertised item or they were considering to purchase it.

MAJOR FINDINGS:

Laczniak and Muehling (1993) used this scale as manipulation check items. In their study, one high-/low-involvement manipulation set (DECIDE) produced the desired levels of discrimination between subjects on all the manipulation check variables. Tests of theoretical relations were not well supported. In fact, the only manipulation set to give consistent results with theory in both high- and low-involvement conditions was the only set that satisfied all the manipulation and confounding check requirements. Their finding emphasizes the need to consider both manipulation and confounding checks in experimental research.

REFERENCE:

Laczniak, Russell N. and Darrel D. Muehling (1993), ''The Relationship Between Experimental Manipulations and Tests of Theory in an Advertising Message Involvement Context,'' *JA*, 22 (3), 59-74.

SCALE ITEMS: ATTENTION TO AD (TASK RELEVANCE)

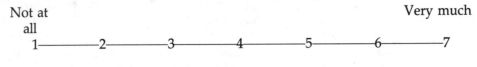

(I paid attention to the 35mm camera ad...)

1. . . . as though I were considering buying a 35mm camera.
2. . . . as though I had an immediate need for a 35mm camera.
3. . . . as though I had no immediate need for a 35mm camera. (r)

SCALE NAME: Attention Toward Advertised Brand (Computer)

SCALE DESCRIPTION:

A four-item, seven-point Likert scale ranging from "not at all" to "very much" measuring how much effort was devoted to evaluating the advertised computer brand.

SCALE ORIGIN:

The scales originally were developed by Laczniak, Muehling, and Grossbart (1989). A slightly modified version of the scales was used with broadcast ads by Bucholz and Smith (1991).

SAMPLES:

Bucholz and Smith (1991) selected a 30-second informational computer commercial for a major national brand from 45 award-winning regional commercials as reviewed by *Advertising Age* (1986). Their test commercial had both strong verbal copy and strong visual elements, making it potentially effective as either a radio or television spot. The commercial was three years old and had been played only on the west coast markets. None of the subjects reported seeing the commercial previous to the experiment. Bucholz and Smith (1991) selected **80** undergraduate students at a large midwestern university and gave course credit for completing the study. Of the total sample, 82.5% currently used personal computers, and 97.5% planned to use a personal computer in the next year.

RELIABILITY:

Cronbach's alpha was reported to be **.90**.

VALIDITY:

No examination of scale validity was reported.

ADMINISTRATION:

Subjects viewed or listened to the program and commercials in groups of ten spaced apart after they arrived at the experiment room. After the media exposure, subjects completed the cognition-listing task and filled out the remaining questionnaire items. The entire procedure took approximately 20 minutes.

MAJOR FINDINGS:

Bucholz and Smith (1991) analyzed scale using ANOVA. Their results indicate that the main effect to the scale was significant between the low- and high-involvement groups ($p < .001$). In addition, group means showed that low-involvement subjects were below the midpoint of the scale (3.01). Conversely, high-involvement subjects were above the midpoint of the scale (5.02).

REFERENCES:

Bucholz, Laura M. and Robert E. Smith (1991), ''The Role of Consumer Involvement in Determining Cognitive Response to Broadcast Advertising,'' *JA*, 20 (1), 4-17.

Laczniak, Russell N., Darrel D. Muehling, and Sanford Grossbart (1989), ''Manipulating Message Involvement in Advertising Research,'' *JA*, 16 (3), 3-12.

SCALE ITEMS: ATTENTION TOWARD THE ADVERTISED BRAND (COMPUTER)

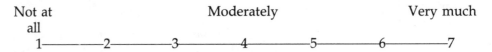

Not at all   Moderately   Very much

1———2———3———4———5———6———7

1. To what extent did you evaluate the advertised computer brand?
2. To what extent did you determine the benefits of the advertised computer brand?
3. To what extent did you rate the quality of the advertised computer brand?
4. To what extent did you examine the attributes of the advertised computer brand?

SCALE NAME: Attitude Toward the Advertiser

SCALE DESCRIPTION:

A six-item, seven-point Likert scale purported to measure perceptions toward the advertiser (perception of professional competence).

SCALE ORIGIN:

It is not clear where the items originated or where they were first used as a multi-item summated scale.

SAMPLES:

Milliman, Fugate, and Afzalurrahim (1991) used telephone survey format to contact 903 potential subjects, of which **650** participated in the survey.

RELIABILITY:

A Cronbach's alpha was reported to be **.81.**

VALIDITY:

No examination of scale validity was reported.

ADMINISTRATION:

Milliman, Fugate, and Afzalurrahim (1991) used an "operator assisted Phone-A-Matic random dialing machine" to contact the participants. Potential subjects were contacted between 7:30 and 9:30 PM, and each call took between 12 and 15 minutes. All interviews were performed by a live, professionally trained interviewer. Subjects were assigned randomly to one of the six treatment types by using a random number table. The questionnaires were administered to respondents following exposure to the advertisement.

MAJOR FINDINGS:

Milliman, Fugate, and Afzalurrahim's (1991) results indicate that only income and age were significantly associated with the attitude toward the advertiser (perception of professional competence). The ads that did not mention price and those that included the free initial consultation resulted in the highest ratings for professional competence, and the ads that stated specific prices resulted in the lowest.

REFERENCE:

Milliman, Ronald E., Douglas L. Fugate, and Afzalur Rahim (1991), "An Empirical Investigation into the Advertising of Legal Services," *JAR*, 31 (5), 51-60.

SCALE ITEMS: ATTITUDE TOWARD THE ADVERTISER

Strongly disagree 1————2————3————4————5————6————7 Strongly agree

1. Professional ability
2. Reputation
3. Quality of service
4. General impression
5. Trust
6. Likability

SCALE NAME: Attitude Toward the Ad

SCALE DESCRIPTION:

A four-point, six-item scale anchored by "no, definitely not" and "yes, definitely" used to measure a person's attitude toward the ad.

SCALE ORIGIN:

It is not clear where the items originated or where they were first used as a multi-item summated scale.

SAMPLES:

Henthorne, LaTour, and Nataraajan (1993) obtained **201** usable responses through the use of mall intercept. The sample consisted of 88 males and 113 females. The total sample had an average education of 13.7 years. The majority of the respondents were white (80 %) and had an average age of 31.5 years.

RELIABILITY:

A Cronbach's alpha of **.77** was reported.

VALIDITY:

No examination of scale validity was reported, though the authors reported that a factor analysis provided evidence of the scale's unidimensionality.

ADMINISTRATION:

Henthorne, LaTour, and Nataraajan (1993) collected the data through the use of mall intercept in a large regional indoor shopping mall in a demographically diverse SMSA in the mid-Atlantic region over a period of seven days during all hours of the mall operation. Trained interviewers varied their locations randomly throughout the mall and allowed some mall traffic to pass between interviews. They performed the stimulus manipulation by the use of print ad. One form of stimulus was an actual black and white ad containing a photograph (appeal with picture) and the other form was the same ad without the photograph (appeal without picture). Questionnaires were shuffled before they were distributed to provide random group assignments. One hundred one subjects were shown the "appeal without picture," and 100 subjects were shown the "appeal with picture." Subjects responded to the questionnaire after viewing the one randomly selected form of stimulus ad presented to them. They were asked to respond to the items in terms of how they felt right after exposure to the ad. Following completion of the arousal items, subjects responded to the items to measure the attitude toward the ad. Higher scores on the scale indicate a more positive attitude.

MAJOR FINDINGS:

> Henthorne, LaTour, and Nataraajan (1993) examined the theoretical supposi-
> tion that increasing tension generates energy up to a certain point and beyond
> that "threshold," increasing tension arouses anxiety, which begins to deplete
> energy. Their findings indicate that print ad induced arousal effects fell short
> of the "threshold" point. The "appeal with picture" stimulus has fallen
> short of the tension generation "threshold" separating the two hypothesized
> models.

REFERENCE:

> Henthorne, Tony L., Michael S. LaTour, and Rajan Nataraajan (1993), "Fear
> Appeals in Print Advertising: An Analysis of Arousal and Ad Response,"
> *JA*, 22 (2), 59-69.

SCALE ITEMS: ATTITUDE TOWARD THE AD

No, definitely not   ____ : ____ : ____ : ____   Yes, definitely
                        1   2   3   4

1. Good
2. Interesting
3. Informative
4. Appropriate
5. Easy to understand
6. Objective

SCALE NAME: Attitude Toward the Ad (Believability)

SCALE DESCRIPTION:

Composed of ten items with a seven-point response format, the scale is purported to measure the perceived believability of the performance claims of an advertised product.

SCALE ORIGIN:

The scale was created by Beltramini (1982, p. 1) to provide researchers with a way to measure the "extent to which an advertisement is capable of evoking confidence in its truthfulness to render it acceptable to consumers." An initial pool of items was generated and then reduced through pretesting to ten scale items and five distractor items. Then, data were collected from college students. The scale was tested on three ads and the alphas were all above .93. Due to the consistently high average inter-item correlations (r ≥ .61), evidence of convergent validity was claimed. Likewise, the lower average inter-item correlations between the scale items and distractor items (r ≤ .47) were provided as evidence of discriminant validity.

SAMPLES:

The data analyzed by Beltramini and Evans (1985) came from a national mail panel. Five thousand surveys were mailed to a probability sample of recently registered car owners. A total of **1994** usable forms were returned. No other demographic description of the sample was provided.

Beltramini (1988) gathered data from students in two large sections of a business course at a major American university. Analysis was based on information from **727** usable questionnaires. The sample was more male (55%) than female and the average age of respodents was 23 years.

The sample used by Beltramini and Stafford (1993) consisted of **330** adults. The sample was drawn from continuing education classes in eight widely separated American cities. In general, the sample was described as evenly divided between males and females and mostly full-time workers who were in their late twenties or thirties.

RELIABILITY:

Alphas of **.90** and **.97** were reported for the scale by Beltramini (1988) and Beltramini and Stafford (1993), respectively. No reliability information was provided by Beltramini and Evans (1985) with regard to the performance of the scale in their main sample.

VALIDITY:

No information was provided by Beltramini and Evans (1985), Beltramini (1988), or Beltramini and Stafford (1993) with regard to the scale's validity.

ADMINISTRATION:

In Beltramini and Evans (1985), the scale was included as part of a questionnaire that was mailed to panel members. Beltramini (1988) included the scale in a larger questionnaire booklet that was administered to college students apparently during class. Beltramini and Stafford (1993) administered the scale as part of a larger self-report questionnaire. Scoring of the scale is such that larger values indicate greater believability.

MAJOR FINDINGS:

The purpose of the field experiment conducted by Beltramini and Evans (1985) was to determine the effects that research results included in ads have on their believability. Four of the five hypotheses were not supported. The one that was supported showed a "threshold effect" on **believability** in research claims such that some evidence, even if legitimate, can be perceived by consumers as "too good to be true."

The believability of warning labels on cigarette packs by young people was investigated by Beltramini (1988). The findings indicated that the degree of **believability** of the warning label information was related to the person's prior attitude about the hazards of smoking.

Beltramini and Stafford (1993) explored the impact of seals of approval on the believability of ads. The authors concluded that seals of approval do not tend to have a substantial positive influence on the **believability** of ad claims.

REFERENCES:

Beltramini, Richard F. (1982), "Advertising Perceived Believability Scale," in *Proceedings of the Southwest Marketing Association*, Daniel R. Corrigan, Frederic B. Kraft, and Robert H. Ross, eds. Cape Girardeau, MO: Southeast Missouri State University, 1-3.

_____ (1988), "Perceived Believability of Warner Label Information Presented in Cigarette Advertising," *JA*, 17 (1), 26-32.

_____ and Kenneth R. Evans (1985), "Perceived Believability of Research Results Information in Advertising," *JA*, 14 (3), 18-24, 31.

_____ and Edwin R. Stafford (1993), "Comprehension and Perceived Believability of Seals of Approval Information in Advertising," *JA*, 22 (3), 3-13.

SCALE ITEMS: ATTITUDE TOWARD THE AD (BELIEVABILITY)

1. Unbelievable   ____ : ____ : ____ : ____ : ____ : ____ : ____ Believable
                     1   2   3   4   5   6   7

2. Untrustworthy   ____ : ____ : ____ : ____ : ____ : ____ : ____ Trustworthy
                     1   2   3   4   5   6   7

3. Not convincing ____ : ____ : ____ : ____ : ____ : ____ : ____ Convincing
                     1   2   3   4   5   6   7

4. Not credible ____ : ____ : ____ : ____ : ____ : ____ : ____ Credible
                  1   2   3   4   5   6   7

5. Unreasonable ____ : ____ : ____ : ____ : ____ : ____ : ____ Reasonable
                  1   2   3   4   5   6   7

6. Dishonest ____ : ____ : ____ : ____ : ____ : ____ : ____ Honest
                  1   2   3   4   5   6   7

7. Questionable ____ : ____ : ____ : ____ : ____ : ____ : ____ Unquestionable
                  1   2   3   4   5   6   7

8. Inconclusive ____ : ____ : ____ : ____ : ____ : ____ : ____ Conclusive
                  1   2   3   4   5   6   7

9. Not authentic ____ : ____ : ____ : ____ : ____ : ____ : ____ Authentic
                  1   2   3   4   5   6   7

10. Unlikely ____ : ____ : ____ : ____ : ____ : ____ : ____ Likely
                  1   2   3   4   5   6   7

SCALE NAME: Attitude Toward the Ad (Brand Reinforcement)

SCALE DESCRIPTION:

A two-item Likert scale, with some versions having up to seven items. The majority of development has been reported in conjunction with the items in Schlinger (1979a) purported to measure consumer attitude toward the ad which relate to the brand in a television advertisement. The items composing each of the scales are changed or modified on a user determined basis. The items reported in this summary represent those available in the published literature used in the development of this compendium.

SCALE ORIGIN:

This scale represents one of seven attitude constructs measured by the Leo Burnett Viewer Response Profile (Schlinger 1979a). An original list of 600 attitudinal statements were culled from verbatim responses of more than 400 viewers of 14 different commercials and story boards. These were reduced to 139 items through deletion of duplications and those items that were commercial specific or "theoretically" inappropriate by the researchers. The remaining statements were analyzed empirically to determine factor structure and discriminant characteristics of individual items. After five separate analyses and refinements, the final version of which represented an analysis of the mean item scores from the first four analyses, a seven-factor solution was achieved. In general, only those items with factor loadings of .5 or higher in at least three of the five factor analyses were retained for the scales. These items were then tested through 18 analyses of variance routines to determine their discrimination capabilities. Only items discriminating at $p < .01$ in at least six of 18 trials were retained. The outcome of these analyses produced the seven-factor, 32-item short version of the Leo Burnett Viewer Response Profile.

SAMPLES:

This scale was developed using post hoc data for the original 600 items. The first factor analysis sample consisted of 20 women per each of 25 tested commercials (n = 500) assumed to be from the Chicago area. The women were selected by age (half more than 35 years of age, half less than 35 years of age) and education level (about one-third had two or more years of college). The second factor analyses utilized a sample of 50 respondents similar to those in the first sample per each of ten of the 25 original commercials (n = 500). The third analysis used a total of 1504 men and women rating 42 different untested commercials. Though authors reported that sample controls remained constant, no indication of the controls is given. Because men were included in this sample, it is not clear that reference is to controls used in previous sampling. The fourth sample totaled 1871 men and women viewing one of 40 different commercials over a period of four years. No subject statistics are available. The fifth factor analysis sample represented all subjects previously used in the study (n = 4375). No sample information is explicitly stated for ANOVA analysis. During the course of the scale development study, 377 different commercials were used (Schlinger 1979a). Zinkhan and Burton (1989) use 26 product class users, each viewing 25 television commercials to attempt replication. Stout and Rust (1993) collected the data through a professional research firm using mall intercepts in several cities throughout the United States. The demographic characteristics of the sample (age, sex, and brand usage) were in the same proportion as they occur in the target population for the product category. Their sample size was 208, of which 50.5% were male.

RELIABILITY:

Individual items were test-retested with a 30-day interval for six different stimuli, resulting in correlations of .87–.97. Test-retest on a modified version of the scale (only five items—specifics not reported) over the same criteria as individual items yielded r = **.86**. Sample for reliability tests is 30 respondents per stimulus (n = 180). Stout and Rust (1993) reported an alpha coefficient of **.74**. As with scale construction, it seems that items are added and deleted at the discretion of the researcher. Caution in interpretation is suggested. The originator claims stability with small samples (Schlinger 1979a). The scale generally replicates in factor analysis in Schlinger (1979b). Coefficient of congruence is .703 for the entire Schlinger profile, and both items of the brand reinforcement scale loaded at less than .20 in replication of Zinkhan and Burton (1989). Scale stability is questionable.

VALIDITY:

Factor structure was similar to that found in previous research (Wells, Leavitt and McConville 1971), and some of items were developed on the basis of theoretical underpinnings, indicating that there is construct validity, face validity is claimed, and predictive validity is demonstrated through case analysis (Schlinger 1979a). Because the scale was developed in a realistic copy testing setting, the measure should be generalizable to that purpose. However, forced exposure to that condition warrants some caution if the scale is used to assess attitudes in less constrained viewing conditions. When used in conjunction with the other three scales developed by Schlinger to represent the viewer response profile that were replicated, Zinkhan and Burton (1989) reported reasonably good nomologic and predictive validity relative to attitude toward the brand (r = .32, p < .01) and choice behavior (r = .30, p < .01). Because this scale did not replicate in this study, its validity is highly questionable.

ADMINISTRATION:

The scale can be administered under typical survey design methodologies in a paper-and-pencil format or recorded response by researcher in personal or telephone interviews, though no use of the scale has been reported with the latter administrations. No time for administration is noted. Unfortunately, the researcher apparently can substitute, add, or delete items at whim, so the exact items to be used in administration may not be clear.

MAJOR FINDINGS:

Using a six-item version of the scale, Olson, Schlinger, and Young (1982) found consumers' mean scale scores were significantly higher (p < .001) when rating commercials for existing products than when rating new ones. However, two individual items were significantly higher for new products and two were higher for existing ones. Stout and Rust (1993) found that older viewers had more descriptive responses than did younger viewers, and overall findings show only limited support for this construct being more important than demographic characteristics such as age, sex, and brand usage in explaining evaluations of commercials.

COMMENTS:

Although the scale appears to be a reliable and valid measure of consumer attitude toward brand reinforcement of an advertisement, arbitrary changes in scale items during development shed some suspicion on the validity and reliability of the scale. Failure to replicate in Zinkhan and Burton (1989) throws serious doubt on this scale as valid measure.

REFERENCES:

Olson, David, Mary Jane Schlinger, and Charles Young (1982), "How Consumers React to New Product Ads," *JAR*, 22 (3), 24-30.

Schlinger, Mary Jane (1979a), "A Profile of Responses to Commercials," *JAR*, 19 (2), 37-48.

_____ (1979b), " Attitudinal Reactions to Advertisements," in *Attitude Research Under the Sun*, John Eighmey, ed. Chicago: American Marketing Association, 171-97.

Stout, Patricia A. and Roland T. Rust (1993), "Emotional Feelings and Evaluative Dimensions of Advertising: Are They Related?" *JA*, 22 (1), 61-71.

Wells, William, Clark Leavitt, and Maureen McConville (1971), "A Reaction Profile for TV Commercials," *JAR*, 11 (6), 11-17.

Zinkhan, George and Scot Burton (1989), "An Examination of Three Multidimensional Profiles for Assessing Consumer Reactions to Advertisements," *JA*, 18 (4), 6-14.

SCALE ITEMS: ATTITUDE TOWARD AD (BRAND REINFORCEMENT)

Instructions: The scale was developed with seven-point Likert anchors, in which 1 = strongly disagree; 2 = disagree; 3 = somewhat disagree; 4 = neutral or no opinion; 5 = somewhat agree; 6 = agree; 7 = strongly agree.

Schlinger (1979a): 1, 2
Schlinger (1979b): 1, 2, 3, 4

Olson, Schlinger, and Young (1982): 1, 2, 3, 4, 5, 6, 7
Stout and Rust (1993): 1, 2, 3, 4, 5, 6, 7

Items identified with an asterisk loaded less than .2 in Zinkhan and Burton (1989).

1. That's a good brand. I wouldn't hesitate recommending it to others.*
2. I know that the advertised brand is a dependable, reliable one.*
3. What they said about the product was dishonest. (r)
4. As I watched, I thought of reasons why I should not buy the product. (r)
5. The commercial described certain specific product characteristics that are undesirable to me. (r)
6. I found myself disagreeing with some things in the commercial. (r)
7. The commercial made exaggerated and untrue claims about the product. (r)

SCALE NAME: Attitude Toward the Ad (Company Image)

SCALE DESCRIPTION:

A two-item, seven-point Likert scale (1 = strongly disagree, 7 = strongly agree) purported image of firms in ads based on sex-role portrayals.

SCALE ORIGIN:

Ford and Latour (1993) indicated that they adapted the scale form previously work by Lundstrom and Sciglimpaglia (1977).

SAMPLES:

Ford and LaTour (1993) used three samples, which consisted of adult females in a large suburban area in the mid-Atlantic region. The first sample was selected form the League of Woman Voters (LOWV) organization. They believed that this sample population would access the more-educated, less-traditional, and higher-income females who tended to be sensitive to female role portrayals. From the mailing list of 276 members of the LOWV, 37 questionnaires were returned with addresses unknown. **Ninety-four** usable responses were obtained for an effective response rate of 39.3%. The majority of the sample were white (87%), were married (54.3%), and had nonmanagerial white-collar professions (42.0%). The second sample was selected from The National Organization for Women (NOW). **One hundred thirty** usable responses were received out of a 300-member list. The sample was 100% white. Most of the participants had nonmanagerial white-collar professions (62.6%) and were divorced or separated (48.6%). The third sample (general area sample) was obtained in a random area prenotification "drop-off-pickup" survey. **One hundred fifty** respondents were selected from a population of 355,900 adult females residing in the same large mid-Atlantic metro suburban area. Most of the sample were white (71.8%), had nonmanagerial white-collar professions (37.6%), and were married (62.3%).

RELIABILITY:

A Cronbach's alpha was reported to be greater than **.80**.

VALIDITY:

No examination of scale validity was reported.

ADMINISTRATION:

In the first and second samples, the questionnaires were mailed to the members of NOW and LOWV. The scale was self-administered by respondents along with other measures. In the third sample, the participants were contacted by telephone. When a respondent declared her intention to participate in the survey, the questionnaire was dropped off at the residence and retrieved after 30 minutes. High scores indicate that respondents expect a negative attitude toward women and minorities in the companies that portray women offensively in their advertising.

MAJOR FINDINGS:

The NOW sample was found to be significantly more in agreement with item 2 than either the LOWV sample or the general area sample. All three of the samples were found to be in agreement with item 1.

REFERENCE:

Ford, John B. and Michael LaTour (1993), "Differing Reactions to Female Role Portrayals in Advertising," *JAR*, 33 (5), 43-52.

SCALE ITEMS: ATTITUDE TOWARD THE AD (COMPANY IMAGE)

Strongly ____ : ____ : ____ : ____ : ____ : ____ : ____ Strongly
disagree   1   2   3   4   5   6   7   agree

1. Companies that portray women offensively in their advertising are more likely to discriminate against women and other minorities in job promotion and advancement, compared to the other companies in the same business or industry.
2. I believe that how women are portrayed in ads merely reflects the general attitude of that company toward women's place in society.

SCALE NAME: Attitude Toward the Ad (Confusion)

SCALE DESCRIPTION:

A five-item, Likert-like scale purporting to measure the cognitive confusion of specific television advertisements to consumers. Stout and Rust (1993) used a modified version as a three-item scale.

SCALE ORIGIN:

The scale was developed in a study by Lastovicka (1983) on the basis of items from a more complete list from the Leo Burnett Storyboard Test (1977). Subjects were exposed by Lastovicka (1983) in small groups to one of six different 60-second television commercials, then answered one open-ended question in which they were asked to list retrospectively the thoughts they had while viewing the commercial. The products advertised were six real, branded products (beer, blue jeans, soft drinks, and automobiles). Results of item measurements were factor analyzed, resulting in three factors representing relevance, confusion and entertainment. Each factor was treated as a scale measuring that respective construct and subjected to multitrait-multimethod testing per Kalleberg and Kluegel (1975). The comparison method was a content analysis of verbatim responses to the open ended question. Written answers to the question were coded as to what degree they indicated an irritation, entertainment, confusion, comprehension, counterargument, source rejection, or message acceptance response by two different coders, who attained a product moment correlation of .70. The relevance scaled factor was paired with rater-summed coded score of verbatims for counterargument, source rejection, and message acceptance.

SAMPLES:

Lastovicka (1983) used a convenience sample of **634** undergraduates from 20 class sections of a university business school. 83% of the sample used or purchased some brand from each of the four product classes in the month prior to the study. Stout and Rust (1993) collected the data through a professional research firm using mall intercepts in several cities throughout the United States. The demographic characteristics of the sample (age, sex, and brand usage) were in the same proportions that they occur in the target population for the product category. Their sample size was **208,** of which 50.5% were male.

RELIABILITY:

Cronbach's alpha was reported to be **.731**. (See "Validity" for an important note on reliability.) Stout and Rust (1993) reported alpha coefficient of **.74**.

VALIDITY:

Construct validity was demonstrated through factor analysis. Of the original 16 items, only those loading at least .30 on this factor alone were retained for the scale. Items expected to load on this factor did so, and those expected to load on other factors did not load on this factor. Confirmatory factor analysis of multitrait-multimethod structure indicate convergent and discriminant validity for this scale. However, analysis of the error variance indicates unacceptable levels of random error associated with this scale when paired with the open-ended measure. This finding draws into question the reliability of this measure.

ADMINISTRATION:

The scale is amenable to most survey research techniques using a paper-and-pencil questionnaire approach. Time for administration is not given but is assumed to be quite short. It is likely that this scale would be integrated into a larger measurement study in application.

MAJOR FINDINGS:

There are no major findings by Lastovicka (1983) associated with this scale beyond those regarding scale validation (discussed previously). Stout and Rust (1993) found that older viewers had more descriptive responses than younger viewers, and overall findings show only limited support for this construct being more important than demographic characteristics such as age, sex, and brand usage in explaining evaluations of commercials.

COMMENTS:

Caution should be exercised with use of this scale, as validation study provides no correlates to assess nomologic validity. Although face and content validity seem reasonable, reliability is unsatisfactory and all validation results could be sample specific. Moreover, subjects were in a forced exposure condition. Consumers in a realistic environment may choose to not expose themselves to commercials that they do see as relevant.

REFERENCES:

Kalleberg, A.L. and J.R. Kluegel (1975), ''Analysis of the Multitrait-Multitrait Matrix: Some Limitations and an Alternative,'' *Journal of Applied Psychology*, 60 (February), 1-9.

Lastovicka, John L. (1983), ''Convergent and Discriminant Validity of Television Rating Scales,'' *JA*, 12 (2), 14-23, 52.

Leo Burnett Company, Inc. (1977), *Manual for the Leo Burnett Storyboard Test System*. Chicago: Leo Burnett Co.

Stout, Patricia A. and Roland T. Rust (1993), ''Emotional Feelings and Evaluative Dimensions of Advertising: Are They Related?'' *JA*, 22 (1), 61-71.

SCALE ITEMS: ATTITUDE TOWARD THE AD (CONFUSION)

Instructions: Subjects are asked to rate each commercial on a six-point Likert scale in which Strongly disagree = 1 and Strongly agree = 6.

1. I clearly understood the commercial. (r)*
2. The commercial was too complex. +
3. I was not sure what was going on in the commercial. +
4. I was so busy watching the screen, I did not listen to the talk.
5. The commercial went by so quickly that it just did not make an impression on me.*
6. It required a lot of effort to follow the commercial.#

* Stout and Rust (1993) did not use these items.
\+ Stout and Rust (1993) combined these items as one.
\# This item used only by Stout and Rust (1993).

SCALE NAME: Attitude Toward the Ad (Empathy)

SCALE DESCRIPTION:

A nine-item, six-point Likert scale measuring the consumer attitudes toward the ad that relate to empathy with the advertisement.

SCALE ORIGIN:

The scale originally was used by Schlinger (1979). Of the 52 scalar items used by Stout and Rust (1993), 44 matched those items used by Schlinger (1979). Schlinger reported six dimensions consumers use to evaluate advertising (Relevant News, Brand Reinforcement, Stimulation, Empathy, Familiarity, and Confusion) and organized 44 scalar items into six groups.

SAMPLES:

Stout and Rust (1993) collected the data through a professional research firm using mall intercepts in several cities throughout the United States. The demographic characteristics of the sample (age, sex, and brand usage) were in the same proportion that they occur in the target population for the product category. Sample size was **208,** of which 50.5% were male. Sixty-eight percent of the sample was between the ages of 18 and 34 years, and 32 percent were between 35 and 49 years of age. Forty-eight percent of the sample were brand users.

RELIABILITY:

LaTour, Pitts, and Snook-Luther (1990) reported a Cronbach's alpha of **.70.**

VALIDITY:

No specific examination of scale validity was reported in the studies.

ADMINISTRATION:

After viewing the commercial, individuals answered an open-ended question assessing the thoughts and feelings evoked by the commercial and indicated his/her agreement with statements about the commercial and product.

MAJOR FINDINGS:

Stout and Rust (1993) found that older viewers had more descriptive responses than younger viewers, and overall findings show only small support that emotional response will be more important than demographic characteristics such as age, sex, and brand usage in explaining evaluations of commercials.

REFERENCES:

LaTour, Michael S., Robert E. Pitts, and D. Snook-Luther (1990), "Female Nudity, Arousal, and Ad-Response: An Experimental Investigation," *JA*, 19 (4), 51-62.

Schlinger, Mary Jane (1979), "A Profile of Responses to Commercials," *JAR*, 19 (2), 37-46.

Stout, Patricia A. and Roland T. Rust (1993), "Emotional Feelings and Evaluative Dimensions of Advertising: Are they Related?" *JA*, 22 (1), 61-71.

SCALE ITEMS: ATTITUDE TOWARD THE AD (EMPATHY)

Strongly disagree	___ : ___ : ___ : ___ : ___ : ___	Strongly agree
	1 2 3 4 5 6	

1. The commercial irritated me—it was annoying.
2. The commercial was in poor taste.
3. I felt as though I was right there in the commercial experiencing the same thing.
4. The commercial was silly.
5. I liked the commercial because it was personal and intimate.
6. That commercial insults my intelligence.
7. I felt the commercial talked down to me.
8. It was an unrealistic commercial—very farfetched.
9. The commercial was very realistic—that is, true to life.

SCALE NAME: Attitude Toward the Ad (Evaluation Judgments)

SCALE DESCRIPTION:

An 11-item, Likert-like scale purporting to measure the evaluation dimension of semantic judgment of a consumer toward specific television advertisements. Zinkhan, Locander, and Leigh (1986) used a three-item scale they maintained was based on the original work. Subjects were asked to rate each of 25 words representing possible characteristics of six advertisements presented as television commercials embedded in programming. The 25 words seem to come from previous research reported in Burke and Edell (1986), and the pool of words was used in construction of Reaction Profile Scales (Wells, Leavitt and McConville 1971). Subjects were exposed to the ad stimuli either once or twice per day for five consecutive days. The television shows in which the commercials were imbedded were the movies *The African Queen* and *Casablanca*, shown in five 30-minute segments. Scale measurements were taken from the same subjects each day. Then data were subjected to factor analysis. Three factors emerged and were labeled by the authors as evaluation, activity, and gentleness. The 11 items in this scale represent the first of those three factors.

SCALE ORIGIN:

The scale was developed for the study reported here.

SAMPLES:

Subjects were **191** people recruited by ads in a newspaper and announcements distributed on a university campus. Other than the fact that subjects were deceived about true purpose of research and were paid for participation, no other description of the sample was given; it would be reasonable to assume it consisted of university students, however. (The scale development subjects were also used for the research reported in "Major Findings.") In Zinkhan, Locander, and Leigh (1986), 420 subjects recruited and compensated by an ad agency were divided evenly among 20 treatment groups.

RELIABILITY:

Cronbach's alpha was reported to be **.89**, although it may be biased upward because the measure was based on 1146 observations (six per subject). Authors used repeated measures of the 191 subjects over six different stimuli. Because of repeated measurement by same subjects, authors claim replicatibility although stimuli were different. Zinkhan, Locander, and Leigh (1986) reported an alpha of **.95** with their version.

VALIDITY:

Content analysis is demonstrated through principle components factor analysis. Of the original 25 items, only those loading at least .50 on this factor alone were retained for the scale. Factors were virtually identical factors found in previous research (Edell and Burke 1987).

ADMINISTRATION:

The scale is a paper-and-pencil instrument amenable to survey research and experimental studies. Although measurement requires an object stimulus, it is not necessary that administration be temporally contingent with stimulus presentation. No time period for administration was reported.

MAJOR FINDINGS:

In Burke and Edell (1989), structural equation analysis indicates evaluation judgments have a significant ($p < .05$) direct effect on attitude toward the ad. They also act as an intermediating variable in channeling significant indirect effects of "upbeat," "warm," and "negative" feelings to attitudes toward the ad, brand attribute evaluations, and attitude toward the brand through attitude toward the ad. Using external single sets components analysis, Zinkhan, Locander, and Leigh (1986) found a "strong" relationship between attitude toward the ad and aided brand recall and ad recognition.

COMMENTS:

Although the authors claim generalizability for their findings, lack of important sample information indicates caution in this respect. See Zinkhan, Locander (1986) and Leigh for a three-item evaluative scale purported to be based upon this scale. It is not clear how the three items were selected.

REFERENCES:

Burke, Marian Chapman and Julie A. Edell (1989), "The Impact of Feelings on Ad-Based Affect and Cognitions," *JMR*, 26 (February), 69-83.
Edell, Julie E. and Marian C. Burke (1987), "The Power of Feelings in Understanding Advertising Effects," *JCR*, 14 (December), 421-33.
Wells, William D., Clark Leavitt, and Maureen McConville (1971), "A Reaction Profile for TV Commercials," *JAR*, 11 (December), 11-17.
Zinkhan, George M., William B. Locander, and James H. Leigh (1986), "Dimensional Relationships of Aided Recall and Recognition," *JA*, 15 (1), 38-46.

SCALE ITEMS: ATTITUDE TOWARD THE AD (EVALUATION JUDGMENTS)*

Instructions: Please tell us how well you think each of the words listed below describes the ad you have just seen by putting a number to the right of the word. Here, we are interested in your thoughts about the ad, not the brand or product class. If you think the word describes the ad extremely well, put a 5; very well, put a 4; fairly well, put a 3; not very well, put a 2; not at all well, put a 1.

1. Believable
2. For me
3. Informative
4. Interesting
5. Irritating (r)
6. Meaningful to me
7. Phony (r)
8. Ridiculous (r)
9. Terrible (r)
10. Valuable
11. Worth remembering
12. Liked the ad
13. Enjoyed the ad
14. Found ad to be good

* Zinkhan, Locander, and Leigh (1986) used an eight-point Likert format with items 12–14.

SCALE NAME: Attitude Toward the Ad (Familiarity)

SCALE DESCRIPTION:

A three-item, seven-point Likert scale, though some versions have more or less items. The majority of development has been reported in conjunction with the items in Schlinger (1979a) purported to measure consumer attitude toward the ad which relate to the familiarity with the advertisement. This scale represents one of seven attitude constructs measured by the Leo Burnett Viewer Response Profile. The items composing each of the scales are changed or modified on a user-determined basis. The items reported here represent those available in the published literature used in the development of this compendium. Stout and Rust (1993) used the six-point version of the scale.

SCALE ORIGIN:

An original list of 600 attitudinal statements were culled from verbatim responses of more than 400 viewers of 14 different commercials and story boards. These were reduced to 139 items through deletion of duplications and those items that were commercial specific or "theoretically" inappropriate by the researchers. The remaining statements were analyzed empirically to determine factor structure and discriminant characteristics of individual items. After five separate analyses and refinements, the final of which represented an analysis of the mean item scores from the first four analyses, a seven factor solution was achieved. In general, only those items with factor loadings of .5 or higher in at least three of the five factor analyses were retained for the scales. These items then were tested through 18 analyses of variance routines to determine their discrimination capabilities. Only items discriminating at $p < .01$ in at least six of 18 trials were retained. The outcome of these analyses produced the seven-factor, 32-item short version of the Leo Burnett Viewer Response Profile (Schlinger 1979a).

SAMPLES:

This scale was developed using post hoc data for the original 600 items. The first factor analysis sample consisted of 20 women per each of 25 tested commercials (n = **500**) assumed to be from the Chicago area. The women were selected by age (half more than 35 years of age, half less than 35 years of age) and education level (about one-third had two or more years of college). The second factor analysis utilized a sample of 50 respondents similar to those in the first sample per each of 10 of the 25 original commercials (n = **500**). The third analysis used a total of **1504** men and women rating 42 different untested commercials. Though authors reported sample controls remained constant, no indication of the controls is given. Because men were included in this sample, it is not clear that the reference is to controls used in previous sampling. The fourth sample totaled **1871** men and women rating viewing one of 40 different commercials over a period of four years. No subject statistics are available. The fifth factor analyses sample represented all subjects previously used in the study (n = **4375**). No sample information is explicitly stated for

ANOVA analysis. During course of the scale development study, 377 different commercials were used (Schlinger 1979a). Zinkhan and Burton (1989) do not test this scale in their work. Stout and Rust (1993) collected the data through a professional research firm using mall intercepts in several cities throughout the United States. The demographic characteristics of the sample (age, sex, and brand usage) were in the same proportion that they occur in the target population for the product category. Their sample size was **208,** of which 50.5% were male.

RELIABILITY:

Test-retest was conducted for the individual items with a 30-day interval for six different stimuli and resulted in correlations of **.87–.97**. A two-item version test-retest over same criteria as individual items yielded r = .62. Sample for reliability tests was 30 respondents per stimulus (n = 180). As with scale construction, it seems that items are added and deleted at the discretion of the researcher. Caution in use is suggested. Author claims stability with small samples. (Schlinger 1979a). Scale generally replicates the factor structure in Schlinger (1979b).

VALIDITY:

Factor structure was similar to structure found in previous research (Wells, Leavitt, and McConville 1971), and some of items were developed on the basis of theoretical underpinnings, indicating that there is construct validity, face validity is claimed, and predictive validity is demonstrated through case analysis (Schlinger 1979a). Because the scale was developed in a realistic copy testing setting, measure should be generalizable to that purpose. However, forced exposure to that condition warrants some caution if scale is used to assess attitudes in less constrained viewing conditions.

ADMINISTRATION:

Scale can be administered under typical survey design methodologies in a paper-and-pencil format or recorded response by researcher in personal or telephone interviews though no use of the scale has been reported with the latter administrations. No time for administration was noted. Unfortunately the researcher can apparently substitute, add, or delete items at whim, so the exact items to be used in administration may not be clear.

MAJOR FINDINGS:

Using a four-item version of the scale, Olson, Schlinger, and Young (1982) found that consumers' mean scale scores were significantly higher (p .001) when rating commercials for existing products than when rating new ones. Stout and Rust (1993) found that older viewers had more descriptive responses than younger viewers, and overall findings show only limited support for this construct being more important than demographic characteristics such as age, sex, and brand usage in explaining evaluations of commercials.

COMMENTS:

Although this scale appears to be a reliable and valid measure of consumer familiarity with an advertisement, arbitrary changes in scale items during development throw some suspicion on the validity and reliability of the scale.

REFERENCES:

Olson, David, Mary Jane Schlinger, and Charles Young (1982), "How Consumers React to New Product Ads," *JAR*, 22 (3), 24-30.

Schlinger, Mary Jane (1979a), "A Profile of Responses to Commercials," *JAR*, 19 (2), 37-48.

———— (1979b), "Attitudinal Reactions to Advertisements," in *Attitude Research Under the Sun*, John Eighmey, ed. Chicago: American Marketing Association, 171-97.

Stout, Patricia A. and Roland T. Rust (1993), "Emotional Feelings and Evaluative Dimensions of Advertising: Are They Related?" *JA*, 22 (1), 61-71.

Wells, William, Clark Leavitt, and Maureen McConville (1971), "A Reaction Profile for TV Commercials," *JAR*, 11 (6), 11-17.

Zinkhan, George and Scot Burton (1989), "An Examination of Three Multidimensional Profiles for Assessing Consumer Reactions to Advertisements," *JA*, 18 (4), 6-14.

SCALE ITEMS: ATTITUDE TOWARD THE AD (FAMILIARITY)

Instructions: Scale was developed with seven-point Likert anchors in which 1 = strongly disagree; 2 = disagree; 3 = somewhat disagree; 4 = neutral or no opinion; 5 = somewhat agree; 6 = agree; 7 = strongly agree.

NOTE: Scale seems to be used without the "neutral" or "no opinion" category as a six-point, forced-choice scale.

Scale items reported here are from Schlinger (1979a), denoted by an "a"; Schlinger (1979b), denoted by a "b"; Olson, Schlinger, and Young (1982), by a "c"; and Stout and Rust (1993) by a "d." It is not clear when specific items should be deleted from any particular scale usage. Item 2 is also included in the entertainment scale assessed elsewhere in this compendium.

1. This kind of commercial has been done many times...it's the same old thing.[a]
2. I've seen this commercial so many times — I'm tired of it.[abcd]
3. I think that this is an unusual commercial. I'm not sure I've seen another one like it.[a]
4. Familiar.[bcd]
5. Saw before.[bcd]

SCALE NAME: Attitude Toward the Ad (Humor)

SCALE DESCRIPTION:

A four-item, nine-point semantic differential scale purporting to measure the subjects' perceptions of humor in an advertisement.

SCALE ORIGIN:

The scale was used originally by Chattopadhyay and Basu (1990).

SAMPLES:

Sample size in Chattopadhyay and Basu (1990) was **80**. No sample specific information was provided.

RELIABILITY:

A Cronbach's alpha of **.91** was reported.

VALIDITY:

No specific examination of the validity was reported.

ADMINISTRATION:

Subjects participated in groups of two to five people. Immediately after the completion of the final filler task, the main study was conducted. All subjects saw a 15-minute segment from a television program on doing business overseas. There were three commercials, during the first commercial break. The first ad in pod was the target ad, which was followed by two filler ads. For half the subjects, the embedded target ad was the humorous version; for the other half it was the nonhumorous version. Before the subjects were handed the main questionnaire, subjects received a one-page questionnaire to seek their opinion of the program.

MAJOR FINDINGS:

The subjects in the positive prior brand evaluation condition had a significantly more favorable ad attitude when exposed to the humorous ad than when exposed to the nonhumorous ad. In contrast, subjects in the negative prior brand evaluation condition tended to have a more favorable ad attitude when exposed to the nonhumorous ad than when exposed to the humorous ad. However, the differences in the means are not statistically significant.

REFERENCE:

Chattopadhyay, Amitava and Kunal Basu (1990), "Humor in Advertising: The Moderating Role of Prior Brand Evaluation," *JMR*, 27 (November), 466-76.

SCALE ITEMS: ATTITUDE TOWARD THE AD (HUMOR)

Pleasant   ___ : ___ : ___ : ___ : ___ : ___ : ___ : ___ : ___   Unpleasant
           1   2   3   4   5   6   7   8   9

Likable   ___ : ___ : ___ : ___ : ___ : ___ : ___ : ___ : ___   Unlikable
           1   2   3   4   5   6   7   8   9

Not
irritating   ___ : ___ : ___ : ___ : ___ : ___ : ___ : ___ : ___   Irritating
           1   2   3   4   5   6   7   8   9

Interesting   ___ : ___ : ___ : ___ : ___ : ___ : ___ : ___ : ___   Uninteresting
           1   2   3   4   5   6   7   8   9

SCALE NAME: Attitude Toward the Ad (Purchase Intention)

SCALE DESCRIPTION:

A three-item, seven-point Likert-type scale (1= strongly disagree, 7 = strongly agree) purported to measure the purchase intention.

SCALE ORIGIN:

Ford and LaTour (1993) indicated that they adapted the scale from previous work by Lundstrom and Sciglimpaglia (1977).

SAMPLES:

Ford and LaTour (1993) had three samples consisting of adult females residing in a large metro suburban area in the mid-Atlantic region. The first sample was selected from League of Women Voters (LOWV) organization. They believed that this sample population would access the more-educated, less-traditional, and higher-income females who tended to be sensitive to female role portrayals. From the mailing list of 276 members of the LOWV 37 questionnaires were returned with addresses unknown. **Ninety-four** usable responses were obtained for an effective response rate of 39.3%. The majority of the sample were white (87%), were married (54.3%), and had nonmanagerial white-collar professions (42.0%). The second sample was selected from The National Organization for Women (NOW). **One hundred thirty** usable responses were received out of a 300-member list. The sample was 100% white. Most of the participants had nonmanagerial white-collar professions (62.6%) and were divorced or separated (48.6%). The third sample (general area sample) was obtained in a random area prenotification "drop-off-pickup" survey. **One hundred fifty** respondents were selected from a population of 355,900 adult females residing in the same large mid-Atlantic metro suburban area. Most of the sample were white (71.8%), had nonmanagerial white-collar professions (37.6%), and were married (62.3 %).

RELIABILITY:

A Cronbach's alpha was reported to be greater than **.80**.

VALIDITY:

No examination of scale validity was reported.

ADMINISTRATION:

In the first and second samples, the questionnaires were mailed to the members of NOW and LOWV. The scale was self-administered by respondents along with other measures. In the third sample, the participants were contacted by telephone. Once a respondent declared her intention to participate

in the survey, the questionnaire was dropped off at the residence and retrieved after 30 minutes.

MAJOR FINDINGS:

Both the NOW and the LOWV samples were found to be significantly more
in disagreement with item 1. The LOWV sample was significantly less in
agreement with item 2 and significantly less in disagreement with item 3
than was the NOW sample. The general area sample was indifferent to item
1, showed slight disagreement with item 2, and slight agreement with item
3.

REFERENCE:

Ford, John B. and Michael LaTour (1993), "Differing Reactions to Female
Role Portrayals in Advertising," *JAR*, (33) 5, 43-52.
Schlinger, M.J. (1979), "A Profile of Responses to Commercials," *JAR*, 19
(2), 37-48.

SCALE ITEMS: ATTITUDE TOWARD THE AD (PURCHASE INTENTION)

Strongly ____ : ____ : ____ : ____ : ____ : ____ : ____ Strongly
disagree   1   2   3   4   5   6   7   agree

1. If a new product is introduced with ads that I find offensive, I might still
   buy it if it offers me benefits which I find attractive.
2. If a new product or service which I use adopts an ad campaign which I
   find offensive, I'll discontinue using it.
3. Even though I may see an ad which is offensive for one product, I would
   continue to purchase other products that I have been using from the same
   company.

SCALE NAME: Attitude Toward the Ad (Relevant News)

SCALE DESCRIPTION:

A five-item Likert scale, with some versions having up to 11 items. The majority of development has been reported in conjunction with the items in Schlinger (1979a) purported to measure consumer attitude toward the relevant news value of a television advertisement. The items composing each of the scales are changed or modified on a user-determined basis. The items reported in this summary represent those available in the published literature used in the development of this compendium.

SCALE ORIGIN:

This scale represents one of seven attitude constructs measured by the Leo Burnett Viewer Response Profile (Schlinger 1979a). An original list of 600 attitudinal statements were culled from verbatim responses of more than 400 viewers of 14 different commercials and story boards. These were reduced to 139 items through deletion of duplications and those items that were commercial specific or "theoretically" inappropriate by the researchers. The remaining statements were analyzed empirically to determine factor structure and discriminant characteristics of individual items. After five separate analyses and refinements, the final version of which represented an analysis of the mean item scores from the first for analyses, a seven-factor solution was achieved. In general, only those items with factor loadings of .5 or higher in at least three of the five factor analyses were retained for the scales. These items then were tested through 18 analyses of variance routines to determine their discrimination capabilities. Only items discriminating at p < .01 in at least six of 18 trials were retained. The outcome of these analyses produced the seven-factor, 32-item short version of the Leo Burnett Viewer Response Profile.

SAMPLES:

This scale was developed using post hoc data for the original 600 items. The first factor analysis sample consisted of 20 women per each of 25 tested commercials (n = **500**) assumed to be from the Chicago area. The women were selected by age (half more than 35 years of age, half less than 35 years of age) and education level (about one-third had two or more years of college). The second factor analyses utilized a sample of 50 respondents similar to those in the first sample per each of 10 of the 25 original commercials (n = **500**). The third analysis used a total of **1504** men and women rating 42 different untested commercials. Though authors reported sample controls remained constant, no indication of the controls is given. Because men were included in this sample, it is not clear that the reference is to controls used in previous sampling. The fourth sample totaled **1871** men and women viewing one of 40 different commercials over a period of four years. No subject statistics are available. The fifth factor analyses sample represented all subjects previously used in the study (n = **4375**). No sample information is explicitly stated for

ANOVA analysis. During the course of the scale development study, 377 different commercials were used (Schlinger 1979a). Zinkhan and Burton (1989) use 26 product class users, each viewing 25 television commercials to attempt replication. Stout and Rust (1993) collected the data through a professional research firm using mall intercepts in several cities throughout the United States. The demographic characteristics of the sample (age, sex, and brand usage) were in the same proportion that they occur in the target population for the product category. Their sample size was **208,** of which 50.5% were male.

RELIABILITY:

Individual items test-retest with 30-day interval for six different stimuli resulted in correlations of **.87–.97.** Test-retest over the same criteria as individual items yielded r = **.87.** Sample for reliability tests = 30 respondents per stimulus (n = 180). Stout and Rust (1993) reported an alpha coefficient of .74. NOTE: as with scale construction, it seems that items are added and deleted at the discretion of the researcher. Caution in interpretation is suggested. The author claims stability with small samples (Schlinger 1979a). The scale generally replicates in factor analysis in Schlinger (1979b). Coefficient of congruence = .703 for entire Schlinger profile, and two of five items of the relevant news scale loaded at less than .20 in replication of Zinkhan and Burton (1989). Scale stability is questionable.

VALIDITY:

Factor structure is similar to structure found in previous research in which the entertainment construct emerged as first factor also (Wells, Leavitt, and McConville 1971), and some of items were developed on the basis of theoretical underpinnings indicating that there is construct validity, face validity is claimed, and predictive validity is demonstrated through case analysis (Schlinger 1979a). Because the scale was developed in a realistic copy testing setting, the measure should be generalizable to that purpose. However, forced exposure to that condition warrants some caution if the scale is used to assess attitudes in less constrained viewing conditions. When used in conjunction with the other three scales developed by Schlinger to represent the viewer response profile that were replicated, Zinkhan and Burton (1989) reported reasonably good nomologic and predictive validity relative to attitude toward the brand (r = .32, p < .01) and choice behavior (r = .30, p < .01).

ADMINISTRATION:

The scale may be administered under typical survey design methodologies in a paper-and-pencil format or recorded response by researcher in personal or telephone interviews, though no use of the scale has been reported with the latter administrations. No time for administration is noted. Unfortunately, the researcher apparently repeatedly substitutes, adds or deletes items at whim, so the exact items to be used in administration may not be clear.

MAJOR FINDINGS:

Using a nine-item version of the scale, Olson, Schlinger, and Young (1982) found consumers' mean scale scores were significantly higher (p < .001) when rating commercials for new products than for existing ones. Six individual items were significantly higher in this test, all at p < .001. Stout and Rust (1993) found that older viewers had more descriptive responses than younger viewers, and overall findings show only limited support for this construct being more important than demographic characteristics such as age, sex, and brand usage in explaining evaluations of commercials.

COMMENTS:

Although the scale appears to be a reliable and valid measure of consumer attitude toward relevant news value of an advertisement, arbitrary changes in scale items during development and use shed some suspicion on the validity and reliability of the scale. Lack of replication for two of five items in Zinkhan and Burton (1989) indicate that caution should be observed in use and interpretation of results of this measure. This research tested only those items reported in Schlinger (1979a).

REFERENCES:

Olson, David, Mary Jane Schlinger, and Charles Young (1982), "How Consumers React to New Product Ads," *JAR*, 22 (3), 24-30.

Schlinger, Mary Jane (1979a), "A Profile of Responses to Commercials," *JAR*, 19 (2), 37-48.

———— (1979b), "Attitudinal Reactions to Advertisements," in *Attitude Research Under the Sun*, John Eighmey, ed. Chicago: American Marketing Association, 171-97.

Stout, Patricia A. and Roland T. Rust (1993), "Emotional Feelings and Evaluative Dimensions of Advertising: Are They Related?" *JA*, 22 (1), 61-71.

Wells, William, Clark Leavitt, and Maureen McConville (1971), "A Reaction Profile for TV Commercials," *JAR*, 11 (6), 11-17.

Zinkhan, George and Scot Burton (1989), "An Examination of Three Multidimensional Profiles for Assessing Consumer Reactions to Advertisements," *JA*, 18 (4), 6-14.

SCALE ITEMS: ATTITUDE TOWARD THE AD (RELEVANT NEWS)

Instructions: Scale was developed with seven-point Likert anchors, in which 1 = strongly disagree; 2 = disagree; 3 = somewhat disagree; 4 = neutral or no opinion; 5 = somewhat agree; 6 = agree; 7 = strongly agree.

NOTE: The scale seems to be used without the neutral or no opinion category as a six-point, forced-choice scale. Scale items reported here are from Schlinger (1979a), denoted by an "a"; Schlinger (1979b), denoted by a "b"; Olson, Schlinger, and Young (1982), denoted by a "c"; and Stout and Rust (1993) by a "d." It is not clear when specific items should be deleted from any particular scale usage. Items identified with an asterisk loaded less than .2 in Zinkhan and Burton (1989).

1. The commercial gave me a new idea.[abc]
2. The commercial reminded me that I'm dissatisfied with what I'm using now and I'm looking for something better.*[abcd]
3. I learned something from the commercial that I didn't know before.[abcd]
4. The commercial told about a new product I think I'd like to try.*[abd]
5. During the commercial I thought how that product might be useful to me.[abcd]
6. I would be interested in getting more information about the product.[bcd]
7. The commercial made me think I might try the brand—just to see if it's as good as they say.[bcd]
8. The commercial showed me the product has certain advantages.[cd]
9. The commercial message was important for me.[cd]
10. The commercial made me feel the product is right for me.[cd]
11. The ad didn't have anything to do with me or my needs.* (r)[cd]

SCALE NAME: Attitude Toward the Ad (Role Portrayals)

SCALE DESCRIPTION:

A 12-item, seven-point Likert-type scale (1 = strongly disagree, 7 = strongly agree) purported to measure the perceptions of advertising sex-role portrayals.

SCALE ORIGIN:

Ford and LaTour (1993) indicated that they adapted the scale from previous work by Lundstrom and Sciglimpaglia (1977).

SAMPLES:

Ford and LaTour (1993) had three samples consisting of adult females residing in a large metro suburban area in the mid-Atlantic region. The first sample was selected from League of Women Voters (LOWV) organization. They believed that this sample population would access the more-educated, less-traditional, and higher-income females who tended to be sensitive to female role portrayals. From the mailing list of 276 members of the LOWV, 37 questionnaires were returned with addresses unknown. **Ninety-four** usable responses were obtained for an effective response rate of 39.3%. The majority of the sample were white (87%), were married (54.3%), and had nonmanagerial white-collar professions (42.0%). The second sample was selected from The National Organization for Women (NOW). **One hundred thirty** usable responses were received out of a 300-member list. The sample was 100% white. Most of the participants had nonmanagerial white-collar professions (62.6%) and were divorced or separated (48.6%). The third sample (general area sample) was obtained in a random area prenotification ''drop-off-pickup'' survey. **One hundred fifty** respondents were selected from a population of 355,900 adult females residing in the same large mid-Atlantic metro suburban area. Most of the sample were white (71.8%), had nonmanagerial white-collar professions (37.6%), and were married (62.3 %).

RELIABILITY:

Cronbach's alpha was reported to be greater than **.80.**

VALIDITY:

No examination of scale validity was reported.

ADMINISTRATION:

In the first and second samples, the questionnaires were mailed to the members of NOW and LOWV. The scale was self-administered by respondents along with other measures. In the third sample, the participants were contacted by telephone. Once a respondent declared her intention to participate in the survey, the questionnaire was dropped off at the residence and re-trieved after 30 minutes.

MAJOR FINDINGS:

By looking at the means of the statements, it is apparent that the NOW and LOWV respondents are significantly more critical of the way women are characterized in ads than are the general area sample respondents. The LOWV and NOW samples were in significantly less disagreement with item 2 and in significantly greater agreement with items 8 and 11 than was the general area sample. In the case of item 9, the NOW sample was in significantly greater agreement than the LOWV sample, which was in significantly greater agreement than the general area sample. The NOW sample was in significantly less disagreement with item 3 than either the LOWV or the general area sample. It also was found that the NOW and LOWV samples were in significantly greater disagreement with items 5 and 6 than was the general area sample. Finally, the NOW sample was found to be significantly more in agreement with item 10 than the LOWV sample, which in turn was significantly more in agreement than was the general area sample.

REFERENCE:

Ford, John B. and Michael LaTour (1993), ''Differing Reactions to Female Role Portrayals in Advertising,'' *JAR*, 33 (5), 43-52.

Lundstrom, William J. and D. Sciglimpaglia (1977), ''Sex Role Portrayals in Advertising,'' *JM*, 41 (3), 72-79.

SCALE ITEMS: ATTITUDE TOWARD THE AD (ROLE PORTRAYALS)

Strongly disagree ____ : ____ : ____ : ____ : ____ : ____ : ____ Strongly agree
  1   2   3   4   5   6   7

1. Ads which I see show women as they really are.
2. Ads suggest that women are fundamentally dependent upon men.
3. Ads which I see show men as they really are.
4. Ads treat women mainly as ''sex objects.''
5. Ads which I see accurately portray women in most of their daily activities.
6. Ads suggest that women make important decisions.
7. Ads which I see accurately portray men in most of their daily activities.
8. Ads suggest that women don't do important things.
9. Ads suggest that a woman's place is in the home.
10. I'm more sensitive to the portrayal of women in advertising than I used to be.
11. I find the portrayal of women in advertising to be offensive.
12. Overall, I believe that the portrayal of women in advertising is changing for the better.

SCALE NAME: Attitude Toward the Ad (Semantic Differential)

SCALE DESCRIPTION:

Various bipolar adjectives presumed to measure the subject's overall evaluation of advertisements. Each scale is not specific to the advertisements under investigation, though certain adjectives may or may not be appropriate for every advertisement one may wish to assess. Many of the scales appear to be overall evaluations of an ad. In contrast, some are purported to measure a component of the overall attitude (e.g., affective, cognitive). Seven-point scales seem to be the most popular response format, but five- and nine-point scales have been commonly used as well.

SCALE ORIGIN:

The source of most of the scales is unclear because of the lack of information provided in the articles. Related investigation, however, suggests that approximately one-third are original with the remaining being either borrowed or modified from previous research (Bruner 1995). In a general sense, the basis for these scales can be traced to the work with semantic differentials pioneered by Osgood, Suci, and Tannenbaum (1957). With specific reference to work in marketing, the most common source is Mitchell and Olson (1981). Their scale is a common form to use when measuring overall evaluative response to an ad. Another source used by several authors, especially those who have wanted to measure the hypothesized affective and cognitive components of an attitude, is Baker and Churchill (1977).

SAMPLES:

Droge (1989) used **178** student subjects, 89 in each of two experimental treatment groups. MacKenzie and Lutz (1989) used **203** student subjects attending a major Midwestern university. Subjects ranged in age from 20 to 25 years, and approximately 50% were male. A validation sample of 120 student subjects from a major university in southern California was also used. Subjects in the validation sample ranged in age from 20 to 32 years, with approximately 60% being male.

Petroshius and Crocker (1989) used **320** white undergraduate student subjects (160 female). Each subject was assigned randomly to one of 16 treatment conditions.

Stout and Burda (1989) used **163** student volunteers as subjects. Subjects were recruited from undergraduate communications classes and offered extra credit for participating. Subjects were assigned randomly to one of four treatment groups (2 × 2 factorial design), with group size ranging from 35 to 47 subjects per group.

Burton and Lichtenstein (1988) used **278** undergraduate business students who were assigned randomly to one of twelve treatment conditions in a 2 × 2 × 3 between-subjects design. It is not clear if the design was balanced or not.

Cox and Cox (1988) used **240** student subjects recruited from MBA classes at a large Southwestern university. Most subjects worked full-time and attended MBA classes on a part-time basis. Ages of subjects ranged from 21 to 62 years, with a median age of 26 years. Forty-five percent of the subjects were female. Cox and Locander (1987) used a convenience sample of **240** adults student subject attending part-time business classes at a large southwestern university. Subjects ranged in age from 21 to 62 years, with the average age approximately 31 years. Forty-five percent of the subjects were women. Each subject was assigned randomly to one of four different ads in each product type.

Kilbourne (1986) used **101** adult subjects (49 male) selected from several communities surrounding a large metropolitan area. Each of the four treatment conditions had at least 24 subjects. The median age of subjects was 30 years, with 79% having attended at least some college. The median income of respondents was $20,700.

Macklin, Bruvold, and Shea (1985) used **127** subjects recruited during a festival at a public elementary magnet school in a large, Midwestern city. Subjects received free tickets to the festival for participation in the study.

Mitchell and Olson (1981) used **71** junior and senior undergraduate students of both sexes who were recruited from an introductory marketing class. Subjects were paid for participation in the study reported here. Kilbourne, Painton, and Ridley (1985) used **238** male and **186** female undergraduate students from a southwestern university. Perrien, Dussart, and Paul (1985) used a sample of **186** members of The Montreal Advertising Club, representing a 26% response rate. All respondents were French speaking. There was some evidence that the sample was not representative of the population.

Madden, Allen, and Twibble (1988) used **143** undergraduate students recruited from an introductory marketing class. Hastak and Olson (1989) used **160** undergraduate students. Janiszewski (1988) used **43** graduate students from two marketing management classes in the first experiment reported. These subjects were paid for participation. In the second experiment, **96** undergraduates from two universities were given extra credit for participating.

Zinkhan and Zinkhan (1985) used **160** part-time MBA students randomly split into two groups of 80. One hundred thirty-four of the students had full time jobs; all had bank accounts and their median income was less than $25,000 per year.

Okechuku and Wang (1988) used subjects recruited at shopping malls and other public places in Detroit and surrounding suburbs in Michigan and in Windsor, London, Sarnia, Toronto, and Hamilton, Ontario. Sample sizes were **27, 27**, and **26** for Chinese ads for three clothes and **29, 30**, and **26** for three North American ads for clothes; **26, 26**, and **30** for three Chinese ads for shoes and **25, 24**, and **26** for three North American ads for shoes. Muehling (1987) used **123** student subjects.

Bucholz and Smith (1991) selected **80** undergraduate students at a large midwestern university and gave course credit for completing the study. Of the total sample, 82.5% currently used personal computers, and 97.5% planned to use a personal computer in the next year.

Burns, Biswas, and Babin (1993) used **377** undergraduate business students in their study. Donthu (1992) used **232** part-time students at a nontraditional, medium sized state university. All of the subjects worked half- to full-time at private and government offices. Sample demographics (average age, sex, marital status, and income) were comparable to the average values for the city, except for their education level.

Homer and Kahle (1990) has a sample of **234** male and female undergraduates volunteered to participate in the study. Subjects were assigned randomly to one of the levels of each experimental manipulation in a 2 × 2 × 2 factorial design. Laczniak and Muehling's (1993) sample consisted of **280** students from an introductory marketing class. Miller and Marks (1992) had **124** undergraduate marketing students from a large midwestern university in their sample.

Peterson, Wilson, and Brown (1992) mailed questionnaires to 2250 members of a mail panel. A total of 1108 questionnaires were returned, of which **999** contained complete data and were usable. Of the total survey participants, 47% were male, 27% had a college degree, and 64% were married. Prakash (1992) had a sample of **85** students (43 males and 42 females) selected at a large university in the southeastern region of the country. Yi (1993) had a sample of **120** students at the business school of a major university.

Whittler and Dimeo (1991) had total of **160** paid white volunteers in their sample. Participants were assigned randomly to receive an ad that had a black or a white actor promoting either a liquid detergent or a fur coat. The sample was selected from several social and civic organizations in a southern city (YWCA, PTA, women's club). Of the total sample, 73% were women. Sample age ranged from 17 to 55 years. One hundred thirty one were married, 19 were single, and nine were divorced. All but one participant obtained a high school diploma, 28% attended college, and 58% had college degrees. Sixty percent earned more than $39,999 per year.

RELIABILITY:

Kilbourne, Painton, and Ridley (1985) reported alphas of **.57, .77,** and **.72** for their cognitive, effective, and sexual attitude scales, respectively. Perrien, Dussart, and Paul reported alphas of **.7832** and **.7957** for the cognitive and effective dimensions, respectively. Madden, Allen, and Twibble (1988) reported an alpha of **.88**. Hastak and Olson (1989) reported an alpha greater than **.90**. Janiszewski (1988) reported alphas of **.93** and **.91** in experiments 1 and 2, respectively.

Cronbach's alphas were **.806** and **.693** for a comparative and a noncomparative treatment group respectively in Droge (1989); **.89** in the main sample and **.88** in the validation sample for MacKenzie and Lutz (1989); **.89** in Stout and Burda (1989); **.90** in Cox and Cox (1988); **.90** in Cox and Locander (1987); **.65** for the cognitive dimension and **.88** for the effective dimension in Kilbourne (1986); **.85** in Macklin, Bruvold, and Shea (1985); **.87** in Mitchell an Olson (1981).

Petroshius and Crocker (1989) used two reliability measures: correlation analysis (only one variable correlated low with its respective group), which indicated that each variable set was statistically significant ($p < .01$); and Cronbach's alpha was **.52** for the cognitive factor and greater than **.75** for the effective factor. Burton and Lichtenstein (1988) reported Cronbach's alphas of

.86 and .73 for the effective and cognitive dimensions, respectively. They also reported a correlation of .67 between the two dimensions, casting some dispersion on the discriminant validity of the two measures.

Okechuku and Wang (1988) reported alphas of .61 and .72 for their cognitive measures and .88 and .86 for their effective measures for clothing and shoe ads respectively. It should be noted that Okechuku and Wang (1988) also combined the cognitive and effective measures with a two-item cognitive measure to assess overall attitude toward the ad, achieving an alpha of .91 and .92 for clothing and shoe ads, respectively.

Bucholz and Smith (1991) reported an alpha of .92. Burns, Biswas, and Babin (1993) reported a reliability coefficient of .88. Donthu (1992) reported a Cronbach's alpha of .88. Homer and Kahle (1990) reported a Cronbach's alpha of 82. Laczniak and Muehling (1993) reported a Cronbach's alpha of .93. Miller and Marks (1992) reported a Cronbach's alpha of .91. Peterson, Wilson, and Brown (1992) reported a Cronbach's alpha of .91. Prakash (1992) reported a Cronbach's alpha of .82. Whittler and Dimeo (1991) reproted a Cronbach's alpha of .87. Yi (1993) reported a Cronbach's alpha of .80. Reliability information was not reported by Zinkhan and Zinkhan (1985) and Muehling (1987).

VALIDITY:

Little validity information was provided per se in most of the studies. Mitchell and Olson (1981) developed the background for using evaluative belief statements as measures of attitude from Fishbein and Ajzen (1975) and Ahtola (1975) and utilized only those four items loading together out of seven original ones in their study. Varimax rotation was used to develop factor structure. Stout and Burda (1989) used a manipulation check to assess the manipulation of brand dominance, but not for attitude toward the ad. Petroshius and Crocker (1989) used factor analysis as a reliability check, noting that the effective and cognitive components in attitude toward the ad constituted 56% of the variance.

Burton and Lichtenstein (1988) did draw their original items from various previous research, including Wells' (1964) early work in this area. They subjected their original 15 items to a confirmatory factor analysis to arrive at the six effective and five cognitive items reported here. They also used a separate sample (n = 44) to see if subjects perceived the effective items as more emotional or ''feeling state'' descriptive than the cognitive items. The results were highly significant in the expected direction. The authors do not address the point that relative differences do not necessarily indicate measures are valid in the absolute sense.

Perrien, Dussart, and Paul (1985) used only those items from a list of items extracted from the literature for 15 marketing experts all agreed belonged in the construct dimension. Madden, Allen, and Twibble (1988) reported substantive discriminant validity between ad evaluation and a measure of positive affect. Marginal discriminant validity between ad evaluation and a measure of negative affect is claimed. Both principle components and confirmatory factor analysis support the unidimensionality of the scale measure of the ad evaluation construct.

Janiszewski (1988) reported unidimensionality (ML Confirmatory Analysis) and support for an assumption of independence of errors in measure. Zinkhan and Zinkhan (1985) attempt to reduce the items in the Response Profile scales (reported elsewhere in this compendium) to four semantic differential scales applicable to print ads for financial services. They factor analyzed data from pretests (sample and items unknown) as an initial validation step. The major findings of their efforts indicate that, of the four factors tested, favorable cognitive and favorable effective scales were moderately successful at discriminating for explaining response to a coupon/postcard use/mail-in request in an advertising.

Okechuku and Wang (1988) drew their measures from Baker and Churchill (1977), in which a principle components factor analysis identified a similar structure for items measuring effective and cognitive components of attitude toward the ad. Okechuku and Wang (1988) factor analyzed their data as per the original and added "interesting" to the effective measure and deleting "try product" from the cognitive component.

ADMINISTRATION:

Kilbourne (1986) used a personal interview procedure to collect data, with 39 of the 101 respondents interviewed at their place of work and the remaining 62 respondents interviewed in their homes. In general, however, paper-and-pencil administration as a part of a longer instrument appears to be the method of choice. Subjects are asked to evaluate a specific advertisement using the adjective listing and mark the scale appropriately. In some instances (Petroshius and Crocker 1989), instructions also may be read aloud by the researchers. Time is of minimal consequence.

In Bucholz and Smith (1991), subjects viewed or listened to the program and commercials in groups of ten spaced apart after they arrived at the experiment room. After the media exposure, subjects completed the cognition-listing task and filled out the remaining questionnaire items. The entire procedure took approximately 20 minutes. Burns, Biswas, and Babin (1993) conducted their study in a classroom setting in which the subjects were assigned randomly to one of the eight treatment groups. The subjects were told that they were selected to evaluate an advertisement of a special automobile purchasing plan for university students. After the subjects read about the plan and the advertisement, they responded to questions on ad believability, imagery processing, attitude toward the ad, attitude toward the brand, and intention. Subjects completed the study with some manipulation checks and demographic questions.

In Donthu (1992), subjects met in batches of 30. After filling out the questionnaire containing demographic information, they viewed a video tape containing a 30-minute situation comedy. Every time the program stopped for commercial breaks, "test ads" were inserted. A total of 12 "test ads" were inserted in the tape. Six of the ads were comparative advertisements and the other six were noncomparative. At the end of the program subjects were asked to recall the advertisements they had seen and describe them in as much detail as possible. Next, they were asked a series of questions to measure their attitude toward the ads. Respondent attitude toward a particular ad was measured by summing, and then scaling, the respondent's score on the ten questions for the ad. The same questions were asked for all 12 of the ads.

Homer and Kahle (1990) administered in small groups (six to 20 per session) with subjects isolated by partitioned walls to prevent awareness of others' behaviors. Subjects read one booklet containing the experimental ad. The booklet contained six professionally produced color advertisements, one of which was the ad of interest, an ad for hypothetical line of skin-care products. After viewing the ad booklet, respondents completed a second booklet containing the dependent measures. All experimental treatments were administered at each session with an approximately equal number of objects.

Laczniak and Muehling (1993) assigned the subjects to one of 12 treatment conditions. Subjects received an ad booklet and were instructed to turn to the inside front cover, read the printed instructions silently, and proceed as directed. After the subjects finished reading, they completed the questionnaires in a pencil-and-paper format.

Miller and Marks (1992) offered students extra credit points in their marketing classes as incentive to participate. The subjects signed up for the day and time that fit to their schedule. They showed the commercials randomly at each session over a period of four days to small groups ranging from 2 to 20 subjects.

Peterson, Wilson, and Brown (1992) mailed advertisements containing one of the six products or services with a questionnaire to members of a national panel. The effective response rate was 44.4%.

Prakash (1992) used the Thematic Apperception Test technique, which involved showing pictures or slides to project a concept to evoke subject response and administered the questionnaires in a laboratory setting.

In Whittler and Dimeo (1991), the participants were organized in groups of three to eight in a large conference room by a white experimenter. Each participant was given a booklet containing the storyboard advertisements and the questionnaire. After viewing all the storyboard advertisements, participants administered the questionnaire in a pencil-and-paper format.

Yi (1993) assigned the subjects to one of the two priming conditions that differed in terms of magazine articles preceding the ad. After the general instructions, each subject read a magazine article that primed one of the two attributes (oil or safety) and administered the questionnaires in pencil-and-paper format.

MAJOR FINDINGS:

In Droge (1989), structural equation modeling via LISREL was utilized to support the dual mediation hypothesis regarding the causal relationship between attitude toward the ad and attitude toward the brand for noncomparative ads (relatively less central processing) and lack thereof for comparative ads (relatively more central processing). It should be noted that the alpha for the noncomparative ad treatment groups measure of attitude toward the ad is relatively low (.693) compared with the comparative group, that no explanation for this difference is offered, and that LISREL is very sensitive to reliability violations.

MacKenzie and Lutz (1989) found that attitude toward the ad is a stronger predictor of brand attitude than ad credibility. Removal of ad attitude from two models predicting brand attitude resulted in a reduction in brand attitude variance of .74 to .58. The removal of ad credibility from these two models resulted only in reductions in brand attitude variance of .13 to .16.

Petroshius and Crocker (1989) found that the physical attractiveness of a spokesperson was significantly related to the subject's effective component of attitude toward the ad ($p = .044$). None of the other tested sources of variation (sex of communicator, race, product, or sex of subject) were significant as predictors of the effective component, and no significant interactions were found. The only significant source of variation in the cognitive component of attitude toward the ad was the sex of the subject ($p = .027$), though an examination of mean responses on individual items indicates inconsistent responses between men and women on dependent variables. No significant interactions were found.

Stout and Burda (1989) studied ''zipped'' television advertisements and their effect on attitudes. They found that the speed of the commercial (i.e., zipped versus. normal) affected attitude toward the ad ($p = .001$) and brand attitudes ($p = .001$). Viewers in the zipped speed condition had more neutral attitudes toward the ad than did viewers in the normal speed condition.

Burton and Lichtenstein (1988) found that price oriented advertising attitudes were affected by the cognitive component as measured but not by the effective component. They also found that after covarying out the effects the deal in the ads, both affect and cognitions affect attitude toward the deal. They conclude a two-factor solution to attitude toward the ad is superior to the single component solution.

Cox and Cox (1988) found that a repeated exposure (two exposures as opposed to one) has a positive and statistically significant ($p < .05$) effect on the evaluations of complex advertisements (attitude toward the ad), and only slight and statistically non-significant effect on the evaluation of simple ads.

Cox and Locander (1987) tested the impact of attitude toward the ad on brand attitude for novel products versus familiar products. They found that for novel products, attitude toward the ad accounted for a greater proportion of the variance in brand attitude ($r^2 = .4$) than for familiar products ($r^2 = .26$). They did not find support for the hypothesis of a difference by attitude toward the ad in the proportion of variance in purchase intention for novel and familiar products.

Kilbourne (1986) found that the use of a model depicting a professional women using a calculator had a statistically significant effect ($p < .05$) on the cognitive dimension of attitude toward the ad in comparison with the use of a model in a similar ad depicting a housewife using the same calculator. The model of a professional woman in the test ad also produced a statistically significant effect ($p < .001$) on the effective dimension of attitude toward the ad in comparison with the use of a model in a similar ad depicting a housewife using the product. Ad content was constant (other than the models) in both test advertisements. Kilbourne, Painton, and Ridley (1985) reported both male and female subjects scored significantly higher on cognitive, affective, and sexual attitudes toward a Scotch whiskey print ad when a sexual embed was present than when it was not. Similar results were not forthcoming when the product was a cigarett. They conclude the product plays an important role in the attitudinal formation process when sexual embeds are present.

Macklin, Bruvold, and Shea (1985) found when the concreteness of verbal messages was held constant, the readability level of the ads made no significant difference on any of the variables examined, including attitude toward the ad (p = .771). However, the subjects' education and the product category had significant effects on all treatments. The authors found that subjects with higher levels of education uniformly liked ads less (p = .0001). As spending per month on the product category increased, favorable attitudes toward the ad also increased (p = .040).

Mitchell and Olson (1981) assessed attitude toward ads for facial tissue. It was a significant contributor to attitude toward the brand and attitude toward the act of purchasing the brand (p < .005) in a regression model including brand evaluative beliefs a la Fishbein and Ajzen (1975) and attitude toward the picture in the ad. The authors conclude this supports what is now termed the dual routes of brand attitude formation.

Perrien, Dussart, and Paul (1985) reported significantly higher (p < .001) attitudinal scores as amounts of factual information increased from one to three factual claims without regard to perceive risk of the product. No differences were found dependent on the respondent's professional category (agency, advertiser, media, service).

Madden, Allen, and Twibble (1988) found processing set to be significantly related to the processing route of ad evaluation. Subjects who were told they were to evaluate ads tended to utilize cognitive response measures and ad evaluation to differentiate among a humorous versus nonhumorous treatment. Subjects who were not told the evaluative purpose of the experiment tend to use effective reactions to discriminate between the humorous and nonhumorous conditions.

Hastak and Olson (1989) used their three-item measure as a part of a cognitive response/structure study. The results relating to attitude toward the ad support the contention that it is mediated processing set through cognitive responses.

Janiszewski (1988) performed two experiments to test the hypothesis that right hemisphere processing of pictorial cues leads to higher ad evaluation than does left hemisphere processing. In general, the results support this hypothesis. However, the researcher cautions that this work is somewhat rudimentary.

Zinkhan and Zinkhan (1985) looked at the discriminant and predictive validity of four measures of attitude toward the ad: Favorable Cognitive Response, Favorable Effective Response, Energy, and Familiarity. Although these construct measures are purported to be developed from various viewer response profiles, they are framed in a semantic differential format and reported here for that reason. Subjects' attitudes toward a financial services ad were measured using the four scales, which were in turn subjected to discriminant analysis as predictors of subject responses to the ads. The response criterion was filling out a postcard for information about the financial services. Response was elicited after two exposures over a three-week period. Favorable Cognitive and Effective measures were both found to be significant predictors of the behavioral response. When the discriminant model developed in the first phase of the research was applied to the responses of a holdout sample, only modest predictive success was achieved over chance (65.0% versus 53.8%).

Okechuku and Wang (1988) compared North American subjects' attitudes toward ads from China and the United States for shoes and clothing. They found no difference in subjects' cognitive attitudes toward the ads but did find a significant (p < .001) difference in effective responses to the ads. Muehling (1987), in each of five comparative formats, found attitude toward the ad to have a significant, positive influence on attitude toward the sponsor and attitude toward purchasing the sponsor while having no influence on attitude toward the competitor or purchasing the competitor.

Burns, Biswas, and Babin (1993) demonstrated that concrete wording is more effective than abstract wording when used in print advertisement in generating visual imagery, positive attitudes, and intentions. They also found that the attitude toward the ad was more positive for low verbal/high visual subjects under the condition of instructions to imagine. Donthu (1992) found that the relationship between intensity and attitude toward the ad increased with lower levels of intensity but dropped at higher levels.

Laczniak and Muehling's (1993) findings indicate that attitude toward the ad is significantly related to brand attitudes under low-involvement conditions. The results of a series of regression analyses (treating the brand attitude index as a dependent variable and index of the attitude toward the ad as an independent variable show different outcomes under different involvement manipulations were used.

Miller and Marks (1992) predicted that ads containing imagery producing sound effects will create stronger attitudes (more favorable or unfavorable, depending on the emotion evoked by the imagery) toward the ad than those without sound effects. In the lawn mower treatment, imagery producing sound effects created stronger feelings of warmth and significantly more favorable attitudes toward the ad. In the tire treatment, the imagery stimuli created a weaker emotional reaction and less favorable attitude toward the ad. However, the attitude toward the ad was not significantly different in the two treatments.

Peterson, Wilson, and Brown's (1992) results indicate that advertised claims of customer satisfaction have little effect on consumer attitudes. Prakash's (1992) results support the conclusion that males are more likely to prefer an ad format depicting competition with others than an ad format showing self competition. Also, males have a preference for large social group. Conversely, females may not be threatened by the situations of competition with others and may feel equally comfortable with scenarios of self-competition and competition with others. Female subjects are flexible about the group size. They are not intimidated by large groups, but they have an equal preference for small ones.

Whittler and DiMeo's (1991) results indicate that high-prejudice whites expressed more favorable evaluations of the ad than low-prejudice whites. Yi (1993) compared the subjects' attitudes toward the ad, which measure specific feelings toward the ad, across the priming conditions. The results indicate that the observed results cannot be attributed to general or specific effect generated by the context.

COMMENTS:

Although these scales represent a generally recognized method for measuring attitude toward an ad, they have relied heavily on researcher judgment with respect to which specific adjective pairs are appropriate for a given situation. In addition, there has been little rigorous testing of validity. Because of this and all of the alternatives that are available, future users are urged to not generate yet more items. Instead, it is suggested that they examine the previously published alternatives and select the one that is most appropriate for their study and has shown the most evidence of validity.

An additional concern is that there seems to be a lack of concern regarding the premise underlying use of the semantic differential. The semantic differential should be constructed so that the items are anchored by adjectives describing opposites on the semantic continuum. It is arguable whether this requirement is being met in those many cases in which researchers have used bi-polar adjectives of the form **X/not X.** Scale items of this form violate the assumption that the midpoint of the scale is meant to be used when the respondent associates the object with neither pole of the adjective pair (Dawes and Smith 1985, p. 534; Osgood, Suci, and Tannenbaum 1957, pp. 29, 83). For example, the midpoint between *interesting* and *boring* would be *neither boring nor interesting.* That is different from the midpoint of a uni-polar set such as *interesting/not interesting,* where the midpoint would be something like *slightly interesting.* The degree to which this violation affects scale scores and interpretation is unknown.

See also Holmes and Crocker (1987) and Rubin, Mager, and Friedman (1982) for related work with attitude-toward-the-ad items. It appears in those two studies that many of the same items as listed subsequently played a role in their analyses but not as summated rating scales.

REFERENCES:

Ahtola, Olli T. (1975), "The Vector Model of PREFERENCES: An Alternative to the Fishbein Model," *JMR*, 12 (February), 52-59.

Baker, Michael J. and Gilbert A. Churchill (1977), "The Impact of Physically Attractive Models on Advertising Evaluations," *JMR*, 14 (November), 538-55.

Bruner II, Gordon C. (1995), "The Psychometric Quality of Aad Scales," *Office of Scale Research Technical Report #9501*, Department of Marketing, Southern Illinois University.

Bucholz, Laura M. and Robert E. Smith (1991), "The Role of Consumer Involvement in Determining Cognitive Response to Broadcast Advertising," *JA*, 20 (1), 4-17.

Burns, Alvin C., Abhijit Biswas, and Laurie A. Babin (1993), "The Operation of Visual Imagery as a Mediator of Advertising Effects," *JA*, 22 (2), 71-85.

Burton, Scot and Donald R. Lichtenstein (1988), "The Effect of Ad Claims and Ad Context on Attitude Toward the Advertisement," *JA*, 17 (1), 3-11.

Cox, Dena Saliagas and Anthony D. Cox (1988), "What Does Familiarity Breed? Complexity as a Moderator of Repetition Effects in Advertisement Evaluation," *JCR*, 15 (June), 111-16.

_____ and William B. Locander (1987), ''Product Novelty: Does It Moderate the Relationship Between Ad Attitudes and Brand Attitudes?'' *JA*, 16 (3), 39-44.

Dawes, Robyn M. and Tom L. Smith (1985), ''Attitude and Opinion Measurement,'' in *Handbook of Social Psychology*, 3rd ed., Vol. 1, Gardner Lindzey and Elliot Aronson, eds. New York: Random House, 509-66.

Donthu, Naveen (1992), ''Comparative Advertising Intensity,'' *JAR*, 32 (6), 53-58.

Droge, Cornelia (1989), ''Shaping the Route to Attitude Change: Central Versus Peripheral Processing Through Comparative Versus Noncomparative Advertising,'' *JMR*, 26 (May), 193-204.

Fishbein, Martin and Icek Ajzen (1975), *Belief, Attitude, Intention and Behavior: An Introduction to Theory and Research*. Reading, MA: Addison-Wesley.

Hastak, Manoj and Jerry C. Olson (1989), ''Assessing the Role of Brand Related Cognitive Responses as Mediators of Communications Effects on Cognitive Structure,'' *JCR*, 15 (March), 444-56.

Holmes, John H. and Kenneth E. Crocker (1987), ''Predispositions and the Comparative Effectiveness of Rational, Emotional, and Discrepant Appeals for Both High Involvement and Low Involvement Products,'' *JAMS*, 15 (Spring), 27-35.

Homer, Pamela M. and Lynn Kahle (1990), ''Source Expertise, Time of Source Identification, and Involvement in Persuasion: An Elaborative Processing Perspective,'' *JA*, 19 (1), 30-39.

Janiszewski, Chris (1988), ''Preconscious Processing Effects: The Independence of Attitude Formation and Conscious Thought,'' *JCR*, 15 (September), 199-209.

Kahle, Lynn R. and Pamela M. Homer (1985), ''Physical Attractiveness of the Celebrity Endorser: A Social Adaption Perspective,'' *JCR*, 11 (March), 954-61.

Kilbourne, William E. (1986), ''An Exploratory Study of the Effect of Sex Role Stereotyping on Attitudes Toward Magazine Advertisements,'' JAMS, 14 (Winter), 43-46.

_____, Scott Painton, and Danny Ridley (1985), ''The Effect of Sexual Embedding on Responses to Magazine Advertisements,'' *JA*, 14 (2), 48-56.

Laczniak, Russell N. and Darrel D. Muehling (1993), ''The Relationship Between Experimental Manipulations and Tests of Theory in an Advertising Message Involvement Context,'' *JA*, 22 (3), 59-74.

MacKenzie, Scott B. and Richard J. Lutz (1989), ''An Empirical Examination of the Structural Antecedents of Attitude Toward the Ad in an Advertising Pretesting Context,'' *JM*, 53 (April), 48-65.

Macklin, M. Carole, Norman T. Bruvold, and Carol Lynn Shea (1985), ''Is It Always as Simple as 'Keep It Simple!'?'' *JA*, 14 (4), 28-35.

Madden, Thomas J., Chris T. Allen, and Jacquelyn L. Twibble (1988), ''Attitude Toward the Ad: An Assessment of Diverse Measurement Indices Under Different Processing Sets,'' *JMR*, 25 (August), 242-52.

Miller, Darryl W. and Lawrence J. Marks (1992), ''Mental Imagery and Sound Effects in Radio Commercials,'' *JA*, 21 (4), 83-93.

Mitchell, Andrew A. and Jerry C. Olson (1981), '' Are Product Attribute

Beliefs the Only Mediator of Advertising Effects on Brand Attitude?'' *JMR*, 18 (August), 318-32.

Muelhing, Darrel D. (1987), "Comparative Advertising: The Influence Attitude-Toward-The-Ad on Brand Evaluation," *JA*, 16 (4), 43-49.

Okechuku, Chike and Gongrong Wang (1988), "The Effectiveness of Chinese Print Advertisements in North America," *JAR*, 28 (October/November), 25-34.

Osgood, Charles E., George J. Suci, and Percy H. Tannenbaum (1957), *The Measurement of Meaning*. Urbana, IL: University of Illinois Press.

Perrien, Jean, Christian Dussart, and Francoise Paul (1985), "Advertisers and the Factual Content of Advertising," *JA*, 14 (1), 30-35, 53.

Peterson, Robert A., William R. Wilson, and Steven P. Brown (1992), "Effects of Advertised Customer Satisfaction Claims on Consumer Attitudes and Purchase Intention," *JAR*, 32 (2), 34-40.

Petroshius, Susan M. and Kenneth E. Crocker (1989), "An Empirical Analysis of Spokesperson Characteristics on Advertisement and Product Evaluations," *JAMS*, 17 (Summer), 217-25.

Prakash, Ved (1992), "Sex Roles and Advertising Preferences," *JAR*, 32 (3), 43-52.

Rubin, Vicky, Carol Mager, and Hershey H. Friedman (1982), "Company President Versus Spokesperson in Television Commercials," *JAR*, 22 (August/September), 31-33.

Stout, Patricia A. and Benedicta L. Burda (1989), "Zipped Commercials: Are They Effective?" *JA*, 18 (4), 23-32.

Wells, William D. (1964), "EQ, Son of EQ, and the Reaction Profile," *JM*, 28 (October), 45-52.

Whittler, Tommy E. and Joan DiMeo (1991), "Viewer's Reaction to Racial Cues in Advertising Stimuli," *JAR*, 31 (6), 37-46.

Yi, Youjae (1993), "Contextual Priming Effects in Print Advertisements: The Moderating Role of Prior Knowledge," *JA*, 22 (1), 1-10.

Zinkhan, George M. and Christian F. Zinkhan (1985), "Response Profiles and Choice Behavior: An Application to Financial Services," *JA*, 14 (3), 39-51, 66.

SCALE ITEMS: ATTITUDE TOWARD THE AD (SEMANTIC DIFFERENTIAL)

Scale items used in specific studies are listed here with an indication of whether item sums or mean of sums were used in the research analysis. If known, the number of response points used for a scale is noted. Although two studies may be shown here to have used one or more of the same items, it should not automatically be concluded that the items were exactly the same. Judgment was used to determine when a bi-polar adjective was similar to one used before or when it was unique. Slight differences in the bi-polar adjectives used, such as *extremely bad* versus *bad* and *uninteresting* versus *interesting*, were counted the same for purposes of the list. If every truly different set of pi-polar adjectives were listed separately, the list of items would have been longer.

Bucholz and Smith (1991): 1, 4, 60 (mean); seven-point.
Burns, Biswas, and Babin (1993): 1, 4, and three unidentified items.

Burton and Lichtenstein (1988) (affective): 13, 18, 27, 28, 29, 30 (mean); nine-point.
Burton and Lichtenstein (1988) (cognitive): 7, 8, 9, 10,23 (mean); nine-point.
Cox and Cox (1988): 1, 2, 18 (sum); nine-point.
Cox and Locander (1987): 1, 2, 22; nine-point.
Donthu (1992): 8, 9, 11, 12, 13, 14, 15, 22, 23, 42 (sum); seven-point.
Droge (1989): 1, 3, 4, 5 (mean); seven-point.
Hastak and Olson (1989): 1, 2, 18, 20 (mean); seven-point.
Homer and Kahle (1990): 4, 61 (mean); nine-point.
Janiszewski (1988): 1, 11, 13, 18, 25 (sum); nine-point.
Kilbourne (1986) (affective): 11, 12, 13; nine-point.
Kilbourne (1986) (cognitive): 6, 8, 9; nine-point.
Kilbourne, Painton, and Ridley (1985) (cognitive): 6, 8, 9 (sum); five-point.
Kilbourne, Painton, and Ridley (1985) (affective): 11, 12, 13 (sum); five-point.
Kilbourne, Painton, and Ridley (1985) (sexual): 31, 32, 33 (sum); five-point.
Laczniak and Muehling (1993): 1, 4, 11, 13, 18, 25, 62, 63, 64 (sum); seven-point.
MacKenzie and Lutz (1989): 1, 22, 26 (mean); seven-point.
Macklin, Bruvold, and Shea (1985): 1, 17, 18, 19, 20, 21; seven-point.
Madden, Allen and Twibble (1988): 1, 18, 25, 37, 45, 46.
Miller and Marks (1992): 1, 2, 3, 4 (mean); five-point.
Mitchell and Olsen (1981): 1, 2, 3, 4 (mean); five-point.
Muehling (1987): 1, 5, 13, 26, 58, 59 (mean); seven-point.
Okechuku and Wang (1988) (cognitive): 8, 9, 15 (mean); nine-point.
Okechuku and Wang (1988) (affective): 4, 11, 12, 13, 14 (mean); nine-point.
Perrien, Dussart, and Paul (1985) (cognitive): 8, 34, 35, 36 (sum); seven-point.
Perrien, Dussart, and Paul (1985) (affective): 13, 18, 37, 38 (sum); seven-point.
Peterson, Wilson, and Brown (1992): 4, 7, 8, 10, 11; five-point.
Petroshius and Crocker (1989) (affective): 4, 11, 12, 13, 14; seven-point.
Petroshius and Crocker (1989) (cognitive): 8, 9, 15; seven-point.
Prakash (1992): 1, 2, 3, 4; seven-point.
Stout and Burda (1989): 2, 16 (mean); seven-point.
Whittler and DiMeo (1991): 7, 13, 16 (mean); 15-point.
Yi (1993): 1, 2, 3, 4; seven-point.
Zinkhan and Zinkhan (1985) (favorable cognition): 23, 47, 48, 49.
Zinkhan and Zinkhan (1985) (favorable affect): 11, 13, 18, 50.
Zinkhan and Zinkhan (1985) (energy): 33, 51, 52, 53.
Zinkhan and Zinkhan (1985) (familiarity): 54, 55, 56, 57.

1. Good   ___ : ___ : ___ : ___ : ___ Bad
         1   2   3   4   5

2. Like   ___ : ___ : ___ : ___ : ___ Dislike
         1   2   3   4   5

3. Irritating   ___ : ___ : ___ : ___ : ___ (Non) not irritating (r)
         1   2   3   4   5

4. Interesting   ___ : ___ : ___ : ___ : ___ (Un) not interesting
         1   2   3   4   5

5. Offensive   ___ : ___ : ___ : ___ : ___   (In) nonoffensive (r)
                          1   2   3   4   5

6. Trustworthy   ___ : ___ : ___ : ___ : ___   Untrustworthy
                          1   2   3   4   5

7. Persuasive   ___ : ___ : ___ : ___ : ___   (Un) not at all persuasive
                          1   2   3   4   5

8. Informative   ___ : ___ : ___ : ___ : ___   Uninformative
                          1   2   3   4   5

9. Believable   ___ : ___ : ___ : ___ : ___   Unbelievable
                          1   2   3   4   5

10. Effective   ___ : ___ : ___ : ___ : ___   Not at all effective
                          1   2   3   4   5

11. Appealing   ___ : ___ : ___ : ___ : ___   Unappealing
                          1   2   3   4   5

12. Impressive   ___ : ___ : ___ : ___ : ___   Unimpressive
                          1   2   3   4   5

13. Attractive   ___ : ___ : ___ : ___ : ___   (Not) attractive
                          1   2   3   4   5

14. Eye-catching   ___ : ___ : ___ : ___ : ___   Not eye-catching
                          1   2   3   4   5

15. Clear   ___ : ___ : ___ : ___ : ___   Not clear
                          1   2   3   4   5

16. Favorable   ___ : ___ : ___ : ___ : ___   Unfavorable
                          1   2   3   4   5

17. Fair   ___ : ___ : ___ : ___ : ___   Unfair
                          1   2   3   4   5

18. Pleasant   ___ : ___ : ___ : ___ : ___   Unpleasant
                          1   2   3   4   5

19. Stale   ___ : ___ : ___ : ___ : ___   Fresh (r)
                          1   2   3   4   5

20. Awful   ___ : ___ : ___ : ___ : ___   Nice (r)
                          1   2   3   4   5

21. Honest   ___ : ___ : ___ : ___ : ___   Dishonest
                          1   2   3   4   5

22. Pleasant   ___ : ___ : ___ : ___ : ___   Unpleasant
                          1   2   3   4   5

23. Convincing   ___ : ___ : ___ : ___ : ___   Unconvincing
                          1   2   3   4   5

24. Overall liking   ___ : ___ : ___ : ___ : ___   Disliking
                 1   2   3   4   5

25. Likable   ___ : ___ : ___ : ___ : ___   (Not) unlikable
                 1   2   3   4   5

26. Favorable   ___ : ___ : ___ : ___ : ___   Unfavorable
                 1   2   3   4   5

27. Soothing   ___ : ___ : ___ : ___ : ___   Not soothing
                 1   2   3   4   5

28. Warm hearted   ___ : ___ : ___ : ___ : ___   Cold hearted
                 1   2   3   4   5

29. Uplifting   ___ : ___ : ___ : ___ : ___   Depressing
                 1   2   3   4   5

30. Affectionate   ___ : ___ : ___ : ___ : ___   Not affectionate
                 1   2   3   4   5

31. Sensual   ___ : ___ : ___ : ___ : ___   Not sensual
                 1   2   3   4   5

32. Erotic   ___ : ___ : ___ : ___ : ___   Not erotic
                 1   2   3   4   5

33. Exciting   ___ : ___ : ___ : ___ : ___   (Un) not exciting
                 1   2   3   4   5

34. Clear   ___ : ___ : ___ : ___ : ___   Imprecise
                 1   2   3   4   5

35. Complete   ___ : ___ : ___ : ___ : ___   Incomplete
                 1   2   3   4   5

36. well structured   ___ : ___ : ___ : ___ : ___   Badly structured
                 1   2   3   4   5

37. Interesting   ___ : ___ : ___ : ___ : ___   Boring
                 1   2   3   4   5

38. Agreeable   ___ : ___ : ___ : ___ : ___   Disagreeable
                 1   2   3   4   5

39. Not credible   ___ : ___ : ___ : ___ : ___   Credible (r)
                 1   2   3   4   5

40. Questionable   ___ : ___ : ___ : ___ : ___   Unquestionable (r)
                 1   2   3   4   5

41. Inconclusive   ___ : ___ : ___ : ___ : ___   Conclusive (r)
                 1   2   3   4   5

42. Not authentic   ___ : ___ : ___ : ___ : ___   Authentic (r)
                 1   2   3   4   5

43. Unlikely   ___ : ___ : ___ : ___ : ___   Likely (r)
                 1   2   3   4   5

44. Reasonable   ___ : ___ : ___ : ___ : ___   Unreasonable
                 1   2   3   4   5

45. Tasteful   ___ : ___ : ___ : ___ : ___   Tasteless
                 1   2   3   4   5

46. Artful   ___ : ___ : ___ : ___ : ___   Artless
                 1   2   3   4   5

47. Meaningful   ___ : ___ : ___ : ___ : ___   Meaningless
                 1   2   3   4   5

48. Valuable   ___ : ___ : ___ : ___ : ___   Not valuable
                 1   2   3   4   5

49. Important to me   ___ : ___ : ___ : ___ : ___   Not important to me
                 1   2   3   4   5

50. Beautiful   ___ : ___ : ___ : ___ : ___   Ugly
                 1   2   3   4   5

51. Lively   ___ : ___ : ___ : ___ : ___   Lifeless
                 1   2   3   4   5

52. Energetic   ___ : ___ : ___ : ___ : ___   Without energy
                 1   2   3   4   5

53. Enthusiastic   ___ : ___ : ___ : ___ : ___   Unenthusiastic
                 1   2   3   4   5

54. Familiar   ___ : ___ : ___ : ___ : ___   Unfamiliar
                 1   2   3   4   5

55. Usual   ___ : ___ : ___ : ___ : ___   Unusual
                 1   2   3   4   5

56. Well known   ___ : ___ : ___ : ___ : ___   Not well known
                 1   2   3   4   5

57. Seen before   ___ : ___ : ___ : ___ : ___   Not seen before
                 1   2   3   4   5

58. Interesting   ___ : ___ : ___ : ___ : ___   Dull
                 1   2   3   4   5

59. Positive   ___ : ___ : ___ : ___ : ___   Negative
                 1   2   3   4   5

60. Pleasing   ___ : ___ : ___ : ___ : ___   Irritating
                 1   2   3   4   5

61. Attention getting   ___ : ___ : ___ : ___ : ___   Not attention getting
                 1   2   3   4   5

62. Dull   ___ : ___ : ___ : ___ : ___   Dynamic (r)
                   1   2   3   4   5

63. Depressing   ___ : ___ : ___ : ___ : ___   Refreshing (r)
                   1   2   3   4   5

64. Enjoyable   ___ : ___ : ___ : ___ : ___   Not enjoyable (r)
                   1   2   3   4   5

SCALE NAME: Attitude Toward the Ad (Stimulation)

SCALE DESCRIPTION:

A ten-item, six-point rating scale ranging from "strongly disagree" to "strongly agree" purported to measure the amount of stimulus created by the advertisement.

SCALE ORIGIN:

The scale was used originally by Schlinger (1979). Of the 52 scalar items used by Stout and Rust (1993), 44 matched to those items used by Schlinger (1979). Schlinger reported six dimensions consumers use to evaluate advertising: Relevant News, Brand Reinforcement, Stimulation, Empathy, Familiarity, and Confusion, and organized 44 scalar items into six groups.

SAMPLES:

Stout and Rust (1993) collected the data through a professional research firm using mall intercepts in several cities throughout the United States. The demographic characteristics of the sample (age, sex, and brand usage) were in the same proportion that they occur in the target population for the product category. Sample size was **208**, of which 50.5% were male. Sixty-eight percent of the sample were between the ages of 18 and 34 years, and 32% were 35 to 49 years of age. Forty eight percent of the sample were brand users.

RELIABILITY:

Stout and Rust (1993) reported a Cronbach's alpha of **.90**.

VALIDITY:

No specific examination of scale validity was reported in the studies.

ADMINISTRATION:

After viewing the commercial, individuals answered an open-ended question assessing the thoughts and feelings evoked by commercial and indicated his/ her agreement with statements about the commercial and product.

MAJOR FINDINGS:

Stout and Rust (1993) found that older viewers had more descriptive responses than did younger viewers, and overall findings show only small support that emotional response will be more important than demographic characteristics such as age, sex, and brand usage in explaining evaluations of commercials.

REFERENCES:

Schlinger, Mary Jane (1979), ''A Profile of Responses to Commercials,'' *JAR*, 19 (2), 37-46.

Stout, Patricia A. and Roland T. Rust (1993), ''Emotional Feelings and Evaluative Dimensions of Advertising: Are They Related?'' *JA*, 22 (1), 61-71.

SCALE ITEMS: ATTITUDE TOWARD THE AD (STIMULATION)

Strongly
disagree   ____ : ____ : ____ : ____ : ____ : ____   Strongly agree

       1   2   3   4   5   6

1. It was dull and boring.
2. The commercial was lots of fun to watch and to listen to.
3. I though it was quite clever and entertaining.
4. The commercial was amusing.
5. The enthusiasm of the commercial is catching—it picks you up.
6. The commercial was tender.
7. The commercial was dreamy. The commercial was playful.
8. The characters (or persons) in the commercial capture your attention.
9. Exciting.
10. The commercial was unique.

SCALE NAME: Attitude Toward the Brand in the Ad

SCALE DESCRIPTION:

Four seven-point bipolar adjectives presumed to measure the subject's attitude toward the brand.

SCALE ORIGIN:

The scale appears to be have been developed by Gardner (1985) and was used by Mitchell (1986).

SAMPLES:

A total of **166** subjects who were business undergraduates enrolled at an eastern university were used in the study. The average age of the sample was 21.7 years, and 49.4% were male.

RELIABILITY:

Cronbach's alpha was reported to be **.93**.

VALIDITY:

No examination of scale validity was reported.

ADMINISTRATION:

Subjects received a manila envelope containing just the four ads and a separate instruction booklet. Subjects worked through the booklet at their own pace. They were free to go earlier pages, but not later ones. After reading the introduction in the booklet that described the four running shoe attributes and levels on them, all subjects completed several tasks related to attitude toward the ad rating for all four brands. Subjects read the choice instructions in the booklet, made their preferred brand choice, gave their attitude toward the brand ratings, and returned the ads to the envelope.

MAJOR FINDINGS:

Biehal, Stephens, and Curlo (1992) examine how attitude toward the ad affects brand choice. The results show that attitude toward the ad has a direct, positive effect on focal brand choice over and above that of attitude toward the brand, as well as an indirect effect through attitude toward the brand. The brand B path coefficients showed that attitude toward the brand was strongly and directly related to brand choice. The total effect of attitude toward the ad on brand choice equaled that of attitude toward the brand.

REFERENCE:

Biehal, Gabriel, Debra Stephens, and Eleonora Curlo (1992), ''Attitude Toward the Ad and Brand Choice,'' JA, 22 (3), 19-36.

Gardner, Meryl P. (1985), ''Does Attitude to the Ad Affect Brand Attitude Under a Brand Evaluation Set?'' *JMR*, 22 (May), 192-98.

Mitchell, Andrew A. (1986), ''The Effect of Verbal and Visual Components of Advertisements on Brand Attitudes and Attitude Toward the Advertisement,'' *JCR*, 13 (1), 12-24.

SCALE ITEMS: ATTITUDE TOWARD THE BRAND IN THE AD

1. Bad   ___ : ___ : ___ : ___ : ___ : ___ : ___   Good
            1   2   3   4   5   6   7

2. Dislike quite a lot   ___ : ___ : ___ : ___ : ___ : ___ : ___   Like quite a lot
            1   2   3   4   5   6   7

3. Unpleasant   ___ : ___ : ___ : ___ : ___ : ___ : ___   Pleasant
            1   2   3   4   5   6   7

4. Poor quality   ___ : ___ : ___ : ___ : ___ : ___ : ___   Good quality
            1   2   3   4   5   6   7

SCALE NAME: Attitude Toward the Company in the Ad

SCALE DESCRIPTION:

A three-item, five-point semantic differential scale measuring the attitude toward the company sponsoring the advertisement.

SCALE ORIGIN:

It is not clear where the items originated or where they were first used as a multi-item summated scale.

SAMPLES:

Peterson, Wilson, and Brown (1992) mailed questionnaires to 2250 members of a mail panel. A total of 1108 questionnaires were returned, of which **999** contained complete data and were usable. Of the total survey participants, 47% were male, 27% had a college degree, and 64% were married.

RELIABILITY:

Peterson, Wilson and Brown (1992) reported a Cronbach's alpha of **.91**.

VALIDITY:

No examination of scale validity was reported.

ADMINISTRATION:

Peterson, Wilson, and Brown (1992) mailed advertisements containing one of the six products or services with a questionnaire to members of a national panel. The effective response rate was **44.4%**.

MAJOR FINDINGS:

Peterson, Wilson, and Brown's (1992) results indicate that advertised claims of customer satisfaction have little effect on consumer attitudes. Also, the source of data supporting the various satisfaction claims had no effect on responses. Participants did not discriminate among personal endorsements. The authors suggest that the recent trend toward including ratings of customer satisfaction in advertisements may not produce the types of responses (favorable attitudes) hoped for in consumer advertising.

REFERENCE:

Peterson, Robert A., William R. Wilson, and Steven P. Brown (1992), ''Effects of Advertised Customer Satisfaction Claims on Consumer Attitudes and Purchase Intention,'' *JAR*, 32 (2), 34-40.

SCALE ITEMS: ATTITUDE TOWARD THE COMPANY IN THE AD

1. Reputable   ____ : ____ : ____ : ____ : ____   Not reputable
                   1   2   3   4   5

2. Customer oriented   ____ : ____ : ____ : ____ : ____   Not customer oriented
                   1   2   3   4   5

3. Unique   ____ : ____ : ____ : ____ : ____   Not unique
                   1   2   3   4   5

SCALE NAME: Attitude Toward the Testimonial

SCALE DESCRIPTION:

A four-item, seven-point Likert scale, purported to measure attitude toward the testimonial.

SCALE ORIGIN:

It is not clear where the items originated or where they were first used as a multi-item summated scale.

SAMPLES:

There are two experiments conducted in this study; this scale was used only in experiment 1. The total sample consisted of **160** MBA students who were enrolled at a northeastern university in the United States. They created two similarity conditions using personal characteristics, education, and occupation The similar endorser (Joan Williams for females and John Williams for males) was described as having received an MBA in 1988 from the same university and having worked since graduation in a management position at a locally based national bank. In the dissimilar endorser condition, the endorser was described as having graduated from high school in 1981 and worked since graduation as a sales clerk at a regional discount chain store. They also created two experience conditions: in the experienced condition, the endorser was described as having been to many of the service providers in the local area, and in the inexperienced condition, the endorser was described as having been only one service provider in the local area.

RELIABILITY

A Cronbach's alpha of **.90** was reported for attitude to testimonial in experiment 1.

VALIDITY:

No examination of scale validity was reported.

ADMINISTRATION:

In experiment 1, Feick and Higie (1992) told the participants that they were doing a research for an advertising agency planning to develop testimonial ads for a few service-providing businesses in the city where the university was located. They also explained that they interviewed some of the customers during the first few weeks of business and recorded their statements about the company, then combined each customer's photograph with his/her testimonial. Female subjects evaluated a testimonial given by Joan Williams, and male subjects evaluated a testimonial given by John Williams. In all conditions, the endorser indicated an identical reaction to the service provider and recommended its use. After examining the ad prototype, each subject completed an evaluation form. High scores indicate that the respondent has a positive attitude toward the testimonial.

REFERENCE:

Feick, Lawrence and Robin A. Higie (1992), ''The Effects of Preference Heterogeneity and Source Characteristics on Ad Processing and Judgments about Endorsers,'' *JA*, 21 (2), 9-24.

SCALE ITEMS: ATTITUDE TOWARD THE TESTIMONIAL

1. Very ineffective testimonial
   ___ : ___ : ___ : ___ : ___ : ___ : ___
     1   2   3   4   5   6   7
   Very effective testimonial

2. Weak advertisement
   ___ : ___ : ___ : ___ : ___ : ___ : ___
     1   2   3   4   5   6   7
   Strong advertisement

3. Not at all persuasive advertisement
   ___ : ___ : ___ : ___ : ___ : ___ : ___
     1   2   3   4   5   6   7
   Very persuasive advertisement

4. Very ineffective for getting people like you to go to [service provider]
   ___ : ___ : ___ : ___ : ___ : ___ : ___
     1   2   3   4   5   6   7
   Very effective for getting people like you to go to [service provider]

SCALE NAME: Beliefs About TV Advertising (Evaluations of How TV Commercials Are Executed)

SCALE DESCRIPTION:

A three-item, five-point Likert scale ranging from ''agree'' to ''disagree.''

SCALE ORIGIN:

The scale appears to be have been developed by Alwitt and Prabhaker (1992) and was only used in their study.

SAMPLES:

Alwitt and Prabhaker (1992) mailed a survey to 1200 randomly selected households with listed phone numbers in the Chicago metropolitan statistical area in March 1990. **Two hundred twenty-eight** usable surveys were returned, a 19% return rate. Compared with the Chicago SMSA population (Bureau of the Census, 1983), this sample is older, is wealthier, and has fewer children. The sample of the respondents to this survey includes fewer respondents between ages 18 and 25 years, more who are older than 65 years of age, fewer with children younger than 18 years of age, and more with annual household incomes of $30,000 or more.

RELIABILITY:

Cronbach's alpha was reported to be **.43**.

VALIDITY:

No examination of scale validity was reported.

ADMINISTRATION:

The scale was self-administered along with other measures in a mail survey format. The possible score range is 3–15. A low score represents negative perceptions of the personal and social benefits or costs of television advertising.

MAJOR FINDINGS:

The goal of the Alwitt and Prabhaker (1992) study was to evaluate why people tend to have unfavorable attitudes about television advertising. They proposed that reasons for attitudes about television are based on what people know about television advertising and how it is relevant to them. What people know about advertising refers to the beliefs that people have toward television advertising, and its relevance refers to the specific function that television advertising serves for a viewer and how it fits into his or her life. To examine

how the beliefs about television advertising are related to how much people like television advertising, the authors had to remove the effects of demographic characteristics and attitudes to television programs. After doing this, the multiple regression model of belief about television advertising is significant and accounts for 15% of the variance. The beta coefficient of the belief about television advertising (Evaluations of how television commercials are executed) is less than –0.3. The more respondents perceive that television advertising is well executed, the more they like it.

REFERENCE:

Alwitt, Linda F. and Paul R. Prabhaker (1992), ''Functional and Belief Dimensions of Attitudes to Television Advertising,'' *JAR*, 32 (5), 30-42.

SCALE ITEMS: BELIEFS ABOUT TV ADVERTISING (EVALUATIONS OF HOW TV COMMERCIALS ARE EXECUTED)

```
Strongly                                                    Strongly
disagree                                                       agree
    1————————————2————————————3————————————4————————————5
```

1. Most TV commercials are in poor taste.
2. A lot of TV advertising is funny or clever.
3. TV ads are more offensive today than they used to be.

SCALE NAME: Beliefs About TV Advertising (Perceptions of Offensive Aspects of Television Advertising)

SCALE DESCRIPTION:

A four-item, five-point Likert scale ranging from "agree" to "disagree."

SCALE ORIGIN:

The scale appears to be have been developed by Alwitt and Prabhaker (1992) and was used only in their study.

SAMPLES:

Alwitt and Prabhaker (1992) mailed a survey to 1200 randomly selected households with listed phone numbers in the Chicago metropolitan statistical area in March 1990. **Two hundred twenty-eight** usable surveys were returned, a 19% return rate. Compared with the Chicago SMSA population (Bureau of the Census, 1983), this sample is older, is wealthier, and has fewer children. The sample of the respondents to this survey includes fewer respondents between ages 18 and 25 years, more older than 65 years of age, fewer with children younger than 18 years of age, and more with annual household incomes of $30,000 or more.

RELIABILITY:

Cronbach's alpha was reported to be **.57**.

VALIDITY:

No examination of scale validity was reported.

ADMINISTRATION:

The scale was self-administered along with other measures in a mail survey format. The possible score range is 4–20. A low score represents negative perceptions of the offensive aspects of television advertising.

MAJOR FINDINGS:

The goal of the Alwitt and Prabhaker (1992) study was to evaluate why people tend to have unfavorable attitudes about television advertising. They proposed that reasons for attitudes about television are based on what people know about television advertising and how it is relevant to them. What people know about advertising refers to the beliefs that people have toward television advertising, and its relevance refers to the specific function that television advertising serves for a viewer and how it fits into his/her life. To examine how the beliefs about television advertising are related to how much people like television advertising, the authors had to remove the effects of demographic characteristics and attitudes to television programs. After doing this, the multiple regression model of belief about television advertising is significant and accounts for 15% of the variance. The beta coefficient of the belief about television advertising (Perception of offensive aspects of television advertising) is less than –0.15.

REFERENCE:

Alwitt, Linda F. and Paul R. Prabhaker (1992), "Functional and Belief Dimensions of Attitudes to Television Advertising," *JAR*, 32 (5), 30-42.

SCALE ITEMS: BELIEFS ABOUT TV ADVERTISING (PERCEPTIONS OF OFFENSIVE ASPECTS OF TELEVISION ADVERTISING)

Strongly   Strongly
disagree   agree
1————————2————————3————————4————————5

1. TV advertising is upsetting to people because it sets goals for the average person that he cannot reach.
2. TV advertising is a main reason our society is so concerned with buying and owning things.
3. There is too much sex in TV advertising.
4. There is too much violence in TV advertising.

SCALE NAME: Beliefs About TV Advertising (Perceptions of the Personal and Social Benefits or Costs of TV Advertising)

SCALE DESCRIPTION:

A ten-item, five-point Likert scale ranging from "agree" to "disagree."

SCALE ORIGIN:

The scale appears to be have been developed by Alwitt and Prabhaker (1992) and was used only in their study.

SAMPLES:

Alwitt and Prabhaker (1992) mailed a survey to 1200 randomly selected households with listed phone numbers in the Chicago metropolitan statistical area in March 1990. **Two hundred twenty-eight** usable surveys were returned, a 19% return rate. Compared with the Chicago SMSA population (Bureau of the Census, 1983), this sample is older, is wealthier, and has fewer children. The sample of the respondents to this survey includes fewer respondents between ages 18 and 25 years, more older than 65 years of age, fewer with children younger than 18 years of age, and more with annual household incomes of $30,000 or more.

RELIABILITY:

Cronbach's alpha was reported to be **.86**.

VALIDITY:

No examination of scale validity was reported.

ADMINISTRATION:

The scale was self administered along with other measures in a mail survey format. The possible score range is 10 to 50. A low score represents negative perceptions of the personal and social benefits or costs of television advertising.

MAJOR FINDINGS:

The goal of the Alwitt and Prabhaker (1992) study was to evaluate why people tend to have unfavorable attitudes about television advertising. They proposed that reasons for attitudes about television are based on what people know about television advertising and how it is relevant to them. What people know about advertising refers to the beliefs that people have toward television advertising, and its relevance refers to the specific function that television advertising serves for a viewer and how it fits into his or her life. To examine

how the beliefs about television advertising are related to how much people like television advertising, the authors had to remove the effects of demographic characteristics and attitudes to television programs. After doing this, the multiple regression model of belief about television advertising is significant and accounts for 15% of the variance. The beta coefficient of the belief about television advertising (perceptions of costs and benefits of television advertising) is less than −0.25. The more that respondents perceive that television advertising has benefits, the more they like it.

REFERENCE:

Alwitt, Linda F. and Paul R. Prabhaker (1992), ''Functional and Belief Dimensions of Attitudes to Television Advertising,'' *JAR*, 32 (5), 30-42.

SCALE ITEMS: BELIEFS ABOUT TV ADVERTISING (PERCEPTION OF THE PERSONAL AND SOCIAL BENEFITS OR COSTS OF TV ADVERTISING)

Strongly   Strongly
disagree   agree
1————————2————————3————————4————————5

1. TV advertising is a good way to learn about what products and services are available.
2. TV advertising results in better products for the public.
3. In general, TV advertising presents a true picture of the product advertised.
4. You can trust brands advertised on TV more than brands not advertised on TV.
5. TV advertising helps raise our standard of living.
6. TV advertisements help me find products that match my personality and interest.
7. TV advertising helps me to know which brands have the features I am looking for.
8. TV advertising gives me a good idea about products by showing the kinds of people who use them.
9. TV advertising helps me buy the best brand for the price.
10. I am willing to pay more for a product that is advertised on TV.

SCALE NAME: Beliefs About TV Advertising (Perceptions that TV Advertisements Are Shown Too Often or Too Much)

SCALE DESCRIPTION:

A three-item, five-point Likert scale ranging from "agree" to "disagree."

SCALE ORIGIN:

The scale appears to be have been developed by Alwitt and Prabhaker (1992) and was used only in their study.

SAMPLES:

Alwitt and Prabhaker (1992) mailed a survey to 1200 randomly selected households with listed phone numbers in the Chicago metropolitan statistical area in March 1990. **Two hundred twenty-eight** usable surveys were returned, a 19% return rate. Compared with the Chicago SMSA population (Bureau of the Census, 1983), this sample is older, is wealthier, and has fewer children. The sample of the respondents to this survey includes fewer respondents between ages 18 and 25 years, more older than 65 years of age, fewer with children younger than 18 years of age, and more with annual household incomes of $30,000 or more.

RELIABILITY:

Cronbach's alpha was reported to be **.58**.

VALIDITY:

No examination of scale validity was reported.

ADMINISTRATION:

The scale was self-administered along with other measures in a mail survey format. The possible score range is 3–15. A low score represents negative perceptions of the personal and social benefits or costs of television advertising.

MAJOR FINDINGS:

The goal of the Alwitt and Prabhaker (1992) study was to evaluate why people tend to have unfavorable attitudes about television advertising. They proposed that reasons for attitudes about television are based on what people know about television advertising and how it is relevant to them. What people know about advertising refers to the beliefs that people have toward television advertising, and its relevance refers to the specific function that television advertising serves for a viewer and how it fits into his or her life. To examine how the beliefs about television advertising are related to how much people like television advertising, they had to remove the effects of demographic characteristics and attitudes to television programs. After doing this, the multiple regression model of belief about television advertising is significant and accounts for 15% of the variance. The beta coefficient of the belief about television advertising (Perceptions that television advertisements are shown too often or too much) is less than 0.15. The more respondents perceive there is a lot of advertising on television, the less they like television advertising.

REFERENCE:

Alwitt, Linda F. and Paul R. Prabhaker (1992), ''Functional and Belief Dimensions of Attitudes to Television Advertising,'' *JAR*, 32 (5), 30-42.

SCALE ITEMS: BELIEFS ABOUT TV ADVERTISING (PERCEPTIONS THAT TV ADVERTISEMENTS ARE SHOWN TOO OFTEN OR TOO MUCH)

Strongly disagree | | | | Strongly agree
1————————2————————3————————4————————5

1. There seems to be more advertising on TV than there used to be.
2. Most commercial breaks on TV have too many commercials in a row.
3. The same TV ads are constantly shown again and again.

SCALE NAME: Beliefs About TV Advertising (Perceptions that TV Advertising Does Not Offer Information)

SCALE DESCRIPTION:

A three-item, five-point Likert scale ranging from ''agree'' to ''disagree.''

SCALE ORIGIN:

The scale appears to be have been developed by Alwitt and Prabhaker (1992) and was used only in their study.

SAMPLES:

Alwitt and Prabhaker (1992) mailed a survey to 1200 randomly selected households with listed phone numbers in the Chicago metropolitan statistical area in March 1990. **Two hundred twenty-eight** usable surveys were returned, a 19% return rate. Compared with the Chicago SMSA population (Bureau of the Census, 1983), this sample is older, is wealthier, and has fewer children. The sample of the respondents to this survey includes fewer respondents between ages 18 and 25 years, more older than 65 years of age, fewer with children younger than 18 years of age, and more with annual household incomes of $30,000 or more.

RELIABILITY:

Cronbach's alpha was reported to be **.61**.

VALIDITY:

No examination of scale validity was reported.

ADMINISTRATION:

The scale was self-administered along with other measures in a mail survey format. The possible score range is 3–15. A low score represents negative perceptions about television advertising offering information.

MAJOR FINDINGS:

The goal of the Alwitt and Prabhaker (1992) study was to evaluate why people tend to have unfavorable attitudes about television advertising. They proposed that reasons for attitudes about television are based on what people know about television advertising and how it is relevant to them. What people know about advertising refers to the beliefs that people have toward television advertising, and its relevance refers to the specific function that television advertising serves for a viewer and how it fits into his or her life. To examine

how the beliefs about television advertising are related to how much people like television advertising, the authors had to remove the effects of demographic characteristics and attitudes to television programs. After doing this, the multiple regression model of belief about television advertising is significant and accounts for 15% of the variance. The beta coefficient of the belief about television advertising (Perception that television advertising does not offer information) is very close to 0.

REFERENCE:

Alwitt, Linda F. and Paul R. Prabhaker (1992), "Functional and Belief Dimensions of Attitudes to Television Advertising," *JAR*, 32 (5), 30-42.

SCALE ITEMS: BELIEFS ABOUT TV ADVERTISING (PERCEPTION THAT TV ADVERTISING DOES NOT OFFER INFORMATION)

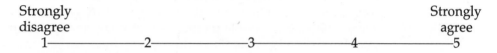

Strongly disagree 1————2————3————4————5 Strongly agree

1. Most TV ads today are not about products themselves, but just create a mood.
2. Today TV ads don't give you as much information as they used to.
3. Today's TV ads tell you more about the people who use a brand than about what the brand does for you.

SCALE NAME: Beliefs About TV Advertising (Perceptions that TV Advertising Is Deceptive)

SCALE DESCRIPTION:

A four-item, five-point Likert scale ranging from "agree" to "disagree."

SCALE ORIGIN:

The scale appears to be have been developed by Alwitt and Prabhaker (1992) and was used only in their study.

SAMPLES:

Alwitt and Prabhaker (1992) mailed a survey to 1200 randomly selected households with listed phone numbers in the Chicago metropolitan statistical area in March 1990. **Two hundred twenty-eight** usable surveys were returned, a 19% return rate. Compared with the Chicago SMSA population (Bureau of the Census, 1983), this sample is older, is wealthier, and has fewer children. The sample of the respondents to this survey includes fewer respondents between ages 18 and 25 years, more older than 65 years of age, fewer with children younger than 18 years of age, and more with annual household incomes of $30,000 or more.

RELIABILITY:

Cronbach's alpha was reported to be **.71**.

VALIDITY:

No examination of scale validity was reported.

ADMINISTRATION:

The scale was self administered along with other measures in a mail survey format. The possible score range is 4–20. A low score represents negative perceptions of the personal and social benefits or costs of television advertising.

MAJOR FINDINGS:

The goal of the Alwitt and Prabhaker (1992) study was to evaluate why people tend to have unfavorable attitudes about television advertising. They proposed that reasons for attitudes about television are based on what people know about television advertising and how it is relevant to them. What people know about advertising refers to the beliefs that people have toward television advertising, and its relevance refers to the specific function that television advertising serves for a viewer and how it fits into his or her life. To examine how the beliefs about television advertising are related to how much people like television advertising, the authors had to remove the effects of demographic characteristics and attitudes to television programs. After doing this, the multiple regression model of six beliefs about television advertising is significant and accounts for 15% of the variance. The beta coefficient of the belief about television advertising (Perception that television advertising is deceptive) is less than –0.05.

REFERENCE:

Alwitt, Linda F. and Paul R. Prabhaker (1992), ''Functional and Belief Dimensions of Attitudes to Television Advertising,'' *JAR*, 32 (5), 30-42.

SCALE ITEMS: BELIEFS ABOUT TV ADVERTISING (PERCEPTIONS THAT TV ADVERTISING IS DECEPTIVE)

Strongly   Strongly
disagree   agree
1————————2————————3————————4————————5

1. Most TV ads try to work on people's emotions.
2. There is a critical need for more truth in today's TV advertising.
3. TV commercials do not show life as it really is.
4. TV advertising mostly tries to create imaginary differences between products that are very similar.

SCALE NAME: Credibility (Source)

SCALE DESCRIPTION:

Various bipolar adjectives measuring the perceived credibility of the source of a message. Specific scale items and number of scale points are indicated subsequently.

SCALE ORIGIN:

Lichtenstein and Bearden (1989) and Ohanian (1990) did not give any information about the origin of their scales. Gotlieb and Sarel (1991) indicated that their scale items were taken from Harmon and Coney (1982).

SAMPLES:

Lichtenstein and Bearden (1989) collected their data from **278** undergraduate business students. The students were assigned randomly to one of 12 treatment conditions in a 2 × 2 × 3 experimental design. There were 21-28 students per cell. Gotlieb and Sarel (1991) collected their data from **156** subjects who were junior and senior students attending a large urban university. The subjects were familiar with the product category (i.e., 147 subjects indicated that they had used a VCR within the past year). Ohanian (1990) used two samples in the exploratory phase of the study. **Two hundred fifty** students in a southern university completed the first version of the questionnaire, in which Madonna was the celebrity promoting a new brand of designer jeans. A different group of **240** students completed the second version, in which John McEnroe was promoting a new line of tennis rackets. In the confirmatory phase, Ohanian (1990) selected the subjects using systematic area-sampling technique. A total of 360 questionnaires (180 using Linda Evans and 180 using Tom Selleck) were delivered, 289 were collected, and **265** were found suitable for analysis. Ohanian (1991) used 40 graduate students to develop a list of celebrities and 38 college students to indicate the most appropriate products these celebrities could endorse. The author then selected the sample from three groups of individuals: one systematically selected from residential neighborhoods (97), a second from the membership of several churches (246), and a third from a student population of graduate and undergraduate students (217). The final sample consisted of **542** respondents.

RELIABILITY:

Lichtenstein and Bearden (1989) reported a Cronbach's alpha of **.78**. Gotlieb and Sarel (1991) reported an alpha of **.84**. Ohanian (1990) reported an alpha greater than **.80**. Ohanian (1991) reported an alpha of **.82**.

VALIDITY:

No examination of scale validity was reported in Lichtenstein and Bearden (1989) and Gotlieb and Sarel (1991). Ohanian (1990) tested nomological validity by relating scores on each dimension of expertise, trustworthiness, and attractiveness to several self-reported behaviors.

ADMINISTRATION:

In Lichtenstein and Bearden (1989), respondents self-administered the scale along with several other measures in an experimental setting. High scores on the scale imply that respondents perceive the source of a message to be highly credible, whereas low scores suggest that respondents believe the source to be untrustworthy. Gotlieb and Sarel (1991) told the subjects that this was a "a survey of consumer reading habits." The information they would be reading came from newspapers and magazines published in America. Subjects then read three print advertisements in a single booklet; two had appeared previously in national magazines, and the third was the test advertisement. After subjects viewed the three advertisements, they closed the first booklet and opened the second, which was used to measure the effects. The scales were administered in paper-and-pencil format. Ohanian (1990) administered the questionnaires in the exploratory phase in paper-and-pencil format and used an interviewing procedure in the confirmatory phase. Ohanian (1991) used trained assistants to monitor each data collection round and read all directions from a prepared script. After the instructions were read, the respondents were asked to complete the first part of the questionnaire, which included the source familiarity and demographic questions. After this phase, the assistant collected the instrument and determined which subjects should continue to the next phases. In the second phase, respondents completed the source credibility scale for one of the four celebrities.

MAJOR FINDINGS:

Lichtenstein and Bearden (1989) examined the influence of merchant-supplied reference prices, ad distinctiveness, and ad message consistency on perception of source credibility, value of the deal, and attitude toward the deal. Among many other findings, perceived credibility was higher for plausible–high merchant-supplied prices than for implausible–high merchant-supplied prices. Gotlieb and Sarel (1991) found that a highly credible source had a more positive impact on the level of construction-motivated involvement than did a low-credibility source. Ohanian (1990) reported that credible sources are more persuasive than are sources of low credibility. Also, highly credible sources induce more behavioral compliance than do less credible sources. However, highly credible sources are not always more effective than less credible ones. Celebrity endorsement in advertising has been increasing. Therefore, a valid instrument measuring the celebrity endorser's credibility is important to understand the impact of using such persons in advertising. Ohanian's (1990) 15-item scale demonstrated high reliability and validity. Ohanian (1991) reported that both female and male respondents across different age categories have similar perceptions of what constitutes expertise, trustworthiness, and attractiveness of a celebrity. Thus, regardless of subjects' age and gender, these constructs can be measured with equal precision. Attractiveness and trustworthiness had minimal effects on source credibility. Only perceived expertise of the celebrity was a significant factor explaining the respondent's intentions to purchase. Therefore, for celebrity persons to be truly effective, they should be knowledgeable, experienced, and qualified to talk about product.

REFERENCES:

Gotlieb, Jerry B. and Dan Sarel (1991), "Comparative Advertising Effectiveness: The Role of Involvement and Source Credibility," *JA*, 20 (1), 38-45.
Lichtenstein, Donald R. and William O. Bearden (1989), "Contextual Influences on Perceptions of Merchant-Supplied Reference Prices," *JCR*, 16 (June), 55-66.
Ohanian, Roobina (1990), "Construction and Validation of a Scale to Measure Celebrity Endorsers' Perceived Expertise, Trustworthiness, and Attractiveness," *JA*, 19 (3), 39-52.
_____ (1991), "The Impact of Celebrity Spokespersons' Perceived Image on Consumer's Intention to Purchase," *JAR*, 31 (1), 46-54.

SCALE ITEMS: CREDIBILITY (SOURCE)

Gotlieb and Sarel (1991): 4, 6, 7, 8, 9, 10 (mean); seven-point
Lichtenstein and Bearden (1989): 1, 2, 3, 4, 5 (mean); nine-point
Ohanian (1990): 1, 2, 3, 4, 8, 9, 11, 12, 13, 14, 15, 16, 17, 18, 19
Ohanian (1991): 1, 2, 3, 4, 8, 9, 11, 12, 13, 14, 15, 16, 17, 18, 19

The (message source) is:

1. Insincere ___:___:___:___:___:___:___ Sincere
   1 2 3 4 5 6 7

2. Honest ___:___:___:___:___:___:___ Dishonest (r)
   1 2 3 4 5 6 7

3. Dependable ___:___:___:___:___:___:___ Not dependable (r)
   1 2 3 4 5 6 7

4. Not trustworthy ___:___:___:___:___:___:___ Trustworthy
   1 2 3 4 5 6 7

5. Not credible ___:___:___:___:___:___:___ Credible
   1 2 3 4 5 6 7

6. Not open-minded ___:___:___:___:___:___:___ Open-minded
   1 2 3 4 5 6 7

7. Good ___:___:___:___:___:___:___ Bad (r)
   1 2 3 4 5 6 7

8. Expert ___:___:___:___:___:___:___ Not expert
   1 2 3 4 5 6 7

9. Experienced ___ : ___ : ___ : ___ : ___ : ___ : ___ Not experienced (r)

1   2   3   4   5   6   7

10. Trained ___ : ___ : ___ : ___ : ___ : ___ : ___ Untrained (r)

1   2   3   4   5   6   7

11. Attractive ___ : ___ : ___ : ___ : ___ : ___ : ___ Unattractive (r)

1   2   3   4   5   6   7

12. Classy ___ : ___ : ___ : ___ : ___ : ___ : ___ Not classy (r)

1   2   3   4   5   6   7

13. Beautiful ___ : ___ : ___ : ___ : ___ : ___ : ___ Ugly (r)

1   2   3   4   5   6   7

14. Elegant ___ : ___ : ___ : ___ : ___ : ___ : ___ Plain (r)

1   2   3   4   5   6   7

15. Sexy ___ : ___ : ___ : ___ : ___ : ___ : ___ Not sexy (r)

1   2   3   4   5   6   7

16. Reliable ___ : ___ : ___ : ___ : ___ : ___ : ___ Unreliable (r)

1   2   3   4   5   6   7

17. Knowledgeable ___ : ___ : ___ : ___ : ___ : ___ : ___ Unknowledgeable (r)

1   2   3   4   5   6   7

18. Qualified ___ : ___ : ___ : ___ : ___ : ___ : ___ Unqaulified (r)

1   2   3   4   5   6   7

19. Skilled ___ : ___ : ___ : ___ : ___ : ___ : ___ Unskilled (r)

1   2   3   4   5   6   7

SCALE NAME: Endorser Attractiveness

SCALE DESCRIPTION:

> A three-item, seven-point Likert scale intended to measure the subjects' perceptions of endorser attractiveness.

SCALE ORIGIN:

> It is not clear where the items originated or where they were first used as a multi-item summated scale.

SAMPLES:

> There are two experiments conducted in this study, though the endorser attractiveness scale was used only in experiment 1. In this experiment, the total sample consisted of **160** MBA students who were enrolled at a northeastern university in the United States. They created two similarity conditions using personal characteristics, education, and occupation. The similar endorser (Joan Williams for females and John Williams for males) was described as having received an MBA in 1988 from the same university and having worked since graduation in a management position at a locally based national bank. In the dissimilar endorser condition, the endorser was described as having graduated from high school in 1981 and as having worked since graduation as a sales clerk at a regional discount chain store. They also created two experience conditions: In the experienced condition, the endorser was described as having been to many of the service providers in the local area, and in the inexperienced condition, the endorser was described as having been to only one service provider in the local area.

RELIABILITY:

> In experiment 1, a Cronbach's alpha of **.96** was reported for endorser's attractiveness .

VALIDITY:

No examination of scale validity was reported.

ADMINISTRATION:

> Feick and Higie (1992) told the participants that they were doing research for an advertising agency planning to develop testimonial ads for a few service-providing businesses in the city where the university was located. They also explained that they interviewed some of the customers during the first few weeks of business and recorded their statements about the company, then combined each customer's photograph with his/her testimonial. Female subjects evaluated a testimonial given by Joan Williams, and male subjects evaluated a testimonial given by John Williams. In all conditions, the endorser

indicated an identical reaction to the service provider and recommended its use. After examining the ad prototype, each subject completed an evaluation form. High scores indicate that endorser is attractive. Authors included this scale only in experiment 1 as a confound check to determine subjects' perceptions of endorser attractiveness.

MAJOR FINDINGS:

The results indicate no significant difference in the perceived physical attractiveness of the endorser across the design.

REFERENCE:

Feick, Lawrence and Robin A. Higie (1992), ''The Effects of Preference Heterogeneity and Source Characteristics on Ad Processing and Judgments About Endorsers,'' *JA*, 21 (2), 9-24.

SCALE ITEMS: ENDORSER ATTRACTIVENESS

Strongly disagree ___ : ___ : ___ : ___ : ___ : ___ : ___ Strongly agree
             1   2   3   4   5   6   7

1. [Endorser] is attractive.
2. In my opinion, [endorser] is good looking.
3. [Endorser] is pretty (handsome).

SCALE NAME: Endorser Experience

SCALE DESCRIPTION:

A five-item, seven-point Likert scale intended to measure the relative importance of an endorser's experience to consumers.

SCALE ORIGIN:

It is not clear where the items originated or where they were first used as a multi-item summated scale.

SAMPLES:

Feick and Higie (1992) conducted two experiments. In experiment 1, the total sample consisted of **160** MBA students who were enrolled at a northeastern university in the United States. They created two similarity conditions using personal characteristics, education, and occupation. The similar endorser (Joan Williams for females and John Williams for males) was described as having received an MBA in 1988 from the same university and having worked since graduation in a management position at a locally based national bank. In the dissimilar endorser condition, the endorser was described as having graduated from high school in 1981, and as having worked since graduation as a sales clerk at a regional discount chain store. They also created two experience conditions: In the experienced condition, the endorser was described as having been to many of the service providers in the local area, and in the inexperienced condition, the endorser was described as having been to only one service provider in the local area. In experiment 2, the sample consisted of **133** undergraduate students enrolled at a northwestern university in the United States. To control for age effects on responses, no students older than 29 years of age were included in the analysis. In addition, those who did not perceive the scenario as realistic were eliminated.

RELIABILITY:

In experiment 1, for endorser's experience a Cronbach's alpha of **.90** was reported. In experiment 2, a Cronbach's alpha for similar-inexperienced endorser was **.89** and for dissimilar-experienced endorser was **.85**.

VALIDITY:

No examination of scale validity was reported.

ADMINISTRATION:

In experiment 1, the authors told the participants that they were doing a research for an advertising agency planning to develop testimonial ads for a few service providing businesses in the city where the university was located. They also explained that they interviewed some of the customers during the first few weeks of business and recorded their statements about the company, then combined each customer's photograph with his/her testimonial. Female subjects evaluated a testimonial given by Joan Williams, and male subjects evaluated a testimonial given by John Williams. In all conditions, the endorser indicated an identical reaction to the service provider and recommended its use. After examining the ad prototype, each subject completed an evaluation form. High scores indicate that endorser is experienced.

In experiment 2, students read a scenario in which they were asked to assume that they just graduated from college and had taken a new job and moved to a new location. Two of their neighbors were described: one of them to be perceived as similar to the subject, but having minimal service-related experience, and the other one to be perceived as dissimilar to the subject, but having substantial service-related experience. After reading the scenario, subjects responded to a pencil-and-paper questionnaire.

MAJOR FINDINGS:

Feick and Higie (1992) have shown that for choices in high preference heterogeneity categories (i.e., choices in which tastes matter and outcomes are likely to be interpreted differently by different consumers), consumers prefer an endorser with similar characteristics, even if the endorser has little service-related experience. Their results indicate that for the high-preference heterogeneity service (night clubs), subjects' reactions to the ad focused more on similarity than on experience. Also, the similar endorser generated more favorable attitudes and intentions than did the dissimilar endorser. As expected, more subjects chose the similar yet inexperienced endorser for the restaurant, night club, and hair salon. For the interior decorator service, which subjects rated highest on preference heterogeneity, only 59% of the subjects chose the similar endorser. The possible explanation for this finding is that interior decoration is a service for which a consumer seeks both expertise and similarity in an endorser.

REFERENCE:

Feick, Lawrence and Robin A. Higie (1992), "The Effects of Preference Heterogeneity and Source Characteristics on Ad Processing and Judgments About Endorsers," *JA*, 21 (2), 9-24.

SCALE ITEMS: ENDORSER EXPERIENCE

Strongly disagree	___ : ___ : ___ : ___ : ___ : ___ : ___	Strongly agree
	1 2 3 4 5 6 7	

1. [Endorser] has been to a lot of [service providers] in the [local] area.
2. [Endorser] seems to have a good sense about the [service providers] in the area.
3. [Endorser] is knowledgeable about [service providers].
4. [Endorser] has experience with [service providers] in the area.
5. [Endorser] knows a lot of [service providers] in this area.

SCALE NAME: Endorser Similarity

SCALE DESCRIPTION:

A three-item, seven-point Likert scale intended to measure the relative importance of an endorser's similarity to consumers.

SCALE ORIGIN:

It is not clear where the items originated or where they were first used as a multi-item summated scale.

SAMPLES:

Feick and Higie (1992) conducted two experiments. In experiment 1, total sample size was **160** (92 males and 68 females). Because endorser similarity required a relatively homogeneous subject sample, MBA students enrolled at a northeastern university in the United States participated in this study as part of a class requirement. They created two similarity conditions using personal characteristics, education, and occupation. The similar endorser (Joan Williams for females and John Williams for males) was described as having received an MBA in 1988 from the same university and having worked since graduation in a management position at a locally based national bank. In the dissimilar endorser condition, the endorser was described as having graduated from high school in 1981, and as having worked since graduation as a sales clerk at a regional discount chain store. In experiment 2, the sample consisted of **133** undergraduate students, enrolled at a northwestern university in the United States. To control for age effects on responses, no students older than 29 years of age were included in the analysis. In addition, those who did not perceive the scenario as realistic were eliminated.

RELIABILITY:

In experiment 1, a Cronbach's alpha was reported to be **.86** for similarity. In experiment 2, Cronbach's alpha for similar-inexperienced endorser was **.82** and for dissimilar-experienced endorser was **.79**.

VALIDITY:

No examination of scale validity was reported.

ADMINISTRATION:

Feick and Higie (1992) conducted two experiments. In experiment 1, they told the participants that they were doing a research for an advertising agency planning to develop testimonial ads for a few service-providing businesses in the city where the university was located. They also explained that they interviewed some of the customers during the first few weeks of business and recorded their statements about the company, then combined each customer's photograph with his/her testimonial. Female subjects evaluated a testimonial given by Joan Williams, and male subjects evaluated a testimonial given by John Williams. In all conditions, the endorser indicated an identical reaction to the service provider and recommended its use. After examining the ad prototype, each subject completed an evaluation form. High scores indicate high similarity between consumers and endorsers.

In experiment 2, students read a scenario in which they were asked to assume that they just graduated from college and had taken a new job and moved to a new location. Two of their neighbors were described: one of them to be perceived as similar to the subject, but having minimal service-related experience, and the other one to be perceived as dissimilar to the subject, but having substantial service-related experience. After reading the scenario, subjects responded to a paper-and-pencil questionnaire.

MAJOR FINDINGS:

Feick and Higie (1992) have shown that for choices in high-preference heterogeneity categories (i.e., choices in which tastes matter and outcomes are likely to be interpreted differently by different consumers), consumers prefer an endorser with similar characteristics, even if the endorser has little service-related experience. Their results indicate that for the high-preference heterogeneity service (night clubs), subjects' reactions to ad focused more on similarity than on experience. Also, the similar endorser generated more favorable attitudes and intentions than did the dissimilar endorser. As expected, more subjects chose the similar yet inexperienced endorser for the restaurant, night club, and hair salon. For the interior decorator service, which subjects rated highest on preference heterogeneity, only 59% of the subjects chose the similar endorser. The possible explanation for this finding is that interior decoration is a service for which a consumer seeks both expertise and similarity in an endorser.

REFERENCE:

Feick, Lawrence and Robin A. Higie (1992), ''The Effects of Preference Heterogeneity and Source Characteristics on Ad Processing and Judgments About Endorsers,'' *JA*, 21 (2), 9-24.

SCALE ITEMS: ENDORSER SIMILARITY

Strongly   ___ : ___ : ___ : ___ : ___ : ___ : ___   Strongly
disagree   1   2   3   4   5   6   7   agree

1. [Endorser] and I probably have similar values and beliefs.
2. [Endorser] is quite a bit like me.
3. It's likely that [Endorser] and I have similar tastes and preferences.

SCALE NAME: Endorser Trustworthiness

SCALE DESCRIPTION:

A four-item, seven-point Likert scale intended to measure the subjects' perceptions of endorser trustworthiness.

SCALE ORIGIN:

It is not clear where the items originated or where they were first used as a multi-item summated scale.

SAMPLES:

There are two experiments conducted in this study. In experiment 1, the total sample consisted of **160** MBA students who were enrolled at a northeastern university in the United States. They created two similarity conditions using personal characteristics, education, and occupation. The similar endorser (Joan Williams for females and John Williams for males) was described as having received an MBA in 1988 from the same university and having worked since graduation in a management position at a locally based national bank. In the dissimilar endorser condition, the endorser was described as having graduated from high school in 1981, and as having worked since graduation as a sales clerk at a regional discount chain store. They also created two experience conditions: In the experienced condition, the endorser was described as having been to many of the service providers in the local area, and in the inexperienced condition, the endorser was described as having been to only one service provider in the local area.

RELIABILITY:

In experiment 1, a Cronbach's alpha of **.85** was reported for endorser's trustworthiness.

VALIDITY:

No examination of scale validity was reported.

ADMINISTRATION:

In experiment 1, Feick and Higie (1992) told the participants that they were doing research for an advertising agency planning to develop testimonial ads for a few service providing businesses in the city where the university was located. They also explained that they interviewed some of the customers during the first few weeks of business and recorded their statements about the company, then combined each customer's photograph with his/her testimonial. Female subjects evaluated a testimonial given by Joan Williams, and male subjects evaluated a testimonial given by John Williams. In all conditions, the endorser indicated an identical reaction to the service provider and recommended its use. After examining the ad prototype, each subject completed an evaluation form. High scores indicate that endorser is experienced. Authors included this scale as a confound check to determine subjects' perceptions of endorser trustworthiness. In experiment 2, only the first two items of the scale were used.

MAJOR FINDINGS:

The results indicate that no significant difference in perceived trustworthiness of the endorser across the design and the endorser was seen as trustworthy.

REFERENCE:

Feick, Lawrence and Robin A. Higie (1992), "The Effects of Preference Heterogeneity and Source Characteristics on Ad Processing and Judgments about Endorsers," *JA*, 21 (2), 9-24.

SCALE ITEMS: ENDORSER TRUSTWORTHINESS

Strongly disagree ___ : ___ : ___ : ___ : ___ : ___ : ___ Strongly agree
           1   2   3   4   5   6   7

1. [Endorser] is trustworthy.
2. [Endorser] would be honest in his recommendation of a [service provider] to me.
3. [Endorser] appears to be dependable.
4. [Endorser] seems to be sincere.

SCALE NAME: Functions of TV Advertising Items (Affirmation of Value Function)

SCALE DESCRIPTION:

A four-item, five-point Likert scale ranging from "agree" to "disagree."

SCALE ORIGIN:

The scale appears to be have been developed by Alwitt and Prabhaker (1992) and was used only in their study.

SAMPLES:

Alwitt and Prabhaker (1992) mailed a survey to 1200 randomly selected households with listed phone numbers in the Chicago metropolitan statistical area in March 1990. **Two hundred twenty-eight** usable surveys were returned, a 19% return rate. Compared with the Chicago SMSA population (Bureau of the Census, 1983), this sample is older, is wealthier, and has fewer children. The sample of the respondents to this survey includes fewer respondents between 18 and 25 years of age, more older than 65 years of age, fewer with children younger than 18 years of age, and more with annual household incomes of $30,000 or more.

RELIABILITY:

Cronbach's alpha was reported to be **.75**.

VALIDITY:

No examination of scale validity was reported.

ADMINISTRATION:

The scale was self-administered along with other measures in a mail survey format. The possible score range is 4–20. A low score represents negative perceptions of the personal and social benefits or costs of television advertising.

MAJOR FINDINGS:

The goal of the Alwitt and Prabhaker (1992) study was to evaluate why people tend to have unfavorable attitudes about television advertising. They proposed that reasons for attitudes about television are based on what people know about television advertising (beliefs that people have toward television advertising) and how it is relevant to them (the specific function that television advertising serves for a viewer and how it fits into his/her life). Alwitt and Prabhaker (1992) examined four functions of advertising in this research: knowledge, hedonic, social learning, and value. They found that these four functions are highly correlated, meaning that the functions of television advertising depend on the specific consumer and situation. To examine how functions of television advertising are related to how much people like television advertising, the authors had to remove the effects of demographic characteristics and attitudes to television programs. The four functions of television advertising account for 25% of the variability in liking of the television advertising when demographics and attitude to television programs have been removed. One outcome of the high intercorrelation among functions of television advertising was that only the hedonic function contributes significantly to the multiple regression model.

REFERENCE:

Alwitt, Linda F. and Paul R. Prabhaker (1992), "Functional and Belief Dimensions of Attitudes to Television Advertising," *JAR*, 32 (5), 30-42.

SCALE ITEMS: FUNCTIONS OF TV ADVERTISING ITEMS (AFFIRMATION OF VALUE FUNCTION)

Strongly disagree 1———2———3———4———5 Strongly agree

1. I like it when advertisements show people like me using my favorite brand.
2. Some products play an important role in my life and I am happy to see they do the same for other people I see in TV commercials.
3. I can really relate to some TV ads because they seem made just for me.
4. TV ads tell things about the product that I can believe in.

SCALE NAME: Functions of TV Advertising Items (Hedonic Function)

SCALE DESCRIPTION:

A five-item, five-point Likert scale ranging from "strongly agree" to "strongly disagree." This scale purports to assess respondents' reaction to TV commercials.

SCALE ORIGIN:

The scale appears to be have been developed by Alwitt and Prabhaker (1992) and was used only in their study.

SAMPLES:

Alwitt and Prabhaker (1992) mailed a survey to 1200 randomly selected households with listed phone numbers in the Chicago metropolitan statistical area in March 1990. **Two hundred twenty-eight** usable surveys were returned, a 19% return rate. Compared with the Chicago SMSA population (Bureau of the Census, 1983), this sample is older, is wealthier, and has fewer children. The sample of the respondents to this survey includes fewer respondents between 18 and 25 years of age, more older than 65 years of age, fewer with children younger than 18 years of age, and more with annual household incomes of $30,000 or more.

RELIABILITY:

Cronbach's alpha was reported to be **.69**.

VALIDITY:

No examination of scale validity was reported.

ADMINISTRATION:

The scale was self-administered along with other measures in a mail survey format. The possible score range is 4–20. A low score represents negative perceptions of the personal and social benefits or costs of television advertising.

MAJOR FINDINGS:

The goal of the Alwitt and Prabhaker (1992) study was to evaluate why people tend to have unfavorable attitudes about television advertising. They proposed that reasons for attitudes about television are based on what people know about television advertising (beliefs that people have toward television advertising) and how it is relevant to them (the specific function that television advertising serves for a viewer and how it fits into his/her life). Alwitt and Prabhaker (1992) examined four functions of advertising in this research:

knowledge, hedonic, social learning, and value. They found that these four functions are highly correlated, meaning that the functions of television advertising depend on the specific consumer and situation. To examine how functions of television advertising are related to how much people like television advertising, the authors had to remove the effects of demographic characteristics and attitudes to television programs. The four functions of television advertising account for 25% of the variability in liking of the television advertising when demographics and attitude to television programs have been removed. One outcome of the high intercorrelation among functions of television advertising was that only the hedonic function contributes significantly to the multiple regression model.

REFERENCE:

Alwitt, Linda F. and Paul R. Prabhaker (1992), ''Functional and Belief Dimensions of Attitudes to Television Advertising,'' *JAR*, 32 (5), 30-42.

SCALE ITEMS: FUNCTIONS OF TV ADVERTISING ITEMS (HEDONIC FUNCTION)

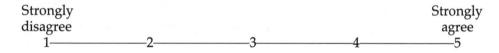

Strongly
disagree

Strongly
agree

1————————2————————3————————4————————5

1. TV ads are fun to watch.
2. TV ads sometimes make me feel good.
3. To me TV commercials are light and entertaining breaks in programs.
4. A lot of TV advertising is funny or clever.
5. Most TV commercials are in poor taste. (r)

SCALE NAME: Functions of TV Advertising Items (Knowledge Function)

SCALE DESCRIPTION:

A three-item, five-point Likert scale that measures the degree to which a person believes TV commercials are a good source of information about products.

SCALE ORIGIN:

The scale appears to be have been developed by Alwitt and Prabhaker (1992) and was used only in their study.

SAMPLES:

Alwitt and Prabhaker (1992) mailed a survey to 1200 randomly selected households with listed phone numbers in the Chicago metropolitan statistical area in March 1990. **Two hundred twenty-eight** usable surveys were returned, a 19% return rate. Compared to the Chicago SMSA population (Bureau of the Census, 1983), this sample is older, is wealthier, and has fewer children. The sample of the respondents to this survey includes fewer respondents between 18 and 25 years of age, more older than 65 years of age, fewer with children younger than 18 years of age, and more with annual household incomes of $30,000 or more.

RELIABILITY:

Cronbach's alpha was reported to be **.66**.

VALIDITY:

No examination of scale validity was reported.

ADMINISTRATION:

The scale was self-administered along with other measures in a mail survey format. The possible score range is 4–20. A low score represents negative perceptions of the knowledge function of television advertising.

MAJOR FINDINGS:

The goal of the Alwitt and Prabhaker (1992) study was to evaluate why people tend to have unfavorable attitudes about television advertising. They proposed that reasons for attitudes about television are based on what people know about television advertising (beliefs that people have toward television advertising) and how it is relevant to them (the specific function that television advertising serves for a viewer and how it fits into his/her life). Alwitt and Prabhaker (1992) examined four functions of advertising in this research: knowledge, hedonic, social learning, and value. They found that these four functions are highly correlated, meaning that the functions of television advertising depend on the specific consumer and situation. To examine how functions of television advertising are related to how much people like television advertising, the authors had to remove the effects of demographic characteristics and attitudes to television programs. The four functions of television advertising account for 25% of the variability in liking of the television advertising when demographics and attitude to television programs have been removed. One outcome of the high intercorrelation among functions of television advertising was that only the hedonic function contributes significantly to the multiple regression model.

REFERENCE:

Alwitt, Linda F. and Paul R. Prabhaker (1992), ''Functional and Belief Dimensions of Attitudes to Television Advertising,'' *JAR*, 32 (5), 30-42.

SCALE ITEMS: FUNCTIONS OF TV ADVERTISING ITEMS (KNOWLEDGE FUNCTION)

```
Strongly                                                    Strongly
disagree                                                      agree
    1——————————2——————————3——————————4——————————5
```

1. TV advertising is a good way to learn about what products and services are available.
2. TV advertising helps me know which brands have the features I am looking for.
3. TV advertising gives me a good idea about products by showing the kinds of people who use them.

SCALE NAME: Functions of TV Advertising Items (Social Learning Function)

SCALE DESCRIPTION:

A four-item, five-point Likert scale that measures the degree to which a person believes TV commercials are a good way to learn who uses what products.

SCALE ORIGIN:

The scale appears to be have been developed by Alwitt and Prabhaker (1992) and was used only in their study.

SAMPLES:

Alwitt and Prabhaker (1992) mailed a survey to 1200 randomly selected households with listed phone numbers in the Chicago metropolitan statistical area in March 1990. **Two hundred twenty-eight** usable surveys were returned, a 19% return rate. Compared with the Chicago SMSA population (Bureau of the Census, 1983), this sample is older, is wealthier, and has fewer children. The sample of the respondents to this survey includes fewer respondents between 18 and 25 years of age, more older than 65 years of age, fewer with children younger than 18 years of age, and more with annual household incomes of $30,000 or more.

RELIABILITY:

Cronbach's alpha was reported to be **.72**.

VALIDITY:

No examination of scale validity was reported.

ADMINISTRATION:

The scale was self-administered along with other measures in a mail survey format. The possible score range is 4–20. A low score represents negative perceptions of the social learning function of television advertising.

MAJOR FINDINGS:

The goal of the Alwitt and Prabhaker (1992) study was to evaluate why people tend to have unfavorable attitudes about television advertising. They proposed that reasons for attitudes about television are based on what people know about television advertising (beliefs that people have toward television advertising) and how it is relevant to them (the specific function that television advertising serves for a viewer and how it fits into his/her life). Alwitt and Prabhaker (1992) examined four functions of advertising in this research: knowledge, hedonic, social learning, and value. They found that these four functions are highly correlated, meaning that the functions of television advertising depend on the specific consumer and situation. To examine how functions of television advertising are related to how much people like television advertising, the authors had to remove the effects of demographic characteristics and attitudes to television programs. The four functions of television advertising account for 25% of the variability in liking of the television advertising when demographics and attitude to television programs have been removed. One outcome of the high intercorrelation among functions of television advertising was that only the hedonic function contributes significantly to the multiple regression model.

REFERENCE:

Alwitt, Linda F. and Paul R. Prabhaker (1992), ''Functional and Belief Dimensions of Attitudes to Television Advertising,'' *JAR*, 32 (5), 30-42.

SCALE ITEMS: FUNCTIONS OF TV ADVERTISING ITEMS (SOCIAL LEARNING FUNCTION)

Strongly   Strongly
disagree   agree
1———————2———————3———————4———————5

1. I like seeing what sort of people use what kinds of brands in TV commercials.
2. TV advertisements help me be more confident in the products I actually use.
3. You can get ideas about fashion and ways to act from watching TV ads.
4. TV commercials tell me that there are other people, like myself, who use the same products.

SCALE NAME: Importance of Information Sources (Independent Experts)

SCALE DESCRIPTION:

A four-item, five-point Likert type scale anchored by "Not Important" and "Very Important," measuring the importance of independent expert information sources.

SCALE ORIGIN:

Strutton and Lumpkin (1992) indicate that the scale had been used previously by Klippel and Sweeny (1974), Lumpkin and Festervand (1987), and Greco, Paskoy, and Robbins (1989).

SAMPLES:

Strutton and Lumpkin (1992) mailed questionnaires to 1000 persons throughout the United States. Of the total sample contacted, **831** responded. Their sample was composed of the following age groups: 50–54 years of age (8%), 55–59 years of age (8%), 60–64 years of age (8%), 65–69 years of age (20%), 70–75 years of age (26%), and older than 75 years of age (30%) The sample had household incomes of $15,000 and more and were living independently.

RELIABILITY:

Strutton and Lumpkin (1992) applied the scale to two different groups of products: generic drugs (continuous innovations) and self-diagnosis devices (discontinuous innovations). For generic drugs, Cronbach's alpha was **.727**, and for self diagnosis devices, the alpha was **.902**.

VALIDITY:

No examination of the validity was reported.

ADMINISTRATION:

Strutton and Lumpkin (1992) collected the data through mail using self administered questionnaires. They identified 18 innovations by examining the geriatric literature and chose generic drugs and self-diagnosis devices to represent the continuous and discontinuous innovations. Generic drugs were classified as continuous because they represent simple changes of an existing product. Self-diagnosis devices such as blood pressure, sugar, cholesterol monitors, calipers, and glucometers were classified as discontinuous because they represent a new product. Respondents were asked to rate the importance of each source "in helping them to make the best choice for shopping for" that innovation.

MAJOR FINDINGS:

Strutton and Lumpkin's (1992) results indicate that adopters and nonadopters differed significantly in their information source usage for generic drugs. Compared with nonadopters, adopters relied significantly on independent expert sources. For self diagnosis devices, adopters and nonadopters differed significantly regarding their information source usage. Adopters relied more on independent sources.

REFERENCE:

Strutten, H. David and James R. Lumpkin (1992), ''Information Sources Used by Elderly Healthcare Product Adopters,'' *JAR*, 32 (4), 20-30.

SCALE ITEMS: IMPORTANCE OF INFORMATION SOURCES (INDEPENDENT EXPERTS)

Not important				Very important
1————————2————————3————————4————————5				

1. Television programs
2. Government reports/approvals
3. Magazine articles
4. Newspaper articles

SCALE NAME: Importance of Information Sources (Interpersonal)

SCALE DESCRIPTION:

A five-item, five-point Likert-type scale anchored by "Not Important" and "Very Important," measuring the importance of the interpersonal information sources.

SCALE ORIGIN:

Strutton and Lumpkin (1992) indicate that the scale had been used previously by Klippel and Sweeny (1974), Lumpkin and Festervand (1987), and Greco, Paksoy, and Robbins (1989).

SAMPLES:

Strutton and Lumpkin (1992) mailed questionnaires to 1000 persons throughout the United States. Of the total sample contacted, **831** responded. Their sample was composed of the following age groups: 50–54 years of age (8%), 55–59 years of age (8%), 60–64 years of age (8%), 65–69 years of age (20%), 70–75 years of age (26%), and older than 75 years of age (30%) The sample had household incomes of $15,000 and more and were living independently.

RELIABILITY:

Strutton and Lumpkin (1992) applied the scale to two different groups of products: generic drugs (continuous innovations) and self-diagnosis devices (discontinuous innovations). For generic drugs, Cronbach's alpha was **.842**, and for self diagnosis devices, the alpha was **.864**.

VALIDITY:

No examination of the validity was reported.

ADMINISTRATION:

Strutton and Lumpkin (1992) collected the data through mail using self-administered questionnaires. They identified 18 innovations by examining the geriatric literature and chose generic drugs and self-diagnosis devices to represent the continuous and discontinuous innovations. Generic drugs were classified as continuous because they represent simple changes of an existing product. Self-diagnosis devices such as blood pressure, sugar, cholesterol monitors, calipers, and glucometers were classified as discontinuous because they represent a new product. Respondents were asked to rate the importance of each source "in helping them to make the best choice for shopping for" that innovation.

MAJOR FINDINGS:

Strutton and Lumpkin's (1992) results indicate that adopters and nonadopters differed significantly in their information source usage for generic drugs. Adopters of the continuous innovation relied significantly more on interpersonal sources. For self-diagnosis devices, adopters and nonadopters differed significantly regarding their information source usage. No relationship was posited to exist between adoption and the use of interpersonal sources.

REFERENCE:

Greco, A.J., C.H. Paksoy, and S.S. Robbins (1989), "Differences in Prepurchase Information Sources Across Age Groups," in *Southern Marketing Association Proceedings*, Robert L. King, ed. Charleston, SC: Southern Marketing Association 69-74.

Klippel, R.E. and T.W. Sweeny (1974), "The Use of Information Sources by the Aged Consumer," *The Gerontologist*, 14 (2), 163-66.

Lumpkin, James R. and T.A. Festervand (1987), "Purchase Information Sources of the Elderly," *JAR*, 27 (6), 31-44.

Strutten, H. David and James R. Lumpkin (1992), "Information Sources Used by Elderly Healthcare Product Adopters," *JAR*, 32 (4), 20-30.

SCALE ITEMS: IMPORTANCE OF INFORMATION SOURCES (INTERPERSONAL)

Not important				Very important
1	2	3	4	5

1. Spouse
2. Family (not spouse)
3. Friends
4. Personal experience
5. Neighbors

SCALE NAME: Importance of Information Sources (Marketing)

SCALE DESCRIPTION:

A four-item, five-point Likert-type scale anchored by "Not Important" and "Very Important," measuring the importance of the marketing information sources.

SCALE ORIGIN:

Strutton and Lumpkin (1992) indicate that the scale had been used previously by Klippel and Sweeny (1974), Lumpkin and Festervand (1987), and Greco, Paksoy, and Robbins (1989).

SAMPLES:

Strutton and Lumpkin (1992) mailed questionnaires to 1000 persons throughout the United States. Of the total sample contacted, **831** responded. Their sample was composed of the following age groups: 50–54 years of age (8%), 55–59 years of age (8%), 60–64 years of age (8%), 65–69 years of age (20%), 70–75 years of age (26%), and older than 75 years of age (30%) The sample had household incomes of $15,000 and more and were living independently.

RELIABILITY:

Strutton and Lumpkin (1992) applied the scale to two different groups of products generic drugs (continuous innovations) and self-diagnosis devices (discontinuous innovations). For generic drugs, Cronbach's alpha was **.888**, and for self-diagnosis devices, the alpha was **.726**.

VALIDITY:

No examination of scale validity was reported.

ADMINISTRATION:

Strutton and Lumpkin (1992) collected the data through mail using self-administered questionnaires. They identified 18 innovations by examining the geriatric literature and chose generic drugs and self-diagnosis devices to represent the continuous and discontinuous innovations. Generic drugs were classified as continuous because they represent simple changes of an existing product. Self-diagnosis devices such as blood pressure, sugar, cholesterol monitors, calipers, and glucometers were classified as discontinuous because they represent a new product. Respondents were asked to rate the importance of each source "in helping them to make the best choice for shopping for" that innovation.

MAJOR FINDINGS:

Strutton and Lumpkin's (1992) results indicate that adopters and nonadopters differed significantly in their information source usage for generic drugs. Adopters of the continuous innovation relied on marketing dominated sources more heavily. For self-diagnosis devices, adopters and nonadopters differed significantly regarding their information source usage. Adopters would evaluate marketing dominated sources as more important.

REFERENCE:

Greco, A.J., C.H. Paksoy, and S.S. Robbins (1989), "Differences in Prepurchase Information Sources Across Age Groups," in *Southern Marketing Association Proceedings*, Robert L. King, ed. Charleston, SC: Southern Marketing Association 69-74.

Klippel, R.E. and T.W. Sweeny (1974), "The Use of Information Sources by the Aged Consumer," *The Gerontologist*, 14 (2), 163-66.

Lumpkin, James R. and T.A. Festervand (1987), "Purchase Information Sources of the Elderly," *JAR*, 27 (6), 31-44.

Strutten, H. David and James R. Lumpkin (1992), "Information Sources Used by Elderly Healthcare Product Adopters," *JAR*, 32 (4), 20-30.

SCALE ITEMS: IMPORTANCE OF INFORMATION SOURCES (MARKETING)

```
Not                                                              Very
important                                                   important
   1————————2————————3————————4————————5
```

1. POS Information (package, label, displays)
2. Salespeople
3. Store reputation
4. Store displays

SCALE NAME: Importance of Information Sources (Mass Media)

SCALE DESCRIPTION:

A five-item, five-point Likert-type scale anchored by ''Not Important'' and ''Very Important,'' measuring the importance of the mass media information sources.

SCALE ORIGIN:

Strutton and Lumpkin (1992) indicate that the scale had been used previously by Klippel and Sweeny (1974), Lumpkin and Festervand (1987), and Greco, Paksoy, and Robbins (1989).

SAMPLES:

Strutton and Lumpkin (1992) mailed questionnaires to 1000 persons over the entire nation. Of the total sample contacted, **831** responded. Their sample composed of the following age groups: 50–54 years of age (8%), 55–59 years of age (8%), 60–64 years of age (8%), 65–69 years of age (20%), 70–75 years of age (26%), and older than 75 (30 percent) The sample had household incomes $15,000 and more and were living independently.

RELIABILITY:

Strutton and Lumpkin (1992) applied the scale to two different groups of products: generic drugs (continuous innovations) and self-diagnosis devices (discontinuous innovations). For generic drugs, Cronbach's alpha was **.723**, and for self diagnosis devices, the alpha was **.832**.

VALIDITY:

No examination of scale validity was reported.

ADMINISTRATION:

Strutton and Lumpkin (1992) collected the data through mail using self-administered questionnaires. They identified 18 innovations by examining the geriatric literature and chose generic drugs and self-diagnosis devices to represent the continuous and discontinuous innovations. Generic drugs were classified as continuous because they represent simple changes of an existing product. Self-diagnosis devices such as blood pressure, sugar, cholesterol monitors, calipers, and glucometers were classified as discontinuous because they represent a new product. Respondents were asked to rate the importance of each source ''in helping them to make the best choice for shopping for'' that innovation.

MAJOR FINDINGS:

Strutton and Lumpkin (1992) results indicate that no relationship exists between adoption use and the use of mass media. Also, no differences were found between adopters and nonadopters. The mean importance for the information sources associated with generic drugs indicated that mass media sources were rated the least influential source by both adopters and nonadopters, and the use of the source did not differ between the groups. Results for the self-diagnosis devices differed significantly between adopters and nonadopters. Adopters relied more on mass media compared with nonadopters. Among the information sources, mass media was the least important, although adopters placed more importance on it.

REFERENCE:

Greco, A.J., C.H. Paksoy, and S.S. Robbins (1989), "Differences in Prepurchase Information Sources Across Age Groups," in *Southern Marketing Association Proceedings*, Robert L. King, ed. Charleston, SC: Southern Marketing Association 69-74.

Klippel, R.E. and T.W. Sweeny (1974), "The Use of Information Sources by the Aged Consumer," *The Gerontologist*, 14 (2), 163-66.

Lumpkin, James R. and T.A. Festervand (1987), "Purchase Information Sources of the Elderly," *JAR*, 27 (6), 31-44.

Strutton, H. David and James R. Lumpkin (1992), "Information Sources Used by Elderly Healthcare Product Adopters," *JAR*, 32 (4), 20-30.

SCALE ITEMS: IMPORTANCE OF INFORMATION SOURCES (MASS MEDIA)

```
Not                                              Very
important                                       important
   1————————2————————3————————4————————5
```

1. Television advertisements
2. Magazine advertisements
3. Newspaper advertisements
4. Celebrity endorsements
5. Catalogs

SCALE NAME: Intrinsic Involvement in the Ad

SCALE DESCRIPTION:

A seven-point, four-item semantic differential scale measuring intrinsic involvement in the ad.

SCALE ORIGIN:

It is not clear where the items originated or where they were first used as a multi-item summated scale.

SAMPLES:

Lord and Burnkrant (1993) had a total sample of **264** undergraduate students. One hundred thirty-four participants viewed the Mobil 1 commercial and the other 130 the drinking and driving ad.

RELIABILITY:

Cronbach's alpha values reported to be **.87** for Mobil 1 and **.85** for drinking and driving ad conditions.

VALIDITY:

No examination of scale validity was reported.

ADMINISTRATION:

Subjects viewed one of the experimental video tapes in a darkened room; then two minutes later, video monitors were turned off and participants completed the appropriate version of the questionnaire. High scores indicate that participants are highly involved with the ad.

MAJOR FINDINGS:

Lord and Burnkrant (1993) found that the topics of the two ads had different involvements. The scale had a higher mean score for the drinking and driving ad than for the Mobil 1 commercial. The observed difference in ad involvement scores is significant but not large. Thus, on the basis of this measure alone, ads would be classified as a slightly involving ad and a moderately involving ad, rather than one low and one high involvement.

REFERENCE:

Lord, Kenneth R. and Robert E. Burnkrant (1993), "Attention Versus Distraction: The Interactive Effect of Program Involvement and Attentional Devices on Commercial Processing," *JA*, 22 (1), 47-60.

SCALE ITEMS: INTRINSIC INVOLVEMENT IN THE AD

1. Important   ___ : ___ : ___ : ___ : ___ : ___ : ___   Unimportant

                    +3   +2   +1   0   −1   −2   −3

2. Irrelevant to me   ___ : ___ : ___ : ___ : ___ : ___ : ___   Relevant to me (r)

                    +3   +2   +1   0   −1   −2   −3

3. Means a lot to me   ___ : ___ : ___ : ___ : ___ : ___ : ___   Means nothing to me

                    +3   +2   +1   0   −1   −2   −3

4. Not needed   ___ : ___ : ___ : ___ : ___ : ___ : ___   Needed (r)

                    +3   +2   +1   0   −1   −2   −3

SCALE NAME: Mood Rating Scale for Advertisement

SCALE DESCRIPTION:

A seven-item, five-point scale anchored by "Does not make me feel at all" and "Makes me feel very strongly. "

SCALE ORIGIN:

The scale was developed originally by Plutchik (1987) and used by Hong, Muderrisoglu, and Zinkhan (1987) and Biswas, Olsen, and Carlet (1992).

SAMPLES:

Biswas, Olsen, and Carlet (1992) selected one news and one women's magazine from each country. The two news magazines were *L'Express* from France and *Time* from the United States, and the two women's magazines were *Madame Figaro* from France and *McCalls* from the United States. Six issues of the magazines were chosen from the time period December 1989–November 1991 for coding purposes. Total sample consisted of **279** American and **259** French advertisements.

RELIABILITY:

Cronbach's alpha was reported to be **.89**.

VALIDITY:

No examination of scale validity was reported.

ADMINISTRATION:

Biswas, Olsen, and Carlet (1992) study has been administered in two phases. In the first phase, the advertisements were coded by two judges. An American judge coded the American advertisements and a French judge coded the French advertisements. In the second phase, a third judge, fluent in English and French, evaluated the advertisements from each country.

MAJOR FINDINGS:

The first hypothesis in Biswas, Olsen, and Carlet (1992) study states that the emotional content of French print advertisements was expected to be higher than that for the American advertisements. Their results indicated that French advertisements did convey more emotion than American advertisements and the difference was significant.

REFERENCE:

Biswas, Abhijit, Janeen E. Olsen, and Valerie Carlet (1992), ''A Comparison of Print Advertisements from the United States and France,'' *JA*, 21 (4), 73-81.

Hong, Jae W., Aydin Muderrisoglu, George M. Zinkhan (1987), ''Cultural Differences and Expression: A Comparative Content Analysis of Japanese and U.S. Magazine Advertising, *JA*, 16 (1), 55-68.

Plutchik, Robert (1980), *Emotion: A Psycho-evolutionary Synthesis*. New York: Harper & Row.

SCALE ITEMS: MOOD RATING SCALE FOR ADVERTISEMENT

Does not make me feel at all				Makes me feel very strongly
1	2	3	4	5

1. Happy
2. Fearful
3. Pleasant
4. Angry
5. Interested
6. Disgusted
7. Surprised

SCALE NAME: Reaction to Ad (Deactivation Sleep, Fatigue)

SCALE DESCRIPTION:

A four-point, three-item activation dimension scale anchored by "Definitely do not feel" and "Definitely feel," purported to measure the fatigue dimension in subjective arousal.

SCALE ORIGIN:

LaTour, Pitts, and Snook-Luther (1990) indicate that this scale had been used previously by Thayer (1978) as a dimension in Activation Deactivation Adjective Checklist.

SAMPLES:

LaTour, Pitts, and Snook-Luther (1990) had a sample of **202** business students who were taking a introductory management class at a southern university. The mean age of the sample was 20.98 years.

RELIABILITY:

LaTour, Pitts, and Snook-Luther (1990) reported a Cronbach's alpha of **.89**.

VALIDITY:

No examination of scale validity was reported.

ADMINISTRATION:

Participants were assigned randomly to one of the three treatment groups (Nude, Semi-nude, Demure). Each group viewed two original ads projected on the screen. The first ad was a perfume ad shown to disguise the nature of the study. The second one was the actual treatment ad shown to the three groups. These ads included the same copy and product image as the first ad, but each was designed to produce different level of arousal. The low-arousal (Demure) ad had a picture containing a fully clothed couple standing apart from each other in a nonsuggestive pose, with a perfume bottle superimposed in the corner of the ad. The moderate-stimulus treatment (Semi-nude) had a picture of a nude female model with her breasts and lower abdomen covered with a perfume bottle image. The high-stimulus treatment (Nude) had a picture of the same nude female model exposing her breasts and lower abdomen without a perfume picture. After viewing the ads, subjects administered the questionnaires in pencil-and-paper format. High scores indicate that participants have a high level of fatigue.

MAJOR FINDINGS:

LaTour, Pitts, and Snook-Luther (1990) found that main effects of high level of nudity on arousal are increasing tension and fatigue, and decreasing calmness. The semi-nude condition has almost the opposite effect of high nudity: less tension, less fatigue, and more calmness. Treatment by gender interactions show that under the condition of high nudity, males feels less tension, more energy, less fatigue, and more calmness. The semi-nude treatment interaction with gender almost has the opposite effects. In this study, fatigue has a direct negative effect on ad impressions.

REFERENCES:

LaTour, Michael S., Robert E. Pitts, and David C. Snook-Luther (1990), ''Female Nudity, Arousal, and Ad Response: An Experimental Investigation,'' *JA*, 19 (4), 51-62.

Thayer, Robert E. (1978), ''Toward a Psychological Theory of Multidimensional Activation (Arousal),'' *Motivation and Emotion*, 2 (1), 1-33.

SCALE ITEMS: REACTION TO AD (DEACTIVATION SLEEP, FATIGUE)

Definitely do not feel ____ : ____ : ____ : ____ Definitely feel
                          0   1   2   3

1. Sleepy
2. Tired
3. Drowsy

SCALE NAME: Reaction to Ad (General Activation, Energy)

SCALE DESCRIPTION:

A four-point, five-item activation dimension scale anchored by "Definitely do not feel" and "Definitely feel," purported to measure the general activation, energy arousal.

SCALE ORIGIN:

Henthorne, LaTour, and Nataraajan (1993) indicate that scales have been used previously by Thayer (1978).

SAMPLES:

Henthorne, LaTour, and Nataraajan (1993) obtained **201** usable responses through mall intercept, 88 males and 113 females. The total sample had an average education 13.7 years. The majority of the sample were white (80 %) and had an average age of 31.5 years. LaTour, Pitts, and Snook-Luther (1990) had a sample of **202** business students who were taking a introductory management class at a southern university. The mean age of the sample was 20.98 years.

RELIABILITY:

Henthorne, LaTour, and Nataraajan (1993) reported a Cronbach's alpha of **.82**. Latour, Pitts, and Snook-Luther (1990) reported an alpha of **.91**.

VALIDITY:

No examination of scale validity was reported.

ADMINISTRATION:

Henthorne, LaTour, and Nataraajan (1993) collected the data through mall intercept in a large regional indoor shopping mall in a demographically diverse SMSA in the mid-Atlantic region over a period of seven days during all hours of the mall operation. Trained interviewers varied their locations randomly throughout the mall and allowed some mall traffic to pass between interviews. They performed the stimulus manipulation by the use of print ad. One form of stimulus was an actual black and white ad containing a photograph (appeal with picture), and the other was the same ad without the photograph (appeal without picture). Questionnaires were shuffled before they were distributed to provide random group assignments. One hundred one subjects were shown the "appeal without picture," and 100 subjects were shown the "appeal with picture." Subjects responded the questionnaire after viewing the one randomly selected form of stimulus ad presented to them. They were asked to respond to the items in terms of how they felt right after exposure to the ad. Following completion of the arousal items, subjects responded to the items to measure the attitude toward the ad.

In LaTour, Pitts, and Snook-Luther (1990), participants were assigned randomly to one of the three treatment groups (Nude, Semi-nude, Demure). Each group viewed two original ads projected on the screen. The first ad was a perfume ad shown to disguise the nature of the study. The second one was the actual treatment ad shown to the three groups. These ads included the same copy and the product image as the first ad, but each was designed to produce different level of arousal. The low-arousal (Demure) ad had a picture containing a fully clothed couple standing apart from each other in a nonsuggestive pose, with a perfume bottle superimposed in the corner of the ad. The moderate-stimulus treatment (Semi-nude) had a picture of a nude female model with her breasts and lower abdomen covered with perfume bottle image. The high-stimulus treatment (Nude) had a picture of the same nude female model exposing her breasts and lower abdomen without a perfume picture. After viewing the ads, subjects administered the questionnaires in pencil-and-paper format. High scores indicate that participants have a high level of energy.

MAJOR FINDINGS:

Henthorne, LaTour, and Nataraajan (1993) intended to study the theoretical supposition that increasing tension generates energy up to a certain point, and beyond that "threshold," increasing tension arouses anxiety, which begins to deplete energy. Their findings indicate that print ad-induced arousal effects fell short of the "threshold" point. The "appeal with picture" stimulus fell short of the tension generation "threshold" separating the two hypothesized models. LaTour, Pitts, and Snook-Luther (1990) found that energy has a direct and positive effect on ad impressions. The correlation between tension and energy is positive. Both energy and calmness increase positive ad impressions, which the authors expected to happen only if the correlation between energy and tension was large and negative; they found that the correlation was positive.

REFERENCES:

Henthorne, Tony L., Michael S. LaTour, and Rajan Nataraajan (1993), "Fear Appeals in Print Advertising: An Analysis of Arousal and Ad Response," *JA*, 22 (2), 59-69.

LaTour, Michael S., Robert E. Pitts, and David C. Snook-Luther (1990), "Female Nudity, Arousal, and Ad Response: An Experimental Investigation," *JA*, (19) 4, 51-62.

Thayer, Robert E. (1978), "Toward a Psychological Theory of Multidimensional Activation (Arousal)," *Motivation and Emotion*, 2 (1) 1-33.

SCALE ITEMS: REACTION TO AD (GENERAL ACTIVATION, ENERGY)

Definitely do not feel ____ : ____ : ____ : ____ Definitely feel

                                     0   1   2   3

1. Active
2. Energetic
3. Vigorous
4. Lively
5. Full of Pep

SCALE NAME: Reaction to Ad (General Deactivation, Calmness)

SCALE DESCRIPTION:

A four-point, five-item activation dimension scale anchored by "Definitely do not feel" and "Definitely feel," purported to measure the calmness dimension in subjective arousal.

SCALE ORIGIN:

LaTour, Pitts, and Snook-Luther (1990) indicate that this scale has been used previously by Thayer (1978) as a dimension in Activation Deactivation Adjective Checklist.

SAMPLES

LaTour, Pitts, and Snook-Luther (1990) had a sample of **202** business students who were taking a introductory management course at a southern university. The mean age of the sample was 20.98 years.

RELIABILITY:

LaTour, Pitts, and Snook-Luther (1990) reported a Cronbach's alpha of **.84**.

VALIDITY:

No examination of scale validity was reported.

ADMINISTRATION:

Participants were assigned randomly to one of the three treatment groups (Nude, Semi-nude, Demure). Each group viewed two original ads projected on the screen. The first ad was a perfume ad shown to disguise the nature of the study. The second one was the actual treatment ad shown to the three groups. These ads included the same copy and product image as the first ad, but each was designed to produce different level of arousal. The low-arousal (Demure) ad had a picture containing a fully clothed couple standing apart from each other in a nonsuggestive pose, with a perfume bottle superimposed in the corner of the ad. The moderate-stimulus treatment (Semi-nude) had a picture of a nude female model with her breasts and lower abdomen covered with perfume bottle image. The high-stimulus treatment (Nude) had a picture of the same nude female model exposing her breasts and lower abdomen without a perfume picture. After viewing the ads, subjects administered the questionnaires in pencil-and-paper format. High scores indicate that participants have a high level of calmness.

MAJOR FINDINGS:

LaTour, Pitts, and Snook-Luther (1990) found that main effects of high level of nudity on arousal are increasing tension, fatigue, and decreasing calmness.

The semi-nude condition has almost the opposite effect of high nudity: less tension, less fatigue, and more calmness. Treatment by gender interactions show that under the condition of high nudity, males feels less tension, more energy, less fatigue, and more calmness. The semi-nude treatment interaction with gender has almost the opposite effects. Both energy and calmness increase positive ad impressions, which the authors expected to happen only if the correlation between energy and tension was large and negative; they found that the correlation was positive.

REFERENCES:

LaTour, Michael S., Robert E. Pitts, and David C. Snook-Luther (1990), ''Female Nudity, Arousal, and Ad Response: An Experimental Investigation,'' *JA*, 19 (4), 51-62.

Thayer, Robert E. (1978), ''Toward a Psychological Theory of Multidimensional Activation (Arousal),'' *Motivation and Emotion*, 2 (1), 1-33.

SCALE ITEMS: REACTION TO AD (GENERAL DEACTIVATION, CALMNESS)

Definitely do not feel ___ : ___ : ___ : ___ Definitely feel

0   1   2   3

1. Placid
2. Calm
3. At rest
4. Still
5. Quiet

SCALE NAME: Reaction to Ad (High Activation, Tension)

SCALE DESCRIPTION:

A four-point, five-item activation dimension scale anchored by "Definitely do not feel" and "Definitely feel," purported to measure the tension arousal.

SCALE ORIGIN:

Henthorne, LaTour, and Nataraajan (1993) indicate that scales have been used previously by Thayer (1978).

SAMPLES:

Henthorne, LaTour, and Nataraajan (1993) obtained **201** usable responses through mall intercept, 88 males and 113 females. The total sample had an average education 13.7 years. The majority of the sample were white (80%) and had an average age of 31.5 years. LaTour, Pitts, and Snook-Luther (1990) had a sample of **202** business students who were taking a introductory management class at a southern university. The mean age of the sample was 20.98 years.

RELIABILITY:

Henthorne, LaTour, and Nataraajan (1993) reported a Cronbach's alpha of **.81**. LaTour, Pitts, and Snook-Luther (1990) reported an alpha of **.84**.

VALIDITY:

No examination of scale validity was reported.

ADMINISTRATION:

Henthorne, LaTour, and Nataraajan (1993) collected the data through mall intercept in a large regional indoor shopping mall in a demographically diverse SMSA in the mid-Atlantic region over a period of seven days during all hours of the mall operation. Trained interviewers varied their locations randomly throughout the mall and allowed some mall traffic to pass between interviews. They performed the stimulus manipulation by the use of a print ad. One form of stimulus was an actual black and white ad containing a photograph (appeal with picture), and the other was the same ad without the photograph (appeal without picture). Questionnaires were shuffled before they were distributed to provide random group assignments. One hundred one subjects were shown the "appeal without picture," and 100 subjects were shown the "appeal with picture." Subjects responded the questionnaire after viewing the one randomly selected form of stimulus ad presented to them. They were asked to respond to the items in terms of how they felt right after exposure to the ad. Following completion of the arousal items, subjects responded to the items to measure the attitude toward the ad.

In LaTour, Pitts, and Snook-Luther (1990), study participants were assigned randomly to one of the three treatment groups (Nude, Semi-nude, Demure). Each group viewed two original ads projected on the screen. The first ad was a perfume ad shown to disguise the nature of the study. The second one was the actual treatment ad shown to the three groups. These ads included the same copy and the product image as the first ad, but each was designed to produce a different level of arousal. The low-arousal (Demure) ad had a picture containing a fully clothed couple standing apart from each other in a nonsuggestive pose, with a perfume bottle superimposed in the corner of the ad. The moderate-stimulus treatment (Semi-nude) had a picture of a nude female model with her breasts and lower abdomen covered with perfume bottle image. The high-stimulus treatment (Nude) had a picture of the same nude female model exposing her breasts and lower abdomen without a perfume picture. After viewing the ads, subjects administered the questionnaires in paper-and-pencil format. High scores indicate that participants have a high level of tension.

MAJOR FINDINGS:

Henthorne, LaTour, and Nataraajan (1993) intended to study the theoretical supposition that increasing tension generates energy up to a certain point, and beyond that "threshold," increasing tension arouses anxiety, which begins to deplete energy. Their findings indicate that print ad-induced arousal effects fell short of the "threshold" point. The "appeal with picture" stimulus has fallen short of the tension generation "threshold" separating the two hypothesized models. LaTour, Pitts, and Snook-Luther (1990) found that main effects of high level of nudity are on arousal, increasing tension and fatigue, and decreasing calmness. The semi-nude condition has almost the opposite effect of high nudity: less tension, less fatigue, and more calmness. They also found that gender has a significant effect on arousal. Males express less tension and more energy than females. The correlation between tension and energy is positive. Both energy and calmness increase positive ad impressions, which the authors expected to happen only if the correlation between energy and tension was large and negative; they found that the correlation was positive.

REFERENCES:

Henthorne, Tony L., Michael S. LaTour, and Rajan Nataraajan (1993), "Fear Appeals in Print Advertising: An Analysis of Arousal and Ad Response," *JA*, 22 (2), 59-69.

LaTour, Michael S., Robert E. Pitts, and David C. Snook-Luther (1990), "Female Nudity, Arousal, and Ad Response: An Experimental Investigation," *JA*, (19) 4, 51-62.

Thayer, Robert E. (1978), "Toward a Psychological Theory of Multidimensional Activation (Arousal)," *Motivation and Emotion*, 2 (1),1-33.

SCALE ITEMS: REACTION TO AD (HIGH ACTIVATION, TENSION)

Definitely do not feel ____ : ____ : ____ : ____ Definitely feel

0　　　1　　　2　　　3

1. Jittery
2. Intense
3. Fearful
4. Clutched-up
5. Tense

SCALE NAME: Realism

SCALE DESCRIPTION:

A three-item, seven-point Likert scale intended to determine how realistic the ad scenario is to consumers.

SCALE ORIGIN:

It is not clear where the items originated or where they were first used as a multi-item summated scale.

SAMPLES:

Feick and Higie (1992) conducted two experiments; this scale was used only in experiment 2. The sample consisted of **133** undergraduate students, enrolled at a northwestern university in the United States. To control for age effects on responses, no students older than 29 years of age were included in the analysis.

RELIABILITY:

A Cronbach's alpha of **.73** was reported for realism in experiment 2.

VALIDITY:

No examination of scale validity was reported.

ADMINISTRATION:

Students read a scenario in which they were asked to assume that they just graduated from college and had taken a new job and moved to a new location. Two of their neighbors were described: one of them to be perceived as similar to the subject, but having minimal service-related experience, and the other one to be perceived as dissimilar to the subject, but having substantial service-related experience. After reading the scenario, subjects responded to a paper-and-pencil questionnaire.

MAJOR FINDINGS:

Feick and Higie (1992), used this scale as a confound check. Their findings indicated that scenarios were realistic and there were no significant differences across services.

REFERENCE:

Feick, Lawrence and Robin A. Higie (1992), ''The Effects of Preference Heterogeneity and Source Characteristics on Ad Processing and Judgments about Endorsers,'' *JA*, 21 (2), 9-24.

SCALE ITEMS: REALISM

Strongly ___ : ___ : ___ : ___ : ___ : ___ : ___ Strongly
disagree   1   2   3   4   5   6   7   agree

1. It is hard to imagine being in the situation described in this study.
2. The scenario is realistic.
3. Something like this situation will probably happen to me.

SCALE NAME: Source Perception (Ability to Identify With the Actor in Ad)

SCALE DESCRIPTION:

A three-item, 15-point Likert scale purported to measure the ability to identify with the actor in a commercial.

SCALE ORIGIN:

Whittler and DiMeo (1991) indicate that the scale had been used previously by Kelman and Eagly (1965).

SAMPLES:

Whittler and Dimeo (1991) had a total of **160** paid white volunteers in their sample. Participants were assigned randomly to receive an ad that had either a black or a white actor promoting either a liquid detergent or a fur coat. The sample was selected from several social and civic organizations in a southern city (YWCA, PTA, women's club). Of the total sample, 73% were women. Sample age ranged from 17 to 55 years. One hundred thirty-one were married, 19 were single, and nine were divorced. All but one participant obtained a high school diploma, 28% attended college, and 58% had college degrees. Sixty percent earned more than $39,999 per year.

RELIABILITY:

Whittler and DiMeo (1991) reported a Cronbach's alpha of .82.

VALIDITY:

No examination of scale validity was reported.

ADMINISTRATION:

In Whittler and Dimeo (1991) study, the participants were organized in groups of three to eight in a large conference room by a white experimenter. Each participant was given a booklet containing the storyboard advertisements and the questionnaire. After viewing all the storyboard advertisements, participants self-administered the questionnaire in a paper-and-pencil format.

MAJOR FINDINGS:

Whittler and DiMeo's (1991) results are consistent with their first hypothesis: High-prejudice whites identified more strongly with white actors than with black actors, whereas low-prejudice whites showed no differences in their identification with a white or black actor.

REFERENCE:

> Whittler, Tommy E. and Joan DiMeo (1991), "Viewer's Reaction to Racial Cues in Advertising Stimuli," *JAR*, 31 (6), 37-46.

SCALE ITEMS: SOURCE PERCEPTION (ABILITY TO IDENTIFY WITH THE ACTOR IN AD)

Strongly ___ : ___ : ___ : ___ : ___ : ___ : ___ : ___ : ___ : ___ : ___ : ___ : ___ : ___ : ___Strongly
disagree   1   2   3   4   5   6   7   8   9   10   11   12   13   14   15   agree

1. A person whom I want to be like.
2. My type of person.
3. A person who speaks for a group

SCALE NAME: Source Perception (Actor's Likability)

SCALE DESCRIPTION:

A four-item, 15-point semantic differential scale purported to measure the actor's likability in a commercial.

SCALE ORIGIN:

The scale appears to have been developed by Whittler and Dime (1991).

SAMPLES:

Whittler and Dimeo (1991) had a total of **160** paid white volunteers in their sample. Participants were assigned randomly to receive an ad that had either a black or a white actor promoting either a liquid detergent or a fur coat. The sample was selected from several social and civic organizations in a southern city (YWCA, PTA, women's club). Of the total sample, 73% were women. Sample age ranged from 17 to 55 years. One hundred thirty-one were married, 19 were single, and nine were divorced. All but one participant obtained a high school diploma, 28% attended college, and 58% had college degrees. Sixty percent earned more than $39,999 per year.

RELIABILITY:

Whittler and Dimeo (1991) reported a Cronbach's alpha of **.87**.

VALIDITY:

No examination of scale validity was reported.

ADMINISTRATION:

In Whittler and Dimeo (1991) study, the participants were organized in groups of three to eight in a large conference room by a white experimenter. Each participant was given a booklet containing the storyboard advertisements and the questionnaire. After viewing all the storyboard advertisements, participants self-administered the questionnaire in a paper-and-pencil format.

MAJOR FINDINGS:

Whittler and Dimeo's (1991) results indicate that low-prejudice whites perceived no difference between their similarity to white or black actors, whereas high-prejudice whites perceived themselves less similar to black actors than to white actors. Also, participants perceived themselves as more similar to actors promoting the liquid laundry detergent than to actors promoting the fur coat.

REFERENCE:

> Whittler, Tommy E. and Joan DiMeo (1991), ''Viewer's Reaction to Racial Cues in Advertising Stimuli,'' *JAR*, 31 (6), 37-46.

SCALE ITEMS: SOURCE PERCEPTION (ACTOR'S LIKABILITY)

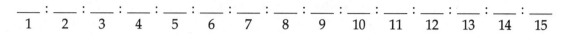

__ :	__ :	__ :	__ :	__ :	__ :	__ :	__ :	__ :	__ :	__ :	__ :	__ :	__ :	__
1	2	3	4	5	6	7	8	9	10	11	12	13	14	15

1. Warm/Cold
2. Likable/Unlikable
3. Sincere/Insincere
4. Friendly/Unfriendly

SCALE NAME: Source Perception (Similarity to the Actor in the Ad)

SCALE DESCRIPTION:

A four-item, 15-point semantic differential scale purported to measure the perceived similarity to the actor in a commercial.

SCALE ORIGIN:

Whittler and DiMeo (1991) indicate that the scale had been used previously by McKirnan, Smith, and Hamayan (1983).

SAMPLES:

Whittler and Dimeo (1991) had a total of **160** paid white volunteers in their sample. Participants were assigned randomly to receive an ad that had either a black or a white actor promoting either a liquid detergent or a fur coat. The sample was selected from several social and civic organizations in a southern city (YWCA, PTA, women's club). Of the total sample, 73% were women. Sample age ranged from 17 to 55 years. One hundred thirty-one were married, 19 were single, and nine were divorced. All but one participant obtained a high school diploma, 28% attended college, and 58% had college degrees. Sixty percent earned more than $39,999 per year. In Whittler's (1991) study 1 he had a sample of **160** white and **140** black undergraduate students. In study 2 he had a sample of **160** southeastern white adults.

RELIABILITY:

Whittler and DiMeo (1991) reported a Cronbach's alpha of **.86**. Whittler (1991) reported Cronbach's alphas of **.72** in study 1 and **.86** in study 2.

VALIDITY:

No examination of scale validity was reported.

ADMINISTRATION:

In Whittler and Dimeo (1991) study, the participants were organized in groups of three to eight in a large conference room by a white experimenter. Each participant was given a booklet containing the storyboard advertisements and the questionnaire. After viewing all the storyboard advertisements, participants self-administered the questionnaires in a paper-and-pencil format. In Whittler (1991), participants rated a professionally prepared storyboard featuring a white or black actor promoting a portable word processor or a liquid laundry detergent. A 2 × 2 (Actor's Race × Product Category) cell design was used, and participants were assigned randomly to one of the four experimental cells. Each participant was given a booklet containing the storyboards and the questionnaire. After viewing all the storyboards, participants administered the questionnaires in a paper-and-pencil format.

MAJOR FINDINGS:

Whittler and Dimeo (1991) results indicate that low-prejudice whites perceived no difference between their similarity to white or black actors, whereas high-prejudice whites perceived themselves as being less similar to black actors than to white actors. Also, participants perceived themselves as more similar to actors promoting the liquid laundry detergent than to actors promoting the fur coat. Whittler's (1991) major findings in study 1 indicate that white participants perceived themselves as less similar to black actors than to white actors, particularly for the portable word processor. Black participants perceived themselves as more similar to black actors than to white actors. In Whittler's (1991) study 2, low-prejudice whites showed no differences between their similarity or ability to identify with black or white actors, whereas high-prejudice whites perceived themselves as less similar to black actors than to white actors.

REFERENCES:

Whittler, Tommy E. (1991), "The Effects of Actors' Race in Commercial Advertising: Review and Extension," *JA*, 20 (1), 54-60.

_____ and Joan DiMeo (1991), "Viewer's Reaction to Racial Cues in Advertising Stimuli," *JAR*, 31 (6), 37-46.

SCALE ITEMS: SOURCE PERCEPTION (SIMILARITY TO THE ACTOR IN THE AD)

Not at all ____ : ____ : ____ : ____ : ____ : ____ : ____ : ____ : ____ : ____ : ____ : ____ : ____ : ____ : ____Very
similar   1   2   3   4   5   6   7   8   9   10   11   12   13   14   15 similar

1. Overall lifestyle
2. Cultural background
3. Dress and appearance
4. Basic values

SCALE NAME: Validity of the Ad Message Claims

SCALE DESCRIPTION:

A four-item, 15-point semantic differential scale purported to measure validity of the message claims of the commercial.

SCALE ORIGIN:

The scale seems to have been created by Whittler and DiMeo (1991) and used in their study.

SAMPLES:

Whittler and Dimeo (1991) had total of **160** paid white volunteers in their sample. Participants were assigned randomly to receive an ad that had either a black or a white actor promoting either a liquid detergent or a fur coat. The sample was selected from several social and civic organizations in a southern city (YWCA, PTA, women's club). Of the total sample, 73% were women. Sample age ranged from 17 to 55 years. One hundred thirty-one were married, 19 were single, and nine were divorced. All but one participant obtained a high school diploma, 28% attended college, and 58% had college degrees. Sixty percent earned more than $39,999 per year. In Whittler's (1991) study 1, he had a sample of **160** white and **140** black undergraduate students. In study 2 he had a sample of **160** southeastern white adults.

RELIABILITY:

Whittler and DiMeo (1991) reported a Cronbach's alpha of **.92**. Whittler (1991) reported Cronbach's alphas of **.87** in study 1 and **.92** in study 2

VALIDITY:

No examination of scale validity was reported.

ADMINISTRATION:

In Whittler and Dimeo (1991), the participants were organized in groups of three to eight in a large conference room by a white experimenter. Each participant was given a booklet containing the storyboard advertisements and the questionnaire. After viewing all the storyboard advertisements, participants administered the questionnaire in a paper-and-pencil format. In Whittler (1991), participants rated a professionally prepared storyboard featuring a white or black actor promoting a portable word processor or a liquid laundry detergent. A 2 × 2 (Actor's Race × Product Category) cell design was used, and participants were assigned randomly to one of the four experimental cells. Each participant was given a booklet containing the storyboards and the questionnaire. After viewing all the storyboards, participants administered the questionnaires in a paper-and-pencil format.

MAJOR FINDINGS:

Whittler and DiMeo's (1991) results indicate that participants rated the message claims in the white actor condition as being stronger than those in black actor condition. Participants also rated the message claims in the detergent advertisement as being stronger than those in the fur coat advertisement. Whittler's (1991) study 1 indicates that participants did not appear to engage in substantial processing of message arguments. None of the measures indicated effects of actor's race or racial orientation toward blacks. In study 2, low-prejudice whites exhibited greater brand name recall than high-prejudice whites. Also, high-prejudice whites' brand name recognition decreased when actors were black but was unaffected when the actors were white.

REFERENCES:

Whittler, Tommy E. (1991), "The Effects of Actors' Race in Commercial Advertising: Review and Extension," *JA*, 20 (1), 54-60.

_____ and Joan DiMeo (1991), "Viewer's Reaction to Racial Cues in Advertising Stimuli," *JAR*, 31 (6), 37-46.

SCALE ITEMS: VALIDITY OF THE AD MESSAGE CLAIMS

1. Strong ___ : ___ : ___ : ___ : ___ : ___ : ___ : ___ : ___ : ___ : ___ : ___ : ___ : ___ : ___Weak
         1   2   3   4   5   6   7   8   9 10 11 12 13 14 15

2. Persuasive ___ : ___ : ___ : ___ : ___ : ___ : ___ : ___ : ___ : ___ : ___ : ___ : ___ : ___ : ___Unpersuasive
         1   2   3   4   5   6   7   8   9 10 11 12 13 14 15

3. Important ___ : ___ : ___ : ___ : ___ : ___ : ___ : ___ : ___ : ___ : ___ : ___ : ___ : ___ : ___Unimportant
         1   2   3   4   5   6   7   8   9 10 11 12 13 14 15

4. Believable ___ : ___ : ___ : ___ : ___ : ___ : ___ : ___ : ___ : ___ : ___ : ___ : ___ : ___ : ___Unbelievable
         1   2   3   4   5   6   7   8   9 10 11 12 13 14 15

Part III

Organizational, Salesforce, and Miscellaneous Scales

SCALE NAME: Commitment (Organizational)

SCALE DESCRIPTION:

A four-item, three-point Likert-type scale assessing the likelihood of an employee leaving a firm for another job if he/she could receive more pay, status, freedom, and so on.

SCALE ORIGIN:

The scale was developed by Hrebiniak and Alutto (1972). The index of 12 items was tested on 318 school teachers and 395 nurses. It was found that the four items listed here had the highest item-total correlations. The reliability (Spearman-Brown) for the scale was .79. Although commitment had some relationship with demographic variables, multivariate analyses showed role-related factors were of primary importance in explaining it.

SAMPLES:

Dubinsky and Hartley (1986) based their analysis on completed questionnaires returned by **120** respondents. Questionnaires were sent to 467 agents who sold lines of a large, multi-insurance company. No nonresponse bias was apparent. The sample had a mean age of 39.1 years, had spent 6.6 years (mean) in their present positions, were mostly male (91%), and more than half were college graduates (56%). The sample used by Hampton, Dubinsky, and Skinner (1986) was based on **116** usable responses from a census of 121 retail salespeople who worked in one of five outlets of a department store chain. The sample had a median age of 23.2 years, had spent 1.4 years (median) in their present positions and 1.1 years (median) with their current supervisors, were mostly female (78%), and 66% had some college education. Skinner, Dubinsky, and Donnelly (1984) collected data from retail salespeople employed by a small departmental store chain. All salespersons employed by the firm participated in the study. Questionnaires were administered to participants at their workplace, and a total of **157** usable questionnaires were received.

RELIABILITY:

Alphas of **.76** and **.80** were reported by Dubinsky and Hartley (1986) and Hampton, Dubinsky, and Skinner (1986), respectively. An alpha of **.78** was reported by Skinner, Dubinsky, and Donnelly (1984).

VALIDITY:

No examination of scale validity was reported in any of the marketing studies.

ADMINISTRATION:

The scale was self-administered by respondents along many other measures in a mail survey format in Dubinsky and Hartley (1986). Hampton, Dubinsky, and Skinner (1986) distributed the survey instrument to respondents in a conference room in each store, where they were self-administered. High scores on the scale indicate that respondents' emotions are very sensitive to the quality of the work they perform in their jobs whereas low scores suggest that their emotions are not significantly influenced by the performance of their jobs. The scale was self-administered by respondents in the study by Skinner, Dubinsky, and Donnelly (1984).

MAJOR FINDINGS:

The purpose of the study by Dubinsky and Hartley (1986) was to investigate several predictors of salesperson performance and the relationships among those predictors. A path analysis indicated that job performance sensitivity had a positive effect on job performance (prior year's commissions). In turn, the former was most significantly affected (positively) by job involvement. A causal model of retail sales supervisor leadership behavior was studied by Hampton, Dubinsky, and Skinner (1986). The results indicated that job satisfaction had a strong positive effect on job performance sensitivity. Skinner, Dubinsky, and Donnelly (1984) studied the relationship between retail sales managers' social bases of power and retail salespeople's job-related outcomes. They used this scale to obtain respondents' feelings about leaving their present company for an increase in pay, an increase in status, more freedom to be creative, or friendlier coworkers. They found that only expert power is significantly related to organizational commitment. It explains about 7% of the variance in organizational commitment.

REFERENCES:

Dubinsky, Alan J. and Steven W. Hartley (1986), ''A Path-Analytic Study of a Model of Salesperson Performance,'' *JAMS*, 14 (Spring), 36-46.

Hampton, Ron, Alan J. Dubinsky, and Steven J. Skinner (1986), ''A Model of Sales Supervisor Leadership Behavior and Retail Salespeople's Job-Related Outcomes,'' *JAMS*, 14 (Fall), 33-43.

Hrebiniak, Lawrence G. and Joseph A. Alutto (1972), ''Personal and Role-Related Factors in the Development of Organizational Commitment,'' *Administrative Science Quarterly*, 17 (December), 555-73.

Skinner Steven J., Alan Dubinsky, and J.H. Donnelly (1984), ''The Use of Social Bases of Power in Retail Sales,'' *JPSSM*, 4 (November), 49-56.

SCALE ITEMS: COMMITMENT (ORGANIZATIONAL)

Assume you were offered a position with another organization. Would you leave your present organization under any of the following conditions? Use the following scale to indicate your response:

3 = yes, definitely would leave
2 = uncertain about leaving

1 = no, definitely would not leave

I would leave my present company:
1. for a slight increase in pay
2. for slightly more freedom to be personally creative
3. for slightly more status
4. to work with people who are a little friendlier

SCALE NAME: Complaint Responsiveness (Probability of Success)

SCALE DESCRIPTION:

A three-item, three-point Likert-type scale ranging from ''Very likely'' to ''Very unlikely'' measuring a person's perception of the response of business to consumer complaints after a dissatisfying experience had reoccurred.

SCALE ORIGIN:

Richins's (1983) study provided the basis for this measure.

SAMPLES:

The sample was taken from 3000 random households who had a dissatisfying experience with the services of a given industry (automotive repair, medical care, or grocery shopping). Questionnaires were sent to a random sample of 1000 households for each industry. The responses received for analysis were as follows: auto repair = 155, medical care = 166, and grocery shopping = 176. Also, 1500 telephone calls were made, 500 for each service category. A contact rate of 80% was achieved, of whom 70% could not recall a dissatisfying experience with the specific service category asked. On the basis of this, an estimate of response rate for the three surveys are as follows: automotive repair = 55%; medical care = 55%; and grocery shopping = 59%.

RELIABILITY:

The composite scale reliability of this three-item measure is **.84** in grocery, **.89** in automotive repair, and **.93** in medical care.

VALIDITY:

Standard operationalizations for most measures were not available in the literature. Focus groups of faculty/staff were conducted to develop and supplement items for the independent constructs. The initial drafts of the questionnaires were pretested, and revisions were made on the basis of these comments.

ADMINISTRATION:

Data were gathered through self-administered mail questionnaires. Per usual practice, the items were modified somewhat to be relevant to the response industry. Telephone callbacks were also made to provide an estimate of the true response rate.

REFERENCES:

Richins, Marsha L. (1983), ''An Analysis of Consumer Interaction Styles in the Marketplace,'' *JCR*, 10 (June), 73-82.

Singh, Jagdip (1990), ''Voice, Exit, and Negative Word-of-Mouth Behaviors: An Investigation Across Three Service Categories,'' *JAMS*, 18 (Winter), 1-15.

SCALE ITEMS: COMPLAINT RESPONSIVENESS (PROBABILITY OF SUCCESS) +

Very likely   ____ : ____ : ____   Very unlikely

                    1   2   3

1. How likely is it that the store would take appropriate action to take care of your problem (refund, etc)?
2. How likely is it that the store would solve your problem and give better service to you in the future?
3. How likely is it that the store would be more careful in the future and everyone would benefit?

Note: This scale also appears in the Consumer Behavior section as Scale #61.

SCALE NAME: Consumer Desires (Desires)

SCALE DESCRIPTION:

A four-item, seven-point Likert-like summated ratings scale measuring the level of picture quality individuals desire, given their photographic needs and desires.

SCALE ORIGIN:

The scale appears to be original to Spreng and Olshavsky (1993).

SAMPLES:

Subjects were recruited from undergraduate and graduate students at a major university, from both the business school and the journalism department. Subjects volunteered and were entered into a drawing for several cash prizes. Usable data were obtained from **128** subjects.

RELIABILITY:

An alpha of .97 was reported for the scale.

VALIDITY:

Convergent validity was indicated by factor coefficients. It was found that 93% of the variance was captured by the construct rather than measurement error. Discriminant validity was demonstrated by conducting a series of chi-square difference tests.

ADMINISTRATION:

Subjects participated in small groups of one to five individuals. A study booklet, containing the four questions (items) that measure the subjects' desires for the picture quality in a new camera, was used. High scores indicate that respondents feel that picture quality was excellent, and low scores indicate that they do not.

MAJOR FINDINGS:

The desires construct is able to subsume some of the other standards or determinants of satisfaction that have been suggested recently in the literature. For example, desires as a standard can encompass Cadotte, Woodruff, and Jenkins' (1987) "experience based norms."

REFERENCES:

Cadotte, Ernest R., Robert B. Woodruff, and Roger L. Jenkins (1987), "Expectations and Norms in Models of Consumer Satisfaction," *JMR*, 24 (August), 305-14.

Spreng, Richard A. and Richard W. Olshavsky (1993), ''A Desires Congruency Model of Consumer Satisfaction,'' *JAMS*, 21 (Summer), 169-77.

SCALE ITEMS: CONSUMERS DESIRES (DESIRES)

Given your individual photographic needs and desires, what would be the level of picture quality you would desire?

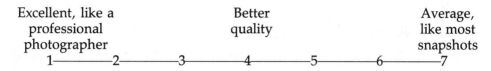

Excellent, like a professional photographer	Better quality	Average, like most snapshots
1———2———3———4———5———6———7		

1. Clarity of the picture
2. Sharpness of the picture
3. Color of the picture
4. Overall picture quality

SCALE NAME: Consumer Desires (Desires Congruency)

SCALE DESCRIPTION:

A four-item, seven-point Likert-like summated ratings scale measuring the performance of a camera with regard to the quality of the picture, given the desires and expectations of the individuals doing the rating.

SCALE ORIGIN:

The scale appears to be original to Spreng and Olshavsky (1993).

SAMPLES:

Subjects were recruited from undergraduate and graduate students at a major university, from both the business school and the journalism department. Subjects volunteered and were entered into a drawing for several cash prizes. Usable data were obtained from **128** subjects.

RELIABILITY:

An alpha of .96 was reported for the scale.

VALIDITY:

Convergent validity was indicated by factor coefficients. It was found that 87% of the variance was captured by the construct rather than measurement error. Discriminant validity was demonstrated by conducting a series of chi-square difference tests.

ADMINISTRATION:

Subjects participated in small groups of one to five individuals. A study booklet, containing the four questions (items) that measure the subjects' desires for the picture quality in a new camera, was used. High scores indicate that respondents feel that picture quality was exactly as they expected, and low scores indicate that they do not.

MAJOR FINDINGS:

Desires congruency has a powerful effect on satisfaction judgments.

REFERENCE:

Spreng, Richard A. and Richard W. Olshavsky (1993), ''A Desires Congruency Model of Consumer Satisfaction,'' *JAMS*, 21 (Summer), 169-77.

SCALE ITEMS: CONSUMERS DESIRES (DESIRES CONGRUENCY)

In comparison to the quality level you desired (expected), how would you rate the performance of this camera with regard to the quality of the picture?

Worse than	Exactly as	Better than
I expected	expected	I expected

1————2————3————4————5————6————7

1. Clarity of the picture
2. Sharpness of the picture
3. Color of the picture
4. Overall picture quality

Note: This scale also appears in the Consumer Behavior section as Scale #84.

SCALE NAME: Consumer Desires (Disconfirmation of Expectations)

SCALE DESCRIPTION:

A four-item, seven-point Likert-like summated ratings scale measuring the performance of a camera with regard to the quality of the picture, given the desires and expectations of the individuals doing the rating.

SCALE ORIGIN:

The scale appears to be original to Spreng and Olshavsky (1993).

SAMPLES:

Subjects were recruited from undergraduate and graduate students at a major university, from both the business school and the journalism department. Subjects volunteered and were entered into a drawing for several cash prizes. Usable data were obtained from **128** subjects.

RELIABILITY:

An alpha of **.96** was reported for the scale.

VALIDITY:

Convergent validity was indicated by factor coefficients. It was found that 90% of the variance was captured by the construct rather than measurement error. Discriminant validity was demonstrated by conducting a series of chi-square difference tests.

ADMINISTRATION:

Subjects participated in small groups of one to five individuals. A study booklet, containing the four questions (items) that measure the subjects' desires for the picture quality in a new camera, was used. High scores indicate that respondents feel that picture quality was exactly as they expected, and low scores indicate that they do not.

MAJOR FINDINGS:

Generally, disconfirmation of expectations has no effect on satisfaction judgments. Confidence in one's expectations may be a requirement for disconfirmation to have an effect on satisfaction. Consumers may not rely on their expectations unless they are held with a fair amount of confidence.

REFERENCE:

Spreng, Richard A. and Richard W. Olshavsky (1993), ''A Desires Congruency Model of Consumer Satisfaction,'' *JAMS*, 21 (Summer), 169-77.

SCALE ITEMS: CONSUMERS DESIRES (DISCONFIRMATION OF EXPECTATIONS)

In comparison to the quality level you desired (expected), how would you rate the performance of this camera with regard to the quality of the picture?

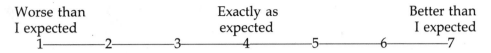

Worse than   Exactly as   Better than

I expected   expected   I expected

1————2————3————4————5————6————7

1. Clarity of the picture
2. Sharpness of the picture
3. Color of the picture
4. Overall picture quality

Note: This scale also appears in the Consumer Behavior section as Scale #87.

SCALE NAME: Consumer Desires (Expectation)

SCALE DESCRIPTION:

A four-item, seven-point Likert-like summated ratings scale measuring the level of picture quality individuals desire, given a choice of five photographs.

SCALE ORIGIN:

The scale appears to be original to Spreng and Olshavsky (1993).

SAMPLES:

Subjects were recruited from undergraduate and graduate students at a major university, from both the business school and the journalism department. Subjects volunteered and were entered into a drawing for several cash prizes. Usable data were obtained from **128** subjects.

RELIABILITY:

An alpha of **.97** was reported for the scale.

VALIDITY:

Convergent validity was indicated by factor coefficients. It was found that 92% of the variance was captured by the construct rather than measurement error. Discriminant validity was demonstrated by conducting a series of chi-square difference tests.

ADMINISTRATION:

Subjects participated in small groups of one to five individuals. A study booklet, containing the four questions (items) that measure the subjects' desires for the picture quality in a new camera, was used. High scores indicate that respondents feel that picture quality was excellent, and low scores indicate that they do not.

MAJOR FINDINGS:

When consumers are dependent on another source for information (e.g., a salesperson, company advertisements or literature) as opposed to direct, personal observation of the product, the beliefs they hold about what the product will do (i.e., their expectations) may be important in forming satisfaction. For example, when expectations about a product's performance are developed from advertising, these persuasion-based expectations can be compared with product performance.

REFERENCE:

Spreng, Richard A. and Richard W. Olshavsky (1993), ''A Desires Congruency Model of Consumer Satisfaction,'' *JAMS*, 21 (Summer), 169-77.

SCALE ITEMS: CONSUMERS DESIRES (EXPECTATIONS)

Given your individual photographic needs and desires, what would be the level of picture quality you would desire?

Terrible, very poor		Average quality			Excellent quality
1———2———3———4———5———6———7					

1. Clarity of the picture
2. Sharpness of the picture
3. Color of the picture
4. Overall picture quality

Note: This scale also appears in the Consumer Behavior section as Scale #108.

SCALE NAME: Customer Orientation—Motivational Direction

SCALE DESCRIPTION:

An 11-item, seven-point Likert-type scale measuring the degree of appropriateness of particular activities into which employee effort is directed and maintained.

SCALE ORIGIN:

The scale appears to be original to Kelley (1992).

SAMPLES:

Kelley (1992) obtained the cooperation of four financial institutions of approximately the same size in four midwestern cities. Questionnaires were administered during regularly scheduled meetings to a total of **249** customer-contact employees. The customer-contact employees responding to the questionnaire included branch managers, assistant branch managers, loan officers, customer service representatives, and tellers. All participating employees completed the questionnaire.

RELIABILITY:

An alpha of **.88** was reported for the scale.

VALIDITY:

LISREL VI (Joreskog and Sorbom 1984) was used to assess the measurement properties of the scale and test for proposed framework relationships. Fit indices provided by the LISREL VI program were used to measure the overall fit of the model and were found to support the measurement properties of the model. The lowest factor loading in the measurement model is .738. All other factor loadings exceed .80. The overall fit indices and the parameter estimates provide evidence supportive of the internal and external consistency of the measures (Gerbing and Anderson 1988).

ADMINISTRATION:

The scale was self-administered in a questionnaire-type format. High scores on the scale indicate that respondents strongly agree with the motivational direction of their jobs (as stated by the items), whereas low scores indicate that they do not.

MAJOR FINDINGS:

The socialization of employees was found to lead to greater motivational direction (among other socialization outcomes). Motivational direction, along with other outcomes, was found to affect the level of customer orientation of service employees. This indicates that managers hoping to increase the customer orientation of their personnel should strive to develop an understanding among their employees of what is expected of them, and increase employee identification and involvement with the organization through the process of organizational socialization.

REFERENCES:

Gerbing, David W. and James C. Anderson (1988), ''An Updated Paradigm for Scale Development Incorporating Unidimensionality and Its Assessment,'' *JMR*, 25 (May), 186-92.

Joreskog, Karl C. and Dag Sorbom (1984), *LISREL VI:Analysis of Linear Structural Relationships by Maximum Likelihood, Instrumental Variables, and Least Squares Methods*. Mooresville, IN: Scientific Software.

Kelley, Scott W. (1992). ''Developing Customer Orientation Among Service Employees,'' *JAMS*, 20 (Winter), 27-36.

SCALE ITEMS: CUSTOMER ORIENTATION—MOTIVATIONAL DIRECTION

With respect to your job, please indicate the degree of your agreement or disagreement with each of the following items:

Strongly
disagree
1————2————3————4————5————6————7
Strongly
agree

1. I plan my work.
2. I think ahead when I am working.
3. Developing a work strategy is important.
4. Being organized is important when I am working.
5. I try to think out beforehand what I am going to do on my job.
6. The way I work is important.
7. I have a game plan for my work.
8. A work plan is important on this job.
9. I have a daily schedule that I follow.
10. I carefully consider how to accomplish my job.
11. I manage my time on the job well.

SCALE NAME: Customer Orientation—Organizational Climate

SCALE DESCRIPTION:

A 22-item, seven-point Likert-type scale measuring the perceptions of individuals in an organization regarding the importance that the organization places on various characteristics of the services it provides.

SCALE ORIGIN:

The scale appears to be original to Kelley (1992).

SAMPLES:

Kelley obtained the cooperation of four financial institutions of approximately the same size in four midwestern cities. Questionnaires were administered during regularly scheduled meetings to a total of **249** customer-contact employees. The customer-contact employees responding to the questionnaire included branch managers, assistant branch managers, loan officers, customer service representatives, and tellers. All participating employees completed the questionnaire.

RELIABILITY:

An alpha of **.95** was reported for the scale.

VALIDITY:

LISREL VI (Joreskog and Sorbom 1984) was used to assess the measurement properties of the scale and test for proposed framework relationships. Fit indices provided by the LISREL VI program were used to measure the overall fit of the model, and were found to support the measurement properties of the model. The lowest factor loading in the measurement model is .738. All other factor loadings exceed .80. The overall fit indices and the parameter estimates provide evidence supportive of the internal and external consistency of the measures (Gerbing and Anderson 1988).

ADMINISTRATION:

The scale was self-administered in a questionnaire-type format. High scores on the scale indicate that respondents strongly agree that the importance the organization places on various characteristics of the services it provides are similar to their the respondents feelings, whereas low scores indicate that they do not.

MAJOR FINDINGS:

Results of this study support the notion that employee perceptions of the organizational climate for service are positively related to their customer orientation.

REFERENCES:

Gerbing, David W. and James C. Anderson (1988), ''An Updated Paradigm for Scale Development Incorporating Unidimensionality and its Assessment,'' *JMR* , 25 (May), 186-92.

Joreskog, Karl C. and Dag Sorbom (1984), *LISREL VI: Analysis of Linear Structural Relationships by Maximum Likelihood, Instrumental Variables, and Least Squares Methods*. Mooresville, IN: Scientific Software.

Kelley, Scott W. (1992), ''Developing Customer Orientation Among Service Employees,'' *JAMS*, 20 (Winter), 27-36.

SCALE ITEMS: CUSTOMER ORIENTATION—ORGANIZATIONAL CLIMATE

With respect to your own feelings about the importance your organization places upon various characteristics of the services it provides, please indicate your degree of agreement or disagreement with each of the following items:

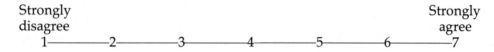

Strongly
disagree

Strongly
agree

1————2————3————4————5————6————7

1. Consistent service performance is important.
2. Dependable service performance is important.
3. Prompt service from its employees is stressed.
4. It is important to honor its promises to customers.
5. The preparation of employees is important.
6. The knowledge of the employees is important.
7. The training of its employees is stressed.
8. Convenient locations are important.
9. It is important to have operating hours that are convenient for its customers.
10. The appearance of its employees is stressed.
11. It is important for employees to be polite to customers.
12. It is important to use language that the customer can understand.
13. It is important to let the customer know how much the service will cost beforehand.
14. It is important to let the customer know what service alternatives are available.
15. Employee honesty is stressed.
16. A reputation for good service is emphasized.
17. The development of customer confidence in the service provided is stressed.
18. The confidentiality of its service is stressed.
19. What the customer needs is important.
20. Individual customer attention is stressed.
21. A nice atmosphere for service is stressed.
22. It is important for employees to have up to date equipment to provide service.

SCALE NAME: Customer Orientation—Organizational Socialization

SCALE DESCRIPTION:

A 20-item, seven-point Likert-type scale measuring the degree of appreciation for the values of an organization on the basis of the employees' experiences.

SCALE ORIGIN:

The scale appears to be original to Kelley (1992).

SAMPLES:

Kelley obtained the cooperation of four financial institutions of approximately the same size in four midwestern cities. Questionnaires were administered during regularly scheduled meetings to a total of **249** customer-contact employees. The customer-contact employees responding to the questionnaire included branch managers, assistant branch managers, loan officers, customer service representatives, and tellers. All participating employees completed the questionnaire.

RELIABILITY:

An alpha of **.87** was reported for the scale.

VALIDITY:

LISREL VI (Joreskog and Sorbom 1984) was used to assess the measurement properties of the scale and test for proposed framework relationships. Fit indices provided by the LISREL VI program were used to measure the overall fit of the model, and were found to support the measurement properties of the model. The lowest factor loading in the measurement model is .738. All other factor loadings exceed .80. The overall fit indices and the parameter estimates provide evidence supportive of the internal and external consistency of the measures (Gerbing and Anderson 1988).

ADMINISTRATION:

The scale was self-administered in a questionnaire-type format. High scores on the scale indicate that respondents strongly agree with the values of the organization, whereas low scores indicate that they do not.

MAJOR FINDINGS:

The process of organizational socialization is extremely important in the development of customer orientation among service employees. Organizational values are conveyed to employees in a variety of implicit and explicit ways through the process of socialization. Regardless of the method or methods of socialization that are implemented, it is extremely important that consistent and appropriate values regarding customer-oriented behaviors are communicated to employees.

REFERENCES:

Gerbing, David W. and James C. Anderson (1988), ''An Updated Paradigm for Scale Development Incorporating Unidimensionality and its Assessment,'' *JMR* , 25 (May), 186-92.

Joreskog, Karl C. and Dag Sorbom (1984), *LISREL VI: Analysis of Linear Structural Relationships by Maximum Likelihood, Instrumental Variables, and Least Squares Methods*. Mooresville, IN: Scientific Software.

Kelley, Scott W. (1992), ''Developing Customer Orientation Among Service Employees,'' *JAMS*, 20 (Winter), 27-36.

SCALE ITEMS: CUSTOMER ORIENTATION—ORGANIZATIONAL SOCIALIZATION

Based upon your experiences, please indicate your degree of agreement or disagreement with each of the following items:

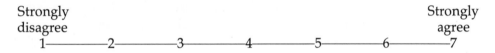

Strongly
disagree

Strongly
agree

1———2———3———4———5———6———7

1. I feel comfortable in this organization.
2. I understand the values that are important to this organization.
3. People in this organization have explained what is expected of me on this job.
4. This organization influences me.
5. I understand the policies of this organization.
6. I get along with my supervisor.
7. This job is what I was looking for when I was searching for a job.
8. I am trusted by the people I work with.
9. Since joining this company, I have learned about the history of this organization.
10. This organization can depend on me.
11. Sometimes I don't feel like I belong in this organization. (r)
12. I am similar to the people that I work with.
13. This organization provides me with the resources that I need to do my job.
14. I am in control of my work situation.
15. The people I work with can count on me to carry out my job.
16. I understand the basic goals of this organization.
17. My responsibilities in this organization are unclear to me. (r)
18. I try to uphold the reputation of this organization.
19. Since joining this organization, my personal values and those of the organization have become more similar.
20. What this organization stands for is important to me.

SCALE NAME: Deontological Norms (DN)

SCALE DESCRIPTION:

A seven-item, seven-point Likert-type summated ratings scale measuring a person's personal values or rules of behavior in conjunction with a predetermined set of guidelines.

SCALE ORIGIN:

The scale appears to be original to Singhapakdi and Vitell (1991). However, reference is made to Hunt and Vitell (1986) on their earlier work on the Comprehensive Theory of Marketing Ethics.

SAMPLES:

This study used an American Marketing Association (AMA) mailing list as the sampling frame. Data were collected through a questionnaire sent to 1998 members. A response rate of 26.54%, or 529 persons, was achieved. Of the 529 responses, **483** were deemed usable. Slightly more than half (55.1%) of the usable responses were from men. Respondents were generally highly educated, and relatively evenly scattered throughout the United States and throughout various industries.

RELIABILITY:

An alpha of **.76** was computed for the scale.

VALIDITY:

Principle components factor analysis was conducted on the seven DN statements, but no details of factor loadings are given.

ADMINISTRATION:

The scale was self-administered by respondents. High scores indicate that the individual is more "ethical" in a deontological sense with regard to relevant guidelines, values, or rules of behavior.

MAJOR FINDINGS:

The results of the study by Singhapakdi and Vitell indicate that there is no significant relationship between the culture of an organization and its employees' deontological norms. A case can be made that organizational culture or "personality" of an individual's organization is too far removed from the deontological norms of the individual compared with his/her personality to have as much impact.

REFERENCES:

Hunt, Shelby D. and Scott Vitell (1986), ''A General Theory of Marketing Ethics,'' *Journal of Macromarketing*, 8 (Spring), 5-16.

Singhapakdi, Anusorn and Scott J. Vitell, Jr. (1991), ''Research Note: Selected Factors Influencing Marketers' Deontological Norms,'' *JAMS* , 19 (Winter), 37-42.

SCALE ITEMS: DEONTOLOGICAL NORMS (DN)

```
Strongly                                              Strongly
disagree                                                 agree
   1————————2————————3————————4————————5————————6————————7
```

DN1: The marketer's professional conduct must be guided by the adherence to all applicable laws and regulations.

DN2: Being honest in serving consumers, clients, employees, suppliers, distributors and the public.

DN3: Communication in a manner that is truthful and forthright.

DN4: All parties intend to discharge their obligations, financial and otherwise, in good faith.

DN5: Rejection of high pressure selling tactics such as the use of associates to mislead or the use of bait and switch to manipulate.

DN6: Not manipulating the availability of a product for purpose of exploitation.

DN7: Meet their obligations and responsibilities in contracts and mutual agreements in a timely manner.

SCALE NAME: Emotional Reactions and Salesperson Motivation (Expectancy Estimates)

SCALE DESCRIPTION:

A 38-item, eight-point ratings scale measuring the extent to which salespeople experience a particular emotion when they fail to meet their monthly quota. The expectancy construct is intended to measure the salesperson's perceived likelihood that he or she would make next month's sales quota.

SCALE ORIGIN:

The items were selected from a comprehensive set of emotional scales used in the measurement of affective responses to advertising (Batra and Holbrook 1986) and from other studies measuring causal attributions and emotions (Russell and McAuley 1986; Weiner, Russell, and Lerman 1978).

SAMPLES:

The sample consisted of sales managers from 49 district sales offices of a leading business forms and supply company. Only salespeople who failed to make their monthly quota were considered. A total of 277 salespeople responded, of which 146 failed to make quota. Of these, 24% were females, 5.1 years was the average job tenure with the company, and 64.7% attained the average quota for the previous month.

RELIABILITY:

An alpha of .75 was reported for this scale.

VALIDITY:

Principle-components factor analysis was performed and factor loadings less than .35 or cross loadings greater than .35 were excluded.

ADMINISTRATION:

The scale was self-administered by respondents and the questionnaires were returned to their managers in a sealed envelope. High scores indicate that respondents have strong feelings for a particular emotion, whereas low scores indicate that they do not.

MAJOR FINDINGS:

The results support the findings that emotional reactions to salesperson failure to make quota will have a significant influence on expectancy estimates of future success. However, feelings of regret were the only emotional reactions to influence expectancy estimates directly.

REFERENCES:

Badovick, Gordon J. (1990), ''Emotional Reactions and Salesperson Motivation: An Attributional Approach Following Inadequate Sales Performance,'' *JAMS*, 18 (2), 123-30.

Batra, Rajeer and Morris B. Holbrook (1986), ''Development of a Set of Scales to Measure Affective Responses to Advertising,'' working paper, Columbia University.

Russell, Dan and Edward McAuley (1986). ''Causal Attributions, Causal Dimensions, and Affective Reactions to Success and Failure,'' *Journal of Personality and Social Psychology*, 50 (June), 1174-85.

Weiner, Bernard, Dan Russell, and David Lerman (1978). ''Affective Consequences of Causal Ascriptions,'' in *New Directions in Attribution Research*, John H. Harvey, William Ickes, and Robert F. Kidd, eds. Hillsdale, NJ: Lawrence Erlbaum and Associates.

SCALE ITEMS: EMOTIONAL REACTIONS AND SALESPERSON MOTIVATION (EXPECTANCY ESTIMATES)

Rate the extent to which you experience each emotion when you fail to make your monthly quota.

No feelings ____ : ____ : ____ : ____ : ____ : ____ : ____ : ____ Extremely strong feelings

1   2   3   4   5   6   7   8

1. Guilty
2. Upset with others
3. Thankful
4. Frustrated
5. Apologetic
6. Concerned
7. Irritated with others
8. Happy
9. Uncheerful
10. Ashamed
11. Confident
12. Dissatisfied with others
13. Astonished
14. Embarrassed
15. Pleased
16. Relieved
17. Surprised
18. Amazed
19. Unhappy
20. Appreciative
21. Sorry
22. Dissatisfied with self
23. Good
24. Proud
25. Irritated at self
26. Grateful
27. Upset with self
28. Capable
29. Satisfied
30. Incompetent
31. Incapable
32. Angry at others
33. Competent
34. Regretful
35. Angry at self
36. Inadequate
37. Disappointed
38. Remorseful

SCALE NAME: Emotional Reactions and Salesperson Motivation (Motivation)

SCALE DESCRIPTION:

A 38-item, eight-point ratings scale measuring the extent to which salespeople experience a particular emotion when they fail to meet their monthly quota. Motivation refers to the amount of effort a salesperson plans to expend on tasks associated with his/her job.

SCALE ORIGIN:

The items were selected from a comprehensive set of emotional scales used in the measurement of affective responses to advertising (Batra and Holbrook 1986) and from other studies measuring causal attributions and emotions (Russell and McAuley 1986; Weiner, Russell, and Lerman 1978).

SAMPLES:

The sample consisted of sales managers from 49 district sales offices of a leading business forms and supply company. Only salespeople who failed to make their monthly quota were considered. A total of **277** salespeople responded, of which 146 failed to make quota. Of these, 24% were females, 5.1 years was the average job tenure with the company, and 64.7% attained the average quota for the previous month.

RELIABILITY:

An alpha of **.88** was reported for this scale.

VALIDITY:

Principle-components factor analysis was performed and factor loadings less than .35 or cross loadings greater than .35 were excluded.

ADMINISTRATION:

The scale was self-administered by respondents and the questionnaires were returned to their managers in a sealed envelope. High scores indicate that respondents have strong feelings for a particular emotion, whereas low scores indicate that they do not.

MAJOR FINDINGS:

The results support the findings that emotional reactions after failure to make quota have a significant influence on subsequent salesperson motivation. The data suggest that feelings of both self-blame and performance satisfaction directly influence motivation but in opposite directions.

REFERENCES:

Badovick, Gordon J. (1990), ''Emotional Reactions and Salesperson Motivation: An Attributional Approach Following Inadequate Sales Performance,'' *JAMS* , 18 (2), 123-30.

Batra, Rajeer and Morris B. Holbrook (1986), ''Development of a Set of Scales to Measure Affective Responses to Advertising,'' working paper, Columbia University.

Russell, Dan and Edward McAuley (1986), ''Causal Attributions, Causal Dimensions, and Affective Reactions to Success and Failure,'' *Journal of Personality and Social Psychology*, 50, (June), 1174-85.

Weiner, Bernard, Dan Russell, and David Lerman (1978). ''Affective Consequences of Causal Ascriptions,'' in *New Directions in Attribution Research*, John H. Harvey, William Ickes, and Robert F. Kidd, eds. Hillsdale, NJ: Lawrence Erlbaum and Associates.

SCALE ITEMS: EMOTIONAL REACTIONS AND SALESPERSON MOTIVATION (MOTIVATION)

Rate the extent to which you experience each emotion when you fail to make your monthly quota.

No feelings ___ : ___ : ___ : ___ : ___ : ___ : ___ : ___ Extremely strong feelings
1   2   3   4   5   6   7   8

1. Guilty
2. Upset with others
3. Thankful
4. Frustrated
5. Apologetic
6. Concerned
7. Irritated with others
8. Happy
9. Uncheerful
10. Ashamed
11. Confident
12. Dissatisfied with others
13. Astonished
14. Embarrassed
15. Pleased
16. Relieved
17. Surprised
18. Amazed
19. Unhappy
20. Appreciative
21. Sorry
22. Dissatisfied with self
23. Good
24. Proud
25. Irritated at self
26. Grateful
27. Upset with self
28. Capable
29. Satisfied
30. Incompetent
31. Incapable
32. Angry at others
33. Competent
34. Regretful
35. Angry at self
36. Inadequate
37. Disappointed
38. Remorseful

SCALE NAME: External and Internal Supplier Influences—Boundary Role Performance (BRP)

SCALE DESCRIPTION:

A five-item, seven-point Likert-like summated ratings scale measuring the extent to which suppliers can generate power in their relationship with dealers through good operating procedures that indirectly translate into desired behavioral responses.

SCALE ORIGIN:

Gassenheimer and Scandura (1993) report that the scale is based on roles of sales personnel identified in a previous study of the industry (Sterling 1985), interviews with dealers, industry experts, and manufacturing representatives. The items are also similar to the noncoercive bases of power used by El-Ansary and Stern (1972).

SAMPLES:

Suppliers in the office systems and furniture industry were used. Eighteen in-depth pretest interviews were conducted. Of the 939 questions sent to the office systems and furniture dealers throughout the United States, **324** responses were received, a response rate of 34.5%. Nearly 90% of the respondents reported that they were the president, vice-president, owner, chief executive officer, or general manager of their dealership.

RELIABILITY:

An alpha of **.85** was reported for the scale.

VALIDITY:

Measures concerning content validity were obtained from a general review of the channels literature and discussions with industry experts, dealers, and manufacturing representatives. The proposed relationships concerning nomologic validity were theoretically based.

ADMINISTRATION:

The scale was self-administered in a mail-survey type format. High scores on the scale indicate that respondents feel high power generation (through good operating procedures and desired behavioral responses), whereas low scores indicate that they do not.

MAJOR FINDINGS:

Results of regression analysis did not support the proposal that boundary role performance by the supplier is positively related to the amount of control the dealer relinquishes to the supplier.

REFERENCES:

El-Ansary, Adel I. and Louis W. Stern (1972), ''Power Measurement in the Distribution Channel,'' *JMR*, 9 (February), 47-52.

Gassenheimer, Jule B. and Terri A. Scandura (1993), ''External and Internal Supplier Influences: Buyer Perceptions of Channel Outcomes,'' *JAMS*, 21 (Spring), 155-60.

Sterling, Jay U. (1985), ''Integrating Customer Service and Marketing Strategies in a Channel of Distribution: An Empirical Study,'' doctoral dissertation, Michigan State University, East Lansing.

SCALE ITEMS: EXTERNAL AND INTERNAL SUPPLIER INFLUENCES— BOUNDARY ROLE PERFORMANCE : (BRP)

Poor   Excellent

1————2————3————4————5————6————7

1. Availability of manufacturer sales reps to participate in customer sales calls and project bids.
2. Timely response to requests for assistance from manufacturer's sales representative.
3. After the sale follow-up by sales reps.
4. Attention to details from order placement to installation.
5. Manufacturer's responsiveness to emergency/unusual needs.

SCALE NAME: External and Internal Supplier Influences—Dealer Satisfaction

SCALE DESCRIPTION:

A nine-item, seven-point Likert-like summated ratings scale measuring over-all dealer satisfaction with his/her major supplier.

SCALE ORIGIN:

The scale appears to be original to Gassenheimer and Scandura (1993). It is based on 18 pretest interviews with dealers and discussions with industry experts and manufacturer representatives.

SAMPLES:

Suppliers in the office systems and furniture industry were used. Eighteen in-depth pre-test interviews were conducted. Of the 939 questions sent to the office systems and furniture dealers throughout the United States, **324** responses were received, a response rate of 34.5%. Nearly 90% of the respondents reported that they were the president, vice-president, owner, chief executive officer, or general manager of their dealership.

RELIABILITY:

An alpha of **.91** was reported for this scale.

VALIDITY:

Measures concerning content validity were obtained from a general review of the channels literature and discussions with industry experts, dealers, and manufacturing representatives. The proposed relationships concerning nomologic validity were theoretically based.

ADMINISTRATION:

The scale was self-administered in a mail-survey type format. High scores on the scale indicate that respondents feel very satisfied overall with their major supplier, whereas low scores indicate that they do not.

MAJOR FINDINGS:

Results of regression analysis support the hypothesis that the boundary role performance by the supplier is positively related to the dealer's satisfaction with the supplier.

REFERENCE:

Gassenheimer, Jule B. and Terri A. Scandura (1993), "External and Internal Supplier Influences: Buyer Perceptions of Channel Outcomes," *JAMS*, 21 (Spring), 155-60.

SCALE ITEMS: EXTERNAL AND INTERNAL SUPPLIER INFLUENCES—DEALER SATISFACTION

```
Very                                                              Very
dissatisfied                                                  satisfied
    1————————2————————3————————4————————5————————6————————7
```

1. Profits generated from manufacturer's product lines.
2. Overall manner you were treated by manufacturer's regional office or headquarters.
3. Overall "sales support/relationship" with the manufacturer's local sales representative.
4. New product market opportunities manufacturer provided you.
5. Sales growth potential from carrying manufacturer's product lines.
6. Overall fairness and honesty of manufacturer.
7. Interest and concern manufacturer has displayed in helping you accomplish your goals and objectives.
8. Manufacturer's commitment to continuing their overall marketing programs (advertising, promotion, selling and distribution).
9. Overall customer service levels provided by the manufacturer.

SCALE NAME: External and Internal Supplier Influences—Supplier Control

SCALE DESCRIPTION:

A ten-item, seven-point Likert-like summated ratings scale measuring the suppliers achieved influence on dealer operations.

SCALE ORIGIN:

The scale appears to be original to Gassenheimer and Scandura (1993). It is based on 18 pretest interviews with dealers and discussions with industry experts and manufacturer representatives. The scale anchors were similar to those used by Keith, Jackson, and Crosby (1990).

SAMPLES:

Suppliers in the office systems and furniture industry were used. Eighteen in-depth pretest interviews were conducted. Of the 939 questions sent to the office systems and furniture dealers throughout the United States, **324** responses were received, a response rate of 34.5%. Nearly 90% of the respondents reported that they were the president, vice-president, owner, chief executive officer, or general manager of their dealership.

RELIABILITY:

An alpha of **.81** was reported for this scale.

VALIDITY:

Measures concerning content validity were obtained from a general review of the channels literature and discussions with industry experts, dealers, and manufacturing representatives. The proposed relationships concerning nomologic validity were theoretically based.

ADMINISTRATION:

The scale was self-administered in a mail-survey type format. High scores on the scale indicate that suppliers have more influence over dealer decisions, whereas low scores indicate that dealers have more influence over their own decisions.

MAJOR FINDINGS:

Results of regression analysis do not support the hypothesis that the supplier's relative market position and the supplier's use of pressure on the dealer interact to affect the amount of control the dealer relinquishes to the supplier.

REFERENCES:

Gassenheimer, Jule B. and Terri A. Scandura (1993), ''External and Internal Supplier Influences: Buyer Perceptions of Channel Outcomes,'' *JAMS*, 21 (Spring), 155-60.

Keith, Janet E., Donald W. Jackson, Jr., and Lawrence A. Crosby (1990), ''Effects of Alternative Types of Influence Strategies Under Different Channel Dependence Structures,'' *JM*, 54 (July), 30-41.

SCALE ITEMS: EXTERNAL AND INTERNAL SUPPLIER INFLUENCES— SUPPLIER CONTROL

After the manufacturer [supplier] tried to influence your [dealer's] decision concerning the various marketing issues, who had the most influence or leverage (the manufacturer [supplier] or yourself, as the dealer) over the actual decision made?

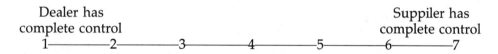

Dealer has complete control ... Suppiler has complete control

1———————2———————3———————4———————5———————6———————7

1. Your margins on contract/projects sales to your customers.
2. Annual minimum volume quotas suggested or requested by the manufacturer.
3. The selection and breadth of the manufacturer's product/line that you actually focused on.
4. Your acceptance and adoption of new products/lines developed or acquired by the manufacturer.
5. Degree of independent/unsolicited participation by the manufacturer in selling new, large accounts/projects.
6. Size, investment, and appearance of your showroom(s).
7. The freedom to buy office systems furniture from competing suppliers.
8. Procedures and techniques used to develop selling skills and account management for your salespeople.
9. The freedom to sell the manufacturer's products outside your implied/ agreed upon sales territory.
10. Order entry and communication methods. (The freedom to develop/use your own system vs. one(s) specified by the manufacturer).

SCALE NAME: External and Internal Supplier Influences—Supplier Pressure

SCALE DESCRIPTION:

A ten- item, eight-point Likert-like summated ratings scale measuring the amount of pressure used by suppliers on dealers to change their decisions on ten key issues.

SCALE ORIGIN:

The scale appears to be original to Gassenheimer and Scandura (1993). It is based on 18 pretest interviews with dealers, and discussions with industry experts and manufacturer representatives.

SAMPLES:

Suppliers in the office systems and furniture industry were used. Eighteen in-depth pre-test interviews were conducted. Of the 939 questions sent to the office systems and furniture dealers throughout the United States, **324** responses were received, a response rate of 34.5%. Nearly 90% of the respondents reported that they were the president, vice-president, owner, chief executive officer, or general manager of their dealership.

RELIABILITY:

An alpha of **.83** was reported for this scale.

VALIDITY:

Measures concerning content validity were obtained from a general review of the channels literature and discussions with industry experts, dealers, and manufacturing representatives. The proposed relationships concerning nomologic validity were theoretically based.

ADMINISTRATION:

The scale was self-administered in a mail-survey type format. High scores on the scale indicate that respondents feel high pressure from suppliers to change their decisions, whereas low scores indicate that they do not.

MAJOR FINDINGS:

Results of regression analysis support the hypothesis that the amount of pressure the supplier uses on the dealer is positively related to the amount of control the dealer relinquishes to the supplier.

REFERENCE:

Gassenheimer, Jule B. and Terri A. Scandura (1993), "External and Internal Supplier Influences: Buyer Perceptions of Channel Outcomes," *JAMS*, 21 (Spring), 155-60.

SCALE ITEMS: EXTERNAL AND INTERNAL SUPPLIER INFLUENCES— SUPPLIER PRESSURE

No   Major
pressure   pressure
1———2———3———4———5———6———7———8

1. Decrease margins on contract/projects sales to your customers.
2. Increase your annual minimum volume quotas suggested or requested by the manufacturer.
3. Increase the selection and breadth of the manufacturer's product line that you actually focus on.
4. Accept new products/lines introduced (developed and/or acquired) by the manufacturer.
5. Accept independent/unsolicited participation by the manufacturer in selling new accounts/projects.
6. Alter the size, investment, and/or appearance of your showroom.
7. Alter your decision and/or ability to buy office systems and furniture from competing suppliers.
8. Alter the procedures and techniques used to develop selling skills and account management for your sales people.
9. Restrict your implied/authorized sales territory for selling the manufacturer's product.
10. Alter your order entry and communication methods.

SCALE NAME: Feelings of Success

SCALE DESCRIPTION:

A seven-item, seven-point Likert-type summated ratings scale measuring the extent to which one feels successful in performing one's job.

SCALE ORIGIN:

The scale was developed originally by Hall and colleagues (1978) and used by Brown, Cron, and Leigh (1993) in their study. The concept of feelings of success also draws on Levin's (1936) assertions that people develop feelings of success and self-esteem when they achieve certain specific goals.

SAMPLES:

Six industrial equipment and supply manufacturers participated in the study. Each of the six companies has a national sales force with geographical territory assignments and multiple product lines. The realized sample included **466** salespeople, for a 54.5% response rate. The sample profile closely matched the sampling frame in demographic terms. The typical respondent was 39 years of age and had 8.7 years' job tenure. Ninety-six percent were male, 72% were married, and 51% had attended college.

RELIABILITY:

Cronbach's alpha for the summated scale was **.84**.

VALIDITY:

No specific examination of scale validity was reported.

ADMINISTRATION:

The scale was self-administered in a mail-survey type format. High scores on the scale indicate that respondents feel very successful in performing their jobs, whereas low scores indicate that they do not.

MAJOR FINDINGS:

The results of the study on the psychological success model by Brown, Cron, and Leigh (1993) provide clear evidence that feelings of success have a mediating effect on the relationship between work performance and job satisfaction. Feelings of success had a much stronger effect on satisfaction than job performance did.

REFERENCES:

Brown, Stephen P., William L. Cron, and Thomas W. Leigh (1993), "Do Feelings of Success Mediate Sales Performance-Work Attitude Relationships?" *JAMS*, 21 (Spring 2), 91-100.

Hall, Douglas T., James Goodale, Samuel Rabinowitz, and Marilyn Morgan (1978), "Effects of Top-Down Departmental and Job Change Upon Perceived Employee Behavior and Attitudes: A Natural Field Experiment," *Journal of Applied Psychology*, 63 (February), 62-72.

Levin, Kurt (1936), "The Psychology of Success and Failure," *Occupations*, 14, 926-30.

SCALE ITEMS: FEELINGS OF SUCCESS

Very
unsuccessful

Very
successful

1————2————3————4————5————6————7

1. I have not been especially proud of my performance in my job lately.
2. Generally, I feel I am achieving my most important personal goals at work.
3. On the basis of my own standards, I feel I have been successful in my work.
4. I get a great sense of accomplishment in my job.
5. My "track record" in my career has been pretty good.
6. I often feel really good about the quality of my work performance.
7. Compared to my peers, I feel quite successful in my career.

SCALE NAME: Index of Services Marketing Excellence (ISME)—Marketing Organization

SCALE DESCRIPTION:

A ten-item, seven-point Likert-type scale measuring the degree to which an organization's (and marketing department's) structure supports and encourages effective marketing.

SCALE ORIGIN:

The scale appears to have been developed originally by Berry, Conant, and Parasuraman (1991).

SAMPLES:

Berry, Conant, and Parasuraman (1991) contacted senior executives and nonmanagerial employees of a large industrial services company. Questionnaires were sent to company managers, employees, and customers (clients). Overall, 45% (**280** of 620) of the clients, 60% (**334** of 561) of the employees, and 59% (**83** of 140) of the managers completed and returned the questionnaires. The 561 employees and 140 managers contacted represented all full-time personnel working for the company at the time of the study.

RELIABILITY:

Cronbach's alphas were reported to be **.67** for managers and **.80** for employees.

VALIDITY:

No specific examination of scale validity was reported.

ADMINISTRATION:

The scale was administered through interviews and mail-survey questionnaires. Separate versions of the questionnaire containing the ISME items were prepared for the three types of respondents: the company's manager's (M), nonmanagerial employees (E), and customers (C). High scores on the scale indicate that respondents strongly agree that the organization's structure supports effective marketing, whereas low scores indicate that they do not.

MAJOR FINDINGS:

The study (1) reinforces the need for, and usefulness of, a services-specific auditing framework such as the ISME; (2) emphasizes the importance of gathering audit information through both qualitative and quantitative research; and (3) suggests that it is worthwhile to collect appropriate data from multiple respondent groups that are capable of providing meaningful inputs.

REFERENCE:

Berry, Leonard L., Jeffrey S. Conant, and A. Parasuraman (1991), ''A Framework for Conducting a Services Marketing Audit,'' *JAMS*, 19 (Summer), 255-68.

SCALE ITEMS: INDEX OF SERVICES MARKETING EXCELLENCE (ISME)— MARKETING ORGANIZATION

Strongly
disagree
1————2————3————4————5————6————7

Strongly
agree

The type of respondent who answered each item in the initial study is noted in parenthesis at the end of each item (e.g. M = Managers; E = Employees; and C = Clients.

1. The senior marketing executive in this company has organizational ''clout'' to influence client satisfaction (M).
2. The Marketing Department does not seem to have enough people to ''get the job done'' (M). (r)
3. The Marketing Department staff has the authority it needs to be effective (M).
4. The Marketing Department does little to help other employees in this company to be effective marketers (M, E). (r)
5. The Marketing Department in this company plays a important role in formulating strategy (M).
6. The relationship between the Marketing Department and the top management of this company is good (M, E).
7. I feel the Marketing Department understands the needs of employees in other departments (M, E).
8. The activities of various departments in this company are well coordinated to insure client satisfaction (M, E, C).
9. The strengths and weaknesses of our Marketing Department are considered when we make strategic decisions (M).
10. The organizational structure of this company facilitates entrepreneurial thinking (M, E).

SCALE NAME: Index of Services Marketing Excellence (ISME)—Marketing Orientation

SCALE DESCRIPTION:

A 17-item, seven-point Likert-type scale measuring the degree to which an organization's activities and decisions reflect a prime focus on the customer.

SCALE ORIGIN:

The scale appears to have been developed originally by Berry, Conant, and Parasuraman (1991).

SAMPLES:

Berry, Conant, and Parasuraman (1991) contacted senior executives and non-managerial employees of a large industrial services company. Questionnaires were sent to company managers, employees, and customers (clients). Overall, 45% (**280** of 620) of the clients, 60% (**334** of 561) of the employees, and 59% (**83** o f140) of the managers completed and returned the questionnaires. The 561 employees and 140 managers contacted represented all full-time personnel working for the company at the time of the study.

RELIABILITY:

Cronbach's alphas were reported to be **.83** for managers, and **.62** for employees.

VALIDITY:

No specific examination of scale validity was reported.

ADMINISTRATION:

The scale was administered through interviews and mail-survey questionnaires. Separate versions of the questionnaire containing the ISME items were prepared for the three types of respondents: the company's manager's (M), nonmanagerial employees (E), and customers (C). High scores on the scale indicate that respondents strongly agree that the organization's activities and decisions reflect a prime focus on the customer, whereas low scores indicate that they do not.

MAJOR FINDINGS:

The study (1) reinforces the need for, and usefulness of, a services-specific auditing framework such as the ISME; (2) emphasizes the importance of gathering audit information through both qualitative and quantitative research; and (3) suggests that it is worthwhile to collect appropriate data from multiple respondent groups that are capable of providing meaningful inputs.

REFERENCE:

Berry, Leonard L., Jeffrey S. Conant, and A. Parasuraman (1991), ''A Framework for Conducting a Services Marketing Audit,'' *JAMS*, 19 (Summer), 255-68.

SCALE ITEMS: INDEX OF SERVICES MARKETING EXCELLENCE (ISME)— MARKETING ORIENTATION

```
Strongly                                                     Strongly
disagree                                                        agree
   1————————2————————3————————4————————5————————6————————7
```

The type of respondent who answered each item in the initial study is noted in parenthesis at the end of each item (e.g. M = Managers; E = Employees; and C = Clients).

1. Decision-making in this company is influenced strongly by client needs (M).
2. Senior managers are always available to speak with clients (M, E).
3. We rarely do formal research about client needs in this company (M). (r)
4. The marketing decisions we make in this company are usually based on market research (M).
5. Written plans for marketing our services are prepared in this company (M).
6. This company engages in comprehensive marketing planning (M).
7. There is little relationship between the new services we develop in the company and genuine client needs (M). (r)
8. The development of new services in this company is more haphazard than systematic (M). (r)
9. We continually monitor client needs in the search for new services to develop (M).
10. In this company, marketing is everyone's responsibility, not just the Marketing Department's (M, E).
11. How we implement marketing strategies in this company is not given sufficient priority (M, E). (r)
12. We do not procrastinate in making needed marketing decisions (M).
13. Everyone in our company understands how their jobs influence client satisfaction (M, E).
14. In our company, senior managers seek suggestions from employees for serving clients better (M, E).
15. The management of this company does not do a good job communicating our strategic goals to employees (M, E). (r)
16. Those of us in management periodically evaluate the company's marketing strategies (M).
17. Everyone in this organization is dedicated to providing high quality client service (M, E).

SCALE NAME: Index of Services Marketing Excellence (ISME)—New Customer Marketing

SCALE DESCRIPTION:

A nine-item, seven-point Likert-type scale measuring the degree to which attracting new customers is given sufficient priority in marketing programming.

SCALE ORIGIN:

The scale appears to have been developed originally by Berry, Conant, and Parasuraman (1991).

SAMPLES:

Berry, Conant, and Parasuraman (1991) contacted senior executives and nonmanagerial employees of a large industrial services company. Questionnaires were sent to company managers, employees, and customers (clients). Overall, 45% (**280** of 620) of the clients, 60% (**334** of 561) of the employees, and 59% (**83** of 140) of the managers completed and returned the questionnaires. The 561 employees and 140 managers contacted represented all full-time personnel working for the company at the time of the study.

RELIABILITY:

Cronbach's alphas were reported to be **.69** for managers, **.68** for employees and **.88** for clients.

VALIDITY:

No specific examination of scale validity was reported.

ADMINISTRATION:

The scale was administered through interviews and mail-survey questionnaires. Separate versions of the questionnaire containing the ISME items were prepared for the three types of respondents: the company's manager's (M), nonmanagerial employees (E), and customers (C). High scores on the scale indicate that respondents strongly agree that the organization's structure supports effective marketing, whereas low scores indicate that they do not.

MAJOR FINDINGS:

The study (1) reinforces the need for, and usefulness of, a services-specific auditing framework such as the ISME; (2) emphasizes the importance of gathering audit information through both qualitative and quantitative research; and (3) suggests that it is worthwhile to collect appropriate data from multiple respondent groups that are capable of providing meaningful inputs.

REFERENCE:

Berry, Leonard L., Jeffrey S. Conant, and A. Parasuraman (1991), ''A Framework for Conducting a Services Marketing Audit,'' *JAMS*, 19 (Summer), 255-68.

SCALE ITEMS: INDEX OF SERVICES MARKETING EXCELLENCE (ISME)—NEW CUSTOMER MARKETING

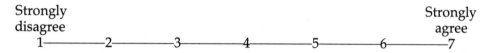

```
Strongly                                                    Strongly
disagree                                                      agree
   1————2————3————4————5————6————7
```

The type of respondent who answered each item in the initial study is noted in parenthesis at the end of each item (e.g. M = Managers; E = Employees; and C = Clients.

1. Formal strategies are in place in this company to attract new clients (M, E).
2. We do not devote sufficient resources to attracting new clients (M, E). (r)
3. In this company we market our services to specific ''market segments'' rather than to one overall market (M).
4. The market segmentation strategy we use in this company seems inappropriate to me (M). (r)
5. Our employees are well-prepared to sell our service to prospective clients (M, E, C). (r)
6. Our employees are poorly motivated to sell our service to prospective clients (M, E, C). (r)
7. We do not do a good enough job differentiating our company from the competition in the eyes of clients (M, C). (r)
8. We have a solid understanding of our competitors' strengths and weaknesses (M).
9. Sometimes I worry that we will not be able to fulfill the promises we make to clients (M, E, C). (r)

SCALE NAME: Job Accomplishment Measure

SCALE DESCRIPTION:

A five-item, nine-point Likert-type scale in which each respondent was to compare himself/herself to all other salespeople in the company doing similar work and to rank himself/herself on a scale varying from "top 10%" to "bottom 10%."

SCALE ORIGIN:

The scale originally was developed and used by Bagozzi (1980). Hafer and Sirgy (1983) modified the scale by eliminating one item from the original six-item scale.

SAMPLES:

Sample consisted of 350 insurance salespeople who were participating in the company's annual meeting at the home office. The respondents were assured of confidentiality of their responses. A total of **336** usable questionnaires were returned, of which 308 were males.

RELIABILITY:

A Cronbach's alpha of **.871** was obtained.

VALIDITY:

No examination of scale validity was reported.

ADMINISTRATION:

The scale was self-administered. The scores ranged from 0 to 45 with a mean of 38.539, median of 39.0, mode of 45, and a standard deviation of 6.828.

MAJOR FINDINGS:

Hafer and Sirgy (1983) found that job accomplishment as an indicator of professional growth was correlated to indicators of personal growth (self-esteem and inner/other-directedness).

REFERENCES:

Bagozzi, Richard P. (1980), "The Nature and Causes of Self-Esteem, Performance, and Satisfaction in the Sales Force: A Structural Equation Approach," *Journal of Business*, 53, 315-31.

Hafer, John (1986), "An Empirical Investigation of The Salesperson's Career Stag Perspective," *JPSSM*, 6 (November), 1-7.

_____ and M. Joseph Sirgy (1983), "Professional Growth Versus Personal

Growth of Salespeople: A General System Model," *JPSSM*, 3 (November), 22-30.

SCALE ITEMS: JOB ACCOMPLISHMENT MEASURE

A nine-point rating scale varying from "top 10%" to "bottom 10%".

1. How do you rate yourself in terms of the quantity of sales you achieve? Overall quantity of volume of sales.
2. How do you rate yourself in terms of the potential you have for reaching the top 10 percent in sales for all salespeople in your company?
3. How do you rate yourself in terms of quality of your performance in regard to management of time, planning ability, and management of expenses?
4. How do you rate yourself in terms of quality of your performance in regard to knowledge of your company, competitors, and client needs?
5. How do you rate yourself in terms of quality of performance in regard to client relations?

SCALE NAME: Job Description Index (JDI)

SCALE DESCRIPTION:

The JDI is a five-measure, composite scale purporting to measure job satisfaction. The five areas are type of work (18 items), opportunities for promotion (nine items), supervision (18 items), pay (nine items), and coworkers (18 items). Each job area measure consists of a list of adjectives or phrases. A summated ratings scale is used ranging from "Y" (yes) to "N" (no), with "?" (cannot decide) between for each job area. Teas (1983) modified the scale somewhat, as is discussed subsequently.

SCALE ORIGIN:

The JDI scales for job satisfaction were originally developed by Smith, Kendall, and Hulin (1969). The research for these scales began in 1959 and was a result of several studies across a wide array of jobs and people. The scales were developed to measure satisfaction on the job within both an "evaluative-general-long-term framework" and a "descriptive-specific-short-term framework," and "to cover the important areas of satisfaction." This wide array of data was used to provide a generally applicable series of measurements of satisfaction (JDI).

SAMPLES:

Busch's (1980) data were obtained from mail questionnaires sent to the sales force of three pharmaceutical companies. The analysis was based on **477** useable questionnaires, for an overall response rate of 53.8%. The response rate of the individual companies were 51.5%, 52.5%, and 57.6%. Of the 477 useable questionnaires 39 respondents were females.

Teas's (1983) data were collected from mail questionnaires sent to two Midwest corporations' sales forces. Included with the questionnaire were cover letters from the researcher and the vice president of sales promising confidentiality and indicating company support for the survey. Usable responses were obtained from 116 salespersons, 49 and 67 salespersons from the two companies respectively (overall response rate was 55%).

Cron and Slocum's (1986) data were obtained from six companies with national sales forces. A total of **466** useable questionnaires were obtained for a response rate of 54.5%. Seventy-two percent of the salespersons were married, 96% were male, and 51% had attended college. Income ranged from $25,000 to $50,000. The average salesperson in the sample was 39 years of age with a tenure of 8.7 years.

Apasu's (1987) data were collected from a U.S.-based multinational firm's sales force. **One hundred fifty-six** useable questionnaires were used for the analysis (the response rate was 60%). The average income of the sample was $30,000, the average sales experience was 7.5 years, and 97% of the respondents were under 40 years of age.

RELIABILITY:

Busch (1980) reported a Spearman-Brown reliability coefficient of **.87** for the job satisfaction with supervision measure of the JDI. Teas (1983) reported an alpha reliability coefficient of **.921** for the modified version of the JDI. (See "Scale Items" for a description of his modifications). Cron and Slocum (1986) reported alpha reliability coefficients for each of the JDI measures of job satisfaction: **.76**, work; **.84**, pay; **.71**, opportunities for promotion; **.86**, supervision; and **.84**, coworkers. Apasu (1987) reported a Cronbach's alpha of **.81** for the satisfaction with pay measure of the JDI.

VALIDITY:

Smith, Kendall, and Hulin (1969) conducted a literature review, which supported the multidimensional notion of job satisfaction. This literature review provided the basis for the original construct of the JDI and its five areas: work, pay, promotions, supervision, and coworkers. An item analysis was conducted, which included item intercorrelations and item validities. All items within each area were intercorrelated (median item intercorrelations exceeded .24). Four individual studies were conducted to evaluate the validity of the JDI using very different samples (Cornell undergraduates, employees of a farmers' cooperative, male employees from two plants of a large electronics manufacturer, and male employees of a bank). Validity was assessed for different forms of the JDI and for different scorings (graphic, interview, triadic scoring, dyadic scoring, direct scoring). The analysis demonstrated that discriminate scores were "obtained from measures directed toward several aspects of the job (discriminate validity for measures and areas), and that several methods of measurement applied to the same aspect show substantial agreement (convergent validity for measures)" (Smith, Kendall, and Hulin 1969, p. 58). These analyses resulted in the final version of the JDI, which has demonstrated discriminant and convergent validity. Moreover, the JDI scales have been shown to be predictive in some situations. No other examination of scale validity was reported or available.

ADMINISTRATION:

Busch (1980), Teas (1983), and Apasu (1987) collected data by mail, the scale being self-administered along with several other measures included in the questionnaire. Cron and Slocrum's (1986) data were collected by two methods: Questionnaires were administered to salespersons during their national sales meeting for three of the companies used in their sample, and the other three companies of the sample were sent questionnaires by mail and were subsequently self-administered. The questionnaires used contained the JDI scales along with several other measures.

The scoring of the JDI scale is as follows:

Response	Weight
Yes to a positive item	3
No to a negative item	3
? to any item	1
Yes to a negative item	0
No to a positive item	0

A high score represents a high level of perceived job satisfaction (e.g., a maximum score of 54 for the satisfaction with work indicates high perceived job satisfaction pertaining to this area). An overall composite score can be used for overall job satisfaction by summating the five areas' summated scores.

MAJOR FINDINGS:

Busch (1980) used only the satisfaction with supervision portion of the JDI. The results indicated that expert ($p < .001$) and referent ($p < .001$) power are significantly related to satisfaction with supervision for all three firms. Coercive power ($p < .01$) was found to be significantly related to satisfaction with supervision for two of the three firms. Legitimate and reward ($p < .05$) were found to be significantly related to satisfaction with supervision for only one of the three firms. No significant differences were found between male/females, and the power bases and job satisfaction. Teas (1983) used a modified version of the JDI (see "Scale Items" for details). The results from the modified JDI measure indicate that a salesperson's perceived role conflict ($p < .001$), consideration ($P < .001$), participation ($p < .001$), and selling experience ($p < .02$) are significantly related to job satisfaction. Role ambiguity was found not to be significantly related to job satisfaction. Cron and Slocum (1986) found that the business strategy of a firm has a significant effect on job satisfaction ($p < .01$). Age was found to be related to job satisfaction ($p < .02$) with older persons being more satisfied. The results indicate that significant main effects of career stages were observed for job satisfaction ($p < .01$). Statistically significant differences were reported for work ($p < .01$), supervision ($p < .01$), and promotion satisfaction ($p < .01$). Salespersons in the exploration stage were the least satisfied, whereas the salespersons in the established and maintenance stages were the most satisfied. The salespersons in the disengagement stage were slightly less satisfied than were salespersons in the established and maintenance stages. Apasu's (1987) study used only the satisfaction with pay measure of the JDI. The results indicate that salespersons with higher achievement-oriented values ($p < .05$), lower value congruence ($p < .01$), and higher dissatisfaction with pay ($p < .01$) perceive pay as an important reward.

COMMENTS:

Also see Teas and Horrell (1981). It appears they used the scale in a study pertaining to job satisfaction.

REFERENCES:

Apasu, Yao (1987), ''The Importance of Value Structures in the Perception of Rewards by Industrial Salespersons,'' *JAMS*, 15 (Spring), 1-10.

Busch, Paul (1980), ''The Sales Manager's Bases of Social Power and Influence Upon the Sales Force,'' *JM*, 44 (Summer), 91-101.

Bush, Ronald F. and Paul Busch (1982), ''The Relationship of Tenure and Age to Role Clarity and Its Consequences in the Industrial Salesforce,'' *JPSSM*, 2 (Fall/Winter), 17-23.

Cron, William L. and John W. Slocum, Jr. (1986), ''The Influence of Career Stages on Salespeople's Job Attitudes, Work Perceptions, and Performance,'' *JMR*, 23 (May), 119-29.

Smith, Patricia C., Lorne M. Kendall, and Charles L. Hulin (1969), *The Measurement of Satisfaction in Work and Retirement*. Chicago: Rand McNally & Company.

Teas, R. Kenneth (1983), ''Supervisory Behavior, Role Stress, and the Job Satisfaction of Industrial Salespeople,'' *JMR*, 20 (February), 84-91.

_____ and James F. Horrell (1981), ''Salespeople Satisfaction and Performance Feedback,'' *Industrial Marketing Management*, 10, 49-57.

SCALE ITEMS: JOB DESCRIPTION INDEX (JDI)

Subjects were instructed for each scale to put Y beside an item if the item described the particular aspect of his/her job (e.g., work, pay), N if the item did not describe that aspect, or ? if he/she could not decide. The response beside each item is the one scored in the ''satisfied'' direction for each scale.

Work	*Pay*	*Coworkers*
Y Fascinating	Y Income adequate for	Y Stimulating
N Routine	normal expenses	N Boring
Y Satisfying	Y Satisfactory profit	N Slow
N Boring	sharing	Y Ambitious
Y Good	N Barely live on income	N Stupid
Y Creative	N Bad	Y Responsible
N Hot	Y Income provides	Y Respected
Y Pleasant	luxuries	Y Fast
N Tiresome	N Insecure	Y Intelligent
Y Challenging	N Less that I deserve	N Easy to make enemies
N Endless	Y Highly paid	Y Useful
Y Gives sense of	N Underpaid	N Talk too much
accomplishment	N On your feet	Y Healthful
N Hard to meet quotas	N Frustrating	Y Smart
		N Lazy
		N Unpleasant
		N No privacy
		N Simple
		Y Active
		N Narrow interests
		Y Loyal

	Supervision		*Promotions*
Y	Asks my advice	Y	Good opportunity for advancement
N	Hard to please	N	Opportunity somewhat limited
N	Impolite	Y	Promotion on ability
Y	Praises good work	N	Dead-end job
Y	Tactful	Y	Good chance for promotion
Y	Influential	N	Unfair promotion policy
Y	Up-to-date	N	Infrequent promotions
N	Doesn't supervise	Y	Regular promotions enough
N	Quick tempered	Y	Fairly good chance for promotion
Y	Tells me where I stand		
N	Annoying		
N	Stubborn		
Y	Knows job well		
N	Bad		
Y	Intelligent		
Y	Leaves me on my own		
N	Lazy		
Y	Around when needed		

Teas (1983) modified the Satisfaction with Supervision measure and added a satisfaction with customers measure (see below). The coding procedure used was "yes" = 3, "could not decide" = 2, and "no" = 1.

Satisfaction with Supervision (b)	*Satisfaction with Customers*
1. Asks my advice	1. Stimulating
2. Unpleasant (r)	2. Hard to please (r)
3. Impolite (r)	3. Boring (r)
4. Praises good work	4. Smart
5. Tactful	5. Impolite (r)
6. Influential	6. Stubborn (r)
7. Up-to-date	7. Intelligent
8. Doesn't supervise enough (r)	8. Talks too much (r)
9. Quick-tempered (r)	9. Narrow interests (r)
10. Tells me where I Stand	10. Hard to meet (r)
11. Annoying (r)	11. Honest
12. Stubborn (r)	12. Quick-tempered (r)
13. Knows job well	13. Tactful
14. Bad (r)	14. Stupid (r)
15. Intelligent	15. Loyal
16. Leaves me on my own	16. Lazy (r)
17. Around when needed	17. Hard to please (r)
18. Lazy (r)	18. Annoying (r)

(a) Only the "satisfaction" portion of the JDI was included. (b) Only items 2, 3, 5, 7, 9, 11, 13, 14, 15, 17, and 18 were used in the modified "satisfaction with supervision" scale.

SCALE NAME: Job Image

SCALE DESCRIPTION:

A 12-item, five-point Likert-type scale measuring what direct salespeople perceive their significant others believe about their jobs.

SCALE ORIGIN:

To date, no reported turnover studies have examined the impact of public image on turnover, propensity to quit, or inactivity-proneness, though Mason (1965) noted that the unsatisfactory image of the selling occupation may reduce salespeople's job satisfaction. Hence, the scale appears to be unique to Wotruba (1990).

SAMPLES:

Four direct selling companies cooperated in supplying respondents for this study. The high turnover experienced by such firms is actually an advantage in this study. Names and addresses were provided of respondents who had begun selling for their company within the previous six months. A mail questionnaire was sent to 1600 direct salespeople from all sections of the United States, and **491** usable responses were obtained (a 30% response rate).

RELIABILITY:

An alpha of **.71** was reported for this scale.

VALIDITY:

The validity of the items was supported with two procedures. One involved a small-sample mail survey of direct salespeople, followed by telephone conversations with each to discuss these and other items in the instrument. The other was a review of the items by executives in the four participating companies. No empirical validation was reported.

ADMINISTRATION:

The scale appears to have been self-administered by respondents. Questionnaire items used to measure each variable differed markedly in format or wording. In addition, the sections of the questionnaire measuring each variable were separated from each other by other questionnaire items not related to this study. These actions were intended to help reduce shared-method variance and its biasing effect on mail questionnaire responses. A high score (after appropriate recoding) indicates a more positive perception.

MAJOR FINDINGS:

There is evidence that direct salespeople perceive that a negative public image of their job exists, with a possible resulting dampening of their job satisfaction and heightening of their inactivity-proneness in their direct selling job.

REFERENCES:

Mason, John L. (1965), ''The Low Prestige of Personal Selling,'' *JM*, 29 (4), 7-10.

Wotruba, Thomas R. (1990), ''The Relationship of Job Image, Performance, and Job Satisfaction to Inactivity-Proneness of Direct Salespeople,'' *JAMS*, 18 (2), 131-41.

SCALE ITEMS: JOB IMAGE

All or nearly all	Most but not all	Just about half	Some but not half	None or almost none
1	2	3	4	5

1. Direct salespeople are too aggressive and will try to sell me something I don't need or want.
2. Products sold by direct salespeople are better in quality than similar products found in retail stores. (r)
3. There is not enough government regulation of direct selling practices.
4. Buying from direct salespeople is much more convenient than buying in regular retail stores. (r)
5. Products sold by direct salespeople are overpriced.
6. Direct salespeople are more knowledgeable about their products than are retail store clerks. (r)
7. It's hard to find the salesperson you bought from when you have a question later or want to reorder.
8. If a product bought from a direct salesperson doesn't work, getting it fixed or replaced is very difficult.
9. Direct salespeople are more helpful than retail store clerks in serving customers' real needs. (r)
10. Some of the policies and practices of direct selling companies are of dubious legality.
11. Products ordered from direct salespeople take too long to be delivered.
12. A job in direct selling is better than most other job opportunities nowadays. (r)

SCALE NAME: Job Performance

SCALE DESCRIPTION:

A 13-item, seven-point summated ratings scale ranging from poor to excellent was used to assess the store managers' job performance in conjunction with the formal performance review process conducted by their supervisors.

SCALE ORIGIN:

A perceptual measure of this type is consistent with the work of Futrell and Parasuraman (1984) and Spencer and Steers (1981) and is generally considered an appropriate measure for managerial positions.

SAMPLES:

A questionnaire was mailed to 294 store managers employed by a national retail chain. A total of **213** usable questionnaires were returned, yielding a highly acceptable 72.4% response rate.

RELIABILITY:

The reliability coefficient alpha for the performance measure was **.92**.

VALIDITY:

A factor analysis of these items produced a single meaningful factor, accounting for 38% of the variation.

ADMINISTRATION:

The scale was self-administered by respondents in a mail survey format.

MAJOR FINDINGS:

The purpose of the study by Lucas, Babakus, and Ingram was to advance the understanding of the relationship between turnover and two of its critical antecedents (Job Satisfaction and Job Performance). The perspective taken here is that studying turnover by considering either Job Satisfaction or Job Performance alone tells an incomplete story.

REFERENCES:

Futrell, C. and A. Parasuraman (1984), "The Relationship of Satisfaction and Performance to Salesforce Turnover," *JM*, 48 (Fall), 33-40.

Lucas, George H. Jr., Emin Babakus, and Thomas N. Ingram (1990), "An Empirical Test of the Job Satisfaction—Turnover Relationship: Assessing the Role of Job Performance for Retail Managers," *JAMS*, 18 (Summer), 199-208.

Spencer, D. and R. Steers (1981), ''Performance as a Moderator of the Job Satisfaction-Turnover Relationship,'' *Journal of Applied Psychology*, 66, 511-14.

SCALE ITEMS: JOB PERFORMANCE

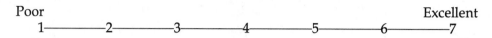

Poor   Excellent

1————2————3————4————5————6————7

1. Manager is a good Salesman.
2. The manager takes charge of the sale, defines the customer's specific wants and needs, and gets him seated.
3. The manager is knowledgeable about (our) products and store program, and translates the product features and our store program into benefits for the consumer.
4. Manager is a self-starter; actively hustles the business outside the store.
5. Customers are greeted politely as they enter the store.
6. Dramatically uses (our) Computerized Fitter and explains importance of fit.
7. Manager makes an effort to try on additional items.
8. Asks customers to send friends to the store.
9. Customer Record system is used properly and dramatically on repeat customers.
10. Has a good, aggressive, findings program—discusses importance and makes sincere effort to sell.
11. Clean store and neatly attired personnel.
12. Has a consistent 13-week advertising program.
13. Knows basic store record-keeping.

SCALE NAME: Job Satisfaction

SCALE DESCRIPTION:

An 18-item, five-point Likert-type scale ranging from "Strongly agree" to "Strongly disagree" purporting to measure job satisfaction.

SCALE ORIGIN:

The scale was originally developed by Brayfield and Rothe (1951) to create an index of job satisfaction. Oliver and Brief (1983) used the same scale in their study to test that goal (sales) commitment is positively related to job satisfaction.

SAMPLES:

Oliver and Brief (1983) collected the data from 114 sales managers employed in eight outlets of a midwestern multiline retailer. After one follow-up, 105 responses (92%) were received. Because the focus of study was on organizationally recognized goals, 31 subjects whose goals were self-assigned or had not been determined were eliminated. The final sample consisted of **74** sales managers, of which 38 had goals assigned to them and 36 participated in a goal-setting process.

RELIABILITY:

A reliability estimate of **.88** was obtained in this study.

VALIDITY:

No examination of scale validity was reported.

ADMINISTRATION:

The scale was self-administered. No scoring was reported, but if the Likert scoring weights for each item ranged from 1 to 5, then the possible total scores could range from 18 to 90 with the undecided point at 54.

MAJOR FINDINGS:

Oliver and Brief (1983) found that job satisfaction is positive and significantly related to goal commitment.

REFERENCES:

Brayfield, A.H. and H.F. Rothe (1951), "An Index of Job Satisfaction," *Journal of Applied Psychology*, 35 (October), 307-11.

Oliver Richard L. and Arthur P. Brief (1983), "Sales Managers' Goal Commitment Correlates," *JPSSM* , 3 (May), 11-17.

SCALE ITEMS: JOB SATISFACTION

Strongly agree	Agree	Undecided	Disagree	Strongly disagree
1	2	3	4	5

1. My job is like a hobby to me.
2. My job is usually interesting enough to keep me from getting bored.
3. It seems that my friends are more interested in their jobs.
4. I consider my job rather unpleasant.
5. I enjoy my work more than my leisure time.
6. I am often bored with my job.
7. I feel fairly well satisfied with my present job.
8. Most of the time I have to force myself to go to work.
9. I am satisfied with my job for the time being.
10. I feel that my job is no more interesting than others I could get.
11. I definitely dislike my work.
12. I feel that I am happier in my work than most other people.
13. Most days I am enthusiastic about my work.
14. Each day of work seems like it will never end.
15. I like my job better than the average worker does.
16. My job is pretty uninteresting.
17. I find real enjoyment in my work.
18. I am disappointed that I ever took this job.

SCALE NAME: Job Satisfaction

SCALE DESCRIPTION:

A nine-item, five-point Likert-type scale ranging from "Strongly disagree" to "Strongly agree" purporting to assess respondents' satisfaction with various aspects of their jobs.

SCALE ORIGIN:

The scale was developed by Johnson (1955). Lucas, Babakus, and Ingram modified the scale, which originally allowed for only a "yes," "no," or "uncertain" response.

SAMPLES:

A questionnaire was mailed to 294 store managers employed by a national retail chain. A total of **213** usable questionnaires were returned, yielding a highly acceptable 72.4% response rate.

RELIABILITY:

An alpha coefficient of **.79** was obtained for this measure.

VALIDITY:

No specific examination of scale validity was reported.

ADMINISTRATION:

The scale was self-administered by respondents in a mail survey format. High scores indicate that store managers find a lot of job satisfaction, whereas low scores suggest that they do not.

MAJOR FINDINGS:

The purpose of the study by Lucas, Babakus, and Ingram was to advance the understanding of the relationship between turnover and two of its critical antecedents (job satisfaction and job performance). The perspective taken here is that studying turnover by considering either job satisfaction or job performance alone tells an incomplete story.

COMMENTS:

The scale constituted the global satisfaction measure for the study. A global satisfaction measure tends to combine very diverse aspects of the job into a single construct fraught with interpretation difficulties.

#390 *Job Satisfaction*

REFERENCES:

Johnson, G. (1955), "An Instrument for the Measurement of Job Satisfaction," *Personnel Psychology*, 8, 27-37.

Lucas, George H., Jr., Emin Babakus, and Thomas N. Ingram (1990), "An Empirical Test of the Job Satisfaction-Turnover Relationship: Assessing the Role of Job Performance for Retail Managers," *JAMS*, 18 (Summer), 199-208.

SCALE ITEMS: JOB SATISFACTION

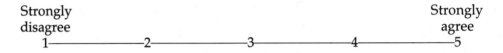

Strongly disagree — 1————2————3————4————5 — Strongly agree

Extrinsic Job Satisfaction (EJS)
1. Given the work I do, I feel that I am not paid fairly.(r)
2. I am relatively well rewarded financially for my work.
3. I am satisfied with the amount of my pay for being a retail store manager.
4. I am satisfied with my working conditions.
5. The benefits (insurance, medical, etc.) provided by my company are not satisfactory.

Intrinsic Job Satisfaction (IJS)
1. I feel a sense of pride and accomplishment as a result of the type of work I do.
2. I very much like the type of work I am doing.
3. My job performance improves from year to year.
4. My job offers me a career path that I am pleased with.

SCALE NAME: Marketing Norms Scale—General Honesty and Integrity

SCALE DESCRIPTION:

A four-item, five-point Likert-like summated ratings scale measuring the marketing-related norms of marketing practitioners as they relate to general honesty, fairness, and integrity.

SCALE ORIGIN:

The scale appears to be original to Vitell, Rallapalli, and Singhapakdi (1993); however, the items were derived from the code of ethics of the American Marketing Association (AMA).

SAMPLES:

A random sample of 2000 individuals was drawn from a mailing list of the American Marketing Association (AMA). Of the 2000 questionnaires mailed, 542 individuals responded for a response rate of 27.1%. Of these responses, **508** were deemed usable. Of these, 52.2% were men, 61.3% were married, and 37.8% were between the ages of 30 and 39 years. More than half of the respondents (63.6%) had at least some graduate education, and 64% reported an annual income of $40,000 or more.

RELIABILITY:

An alpha of **.67** was reported for the scale.

VALIDITY:

To test the validity of the dimensions of the marketing norms scale, each scale was correlated with the two dimensions of the Ethics Position Questionnaire (EPQ), idealism and relativism. The correlations represent a test of the convergent as well as discriminant validity of the norms scale. The general honesty and integrity scale was positively correlated with idealism (.34) and negatively correlated with relativism (−.20). This shows that the scale represents measures of marketing-related norms and not teleological considerations.

ADMINISTRATION:

The scale was a self-administered paper-and-pencil measure used as part of a larger mail survey questionnaire. High scores indicate that respondents strongly agree to general honesty and integrity norms, whereas low scores indicate that they do not.

MAJOR FINDINGS:

The results of the study by Vitell, Rallapalli, and Singhapakdi (1993) indicate that the general honesty and integrity norms are strongly accepted by respondents.

REFERENCES:

American Marketing Association (1986), ''AMA Again Seeks Input on Proposed Code Ethics,'' *Marketing News*, 18 (December 5), 6.

Vitell, Scott J., Kumar C. Rallapalli, and Anusorm Singhapakdi (1993), ''Marketing Norms: The Influence of Personal Moral Philosophies and Organizational Ethical Culture,'' *JAMS* , 21 (Fall), 331-38.

SCALE ITEMS: MARKETING NORMS SCALE—GENERAL HONESTY AND INTEGRITY

```
Strongly                                                    Strongly
disagree                                                       agree
  1——————————2——————————3——————————4——————————5
```

1. One should always adhere to all applicable laws and regulations.
2. One should always accurately represent one's education, training and experience.
3. One must always be honest in serving consumers, clients, employees, suppliers, distributors, and public.
4. One should not knowingly participate in a conflict of interest without prior notice to all parties involved.

SCALE NAME: Marketing Norms Scale—Information and Contract Norms

SCALE DESCRIPTION:

A six-item, five-point Likert-like summated ratings scale measuring the marketing-related norms of marketing practitioners as they relate to the honest disclosure of marketing-related information and contractual agreements.

SCALE ORIGIN:

The scale appears to be original to Vitell, Rallapalli, and Singhapakdi (1993); however, the items were derived from the code of ethics of the American Marketing Association (AMA).

SAMPLES:

A random sample of 2000 individuals was drawn from a mailing list of the American Marketing Association (AMA). Of the 2000 questionnaires mailed, 542 individuals responded for a response rate of 27.1%. Of these responses, **508** were deemed usable. Of these, 52.2% were men, 61.3% were married, and 37.8% were between the ages of 30 and 39 years. More than half of the respondents (63.6%) had at least some graduate education, and 64% reported an annual income of $40,000 or more.

RELIABILITY:

An alpha of **.81** was reported for the scale.

VALIDITY:

To test the validity of the dimensions of the marketing norms scale, each scale was correlated with the two dimensions of the Ethics Position Questionnaire (EPQ), idealism and relativism. The correlations represent a test of the convergent as well as discriminant validity of the norms scale. The information and contract scale was positively correlated with idealism (.43) and negatively correlated with relativism (-.07). This shows that the scale represents measures of marketing-related norms and not teleological considerations.

ADMINISTRATION:

The scale was a self-administered paper-and-pencil measure used as part of a larger mail survey questionnaire. High scores indicate that respondents strongly agree to information and contractual norms, whereas low scores indicate that they do not.

MAJOR FINDINGS:

The results of the study by Vitell, Rallapalli, and Singhapakdi (1993) indicate that the information and contract norms are generally accepted to a larger degree than the price and distribution norms.

REFERENCES:

American Marketing Association (1986), ''AMA Again Seeks Input on Proposed Code Ethics,'' *Marketing News*, 18 (December 5), 6.

Vitell, Scott J., Kumar C. Rallapalli, and Anusorm Singhapakdi (1993), ''Marketing Norms: The Influence of Personal Moral Philosophies and Organizational Ethical Culture,'' *JAMS* , 21 (Fall), 331-38.

SCALE ITEMS: MARKETING NORMS SCALE—INFORMATION AND CONTRACT NORMS

```
Strongly                                                    Strongly
disagree                                                      agree
    1——————————2——————————3——————————4——————————5
```

1. Information regarding all substantial risks associated with product or service usage should be disclosed.
2. Any product component substitution that might materially change the product or impact on the buyer's purchase decision should be disclosed.
3. Outside clients and suppliers should be treated fairly.
4. Confidentiality and anonymity in professional relationships should be maintained with regard to privileged information.
5. Obligations and responsibilities in contracts and mutual agreements should be met in a timely manner.
6. The practice and promotion of a professional code of ethics must be actively supported.

SCALE NAME: Marketing Norms Scale—Obligation and Disclosure Norms

SCALE DESCRIPTION:

A four-item, five-point Likert-like summated ratings scale measuring the marketing-related norms of marketing practitioners as they relate to one's ethical obligations and the disclosure of pertinent information.

SCALE ORIGIN:

The scale appears to be original to Vitell, Rallapalli, and Singhapakdi (1993); however, the items were derived from the code of ethics of the American Marketing Association (AMA).

SAMPLES:

A random sample of 2000 individuals was drawn from a mailing list of the American Marketing Association (AMA). Of the 2000 questionnaires mailed, 542 individuals responded for a response rate of 27.1%. Of these responses, **508** were deemed usable. Of these, 52.2% were men, 61.3% were married, and 37.8% were between the ages of 30 and 39 years. More than half of the respondents (63.6%) had at least some graduate education, and 64% reported an annual income of $40,000 or more.

RELIABILITY:

An alpha of **.70** was reported for the scale.

VALIDITY:

To test the validity of the dimensions of the marketing norms scale, each scale was correlated with the two dimensions of the Ethics Position Questionnaire (EPQ), idealism and relativism. The correlations represent a test of the convergent as well as discriminant validity of the norms scale. The obligation and disclosure scale was positively correlated with idealism (.21) and negatively correlated with relativism (-.13). This shows that the scale represents measures of marketing-related norms and not teleological considerations.

ADMINISTRATION:

The scale was a self-administered paper-and-pencil measure used as part of a larger mail survey questionnaire. High scores indicate that respondents strongly agree to obligation and disclosure norms, whereas low scores indicate that they do not.

MAJOR FINDINGS:

The results of the study by Vitell, Rallapalli, and Singhapakdi (1993) indicate that the obligation and disclosure norms are almost overwhelmingly agreed upon by the respondents.

REFERENCES:

American Marketing Association (1986), ''AMA Again Seeks Input on Proposed Code Ethics,'' *Marketing News*, 18 (December 5), 6.

Vitell, Scott J., Kumar C. Rallapalli, and Anusorm Singhapakdi (1993). ''Marketing Norms: The Influence of Personal Moral Philosophies and Organizational Ethical Culture,'' *JAMS*, 21 (Fall), 331-38.

SCALE ITEMS: MARKETING NORMS SCALE—OBLIGATION AND DISCLOSURE NORMS

Strongly   Strongly
disagree   agree
1————————2————————3————————4————————5

1. One should discharge one's obligations, financial and otherwise, in good faith.
2. The full price associated with any purchase should be disclosed.
3. Selling or fund raising under the guise of conducting research should be avoided.
4. Research integrity should be maintained by avoiding the misrepresentation and omission of pertinent research data.

SCALE NAME: Marketing Norms Scale—Price and Distribution Norms

SCALE DESCRIPTION:

> A six-item, five-point Likert-like summated ratings scale measuring the marketing-related norms of marketing practitioners as they relate to pricing and distribution decisions.

SCALE ORIGIN:

> The scale appears to be original to Vitell, Rallapalli, and Singhapakdi (1993); however, the items were derived from the code of ethics of the American Marketing Association (AMA).

SAMPLES:

> A random sample of 2000 individuals was drawn from a mailing list of the American Marketing Association (AMA). Of the 2000 questionnaires mailed, 542 individuals responded for a response rate of 27.1%. Of these responses, **508** were deemed usable. Of these, 52.2% were men, 61.3% were married, and 37.8% were between the ages of 30 and 39 years. More than half of the respondents (63.6%) had at least some graduate education, and 64% reported an annual income of $40,000 or more.

RELIABILITY:

> An alpha of **.82** was reported for the scale.

VALIDITY:

> To test the validity of the dimensions of the marketing norms scale, each scale was correlated with the two dimensions of the Ethics Position Questionnaire (EPQ), idealism and relativism. The correlations represent a test of the convergent as well as discriminant validity of the norms scale. The price and distribution scale was positively correlated with idealism (.42) and negatively correlated with relativism (−.12). This shows that the scale represents measures of marketing-related norms and not teleological considerations.

ADMINISTRATION:

> The scale was a self-administered paper-and-pencil measure used as part of a larger mail survey questionnaire. High scores indicate that respondents strongly agree to pricing and distribution norms, whereas low scores indicate that they do not.

MAJOR FINDINGS:

> The results of the study by Vitell, Rallapalli, and Singhapakdi (1993) indicate that the price and distribution norms are generally accepted, but to a lessor degree than for the other factors.

REFERENCES:

American Marketing Association (1986), ''AMA Again Seeks Input on Proposed Code Ethics,'' *Marketing News,* 18 (December 5), 6.

Vitell, Scott J., Kumar C. Rallapalli, and Anusorm Singhapakdi (1993), ''Marketing Norms: The Influence of Personal Moral Philosophies and Organizational Ethical Culture,'' *JAMS,* 21 (Fall), 331-38.

SCALE ITEMS: MARKETING NORMS SCALE—PRICE AND DISTRIBUTION NORMS

Strongly   Strongly

disagree   agree

1————————2————————3————————4————————5

1. All extra-cost added features should be identified.
2. One should not manipulate the availability of a product for the purpose of exploitation.
3. Coercion should not be used within the marketing channel.
4. Undue influence should not be exerted over the resellers' choice to handle a product.
5. One should not engage in price fixing.
6. Predatory pricing should not be practiced.

SCALE NAME: Marketing Norms Scale—Product and Promotion Norms

SCALE DESCRIPTION:

A five-item, five-point Likert-like summated ratings scale measuring the marketing-related norms of marketing practitioners as they relate to product design, advertising, and sales promotion.

SCALE ORIGIN:

The scale appears to be original to Vitell, Rallapalli, and Singhapakdi (1993); however, the items were derived from the code of ethics of the American Marketing Association (AMA).

SAMPLES:

A random sample of 2000 individuals was drawn from a mailing list of the American Marketing Association (AMA). Of the 2000 questionnaires mailed, 542 individuals responded for a response rate of 27.1%. Of these responses, **508** were deemed usable. Of these, 52.2% were men, 61.3% were married, and 37.8% were between the ages of 30 and 39. More than half of the respondents (63.6%) had at least some graduate education, and 64% reported an annual income of $40,000 or more.

RELIABILITY:

An alpha of **.87** was reported for the scale.

VALIDITY:

To test the validity of the dimensions of the marketing norms scale, each scale was correlated with the two dimensions of the Ethics Position Questionnaire (EPQ), idealism and relativism. The correlations represent a test of the convergent as well as discriminant validity of the norms scale. The product and promotion scale was positively correlated with idealism (.24) and negatively correlated with relativism (−.12). This shows that the scale represents measures of marketing-related norms and not teleological considerations.

ADMINISTRATION:

The scale was a self-administered paper-and-pencil measure used as part of a larger mail survey questionnaire. High scores indicate that respondents strongly agree to product and promotion norms, whereas low scores indicate that they do not.

MAJOR FINDINGS:

The results of the study by Vitell, Rallapalli, and Singhapakdi (1993) indicate that the product and promotion norms are generally accepted to a larger degree than any of the other factors.

REFERENCES:

American Marketing Association (1986), ''AMA Again Seeks Input on Proposed Code Ethics,'' *Marketing News*, 18 (December 5), 6.

Vitell, Scott J., Kumar C. Rallapalli, and Anusorm Singhapakdi (1993), ''Marketing Norms: The Influence of Personal Moral Philosophies and Organizational Ethical Culture,'' *JAMS*, 21 (Fall), 331-38.

SCALE ITEMS: MARKETING NORMS SCALE—PRODUCT AND PROMOTION NORMS

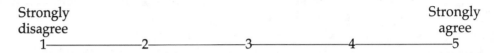

Strongly disagree 1————————2————————3————————4————————5 Strongly agree

1. Products and services offered should be safe and fit for their intended uses.
2. Communications about products and services offered should not be deceptive.
3. False and misleading advertising should be avoided.
4. High pressure manipulations or misleading sales tactics should be avoided.
5. Sales promotions that use deception or manipulation should be avoided.

SCALE NAME: Motivation to Work (Generalized)

SCALE DESCRIPTION:

An eight-item, five-point Likert-type summated ratings scale measuring an employee's enjoyment of his/her work and motivation to engage in it rather than other activities. It is referred to by Duncan (1969) as Commitment to Work, and it is called Achievement Motivation by Bagozzi (1980), Hafer and Sirgy (1983) and Hart, Moncrief, and Parasuraman (1989).

SCALE ORIGIN:

The items composing the scale apparently were used first by Westoff and colleagues (1961, pp. 385, 386). However, the items were not used together as a summated scale until the research of Duncan (1969). The latter reports a reliability (KR-20) of .7755 on the basis of a sample of 941 men. An extended discussion of the scale's validity is provided.

SAMPLES:

The analysis made by Bagozzi (1980) was based on **122** completed questionnaires from industrial salespeople assigned to exclusive geographic territories. Hart, Moncrief, and Parasuraman (1989) mailed questionnaires to 149 salespeople who worked for 25 independent brokers representing a major food producer. After two follow-up mailings, usable responses were received from **84** sales representatives. Hafer and Sirgy (1983) collected the data from 350 insurance salespeople who were participating in company's annual meeting at the home office. A total of **336** usable questionnaires were obtained, of which 308 were from male participants.

RELIABILITY:

Alphas of **.60** and **.74** were reported for the scale by Bagozzi (1980) and Hart, Moncreif, and Parasuraman (1989). Hafer and Sirgy (1983) reported an alpha of .231, indicating low item interconsistency. However, on deleting items 3 and 8, an alpha of **.6421** was obtained.

VALIDITY:

No specific examinations of validity were conducted by Bagozzi (1980), Hafer and Sirgy (1983), or Hart, Moncrief, and Parasuraman (1989).

ADMINISTRATION:

The scale was self-administered by respondents in the form of a mail survey questionnaire (Hart, Moncrief, and Parasuraman 1989). The setting of the scale's administration was not specified by Bagozzi (1980). High scores on the scale indicate that employees have high motivation toward their work, whereas low scores suggest that they derive little pleasure from their work and would rather be doing other things. Scores, in the case of Hafer and Sirgy (1983) with all eight items, ranged from 14 to 32 with a mean of 27.289, median of 17.457, mode of 27.0, and a standard deviation of 3.318. After deleting items 3 and 8, scores ranged from 9.0 to 30.0 with a mean of 23.289, median of 23.597, mode of 25.0, and standard deviation of 3.736.

MAJOR FINDINGS:

Bagozzi (1980) investigated the relationship between performance and satisfaction for an industrial sales force using causal modeling. The results indicated that job satisfaction was influenced to a significant degree by motivation to work. The purpose of the study by Hart, Moncrief, and Parasuraman (1989) was to investigate goal theory as it relates to sales contests. When used as a moderator variable, the results provided evidence that for those with low work motivation, goal difficulty was related positively to work effort. The objective of Hafer and Sirgy (1983) was to test the hypothesis that "personality traits reflective of personal growth are related to indicators of professional growth for salespeople." They found that achievement motivation measure as an indicator of professional growth was correlated to indicators of personal growth (self-esteem and inner/other-directedness).

COMMENTS:

See also Joreskog and Sorbom (1982) for a reanalysis of the Bagozzi (1980) data.

REFERENCES:

Bagozzi, Richard P. (1980), "Performance and Satisfaction in an Industrial Salesforce: An Examination of Their Antecedents and Simultaneity," *JM*, 44 (Spring), 65-77.

Duncan, Otis D. (1969), "Contingencies in Constructing Causal Models," in *Sociological Methodology*, Edgar F. Borgatta and George W. Bohrnstedt, eds. San Francisco: Jossey-Bass, Inc.

Hafer, John (1986), "An Empirical Investigation of the Salesperson's Career Stage Perspective," *JPSSM*, 6 (November), 1-7 .

_____ and Joseph M. Sirgy (1983), "Professional Growth Versus Personal Growth of Salespeople: A General System Model," *JPSSM*, 3 (November), 22-30.

Hart, Sandra Hile, William C. Moncrief, and A. Parasuraman (1989), "An Empirical Investigation of Salespeople's Performance, Effort and Selling Method During a Sales Contest," *JAMS*, 17 (Winter), 29-39.

Joreskog, Karl G. and Dag Sorbom (1982), "Recent Developments in Structural Equation Modeling," *JMR*, 19 (November), 404-16.

Westoff, Charles F., Robert G. Potter, Jr., Philip C. Sagi, and Elliot G. Mishler (1961), *Family Growth in Metropolitan America*. Princeton, NJ: Princeton University Press.

SCALE ITEMS: MOTIVATION TO WORK (GENERALIZED)

Sales people differ in their attitude and preferences toward work, their job, leisure activities, and so on. So that I may learn more about how salespeople feel about things, please indicate for each of the following questions if you strongly agree, agree, are undecided, disagree, or strongly disagree. Since there are really no correct or wrong answers and since some salespeople will agree with a particular question while others may disagree with it, please answer with the first response that comes to mind.

Strongly agree	Agree	Undecided	Disagree	Strongly disagree
1—————	—2————	——3————	—4————	—5

1. I would much rather relax around the house all day than go to work. (r)
2. My work is more satisfying to me than the time I spend around the house.
3. If I inherited so much money that I didn't have to work, I would still continue to work at the same thing I am doing now.
4. Some of my main interests and pleasures in life are connected with my work.
5. I have sometimes regretted going into the kind of work I am now in. (r)
6. The work I do is one of the most satisfying parts of my life.
7. I enjoy my spare-time activities much more than my work. (r)
8. To me my work is just a way of making money. (r)

SCALE NAME: Organizational Structure and Climate—Concentration of Authority (CONT)

SCALE DESCRIPTION:

A two-item, six-point Likert-like summated ratings scale measuring the concentration of authority and the ability to act without obtaining prior approval.

SCALE ORIGIN:

Song and Parry (1993) indicated that they used items selected by Gupta (1984) in their study. Gupta, in turn, selected the items from scales developed by Aiken and Hage (1968).

SAMPLES:

Song and Parry (1993) identified 801 Japanese companies from trade association mailing lists and published sources that satisfied their criteria that the companies are (1) publicly held and traded on the stock exchange, (2) in a high-tech industry, (3) domiciled in Japan and managed by Japanese nationals, and (4) devoted to spending at least 2% of their annual sales on R&D expenditures. Of the 801 firms, a questionnaire was mailed to 411 firms, of which **264** usable responses were received, indicating a response rate of 64%.

RELIABILITY:

An alpha of **.70** was reported for the scale.

VALIDITY:

No specific examination of scale validity was reported.

ADMINISTRATION:

The scale was self-administered in a mail-survey type format. High scores on the scale indicate that respondents feel that there is strong concentration of authority, whereas low scores indicate that they do not.

MAJOR FINDINGS:

The results of the study on Japanese firms by Song and Parry (1993) indicate that higher levels of centralization were associated with higher levels of achieved integration and information-sharing. This effect differs from that reported in studies of U.S. firms and may reflect the fact that, in Japan, firms with more decentralized decision processes tend to be older and more mature than firms with more centralized decision processes (Clark 1979).

REFERENCES:

Aiken, Michael and Jerald Hage (1968), "Organizational Interdependence and Intraorganizational Structure," *American Sociological Review*, 33 (December), 912-31.

Clark, Rodney (1979), *The Japanese Company*. New Haven, CT: Yale University Press.

Gupta, Ashok K. (1984), "A Study of the R&D/Marketing Interface and Innovation Success in High Technology Firms," doctoral dissertation, Syracuse University.

Song, X. Michael and Mark E. Parry (1993), "R&D Marketing Integration in Japanese High-Technology Firms: Hypothesis and Empirical Evidence," *JAMS*, 21 (Spring), 125-33.

SCALE ITEMS: ORGANIZATIONAL STRUCTURE AND CLIMATE— CONCENTRATION OF AUTHORITY (CONT)

Strongly
disagree

Strongly
agree

1————2————3————4————5————6

1. In this organization, very few actions are taken without the approval of a supervisor.
2. Even small matters on the job have to be referred to someone higher up for a final answer.

SCALE NAME: Organizational Structure and Climate—Encouragement of Risk Taking (RISK)

SCALE DESCRIPTION:

A three-item, six-point Likert-like summated ratings scale measuring management's preference for high-risk projects and reaction to new product failure.

SCALE ORIGIN:

Song and Parry (1993) indicated that they used items selected by Gupta (1984), based partly on the work of Khandwalla (1974).

SAMPLES:

Song and Parry identified 801 Japanese companies from trade association mailing lists and published sources that satisfied their criteria that the companies are (1) publicly held and traded on the stock exchange, (2) in a high-tech industry, (3) domiciled in Japan and managed by Japanese nationals, and (4) devoted to spending at least 2% of their annual sales to R&D expenditures. Of the 801 firms, a questionnaire was mailed to 411 firms, of which **264** usable responses were received, indicating a response rate of 64%.

RELIABILITY:

An alpha of **.75** was reported for the scale.

VALIDITY:

No specific examination of scale validity was reported.

ADMINISTRATION:

The scale was self-administered in a mail-survey type format. High scores on the scale indicate that respondents feel that management strongly supports risk-taking, whereas low scores indicate that they do not.

MAJOR FINDINGS:

The results of the study on Japanese firms by Song and Parry (1993) indicate that risk tolerance affected integration in the budgeting process, but did not affect information-sharing or integration in the early stages of the new product development process. This suggests that case-specific accounts of the relationship between a high-risk orientation and the success of interdisciplinary teams (Takeuchi and Nonaka 1986) may not be representative of the majority of Japanese firms.

REFERENCES:

Gupta, Ashok K. (1984), ''A Study of the R&D/Marketing Interface and Innovation Success in High Technology Firms,'' doctoral dissertation, Syracuse University.

Khandwalla, Prandip N. (1974), *The Design of Organizations.* New York: Harcourt Brace Jovanovich.

Song, X. Michael and Mark E. Parry (1993), ''R&D Marketing Integration in Japanese High-Technology Firms: Hypothesis and Empirical Evidence,'' *JAMS*, 21 (Spring), 125-33.

Takeuchi, Hirotaka and Ikujiro Nonaka (1986), ''The New Product Development Game,'' *Harvard Business Review*, 64 (January), 137-46.

**SCALE ITEMS: ORGANIZATIONAL STRUCTURE AND CLIMATE—
ENCOURAGEMENT OF RISK TAKING (RISK)**

```
Strongly                                                        Strongly
disagree                                                          agree
  1————————2————————3————————4————————5————————6
```

1. The management provides enough incentives to work on new ideas despite the uncertainty of their outcomes.
2. The management has a strong desire for high-risk, high-return investments.
3. If you fail in the process of creating something new, management encourages you to keep trying. Initial failures don't reflect on your competence.

SCALE NAME: Organizational Structure and Climate—Formalization (FORM)

SCALE DESCRIPTION:

A three-item, six-point Likert-like summated ratings scale measuring the importance of written documentation in the specification of responsibility and accountability and in the evaluation of performance.

SCALE ORIGIN:

Song and Parry (1993) indicated that they used items selected by Gupta (1984) in their study. Gupta, in turn, selected the items from scales developed by House and Rizzo (1972).

SAMPLES:

Song and Parry identified 801 Japanese companies from trade association mailing lists and published sources that satisfied their criteria that the companies are (1) publicly held and traded on the stock exchange, (2) in a high-tech industry, (3) domiciled in Japan and managed by Japanese nationals, and (4) devoted to spending at least 2% of their annual sales to R&D expenditures. Of the 801 firms, a questionnaire was mailed to 411 firms, of which **264** usable responses were received, indicating a response rate of 64%.

RELIABILITY:

An alpha of **.80** was reported for the scale.

VALIDITY:

No specific examination of scale validity was reported.

ADMINISTRATION:

The scale was self-administered in a mail-survey type format. High scores on the scale indicate that respondents feel employees strongly agree on the importance of written documentation, whereas low scores indicate that they did not.

MAJOR FINDINGS:

The results of Song and Parry (1993) indicate that the negative effects of formalization (the attenuation of information flows) outweighed the positive effects (reductions in role ambiguity). The study also failed to confirm the reasoning of Zaltman, Duncan, and Holbeck (1973), who suggested that the negative effects of formalization (relative to the positive effects) may be greatest in the early stages of the new product development process.

REFERENCES:

Gupta, Ashok K. (1984), ''A Study of the R&D/Marketing Interface and Innovation Success in High Technology Firms,'' doctoral dissertation, Syracuse University.

House, Robert and John R. Rizzo (1972), ''Toward the Measurement of Organizational Practices: Scale Development and Validation,'' *Journal of Applied Psychology*, 56 (October), 388-96.

Song, X. Michael and Mark E. Parry (1993), ''R&D Marketing Integration in Japanese High-Technology Firms: Hypothesis and Empirical Evidence,'' *JAMS*, 21 (Spring), 125-33.

Zaltman, Gerald, Robert Duncan, and Jonny Holbeck (1973), *Innovations and Organizations*. New York, John Wiley & Sons.

SCALE ITEMS: ORGANIZATIONAL STRUCTURE AND CLIMATE— FORMALIZATION (FORM)

1. Performance appraisals in our organization are based on written performance standards.
2. Duties, authority, and accountability of personnel are documented in policies, procedures, or job descriptions.
3. Written procedures and guidelines are available for most of the work situations.

SCALE NAME: Organizational Structure and Climate—Participation in Decision Making (PART)

SCALE DESCRIPTION:

A four-item, six-point Likert-like summated ratings scale measuring the level of employee participation in decisions to introduce, modify, and delete products.

SCALE ORIGIN:

Song and Parry (1993) indicated that they used items selected by Gupta (1984) in their study. Gupta, in turn, selected the items from scales developed by Aiken and Hage (1968).

SAMPLES:

Song and Parry (1993) identified 801 Japanese companies from trade association mailing lists and published sources that satisfied their criteria that the companies are (1) publicly held and traded on the stock exchange, (2) in a high-tech industry, (3) domiciled in Japan and managed by Japanese nationals, and (4) devoted to spending at least 2% of their annual sales to R&D expenditures. Of the 801 firms, a questionnaire was mailed to 411 firms, of which **264** usable responses were received, indicating a response rate of 64%.

RELIABILITY:

An alpha of **.85** was reported for the scale.

VALIDITY:

No specific examination of scale validity was reported.

ADMINISTRATION:

The scale was self-administered in a mail-survey type format. High scores on the scale indicate that respondents feel employees strongly participated in decisions regarding the product, whereas low scores indicate that they did not.

MAJOR FINDINGS:

The results of the study on Japanese firms by Song and Parry (1993) indicate that high levels of participative decision-making are associated with high levels of R&D-marketing integration. Also, the perceived degree of participative decision making was positively related to (1) perceptions of integration in the early stages of product development, and (2) perceptions of the level of information-sharing between R&D and marketing. These results are consistent with those reported by Gupta, Raj, and Wilemon (1987) in their study of U.S. firms.

REFERENCES:

Aiken, Michael and Jerald Hage (1968), "Organizational Interdependence and Intraorganizational Structure," *American Sociological Review*, 33 (December), 912-31.

Gupta, Ashok K. (1984), "A Study of the R&D/Marketing Interface and Innovation Success in High Technology Firms," doctoral dissertation, Syracuse University.

_____, S. P. Raj, and David Wilemon (1986), "A Model for Studying R&D-Marketing Interface in the Product Innovation Process," *Journal of Marketing*, 50 (April), 7-17.

Song, X. Michael and Mark E. Parry (1993), "R&D Marketing Integration in Japanese High-Technology Firms: Hypothesis and Empirical Evidence," *JAMS*, 21 (Spring), 125-33.

SCALE ITEMS: ORGANIZATIONAL STRUCTURE AND CLIMATE— PARTICIPATION IN DECISION MAKING (PART)

Please indicate your perception of the degree of participation of various levels of employees in your department:

No participation 1————2————3————4————5————6 Strong participation

1. Decisions to develop new products.
2. Decisions to adopt a new idea or program.
3. Decisions to modify an existing product.
4. Decisions to delete existing products.

SCALE NAME: Organizational Structure and Climate—Quality of R&D-Marketing Relations (RELATE)

SCALE DESCRIPTION:

A three-item, six-point Likert-like summated ratings scale measuring the nature of R&D-marketing interactions, the method of conflict resolution, and the extent to which R&D and marketing are both involved early in the new product development process.

SCALE ORIGIN:

Song and Parry (1993) indicated that they used items selected by Gupta (1984) in their study. Gupta, in turn, used the research of Souder and colleagues (1977) to construct the scales.

SAMPLES:

Song and Parry (1993) identified 801 Japanese companies from trade association mailing lists and published sources that satisfied their criteria that the companies are (1) publicly held and traded on the stock exchange, (2) in a high-tech industry, (3) domiciled in Japan and managed by Japanese nationals, and (4) devoted to spending at least 2% of their annual sales to R&D expenditures. Of the 801 firms, a questionnaire was mailed to 411 firms, of which 264 usable responses were received, indicating a response rate of 64%.

RELIABILITY:

An alpha of .65 was reported for this scale.

VALIDITY:

No specific examination of scale validity was reported.

ADMINISTRATION:

The scale was self-administered in a mail-survey type format. High scores on the scale indicate that respondents feel that there exists strong R&D-marketing relations, whereas low scores indicate that they do not.

MAJOR FINDINGS:

The results of Song and Parry (1993) indicate that perceived levels of R&D-marketing integration are positively related to (1) the perceived harmony of R&D-marketing relations and (2) the perceived value placed by senior management on integration.

REFERENCES:

Gupta, Ashok K. (1984), ''A Study of the R&D/Marketing Interface and Innovation Success in High Technology Firms,'' doctoral dissertation, Syracuse University.

Song, X. Michael and Mark E. Parry (1993), ''R&D Marketing Integration in Japanese High-Technology Firms: Hypothesis and Empirical Evidence,'' *JAMS*, 21 (Spring), 125-33.

Souder, William E. et al. (1977), ''An Exploratory Study of the Coordinating Mechanisms between R&D and Marketing as an Influence on the Innovation Process,'' Final Report to the National Science Foundation, NTIS PB-279- 366/AS.

SCALE ITEMS: ORGANIZATIONAL STRUCTURE AND CLIMATE—QUALITY OF R&D-MARKETING RELATIONS (RELATE)

```
Strongly                                                      Strongly
disagree                                                        agree
   1————————2————————3————————4————————5————————6
```

1. There is a give-and-take relationship between R&D and marketing. Each challenges the other in their meetings and discussions and tries to understand each other's point of view.
2. Marketing and R&D are always involved from the very early stages of discussions about a new product.
3. Conflicts between R&D and marketing are resolved at lower levels of the organization.

SCALE NAME: Organizational Structure and Climate—Senior Management Values Integration (VALUE)

SCALE DESCRIPTION:

A three-item, six-point Likert-like summated ratings scale measuring the degree to which senior management values and promotes R&D-marketing integration.

SCALE ORIGIN:

Song and Parry (1993) indicated that they used items selected by Gupta (1984) in their study. Gupta, in turn, used the research of Souder and colleagues (1977) to construct the scales.

SAMPLES:

Song and Parry identified 801 Japanese companies from trade association mailing lists and published sources that satisfied their criteria that the companies are (1) publicly held and traded on the stock exchange, (2) in a high-tech industry, (3) domiciled in Japan and managed by Japanese nationals, and (4) devoted to spending at least 2% of their annual sales to R&D expenditures. Of the 801 firms, a questionnaire was mailed to 411 firms, of which 264 usable responses were received, indicating a response rate of 64%.

RELIABILITY:

An alpha of .65 was reported for this scale.

VALIDITY:

No specific examination of scale validity was reported.

ADMINISTRATION:

The scale was self-administered in a mail-survey type format. High scores on the scale indicate that respondents feel that senior management strongly supports R&D-marketing integration, whereas low scores indicate that they do not.

MAJOR FINDINGS:

The results of Song and Parry (1993) indicate that perceived levels of R&D-marketing integration are positively related to (1) the perceived harmony of R&D-marketing relations and (2) the perceived value placed by senior management on integration.

REFERENCES:

Gupta, Ashok K. (1984), ''A Study of the R&D/Marketing Interface and Innovation Success in High Technology Firms,'' doctoral dissertation, Syracuse University.

Song, X. Michael and Mark E. Parry (1993), ''R&D Marketing Integration in Japanese High-Technology Firms: Hypothesis and Empirical Evidence,'' *JAMS*, 21 (Spring), 125-33.

Souder, William E. et al. (1977), ''An Exploratory Study of the Coordinating Mechanisms between R&D and Marketing as an Influence on the Innovation Process,'' Final Report to the National Science Foundation, NTIS PB-279-366/AS.

SCALE ITEMS: ORGANIZATIONAL STRUCTURE AND CLIMATE—SENIOR MANAGEMENT VALUES INTEGRATION (VALUE)

Strongly   Strongly
disagree   agree
1———————2———————3———————4———————5———————6

1. This organization values cooperation and collaboration between R&D and marketing.
2. This organization provides opportunities to marketing personnel to understand and appreciate the technological aspects of the business through training programs, seminars, and get-togethers.
3. In this organization marketing gets the blame for new product failures, while R&D gets the credit for success.

SCALE NAME: Perceived Fairness

SCALE DESCRIPTION:

A six-item, five-point summated ratings scale measuring a salesperson's perception regarding the way rewards such as pay and promotion are allocated and general supervisory practices of the sales manager connote perceived fairness.

SCALE ORIGIN:

The scale was developed by Sager (1991) for this study.

SAMPLES:

The sample studied was composed of detail sales representatives employed by a national manufacturer of branded consumer products. A self-report questionnaire (t 1) was distributed to 156 sales representatives and trainees. Nine months later, a second questionnaire (t 2) was distributed. A total of **96** sales representatives and trainees responded to both t 1 and t 2 .

RELIABILITY:

An alpha coefficient of **.70** and **.77** was reported for t 1 and t 2 respectively.

VALIDITY:

No specific examination of scale validity was reported.

ADMINISTRATION:

The questionnaire was self-administered by sales representatives. High scores indicate that respondents strongly agree managerial incentives and rewards connote perceived fairness, whereas low scores indicate that they do not.

MAJOR FINDINGS:

The role of the fairness construct was found to be difficult to interpret. Theory is lacking regarding the relationship between fairness and turnover. Yet it appears that some type of alteration in perceived fairness of manager and organization policies accompanies turnover from a sales organization.

REFERENCE:

Sager, J. K. (1991), ''A Longitudinal Assessment of Change in Sales Force Turnover,'' *JAMS*, 19 (Winter), 25-36.

SCALE ITEMS: PERCEIVED FAIRNESS

Strongly
disagree
                                                                    Strongly
                                                                    agree

1————————2————————3————————4————————5

1. Find my sales manager is fair in dealing with me.
2. Feel job promotion policies are unfair.
3. Find my boss treats me fairly.
4. Have promotion system that helps the best men rise to the top.
5. Find a close relationship between excellence of job performance and rewards received.
6. Feel if I increase my performance I will receive extra rewards for it.

SCALE NAME: Performance (Behavioral Aspects)

SCALE DESCRIPTION:

A six-item, five-point Likert-type summated ratings scale measuring the degree to which salespersons ranked behavioral performance dimensions in importance.

SCALE ORIGIN:

The scale was developed by Ingram, Lee, and Lucas (1991), but the scale items correspond closely to the four behavioral dimensions of the Behrman and Perreault (1982) self-report salesperson performance scale.

SAMPLES:

In an effort to devise a performance scale suited to the variety of participating companies, in-depth interviews with 15 out of a pool of 250 industrial sales managers were conducted. The consensus of this group of participants was that any such measure should focus on the behavioral aspects of performance, due to the degree to which the salespeople can influence these dimensions.

RELIABILITY:

An alpha of .78 was reported for this scale.

VALIDITY:

No specific examination of scale validity was reported.

ADMINISTRATION:

The scale was self-administered by respondents in a mail questionnaire format. Two responses were required for each item. First, respondents indicated their ranking within their own company on the performance dimension in question (range from top 10% to bottom 10%). Next, the importance ranking for that behavioral performance dimension was indicated. The two responses were multiplied for each of the six items, and their products were summed to achieve an overall performance score for each respondent.

MAJOR FINDINGS:

The purpose of this study was to assess differences in salesperson performance and effort for varying levels of importance of behavioral performance dimensions. Salespersons who ranked behavioral performance dimensions highly in importance generally showed high performance and effort towards the company. These types of salespeople were termed institutional stars. Institutional stars are likely to be seen by most sales organizations as the most desirable type of people to employ and retain.

REFERENCES:

Behrman, Douglas N. and William D. Perreault, Jr. (1982), ''Measuring the Performance of Industrial Salespersons,'' *Journal of Business Research*, 10 (September), 355-70.

Ingram, Thomas N., Keun S. Lee, and George H. Lucas, Jr. (1991), ''Commitment and Involvement: Assessing a Salesforce Typology,'' *JAMS*, 19 (Summer), 187-97.

SCALE ITEMS: PERFORMANCE (BEHAVIORAL ASPECTS)

Unimportant   Important

1————————2————————3————————4————————5

1. Customer relations.
2. Controlling expenses.
3. Sales presentation effectiveness.
4. Providing information to and effective communication with the management.
5. Planning and Management of time in carrying out selling activities.
6. Technical knowledge related to our products, competitors' products, and customers' needs.

SCALE NAME: Performance Sensitivity (Job)

SCALE DESCRIPTION:

A six-item, seven-point Likert-type scale assessing the degree to which an employee's emotions are influenced by the quality of work he/she performs. The scale was called Work Motivation by Dubinsky and Hartley (1986), Skinner, Dubinsky, and Donnelly (1984) and Hampton, Dubinsky, and Skinner (1986). The short form of the scale with four items was used by Dubinsky and colleagues (1986) and was referred to as Internal Work Motivation.

SCALE ORIGIN:

The scale used by Dubinsky and colleagues (1986) is apparently the short version of the Internal Work Motivation scale developed by Hackman and Oldham (1974, 1975). No specific psychometric information is provided concerning the four-item version, but the six-item version is indicated to be reasonably reliable and valid. Specifically, the internal consistency of the scale is reported to be .76. Evidence of convergent validity is that the scale has high positive correlations with several other related but conceptually different measures such as job satisfaction, growth satisfaction, and work meaningfulness.

SAMPLES:

Analysis in Dubinsky and colleagues (1986) was based on data collected from **189** salespeople. Letters were sent to a national sample of 2000 senior-level executives asking them to have their least experienced salesperson complete the questionnaire. The respondents represented 189 different companies that marketed 50 different product categories. The sample had a median age of 30.5 years, had spent 1.4 years (median) in their present positions, and were mostly male (86%). Dubinsky and Hartley (1986) based their analysis on completed questionnaires returned by **120** respondents. Questionnaires were sent to 467 agents who sold lines of a large, multi-insurance company. No nonresponse bias was apparent. The sample had a mean age of 39.1 years, had spent 6.6 years (mean) in their present positions, were mostly male (91%), and more than half were college graduates (56%). The sample used by Hampton, Dubinsky, and Skinner (1986) was based on **116** usable responses from a census of 121 retail salespeople who worked in one of five outlets of a department store chain. The sample had a median age of 23.2 years, had spent 1.4 years (median) in their present positions and 1.1 years (median) with their current supervisors, were mostly female (78%), and 66% had some college education. Skinner, Dubinsky, and Donnelly (1984) collected data from retail salespeople employed by a small departmental store chain. All salespersons employed by the firm participated in the study, Questionnaires were administered to participants at their work place, and a total of **157** usable questionnaires were received.

RELIABILITY:

A LISREL estimate of reliability was **.54** (Dubinsky et al. 1986) and alphas of **.60** and **.81** were reported by Dubinsky and Hartley (1986) and Hampton, Dubinsky, and Skinner (1986), respectively. Skinner, Dubinsky, and Donnelly (1984) reported an alpha of **.81**.

VALIDITY:

No examination of scale validity was reported in any of the marketing studies.

ADMINISTRATION:

The scale was self-administered by respondents along with many other measures in a mail survey format in the studies by Dubinsky (et al. 1986; and Hartley 1986). Hampton et al. (1986) distributed the survey instrument to respondents in a conference room in each store, where they were self-administered. High scores on the scale indicate that respondent's emotions are very sensitive to the quality of the work they perform in their jobs, whereas low scores suggest that their emotions are not significantly influenced by the performance of their jobs. The scale was self-administered by respondents in the study by Skinner, Dubinsky, and Donnelly (1984).

MAJOR FINDINGS:

Dubinsky and colleagues (1986) examined a model of sales force assimilation. Acceptance by coworkers was the main variable found to have a significant positive impact on job performance sensitivity. The purpose of Dubinsky and Hartley (1986) was to investigate several predictors of salesperson performance and the relationships among those predictors. A path analysis indicated that job performance sensitivity had a positive effect on job performance (prior year's commissions). In turn, the former was most significantly affected (positively) by job involvement. A causal model of retail sales supervisor leadership behavior was studied by Hampton, Dubinsky, and Skinner (1986). The results indicated that job satisfaction had a strong positive effect on job performance sensitivity. Skinner, Dubinsky, and Donnelly (1984) studied the relationship between retail sales managers' social bases of power and retail salespeople's job related outcomes. They found that expert power and legitimate power are positively related to work motivation. These two bases of power explain about 13% of the variance in work motivation.

COMMENTS:

The internal consistency of the short version of the scale is low, and the slightly longer version should be used because of its apparently better reliability.

REFERENCES:

Dubinsky, Alan J. and Steven W. Hartley (1986), ''A Path-Analytic Study of a Model of Salesperson Performance,'' *JAMS*, 14 (Spring), 36-46.

_____, Roy D. Howell, Thomas N. Ingram, and Danny Bellenger (1986), "Salesforce Socialization," *JM*, 50 (October), 192-207.

Hackman, J. Richard and Greg R. Oldham (1974), *The Job Diagnostic Survey: An Instrument for the Diagnosis of Jobs and the Evaluation of Job Redesign Projects, Technical Report #4*. New Haven, CT: Department of Administrative Sciences, Yale University.

_____ and _____ (1975), "Development of the Job Diagnostic Survey," *Journal of Applied Psychology*, 60 (2), 159-70.

Hampton, Ron, Alan J. Dubinsky, and Steven J. Skinner (1986), "A Model of Sales Supervisor Leadership Behavior and Retail Salespeople's Job-Related Outcomes," *JAMS*, 14 (Fall), 33-43.

Skinner, Steven J., Alan Dubinsky, and J.H. Donnelly (1984), "The Use of Social Bases of Power in Retail Sales," *JPSSM*, 4 (November), 49-56 .

SCALE ITEMS: PERFORMANCE SENSITIVITY (JOB)*

Strongly disagree	Disagree	Slightly disagree	Neutral	Slightly agree	Agree	Strongly agree
1	2	3	4	5	6	7

1. My opinion of myself goes up when I do this job well.
2. I feel a great sense of personal satisfaction when I do this job well.
3. I feel bad and unhappy when I discover that I have performed poorly on this job.
4. My own feelings are generally not affected much one way or the other by how well I do on this job. (r)
5. Most people on this job feel a great sense of personal satisfaction when they do the job well.
6. Most people on this job feel bad or unhappy when they find that they have performed the work poorly.

* Items 1-4 compose the short form of the scale and are the ones used by Dubinsky and colleagues (1986).

SCALE NAME: Power Bases (Sales Manager)

SCALE DESCRIPTION:

A five-item, seven-point Likert-type scale ranging from strongly disagree to strongly agree. It measures the sales managers' bases of power.

SCALE ORIGIN:

Skinner, Dubinsky, and Donnelly (1984) developed this scale on the basis of prior studies by Bachman, Smith, and Slesinger (1966), Burke and Wilcox (1971), Busch (1980), Ivancevich and Donnelly (1970), and Student (1968).

SAMPLES:

Data were collected from retail salespeople employed by a small departmental store chain. All sales personnel employed by the firm participated in the study. Questionnaires were administered to participants at their work place and a total of 157 usable questionnaires were received.

RELIABILITY:

Alpha was not reported for this scale.

VALIDITY:

No specific examination of the scale validity was reported.

ADMINISTRATION:

The scale was self administered by respondents.

MAJOR FINDINGS:

This scale is part of a larger study by Skinner, Dubinsky, and Donnelly (1984), which explores the relationships between retail sales managers' social bases of power and retail salespeople's job-related outcomes. The authors found higher correlation between expert and referent power and reward and coercive power. Also, sales managers' legitimate and expert power bases are positively related to retail salespeople's overall job satisfaction. Reward, referent, and expert power are related positively to satisfaction with supervisor, and coercive power is related negatively.

COMMENTS:

See also following scales—Commitment (Organizational), Role Ambiguity (Salesperson and Product Manager), and Satisfaction with Job (Generalized).

REFERENCES:

Bachman, J.G., C.G. Smith, and J.A. Slesinger (1966), "Control, Performance, and Satisfaction: An Analysis of Structural and Individual Effects," *Journal of Personality and Social Psychology*, 4 (August), 127-36.

Burke, R.J. and D.S. Wilcox (1971), "Bases of Supervisory Power and Subordinate Job Satisfaction," *Canadian Journal of Behavioral Science*, 3, 182-93.

Busch, P. (1980), "The Sales Managers' Bases of Social Power and Influence Upon the Sales Force," *JM*, 44 (Summer), 91-101.

Ivancevich, J.M. and J.H. Donnelly (1970), "Leader Influence and Performance," *Personal Psychology*, 23 (Winter), 534-49.

Skinner, Steven J., Alan Dubinsky, and J. Donnelly (1984), "The Use of Social Bases of Power in Retail Sales," *JPSSM*, 4 (November), 49-56.

Student, K.R. (1968), "Supervisory Influence and Work Group Performance," *Journal of Applied Psychology*, (June), 188-94.

SCALE ITEMS: POWER BASES (SALES MANAGER)

1 = Strongly disagree   7 = Strongly agree

1. Reward Power: "I do the things my immediate supervisor suggests or wants me to do because he/she is in a good position to recommend promotions or permit special privileges for me."
2. Coercive Power: "I do the things my immediate supervisor suggests or wants me to do because he/she can apply pressure to enforce his/her suggestions if they are not carried out fully and properly."
3. Legitimate Power: "I do the things my immediate supervisor suggest or wants me to do because he/she has a legitimate right because of his/her position to expect that his/her suggestions will be followed."
4. Referent Power: "I do the things my immediate supervisor suggest or wants me to do because I like him/her personally, and I regard him/her as a friend."
5. Expert Power: "I do the things my immediate supervisor suggest or wants me to do, since I respect his/her knowledge and good judgment because he/she is well trained and experienced."

SCALE NAME: Psychological Climate: Franchisee–Autonomy

SCALE DESCRIPTION:

A five-item, seven-point Likert-type ratings scale measuring the effects of autonomy on the psychological climate within the franchise channel. *Autonomy* refers to the closeness of the (franchise) manager's supervision, individual responsibility delegated (to the franchisee) and the absence of (franchisor) initiated structure (Joyce and Slocum 1984).

SCALE ORIGIN:

Strutton, Pelton, and Lumpkin (1993) indicated that they used statements taken from Koys and DeCotiis (1991) to measure the psychological climate within the franchise channel.

SAMPLES:

The sampling domain included four primary metropolitan statistical areas (PMSA) contiguous to a major city. A stratified random sampling procedure was used. Franchise categories were selected from the *Franchise Opportunities Handbook*, and a comprehensive list of franchises for each category was prepared from the latest telephone directory. A total of 311 franchises were contacted, and **239** usable questionnaires were received, indicating a response rate of 76.8%.

RELIABILITY:

An alpha of **.70** was reported for the scale.

VALIDITY:

No specific examination of scale validity was reported.

ADMINISTRATION:

The scale was self-administered in a mail-survey type format. High scores indicate that respondents strongly agree that the organization is autonomous, whereas low scores indicate that they do not feel that the organization is autonomous.

MAJOR FINDINGS:

Franchisors rather uniformly feel comfortable in implicitly providing franchisees substantial rein under their umbrella of legitimate control. Therefore, as a descriptor of the channel climate, autonomy has little discriminating power across the conflict resolution strategy classifications.

REFERENCES:

Joyce, William F. and John W. Slocum (1984), ''Collective Climate: Agreement as a Basis for Defining Climates in Organizations,'' *Academy of Management Journal*, 27 (December), 721-42.

Koys, Daniel J. and Thomas A. DeCotiis (1991), ''Inductive Measures of Psychological Climate,'' *Human Relations*, 44 (March), 265-85.

Strutton, David, Lou E. Pelton, and James R. Lumpkin (1993), ''The Influence of Psychological Climate on Conflict Resolution Strategies in Franchise Relationships,'' *JAMS*, 21 (Summer), 207-16.

SCALE ITEMS: PSYCHOLOGICAL CLIMATE: FRANCHISEE—AUTONOMY

Strongly disagree			Neutral			Strongly agree
1	2	3	4	5	6	7

1. I organize the franchise as I see fit.
2. I set the work standards for my franchise.
3. I make most of the decisions that affect the way my franchise performs.
4. I schedule my own work activities.
5. I determine my own operational routine.

SCALE NAME: Psychological Climate: Franchisee–Cohesion

SCALE DESCRIPTION:

A five-item, seven-point Likert-type ratings scale measuring the effects of cohesion on the psychological climate within the franchise channel. *Cohesion* refers to the presence of team spirit and cooperation within the franchisees organizational setting.

SCALE ORIGIN:

Strutton, Pelton, and Lumpkin (1993) indicated that they used statements taken from Koys and DeCotiis (1991) to measure the psychological climate within the franchise channel.

SAMPLES:

The sampling domain included four primary metropolitan statistical areas (PMSA) contiguous to a major city. A stratified random sampling procedure was used. Franchise categories were selected from the *Franchise Opportunities Handbook*, and a comprehensive list of franchises for each category was prepared from the latest telephone directory. A total of 311 franchises were contacted, and **239** usable questionnaires were received, indicating a response rate of 76.8%.

RELIABILITY:

An alpha of **.74** was reported for the scale.

VALIDITY:

No specific examination of scale validity was reported.

ADMINISTRATION:

The scale was self-administered in a mail-survey type format. High scores indicate that respondents strongly agree that cohesion exists in the organization, whereas low scores indicate that they do not feel the presence of strong cohesion.

MAJOR FINDINGS:

Franchisors can influence conflict resolution strategies used by franchisees through selectively administering their franchising system's psychological climate. Results indicate that a franchising system characterized by, among other things, cohesion should confer a greater willingness to listen openly, exchange information, and undertake reasonably risky ventures.

REFERENCES:

Koys, Daniel J. and Thomas A. DeCotiis (1991), ''Inductive Measures of Psychological Climate,'' *Human Relations*, 44 (March), 265-85.

Strutton, David, Lou E. Pelton, and James R. Lumpkin (1993), ''The Influence of Psychological Climate on Conflict Resolution Strategies in Franchise Relationships,'' *JAMS*, 21 (Summer), 207-216.

SCALE ITEMS: PSYCHOLOGICAL CLIMATE: FRANCHISEE—COHESION

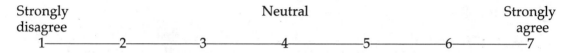

Strongly disagree			Neutral			Strongly agree
1	2	3	4	5	6	7

1. In this company, franchisees pitch in to help each other out.
2. In this company, franchisees take a personal interest in each other.
3. There is a lot of team spirit in this company.
4. Franchisees tend to get along well with each other.
5. I feel like I have a lot in common with other franchisees.

SCALE NAME: Psychological Climate: Franchisee–Fairness

SCALE DESCRIPTION:

A four-item, seven-point Likert-type ratings scale measuring the effects of fairness on the psychological climate within the franchise channel. *Fairness* refers to the presence of two forms of justice: procedural and outcome (Konovosky and Cropanzano 1991). Procedural justice relates to the impartiality of the means used to determine the outcomes of conflicts, whereas outcome justice addresses the objectivity of the ends achieved.

SCALE ORIGIN:

Strutton, Pelton, and Lumpkin (1993) indicated that they used statements taken from Koys and DeCotiis (1991) to measure the psychological climate within the franchise channel.

SAMPLES:

The sampling domain included four primary metropolitan statistical areas (PMSA) contiguous to a major city. A stratified random sampling procedure was used. Franchise categories were selected from the *Franchise Opportunities Handbook,* and a comprehensive list of franchises for each category was prepared from the latest telephone directory. A total of 311 franchises were contacted, and **239** usable questionnaires were received, indicating a response rate of 76.8%.

RELIABILITY:

An alpha of **.68** was reported for the scale.

VALIDITY:

No specific examination of scale validity was reported.

ADMINISTRATION:

The scale was self-administered in a mail-survey type format. High scores indicate that respondents strongly agree that fairness is practiced in the organization, whereas low scores indicate that they do not feel strongly that fairness is present.

MAJOR FINDINGS:

Franchisors can influence conflict resolution strategies used by franchisees through selectively administering their franchising system's psychological climate. Results indicate that a franchising system characterized by, among other things, fairness should confer a greater willingness to listen openly, exchange information, and undertake reasonably risky ventures.

REFERENCES:

Konovosky, Mary A. and Russell Cropanzano (1991), ''Perceived Fairness of Employee Drug Testing as a Predictor of Employee Attitudes and Job Performance,'' *Journal of Applied Psychology*, 76 (October), 698-707.

Koys, Daniel J. and Thomas A. DeCotiis (1991), ''Inductive Measures of Psychological Climate,'' *Human Relations*, 44 (March), 265-85.

Strutton, David, Lou E. Pelton, and James R. Lumpkin (1993), ''The Influence of Psychological Climate on Conflict Resolution Strategies in Franchise Relationships,'' *JAMS*, 21 (Summer), 207-16.

SCALE ITEMS: PSYCHOLOGICAL CLIMATE: FRANCHISEE—FAIRNESS

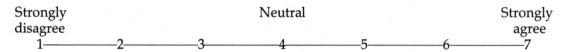

Strongly disagree   Neutral   Strongly agree

1————2————3————4————5————6————7

1. I can count on a fair shake from my franchisor.
2. The objectives my franchisor sets for me are reasonable.
3. If my franchisor terminates a franchise relationship, the franchisee was probably at fault.
4. My franchisor does not play favorites.

SCALE NAME: Psychological Climate: Franchisee–Innovation

SCALE DESCRIPTION:

A five-item, seven-point Likert-type ratings scale measuring the effects of innovation on the psychological climate within the franchise channel. *Innovation* refers to the opportunity to improve on established work procedures and affect performance outcome within the franchisee's organizational setting.

SCALE ORIGIN:

Strutton, Pelton, and Lumpkin (1993) indicated that they used statements taken from Koys and DeCotiis (1991) to measure the psychological climate within the franchise channel.

SAMPLES:

The sampling domain included four primary metropolitan statistical areas (PMSA) contiguous to a major city. A stratified random sampling procedure was used. Franchise categories were selected from the *Franchise Opportunities Handbook*, and a comprehensive list of franchises for each category was prepared from the latest telephone directory. A total of 311 franchises were contacted, and **239** usable questionnaires were received, indicating a response rate of 76.8%.

RELIABILITY:

An alpha of **.82** was reported for the scale.

VALIDITY:

No specific examination of scale validity was reported.

ADMINISTRATION:

The scale was self-administered in a mail-survey type format. High scores indicate that respondents strongly agree that innovation is encouraged in the organization, whereas low scores indicate that they do not feel strongly encouraged to innovate.

MAJOR FINDINGS:

Franchisors can influence conflict resolution strategies used by franchisees through selectively administering their franchising system's psychological climate. Results indicate that a franchising system characterized by, among other things, innovation should confer a greater willingness to listen openly, exchange information, and undertake reasonably risky ventures.

REFERENCES:

Koys, Daniel J. and Thomas A. DeCotiis (1991), ''Inductive Measures of Psychological Climate,'' *Human Relations*, 44 (March), 265-85.

Strutton, David, Lou E. Pelton, and James R. Lumpkin (1993), ''The Influence of Psychological Climate on Conflict Resolution Strategies in Franchise Relationships,'' *JAMS*, 21 (Summer), 207-16.

SCALE ITEMS: PSYCHOLOGICAL CLIMATE: FRANCHISEE—INNOVATION

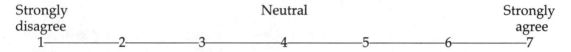

1. My franchisor encourages me to find new ways around old problems.
2. My franchisor encourages me to develop my own ideas.
3. My franchisor encourages me to improve upon its methods.
4. My franchisor talks up new ways of doing things.
5. My franchisor likes me to try new ways of doing things.

SCALE NAME: Psychological Climate: Franchisee–Pressure

SCALE DESCRIPTION:

A four-item, seven-point Likert-type ratings scale measuring the effects of pressure on the psychological climate within the franchise channel. *Pressure* refers to externally imposed constraints that limit an organization's opportunity for self-determination.

SCALE ORIGIN:

Strutton, Pelton, and Lumpkin (1993) indicated that they used statements taken from Koys and DeCotiis (1991) to measure the psychological climate within the franchise channel.

SAMPLES:

The sampling domain included four primary metropolitan statistical areas (PMSA) contiguous to a major city. A stratified random sampling procedure was used. Franchise categories were selected from the *Franchise Opportunities Handbook,* and a comprehensive list of franchises for each category was prepared from the latest telephone directory. A total of 311 franchises were contacted, and 239 usable questionnaires were received, indicating a response rate of 76.8%.

RELIABILITY:

An alpha of .76 was reported for the scale.

VALIDITY:

No specific examination of scale validity was reported.

ADMINISTRATION:

The scale was self-administered in a mail-survey type format. High scores indicate that respondents strongly agree that pressure exists in the organization, whereas low scores indicate that they do not feel strongly pressured.

MAJOR FINDINGS:

As semi-autonomous, entrepreneurial-oriented businesspeople, most franchisees understand and tacitly accept that some baseline level of pressure will always accompany the franchisee role. Often such pressures emanate from within the individual, and the franchisees are able to use them as an intrinsic motivational force.

REFERENCES:

Koys, Daniel J. and Thomas A. DeCotiis (1991), ''Inductive Measures of Psychological Climate,'' *Human Relations*, 44 (March), 265-85.

Strutton, David, Lou E. Pelton, and James R. Lumpkin (1993), ''The Influence of Psychological Climate on Conflict Resolution Strategies in Franchise Relationships,'' *JAMS*, 21 (Summer), 207-16.

SCALE ITEMS: PSYCHOLOGICAL CLIMATE: FRANCHISEE—PRESSURE

Strongly disagree			Neutral			Strongly agree
1—————	2—————	3—————	4—————	5—————	6—————	7

1. I have too much work and too little time to do it.
2. The franchise arrangement provides a relaxed working environment.
3. I feel like I never have a day off.
4. In this franchise, too many people get ''burned out'' by demands of the job.

SCALE NAME: Psychological Climate: Franchisee–Recognition

SCALE DESCRIPTION:

A four-item, seven-point Likert-type ratings scale measuring the effects of recognition on the psychological climate within the franchise channel. *Recognition* refers to rewards associated with franchisor awareness of franchisee successes and/or levels of effort.

SCALE ORIGIN:

Strutton, Pelton, and Lumpkin (1993) indicated that they used statements taken from Koys and DeCotiis (1991) to measure the psychological climate within the franchise channel.

SAMPLES:

The sampling domain included four primary metropolitan statistical areas (PMSA) contiguous to a major city. A stratified random sampling procedure was used. Franchise categories were selected from the *Franchise Opportunities Handbook,* and a comprehensive list of franchises for each category was prepared from the latest telephone directory. A total of 311 franchises were contacted, and 239 usable questionnaires were received, indicating a response rate of 76.8%.

RELIABILITY:

An alpha of .74 was reported for the scale.

VALIDITY:

No specific examination of scale validity was reported.

ADMINISTRATION:

The scale was self-administered in a mail-survey type format. High scores indicate that respondents strongly agree that recognition is present in the organization, whereas low scores indicate that they do not feel strong recognition within the organization.

MAJOR FINDINGS:

Franchisors can influence conflict resolution strategies used by franchisees through selectively administering their franchising system's psychological climate. Results indicate that a franchising system characterized by, among other things, recognition should confer a greater willingness to listen openly, exchange information, and undertake reasonably risky ventures.

REFERENCES:

Koys, Daniel J. and Thomas A. DeCotiis (1991), ''Inductive Measures of Psychological Climate,'' *Human Relations*, 44 (March), 265-85.

Strutton, David, Lou E. Pelton, and James R. Lumpkin (1993), ''The Influence of Psychological Climate on Conflict Resolution Strategies in Franchise Relationships,'' *JAMS*, 21 (Summer), 207-16.

SCALE ITEMS: PSYCHOLOGICAL CLIMATE: FRANCHISEE—RECOGNITION

Strongly disagree			Neutral			Strongly agree
1	2	3	4	5	6	7

1. I can count on a pat on the back when the franchise performs well.
2. The only time I hear about my franchise performance is when I make a mistake.
3. My franchisor knows what my strengths are and lets me know it.
4. My franchisor is quick to recognize good performance.

SCALE NAME: Role Ambiguity (Salesperson and Product Manager)

SCALE DESCRIPTION:

A six-item, seven-point Likert-type summated scale ranging from "Very False" to "Very True" purporting to measure the degree of perceived role ambiguity by noting the reported amount of certainty a salesperson has about his/her responsibilities.

SCALE ORIGIN:

The scale was developed originally by Rizzo, House, and Lirtzman (1970). The scale was found to demonstrate internal consistency reliability exceeding .70 along with high concurrent validity (Schuler, Aldag, and Brief 1977).

SAMPLES:

Teas (1980) used a questionnaire mailed out in 1978 to a midwestern corporation's industrial sales force. A cover letter was sent along with the questionnaire requesting a prompt response and promising anonymity. In addition, a letter from the firm's vice president of sales was included indicating support for the survey. Usable responses were obtained from **127** out of 184 salespeople surveyed (response rate was 69%). Teas's (1983) data were obtained by a mail survey of two midwestern corporations' sales forces. Included with the questionnaire were cover letters from the researcher and the vice president of sales promising confidentiality and indicating company support for the survey. Usable responses were obtained from **116** salespersons, 49 and 67 salespersons from each company (response rate was 55%).

Lysonski's (1985) data were obtained from questionnaires mailed to 449 product managers in consumer packaged goods industries. A second mailing to nonrespondents yielded a final return rate of 55%, or 224 completed questionnaires, of which 54 were unusable. The final sample for analysis was **170**.

Dubinsky and Hartley's (1986) data were obtained through a questionnaire mailed to insurance agents located throughout the United States. Included with the questionnaire were cover letters from the company's divisional vice president indicating support for the project and a cover letter from the researchers promising confidentiality. A total of 467 questionnaires were sent out. Usable questionnaires were returned by **120** agents (response rate of 25.7%). Ninety-one percent of the respondents were male. The mean age was 39.1 years. Approximately 56% had earned at least a bachelor's degree. Mean job tenure was 6.6 years.

Hampton, Dubinsky, and Skinner's (1986) data were obtained from a census of (n = 121) retail salespeople employed in a department store chain (five outlets). Usable questionnaires were obtained from **116** of the salespeople (response rate of 95.9%), 91 of which were female. The median age was 23.2 years. Approximately 66% had at least some college education. Median job tenure was 1.4 years, and median time spent working with the current sales supervisor was 1.1 years.

Fry and colleagues' (1986) data were obtained by a mail survey of a national pharmaceutical manufacturer's sales force. Questionnaires were returned by 216 of 347 salespeople surveyed (response rate of 62%). The data analyzed were from men only. Data on age, income, tenure, and education were not specified.

Michaels and colleagues' (1986) data were obtained by self-administered questionnaires distributed to 255 full-line salespeople of an industrial building materials manufacturer. Usable questionnaires were returned by **215** salespeople (response rate of 84.3%). Mean respondent age was 43.9 years, mean job tenure 12.9 years, mean organization tenure 15.2 years, and mean sales experience 18.1 years. Data were also collected from a randomly selected sample of 554 members of the National Association of Purchasing Management. Data were collected by self-administered mail questionnaire. Of the 335 questionnaires returned, **330** were usable (59.6%). Mean respondent age was 42.2 years, mean job tenure 5.7 years, mean organization tenure 10.6 years, and mean purchasing experience 12.5 years.

Cummings, Jackson, and Ostrom's (1989) data were obtained by self-administered questionnaires which were distributed by mail to firms selected from the American Marketing Association Membership Directory. One hundred fifty six firms agreed to participate in the study, providing a potential sample of 624 product managers. A total of **201** usable questionnaires were returned.

Skinner, Dubinsky and Donnelly (1984) collected data from retail salespeople employed by a small departmental store chain. All salespeople employed by the firm participated in the study. Questionnaires were administered to participants at their workplace, and a total of **157** usable questionnaires were received.

RELIABILITY:

The following Cronbach's alphas were reported for the scale: **.797** (Teas 1980); **.824** (Teas 1983); **.85** (Lysonski 1985); **.76** (Dubinsky and Hartley 1986); **.74** (Hampton, Dubinsky, and Skinner 1986); **.90** (Fry et al. 1986); **.85** (Michaels et al. 1988); **.813** (Cummings, Jackson, and Ostrom 1989); and **.75** (Skinner, Dubinsky, and Donnelly 1984).

VALIDITY:

Dubinsky and Hartley (1986) noted that the scale has demonstrated discriminant and predictive validity (Rizzo, House, and Lirtzman 1970) and construct and concurrent validity (Schuler, Aldag, and Brief 1977); in addition, it has shown to be free from semantic confusion (House, Schuler, and Levanoni 1983).

ADMINISTRATION:

The scale was self-administered in most of the studies along with several other measures in mail questionnaires. Accompanying the questionnaires were a cover letter from the chain's president indicating company support for the project and a cover letter from the researchers promising confidentiality.

Hampton, Dubinsky, and Skinner (1986) used a different approach by administering the questionnaires to the respondents in a conference room at each store. The scores from each item of the scale are summated. The possible score range is 6 to 42. A low score (lowest possible score is 6) indicates a high degree of perceived role ambiguity.

MAJOR FINDINGS:

Teas's (1980) results indicate that participation and closeness of supervision are significantly (p < .05) related to role ambiguity. However, the hypothesis that experience is negatively related to role ambiguity was not supported by the results. Role ambiguity was found to be related to job satisfaction (p < .05). Teas (1983) found that leader consideration and sales force participation are negatively related to the salesperson's perception of both role conflict (p < .001 and p < .05) and role ambiguity (p < .005). Feedback also was found to be negatively related to role ambiguity (p < .025). The results indicated that role ambiguity was not a significant predictor of sales force job satisfaction. In addition, role ambiguity and role conflict were found to have a high correlation (r = .515).

Lysonski's (1985) results indicate that perceived uncertainty is associated with role conflict and ambiguity (p < .001). Role ambiguity was found not to be associated with boundary spanning except for internal organizational boundary spanning (p < .05). Role autonomy was found to influence only the role ambiguity-satisfaction relationship (F = 9.38, p < .001). Need for affiliation was found to have a definite moderating influence; it lowered the role conflict-perceived performance relationship (F = 7.02, p < .001), increased the role ambiguity-job related tension relationship (F = 5.83, p < .01), and lowered the role ambiguity-perceived performance relationship (F = 3.83, p < .05). Education was found to reduce the role conflict-job satisfaction relationship (F = 6.04, p < .01) and role ambiguity-job tension relationship (F = 7.25, p < .001). Moreover, it was found that experience as a product manager increased the role conflict-job tension relationship (F = 7.42, p < .001) and lowered the role ambiguity-perceived performance relationship (F = 4.85, p. < .05). However, experience with the present product as a product manager increased the role conflict-job tension (F = 6.50, p < .01) and role ambiguity-job tension relationships (F = 6.20, p < .001).

Dubinsky and Hartley's (1986) results indicate that role ambiguity explains 18% of the variance in job satisfaction. Self-monitoring did not appear to be related to role conflict or role ambiguity. Moreover, it was found that role ambiguity is negatively related to job performance (p < .01).

Hampton, Dubinsky, and Skinner's (1986) results indicate that both initiating structure (p < .03) and consideration (p < .04) are inversely related to role ambiguity.

Fry and colleagues' (1986) results indicate that role ambiguity (p < .05) has a negative influence on satisfaction with job, company policy and support, and customers. Michaels and colleagues (1988) results indicate that higher levels of organizational formalization are associated with lower levels of role ambiguity among salespeople (p < .001) and buyers (p < .001). Higher levels of role conflict (p < .001) and ambiguity (p < .001) are associated with lower levels of organizational commitment. Also, higher levels of role ambiguity are associated with higher levels of work alienation (p < .01). This pattern of results is identical in the two samples (salespersons and industrial buyers).

Cummings, Jackson, and Ostrom (1980) did not find a significant relationship between role ambiguity and job structure or job performance However, role ambiguity was found to be inversely related to job satisfaction (p < .0001).

Skinner, Dubinsky, and Donnelly (1984) studied the relationship between retail sales managers' social bases of power and retail salespeople's job related outcomes. They found that legitimate, expert, and coercive power are negatively related to role ambiguity.

COMMENTS:

See also Futrell (1980) for another apparent use of this or a similar scale.

REFERENCES:

Cummings, W. Theodore, Donald W. Jackson, Jr., and Lonnie L. Ostrom (1989), "Examining Product Managers' Job Satisfaction and Performance Using Selected Organizational Behavior Variables," *JAMS*, 17 (2), 147-56.

Dubinsky, Alan J. and Steven W. Hartley (1986), "A Path-Analytic Study of a Model of Salesperson Performance," *JAMS*, 14 (Spring), 36-46.

Fry, Louis W., Charles M. Futrell, A. Parasuraman, and Margaret A. Chmielewski (1986), "An Analysis of Alternative Causal Models of Salesperson Role Perceptions and Work-Related Attitudes," *JM*, 23 (May), 153-63.

Futrell, Charles M. (1980), "Salesmen and Saleswomen Job Satisfaction," *Industrial Marketing Management*, 9, 27-30.

Hampton, Ron, Alan J. Dubinsky, and Steven J. Skinner (1986), "A Model of Sales Supervisor Leadership Behavior and Retail Salespeople's Job-Related Outcomes," *JAMS*, 14 (Fall), 33-43.

House, R.L., R.S. Schuler, and E. Levanoni (1983), "Role Conflict and Ambiguity Scales: Reality on Artifact?" *Journal of Applied Psychology*, 68 (May), 334-37.

Lysonski, Steven (1985), "A Boundary Theory Investigation of the Product Manager's Role," *JM*, 49 (Winter), 26-40.

Michaels, Ronald E., William L. Cron, Alan J. Dubinsky, and Erich A. Joachimsthaler (1988), "Influence of Formalization on the Organizational Commitment and Work Alienation of Salespeople and Industrial Buyers," *JMR*, 25 (November), 376-83.

Rizzo, John R., Robert J. House, and Sidney I. Lirtzman (1970), "Role Conflict and Ambiguity in Complex Organizations," *Administration Science Quarterly*, 15 (June), 150-63.

Schuler, R.S., R.J. Aldag, and A.P. Brief (1977), "Role Conflict and Ambiguity: A Scale Analysis," *Organizational Behavior and Human Performance*, 20 (October), 111-28.

Skinner Steven J., Alan Dubinsky, and J.H. Donnelly (1984), "The Use of Social Bases of Power in Retail Sales," *JPSSM*, 4 (November), 49-56 .

Teas, R. Kenneth (1980), "An Empirical Test of Linkages Proposed in the

Walker, Churchill, and Ford Model of Salesforce Motivation and Performance,'' *JAMS*, 8 (Winter), 58-72.

_____ (1983), ''Supervisory Behavior, Role Stress, and the Job Satisfaction of Industrial Salespeople,'' *JMR*, 20 (February), 84-91.

SCALE ITEMS: ROLE AMBIGUITY (SALESPERSON AND PRODUCT MANAGER)*

Very false   Very true

1———2———3———4———5———6———7

1. I feel certain about how much authority I have in my selling position.
2. I have clear, planned goals and objectives for my selling position.
3. I know that I have divided my time properly while performing the tasks connected with my selling.
4. I know what my responsibilities are in my selling position.
5. I know exactly what is expected of me in my selling position.
6. I receive clear explanations of what has to be done in my selling position.

* Michaels and colleagues (1988) used a modified version of Rizzo, House, and Lirtzman's (1970) original scale. The modified version consisted of a nine-item, seven-point Likert-type summated scale, in which 7 = high and 1 = low. No specific information was available as to the actual scale items used. Similarly, Cummings, Jackson, and Ostrom (1989) used a modified version of Rizzo, House, and Lirtzman's (1970) original scale. The modified version consisted of a four-item, five-point Likert-type summated scale. No specific information was available as to the actual scale items used.

SCALE NAME: Role Clarity (Salesperson)

SCALE DESCRIPTION:

A five-item, five-point summated ratings scale measuring a salesperson's perceived role clarity. The scale has also been referred to as the Role Clarity Index.

SCALE ORIGIN:

There is no information indicating that the scale originated elsewhere than in the study by Busch (1980). His is the only known use of the scale in the marketing literature reviewed here.

SAMPLES:

Analysis was based on data collected from **477** usable questionnaires from the salespeople of three pharmaceutical companies. The overall response rate was 53.8%. The database consisted of 436 male respondents and 39 female respondents.

RELIABILITY:

A Cronbach's alpha of **.81** was reported for the scale.

VALIDITY:

No examination of scale validity was reported for the scale.

ADMINISTRATION:

The scale was self-administered along with several other measures included in the mail questionnaire. No information was available as to the actual scoring to be used for the scale items. Assuming 1 to represent the "Not at all Clear" anchor and 5 to represent the "Perfectly clear" anchor, the possible summated scores range from 5 to 25. A low score (5 being the lowest possible score) represents a low degree of perceived role clarity.

MAJOR FINDINGS:

The results indicated that expert power was positively related to role clarity in all three firms (firm 1, $p < .001$, and firm 3, $p < .002$). It was found that referent power was positively related to role clarity within all three firms. Moreover, it was found that two male-female differences exist for the relationship between role clarity and the sales managers' power bases: expert power (male, $r = .33$, $p < .05$; female, $r = -.05$) and legitimate power (males, $r = .12$; females, $r = -.15$).

REFERENCES:

Busch, Paul (1980), ''The Sales Manager's Bases of Social Power and Influence Upon the Sales Force,'' *JM*, 44 (Summer), 91-101.

Bush, Ronald F. and Paul S. Busch (1982), ''The Relationship of Tenure and Age to Role Clarity and Its Consequences in the Industrial Salesforce,'' *JPSSM*, (Fall/Winter), 17-23.

SCALE ITEMS: ROLE CLARITY* (SALESPERSON)

Please read the following questions. After carefully reading the questions, CHECK THE SPACE BELOW THE QUESTION WHICH MOST ACCU-RATELY REFLECTS YOUR FEELINGS. Remember that there are no right or wrong answers to the questions. The main interest is in your own personal feelings. Place a check in one of the spaces after each question.

```
Not at                                              Perfectly
all clear                                              clear
   1————————2————————3————————4————————5
```

1. How clear are you about the limits of your authority in your present job?
2. Do you feel you are always as clear as you would like to be about what you have to do on your job?
3. Do you feel you are always as clear as you would like to be about how you are supposed to do things on your job?
4. In general, how clearly defined are the policies and the various rules, procedures, and regulations of the company that affect your job?
5. In general, how clearly defined are the rules, policies, and procedures of your department that affect your job?

* The same findings are reported in Bush and Busch (1982).

SCALE NAME: Role Conflict (Ethical Situations)

SCALE DESCRIPTION:

A 27-item, five-point Likert-type scale ranging from "Complete agreement" to "No agreement." It measures the role conflict between (1) sales representatives and their sales supervisors, (2) their job expectations and the actual job, (3) themselves and their customers regarding various sales activities, (4) themselves and their families regarding various sales activities, and (5) their personal principles and various sales activities.

SCALE ORIGIN:

Chonko and Burnett (1983) developed this scale.

SAMPLES:

Chonko and Burnett (1983) collected data from a larger study involving industrial sales force behavior. Data were solicited from 143 sales representatives, 23 sales managers and 94 sales support personnel of a *Fortune* 500 firm. The research package consisted of two cover letters (one from the researcher and one from the president of the company) and a questionnaire. The questionnaire was initially pretested by six sales managers and 30 salespeople at another firm. The host firm's major line of business was energy-related products. Out of 260 questionnaires mailed, **215** (83%) usable questionnaires were obtained in two separate mailings. A total of 122 (85%) sales representatives, 19 (83%) area managers, and 74 (79%) sales support staff personnel responded.

RELIABILITY:

Cronbach's alpha coefficients for each source of conflict were found to be **.89** for supervisor, **.90** for job, **.81** for customer relations, **.85** for family, and **.86** for ethics.

VALIDITY:

The 31 role conflict items were factor analyzed, using principle factoring with iterations. Factors were rotated, using Varimax technique. Two separate analyses were run, one on the sample of salespeople and one on the sample of sales managers and support personnel. For both groups, four role conflict factors were obtained—job, family, ethics, and customer relations. A factor loading of .40 was considered sufficient for retaining an item, and in only four cases this criterion was not met.

ADMINISTRATION:

The scale was self-administered by respondents. The scores ranged from 2.22 to 3.42. A high score represents a high perceived role conflict.

MAJOR FINDINGS:

Chonko and Burnett's (1983) results indicate that conflict was greatest with ethical situations followed by job, customer relations, and family conflict. Results also indicate that the degree of role conflict perceived from each of the four sources is significantly different.

REFERENCE:

Chonko, Lawrence B. and John J. Burnett (1983), ''Measuring the Importance of Ethical Situations as a Source of Role Conflict: A Survey of Salespeople, Sales Managers, and Sales Support Personnel,'' *JPSSM*, 3 (May), 41-47.

SCALE ITEMS: ROLE CONFLICT (ETHICAL SITUATIONS)

Complete agreement	Very much agreement	Moderate agreement	Some agreement	No agreement
1	2	3	4	5

FACTOR 1: Customer Orientation
HOW MUCH AGREEMENT WOULD YOU SAY THERE IS BETWEEN YOU AND YOUR SUPERVISOR ON.....
1. How much maintenance service you should provide for your customers.
2. How much authority you should have regarding delivery adjustments for your customers.
3. How much authority you should have regarding price negotiations with customers.
4. How much training you should provide your customers.

HOW MUCH AGREEMENT WOULD YOU SAY THERE IS BETWEEN YOU AND YOUR CUSTOMER ON.....
5. Your performance of field tests for customers.
6. How much training you should provide customers.
7. When you should be available to your customers.
8. The extent to which you should develop personal relations with your customers.
9. How you should handle competition in your sales presentations.
10. How you should present the benefits of your firm's products to your customers.
11. How much maintenance service you should provide for your customers.

FACTOR 2: Job
HOW MUCH AGREEMENT WOULD YOU SAY THERE IS BETWEEN .....
12. The amount of sales territory I expect to cover and the territory I actually cover.
13. The number of customers I expect to have and the number of customers I actually have.
14. The non-selling tasks I expected to perform and the non-selling tasks I actually perform.

15. The amount of leisure time I expected to have and the leisure time I actually have.

HOW MUCH AGREEMENT WOULD YOU SAY THERE IS BETWEEN YOU AND YOUR SUPERVISOR ON.....
16. How much customer research I should provide.
17. How much troubleshooting I should do for my customers.

FACTOR 3: Family
HOW MUCH AGREEMENT WOULD YOU SAY THERE IS BETWEEN YOU AND YOUR FAMILY ON.....
18. The time you spend working.
19. The time you spend socializing with customers.
20. The time you spend socializing with other salespeople.
21. How much you travel on your job.

FACTOR 4: Ethics
HOW MUCH AGREEMENT WOULD YOU SAY THERE IS BETWEEN YOUR PERSONAL PRINCIPLES AND.....
22. How far I should stretch the truth to make a sale.
23. How often your customers offer you favors to bend the rules of your company.
24. How often your customers offer you favors to bend government laws and regulations.
25. How often you try to sell a product to a customer even if you feel the product has little or no value to that customer.
26. How often you feel pressure to stretch the truth in order to make a sale.
27. How often you feel pressure to apply the "hard sale" in order to make a sale.

SCALE NAME: Role Conflict (Salesperson and Product Manager)

SCALE DESCRIPTION:

An eight-item, seven-point Likert-type summated ratings scale ranging from ''Very true'' to ''Very false'' purporting to measuring a person's perceived role conflict.

SCALE ORIGIN:

The scale was developed originally by Rizzo, House, and Lirtzman (1970).

SAMPLES:

Teas's (1983) data were obtained by a mail survey of two midwestern corporations' sales forces. Included with the questionnaires were cover letters from the researcher and the vice president of sales promising confidentiality and indicating company support for the survey. Usable responses were obtained from **116** salespersons, 49 and 67 salespersons from each company (response rate was 55%).

Lysonski's (1985) data were obtained from questionnaires mailed to 449 product managers in consumer package goods industries. A second mailing to nonrespondents yielded a final return rate of 55%, or 224 completed questionnaires, of which 54 were unusable. The final sample for analysis was **170**.

Dubinsky and Hartley's (1986) data were collected by a questionnaire mailed to insurance agents located throughout the United States. Included with the questionnaires were cover letters from the company's divisional vice president indicating support for the project and a cover letter from the researchers promising confidentiality. A total of 467 questionnaires were sent out. Usable questionnaires were returned by **120** agents (response rate of 25.7%). Ninety-one percent of the respondents were male. The mean age was 39.1 years. Approximately 56% had earned at least a bachelor's degree. Mean job tenure was 6.6 years.

Fry and colleagues' (1986) data were obtained by a mail survey of a national pharmaceutical manufacturer's sales force. Questionnaires were returned by 216 of 347 salespeople surveyed (response rate of 62%). The data analyzed was from men only. Data on age, income, tenure, and education was not specified.

Hampton, Dubinsky, and Skinner's (1986) data were obtained from a census of (n = 121) retail salespeople employed in a department store chain (five outlets). Usable questionnaires were obtained from **116** of the salespeople (response rate of 95.9%), 91 of which were female. The median age was 23.2 years. Approximately 66% had at least some college education. Median job tenure was 1.4 years, and median time spent working with the current sales supervisor was 1.1 years.

Michaels and colleagues' (1988) data were obtained by self-administered questionnaires distributed to 255 full-line salespeople of an industrial building materials manufacturer. Usable questionnaires were returned by **215** salespeople (response rate of 84.3%). Mean respondent age was 43.9 years, mean job tenure 12.9 years, mean organization tenure 15.2 years, and mean sales experience 18.1 years. Data also were collected from a sample of industrial buyers. A randomly selected sample of 554 members of the National Association of Purchasing Management constituted the industrial buyer sample. Data were collected by self-administered mail questionnaire. Three hundred thirty five of the questionnaires were returned, **330** usable (59.6%). Mean respondent age was 42.2 years, mean job tenure 5.7 years, mean organization tenure 10.6 years, and mean purchasing experience 12.5 years.

Cummings, Jackson, and Ostrom's (1989) data were obtained by self-administered questionnaires distributed by mail to firms selected from the American Marketing Association Membership Directory. One hundred fifty six firms agreed to participate in the study, providing a potential sample of 624 product managers. A total of **201** usable questionnaires were returned.

Skinner, Dubinsky, and Donnelly (1984) collected data from retail salespeople employed by a small departmental store chain. All salespeople employed by the firm participated in the study. Questionnaires were administered to participants at their workplace, and a total of **157** usable questionnaires were received.

RELIABILITY:

The following Cronbach's alphas values were reported for the scale: **.881** (Teas 1983); **.84** (Lysonski 195); **.86** (Fry et al. 1986); **.78** (Hampton, Dubinsky, and Skinner 1986); **.85** (Michaels et al. 1988); **.791** (Cummings, Jackson, and Ostrom 1989); and **.79** (Skinner, Dubinsky and Donnelly 1984).

VALIDITY:

Dubinsky and Hartley (1986) noted that the scale has demonstrated discriminant and predictive validity (Rizzo, House, and Lirtzman 1970), and construct and concurrent validity (Schuler, Aldag, and Brief 1977); in addition, it has proven to be free from semantic confusion (House, Schuler, and Levanoni 1983).

ADMINISTRATION:

The scale was self-administered along with several other measures included in the mail questionnaire in most of the studies. Accompanying the questionnaires were a cover letter from the chain's president indicating company support for the project and a cover letter from the researchers promising confidentiality. Hampton, Dubinsky, and Skinner (1986) used a different approach by administering the questionnaires to the respondents in a conference room at each store. The scores from each item are summated. The possible score range is 8 to 56. A low score (8 being the lowest possible score) represents high perceived role conflict.

MAJOR FINDINGS:

Teas's (1983) results indicate that the following predictor variables are related to a salesperson's perception of role conflict: consideration, negatively related (p < .001); initiation of structure, positively related (p < .05); participation, negatively related (p < .05); and experience, negatively related (p < .01). Moreover, it was found that the salesperson's perceived role conflict is found to be significantly (p < .001) negatively related to a salesperson's job satisfaction.

Lysonski's (1985) results indicate that the correlations are significant for perceived uncertainty (role conflict (p < .001); person-role conflict (p < .001), intersender conflict (p < .001), intrasender conflict (p < .01), and role-overload conflict (p < .01)), whereas only objective uncertainty is related to intersender conflict (p < .05). Therefore, the results indicate that uncertainty is associated with role conflict only for perceived uncertainty. The correlations between the dimensions of role conflict and measures of boundary spanning aggregate boundary spanning (p < .001); informal (p < .05), formal (p < .001), internal (p < .001) and external (p < .05) are all statistically significant. The correlations between role pressures and personal outcomes states in nearly every case, role conflict including its dimensions and role ambiguity is adversely associated with job satisfaction, job-related tension, and perceived performance (p ranged from less than .001 to less than .05). The results indicate that environmental uncertainty links strongly to role conflict (path coefficient, p = .251). Boundary spanning was found to be related to role conflict (path coefficient, p = .181). Role conflict was found to lead to adverse psychological reactions (tension, p = .052; dissatisfaction; and reduced perceived performance, p = -.066). The following were found to be related to role conflict: role conflict-satisfaction relationship, education = increased satisfaction (p < .01); role conflict-job related tension relationship, tolerance of ambiguity = decreased tension (p < .05), experienced as a product manager = increased tension (p < .001), experience with present product as a product manager = increased tension (p < .001); role conflict-perceived performance relationship, need for affiliation = increased performance (p < .001).

Dubinsky and Hartley's (1986) results indicate that self-monitoring and work motivation do not to appear to be related to role conflict or role ambiguity (they were not found to be significant). In addition, role conflict was not found to be related to job satisfaction. However, role conflict was found to be associated with job performance (p < .01).

Fry and colleagues (1986) results indicate role conflict and ambiguity have a direct negative impact on satisfaction (p < .05). Role conflict is positively related to job anxiety (p < .05). Also, a supervisor's consideration affects role conflict (p < .05). Role conflict has a negative effect (p < .05) on all job satisfaction dimensions (e.g., job, fellow workers, supervisor, pay promotion and development, company policy and support) except satisfaction with customer.

Hampton, Dubinsky, and Skinner's (1986) results indicate initiating structure does not impact role conflict (was found not to be significant), which supports the findings of Szilagyi and Keller (1976) and Walker, Churchill, and Ford (1975). Consideration was found to be inversely related to role conflict (p < .05). Moreover, role conflict was found to have a strong inverse relationship with overall job satisfaction (p < .0001).

Michaels and colleagues (1988) results indicate that higher levels of role conflict and ambiguity are associated with lower levels of organizational commitment (p < .001). In addition, in both samples (industrial buyer sample and salesperson sample) the relationship between formalization and role conflict is negative (p < .001).

Cummings, Jackson, and Ostrom's (1989) results indicated a direct relationship between job structure and role conflict (p < .007). However, job structure explained only 5% of the variance in role conflict. Role conflict was not found to be significantly related to job satisfaction or job performance.

Skinner, Dubinsky, and Donnelly (1984) studied the relationship between retail sales managers' social bases of power and retail salespeople's job related outcomes. They found that legitimate and expert power are inversely related to role conflict. Together, these two measures explain over 8% of the variance in role conflict. Reward, coercive and referent power do not explain any additional variance in role conflict.

COMMENTS:

Also see Futrell (1980) for an apparent use of the scale in a study pertaining to job satisfaction.

REFERENCES:

Cummings, W. Theodore, Donald W. Jackson, Jr., and Lonnie L. Ostrom (1989), "Examining Product Managers' Job Satisfaction and Performance Using Selected Organizational Behavior Variables," *JAMS*, 17 (2), 147-156.

Dubinsky, Alan J. and Steven W. Hartley (1986), "A Path-Analytic Study of a Model of Salesperson Performance," *JAMS*, 14 (Spring), 36-46.

Fry, Louis W., Charles M. Futrell, A. Parasuraman, and Margaret A. Chmielewski (1986), "An Analysis of Alternative Causal Models of Salesperson Role Perceptions and Work-Related Attitudes," *JMR*, 23 (May), 153-63.

Futrell, Charles M. (1980), "Salesmen and Saleswomen Job Satisfaction," *Industrial Marketing Management*, 9, 27-30.

Hampton, Ron, Alan J. Dubinsky, and Steven J. Skinner (1986), "A Model of Sales Supervisor Leadership Behavior and Retail Salespeople's Job-Related Outcomes," *JAMS*, 14 (Fall), 33-43.

House, R. L., R. S. Schuler, and E. Levanoni (1983), "Role Conflict and Ambiguity Scales: Reality on Artifacts?" *Journal of Applied Psychology*, 68 (May), 334-37.

Lysonski, Steven (1985), "A Boundary Theory Investigation of the Product Manager's Role," *JM*, 49 (Winter), 26-40.

Michaels, Ronald E., William L. Cron, Alan J. Dubinsky, and Erich A. Joachimsthaler (1988), "Influence of Formalization on the Organizational Commitment and Work Alienation of Salespeople and Industrial Buyers," *JMR*, 25 (November), 376-83.

Rizzo, J., R.J. House, and S.I. Lirtzman (1970), "Role Conflict and Ambiguity in Complex Organizations," *Administrative Science Quarterly*, 15 (June), 150-63.

Schuler, Randall S., Ramon J. Aldag, and Arthur P. Brief (1977), "Role Conflict and Ambiguity: A Scale Analysis," *Organizational Behavior and Human Performance*, 16, 111-128.

Skinner S.J., A. Dubinsky, and J.H. Donnelly (1984), ''The Use of Social Bases of Power in Retail Sales,'' *JPSSM*, 4 (November), 49-56.

Szilagyi, A.D. and R.T. Keller (1976), ''A Comparative Investigation of the Supervisory Behavior Description Questionnaire (SBDQ) and the Revised Leader Behavior Description Questionnaire (LBDQ-Form XII),'' *Academy of Management Journal*, 19 (December), 642-49.

Teas, R. Kenneth (1983), ''Supervisory Behavior, Role Stress, and the Job Satisfaction of Industrial Salespeople,'' *JMR*, 20 (February), 84-91.

Walker, O.C., G.A. Churchill, and N.M. Ford (1975), ''Organizational Determinants of the industrial Salesman's Role Conflict and Ambiguity,'' *JM*, 39 (January), 32-39.

SCALE ITEMS: ROLE CONFLICT (SALESPERSON AND PRODUCT MANAGER)*

The following is Rizzo, House, and Lirtzman's (1970) original scale used to measure role conflict. (1 = ''Very True''; 7 = ''Very False'')

1. I have to do things that should be done differently.
2. I receive an assignment without the manpower to complete it.
3. I have to buck a rule or policy in order to carry out an assignment.
4. I work with two or more groups who operate quite differently.
5. I receive incompatible requests from two or more people.
6. I do things that are apt to be accepted by one and not accepted by others.
7. I receive an assignment without adequate resources and materials to execute it.
8. I work on unnecessary things.

* Teas (1983) used a five-point scale instead of this seven-point scale. Lysonski (1985) used a ten-item version of the above scale. There was no description available as to the number of points or the actual items this above scale with no description available as to the actual items used. Cummings, Jackson, and Ostrom (1989) used a modified version of Rizzo, House, and Lirtzman's (1970) original scale. The modified version consisted of a six-item, five-point Likert-type summated type scale. No information was available as to the actual anchors used.

SCALE NAME: Sales Training Index (Directing)

SCALE DESCRIPTION:

A five-item, five-point Likert type scale measuring the level of sales training in a bank. It is a part of a larger study consisting of a 20-item Sales Training Index scale used in the banking industry.

SCALE ORIGIN:

The scale was developed by Futrell, Berry, and Bowers (1984).

SAMPLES:

The sample was drawn from the roster of the Bank Marketing Association. Two thousand members were selected randomly for this study. Of these, 1000 each were placed randomly in "retail" and "wholesale" subsamples. All members were mailed identical questionnaires. Retail sample members were asked to respond in the context of selling to consumers, and wholesale sample members were asked to answer in terms of selling to institutions. A response rate of 37% for the retail group and 34.4% for the wholesale group was reported.

RELIABILITY:

An alpha of .87 was reported for this scale.

VALIDITY:

No specific examination of scale validity was reported.

ADMINISTRATION:

The scale was self-administered by respondents in a mail survey format. The higher the score, the higher the level of sales training in the bank.

MAJOR FINDINGS:

Futrell, Berry, and Bowers (1984) examined sales training in the banking industry using a scale divided into three categories—Planning and Evaluation, Organizing and Directing. The authors found that planning and evaluation in a bank's sales training effort receive less attention than organizing and directing.

COMMENTS:

Also see STI—Planning and Evaluation and STI—Organizing scales (#418 and #419).

REFERENCE:

Futrell, Charles M., Leonard L. Berry, and Michael R. Bowers (1984), ''An Evaluation of Sales Training in the U.S. Banking Industry,'' *JPSSM*, 4, 41-47.

SCALE ITEMS: SALES TRAINING INDEX (DIRECTING)

Strongly   Strongly
disagree   agree
1————————2————————3————————4————————5

1. Sales training is performed in a positive manner that encourages our sales-people.
2. The personnel who lead our sales training sessions have the necessary background and experience.
3. There is an individual or department in our bank responsible for developing and coordinating sales training programs.
4. The personnel who lead our sales training sessions are effective in communicating salesmanship techniques to others.
5. The personnel who conduct our sales training are themselves skilled sales-people.

SCALE NAME: Sales Training Index (Organization)

SCALE DESCRIPTION:

A seven-item, five-point Likert-type scale measuring the level of sales training in a bank. It is a part of a larger study consisting of a 20-item Sales Training Index scale used in the banking industry.

SCALE ORIGIN:

The scale was developed by Futrell, Berry, and Bowers (1984).

SAMPLES:

The sample was drawn from the roster of the Bank Marketing Association. Two thousand members were selected randomly for this study. Of these, 1000 each were placed randomly in "retail" and "wholesale" subsamples. All members were mailed identical questionnaires. Retail sample members were asked to respond in the context of selling to consumers, and wholesale sample members were asked to answer in terms of selling to institutions. A response rate of 37% for retail group and 34.4% for wholesale group was reported.

RELIABILITY:

An alpha of **.86** was reported for this scale.

VALIDITY:

No specific examination of scale validity was reported.

ADMINISTRATION:

The scale was self-administered by respondents in a mail survey format. The higher the score, the higher the level of sales training in the bank as perceived by respondents.

MAJOR FINDINGS:

Futrell, Berry, and Bowers (1984) examined sales training in the banking industry using a 20-item Sales Training Index scale divided into three categories—Planning and Evaluation, Organizing and Directing. The authors found that planning and evaluation in a bank's sales training effort receive less attention than organizing and directing.

COMMENTS:

Also see STI—Directing and STI—Planning and Evaluation scales (#417 and #419).

REFERENCE:

Futrell, Charles M., Leonard L. Berry, and Michael R. Bowers(1984),"An Evaluation of Sales Training in the U.S. Banking Industry," *JPSSM*, 4, 41-47.

SCALE ITEMS: SALES TRAINING INDEX (ORGANIZATION)

Strongly disagree
1————2————3————4————5
Strongly agree

1. Sales training takes place on a regular basis in our bank.
2. Management provides the necessary budget for sales training.
3. Most bank personnel in selling roles seem to make use of the information provided them in sales training sessions.
4. We have good sales training facilities.
5. The bank's management supports the sales training program.
6. The degree of managerial support for the sales training program is recognized by the bank's staff.
7. The bank's sales training program motivates our employees to want sales success.

SCALE NAME: Sales Training Index (Planning and Evaluation)

SCALE DESCRIPTION:

> An eight-item, five-point Likert type scale measuring the level of sales training in a bank. It is a part of a larger study consisting of a 20-item Sales Training Index scale used in the banking industry.

SCALE ORIGIN:

> The scale was developed by Futrell, Berry, and Bowers (1984).

SAMPLES:

> The sample was drawn from the roster of the Bank Marketing Association. Two thousand members were selected randomly for this study. Of these, 1000 each were placed randomly in "retail" and "wholesale" subsamples. All members were mailed identical questionnaires. Retail sample members were asked to respond in the context of selling to consumers, and wholesale sample members were asked to answer in terms of selling to institutions. A response rate of 37% for retail group and 34.4% for wholesale group was reported.

RELIABILITY:

> An alpha of **.90** was reported for this scale.

VALIDITY:

> No specific examination of scale validity was reported.

ADMINISTRATION:

> The scale was self-administered by respondents in a mail survey format. The higher the score, the higher the level of sales training in the bank as perceived by respondents.

MAJOR FINDINGS:

> Futrell, Berry, and Bowers (1984) examined sales training in the banking industry using a 20-item Sales Training Index scale divided into three categories—Planning and Evaluation, Organizing and Directing. The authors found that planning and evaluation in a bank's sales training effort receive less attention than organizing and directing.

COMMENTS:

Also see STI—Organizing and STI—Directing scales (#417 and #418).

REFERENCE:

Futrell, Charles M., Leonard L. Berry, and Michael R. Bowers(1984),"An Evaluation of Sales Training in the U.S. Banking Industry," *JPSSM*, 4, 41-47.

SCALE ITEMS: SALES TRAINING INDEX (PLANNING AND EVALUATION)

```
Strongly                                                    Strongly
disagree                                                      agree
    1—————————2—————————————3—————————4—————————5
```

1. Job description for our sales positions are considered when developing sales training programs.
2. We have specific goals which our sales training program is expected to meet.
3. Sales training goals are related directly to the goals of the bank.
4. We analyze our salespeople's jobs in order to determine their sales training needs.
5. We regularly evaluate the results of our sales training program.
6. At the same time sales training goals are determined, methods are established to evaluate the effectiveness of the training.
7. We use specific items (increase in sales, call/order ratio) to evaluate sales training results.
8. Information used for evaluating the sales training program is gathered before and after training takes place.

SCALE NAME: Satisfaction With Job (General)

SCALE DESCRIPTION:

A five-item, seven-point Likert-type scale assessing the degree to which an employee is generally satisfied with the kind of work he/she does. The scale is "general" in the sense that the items do not get into specific issues such as pay, supervision, co-workers, and so on. The short form of the scale with three items was used by Dubinsky and colleagues (1986).

SCALE ORIGIN:

The scale used by Dubinsky and colleagues (1986) is apparently the short version of the job satisfaction scale developed by Hackman and Oldham (1974, 1975). No specific psychometric information is provided regarding the three-item version, but the five-item version is indicated to be reasonably reliable and valid. Specifically, the internal consistency of the scale is reported to be .76. Evidence of convergent validity is that the scale has high positive correlations with several other related but conceptually different measures such as social satisfaction, supervisory satisfaction, growth satisfaction, and work meaningfulness.

SAMPLES:

Analysis in Dubinsky and colleagues (1986) was based on data collected from **189** salespeople. Letters were sent to a national sample of 2000 senior-level executives asking them to have their least experienced salesperson complete the questionnaire. The respondents represented 189 different companies marketing 50 different product categories. The sample had a median age of 30.5 years, had spent 1.4 years (median) in their present positions, and were mostly male (86%).

Dubinsky and Hartley (1986) based their analysis on completed questionnaires returned by **120** respondents. Questionnaires were sent to 467 agents who sold lines of a large, multi-insurance company. No nonresponse bias was apparent. The sample had a mean age of 39.1 years, had spent 6.6 years (mean) in their present positions, were mostly male (91%), and more than half were college graduates (56%).

The sample used by Hampton, Dubinsky, and Skinner (1986) was based on **116** usable responses from a census of 121 retail salespeople who worked in one of five outlets of a department store chain. The sample had a median age of 23.2 years, had spent 1.4 years (median) in their present positions and 1.1 years (median) with their current supervisors, were mostly female (78%), and 66% had some college education.

Skinner, Dubinsky, and Donnelly (1984) collected data from retail salespeople employed by a small departmental store chain. All salespeople employed by the firm participated in the study. Questionnaires were administered to participants at their workplace, and a total of **157** usable questionnaires were received.

RELIABILITY:

A LISREL estimate of reliability was **.83** (Dubinsky et al 1986), and alphas of **.73** and **.81** were reported by Dubinsky and Hartley (1986) and Hampton, Dubinsky, and Skinner (1986), respectively. Skinner, Dubinsky, and Donnelly (1984) reported an alpha of **.82**.

VALIDITY:

No examination of scale validity was reported in any of these studies.

ADMINISTRATION:

The scale was self-administered by respondents in the studies by Dubinsky (et al. 1986; and Hartley 1986) along with many other measures in a mail survey format. Hampton, Dubinsky, and Skinner (1986) distributed the survey instrument to respondents in a conference room in each store where they were self-administered. In the study by Skinner, Dubinsky, and Donnelly (1984), the scale was self-administered by respondents. High scores on the scale indicate that respondents have a high level of general satisfaction with the work they perform in their jobs, whereas low scores indicate respondents are very dissatisfied with their jobs.

MAJOR FINDINGS:

Dubinsky and colleagues (1986) examined a model of sales force assimilation. Job suitability and dealing with conflicts at work were both found to have significant positive impacts on general job satisfaction. The purpose of Dubinsky and Hartley (1986) was to investigate several predictors of salesperson performance and the relationships among those predictors. A path analysis indicated that though job satisfaction had some effect on job involvement, it had a stronger (positive) effect on organizational commitment. In turn, it was most significantly affected (negatively) by role ambiguity. A causal model of retail sales supervisor leadership behavior was studied by Hampton, Dubinsky, and Skinner (1986). The results indicated that job satisfaction had strong positive effects on organizational commitment and "work motivation." In turn, role conflict had a strong negative impact on job satisfaction. Skinner, Dubinsky, and Donnelly (1984) studied the relationship between retail sales managers' social bases of power and retail salespeople's job related outcomes. They found that sales managers' legitimate and expert power bases are positively related to retail salespeople's overall job satisfaction.

REFERENCES:

Dubinsky, Alan J. and Steven W. Hartley (1986), "A Path-Analytic Study of a Model of Salesperson Performance," *JAMS*, 14 (Spring), 36-46.
_____, Roy D. Howell, Thomas N. Ingram, and Danny Bellenger (1986), "Salesforce Socialization," *JM*, 50 (October), 192-207.
Hackman, J. Richard and Greg R. Oldham (1974), *The Job Diagnostic Survey:*

An Instrument for the Diagnosis of Jobs and the Evaluation of Job Redesign Projects, Technical Report #4. New Haven, CT: Department of Administrative Sciences, Yale University.

_____ and _____ (1975), "Development of the Job Diagnostic Survey," *Journal of Applied Psychology*, 60 (2), 159-70.

Hampton, Ron, Alan J. Dubinsky, and Steven J. Skinner (1986), "A Model of Sales Supervisor Leadership Behavior and Retail Salespeople's Job-Related Outcomes," *JAMS*, 14 (Fall), 33-43.

Skinner, Steven J., Alan Dubinsky, and J.H. Donnelly (1984), "The Use of Social Bases of Power in Retail Sales," *JPSSM*, 4 (November), 49-56.

SCALE ITEMS: SATISFACTION WITH JOB (GENERAL)*

Strongly disagree	Disagree	Slightly disagree	Neutral	Slightly agree	Agree	Strongly agree
1	2	3	4	5	6	7

1. Generally speaking, I am very satisfied with this job.
2. I frequently think of quitting this job. (r)
3. I am generally satisfied with the kind of work I do in this job.
4. Most people on this job are very satisfied with the job.
5. People on this job often think of quitting. (r)

* Items 1-3 compose the short form of the scale and are the ones used by Dubinsky and colleagues (1986).

SCALE NAME: Satisfaction With Job (Generalized)

SCALE DESCRIPTION:

An eight-item, six-point Likert-type summated ratings scale measuring the degree of satisfaction a salesperson expresses having with his/her work. Hafer and Sirgy (1983) used the eight-item version and a modified version obtained by deleting item 1.

SCALE ORIGIN:

The first four items of the scale originate from the work of Pruden and Reese (1972), and the last four were designed for the specific sales situation under study in the dissertation by Bagozzi (1976).

SAMPLES:

The analysis made by Bagozzi (1980) was based on **122** completed question-naires from industrial salespeople assigned to exclusive geographic territor-ies. Hafer and Sirgy (1983) collected the date from 350 insurance salespeople who were participating in their company's annual meeting at the home office. A total of **336** usable questionnaires were obtained, of which 308 were male.

RELIABILITY:

An alpha of **.78** was reported for the scale by Bagozzi (1980). Hafer and Sirgy (1983) reported an alpha of **.549;** however, on deleting item 1, alpha increased to **.6709.**

VALIDITY:

No specific examination of scale validity was reported.

ADMINISTRATION:

The scale was apparently self-administered in an unspecified setting as part of a larger survey instrument. High scores on the scale suggest that respon-dents are very satisfied with several aspects of their jobs, whereas low scores indicate that they are very dissatisfied with their work. Scores, in the case of Hafer and Sirgy's (1983) seven-item scale, ranged from 22.0 to 42.0, with a mean of 36.914, median of 37.682, mode of 42.0, and standard deviation of 4.415.

MAJOR FINDINGS:

Bagozzi (1980) investigated the relationship between performance and satis-faction for an industrial sales force using causal modeling. The results indi-cated that job satisfaction was influenced to a significant degree by motivation to work and sales performance. The objective of Hafer and Sirgy (1983) was to test the hypothesis that "personality traits reflective of personal growth are related to indicators of professional growth for salespeople." They found that the job satisfaction measure as an indicator of professional growth was correlated to indicators of personal growth (self-esteem and inner/other-directedness).

COMMENTS:

See also a reanalysis of Bagozzi's (1980) data made by Joreskog and Sorbom (1982).

REFERENCES:

Bagozzi, Richard P. (1976), "Toward a General Theory for the Explanation of the Performance of Salespeople," doctoral dissertation, Northwestern University.

_____ (1980), "Performance and Satisfaction in an Industrial Salesforce: An Examination of Their Antecedents and Simultaneity," *JM*, 44 (Spring), 65-77.

Hafer, John (1986), "An Empirical Investigation of the Salesperson's Career Stage Perspective," *JPSSM*, 6 (November), 1-7.

_____ and Joseph M. Sirgy (1983), "Professional Growth Versus Personal Growth of Salespeople: A General System Model," *JPSSM*, 3 (November), 22-30 .

Joreskog, Karl G. and Dag Sorbom (1982), "Recent Developments in Structural Equation Modeling," *JMR*, 19 (November), 404-16.

Pruden, H.O. and R.M. Reese (1972), "Interorganizational Role-Set Relations and the Performance and Satisfaction of Industrial Salesmen," *Administrative Science Quarterly*, 17 (December), 601-609.

SCALE ITEMS: SATISFACTION WITH JOB (GENERALIZED)

Use the following scale to indicate responses to the first six statements.

Definitely yes	Probably yes	Maybe yes	Maybe no	Probably no	Definitely no
6	5	4	3	2	1

1. Do you feel promotion opportunities are wider in jobs other than yours?
2. Do you feel it is as easy to demonstrate ability and initiative in your job as in others?
3. Would you advise a friend looking for a new job to take one similar to yours?
4. Do you think that there is as much a feeling of security in your job as in others?
5. Do you feel your pay is as high in comparison with what others get for similar work in other companies?
6. Do you find your work challenging, exciting, and giving you a sense of accomplishment?

7. How satisfied are you with your general work situation?

Extremely satisfied	Moderately satisfied	Somewhat satisfied	Somewhat dissatisfied	Moderately dissatisfied	Extremely dissatisfied
6	5	4	3	2	1

8. How much control do you feel you have over your work activities such as number of calls required in a week, etc.?

No control	Very little control	Slight amount of control	Moderate amount of control	Very much control	Total control
1	2	3	4	5	6

SCALE NAME: Satisfaction With Supervisor

SCALE DESCRIPTION:

A three-item, seven-point Likert-type scale assessing the degree to which an employee is satisfied with the treatment, respect, and guidance received from a supervisor at work.

SCALE ORIGIN:

The scale was developed by Hackman and Oldham (1974, 1975) and is indicated to be reasonably reliable and valid. Specifically, the internal consistency of the scale is reported to be .79. Evidence of convergent validity is that the scale has moderate positive correlations with several other related but conceptually different measures such as general job satisfaction, social satisfaction, and growth satisfaction.

SAMPLES:

The sample used by Hampton, Dubinsky, and Skinner (1986) was based on **116** usable responses from a census of 121 retail salespeople who worked in one of five outlets of a department store chain. The sample had a median age of 23.2 years, had spent 1.4 years (median) in their present positions and 1.1 years (median) with their current supervisors, were mostly female (78%), and 66% had some college education. Skinner, Dubinsky, and Donnelly (1984) collected data from retail salespeople employed by a small departmental store chain. All salespeople employed by the firm participated in the study. Questionnaires were administered to participants at their workplace, and a total of **157** usable questionnaires were received.

RELIABILITY:

Alphas of **.81** and **.83** were reported by Hampton, Dubinsky, and Skinner (1986) and Skinner, Dubinsky, and Donnelly (1984), respectively.

VALIDITY:

No examination of scale validity was reported.

ADMINISTRATION:

Hampton, Dubinsky, and Skinner (1986) distributed the survey instrument to respondents in a conference room in each store, where they were self-administered. High scores on the scale indicate that respondents have a high level of satisfaction with the supervision they receive in their jobs, whereas low scores indicate respondents are very dissatisfied with their supervisors. In Skinner, Dubinsky, and Donnelly (1984) the scale was self-administered by respondents.

MAJOR FINDINGS:

A causal model of retail sales supervisor leadership behavior was studied by Hampton, Dubinsky, and Skinner (1986). The strongest model found in the study involved satisfaction with supervision; its greatest predictor was the sales supervisor being perceived to have a ''considerate'' leadership style. Skinner, Dubinsky, and Donnelly (1984) studied the relationship between retail sales managers' social bases of power and retail salespeople's job related outcomes. They found that reward, referent, and expert power are related positively to satisfaction with supervisor, whereas coercive power is related negatively.

REFERENCES:

Hackman, J. Richard and Greg R. Oldham (1974), *The Job Diagnostic Survey: An Instrument for the Diagnosis of Jobs and the Evaluation of Job Redesign Projects, Technical Report #4*. New Haven, CT: Department of Administrative Sciences, Yale University.

_____ and _____ (1975), ''Development of the Job Diagnostic Survey,'' *Journal of Applied Psychology*, 60 (2), 159-70.

Hampton, Ron, Alan J. Dubinsky, and Steven J. Skinner (1986), ''A Model of Sales Supervisor Leadership Behavior and Retail Salespeople's Job-Related Outcomes,'' *JAMS*, 14 (Fall), 33-43.

Skinner, Steven J., Alan Dubinsky, and J.H. Donnelly (1984), ''The Use of Social Bases of Power in Retail Sales,'' *JPSSM*, 4 (November), 49-56.

SCALE ITEMS: SATISFACTION WITH SUPERVISOR

Strongly disagree	Disagree	Slightly disagree	Neutral	Slightly agree	Agree	Strongly agree
1	2	3	4	5	6	7

1. I am satisfied with the degree of respect and fair treatment I receive from my immediate supervisor.
2. I am satisfied with the amount of support and guidance I receive from my immediate supervisor.
3. I am very satisfied with the overall quality of supervision I receive from my immediate supervisor.

SCALE NAME: Sex-Role Inventory (BSRI)

SCALE DESCRIPTION:

A 60-item, seven-point Likert-type scale measuring the masculine, feminine, and neutral personality characteristics of an individual.

SCALE ORIGIN:

The scale used in Lucette and Marvin (1985) was developed originally by Bem (1974).

SAMPLES:

Respondents in Lucette and Marvin (1985) were **96** undergraduate students about to complete a sales management class at a large university in the mid-Atlantic area.

RELIABILITY:

Lucette and Marvin reported an alpha of **.873** for masculine items and **.792** for feminine items.

VALIDITY:

No specific examination of scale validity was reported.

ADMINISTRATION:

The scale was self-administered by respondents.

MAJOR FINDINGS:

Lucette and Marvin (1985) examined the sex-labeling of selling jobs. They divide the selling jobs into five broad categories—three male oriented and two female oriented: (1) Industrial or organizational end user, (2) resellers, (3) Direct-to-home (Large-ticket items), (4) In-Store selling, and (5) Direct-to-home (small-ticket items). Findings indicate the desire of female undergraduates to move into male-dominated selling domains. It is indicated that 34 of 41 male students (83%) are masculine typed, and 80% of the females are classified as either masculine typed or androgynous.

REFERENCES:

Bem, Sandra L. (1974), ''The Measurement of Psychological Androgyny,'' *Journal of Consulting and Clinical Psychology*, 42, 155-62.
Comer, Lucette B. and Marvin A. Jolson (1985), ''Sex-Labeling of Selling Jobs and Their Applicants,'' *JPSSM*, 5 (May), 15-22.

SCALE ITEMS: SEX-ROLE INVENTORY (BSRI)

Respondents scored themselves on a seven-point scale.

Masculine Items	Feminine Items	Neutral Items
Acts as a leader	Affectionate	Adaptable
Aggressive	Cheerful	Conceited
Ambitious	Childlike	Conscientious
Analytical	Compassionate	Conventional
Assertive	Does not use harsh language	Friendly
Athletic	Happy	
Competitive	Eager to soothe hurt feelings	Helpful
Defends own beliefs	Inefficient	
Dominant	Feminine	Jealous
Forceful	Flatterable	Likeable
Has leadership abilities	Gentle	Moody
Independent	Gullible	Reliable
Individualistic	Loves children	Secretive
Makes decisions easily	Loyal	Sincere
Masculine	Sensitive to the	Solemn
Self-reliant	needs of others	Tactful
Self-sufficient	Shy	Theatrical
Strong personality	Soft spoken	Truthful
Willing to take a stand	Sympathetic	Unpredictable
Willing to take risks	Tender	Unsystematic
	Understanding	Yielding
	Warm	

Note: The items in this scale have been used as two separate scales and are reported in the Consumer Behavior section as Scales #116 and #167.

Reading List For
Scale Development and Use
••••••••••••••••••••••••••••••

Ballard, Rebecca, Michael D. Crino, and Stephen Rubenfeld (1988), "Social Desirability Response Bias and the Marlowe-Crowne Social Desirability Scale," *Psychological Reports*, 63, 227-37.

Bocker, Franz (1988), "Scale Forms and Their Impact on Ratings' Reliability and Validity," *JBR*, 17 (August), 15-26.

Boyle, Gregory J. (1991), "Does Item Homogeneity Indicate Internal Consistency or Item Redundancy in Psychometric Scales?" *Personality & Individual Differences*, 12 (3), 291-94.

Bruner II, Gordon C. and Paul J. Hensel (1993), "Multi-Item Scale Usage in Marketing Journals: 1980 to 1989," *JAMS*, 21 (Fall), 339-44.

Campbell, Donald T. and Donald W. Fiske (1959), "Convergent Validity and Discriminant Validity by the Multitrait-Multimethod Matrix," *Psychological Bulletin*, 56 (March), 81-105.

Churchill, Gilbert A., Jr. (1979), "A Paradigm for Developing Better Measures of Marketing Constructs," *JMR*, 16 (February), 64-73.

———— (1992), "Better Measurement Practices are Critical to Better Understanding of Sales Management Issues," *JPSSM*, 12 (Spring), 73-80.

———— and J. Paul Peter (1984), "Research Design Effects on the Reliability of Rating Scales: A Meta-Analysis," *JMR*, 21 (November), 360-75.

Comrey, Andrew L. (1988), "Factor Analytic Methods of Scale Development in Personality and Clinical Psychology," *Journal of Consulting and Clinical Psychology*, 56 (October), 754-61.

Cortina, Jose M. (1993), "What is Coefficient Alpha? An Examination of Theory and Applications," *Journal of Applied Psychology*, 78 (1), 98-104.

Cox III, Eli P. (1980), "The Optimal Number of Response Alternatives For a Scale: A Review," *JMR*, 17 (November), 407-422.

Cronbach, Lee J. (1951), "Coefficient Alpha and the Internal Structure of Tests," *Psychometrika*, 16 (September), 297-334.

———— (1955), "Construct Validity in Psychological Tests," *Psychological Bulletin*, 52 (July), 281-302.

Crowne, Douglas P. and David Marlowe (1960), "A New Scale of Social Desirability Independent of Psychopathology," *Journal of Consulting Psychology*, 24 (August), 349-54.

DeVellis, Robert F. (1991), *Scale Development: Theory and Applications.* Newbury Park, CA: Sage Publications, Inc.

Didow, Jr., Nicholas M., Kevin Lane Keller, Hiram C. Barksdale, Jr., and George R. Franke (1985), "Improving Measure Quality by Alternating Least Squares Optimal Scaling," *JMR*, 22 (February), 30-40.

Edris, Thabet A. and A. Meidan (1990), "On the Reliability of Psychographic Research: Encouraging Signs for Measurement Accuracy and Methodology in Consumer Research," *European Journal of Marketing*, 24 (3), 23-41.

Gerbing, David W. and James C. Anderson (1988), "An Updated Paradigm for Scale Development Incorporating Uni-dimensionality and Its Assessment," *JMR*, 25 (May), 186-92.

Givon, Moshe M. and Zur Shapira (1984), "Response to Rating Scales: A Theoretical Model and Its Application to the Number of Categories Problem," *JMR*, 21 (November), 410-19.

Green, Paul E. and Vithala R. Rao (1970), "Rating Scales and Information Recovery: How Many Scales and Response Categories to Use?" *JM*, 34 (July), 33-39.

Heeler, Roger M. and Michael L. Ray (1972), "Measure Validation in Marketing," *JMR*, 9 (November), 361-70.

Hensel, Paul J. and Gordon C. Bruner II (1992), "Multi-Item Scaled Measures in Sales-Related Research," *JPSSM*, 12 (Summer), 77-82.

Jacoby, Jacob (1978), "Consumer Research: A State of the Art Review," *JM*, 42 (April), 87-96.

Kline, Paul (1986), *A Handbook of Test Construction: Introduction to Psychometric Design.* New York: Methuen, Inc.

Komorita, S. S. (1963), "Attitude Content, Intensity, and the Neutral Point on a Likert Scale," *Journal of Social Psychology*, 61 (December), 327-34.

Martin, Warren S. (1973), "The Effects of Scaling on the Correlation Coefficient: A Test of Validity," *JMR*, 10 (August): 316-18.

———— (1978), "Effects of Scaling on the Correlation Coefficient: Additional Considerations," *JMR*, 15 (May), 304-308.

Nunnally, Jum C. and Ira H. Bernstein (1994), *Psychometric Theory.* New York: McGraw-Hill.

Peter, J. Paul (1979), "Reliability: A Review of Psychometric Basics and Recent Marketing Practices," *JMR*, 16 (February), 6-17.

———— (1981), "Construct Validity: A Review of Basic Issues and Marketing Practices," *JMR*, 18 (May), 133-45.

———— and Gilbert A. Churchill, Jr. (1986), "Relationships Among Research Design Choices and Psychometric Properties of Rating Scales: A Meta-Analysis," *JMR*, 50 (February), 1-10.

Peterson, Robert A. (1994), "A Meta-Analysis of Cronbach's Coefficient Alpha," *JCR*, 21 (September), 381-91.

Rentz, Joseph O. (1988), "An Exploratory Study of the Generalizability of Selected Marketing Measures," *JAMS*, 16 (Spring), 141-50.

Revelle, William (1979), "Hierarchical Cluster Analysis and the Internal Structure of Tests," *Multivariate Behavioral Research*, 14 (January), 57-74.

Silva, Fernando (1993), *Psychometric Foundations and Behavioral Assessment.* Newbury Park, CA: Sage Publications, Inc.

Singh, Jagdip, Roy D. Howell, and Gary K. Rhoads (1990), "Adaptive Designs for Likert-Type Data: An Approach for Implementing Marketing Surveys," *JMR*, 27 (August), 304-321.

Spector, Paul E. (1992), *Summated Ratings Scale Construction.* Newbury Park, CA: Sage Publications, Inc.

AUTHOR INDEX

•••••••••••••••••••••••

The numbers following author names refer to the *scale number* located at the top of each page.

Note: Alphabetically listed by first author for multiple authored references.

SUBJECT INDEX

· ·

The numbers following the key word refer to the *scale number* located at the top of each page.